THE EXCLUSION OF IMMIGRANTS FROM WELFARE PROGRAMS

The Exclusion of Immigrants from Welfare Programs

Cross-National Analysis and Contemporary Developments

EDITED BY EDWARD A. KONING

UNIVERSITY OF TORONTO PRESS
Toronto Buffalo London

Toronto Buffalo London
utorontopress.com

ISBN 978-1-4875-4634-2 (cloth)
ISBN 978-1-4875-4523-9 (EPUB)
ISBN 978-1-4875-4435-5 (PDF)

Library and Archives Canada Cataloguing in Publication

Title: The exclusion of immigrants from welfare programs : cross-national analysis and contemporary developments / edited by Edward A. Koning.
Names: Koning, Edward Anthony, 1982– editor.
Description: Includes bibliographical references.
Identifiers: Canadiana (print) 20220245789 | Canadiana (ebook) 20220245851 | ISBN 9781487546342 (hardcover) | ISBN 9781487545239 (EPUB) | ISBN 9781487544355 (PDF)
Subjects: LCSH: Immigrants – Services for – Case studies. | LCSH: Immigrants – Social conditions – Case studies. | LCSH: Welfare state – Political aspects – Case studies. | LCSH: Emigration and immigration – Government policy – Case studies. | LCSH: Immigrants – Government policy – Case studies.
Classification: LCC HV4005 .E93 2022 | DDC 362.89/912 – dc23

We wish to acknowledge the land on which the University of Toronto Press operates. This land is the traditional territory of the Wendat, the Anishnaabeg, the Haudenosaunee, the Métis, and the Mississaugas of the Credit First Nation.

University of Toronto Press acknowledges the financial support of the Government of Canada, the Canada Council for the Arts, and the Ontario Arts Council, an agency of the Government of Ontario, for its publishing activities.

Canada Council for the Arts
Conseil des Arts du Canada

Funded by the Government of Canada
Financé par le gouvernement du Canada
Canada

Contents

Section Three: Case Studies

Section Four: Concluding Reflections

Figures and Tables

Figures

Tables

Acknowledgments

First of all, I would like to thank the contributors to this volume, not only for agreeing to participate but also for sharing insightful feedback on the project as a whole, for putting up with my occasional micro-managing tendencies, and above all else, of course, for delivering such excellent chapters. It has been a humbling and rewarding experience to work with this group of stellar scholars. Many, many thanks to Keith Banting, Liv Bjerre, Grete Brochmann, Adam Butz, Markus Crepaz, Anil Duman, Oliver Gruber, Christian Joppke, Martin Kahanec, Neeraj Kaushal, Jason Kehrberg, Lucia Mýtna Kureková, Will Kymlicka, Catarina Reis Oliveira, João Peixoto, Tsewang Rigzin, Friederike Römer, and Mikhala West.

I owe thanks as well to the two anonymous reviewers who provided lengthy and generous comments on a first draft of this volume. Their feedback was insightful and constructive and improved the overall quality of this book.

This project simply would not have existed without the excellent work of a large number of research assistants. Many thanks to Silvina Antunes, Zina Bibanovic, Yuriko Cowper-Smith, Besarta Kajmolli, David Markle, Matt McBurney, Madison Milne-Ives, Gloria Novovic, Joshua Pedersen, Camila Rivas-Garrido, Liam Thompson, and Daniel Waring for helping me collect key information on immigrants' access to social programs. I am grateful as well to Sibena Peters, who prepared a careful literature review as a first step toward collecting that information, and to Aidan Hughes, who helped me plan and run a workshop in which all contributors presented a first draft of their chapters.

Hiring this great team of research assistants was made possible by a generous Insight Development Grant from the Social Sciences and Humanities Research Council of Canada. I am also thankful to the University of Guelph; not only does it continue to offer a productive and collegial work environment, but it also provided funding for hiring two research assistants and subsidizing the publication of this book.

Next, I wish to express my sincere gratitude to the Montreal artist Dawson, who generously agreed to let me use his striking painting *Quarrel* for the cover. His depiction of conflicting views that are forced to coexist beautifully accompanies our analysis of the controversial subject of immigrant welfare exclusion.

At the University of Toronto Press, I would like to thank Daniel Quinlan for his consistently timely and careful editorial assistance. My thanks as well to Matthew Kudelka for the detailed and thorough copy editing of this lengthy volume, and to Leah Connor for overseeing the editorial and production process.

Finally, I want to thank Léon, Oscar, and Caroline. Your love and support mean more than I can express in words.

SECTION ONE

Setting the Stage

1 Introduction

EDWARD A. KONING

Few immigration-related issues are as politically combustible as newcomers' access to social benefits and programs. In most Western democracies, immigrants experience more economic difficulties than native-born citizens, and as a result they are overrepresented among the recipients of some transfer benefits. Some politicians and public commentators respond to such patterns with accusations that immigrants are lazy and prone to taking advantage of the system, and thus with proposals for limiting newcomers' welfare access. Others take these patterns as revealing of a much larger problem of immigrant economic marginalization and therefore advocate more inclusion. Unsurprisingly, academic literature has paid much attention to the connection between immigration and welfare. Recent scholarship has revealed several insights, for example, that a sizable share of the public favours privileging native-born citizens in the extension of benefits, that fostering widespread support for social programs is harder where concerns about immigrants' welfare access are more widespread, and that calls for policy change this tension generates most frequently focus on introducing stricter eligibility requirements for newcomers.

What so far seems missing in this large body of literature is a bird's eye view of the extent to which existing policy arrangements in Western welfare states exclude immigrants from social programs and benefits. This lack of systematic comparative evidence has prevented existing research from making general claims about the overall direction of change, about why some countries have pursued more exclusionary approaches than others, and about the consequences that exclusionary approaches may have for immigrant-receiving societies.

This volume contributes to the literature by pursuing exactly these types of general claims. It takes advantage of a novel dataset that compares the extent to which welfare states differentiate between immigrants and native-born in granting access to social benefits and programs using 25 indicators related to seven social programs (tax-paid pensions, health care benefits, contributory pensions, contributory unemployment benefits, housing benefits, social assistance, and active labour market policies) for 22 countries (Australia, Austria, Belgium, Canada, Denmark, Finland, France, Germany, Iceland, Ireland, Italy, Luxembourg, Malta, Netherlands, New Zealand, Norway, Portugal, Spain, Sweden, Switzerland, United Kingdom, and the United States) at four moments in time (1990, 2000, 2010, and 2015). As discussed in more detail in chapter 2, this empirical domain enables us to paint a comprehensive picture of the welfare exclusion immigrants have faced over the last three decades in Western immigrant-receiving welfare states. We trace general developments; investigate explanations for variation; probe the implications of welfare exclusion for nativist backlash, socio-economic integration, and social spending; and zoom in on four countries that stand out in the cross-national comparisons: Austria – the most exclusionary case under consideration; Norway – the most inclusionary system; the United States – a country that has undergone a dramatic exclusionary change during the period we consider; and Portugal – which has witnessed a remarkable inclusionary transformation during this time.

While we find support for some theoretical propositions that have been generated by the existing literature, our findings also challenge often taken-for-granted assumptions on this subject. Four conclusions are most important to emphasize here. First, while extremely exclusionary measures seem to have become less common, many countries have thrown up new barriers to immigrant access in recent years. More generally, the overall longitudinal pattern is one of consistently large cross-national variation in levels of immigrant welfare exclusion yet significant within-country change over time. This high level of variability – even among 22 Western, liberal democracies, many of them member states of the same supranational organization of the European Union – casts serious doubt on any suggestion that forces of globalization, human rights legislation, and supranational governance are somehow leading to cross-national convergence or the indefinite "locking in" of immigrants' social rights.

Second, our findings largely confirm previous insights about the importance of the pre-existing welfare regime for patterns of welfare inclusion but are more equivocal regarding the importance of other institutional and socio-economic factors that are commonly invoked in existing research. Quantitatively, we are not able to confirm a clear effect of migration patterns, political parties, or legal protections on levels of immigrant exclusion from welfare programs. On the other hand, each of these factors does appear to be consequential in our qualitative investigations. Our tentative interpretation of these mixed findings is that the exclusion of immigrants from welfare programs is not only shaped by nomothetic patterns but also driven by relatively contingent political dynamics.

Third, the empirical arguments that are most commonly invoked to justify welfare exclusion find little support in our analyses. For one thing, we find no evidence that throwing up restrictions to immigrants' access to the welfare state will somehow appease a native-born population that would otherwise feel that newcomers are treated too generously. Instead, welfare exclusion seems associated with more *negative* public attitudes about immigrants. Neither do we find evidence that welfare exclusion improves immigrants' labour market integration. On aggregate, we find that immigrants are less likely to be in the labour force, and more likely to be unemployed, in countries that pursue more exclusion. And perhaps most surprisingly, exclusion does not seem to result in significant reductions in social spending. Even when we zoom in on short-term effects, where we would most expect exclusion to reduce government expenditure, we find only very small and statistically insignificant effects.

Our final main conclusion is mostly a warning: welfare inclusion in and of itself is not a panacea for all of the challenges that incorporating immigrants might pose. Despite the vast differences in how they are treated by the welfare system to which they have migrated, immigrants in Norway, Portugal, Austria, and the United States experience some of the same difficulties in their (economic) integration, with similar broader societal implications.

To be clear, some of these conclusions are more tentative and qualified than others, and by no means do we pretend we can reach final and definitive conclusions about the politics and policies of immigrant welfare exclusion. Our aim here is to pursue answers to questions that so far have been difficult to investigate systematically, as well as to pave the way for other researchers to further probe our line of enquiry and take advantage of the dataset that is launched in this book.

This introductory chapter provides a quick survey of the existing literature and a description of the theoretical framework that underpins this volume. It closes with a brief overview of the twelve chapters that follow.

Existing Literature and Theoretical Framework

The connection between immigration and welfare systems has long attracted scholarly attention. More than three decades ago, Gary Freeman (1986) already worried that large-scale migration would lead to the "Americanization" of European welfare states. More generally, much of the early literature depicted immigration as a potential threat to social policies and programs, primarily because it was expected to overburden the system and reduce the support from voters who did not wish to share redistributive policies with newcomers.

By now, it is clear that immigration did not make European welfare systems disappear. More generally, the massive literature on this topic has produced only limited evidence of aggregate negative effects. Most studies conclude that the net economic effects of immigration are small and positive (Spencer 2003; Venturini 2004; Zimmerman 2005; Franchino 2009), though studies that look exclusively at taxes and transfers do tend to find that especially recent immigrants generally contribute less in tax-generated revenue than they incur in benefit-related costs (House of Lords 2008; Van der Geest and Dietvorst 2010; Kapsalis 2020). Similarly, while some studies find evidence that immigration may reduce support for social programs (Eger 2010) or dampen social spending (Soroka et al. 2016), many others do not (Van Oorschot and Uunk 2007; Finseraas 2012; Crepaz 2008; Gerdes 2011). All in all, a persistent finding is that institutionalized welfare systems are relatively resistant to the pressures immigration may pose. While it is true that in many countries immigrants are overrepresented among welfare recipients and that a sizable part of the electorate is concerned about this, the outcome has not been large-scale retrenchment.

Instead, recent scholarship tends to conclude that a more common manifestation of any tension between immigration and redistribution has been support for reducing the entitlements of immigrants in particular. There is now a wealth of public opinion research on this subject, investigating just how popular the sentiment is that welfare state systems should privilege native-born citizens over newcomers in the extension of social programs, why some individuals but not others share this sentiment, and why it is more pervasive in some contexts than in others (Cappelen and Peters 2018; Gorodzeisky 2013; Kros and Coenders 2019; Mewes and Mau 2013).

More important for our purposes is research that examines whether this sentiment has been reflected in actual policy, or in other words, research that examines to what extent immigrants are included or excluded in social programs and policies. Addressing this question often requires rather technical descriptions of the interaction of admission, residence, and welfare policies, and as a result, most existing studies have a relatively narrow empirical scope and consider only one country, one social program, and/or one class of immigrants (Fix 2009; Boucher 2014; J.G. Andersen 2007; Boso and Vancea 2016). Only in recent years have we seen comparative case studies that compare the inclusion of immigrants in different welfare states more comprehensively (Sainsbury 2012; Koning 2019). There are also some quantitative comparisons with a broader scope in terms of the countries they consider, even though these still tend to focus on only a subset of social programs and/or categories of migrants (Eugster 2018; Huddleston et al. 2015; Bjerre et al. 2016).

Availing ourselves of existing insights in the literature generated by case studies, comparative case studies, and studies of specific programs or classes of migrants, as well as more general literature on immigration and social policy, we can formulate several expectations regarding the origins and consequences of immigrant welfare exclusion. The theoretical framework of this volume incorporates seven hypotheses that have received most of the attention.

To begin, we consider four possible explanations for cross-national variation in the degree to which immigrants are included or excluded in welfare state systems. First, following the insights of institutionalist theory on comparative social policy (Korpi 1980; Rothstein 1998; Larsen 2008), many scholars have hypothesized that the structure of a welfare regime shapes the entitlements of immigrants as well. More specifically, the expectation is that universal welfare systems will be more inclusionary because they are committed to the activation of those who are struggling in the labour market and encourage solidarity among taxpayers and benefit recipients. In this account, immigrants are expected to be worse off in conservative welfare regimes that depend on contributory programs that penalize those with a short work history in the country, and in an even more precarious position in liberal welfare systems where their heavy reliance on targeted programs frequently leads to the politicization of recipients' deservingness (Banting 2000; Sainsbury 2006; Crepaz and Damron 2009; Sciortino 2013). In sharp contrast, a minority of scholars argue that generous welfare systems are more likely to implement immigrant-exclusionary welfare reforms because the financial implications of inclusion are larger (Nannestad 2004; Razin, Sadka, and Suwankiri 2011; Kremer 2013). However, this seemingly functionalist expectation has found little support in existing research (Römer 2017).

Second, some suggest that migration patterns shape the level of immigrant exclusion from social programs. More specifically, this line of reasoning expects that a large inflow of immigrants, especially of those who are likely to struggle economically and to be perceived as different by the majority population, will result in exclusionary responses. This hypothesis is pervasive in political discourse and often seems tacitly assumed in academic literature (O'Connell 2005; Freeman 2009; Harris 2016). However, it is rarely subjected to empirical investigation. From other literature, we know that objective economic facts rarely affect the development of social policy and other public policies directly (Kingdon and Thurber 1984; Cox 2001; Kuipers 2006). And an investigation with admittedly low external validity found little support for this hypothesis (Koning 2019). Nevertheless, considering that many academics and political commentators seem to treat it as almost self-evident, it is an important expectation to test systematically.

Third, a common hypothesis in the literature on immigration is that a political environment in which politicians are encouraged to take a hard line on migration issues will likely lead to exclusionary policies. This seems particularly likely in countries where public concern over immigration and immigrant integration is widespread and where anti-immigrant parties have had strong electoral success. There is considerable empirical support for this line of reasoning in other areas than immigrant welfare exclusion (Heinisch 2003; Fallend 2004; Zaslove 2004; Albertazzi 2009; Howard 2010), although it is worth noting that there is more evidence that anti-immigrant parties shape policies indirectly (by incentivizing mainstream parties to adopt more restrictive positions, or by introducing policy suggestions that were not taken seriously before their arrival) than directly (Akkerman 2012; Bale 2003). On our specific subject of interest, some case studies and comparative case studies indeed suggest that exclusionary approaches to immigrants' welfare access are more likely in these types of hostile political environments and that, more generally, immigrant-excluding welfare reforms are typically premised on anti-immigrant sentiment (Cuttitta 2014; J. Andersen, Larsen, and Møller 2009; Banting and Koning 2017; Koning 2019; Wilkinson and Craig 2012).

The final factor we consider as a possible explanation for variation in welfare exclusion is the scope and robustness of legal protections. Many scholars have noted that immigrant inclusion, rather than being the product of deliberate policy-making by legislators, more likely results from judicial interpretations of human rights legislation and the proliferation of international rights protection (Joppke 2001; Guiraudon 2000; Soysal 1994; Banting and Koning 2017). This seems to be the case especially for member states of the European Union: the key principle of *lex loci laboris* stipulates that these countries should extend the same social rights to migrants from other member states who work on their territory as to their own citizens, and over time interpretations from the European Court of Justice have expanded the scope of this principle (Conant 2006; Barbalescu and Favell 2019; Koning 2021). The expectation here, then, is that immigrants will face more exclusion from social programs and benefits in contexts where these kinds of legal protections are either limited or easily circumvented.

The fifth hypothesis considers public opinion, the role of which is somewhat difficult to theorize. On the one hand, and as mentioned earlier, we could think of public attitudes as a key component of a political climate and as such of importance in shaping how politicians decide to accommodate immigrants in a welfare state. Moreover, a persistent argument in the more general literature is that the political culture of a community has a strong impact on immigration policy-making (Greenfeld 1992; Koopmans and Statham 2000). On the other hand, however, there are also good reasons to expect that existing arrangements on immigrants' welfare access shape public opinion. First, the institutionalist insistence that public opinion is status-quo–oriented and likely takes existing policy configurations for granted or believes them to be the legitimate way of doing things leads us to expect that exclusionary arrangements foster public attitudes that immigrants are undeserving (Jepperson 1991; March and Olsen 1984). A similar expectation relates to what Markus Crepaz (see chapter 4) calls a stigmatization effect: the exclusion of migrants from benefits likely makes their economic difficulties more visible and as such can be expected to encourage xenophobic sentiment. Interestingly, many critics of immigration formulate the exact opposite expectation, namely that generous approaches generate a nativist backlash. Following the literature that criticizes affirmative action programs for leading to widespread concern about positive discrimination (Barry 2001; Sowell 2004; De Zwart 2005), some suggest that immigrant welfare inclusion likely exacerbates xenophobic sentiment (Engelen 2003). This is a common line of reasoning among politicians as well, who frequently justify exclusionary approaches as a way to foster peaceful intergroup relations. In this account, then, exclusion leads to more positive attitudes about immigration. Considering the difficulty of disentangling cause and effect, in this volume we will primarily be interested in the nature of the association between immigrant welfare exclusion and public attitudes about immigration without venturing definitive statements about the direction of causality.

Finally, we will consider two hypotheses about the possible consequences of immigrant exclusion from social programs. The first regards the effect of welfare exclusion on immigrant integration. On the one hand, some have argued that exclusion hinders immigrants' chances of economic integration, because it leaves them on the margins of the labour market with little opportunity to pursue upward social mobility. In support of this line of reasoning, Beatrice Eugster (2018) finds evidence that exclusionary arrangements are more likely to result in widespread poverty among immigrants. In sharp contrast, however, other commentators worry that inclusion discourages economic activity, based either on the more general neoliberal argument that transfer benefits disincentivize employment or the more specific suggestion that immigrants are particularly likely to take advantage of benefits when possible because of the generosity of those benefits compared to the standard of living in their country of origin (Mollenkopf 2000; Hagelund 2005; Koopmans 2010). And while several studies have falsified some of the assumptions on which this line of reasoning seems to be based – namely, that immigrants have a welfare penchant or that inclusionary approaches attract immigrants who are likely to turn to social support (Barrett and McCarthy 2008; Yang and Wallace 2007; Castronova et al. 2001; Moon, Lubben, and Villa 1998; Tienda and Jensen 1986; Kaushal 2005; Huang, Kaushal, and Wang 2020) – this overall expectation still enjoys currency in academic literature and, especially, in political discourse.

Second, we investigate the at least equally controversial effect of welfare exclusion on social spending. For many advocates of exclusion, the expectation that exclusionary approaches will reduce costs barely needs explanation (Grubel and Grady 2011). Some argue, however, that inclusion will likely result in positive economic effects, especially in the long run. This argument is related not only to the above-mentioned expectation that inclusionary approaches will ameliorate immigrants' economic integration and thereby reduce their long-term dependence on the state, but also to the worry that excluding immigrants from mainstream welfare programs will increase the caseloads of other, potentially more costly, programs (Kahanec, Kim, and Zimmerman 2013; Doctors Without Borders 2005). This is a particularly common argument in the area of health care: failing to offer relatively cheap treatment at an early stage may necessitate much more expensive emergency care (which few countries deny to any category of newcomers) at a later time.

Figure 1.1. Overview of theoretical framework

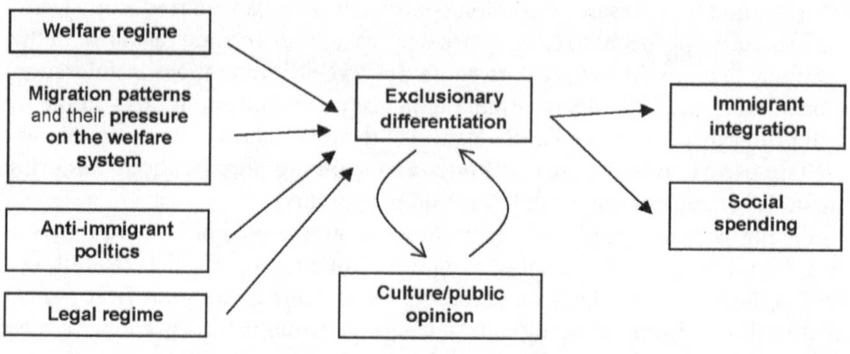

Figure 1.1 summarizes the seven hypotheses that make up the guiding theoretical framework of this volume. It lists four explanatory factors (welfare regime, migration patterns, anti-immigrant politics, and legal regime), one endogenous factor (culture/public opinion), and two outcome variables (integration and social spending). To be clear, this figure only describes the variables that receive central attention in this volume and should *not* be read as a summary of the conclusions we reach about them. As mentioned earlier, the chapters in this volume give us reason to doubt the veracity of some of the hypotheses in this figure.

Similarly important to point out are two limitations to our theoretical model. First, while Figure 1.1 draws attention to those factors that existing literature would lead us to consider most important, it is not comprehensive. Some of the variables that are not included here will be discussed in country chapters for idiosyncratic reasons, but it is also worth stressing that the importance of many variables one might consider is indirect: such factors might explain immigration politics, the welfare regime, or immigrant admission policies and as such primarily help us understand variation in the explanatory variables in the figure.

The second limitation is more intractable: not all variables in Figure 1.1 can easily be separated from one another in empirical terms. Most crucially, the outcome variable "immigrant integration" is closely related to the explanatory variable "migration patterns and their pressure on the welfare system" (after all, the pressure on the welfare system likely increases when immigrants' socio-economic integration deteriorates), and the outcome variable "social spending" is not independent from the explanatory variable "welfare regime" (after all, more universal welfare systems are likely to have higher levels of social expenditure). The empirical analyses have taken up deliberate strategies to address these problems of endogeneity as well as possible, for example by employing lags in the measurement of independent and dependent variables, leveraging both cross-national and cross-temporal variation in the key variables, and employing different operationalizations of the same concepts. (These strategies are discussed in more detail in the chapters where the challenge of endogeneity is most acute – see chapters 3, 5, and 6.)

In assessing the merit of this framework, this volume takes full advantage of the relative strengths of quantitative and qualitative approaches. Each arrow in Figure 1.1 is subjected explicitly to a quantitative investigation: chapter 3 focuses on the first part of the figure (explanatory factors); chapter 4 investigates the role of culture/public opinion (endogenous factor); chapter 5 focuses on the first outcome variable (integration); and chapter 6 on the second outcome variable (social spending). These chapters offer a systematic analysis of what each of these relationships looks like in general. At the same time, this quantitative approach inherently raises challenges related to data availability, degrees of freedom, reliable operationalization, and – as mentioned earlier – endogeneity.

This is where the qualitative chapters come in, which can assess the full picture with more nuance in cases of particular interest and dig a bit deeper into the relevance of some variables for the particular case under investigation than what is feasible to do quantitatively. For example, "anti-immigrant politics" is operationalized in the quantitative cross-national analysis as the participation of right-wing parties in government and the electoral success of the radical right, but is unpacked further in the qualitative analysis of the United States to reveal the importance of bipartisan package deals in which immigrant exclusion is tacked onto large-scale reforms as a way to increase support for the latter in Congress. Similarly, data availability may dictate that "migration patterns" be considered in aggregate terms in some quantitative analyses, but the country chapters demonstrate relevant differences between, for example, EU and non-EU migrants. Moreover, idiosyncratic features, such as Portugal's status as an emigration country and the importance of its colonial history in attracting migrants with a similar linguistic and religious background assume more importance in the case studies than in the quantitative investigation. And finally, the qualitative chapters can dig deeper than what the dataset of welfare differentiation between immigrants and native-born is able to do – the chapter on Norway, for example, reveals forms of exclusion that the quantitative index misses because even general welfare reforms can have an immigrant-targeted flavour to them, considering immigrants' widespread dependence on benefits in that particular context.

Organization of the Volume

The next chapter introduces the database on which much of the analysis in this volume is based: the Immigrant Exclusion from Social Programs Index (IESPI). It describes the conceptualization and operationalization of this index in detail and presents basic descriptive findings. We will see that the level of exclusion from welfare benefits varies dramatically between countries and that there have been large changes over time within countries as well. While the most dramatic forms of exclusion seem less likely today than three decades ago, the overall pattern is one of persistently large cross-national differences and wildly different within-country trajectories. Equally noteworthy is that patterns of inclusion and exclusion seem to differ between social programs – most countries have gradually become less exclusionary in the areas of health care and active labour market policies, yet many have become *more* exclusionary when it comes to extending social assistance benefits.

In chapter 3, Friederike Römer and Liv Bjerre investigate possible explanations for these descriptive findings. Their quantitative investigation considers the extent to which welfare generosity, migration patterns, anti-immigrant politics, and legal safeguards can explain cross-national and longitudinal variation. Their bivariate and multivariate analyses show ample support for the hypothesis that more general welfare generosity drives inclusionary approaches to immigrant welfare access but find no clear evidence that any of the other factors matter. As such, the chapter suggests that national idiosyncrasies may make it difficult to detect aggregate patterns in the drivers of exclusion.

In chapter 4, Markus Crepaz investigates public opinion. Both in bivariate and multivariate analyses that control for a range of relevant factors, his findings consistently show that exclusionary approaches are associated with more negative public attitudes toward immigrants. And while it may be hard to disentangle cause and effect in this type of investigation, these findings cast serious doubt on the suggestion that exclusionary approaches will appease a public that otherwise might feel that immigrants' entitlements are unreasonably generous.

In chapter 5, Anil Duman, Martin Kahanec, and Lucia Mýtna Kureková use the IESPI dataset to analyse the possible consequences of welfare exclusion for immigrant integration. Their multivariate investigation reveals that social policy inclusiveness supports economic integration both in terms of accessing the labour market (measured by labour force participation) and in terms of finding employment (measured by unemployment rates). However, their chapter also shows that the effects vary across different social programs. Inclusion in housing benefits seems to generate particularly positive outcomes, whereas inclusion in social assistance programs seems to "trap" immigrants in substandard labour market outcomes.

Chapter 6 examines the effects of welfare exclusion on social spending. Reasoning that any cost savings generated by welfare exclusion would most likely manifest themselves in the short term, Tsewang Rigzin and Neeraj Kaushal investigate short-term effects and find little evidence to justify welfare exclusion grounded in reducing social expenditure. The savings their models predict are very small and statistically insignificant. Moreover, Kaushal and Rigzin find no evidence that inclusionary approaches attract more newcomers who are likely to turn to the state for support.

After these quantitative investigations, the volume turns to case study research. Chapter 7 tackles the case of Austria, which for the latest data point is the most exclusionary country in the database. Oliver Gruber details the various barriers immigrants face in accessing social benefits and programs in the country and demonstrates that a combination of economic and political variables help explain this outcome. More specifically, a rapid increase in partly uncontrollable migration flows coupled with a hardening political climate drove Austria to craft an overall exclusionary policy apparatus, albeit with very different implications for different categories of immigrants.

Chapter 8 turns to Norway, the most inclusionary case according to the database. Grete Brochmann demonstrates that the country's egalitarian and universal welfare state resulted almost naturally in an inclusionary approach to immigrant entitlements. However, the chapter also shows that this inclusionary approach has depended on a relatively strict admission policy and has come under pressure now that admission control is being circumvented by EEA regulations on free movement: immigrants have struggled to find employment in the skill-demanding economy, opportunities for equal interactions between native-born and immigrant Norwegians are limited, and the anti-immigrant Progress Party has been able to play a larger role in politics and policy-making. Thus her analysis concludes that it would be misleading to characterize the Norwegian experience as an unreserved success story and that some exclusionary adjustments are likely on the horizon.

Chapter 9 tackles the remarkable case of the United States, which simultaneously ranks as the second-most exclusionary case today (after Austria) and as the country that has undergone the second-most exclusionary turn during the time period under investigation (after the Netherlands). Jason Kehrberg, Adam Butz, and Mikhala West review how the politics of immigrant welfare have played out in a country that has long resisted redistributive and universal approaches to social entitlements. The chapter demonstrates that the welfare reforms of the mid-1990s made the already exclusionary nature of the American welfare system even more pronounced; it also highlights the importance of federalism, legislative gridlock, and racial politics in the politics of welfare exclusion in that country.

Chapter 10 analyses the case of Portugal, which is equally unique for the opposite reasons: it ranks as the second-most inclusionary case today (after Norway) and has experienced the most inclusionary turn by far of all cases under investigation (from an aggregate score of 70 on the exclusion index in 1990 to only 23 in 2015). Catarina Reis Oliveira and João Peixoto demonstrate that the combination of a legal regime that protects the rights of minorities, a national narrative that is largely pro-migrant because of Portugal's rich emigration history, and the absence of divisive political actors have together made policy-makers keen to remove any barriers to immigrants' social entitlements. At the same time, Reis Oliveira and Peixoto stress that the large strides toward formal equality have (so far) not resulted in equal outcomes: immigrants in Portugal are still more likely to live in vulnerable economic conditions than their native-born counterparts.

The final three chapters subject the findings from this volume to overall reflections. In chapter 11, Christian Joppke considers the developments in immigrant welfare exclusion in light of the more general developments of globalization and the spread of neoliberalism. His argument revisits the long-standing discussion about whether rising cross-border mobility necessitates a smaller role for redistribution.

Will Kymlicka pursues a normative evaluation of the volume's key findings in chapter 12. His analysis demonstrates that normative political philosophy tends to struggle in theorizing a just approach to immigrants' access to social programs and benefits, because this subject seems to fall within "a grey zone between humanitarian and citizenship-based conceptions of fairness." He suggests that barriers to welfare access are particularly problematic in jurisdictions that do not provide newcomers with an effective ladder to full inclusion. The moral significance of welfare exclusion depends not only on the size of the benefits being denied at a given point in time but also on whether this status is "sticky," relegating newcomers to long periods of disadvantage or precarity. This in turn raises questions about how welfare exclusion interacts with broader policies of immigrant integration and citizenship.

The volume closes with a summary of the key conclusions that the analyses in this volume seem to suggest. Keith Banting pulls the various threads of the volume together to consider what they mean for the political feasibility of an inclusive welfare state. Overall, Banting concludes that the volume offers grounds for optimism, suggesting that the prospects for inclusion in an era of immigration are not as bleak as political rhetoric tends to suggest.

2 The IESPI and Descriptive Findings

EDWARD A. KONING

This chapter introduces the Immigrant Exclusion from Social Programs Index (hereafter: IESPI). It outlines the underlying conceptualization that distinguishes different ways in which a welfare system can differentiate in benefit extension between native-born citizens and immigrants, describes the process of data collection, elaborates on the coding of each indicator, and presents basic descriptive findings. Readers who are interested primarily in the key questions that motivate this volume, such as why some countries pursue more exclusionary approaches than others, which kinds of approaches seem most conducive to favourable outcomes, or how immigrant welfare inclusion or exclusion plays out in concrete cases, can move straight to the next chapters. My main goals here are to clarify the methodology that produced the IESPI and to demonstrate that it captures striking variation across time, place, and social programs in the extent to which immigrants are excluded from social programs and services.

The overall pattern of immigrant welfare exclusion the database reveals can be summarized with three observations. First, there are very large differences between countries regarding the extent to which they differentiate between immigrants and native-born in the extension of social programs and benefits. Second, on aggregate there has been a slight reduction over time in exclusionary practices, especially their most extreme manifestations. Third, there is no sign of cross-national convergence. Many countries have moved in an inclusionary direction over time, but others have followed the opposite trajectory of throwing up more hurdles for immigrants' access to social programs, and yet others have simultaneously implemented inclusionary and exclusionary policy changes. As a result, cross-national variation is still as large as it was in the 1990s. It is worth underscoring the importance of these observations. Considering that the countries being investigated are all Western liberal democracies and that many are member states of a powerful supranational organization – the European Union – the lack of policy convergence is striking indeed. This chapter discusses the conceptualization of the IESPI, the methods of data collection, and the components of the index in some detail; it then turns to what the data suggest about cross-national and cross-temporal patterns of immigrant welfare exclusion.

Conceptualization and Purpose

The IESPI measures the level of differentiation between immigrants and native-born citizens in the extension of social programs. Following the theoretical framework I developed elsewhere (Koning 2019), it considers four different mechanisms by which social programs may be less accessible to newcomers than to individuals who have resided in the country all their lives.[1] First, a program may pose *length of residence* requirements, demanding that applicants have resided in the country (or, as is sometimes the case with housing benefits, the municipality) for a minimum period. Second, it may set *status* requirements, including certain classes of migrants (for example, permanent residents) while excluding others (e.g., individuals on an international student permit). Third, it may pose *integration* requirements, requiring newcomers to demonstrate "successful integration" (typically by participating in or completing language and/or integration programs) as a condition for benefit access. And finally, a program may set restrictions on the *location of residence*, meaning that immigrants may become ineligible if they return to their country of origin.

In addition to these mechanisms by which a welfare state may be less accessible to immigrants, the index considers the presence of targeted policies designed specifically to ameliorate newcomers' interactions with the welfare state in particular or socio-economic integration in general, such as funded language training or culturally sensitive health care delivery. Of course, one might argue that a failure to offer such programs does not constitute welfare exclusion. Whether such an argument seems persuasive likely depends on one's more general views about the merits of affirmative action programs, a discussion I cannot engage here. All that matters for our current purposes is that including these programs allows for a more fine-grained assessment of the extent to which a welfare system adopts an inclusionary or exclusionary approach to newcomers. At the very least, it seems reasonable to view a welfare state that offers such programs as less exclusionary than a welfare state that does not.

By incorporating a variety of differentiating policy features, the index captures just how important the personal characteristics of individual migrants are for their place in a welfare system. After all, no immigration regime treats all immigrants equally. Undocumented migrants and asylum claimants, for example, are faced with a wildly different policy response than high-skilled labour migrants. Newly arrived immigrants are in a very different position than those who have lived in the country for a long time. And migrants who intend to stay for a couple of years of employment have different rights than those who plan to settle permanently. In other words, the index recognizes explicitly that some categories of migrants face more exclusion than others, documents variation in the number of categories that are excluded, and considers how badly excluded the worst-off categories are.

The IESPI includes 25 indicators related to seven publicly funded[2] social programs: tax-paid pension programs, public health care services or health care subsidies, contributory unemployment benefits, contributory pension programs, housing benefits, social assistance, and active labour market policies (including immigrant-targeted programs such as integration assistance). Three criteria informed the selection of these seven programs. First, they exist in almost every welfare system and therefore lend themselves well to cross-national analysis. It would be difficult to make clean comparisons between countries based on differentiation in access to sickness benefits, for example, because some welfare states offer such benefits but others do not. Second, they commonly exhibit differentiation between immigrants and native-born. Introducing public education for children, for example, would introduce no variation in the index because all countries are required to offer schooling to underaged children regardless of immigrant status. Third, these programs can be isolated both analytically and empirically with relative ease. Including parental benefits, for example, would create redundancy (Bjerre et al. 2015) considering that many countries tie such benefits to contributory unemployment programs. An elaborate discussion of each indicator is provided below.

High scores on the index indicate that immigrants have considerably less access to these programs than native-born citizens. Low scores suggest that the welfare system is inclusionary of immigrants. In other words, the key concept the index measures is *social policy differentiation*: the degree to which access to social programs is different for immigrants than for native-born citizens. This means that the indicators do not convey any information about the generosity of the programs in absolute terms: a generous welfare system that throws up many barriers for immigrants would receive a higher score than a leaner system that treats immigrants the same as native-born citizens. Indeed, a country could offer many programs and services to immigrants and still receive a high score on this index if the services it offers to native-born citizens are even more generous. This approach has the considerable advantage of avoiding conceptual conflation with a country's welfare system in general. As has been well-documented, the welfare state has undergone considerable change over the last three decades (Huber and Stephens 2001; Kvist et al. 2012). Because the IESPI exclusively measures whether immigrants have access to fewer or lower benefits than native-born citizens, any changes it documents cannot be conflated with more general welfare state change. Moreover, this approach allows one to empirically investigate (rather than theoretically hypothesize) how, if at all, welfare generosity and welfare inclusiveness are related – a particularly interesting line of inquiry considering the ongoing controversy over whether welfare generosity and inclusiveness go hand and hand, or conversely, whether an inclusive approach to immigrants' welfare rights necessitates across-the-board welfare retrenchment (see also chapters 3, 11, and 13).

A similarly important clarification is that the index does not directly measure a country's residence or admission policy. For example, some indicators capture which types of permits make migrants ineligible for a program but do not contain information on how many individuals are on such a permit. Indirectly, however, the index does capture aspects of a country's immigration regime. If, for example, a program is available only to permanent residents and the country only allows newcomers to apply for permanent residence status after five years, the program will be considered as having a residence requirement of five years as well.

A final cautionary note is that in measuring policy, the index is unable to capture how benefit extension plays out in practice. Several studies have documented that some immigrants do not access the programs to which they are entitled, either because they are not aware of their entitlement or because they face unhelpful or hostile service providers (Ma and Chi 2005; Capps, Hagan, and Rodriguez 2004). Conversely, sometimes immigrants can access services to which they are not legally entitled, for example, when health care professionals treat undocumented migrants they are technically supposed to refuse or when the authorities who determine benefit eligibility are unable to verify residence status (Alexander 2010; Koning and Banting 2013). There are two main reasons to focus on formal policy rather than actual practice. The first is admittedly pragmatic: it is much more challenging to find cross-nationally and longitudinally reliable information on actual patterns of benefit extension as opposed to formal policy features. But the second and more important reason, again, is that including indicators on the practical extension of benefits to immigrants would lead to conceptual conflation and make it impossible to use the index to investigate the relationship between policy and practice (and explore, for example, whether the actual use of benefits by immigrants as documented in household surveys is greater in countries where those benefits are more formally accessible as measured in the IESPI).

The key purpose of the IESPI is to offer a general and comparable overview of immigrants' inclusion in welfare systems and, as such, to enable comparative assessments of the level of exclusion in any given welfare regime. Certainly, there are several existing studies that help in making such assessments. However, much of the literature has so far consisted of case studies and comparative case studies (Fix 2009; Boucher 2014; Sainsbury 2012; Banting and Koning 2017). Quantitative comparisons have been less common, although not entirely absent. Beatrice Eugster (2018) has compared immigrants' access to unemployment, social assistance, and family benefits in 19 countries in 2007. The Migrant

Integration Policy Index, which describes policies and policy outcomes in 38 countries between 2004 and 2020, includes information on immigrants' access to active labour market policies and health care (Huddleston et al. 2015). And the even more impressive Immigration Policies in Comparison Project, which measures a wide range of immigration-related policy indicators for a large number of countries since 1990, includes some indicators on migrants' access to social and unemployment insurance (Bjerre et al. 2016). These databases are invaluable, but they are not fully suited for the purposes of this volume. They include fewer programs, fewer forms of exclusion, and fewer categories of migrants than the IESPI; they also tend to measure immigrants' entitlements in absolute terms instead of comparing them to the entitlements of native-born citizens (and as such, they risk conflating the generosity and the inclusivity of a welfare system; see the preceding discussion).

More than any existing index, then, the IESPI can ground the typically heated arguments about whether a welfare system is overly inclusionary or exclusionary toward immigrants in empirical reality. In addition, the index allows an investigation of best practices. As several chapters in this volume illustrate, there are tangible consequences to pursuing an inclusionary or exclusionary approach, and the IESPI makes it possible to document them. This means we can also use the index to investigate explanations for divergence from those practices – in other words, to identify barriers to effective policy-making in the area of immigration and welfare.

This volume hopes to bring existing literature forward by engaging exactly these questions. Of course, future researchers can use the IESPI for other investigations as well. For example, rather than assessing levels of welfare exclusion in general terms, one could pursue targeted investigations of exclusion in particular policies. Similarly, the index could be used in tandem with other data to pursue a range of other investigations. For example, researchers might combine the IESPI with permit data to measure the number of individuals who are affected by exclusionary measures, with data on uptake levels to compare policy and practice, or with data on welfare generosity to measure the overall reach of a welfare state.

Methods of Data Collection

Data collection proceeded in three stages. First, based on the conceptualization described above I established a list of policy features by which we might expect the seven social programs under study to differentiate between native-born and immigrant residents. A large research team of undergraduate and graduate students[3] then collected information on each of these features by reviewing existing scholarly literature, analysing government and policy documents, and conducting follow-up interviews with civil servants. In the second stage,

I coded the data using a range from 0 to 4 for each indicator. To maximize variation in the index, I determined the coding scheme inductively: for every policy feature, I compared approaches in all the countries and time periods for which the research team had collected data and then assigned a value of 0 to the most inclusionary approach, a value of 4 to the most exclusionary approach, and the values of 1, 2, and 3 for approaches that fell somewhere between these extremes. This means – as will be discussed in more detail in the following section – that the codes for each program vary from one another based on the range of variation in the 22 countries and the four points in time under investigation. For example, when it comes to health care, housing benefits, and social assistance, we encountered instances where undocumented migrants were granted access, and therefore the most inclusionary score on the indicators regarding status requirements indicates a regime that includes undocumented migrants. This category of immigrants has invariably been excluded from the other four programs, however, and therefore the indicators on status requirements for those programs do not consider them (see also note 7).

In the third stage, I assigned the codes by following the original data collection, double-checking the original sources, and cross-validating the information with additional sources and email inquiries. This final step aimed to ensure that the codes were consistently applied and accurately described the policy regimes under study. When constructing policy indexes, researchers sometimes rely on multiple coders as a further test of validation, especially when the codes are open to interpretation. The reason this approach was not followed here is that most coding decisions were unambiguous once the relevant sources had been identified – for example, the duration of a formal residence requirement would not be coded differently by different researchers using the same codebook. In any event, it is worth noting that for as far as we can assess, the face validity and convergent validity of the IESPI data are high. The results presented below (see Figure 2.1) match up well with the findings of comparative case study research (Sainsbury 2012; Koning 2019) and correlate strongly with existing quantitative indicators of immigrants' social rights. The correlation between IESPI data from 2010 and the data Eugster (2018) collected on immigrants' access to unemployment and social assistance benefits in 2007 is 0.76 ($p < 0.001$); the correlation between IESPI data from 2010 and IMPIC (Bjerre et al. 2016) data from 2010 is 0.60 ($p = 0.014$); and the correlation between IESPI data and MIPEX (Huddleston et al. 2015) data from 2010 on active labour market policies, social security, and health care is 0.64 ($p < 0.001$) (see Koning 2020). Of course, we would not expect anything resembling perfect relationships here considering the differences between the IESPI and these indicators, but these findings nevertheless increase confidence in the validity of our data.

Data have been collected for 22 countries (Australia, Austria, Belgium, Canada, Denmark, Finland, France, Germany, Iceland, Ireland, Italy, Luxembourg,

Malta, Netherlands, New Zealand, Norway, Portugal, Spain, Sweden, Switzerland, United Kingdom, and United States) and four time periods (1990, 2000, 2010, and 2015). Two considerations motivated the selection of these countries. First, they are similar enough to enable reliable comparisons: they are all established liberal democracies with an institutionalized welfare apparatus (which is why they are typically included in investigations of social policy in Western democracies). At the same time, and as will be amply demonstrated in the remainder of this volume, they differ from one another on the key variables of interest (see Figure 1.1) – for example, the sample includes social democratic, conservative, and liberal welfare regimes; countries with very different migration patterns in terms of history, volume, and categories of migrants; countries with wildly different experiences regarding the success of anti-immigrant politicians and parties; and countries in which governments face varying levels of constraint by national and supranational legal structures. Of course, this sample could theoretically be expanded: future research might take the indicators of the IESPI and apply them to democracies in Central and Eastern Europe, Central and South America, and/or South and East Asia. The only qualification is that because the coding has been determined inductively based on variation among Western welfare states, some of the codes might have to be adjusted to accommodate policy features in countries that are currently not included.

Two issues deserve separate attention. First, in some countries some of the programs are operated at the subnational level, which makes establishing a country-wide regime somewhat challenging. As chapter 9 illustrates, in the extreme example of the United States just how much access immigrants have to social programs differs considerably from one state to another. To address this complication, the IESPI measures immigration policies and frameworks at the national/federal level. National-level policies have a large imprint on immigrants' eligibility even in countries where social programs are run by subnational authorities. Even in the most federalized systems, the national/federal government tends to determine the residence status of newcomers and as such often sets eligibility criteria indirectly. Also, it is usually in charge of the accommodation and treatment of refugees and asylum seekers and therefore determines the services and programs these categories of migrants can access. And finally, it frequently establishes frameworks within which subnational policies are allowed to differ or that at the very least can serve as an "average" of the variation between subnational units (Koning 2018).[4]

A second issue to highlight is the special privilege EU citizens enjoy in all member states. They not only are free to move from one member state to another but also enjoy largely the same entitlements to social programs and benefits as native-born citizens, at least if they are employed (Stokke 2007; Barbalescu and Favell 2019). Fortunately, the unique position of EU citizens did not pose serious complications for the systematic comparisons this dataset pursues. As mentioned earlier, one of the indicators for every program under study concerns status requirements, that is, what type of permit would make a newcomer eligible. Many welfare systems treat EU migrants as permanent residents, and their privileged position is therefore captured in the index as such. In a few instances, EU citizens are treated better than permanent residents from outside the union, in which case the status requirements are coded as more exclusionary (see for example, indicator TPP3 and ALM2 in Table 2.1).

The main reason to start the investigation of policy developments in 1990 is that in most of the countries under study, immigrants' place in the welfare system did not attract much attention and was not even explicitly legislated before that year. A related and more practical reason is the challenge of collecting pre-1990 data: policy documents are less accessible, and it is harder to identify civil servants who can speak about the policy regime. Again, of course, future research might expand the time span of the dataset and apply the indicators to developments before 1990 or after 2015.

Components of the IESPI

As mentioned earlier, the IESPI consists of 25 indicators that measure social policy differentiation between immigrants and native-born citizens. These indicators, and the associated values, are summarized in Table 2.1 and discussed in more detail below. See the appendix to this volume for the scores for each country and each point in time on each of these indicators.

Four indicators measure the level of differentiation in *tax-paid pension benefits.* The first considers how many years of residence are required to access a universal pension program (where such a program exists). Such residence requirements can differ considerably from one place to another – for example, New Zealand only requires 10 years of residence, whereas in the Netherlands pensioners can access a complete benefit only if they have resided in the country for at least 50 years. The second indicator measures whether the country offers a means-tested pension that can partly compensate for a low pension income resulting from a short history of residence in the country. Some countries, such as Luxembourg, do not and consequently force low-income elderly to resort to social assistance. Others do, but among them some set lengthy residence requirements to access means-tested pensions (in Australia, for example, 10 years of residence are required), while others make them immediately available (such as Germany since 2001).[5] The third indicator considers the status requirements for accessing (universal or means-tested) tax-paid pension programs. While some countries (such as Iceland) make them available to all legal residents, others exclude immigrants on temporary permits or, in extreme cases, all foreigners (Malta, for example, only extends its tax-paid pension benefit to Maltese citizens and, since it joined the EU, to citizens of other EU states

Table 2.1. Indicators and values of the IESPI

Tax-paid Pension

Residence requirement (TPP1): 0: Less than 5 years; 1: Between 5 and 10 years; 2: More than 10 but less than 40 years, with pro-rating; 3: 40 years, with pro-rating; 4: More than 40 years, with pro-rating

Availability of top-up (TPP2): 0: With residence of less than a year; 1: With residence between 1 and 3 years; 2: With residence of more than 3 but less than 10 years; 3: With residence of at least 10 years; 4: Not available

Status requirement (TPP3): 0: All legal residents; 1: Citizens and all permanent residents; 2: Citizens and most permanent residents; 3: Citizens and specially designated groups only; 4: Citizens only

Export possibilities (TPP4):* 0: Without restrictions; 1: With additional residence requirements; 2: With cuts in benefits; 3: During very short stay abroad only; 4: Not possible

Health Care (Subsidies)

Residence requirement (HC1): 0: No waiting period; 1: Less than 6 weeks; 2: More than 6 weeks but less than 1 year; 3: 1 year of residence or contributions; 4: More than 1 year of residence or contributions

Status requirement (HC2): 0: Access for all; 1: Restrictions for undocumented; 2: Restrictions for undocumented and some other; 3: Undocumented excluded entirely; 4: Undocumented and some others excluded entirely

Accessibility services (HC3): 0: State-funded translation and cultural sensitivity; 1: State-funded translation; 2: Services exist but are not fully funded; 3: Incidental programs or translated written documents; 4: Nothing available

Additional benefits (HC4): 0: Expanded coverage for refugees and claimants; 1: Expanded coverage for some refugees or claimants; 2: Specialized services for refugees; 3: Incidental services; 4: Nothing available

Contributory Unemployment Benefits

Status requirement (CUB1): 0: All legal residents; 1: International students and/or seasonal workers excluded; 2: Asylum seekers excluded; 3: Most temporary residents excluded; 4: Permanent residents and citizens only

Integration requirement (CUB2): 0: No integration requirements; 1: Integration requirements exist but are not enforced; 2: Access tied to permits with integration requirements; 4: Integration and language requirements

Export possibilities (CUB3): 0: With cuts in benefits; 2: During short stay abroad only; 4: Not possible

Contributory Pension

Status requirement (CP1): 0: All legal residents; 1: Temporary excluded but can opt out of premium payments; 3: Some temporary excluded; 4: All temporary excluded

Export possibilities (CP2):* 0: Without restrictions; 1: With additional restrictions; 2: With cuts in benefits; 3: Only possible for citizens; 4: Not possible

(*Continued*)

Table 2.1. Indicators and values of the IESPI (*Continued*)

Housing Benefits

Residence requirement (HB1): 0: None; 1: 1 year or less; 2: 2 years; 3: 3 or 4 years; 4: More than 4 years

Status requirement (HB2): 0: All residents; 1: All legal residents; 2: Some temporary migrants excluded; 3: Only citizens and permanent residents; 4: Some permanent residents excluded

Integration requirement (HB3): 0: No integration requirement; 2: Access tied to permit with integration requirements; 4: Integration and/or language requirements

Privileged access (HB4): 0: Earmarked housing for various groups of migrants; 1: Earmarked housing for refugees; 2: Housing assistance for refugees; 3: Services exist but are not fully funded; 4: No privileged access

Social Assistance

Residence requirement (SA1): 0: None; 1: Only for some categories, such as family migrants; 2: 1 year or less; 3: 5 years or less (but more than 1 year); 4: More than 5 years

Status requirement (SA2): 0: All residents; 1: All legal residents; 2: Some temporary migrants excluded; 3: All permanent residents; 4: Only citizens and some permanent residents

Consequences of uptake (SA3): 0: No consequences; 1: Delayed access to permanent residence or citizenship; 2: Inaccessible permanent residence or citizenship; 3: Non-renewal of permit; 4: Revocation of permit

Integration requirements (SA4): 0: None; 1: Can be requested at discretion; 2: Only for refugee-targeted assistance benefits; 3: Access tied to permits with integration requirements; 4: Compulsory integration

Active Labour Market Policies

Residence requirement (ALM1): 0: None; 2: Access tied to benefits requiring work or residence history; 4: More than 1 year

Status requirement (ALM2): 0: All legal residents; 1: Some temporary excluded; 2: All citizens and permanent residents; 4: Citizens and privileged non-nationals only

Immigrant-targeted language programs (ALM3): 0: Fully funded for all; 1: Existing, but not freely available to all; 2: Visa fee levied for access to language programs; 3: Some rebate upon successful completion; 4: None

Immigrant-targeted employment assistance (ALM4): 0: Available to all; 1: Available for refugees and some other migrants; 2: Only for refugees and/or asylum seekers; 3: Programs offered incidentally or unevenly; 4 None

Missing values are assigned where the program does not exist, unless the very absence of the program signals lack of accommodation (as is the case for indicators TPP2, HC3, HC4, HB4, ALM3, ALM4).* If the rules differ depending on the country to which the benefit is exported, the values are weighted by the relative size of the foreign-born population from those countries, for as far as data availability in the OECD International Migration Database permits.

as well). The final indicator considers the possibilities to enjoy the pension benefit while residing abroad. Some countries set no restrictions in that regard if applicants meet the status and residence requirements, while others pose additional requirements, reduce the benefit level, or even make export impossible. In many countries, the rules for exporting benefits are determined by bilateral and multilateral social security agreements and therefore differ depending on the citizenship of the applicant or the country to which the benefit is exported. For example, exporting the Finnish pension is possible without restrictions to Switzerland and all EU and EEA member states, requires additional residence requirements for the United States, Canada, Chile, and Israel, will result in benefit cuts for Australia, and is only possible for a period of up to one year to other countries. Whenever a country employs such complicated rules, the score on this indicator is weighted by the relative size of the immigrant population from each category of countries according to the OECD International Migration Database (OECD 2020).[6]

Regarding public *health care*, the index measures four possible vectors of differentiation. First, it considers residence requirements. In many countries, newcomers are immediately eligible for public health care services or health care subsidies, but some countries (such as Canada) mandate short waiting periods and some even set lengthy residence requirements (e.g., since 2004 most non-EU migrants in the United Kingdom have been unable to access health care during their first five years in the country). A second indicator measures status requirements. While some countries (such as Portugal since 2001) open their health care system to all residents, others are more restrictive. Some regimes exclude not only undocumented but also some categories of legal residents from regular public health care, and in extreme cases, from emergency care as well. Third, the index measures whether the health care system undertakes targeted efforts to make services more accessible to immigrants. Some countries (such as Australia) go quite far in this respect, offering not only funded translation services but also opportunities for culturally sensitive health care service delivery. In other countries, such as Italy, no such services exist, at least not in the public sphere (see also note 2). The fourth indicator considers the presence of additional health care services that are exclusively available to immigrants. Some countries (such as Canada and Norway) offer refugees and refugee claimants health care services that are not freely available to other residents, such as dental care, ophthalmological care, or refugee-targeted mental health programs. Many other countries, however, do not offer any such programs.

To measure differentiation in *contributory unemployment benefits*, the index employs three indicators.[7] First, it considers status requirements. In some places (such as France), all legal residents become eligible under the same conditions as native-born citizens as soon as they take up work, but most countries place more restrictions, barring some or all categories of residents who hold a temporary permit. Second, it considers whether immigrants must satisfy certain criteria of successful integration before they can access these benefits. Most countries do not, but since the turn of the century Iceland, the Netherlands, and the United Kingdom have imposed such requirements, either directly or indirectly (i.e., the benefits are available only for migrants on permits that come with integration requirements). Third, the index measures the possibilities for retaining built-up entitlement to these benefits when moving abroad. Most countries either do not or only allow it for a short time to a limited number of countries. Since 2008, however, immigrants in Spain can receive 60% of their accrued benefits up front if they leave the country when they fall unemployed.

Two indicators consider the program under study that usually features the least differentiation between immigrant and native-born residents, *contributory pension benefits.* First, it measures status requirements. Most countries only require a legal work history and do not make any demands in this respect, but some countries (such as Austria and Denmark) throw up additional hurdles for some or all residents on a temporary permit. Second, it considers export possibilities. Again, in most cases immigrants can retain the pension benefits they accrued if they move abroad, but some countries pose additional restrictions, for example, reducing the benefit level or prohibiting the practice for non-citizens. And as was the case with the export of universal benefits, often these types of restrictions differ depending on the country to which the benefit is exported; therefore the value of this indicator is weighted to account for the origins of the foreign-born population (see also note 6).

Next, four indicators measure differentiation in the extension of housing benefits, such as rent subsidies, housing allowances, and/or access to social housing. First, the index considers residence requirements: some countries (such as Belgium) do not pose these at all, while others only extend benefits to newcomers who have been in the country for a long time (Austria, for example, demands as much as five years of residence). The second indicator measures status requirements, for which there is also significant cross-national variation: in some regimes even undocumented migrants can be eligible (as was the case in the Netherlands before 1998), whereas in others not even all permanent residents can avail themselves of these benefits (in Malta, for example, only EU citizens and recognized refugees can access them). The third indicator considers whether access to these benefits depends on successful integration, which a small number of countries have recently started demanding. Fourth, the index measures whether (some groups of) immigrants have privileged access to social housing. Some countries (such as Portugal) reserve portions of their social housing for refugees or temporary foreign workers, and others (such as New Zealand) offer extensive housing assistance to recognized refugees when they first arrive in the country. Other countries, however, offer no such services.

Differentiation in probably the most contentious program, *social assistance*, is measured by four indicators. The first indicator considers residence requirements, which can differ considerably from one context to another. For example, in Norway all newcomers are immediately eligible if they satisfy the other eligibility criteria, whereas in the Netherlands immigrants are in most cases ineligible during their first five years in the country. Second, the index measures status requirements, which can vary considerably, from granting welfare even to undocumented migrants at one extreme to excluding some categories of permanent residents at the other. Third, it considers whether taking up social assistance can have negative consequences for immigrants' residence status. For example, immigrants who go on welfare will become ineligible for citizenship in Denmark, may be denied renewal of their residence status in Finland, and can even lose their existing status in Germany. The fourth indicator measures integration requirements. As discussed in the context of unemployment and housing benefits, some countries require immigrants to satisfy certain standards of integration to access welfare, either directly or indirectly (i.e., by tying such requirements to the necessary permits). Norway and Sweden employ a less punitive variation of such requirements: refugees and asylum seekers receive a targeted social assistance benefit at a slightly higher level if they participate in an integration trajectory but lose it if they do not.

A final set of indicators measures differentiation in active labour market policies (ALMPs). The first indicator considers residence requirements. Whereas some countries allow immigrants to enrol in ALMPs as soon as they arrive, others grant immigrants access only after a waiting period. Many countries tie access to these programs to contributory unemployment programs and thus indirectly pose a requirement of prolonged residence (or, more accurately, work history). Second, the index considers status requirements. We again see much cross-national variation, with some countries opening ALMPs to any legal residents but others excluding some categories of temporary or even permanent residents. Finally, the index considers the presence of programs that are not often treated as active labour market policies in existing literature but that certainly perform the function of encouraging employment and upward social mobility: immigrant-targeted language programs and immigrant-targeted employment programs. Some countries do not offer any such programs, while others offer a wide range of freely available programs specifically designed to assist immigrants with language training, job-seeking, reschooling, or internship opportunities.

In the existing literature, such integration policies are sometimes described as punitive arrangements (Schierup and Ålund 2011; Gebhardt 2016), and it might therefore seem curious that the IESPI treats them as indicators of inclusion. Such an evaluation, however, depends largely on whether participation in these programs is mandatory. A publicly funded program that aims to assist

Figure 2.1. Summary scores of the IESPI, 2015

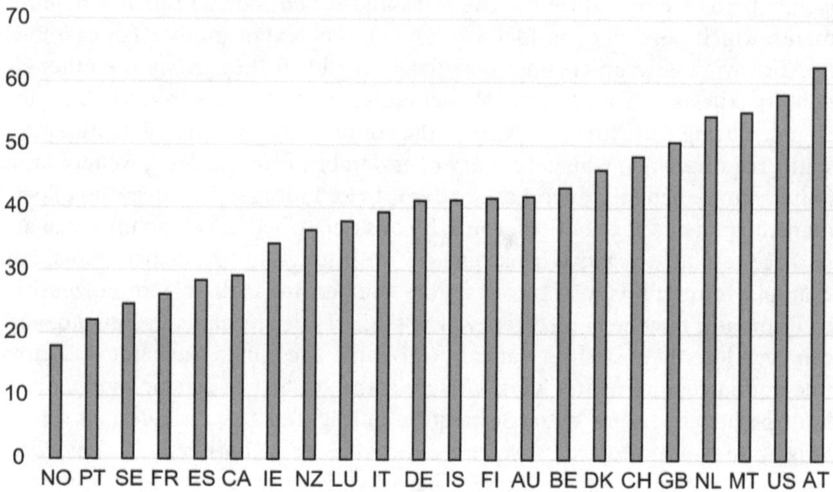

immigrants' language acquisition and employment opportunities can hardly be described as exclusionary if immigrants can decide whether they want to participate or not. The situation is different, of course, if non-participation has consequences such as a loss of benefit access. In such instances, the punitive nature is captured elsewhere in the index (in particular, by indicators CUB2, HB3, and SA4).

Descriptive Findings

Before we move to the subsequent chapters that analyse the data from the IESPI in detail, this section presents some basic and descriptive findings. Figure 2.1 reports the summary scores of all 22 countries under study for the year 2015.

These scores are calculated by taking the average score of all indicators for each program, then taking the average of all program averages, and then multiplying the value by 25 to end up with a score between 0 and 100. This results in a straightforward numerical summary of the extent to which the welfare system excludes immigrants. The reasons to use program averages (instead of, for example, adding up the values for all 25 indicators) are twofold. First, in cases where specific programs or program features do not exist in a country this technique ensures that the missing values do not artificially lower the summary score. Second, this technique recognizes that the social program (and not the individual indicator) is the most relevant unit of analysis and ensures that programs with many indicators (such as social assistance) will not weigh more heavily than those with fewer (such as contributory pension benefits).[8]

As becomes obvious, the cross-national differences are large. Some welfare systems, such as those in Norway and Portugal, are highly inclusionary of immigrants, whereas others, such as those in the United States and Austria, are much more difficult to access. In other words, while the former obtain low scores on almost all indicators discussed in the previous section, the latter adopt an exclusionary approach in almost all these respects. Chapters 7 to 10, which pursue detailed investigations of these four extreme cases, offer further illustration of what the differences in these scores mean in practical terms.

Table 2.2 presents a more fine-grained overview of each country's approach to incorporating immigrants in its welfare system. It presents the average scores for each of the seven programs in 2015 separately. Two observations stand out. First, and much in line with what we saw earlier, we see very large differences between countries in the extent to which they open these seven social programs to immigrants. Second, we also see striking variation in the degree to which different programs within one country differentiate between immigrants and native-born citizens. Overall, it is true that the scores on separate indicators and program averages are positively correlated with each other. But these correlations are far from perfect: a reliability analysis of all program averages results in only a moderately high Cronbach's alpha of 0.76, and a principal component analysis suggests that while the best solution is to extract a single component, its explained variance is only 44%. In other words, while there is empirical support for combining these indicators in a single index, it is clearly important to distinguish different social programs and policy features. After all, the separate components of this index can vary relatively independently from one another. An inclusionary approach in one area can mitigate exclusion in another – for example, the availability of free language and integration courses in Belgium makes the integration requirements for accessing social assistance there less onerous. Existing research that compares immigrants' welfare rights across many countries tends to focus on a single policy or program characteristic (see also above). The findings in Table 2.2 demonstrate that using such research to generalize about the social rights of immigrants in general could be highly misleading.

Besides measuring cross-national variation, the IESPI captures developments over time. Figure 2.2 plots the overall trajectory of immigrant welfare exclusion in the countries under study. More specifically, the box-and-whisker plot shows the quartile range (depicted by the box) and the full range (portrayed by the whiskers) of the 22 countries for each of the four time periods for which data have been collected (1990, 2000, 2010, and 2015). For example, Figure 2.2 shows that in 1990, the highest score any country obtained on the IESPI was 74, the minimum score was 26, and the middle 50% of cases had scores between

Table 2.2. IESPI scores by program, 2015

Country	TPP	HC	CUB	CP	HB	SA	ALM	Mean
Norway (NO)	21	19	42	0	13	25	6	18
Portugal (PT)	42	31	25	0	6	44	6	22
Sweden (SE)	35	44	25	0	38	25	6	25
France (FR)	59	56	17	2	13	38	0	26
Spain (ES)	50	56	8	9	31	25	19	28
Canada (CA)	50	44	42	0	31	19	19	29
Ireland (IE)	50	31	33	0	38	38	50	34
New Zealand (NZ)	31	25	n/a	38	44	38	44	36
Luxembourg (LU)	100	69	33	0	6	44	13	38
Italy (IT)	58	63	42	0	63	38	13	39
Germany (DE)	42	50	42	11	38	81	25	41
Iceland (IS)	39	69	58	n/a	19	38	25	41
Finland (FI)	43	44	42	38	19	81	25	42
Australia (AU)	57	38	n/a	13	56	31	56	42
Belgium (BE)	67	44	50	14	31	56	41	43
Denmark (DK)	56	50	42	38	31	81	25	46
Switzerland (CH)	50	44	33	11	100	63	38	48
United Kingdom (GB)	50	63	58	14	69	56	44	51
Netherlands (NL)	43	38	67	n/a	31	81	69	55
Malta (MT)	92	63	33	38	75	38	50	55
United States (US)	67	75	58	51	38	69	50	58
Austria (AT)	58	69	42	50	94	81	44	63

34 and 55. All in all, the graph offers an easily interpretable overview of the aggregate trend in immigrant welfare exclusion, both in terms of direction (i.e., whether countries are on average becoming more exclusionary or inclusionary) and variation (i.e., whether we are witnessing cross-national convergence or divergence).

Two observations are worth emphasizing. First, the overall direction of change seems to be inclusionary, although the changes over time are not dramatic and the trend does not seem to continue after 2010. Much of this pattern can be explained by inclusionary developments in some of the countries with the highest scores in 1990 (the IESPI score for Malta, for example, decreased from 74 in 1990 to 55 in 2015, and the value for Portugal dropped even more dramatically, from 70 in 1990 to 23 in 2015). Second, there is no sign of policy convergence: the differences between countries remain roughly equally large over time. Indeed, the graph shows relatively little change in the size of the boxes (spanning 21 points in 1990, 18 in 2000, 19 in 2010, and 20 in 2015) and the whiskers (indicating a range of 48 points in 1990, 47 in 2000, 48 in 2010, and 45 in 2015).

Setting aside the relative stability in the overall size of cross-national differences, there has been much change within individual countries. Closer inspection reveals that the policy trajectories in the 22 countries follow one of four

Figure 2.2. Overall trajectory of change in welfare exclusion, 1990–2015

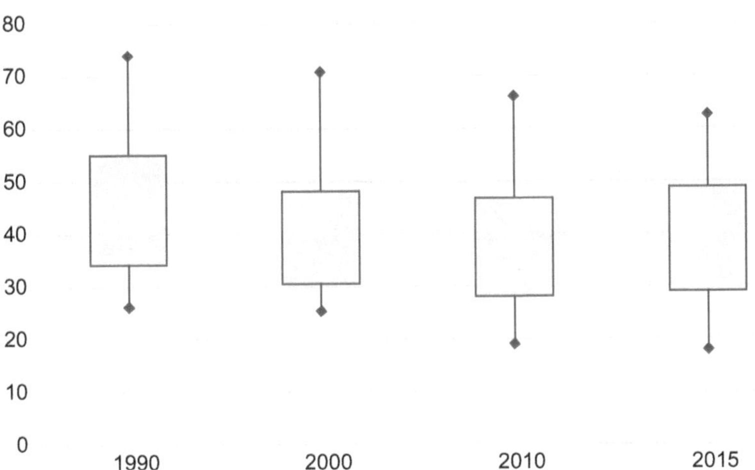

Graph shows quartile range (box) and full range (whiskers) of IESPI scores for all 22 countries.

trends. In nine of these countries (Finland, France, Germany, Luxembourg, Malta, New Zealand, Norway, Portugal, and Switzerland), social programs have steadily become more accessible to immigrants over time. In four others (Australia, the Netherlands, the United Kingdom, and the United States) the development has been the opposite, with the summary score increasing for each point in time. In a third set of countries (Austria, Canada, Denmark, and Sweden), the summary scores have remained relatively unchanged over time, reflecting either policy stability or the simultaneous adoption of offsetting inclusionary and exclusionary policy changes. And finally, five countries (Belgium, Iceland, Ireland, Italy, and Spain) have followed a pattern of what we might call "truncated inclusion": beginning at a comparatively exclusionary starting point in 1990, each of these countries' welfare systems quickly became more inclusionary but then moved in an exclusionary direction again. Figure 2.3 summarizes the above discussion: for each cluster of countries, it shows the average summary score for each of the four data points.

The trajectory of change, then, has been very different from one country to another. Moreover, the *way* the level of exclusion has changed in different programs is also far from uniform, as is illustrated in Figure 2.4, which shows the average score of all 22 countries under study for different social programs. Some programs, such as health care and active labour market policies, have become more inclusive of immigrant populations over time. When it comes to

Figure 2.3. Four trajectories of change in immigrant welfare exclusion, 1990–2015

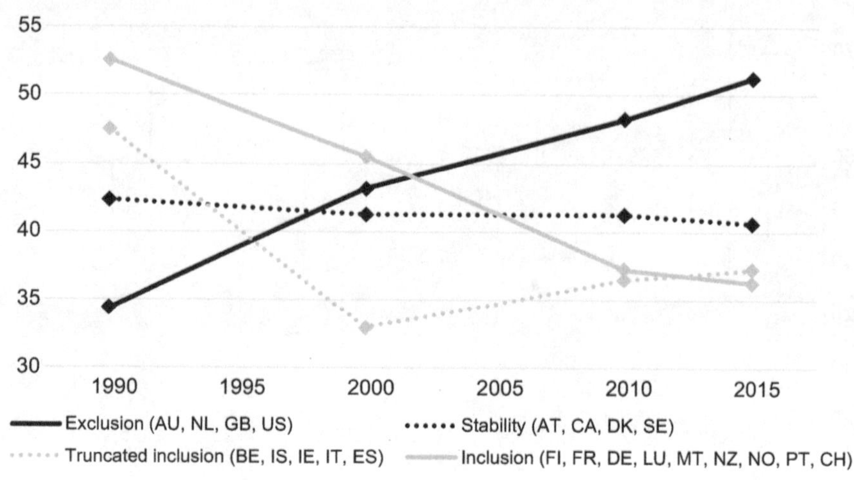

Figure 2.4. Level of immigrant exclusion by social program, 1990–2015

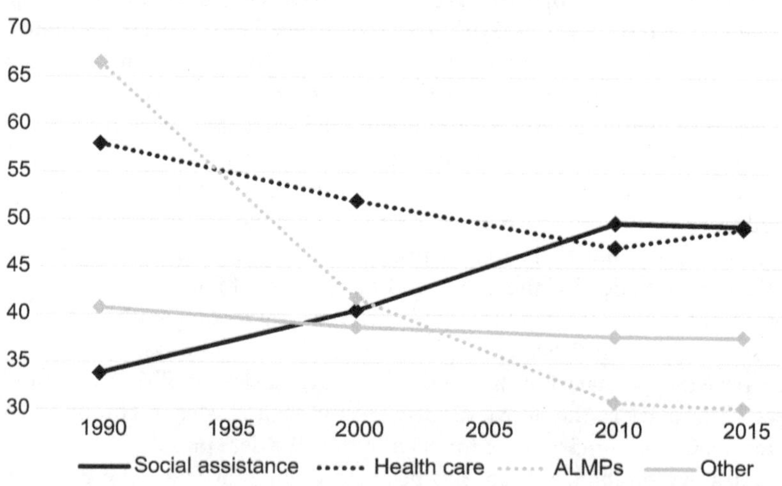

social assistance, by contrast, we observe an overall trend in an exclusionary direction. For the other programs (tax-paid pensions, contributory unemployment benefits, contributory pension benefits, and housing benefits), the aggregate picture shows little change overall.[9]

All in all, the IESPI reveals a striking level of variation between countries, time periods, and programs. In sharp contrast to arguments that forces of Europeanization and globalization are reducing the scope for national decision-making (Sassen 1996; Caminada, Goudswaard, and van Vliet 2010), the IESPI shows no evidence of policy convergence at all. These descriptive findings of course raise several questions. Why do different countries adopt such different approaches to tackle more or less the same policy challenge, that is, how to incorporate newcomers into systems of redistribution and social rights protection? And what explains the contrasting developments over the past three decades in countries such as the United States and the Netherlands on the one hand and Portugal and New Zealand on the other? Why do some programs seem more affected by inclusionary developments, while others have mostly become more restricted over time? And finally, does any of this matter? What are the consequences of these differences across time, place, and social programs for the integration of immigrants, tensions between native-born and immigrant groups, and the sustainability of the welfare state in general? The following chapters pursue answers to these questions.

NOTES

1 As this formulation aims to make clear, the IESPI follows the definition of a "migrant'" as any person who crosses national borders for the purpose of residing elsewhere. It includes, therefore, "remigrants": individuals who return to their country of birth after a prolonged period of residence abroad. While these individuals are sometimes not considered "immigrants" in public parlance, they are affected by many of the same differentiations that affect newcomers who were born abroad. In particular, both groups face length of residence requirements when accessing tax-paid pension benefits (for other programs, such residence requirements do not always apply to native-born citizens). Parenthetically, based on the definition employed here we should technically juxtapose "migrants" with "native-born citizens who have resided in the country all their lives," but for reasons of narrative flow the remainder of the text simply distinguishes between "immigrants" and "native-born citizens."

2 The index therefore does not capture possible differentiation in social programs that are run by the private sector or non-governmental organizations. Considering the trend toward privatization of social programs in some countries (Van Slyke 2003, Benish and Levi-Faur 2020), as well as the heavy reliance on private or occupational pensions in some countries' pension regimes (Ginn and Arber 1999), this is an admittedly important omission. Since some of the decisions about non-public programs are made by sectoral or private organizations, however, including them would be difficult not only because the theoretical framework summarized in

Figure 1.1 would be less applicable but also because the rules could vary from one sector or organization within a country to another.

3 Many thanks again to Silvina Antunes, Zina Bibanovic, Yuriko Cowper-Smith, Besarta Kajmolli, Matt McBurney, David Markle, Madison Milne-Ives, Gloria Novovic, Josh Pedersen, Sibena Peters, Camila Rivas-Garrido, Liam Thompson, and Daniel Waring for their excellent assistance.

4 Nevertheless, there are a limited number of instances for which it was impossible to assign a country-wide score. The most extreme case is that of Belgium, where the policies in Flanders differ from those in Wallonia on 8 of the 25 indicators. In aggregate scores, the index reports the average of these two values. The other instances are relatively minor and only involve variation between subnational units for one or two indicators for only one or two moments in time. In those instances, the index describes the regime in the sub-national unit that is both the most populated and host to the largest immigrant population: New South Wales in Australia, North Rhine-Westphalia in Germany, and Lombardy in Italy.

5 The first and second indicators need to be considered in tandem. Where the universal pension has a very short residence requirement, the absence of a means-tested pension program cannot be considered an exclusionary feature. In such cases, the value on the second indicator is scored as missing.

6 In the Finnish example, OECD data suggest that in 2015, about 36% of the foreign-born population was from Switzerland or EU/EEA member states, about 2% from Canada, Chile, Israel, and the United States, about 0.3% from Australia, and the remaining 62% from other countries. As such, Finland's score on this indicator for this year is 0.36*0+0.02*1+0.003*2+0.62*3=1.9. Of course, this weighting exercise only produces a tentative approximation of the extent to which export is restricted (after all, not all migrants are equally likely to aspire retirement in their country of origin), but it nevertheless seems preferable over alternatives (such as using the score for the most restrictive or least restrictive policy).

7 The index does not include any measurement of residence requirements for contributory benefits, because none of the countries under study directly require a longer history of contributions from migrants than from other residents to access these benefits.

8 A related point is that the accessibility of a program can only be properly assessed when considering all characteristics simultaneously. After all, a program might be accessible in one respect but not in another.

9 In interpreting Figure 2.4, it is important to remember that coding has been determined inductively based on variation in each program across countries and time periods. For that reason, one cannot directly compare the level of inclusion across programs and read Figure 2.4 as suggesting, for example, that in the year 2000 health care programs were more exclusionary than social assistance programs.

SECTION TWO

Quantitative Analyses

3 The Drivers of Exclusion

FRIEDERIKE RÖMER AND LIV BJERRE

What explains variation in immigrant welfare access between countries and over time? Why do some countries pursue more exclusionary approaches than others, and why have some changed their approach over time? This chapter contributes to the growing literature on the drivers of restrictions and expansions in immigrant welfare rights by investigating the left-hand side of the theoretical framework presented in the introduction to this volume (cf. chapter 1, Figure 1.1). The chapter pays particular attention to three explanatory factors. First, it considers the influence of the welfare state itself. Two competing rationales are formulated regarding the relationship between regime types/welfare state size and entitlements of immigrants, as also discussed in the introduction to this volume. Several scholars have shown that the structure of the welfare state correlates with how immigrants are treated by that system, finding that regimes that are more generous in general tend be more inclusionary toward immigrants as well. Yet there is also reason to question this assumption, arguing that more robust welfare systems may have the strongest incentives to shield their generous entitlements from immigrants.

The second factor assessed in this chapter is the level of immigrant welfare dependence, that is, the idea that "migration patterns and their pressure on the welfare system" shape the level of immigrant exclusion (cf. chapter 1, Figure 1.1). Cuts in immigrant welfare rights are often justified politically as necessary adjustments to an overburdened system, but for now there is no empirical evidence that these reforms are indeed most likely to be adopted where and when immigrants disproportionally rely on benefits.

Third, this chapter investigates the extent to which restrictions (and expansions) in immigrants' welfare access are driven by certain political parties (cf. the factor termed "anti-immigrant politics" in chapter 1, Figure 1.1). "Welfare chauvinism" – that is, the belief that welfare benefits should be reserved for the "native" population (see, e.g., Kitschelt and McGann 1997, 22) – is an important platform for populist radical right parties and has been shown to impact policy-making as well. At the same time, it has been argued that a large number of supporters of left parties support cuts in immigrant welfare rights, too. It is thus possible that exclusions from social programs could be pushed by both parties of the radical right and parties on the left of the political spectrum.

The fourth explanatory factor highlighted in the introduction to this volume, "legal regime," is included in the analysis in the form of control variables measuring the legal protection of immigrants in the form of veto points and EU integration (cf. control variables below). The chapter does not include measures of public opinion in the analyses, since this factor is likely deeply endogenous with IESPI scores (cf. chapter 1).

The emerging comparative literature on the topic has shown the importance of welfare generosity; it has also found evidence that political parties have an impact (Chueri 2020; Schmitt and Teney 2018; Römer 2017; Sainsbury 2012). These studies, however, have mostly been limited to analysing access to one or two welfare benefit types only (e.g., Römer 2017). Others have assessed restrictive or liberalizing changes within countries over time (e.g., Chueri 2020; Schmitt and Teney 2018), a strategy that does not allow an assessment of the level of restrictiveness across countries. The IESPI data we rely on in this chapter measure immigrant access to different benefit types across 22 countries and for four points in time. They thus allow us to test the explanatory power of these factors across a wider set of benefit types, countries, and years as well as to compare the relative importance of these different factors. Taking advantage of the IESPI's coverage, we find strong support for the claim that more generous welfare systems are more inclusionary across all types of benefits (with the exception of social pensions). Regarding the other two factors, our findings neither clearly support nor contradict hypotheses about the importance for immigrant welfare exclusion of migration patterns and the pressures they exert on the welfare system and anti-immigrant politics.

In the next section we discuss the above-mentioned theoretical perspectives in greater detail and derive hypotheses regarding how the three factors may matter for welfare exclusion. We then present our methodology and operationalization of variables. In the empirical part of the chapter, we assess the effect of the three factors on immigrant exclusion from social programs.

Explanations of Variation in Immigrant Welfare Access

For a long time, the welfare entitlements of immigrants were not a prominent topic in comparative welfare state research. One strand of the literature that engaged with questions at the nexus of immigration and welfare focused on the – potentially negative – effects of immigration and diversity on welfare states in general, namely welfare provisions for citizens (e.g., Alesina and Glaeser 2004). Another strand of the literature on migration and welfare states examined the role that labour migrants play in the provision of care, both formally and informally (e.g., Yeates 2009). The few studies that were concerned with immigrants' welfare access specifically asserted that there was relatively little variation in immigrants' welfare access across countries and that especially immigrants with long-term residency status could access many benefits on the same footing as citizens, a status termed "denizenship" (Hammar 1994; see also Brubaker 1989). Soysal (1994) explained this convergence in terms of the increased influence of supranational institutions and global human rights norms.

Because of the assumption that immigrants' welfare access is relatively far-reaching, and restrictions only of a temporary nature, the comparative literature showed little interest in explaining cross-country differences in the extent to which immigrants were being granted or denied access to welfare provisions. It is important to note, though, that case studies of individual countries started to pick up on variations (e.g., Morris 2002; Gal 2008; Timonen and Doyle 2008; Valenta and Bundar 2010). More recently, the wide variety of legal categories of entry and residence that determine immigrants' eligibility for benefits has also been acknowledged by comparative approaches (see chapter 2; Sainsbury 2012; Römer 2017). This includes acknowledgment of the fact that different benefit types often have different sets of eligibility requirements. The term "immigrant welfare rights" is thus increasingly understood as an umbrella term that encompasses a multitude of differently restricted entitlements to different benefits for different groups of immigrants.

In line with this development, in recent years a growing number of datasets have emerged that allow us to measure differences between immigrant and citizen welfare rights and thus to quantitatively assess immigrants' welfare access over time and across countries. The Migrant Integration Policy Index (MIPEX) measures the inclusion of immigrants for 38 countries (Huddleston et al. 2015); the Immigration Policy in Comparison (IMPIC) database encompasses social rights across 18 countries (Bjerre et al. 2016); the Migrant Social Protection Database expands this to 38 countries, including countries in the Global South (Römer et al. 2021); and the International Migration Policy and Law Analysis (IMPALA) database includes the rights granted to immigrants in 25 countries (Beine et al. 2016). Finally, the DEMIG policy database (2015) in its integration section lists policy changes in regard to social rights for 45 countries for the years 1945 to 2013 (de Haas, Natter, and Vezoli 2014). All of these datasets show that there is substantial variation in immigrants' welfare access both between countries and over time.

Among these datasets, the IESPI stands out as the first dataset that allows us to systematically assess immigrant welfare rights across a larger set of benefit types, namely tax-paid pension programs, public health care services or health care subsidies, contributory unemployment benefits, contributory pension programs, housing benefits, social assistance, and active labour market policies (including immigrant-targeted programs such as integration assistance) (cf. the conceptualization of IESPI in chapter 2 of this volume). Other existing datasets focus on only one or two benefits, or on changes within countries, which does not allow us to make meaningful comparisons between countries.

As discussed in more detail in chapter 2 of this volume, the IESPI echoes previous studies that reject the assumption that there is little to no variance in immigrant rights. Indeed, it shows "striking variation across time, place, and social programs." The picture emerging from IESPI, being more fine-grained and covering more programs than existing datasets measuring immigrant welfare access, thus reinforces the need to uncover the causes of these variations.

Welfare State Characteristics

Among the three drivers discussed in this chapter, welfare state characteristics have received the most attention in the comparative literature (Schmitt and Teney 2018; Römer 2017; Sainsbury 2012). This is not by coincidence. Immigrant access to welfare is by definition always situated within a broader system of welfare benefits and services. It seems obvious that immigrants' welfare access will be affected by the institutional and normative frame this larger system provides. But just as important for scholarly interest in this relationship, there are theoretical grounds to formulate two competing hypotheses regarding the association between welfare regime type (or generosity) and immigrants' welfare access. Depending on the consulted literature, we could expect generous welfare states to be *more* exclusionary or *less* exclusionary. These two competing hypotheses have been discussed in a number of variations using different terminologies.[1]

In an early contribution, Banting (2000: 25) argued that stronger welfare states had succeeded better at incorporating immigrants than weaker welfare states; thus, he argued that there was a positive relationship between generosity and immigrant inclusion. Banting, however, did not discuss the underlying mechanisms in depth. Other studies have elaborated on this hypothesis by explicating the reasons *why* generous welfare states may be more inclusive toward immigrants. Boräng (2015) has argued that because they increase social solidarity and trust, generous welfare states should be more likely to extend rights to foreigners. Furthermore, in generous welfare states, public opinion tends to approve of the state taking responsibility for vulnerable populations (Boräng 2015: 216).

In addition to these normative foundations, generous welfare states may be more likely to be inclusionary of foreigners for material and institutional reasons as well. Materially, in systems where generous and decommodifying policies protect workers from the risks of the market, immigrants are less likely to be seen as a threat by citizens, which translates into lower levels of welfare chauvinism among the population (Van der Waal, De Koster, and Van Oorschot 2013). Furthermore, institutionally generous and egalitarian systems tend to resort less to screening and targeting. For generous welfare states to be able to identify immigrants for the purpose of excluding them would hence require the erection of some sort of screening infrastructure, a costly and thus unlikely option (Römer 2017: 176–7). In comparative empirical studies, the generosity hypothesis has been largely confirmed. Both Römer (2017) and Schmitt and Teney (2018) have found that immigrants are more likely to be granted access to benefits in countries where social protection systems are more generous. We thus formulate *hypothesis 1a* as "*The more generous the welfare regime, the less exclusionary toward immigrants.*"

The competing hypothesis, namely that more generous systems will do the most to exclude immigrants, has to our knowledge not been empirically verified. Nevertheless, there are theoretical reasons to expect such a relationship. The argument is based on two assumptions. The first is the "welfare magnet hypothesis," which posits that more generous welfare provisions attract migrants who are more likely to use such provisions, that is, low-skilled migrants with low earning potential (Borjas 1999). The second assumption, which logically follows, is that if access to benefits remains unrestricted, then higher numbers of immigrant welfare recipients will increase the fiscal pressure on generous welfare states (Barrett and Maître 2011; Koopmans 2010; Razin and Sadka 2000). To counteract this fiscal pressure while keeping generosity for citizens at a high level, welfare states will thus restrict immigrants' access to benefits. Based on this we formulate *hypothesis 1b* as "*The more generous the welfare regime, the more exclusionary toward immigrants.*"

Levels of Immigrant Welfare Dependence

The second explanatory factor assessed in this chapter is the level of immigrant welfare dependence. The argument here is relatively straightforward. For a long time, authors have argued that there is an inherent tension between immigration and welfare state viability (see also chapter 11 in this volume). Restricting immigrants' access to benefits is an inevitable outcome of welfare states' fundamental logic of demarcating eligible insiders from outsiders, because if everyone were considered eligible, the demand for benefits would exceed welfare states' resources (Freeman 1986). This outcome is especially obvious in cases where outsiders would take up benefits disproportionally.

The expectation that immigrants will take up benefits disproportionately is on the one hand based on the welfare magnet hypothesis outlined earlier. Generally, little support for the welfare magnet is found in the literature (for a discussion, see Ponce 2019), and "welfare inclusiveness does not trap immigrants in inactivity or unemployment" (see chapter 5 of this volume). But whether or not such a "magnet" exists, there is agreement in the literature that immigrants on average have lower levels of formally acknowledged education and domestic language skills than non-immigrants. Furthermore, they face a higher risk of labour market discrimination. Taken together, these factors make it more likely that immigrants will be unemployed and thus dependent on welfare benefits (Burgoon 2014; see also Barrett and Maître 2011). The higher the fiscal pressures stemming from immigrants claiming benefits, the more likely restrictions will occur. Furthermore, public opinion may shift toward welfare chauvinism if immigrants are perceived as the main beneficiaries of the welfare system, even if the objective fiscal costs are small. Based on this literature, we formulate *hypothesis 2: "The higher relative immigrant unemployment, the more immigrant welfare exclusion."*

Several studies, however, have cast doubt on the assumption that there is a relationship between immigration and increased social expenditure, and between immigrant unemployment and an increase in chauvinist attitudes toward welfare. Generally, it has been found that immigrants add to the budget as much as they take (OECD 2013; see also chapter 6 in this volume). Furthermore, the link between relative immigrant unemployment and an increase in welfare chauvinist attitudes has not been supported – indeed, immigrant welfare exclusion has been found to have little to do with economic factors and more to do with general opposition to immigration and multiculturalism (Koning 2019). It seems that the missing link here is the absence or presence of populist radical-right parties, the final factor we will look at in this chapter.

Political Parties

The third factor this chapter will look at in more detail is the influence of political parties. Including this factor with the other two seems important for at least two reasons. The importance of regime generosity notwithstanding, there is variation within countries over time, which fluctuates more than the more stable regime characteristics. Furthermore, as was already touched upon in the previous section, policy rarely follows direct objective pressures, but rather is mediated through politics. Thus for policy to become more restrictive, the impact of the alleged "burden" of immigrant dependency must first be recognized and politicized by political actors. In fact, any change in policy must originate in political parties in their role as "office holders and policy makers … drawing up and implementing measures for inclusion or exclusion" (Schmitt and Teney 2018: 47).

Immigrant populations were not a central political issue in most Western European countries before the early 1990s. Indeed, during the 1960s and 1970s civil society had successfully lobbied *for* inclusion, backed by the courts (see, e.g., Guiraudon 1999). Since the early 1990s, however, immigration has become a focal point of political and public debate (Messina 2007). This has been accompanied by the rise of populist radical-right parties (PRRPs), which only two decades earlier were marginal in the political arena (de Lange 2008) but today are established in most advanced industrialized European democracies. A nascent literature concerns itself with the impact of PRRPs on immigrant welfare rights (Chueri 2020). An important observation in this literature is that PRRPs have become more successful and that their agendas have evolved considerably over time. At least since the late 1990s, a uniting feature of PRRPs has been a turn away from anti-statist positions toward welfare chauvinism. A welfare chauvinist agenda offers an ideal intersection between a cultural nativist agenda and a social policy based on deservingness, and this has helped unite PRRP supporters on the socio-economic dimension. Cutting immigrants' access to welfare is a key plank among PRRPs, which view this as a means to foster the recognition of their native-born core voter groups. PRRPs are seldom in a position to govern by themselves. However, the centre-right, the party they most commonly coalition with, will not oppose immigrant exclusion from welfare either, as such a policy is neither economically nor electorally costly[2] for them (Koning 2019). We thus formulate *hypothesis 3: "The stronger populist radical-right parties are, the more immigrant welfare exclusion."*

In contrast to that, parties on the left are commonly expected to favour an expansion of immigrant welfare rights. Generally, left parties advocate generous and comprehensive benefit schemes (Allan and Scruggs 2004; Huber and Stephens 2001; Korpi and Palme 2003). Furthermore, previous research suggests that compared to conservative and right-wing parties, left-wing parties support extending immigrant rights (Koopmans Michalowski, and Waibel 2012: 1209; Lahav 1997). In line with this, Sainsbury (2012) has found that left governments tend to implement more inclusive policies regarding immigrants' social rights than do right-wing governments. Yet there is also reason to doubt that left parties' commitment to immigrant welfare inclusion is strong and consistent. Even though a growing proportion of their supporters are middle-class voters, the working class remains important for the electoral success of left parties (Gingrich and Häusermann 2015). Substantial evidence points to a polarization in attitudes between middle- and working-class voters on immigration in general and welfare chauvinism in particular (Brady and Finnigan 2014; Kriesi et al. 2012). Working-class voters are more likely to perceive immigrants as competitors for scarce economic resources (Kriesi et al. 2008), and the literature on welfare chauvinist attitudes has found that education level explains support for excluding immigrants from welfare (e.g., Mewes and Mau 2013; Oesch 2008). Since blue-collar workers still make up a large proportion of left-wing parties' voters, left-wing parties may endorse cuts in immigrant welfare rights to appeal to those voters. Given these diverging arguments, we will leave open the question of the role of left parties and here simply note that we test for the potential impact.

Data

We rely on data from a variety of sources to assess the importance of the welfare regime, the level of immigrant welfare dependence, and political parties in explaining variation in immigrants' exclusion from social programs. The dependent variables measuring immigrants' exclusion from social programs are drawn from the IESPI. The proximate source for all explanatory variables is the Comparative Welfare States Dataset (Brady, Huber, and Stephens 2020), with the exception of data on PRRP vote share, which come from Koning (2020), and on (relative) immigrant unemployment, which are calculated based on data from the OECD (2020).

Dependent Variable

Immigrant exclusion from social programs is measured by the IESPI, as mentioned earlier. As described in more detail in chapter 2 of this volume, IESPI measures immigrant welfare exclusion in regard to seven benefit types: tax-paid pension benefits, public health care or health care subsidies, contributory unemployment benefits, contributory pension benefits, housing benefits, social assistance, and active labour market policies. The dataset consists of 25 indicators that capture how these programs may differentiate between native-born citizens and immigrants. The index for each program varies from 0 to 100 (0: extreme inclusivity; 100: extreme exclusivity). The aggregate index is constructed as the average of the seven indices and varies from 0 to 100. In the analyses, we use both the aggregated measure and all seven sub-indices.

Explanatory Variables

To test the influence of the welfare regime, we use three different measures of the welfare state: *social welfare expenditures* as a percentage of GDP, welfare *generosity,* and *regime type.* In the multivariate analyses we focus on a measure of *social welfare expenditures* to capture welfare state size, which we consider an adequate albeit not perfect proxy for welfare regime generosity. This is measured as spending on social cash and non-cash transfers and social services as a percentage of the GDP. Second, we use index generosity as constructed by Scruggs, Jahn, and Kuitto (2014: Version 2014–03). Higher values indicate higher degrees of generosity. This index builds on Esping-Andersen's (1990) original index. It combines information on coverage, qualifying periods for eligibility, and replacement rates for unemployment, sickness, and pension welfare programs for an average production worker in the manufacturing sector who is 40 years old and has been working for 20 years preceding the benefit period (Scruggs Jahn, and Kuitto 2014). Specific conditions for immigrants are not accounted for. The generosity variable has been collected only up until 2010, which reduces our sample considerably. We thus employ it only in the bivariate analyses and for a robustness check. Finally, as a robustness check we use a categorical measure of regime type based on the four classic welfare regimes: "liberal," "social democratic," "conservative" (Esping-Andersen 1990), and a "southern" regime type (Ferrera 1996).

To capture the impact of immigrant welfare dependency, we rely on the relatively straightforward measure of the *unemployment gap* between native-born and foreign-born[3]. We chose this measure because comparable data on unemployment are available for all countries in the sample (and for all years after 1999), unlike data on benefits received by immigrants and non-immigrants. In robustness checks we also included the proxy *relative unemployment rate* of foreign-born to native-born.[4] We also included interaction effects of these measures with size of the migrant population, to account for differences in a potential burden effect. (As we will see, however, applying these measures did not yield different results.)

To account for the strengths of left and right parties we use four measures in total. We use measures of respective *vote share* for left parties and PRRPs, that is, populist nativist parties following Koning (2020). Such figures are available for all countries in the sample except the US (due to the two-party system). In robustness checks we also include the variables *left cabinet* and *right cabinet*, following Brady, Huber, and Stephens's (2014) coding of parties.

Control Variables

Variation in welfare exclusion is potentially driven by several other factors. In addition to the explanatory variables we thus include three control variables: migrant stock, veto points, and EU integration. *Migrant stock* refers to the international migrant stock as a percentage of the population. Data come from the World Bank (World Bank 2020), the OECD (2020), and the United Nations Department of Economic and Social Affairs Population Division (2017). Data are interpolated based on a linear approximation for the years 1990 to 2008, where data is only available for every fifth year. This measure is included based on the argument also presented in the introduction to this volume, namely that large inflows of immigrants may result in exclusionary responses due to a perceived "difference" from the majority population and burden to the welfare state (cf. chapter 1). To account for "liberal constraints" we include legal protection in the form of veto points and EU integration. *Veto points* is the sum of measures of federalism, presidential system, single-member district plurality electoral systems, the strength of bicameralism, the frequency of referendums, and judicial review. This follows Huber and Stephens (2001), who refer to the same measure as "constitutional structure." For a further robustness check we also include a measure of *EU integration* measured by a proxy of EU membership, following König and Ohr (2013).[5]

For reasons of data availability on the explanatory and control variables, the final sample does not include Iceland, Malta, and Luxembourg. Furthermore, for parts of the analyses that include the generosity measure from Scruggs, Jahn, and Kuitto (2014), our sample is restricted to the years 1990, 2000, and 2010, because data are only available for these years. Similarly, the data on EU integration was available only for the years 1990, 2000, and 2010. Data on relative unemployment and the unemployment gap are only available for the years 2000 to 2015.

Method and Results

We assess variation in immigrant exclusion from social programs in two steps. First, to explore the relationship, we plot the bivariate relationship between immigrants' access to social programs and the three explanatory factors: welfare state size, relative immigrant unemployment, and political parties. Given the data availability of the respective variables, we analyse the bivariate relationship for two, three, and four years. For the bivariate analyses, we employ the summary score of the IESPI. Ideally, we would lag the explanatory variables, as one might reasonably expect that it is the performance of these indicators at t – 1, and not current performance, that affects the exclusion of immigrants from social programs; however, given the structure of IESPI, which is collected for the four years 1990, 2000, 2010, and 2015, the baseline for the lag is unclear, as we do not know in which year(s) IESPI changed. Therefore, we take the average of the explanatory variables across the respective 10-year intervals.

Figure 3.1 shows the bivariate relationship between welfare generosity and immigrant exclusion from welfare. Recall that data for welfare generosity are only available for three of the years in our sample, namely 1990, 2000, and 2010.

Bearing in mind that higher scores on the IESPI denote more restrictiveness, the figure shows that higher levels of generosity are associated with lower levels of exclusion. This relationship grows stronger over time. The relationship is even stronger when Austria is excluded from the sample. This same finding is confirmed when we plot the bivariate relationship between the IESPI and social expenditures (see Figure A3.1) and when we plot the relationship between the IESPI and regime type (see Figure A3.2). In line with the findings of previous studies, these graphs lend support to *hypothesis 1a*: more generous welfare states are more inclusive toward immigrants.

Figure 3.2 depicts the bivariate relationship between the unemployment gap and immigrant exclusion from welfare. A value of 0 means that immigrant and native unemployment are exactly the same, whereas negative values denote that foreign-born unemployment is higher, and positive values that it is lower.

Figure 3.1. Welfare generosity and immigrant exclusion from social programs in 18 welfare states in 1990 (Pearson's r = -.14), 2000 (Pearson's r = -.23), and 2010 (Pearson's r = -.29)

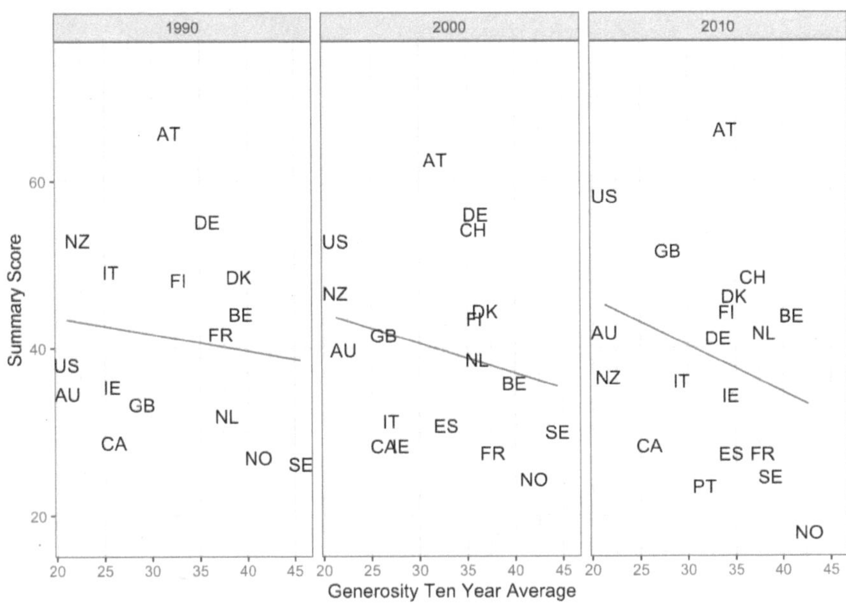

Figure 3.2. Unemployment gap and immigrant exclusion from social programs in 18 welfare states in 2010 (Pearson's r = .06) and 2015 (Pearson's r = .22)

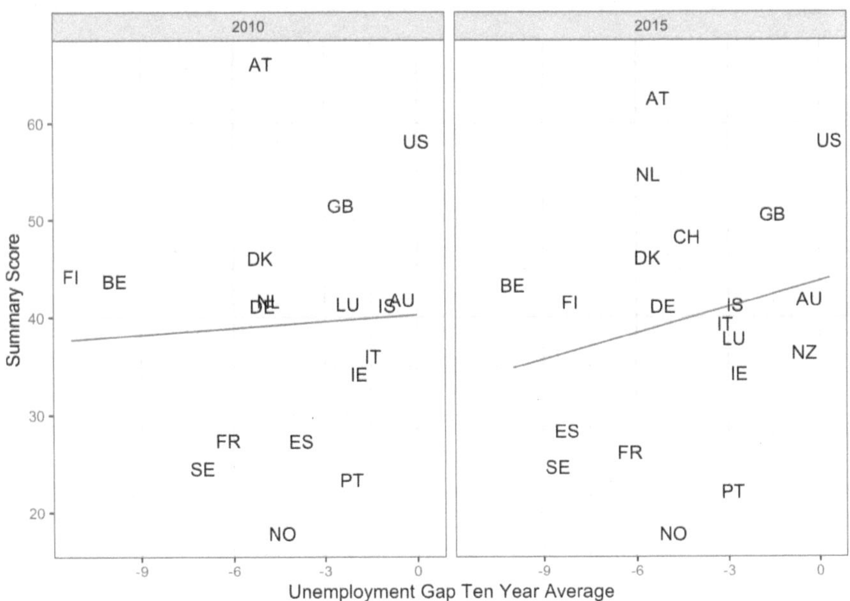

Figure 3.3. Left vote share and immigrant exclusion from social programs in 18 welfare states in 1990 (Pearson's r = .26), 2000 (Pearson's r = -.08), 2010 (Pearson's r = -.36), and 2015 (Pearson's r = -.46)

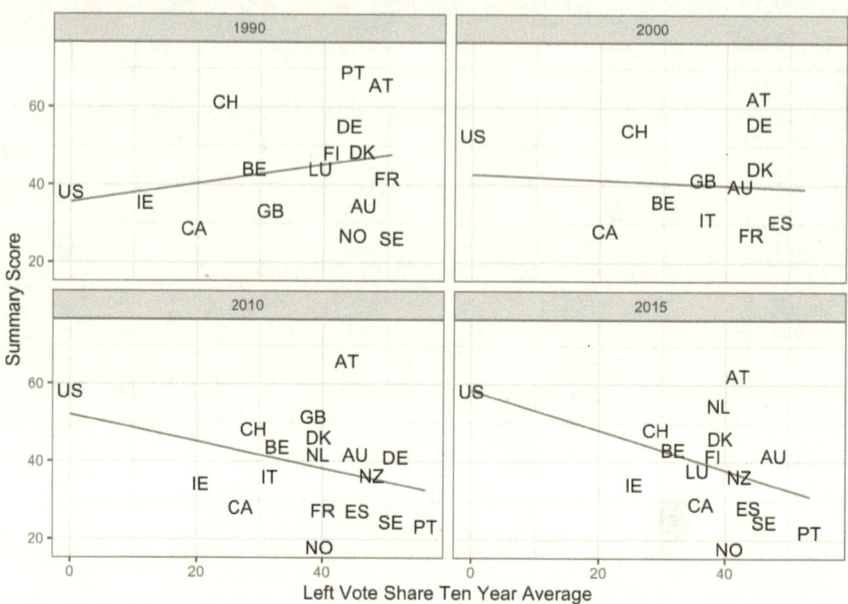

Recall that data on immigrant unemployment are only available for the years 2000 to 2015, so 10-year averages of the previous decade are only available for two points in time, namely 2010 and 2015. The fitting line suggests a positive relationship, meaning that when the unemployment rate among immigrants is higher than among citizens, there are fewer restrictions in immigrant welfare rights. This is contrary to the theoretical expectations. However, the distribution of countries gives reason to doubt that this is a true association. There is thus no clear evidence in favour of or against *hypothesis 2.*

Figure 3.3 and 3.4 show the bivariate relationships between immigrant exclusion from welfare and the vote shares of left parties and PRRPs, respectively. Figure 3.3 shows that there is no clear-cut relationship between left vote share and restrictions in immigrants' access to welfare. In 1990, the relationship is slightly positive, but in later years there is evidence of a negative relationship, which grows more pronounced over time, thus lending support to the hypothesis that left parties favour expansions in immigrants' access to welfare. The relationship between right vote share and immigrant welfare rights is also not pronounced, but it seems to be positive, and growing more so over time. Interesting outliers are Malta and Norway. In Norway, the vote share of a PRRP is

Figure 3.4. PRRP vote share and immigrant exclusion from social programs in 18 welfare states in 1990 (Pearson's r = .07), 2000 (Pearson's r = 0.06), 2010 (Pearson's r = .13), and 2015 (Pearson's r = .18)

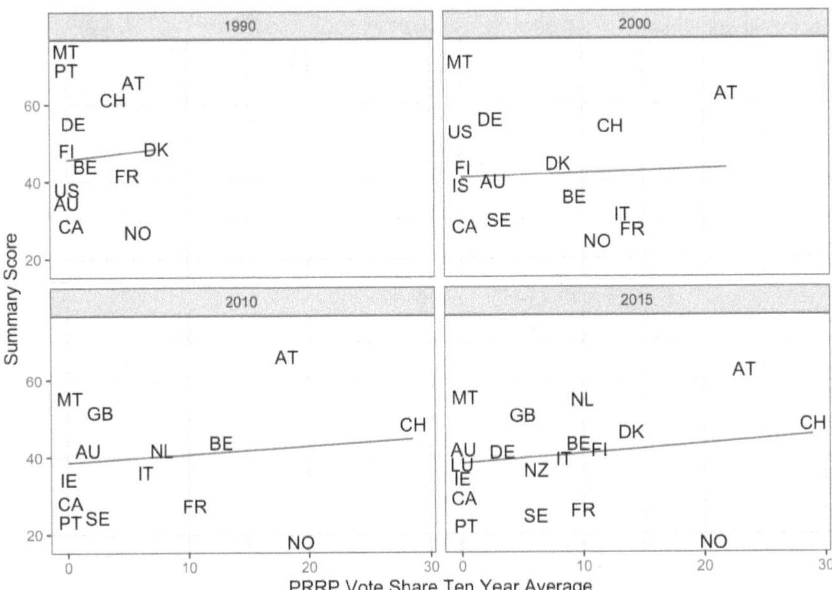

relatively high, but rights are not very restricted. In Malta, by contrast, the vote share is zero, but rights are relatively curtailed. Excluding these cases in the multivariate analyses, however, did not yield different results.

We also looked at the bivariate relationship between left cabinet and immigrant welfare exclusion and right cabinet and immigrant welfare exclusion (see Figures A3.3 and A3.4). There is no conclusive relationship between left cabinet and immigrants' exclusion from welfare. Whereas for the year 1990 there seems to be a positive relationship, which would not support the hypothesis that left parties protect immigrant welfare rights, the years 2000, 2010, and 2015 exhibit a negative relationship. Surprisingly, and contrary to theoretical expectations, for both 1990 and 2015 there is a slight indication of a negative relationship between right cabinet and restrictions of immigrants' welfare rights (which, however, is not robust in the multivariate analyses).

The bivariate descriptive analyses provide a helpful first assessment of the relationship between immigrant exclusion from welfare and the respective explanatory factors. However, to ensure that these are not confounded, we proceed with multivariate analyses in a second step. In the multivariate analyses we employ not only the summary score of the IESPI but also all sub-indices of

Table 3.1. Country- and year-fixed effects stepwise models for the IESPI overall score (standardized coefficients)

	(1)	(2)	(3)	(4)
Social expenditures	−0.684***	−0.777***	−0.813***	−0.810***
	(−3.934)	(−4.272)	(−4.328)	(−4.270)
PRRP vote		−0.243	−0.278	−0.283
		(−1.437)	(−1.588)	(−1.595)
Left vote		−0.252	−0.267	−0.267
		(−0.930)	(−0.980)	(−0.972)
Migrant stock			−0.375	−0.365
			(−0.808)	(−0.778)
Veto points				0.145
				(0.294)
N	78	78	78	78
Within-R^2	0.30	0.33	0.34	0.34

Z-statistics in parentheses. *** $p < 0.001$, ** $p < 0.01$, * $p < 0.05$, + $p < 0.1$. All explanatory variables are ten-year averages.

the dataset. Here again, we take the 10-year average of the independent variables and all models include year- and country-fixed effects. Country-fixed effects control for time-invariant country-specific factors, whereas year-fixed effects take into account specific circumstances unique to a given year. This seems especially relevant given that the data cover only four points in time and do not allow for full time-series analyses. Given the relatively low number of observations, the explanatory variables are included in stepwise fashion in order to avoid overfitting. For additional robustness checks we also ran the analyses including a lagged dependent variable, as dynamic panel models have been suggested to address the endogeneity problem caused by reverse causality (Leszczensky and Wolbring 2019: 8). These estimates may be biased, but including lags of the dependent variable as instrument(s) to resolve the issue of bias is not possible because the IEPSI data are available for only four points in time. Moreover, all models in Table 3.1 were re-estimated while dropping one country at a time. For both robustness specifications, the results remain unchanged.[6]

Table 3.1 presents the results of the stepwise regression for the aggregate IESPI index but does not include the measure of relative foreign-born unemployment, as this would result in a more restricted sample. Similarly, instead of generosity, social expenditure is used to test *hypotheses 1a* and *1b*, to ensure that data availability does not restrict the sample further. This results in a sample of 78 country-years. Model 1 in Table 3.1 includes only social expenditures and country and year dummies. Model 2 introduces the political variables, and in models 3 and 4 the control variables migrant stock and veto points are added.

The full model 4 has a within-R^2 of 0.34 (meaning that the five variables help us explain 34% of the variation within countries in immigrant welfare exclusion).

In all four models, the coefficient of social expenditure is negatively and significantly associated with restrictions in immigrant welfare rights, lending further support to *hypothesis 1a*. Holding all other variables at their means and moving from the minimum of the 10-year-average of social expenditure in our sample, roughly 10% of GDP, to the maximum, roughly 30% of GDP, amounts to a large change in the predicted value of the overall IESPI from 62 to 21. It seems, then, that welfare state size is a relevant predictor of immigrant inclusion. This is in line with the findings of previous studies. Interestingly, none of the other variables included in the model show robust and significant results. The most important implication is that we cannot confirm the hypotheses on the influence of political parties. It is important to note, however, that especially in the context of analysing political mechanisms, a careful modelling of temporal dynamics is of utmost importance. So it is highly likely that the 10-year aggregates fail to account for the ways political parties influence policy-making on immigrant welfare exclusion.

We also ran robustness checks including generosity and the measure of EU integration (see Table A3.1). Including these variables in the analyses resulted in a reduced sample of only 53 observations. In this reduced sample, neither generosity nor EU integration proved to be significant. As is the case with political parties, however, it is important to note that the positive relationship between generosity and immigrant welfare rights found in previous studies in part also stems from within-country mechanisms, as cuts in immigrant welfare rights often occurred in the context of larger-scale retrenchment reforms. Temporality is hard to tease out because of the set-up of the IESPI data, which could explain the lack of significant results here. Furthermore, even though the coefficient for social expenditure ceased to be significant in the restricted sample, it remained negative in both specifications.

A significant advantage of the IESPI over other indices measuring immigrant welfare exclusion is that it allows us to differentiate between different types of benefits. We thus ran models for all seven sub-indicators, with the results depicted in Table 3.2. Those results again lend support to *hypothesis 1a*. In five of seven models the coefficient of social expenditure is negative and significant. Interestingly, for both types of pensions – that is, contributory and social pensions – welfare state size does not seem to be a relevant predictor. For some of the sub-indicators there is evidence of influence by political parties. Housing benefits seem to be more inclusive when the vote share of left parties is high (cf. model 5). Surprisingly, a negative coefficient for PRRP vote share was found in model 2, which relied on exclusion in health care. In the same model the control variable of immigration (migrant stock) has a significant negative effect, indicating that the more migrants live in a given country, the

Table 3.2. Country- and year-fixed effects stepwise models for the seven IESPI sub-indicators (standardized coefficients)

	(1) Social pensions	(2) Health care	(3) Contr. unempl.	(4) Contr. pens.	(5) Housing benefits	(6) Social assist.	(7) ALMPs
Social	−0.118	−0.475**	−1.065***	−0.100	−0.611***	−0.433*	−0.563**
expenditures	(−0.526)	(−2.709)	(−5.025)	(−0.610)	(−3.849)	(−2.206)	(−2.744)
PRRP vote	−0.252	−0.375*	−0.370+	−0.075	−0.048	0.016	−0.204
	(−1.200)	(−2.288)	(−1.827)	(−0.547)	(−0.327)	(0.090)	(−1.065)
Left vote	0.042	−0.426+	0.110	0.275	−0.560*	−0.101	−0.166
	(0.130)	(−1.676)	(0.356)	(1.318)	(−2.437)	(−0.356)	(−0.559)
Migrant	0.205	−0.852*	−0.102	−0.100	−0.352	−0.030	−0.225
stock	(0.368)	(−1.963)	(−0.203)	(−0.277)	(−0.898)	(−0.062)	(−0.444)
Veto points	−0.279	0.613	1.767*	−1.350*	−0.048	0.092	−0.164
	(−0.477)	(1.340)	(2.334)	(−2.484)	(−0.116)	(0.179)	(−0.306)
N	78	78	69	72	78	78	78
Within-R^2	.09	.34	.46	.21	.28	.36	.55

Z-statistics in parentheses. *** $p < 0.001$, ** $p < 0.01$, * $p < 0.05$, + $p < 0.1$. All explanatory variables are ten-year averages.

fewer restrictions in immigrant rights to health care. To summarize, together Tables 3.1 and 3.2 offer clear evidence in favour of *hypothesis 1a*, but offer little basis to make definitive statements about *hypothesis 3* and the role of political parties more generally.

Let us now turn to *hypothesis 2*, regarding the effect of immigrant unemployment. Table 3.3 presents the results for the aggregate IESPI index and includes several measures of immigrant unemployment: the unemployment gap, relative immigrant unemployment, and the interaction of these two measures with migrant stock. Furthermore, we include interactions between PRRP vote share and relative unemployment share and the unemployment gap to test whether PRRPs use higher immigrant unemployment rates as an opportunity to cut immigrants' rights. Introducing these measures results in a starkly reduced sample of only 36 observations. While the coefficient for social expenditure remains negative, it is not significant in any of the models.

None of the immigrant unemployment measures, including the interaction effects, show a significant association with immigrant exclusion from welfare for the overall IESPI index. In robustness checks we also ran these for the seven sub-indicators. For six of the seven sub-indicators we found no significant association. A negative relationship was, however, found between the unemployment gap and exclusion in regard to tax-based pensions (see Table A3.2), indicating that higher immigrant unemployment went along with more restrictions. This could be interpreted as some support for *hypothesis 2*, but such a conclusion clearly warrants further analysis.

Table 3.3. Country- and year-fixed effects stepwise models for the IESPI overall score and different measures of immigrant unemployment (standardized coefficients)

	(1)	(2)	(3)	(4)	(5)	(6)
Social expenditures	−0.152	−0.153	−0.349	−0.399	−0.224	−0.422
	(−0.703)	(−0.674)	(−1.366)	(−1.503)	(−0.907)	(−1.531)
PRRP vote	0.080	0.068	−0.051	−0.001	0.69	0.371
	(0.358)	(0.269)	(−0.230)	(−0.005)	(0.736)	(0.642)
Left vote	0.507	0.535	0.538	0.415	0.653+	0.584+
	(1.630)	(1.405)	(1.626)	(1.135)	(1.690)	(1.710)
Migrant stock	−1.076+	−1.157	−0.402	−0.040	−1.168+	−0.395
	(−1.841)	(−1.389)	(−0.635)	(−0.051)	(−1.899)	(−0.613)
Veto points	0.995	−0.980	1.760+	1.816+	1.319	1.948*
	(1.216)	(1.135)	(1.867)	(1.896)	(1.362)	(1.972)
Unemployment gap	−0.272	−0.230			−0.307+	
	(−1.640)	(−0.676)			(−1.725)	
Unempl. gap * migr. stock		−0.056				
		(−0.143)				
Relative unemployment			0.389	0.004		0.168
			(1.183)	(0.007)		(0.386)
Rel. unemp. * migr. stock				0.575		
				(0.837)		
Unemp. Gap * PRRP vote					0.460	
					0.671)	
Rel. unemp. * PRRP						0.500
						(0.793)
N	36	36	36	36	36	36
Within-R^2	.40	.34	.38	.40	.42	.38

Z-statistics in parentheses. *** $p < 0.001$, ** $p < 0.01$, * $p < 0.05$, + $p < 0.1$. All explanatory variables are ten-year averages.

Conclusion and Discussion

With this chapter, we set out to investigate the relative importance of three independent variables in explaining variation in immigrants' access to social programs, namely welfare state size, immigrant welfare dependence, and the influence of political parties. The chapter thus offers a (partial) test of the explanatory factors outlined in the theoretical framework of this volume (cf. chapter 1; Figure 1.1). We analysed the association between the three factors and immigrant exclusion from seven social programs: tax-paid pension benefits, public health care or health care subsidies, contributory unemployment benefits, contributory pension benefits, housing benefits, social assistance, and active labour market policies. Even with a very limited number of observations, our findings show a robust, sizable, and significant effect of the level of social expenditure on the aggregate measure of immigrant exclusion from social benefits and programs. When analysing the subdimensions, it became clear that this relationship also holds for the individual benefits, with the exception of contributory and social pensions.

We did not find a systematic, significant effect of migration patterns and their pressure on the welfare system for the overall IESPI and six of the seven sub-indicators. This is not especially surprising. Although an inherent tension between welfare state viability and disproportionate uptake of benefits by immigrants has been asserted by many, empirically, the welfare magnet hypothesis as well as the link between immigrant relative uptake and welfare chauvinist attitudes is not very well established (see among others Ponce 2019, Koning 2019). The findings of chapter 5 in this volume further support the "lack of a link" by showing that immigrant unemployment or inactivity is not associated with inclusive policies. Nevertheless, the fact that there was some support for an association between exclusion from tax-paid pensions and the unemployment gap warrants further analysis.

Finally, little support was found for the influence of political parties, but we would conclude that this should not lead to a rejection of the assumption that parties as policy-makers are influential in explaining immigrant exclusion from welfare benefits. Instead, we would conclude that there is some evidence that different benefits may be differently affected by the influence of political parties. These relationships should be further tested with additional time series data.

Returning to the question at the beginning of the chapter, "What explains variation in immigrant welfare rights between countries and over time?," our chapter offers one clear answer and two "maybes." Clear evidence was found for the importance of welfare state size, with larger welfare states adopting more inclusionary approaches. The two "maybes" relate to the potential effects of both right and left parties, which were not contradicted by our findings, but also not supported, as well as the relationship between immigrant unemployment and exclusion from certain benefits. In the same way that the coverage of IEPSI across social programs has allowed for new insight into the variation in migrants' welfare access, extended coverage across time may shed further light on the impact of these – and other – factors.

NOTES

1 E.g. Römer (2017) calls these the "generosity" versus "dualization" hypotheses, whereas Schmitt and Teney (2018) refer to them as the "postnational" versus "welfare chauvinism" hypotheses.

2 Cutting back welfare rights for immigrants is not a risky strategy in electoral terms for two reasons. Survey data show that in the beginning of the 2000s in European

countries the public at large considered immigrants to be less deserving of welfare benefits than the native population (Van Oorschot 2006). Furthermore, immigrants often do not enjoy formal voting rights (Blatter, Schmid, and Blättler 2015). Cutting immigrant welfare rights is thus a means to reduce social spending at the expense of a segment of the population that is not an important part of the electorate.

3 Calculated as the unemployment rate of foreign-born subtracted from the unemployment rate of native-born.

4 The relative unemployment rate of foreign-born to native-born is calculated as (percentage unemployed natives – percentage unemployed foreigners) / percentage unemployed natives * 100.

5 König and Ohr (2013) measure the level of integration in the EU of all EU member states on a 0–100 scale. We have assigned a value of 0 to the non-member states in our sample.

6 These results are not shown but can be made available upon request.

APPENDIX

Appendix Figure 3.1. Social expenditures and immigrant exclusion from social programs in 18 welfare states in 1990 (Pearson's r = –.34), 2000 (Pearson's r = –.17), 2010 (Pearson's r = –.11), and 2015 (Pearson's r = –.19)

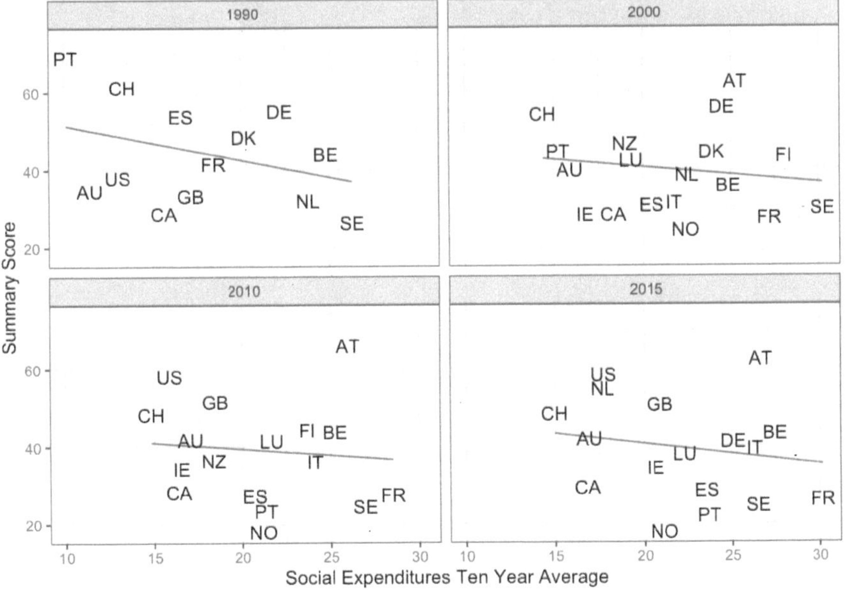

Appendix Figure 3.2. Regime types and immigrant exclusion from social programs in 18 welfare states in 1990, 2000, 2010, and 2015

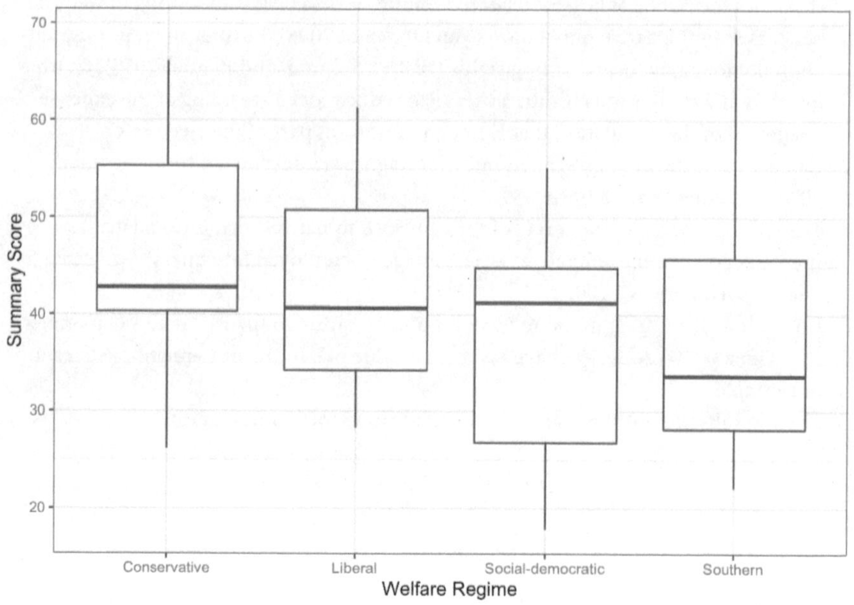

Appendix Figure 3.3. Left cabinet share and immigrant exclusion from social programs in 18 welfare states in 1990 (Pearson's r = .16), 2000 (Pearson's r = –.30), 2010 (Pearson's r = –.23), and 2015 (Pearson's r = –.28)

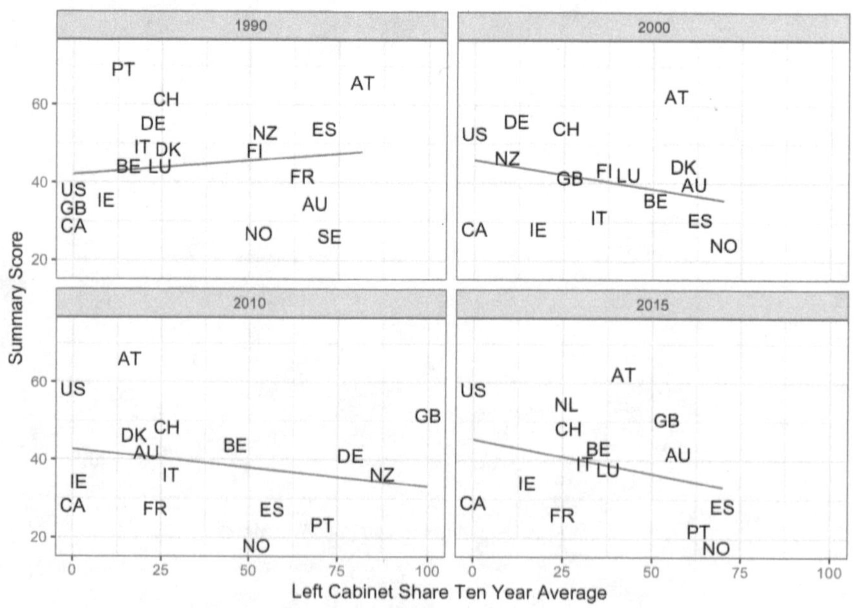

Appendix Figure 3.4. Right cabinet share and immigrant exclusion from social programs in 18 welfare states in 1990 (Pearson's r = –.44), 2000 (Pearson's r = –.05), 2010 (Pearson's r = .10) and 2015 (Pearson's r = –.19)

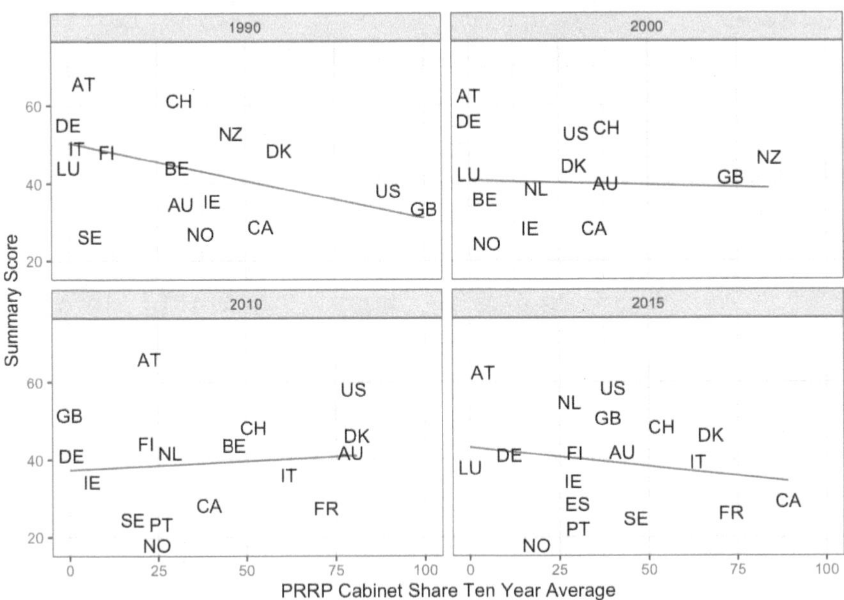

Appendix Table 3.1. Country- and year-fixed effects stepwise models for the IESPI overall score including generosity and EU integration (standardized coefficients)

	(1)	(2)
Social expenditures	–0.313	
	(–1.362)	
PRRP vote	–0.129	–0.218
	(–0.615)	(–1.197)
Left vote	–0.147	0.372
	(–0.528)	(1.002)
Migrant stock	0.011	0.427
	(0.023)	(0.873)
Veto points		0.204
		(0.445)
EU integration	0.299	
	(0.413)	
Generosity		0.033
		(0.089)
N	53	53
Within-R^2	.10	.16

Z-statistics in parentheses. *** p < 0.001, ** p < 0.01, * p < 0.05, + p < 0.1. All explanatory variables are ten-year averages

Appendix Table 3.2. Country- and year-fixed effects stepwise models for the IESPI tax-paid pensions and different measures of immigrant unemployment (standardized coefficients)

	(1)	(2)	(3)	(4)
Social expenditures	−0.329*	−0.322*	−0.424*	−0.479*
	(−2.037)	(−2.318)	(−2.002)	(−2.222)
PRRP vote	−0.381*	−0.260+	−0.505**	−0.452*
	(−2.271)	(−1.689)	(−2.752)	(−2.404)
Left vote	0.075	−0.190	0.061	−0.070
	(0.325)	(−0.818)	(0.223)	(−0.237)
Migrant stock	−0.190	0.572	0.243	0.633
	(−0.436)	(1.123)	(0.461)	(1.007)
Veto points	0.356	0.496	0.763	0.824
	(0.584)	(0.938)	(0.975)	(1.061)
Unemployment gap	−0.258*	−0.653**		
	(−2.089)	(−3.137)		
Unemp. gap * migr. stock		0.530*		
		(2.207)		
Relative unemployment			0.121	−0.293
			(0.442)	(−0.637)
Rel. unempl. * migr. stock				0.619
				(1.109)
N	36	36	36	36
Within-R^2	.68	.56	.60	.78

Z-statistics in parentheses. *** $p < 0.001$, ** $p < 0.01$, * $p < 0.05$, + $p < 0.1$. All explanatory variables are ten-year averages.

4 Appeasement via Exclusion? Differential Access to Social Programs and Their Effects on Xenophobia, Racism, and Perceived Welfare System Abuse

MARKUS M.L. CREPAZ

How does differential access to social programs between immigrants and the native-born affect xenophobia, racism, and public views about whether immigrants abuse the welfare system? Could nativists be appeased once they grasp that immigrants have less access to social programs than they do? Or does more restrictive access to social programs broaden the gulf between natives and newcomers by making it more difficult for the latter to find work, housing, health care, and other social supports? Might the consequences of this sharpen the divide between "them" and native-born citizens and thereby generate still more xenophobia and racism?

Investigating the relationship between immigrant exclusion from welfare programs and public opinion (and as such, scrutinizing the middle part of Figure 1.1), this chapter mostly finds evidence for the latter proposition. Differential exclusion to social programs is associated with higher levels of racism, higher levels of xenophobia, and more widespread perceptions that immigrants are welfare cheats. As such, the findings in this chapter do not support the claim that welfare exclusion could appease nativists; indeed, they suggest that it only encourages divisive sentiment.

A fundamental assumption in democratic politics is that people's personal beliefs – or, as supporters of rational choice theories are wont to say, preferences – are transmitted through either political parties or interest groups, thus creating a set of rules for governing the body politic. It is asserted that this churning process, while not always pretty and likened by Bismarck to "sausage-making" better not to be seen, produces public outcomes that are more or less congruent with citizens' desires. This establishes the sequence of how democratic politics supposedly unfolds: beliefs and attitudes are prior and political outcomes such as laws and regulations are consequent.

Institutionalists, however, have turned this logic on its head, arguing that institutions and their attendant rules and regulations shape how people think about the world around them. In the words of Douglass North (1990, 3), "institutions are the rules of the game in a society or, more formally, the humanly devised constraints that shape human interaction." Focusing more on welfare regimes, Christian A. Larsen (2008, 148) describes the institutional mechanism as follows: "The institutional structure of the different welfare regimes influences ... the way the public perceives the poor and unemployed. Thus the political preferences of individuals are not exogenous ... but are highly influenced by the institutional structures." Larsen (2020) has found that the programmatic features of welfare schemes shape public perceptions of migrants' entitlement to social benefits in Denmark, Germany, and the Netherlands.

If institutional rules are a reflection of people's beliefs and desires, then political culture should matter in understanding how not only citizens but also newcomers are treated. To be sure, national narratives supporting the rights of immigrants do not protect them from outbreaks of populist episodes as occurring right now in the United States and in a number of other modern, post-industrial countries, which may temporarily or even permanently reduce their access to social benefits.[1]

Generally, however, political cultures and national identities tend to set the broad parameters of laws, and, once created, they have their own sticking power, even if political cultures change, creating a dynamic process between values and laws, agency and culture. In this vein, then, it is assumed that the Immigrant Exclusion from Social Policies Index (IESPI) is a broad reflection of national political cultures. While the argument in this chapter is primarily about the opposite effects, namely how the IESPI affects attitudes, it is useful to keep in mind that the differential treatment of migrants may not be detached from the broader political culture that shaped this index in the first place. If that is the case, and the causal arrow indeed runs the other way, examining how the index might affect attitudes such as racism, xenophobia, and broader integration outcomes is not independent from the initial conditions that produced the variations of the index across different countries.

Overview: Social Programs and Their Effect on Crafting National Identities

It is now well-understood that redistributive welfare institutions can transcend local loyalties and shape broader, national identities.[2] Kevins and Kersbergen (2019, 115) write that, "social policy has thus been a tool of statecraft, pushing forward integration on the basis of territorial bonds while at the same time diffusing inter-class tensions." There is indeed strong evidence that the creation of the welfare state was part and parcel of the nation-building process in European countries such as the UK, Germany, France, and Austria (Weber 1976; Beveridge 1942).[3] The development of the welfare state can thus be understood as a functionalist response to class conflict, ethnic conflict, or even inter-state wars.[4]

This sense of identity and belonging to a nation may indeed be construed as a function of the scope of welfare provision, be it targeted or universal. Richard Titmuss, a pioneer of the welfare state, recognized early on that differential treatment of people can lead to stigmatization, with adverse effects on social cohesion, and can foster individual pathologies such as lack of self-esteem and a sense of dependence.[5] In G.J. Room's interpretation of Richard H. Tawney, the collective commitment to a more egalitarian society "could secure popular acquiescence ... which would involve citizens as a collective force for social transformation" (Room 1981, 410). Flora and Heidenheimer (1981, 24) argued similarly for the integrative capacity of the welfare state, claiming that it "may be understood to *create* [italics added] a new kind of solidarity in highly differentiated societies."

Similarly, examining welfare chauvinist attitudes as a function of the type of welfare provision, Esping-Andersen (1990, 24) concludes that there is "more welfare chauvinism in means-tested than in universal welfare states." Bo Rothstein and Dietlind Stolle (2003, 196) have argued that "the basic principle of a universal welfare policy is not to discriminate between citizens." Following that principle by avoiding onerous means-testing and discriminatory rules and regulations, and by adopting administrative mechanisms that blur the distinction between "us" and "them," results in institutions that are "undivisive, encompassing, and inclusionary in character." People's "perceived experiences" with welfare delivery systems, be they universal or means-tested, can have wide-ranging effects. Kumlin and Rothstein (2005) found evidence, based on Swedish survey data, that universal welfare institutions tend to create social trust, whereas the opposite is true for means-tested welfare institutions. Much of this broad literature, which could be summarized as "citizen making through social benefits" (Leibfried and Pierson 2000, 279), assumes that the recipients of social benefits are citizens.

An unspoken assumption among the early pioneers of the welfare state and even their more recent followers is that its institutional configuration affects only the *citizens* of the country they are investigating. Citizens' reactions to various welfare state policies may be quite different depending on whether the recipients of the benefits are themselves or the "others" which broaches, of course, the very idea of welfare chauvinism (Andersen and Bjorklund 1990). Whether native-born individuals see immigrants as deserving and/or belonging to their community or not may affect their attitudes and beliefs and thus their support for various welfare state arrangements.[6]

Examining whether the IESPI affects the attitudes of native-born citizens toward migrants raises two questions. First, do national cultures of social cohesion and solidarity extend beyond the orbit of citizens to include foreigners? And second, do native-born citizens know the degree to which there is differential access to welfare benefits?

Trading Off Universal Protection in a Closed Immigration System with Selective Protection in an Open Immigration System?

The arguments about the effects of universal welfare provision sound quite plausible in a closed system in which there are few immigrants or none. Yet it is also quite plausible that in open systems, universal welfare programs may generate strong nativism and welfare chauvinism; that is, the native-born may perceive that the "universalism" of their welfare protection unjustly includes people(s) who are *not* deserving, because they have not contributed enough and/or do not culturally belong to their nation. Crepaz (2008, 151) has suggested that "precisely because a welfare regime is universal, and *widely known to be universal by members of the host society* [italics added] welfare chauvinism should be more pronounced than in means-tested ones." Conversely, less desire to disentitle foreigners from welfare benefits should be observable in means-tested systems since "natives may feel that means testing will ensure that only those that are deserving are in fact receiving the meager support" (Crepaz 2008, 151).

A very similar argument has been made more recently by Kevins and Kersbergen (2019), who have in important ways extended the discussion about the effects of welfare systems by distinguishing between "community perks," that is, the level of welfare protection citizens receive, and "community scope," that is, who is perceived by the native majority not only as deserving but also as belonging. What motivates their paper is their observation that welfare chauvinism is higher in universalist Denmark than in relatively selectivist Canada. Their central argument is that in the face of immigration-induced diversity, universalist systems "may go hand in hand with a push toward welfare chauvinism as more generous universal benefits stoke increased fears about the motivation and disposition of newcomers – in the process undercutting the ability of the welfare state to generate links of solidarity between newcomers and native-born citizens" (Kevins and Kersbergen 2019, 120).

There appears to be an inverse relationship between the universality of welfare support (community perks) and a more exclusionary view as to who counts as members of the community (community scope). In other words, when faced with immigration-induced diversity, the more universal the welfare system, the more welfare chauvinist and exclusionary native-born citizens become; conversely, the more open and less restrictive a country is to immigration, the more selective (i.e., less generous) its welfare system tends to be, which is "why 'classically universalist' Denmark is facing threats to solidarity that are much more intense than those found in 'classically selectivist' Canada" (Kevins and Kersbergen 2019, 127).

This is a highly plausible argument, yet it rests on a rather heroic assumption, namely that native-born citizens are aware of the degree of differential access to welfare programs. There is no evidence that the native-born are that sophisticated. Quite the opposite – there is a fascinating, and perhaps troubling, literature on "innumeracy" showing the extent to which native-born respondents misjudge the number of migrants or Muslims in their country (Herda 2010, 2018; Kunovich 2017). This does not prevent native-born individuals, however, from having very strong opinions about immigrants, their impact on the welfare state, and how welfare state rules differentiate access between native-born and immigrants.

These opinions, then, must spring from somewhere else. So it is important to briefly examine the role of the mass media, political leaders, and parties and to reflect on how their statements shape the discourse about immigrants and how they supposedly affect access to social benefits. As will be shown in the next section, some politicians quite blatantly highlight the differences in treatment in terms of access to social programs between native-born and immigrants in order to justify cuts to welfare programs in general. A case in point is the passing of the 1996 Personal Responsibility and Work Opportunity Reconciliation Act (PRWORA), which attempted to make drastic cuts in social benefits for native-born citizens more palatable by highlighting that immigrants would be treated even more harshly (see also chapter 9).

The Relevance of Political Discourse on Welfare Access

In August 2019, Ken Cucinelli, the Deputy Director of US Citizenship and Immigration Services, suggested a revision to Emma Lazarus's famous poem chiselled into the pedestal of the Statue of Liberty from "Give me your tired, your poor, your huddled masses, yearning to be free, the wretched refuse of your teeming shore," to "Give me your tired and your poor who can stand on their own two feet and who will not become a public charge" (NBC News, 13 August 2019). Cucinelli's statement reveals a "narrative script" that says only those who can look after themselves should be allowed to enter the United States.

"Narrative scripts" are common stereotypical beliefs about the characteristics of other people(s) that are generated and amplified by the mass media, which have the power to determine what people pay attention to and how they think about social problems (Gilliam 1999). Given the general lack of political sophistication and the unreasonable assumption that individuals are aware of the degree of differential access to social benefits between native-born and immigrants, people's beliefs and attitudes are driven to a large extent by the discourse on immigrants and their effects on the welfare state as it is shaped by policy-makers, governments, interest groups, social movements, political parties, and other influential individuals and groups whose messages leave a public trace on various media platforms.

Martin Gilens (1999, 3) argued that "racial stereotypes [as propagated by the mass media] play a central role in generating opposition to welfare in America."

He shows that two particular stereotypes are powerful drivers of opposition to welfare in America: "First, the American public thinks that most people who receive welfare are black, and second, the public thinks that blacks are less committed to the work ethic than other Americans." Frank Gilliam, in a creative "Welfare Queen Experiment," has found empirical support for Gilens's argument and extends it not only to a racial dimension but also to a gender dimension, namely the widespread belief that welfare recipients are mostly women who "choose to be on welfare because they fail to adhere to a core set of American values" (Gilliam 1999).

Unsurprisingly, similar stereotypes exist about immigrants in Europe. One of the greatest concerns uttered by many observers and policy-makers in the wake of the 2015 migration "crisis," as it was dubbed in Germany, was that migrants were coming to Europe in order to take advantage of the welfare states as "parasites" (Heitmeyer 2018, 352) – that is, to enjoy the "social hammock of the welfare state" (EU-Infothek, 12 June 2020). The former conservative Austrian chancellor Sebastian Kurz recently stated that "many [immigrants] receive basic social benefit payments … without having paid into the social system yet. Those who work and pay taxes must not be disadvantaged," and reminded everybody that the welfare state only functions if everybody works and pays taxes (Nasralla 2017). Research uncovered that the more media report on immigration issues, the more people tend to vote for far-right political parties (Vliegenthart and Boomgaarden 2007).

These findings have influenced popular beliefs about who "deserves" welfare support. A leading scholar in this area, Wim van Oorschot, has found that Europeans share a common "deservingness culture": elderly people are considered most deserving of welfare support, followed by sick and disabled people, then the unemployed, and, last, immigrants (van Oorschot 2006; van Oorschot et. al. 2017). These bases of support are constructed daily in the media and shape, in Walter Lippmann's (1922) famous phrase, "the images in our head."

In a qualitative content analysis, Dorota Lepianka examined 55 newspaper articles that appeared in six Dutch dailies. She found that the primary frames used to depict immigrants in the Netherlands are that they are responsible for their own need; they are also presented as guilty of draining the welfare state and as partly responsible for the discrimination they encounter. Their perceived non-deservingness may be "related to their insufficient contribution or failure to change their cultural and behavioral patterns" (Lepianka 2017, 142). The message these frames convey is that immigrants are not as deserving of welfare support because they have not contributed to the welfare state and are not willing to assimilate into the national culture.

Politicians sometimes declare that there is a significant difference in access to social programs between the native-born and immigrants in order to justify the meagre welfare support for which the native-born are eligible. A case in point is the PRWORA, which was signed into law in the US on 22 August 1996 and was a cornerstone of the Republican Party's "Contract with America." It sharply reduced social benefits to American citizens, but at the same time it went to great lengths to distinguish between welfare support for the native-born and for immigrants, emphasizing that it ended "an era of increasingly generous welfare benefits that had made no distinction between U.S. citizens and legal permanent residents" (Gerken 2007, 80).

Consistent with the appeasement hypothesis, Republican proponents of the PRWORA emphasized the differential access to welfare support between immigrants and the native-born. For instance, Republican Senator Richard Shelby stated that politicians "have a moral obligation to take care of American citizens first" (US Congress, Senate, 25 April 1996; (qtd. in Gerken, 2007, 128). Similarly, Dana Rohrabacher (R-CA) argued that "those millions of illegal immigrants that have come here, they may be fine people," but what really counted was the fact that "they are consuming resources and benefits that are meant for the people of the United States of America" (US Congress, House, 25 September 1996) (qtd. in Gerken 2007, 140). Rohrabacher continued: "It is absolutely wrong to spend $2 billion on the children of foreigners who have come here illegally ... Our priorities should be what is in the interest of the people of the United States. We can care for the children of foreigners, we can care about their well-being, but we must first care about our own children, our own families" (US Congress, House, 25 September 1996) (qtd. in Gerken 2007, 67). The uptake of public services by undocumented migrants was regularly highlighted by Elton Gallegly (R-CA), the chair of the Congressional Task Force on Immigration Reform, who stated that undocumented immigrants "consume precious social benefits that are denied every day to legal residents who are truly entitled to those benefits" (US Congress, House, 25 September 1996) (qtd. in Gerken 2007, 67).

The PRWORA significantly reduced welfare benefits for native-born citizens but reduced them even more sharply for immigrants. Bipartisan support for the PRWORA was reached at the expense of and on the backs of welfare support for immigrants, many of whom either were not allowed to vote or turned out in small numbers. Peter Edelmann, a Clinton appointee who resigned in protest over the bill, states that "the view expressed by the White House and by Hill Democrats, who wanted to put their votes for the bill in the best light, was that the parts of the bill affecting immigrants was awful ... but that the welfare-reform part of the bill was basically all right. The immigrant and food-stamp parts of the bill *are* awful, but so is the welfare part" (Edelmann 1997). What was particularly attractive to both sides of the aisle was that excluding non-citizens from participation in federal welfare supports generated massive savings, to the tune of more than $54 billion over six years. "The largest savings – $23.8 billion or 44 percent of the net savings – was to come from slashing benefits to legal permanent residents (green card holders)" (Singer 2004, 25).

The purpose of this brief excursion into the role of the mass media and how it uses frames to shape political discourse and individual opinions is to shed light on the origins of individual attitudes. As mentioned earlier, it is unreasonable to assume that citizens are aware of the degree of differential access to welfare benefits between native-born individuals and immigrants. Still, as the example of the PRWORA shows, politicians sometimes focus quite explicitly on the differential access to social programs between the native-born and immigrants; the latter are, in general, an easy constituency to discriminate against given their relative lack of political influence and participation. Thus, people *do* have beliefs, no matter how misguided sometimes, about how the native-born are treated differently from newcomers when it comes to social benefits. The origins of these beliefs are found in the way frames and other tropes are used to shape the national discourse, which in turn shapes individual attitudes. The utterances of opinion leaders, politicians, political parties, newspaper editors, and others – some of whom do have a good understanding of how welfare benefits are differentially structured between native-born and newcomers – eventually manifest themselves in the attitudes of the native-born.

Research Design and Variables

The central predictor of this research design is the IESPI, which measures "the extent to which a welfare system differentiates between immigrants and native-born citizens in granting access to social programs" (see chapter 2). This index measures the variation in access to social programs between immigrants and native-born citizens and is not a measure of the generosity of the welfare system.

The panel structure of the data (t = 4, x = 22) calls for a random effects model as the within-variation of each unit is not of central interest. A Hausmann specification indeed confirms that given the nature of the panel structure, a random effects model is the appropriate model.[7] To handle possible autocorrelation of the within-observations, clustering was applied (Rogers 1993), since the assumption is that the standard errors are not independent within each cluster of countries but are random between the clusters of countries.

There are three dependent variables. First, "xenophobia" is operationalized as the percentage of those who have affirmatively indicated "immigrants/foreign workers" in the following query: "Who would you not like to have as neighbors" (sources: ISSP and WVS). The second dependent variable is a composite score of two variables: (a) the percentage of respondents who answered "allow a few" or "allow none" when asked: "How many immigrants of the *same* race/ethnic group as the majority should be allowed into the country?"; and (b) the percentage of respondents who answered "allow a few" or "allow none" when asked: "How many immigrants of a *different* race/ethnic group as the majority should be allowed into the country?" A factor analysis revealed a strong commonality between these two measures with a Cronbach's Alpha of .93. So a new combined variable, based on factor scores and weighted by each individual factor loading was created and termed "racism."[8] The sources for this variable are the various editions of the European Social Survey.

The third dependent variable can be termed "welfare cheats" and is operationalized by the following query: "Taxes and Services: A lot of people who come to live in [country] from other countries pay taxes and make use of social benefits and services. On balance, do you think people who come to live in [country] receive more than they contribute or contribute more than they receive?" The answer options ranged from 0 to 10, with 0 meaning "generally take out more" and 10 meaning "generally contribute more." The measure applied was the sum of the percentages of answer categories 0, 1, and 2.

Hypotheses

There are two competing theories that could explain an association between the IESPI and racism, xenophobia, and the view that immigrants are welfare cheats. First, if it is true that the IESPI can be considered an outgrowth of the national culture of solidarity, we should expect low levels of racism, xenophobia, and the view that immigrants are welfare cheats in countries with a low IESPI (more inclusive), for presumably, these policies are the result of the electorate's desire to be welcoming to immigrants. Conversely, countries with a high IESPI should see higher levels of xenophobia, racism, and sentiments that immigrants are welfare cheats. Second, as mentioned earlier, it is also plausible that the lower the IESPI, that is, the more equal the treatment between native-born and immigrants, the more widespread the racism, xenophobia, and beliefs that immigrants are welfare cheats (as suggested by Crepaz 2008 and Kevins and Kersbergen 2019), because native-born citizens are upset that, in their estimation, the government is too friendly to immigrants. Conversely, a high IESPI should mollify public opinion as people should be satisfied that a clear demarcation has been drawn between them, the deserving receivers of welfare, and the "others," the undeserving receivers of welfare. Thus, a higher IESPI, that is, more exclusive access to social programs, should be associated with less xenophobia and racism. Similarly, a high IESPI should lower the sentiment among native-born that immigrants are welfare cheats, for they believe that immigrants are already treated rather meagrely and that there is little to "chisel" away from welfare programs in the

Figure 4.1. Link between the IESPI and xenophobia (N = 88; p-value: < .000; slope: .23; R-square: .21)

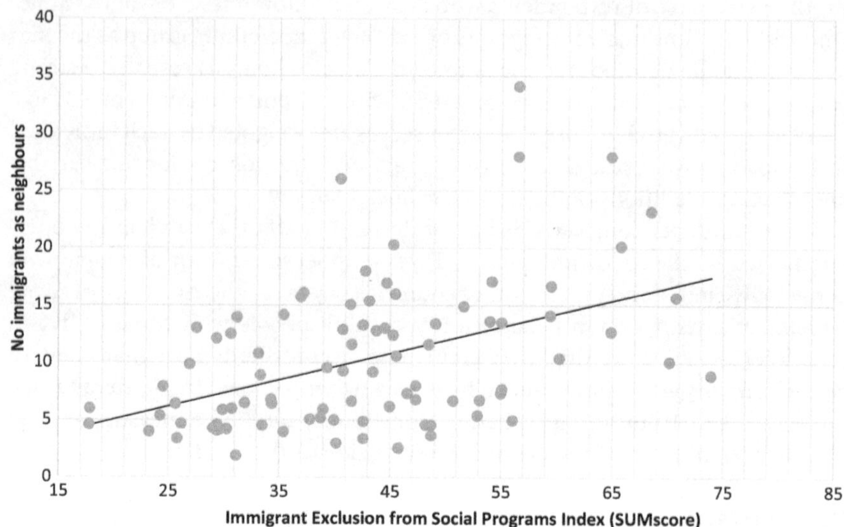

first place. I will call this the "appeasement hypothesis," which leads to three expectations:

h1: The higher the IESPI the lower the levels of racism.
h2: The higher the IESPI the lower the levels of xenophobia.
h3: The higher the IESPI the less widespread the sentiment that immigrants are welfare cheats.

Results

Figures 4.1 and 4.2 show the bivariate associations between the aggregate score on the IESPI and the first two dependent variables. Inspection of Figure 4.1 shows that xenophobia is higher where access to social benefits is more unequal or selective. This positive, linear relationship is statistically significant, with a t-value of 4.75 (p-value < .000) and can explain roughly 20% of the variance of the dependent variable (N = 88).

Figure 4.2 shows a similar, positive relationship between the IESPI and racism as measured by the factor scores of the two race measures indicated earlier.

The bivariate analysis of the relationship between the IESPI and views that immigrants are welfare cheats is not shown here. It suggests this relationship is

Figure 4.2. Link between the IESPI and racism (factor scores) (N = 59; p-value: .001; slope: .034; R-square: .18)

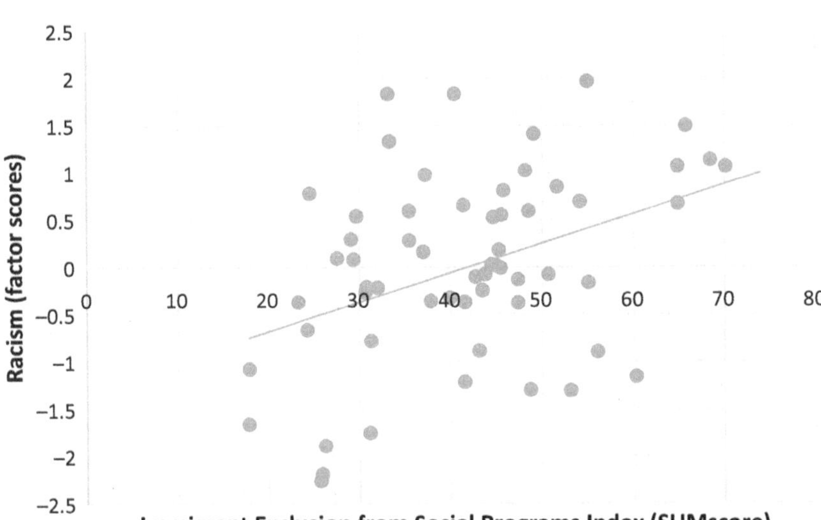

positive but statistically insignificant. However, this relationship does turn out to be highly statistically significant in multivariate analyses.

Multivariate Analyses

The bivariate results indicated in Figures 4.1 and 4.2 hint at a systematic association between the IESPI and the racism, xenophobia, and welfare cheat variables that does not conform to the preceding hypotheses. To explore this further, it is important to test whether these links hold up in a multivariate model that introduces relevant control variables. Five control variables are introduced:

First: Percentage of foreign-born in a country. A well-trodden argument in this field of research is that as societies become more diverse, racism, xenophobia, and nativism in general should rise (Alesina and Glaeser 2004; Sanderson 2004; Wright and Reeskens 2013; Markaki and Longhi 2013; Putnam 2007; Goodhart 2004, and many others), since increasing diversity supposedly brings into sharper relief the difference between "us" and "them."

Second: Multicultural policies. There is a vibrant literature on the effects of multiculturalism on the "cement of society." Some have argued that multicultural policies lead to greater cohesion, tolerance, and democracy (Banting and

Kymlicka 2006, 2017; Levin et al. 2012; Verkuyten 2005), while others have argued that emphasizing "difference" undermines the sense of belonging and generates nativist, racist, and xenophobic responses (Stenner and Haidt 2018; Haidt 2016; Barry 2000; Vorauer and Sasaki 2011).

Third: Total welfare generosity, an index developed by Lyle Scruggs and colleagues (2017) that takes into account programmatic features of the welfare state such as benefit duration and replacement rates in addition to the monetary extent of social benefits.

Fourth: Social expenditures as a percentage of GDP from the OECD Social Expenditures database. If the preceding argument is correct that the IESPI is largely a manifestation of the national culture of solidarity, then this broader measure of welfare protection should also be linked to the dependent variables, allowing us to explore the independent effect of the narrower IESPI in comparison with the social expenditure measure.

Fifth: Types of welfare regimes. These have been linked to different outcomes at least since Esping-Andersen's well-known *The Three Worlds of Welfare Capitalism* in 1990. There has since been a proliferation of "regime types" that broadly distinguish between "liberal," "conservative," and "social democratic." This study adds a fourth, recent innovation, namely the "southern" type of welfare regime, following Maurizio Ferrera's (2005) categorization of "welfare regions." This regime variable will be measured with a series of dummy variables, with the "conservative" type of welfare regime as the reference category.

Figures 4.3 to 4.5 show in graphic form the marginal effects of the various independent variables on the three dependent variables. The appendix shows the same models in more detailed tabular form.

Figure 4.3 shows the marginal effects of the random effects model with clustered, robust standard errors on xenophobia, indicating that the IESPI is positively and significantly linked ($p = .012$) with xenophobia whereas multiculturalism, percentage foreign-born, and Scruggs's measure of total welfare generosity are not significant. The social expenditures variable, however, just barely misses the significance threshold of .1, suggesting a small chance that as social expenditures increase, so does xenophobia. The regime variables demonstrate that social democratic regimes significantly depress xenophobia compared to conservative regimes (the reference category), whereas liberal and southern regimes do not vary significantly from conservative welfare regimes.

Figure 4.4 applies the same random effects model to the composite measure of racism (factor scores) and again finds a statistically positive relationship between the IESPI and racism. It also finds, quite counter-intuitively, that a higher percentage of foreign-born individuals in a country is associated with lower racism, whereas higher levels of social expenditures have a positive effect on racism. Interpreting this latter finding with inverse polarity means that as social expenditures decline, so would racism. This finding gives credence to the

Figure 4.3. Linear regression with clustered, robust standard errors with xenophobia as the dependent variable (N = 76, R-square: .36)

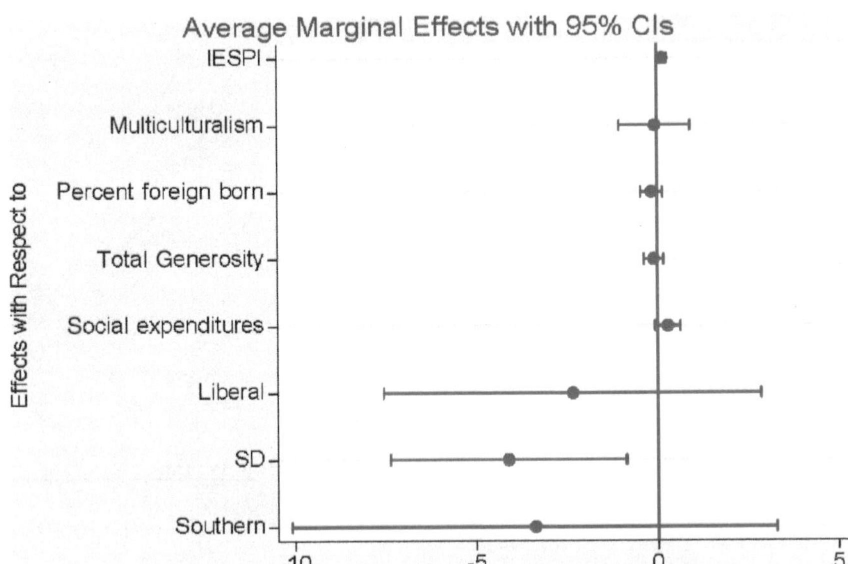

appeasement hypothesis and is consistent with Crepaz (2008) and Kevins and Kersbergen (2019), who claim that more generous welfare states are linked with higher levels of racism. And again, social democratic regimes experience significantly less racism as a function of the IESPI compared to their conservative counterparts, whereas liberal and southern regimes do not vary significantly from conservative welfare regimes.

Higher levels of exclusion are connected to a sentiment among some respondents in developed democracies that immigrants are welfare cheats. Figure 4.5 shows a significant relationship between the IESPI and the welfare cheat variable. Unequal access to welfare programs is associated with a significant increase in respondents who think that immigrants take out more than they put in. The same direction of this relationship pertains to total welfare generosity and to social expenditures. As these measures increase so does the sentiment that immigrants are welfare cheats – an observation that is inconsistent with the appeasement hypothesis. Not surprisingly, social democratic welfare regimes have a significantly depressing effect on welfare cheat sentiments compared to conservative regimes, and perhaps also unsurprisingly, in liberal regimes welfare cheat sentiments are significantly higher than in conservative regimes.

Figure 4.4. Linear regression with clustered, robust standard errors with racism (factor scores) as the dependent variable (N = 76, R-square: .22)

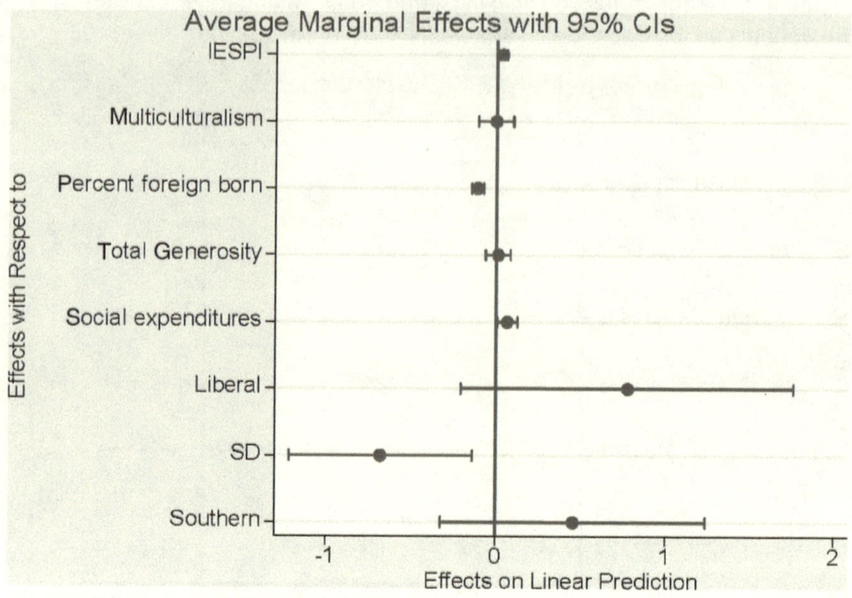

Figure 4.5. Linear regression with clustered, robust standard errors with welfare cheats as the dependent variable (N = 56, R-square within: .13; between: .73; overall: .35)

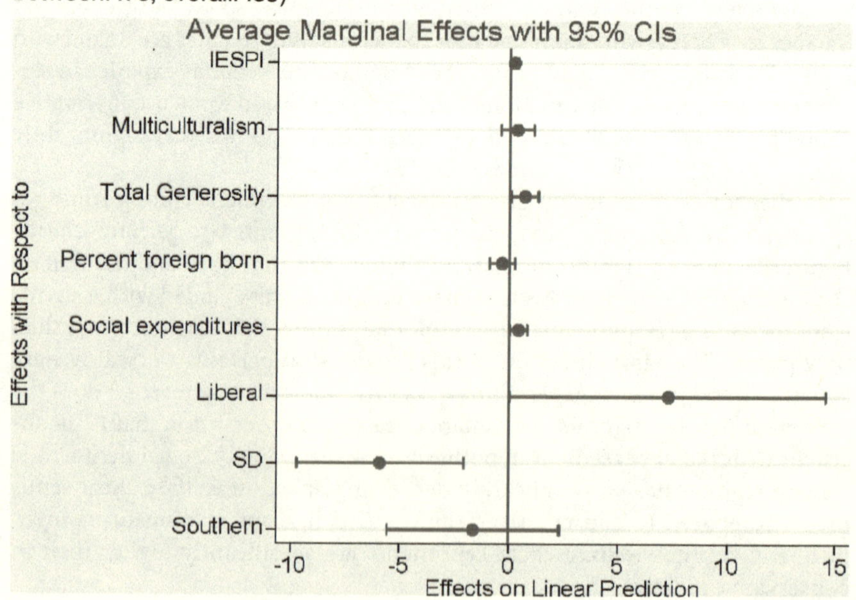

Conclusions and Implications

If the IESPI were to be applied to a dimension called "solidarity with immigrants," the higher end of the index might be described as "exclusive solidarity," since there the difference in access to social programs is the widest while the lower end might be described as "inclusive solidarity." The results broadly do not correspond to the hypotheses laid out earlier. In fact, the bigger the difference in access to social programs, the less it appeases native-born respondents. Rather, the opposite seems to be the case: exclusive solidarity is linked to increased racism, xenophobia, and the sentiment that immigrants are welfare cheats. These results may be explained with a logic similar to what is applied to the difference between universal and means-tested welfare regimes. Less access to social programs means fewer chances to succeed in finding employment and housing and receiving needed health care and job and language training, which makes migrants both more visible and more socio-economically insecure in their immigrant enclaves. As ethnic and socio-economic cleavages begin to reinforce each other, right-wing politicians and allied social media outlets spin a narrative that paints them as neither belonging to the host society nor deserving of public support. This constructed narrative may explain why beliefs that immigrants are welfare cheats increase as a function of them being excluded from social programs.

One might reasonably assume that it should be the opposite: the more meagre, that is, the more exclusive, immigrants' access to social programs is, the less native-born should think that they are welfare cheats. It may very well be that even if immigrants had no access to social programs at all, such attitudes would still be observable, which would only serve as a testament to the power of politicians and the mass media to shape the narrative on migrants and the welfare state. The positive effect of the liberal welfare regime as compared to the conservative regime (its reference category) on beliefs that immigrants are welfare cheats demonstrates that views about community and the responsibility for one another's welfare are to be found in the broad political cultures in the various welfare regime types. It is remarkable to see the consistent and significant negative effect the social democratic regime type has on racism, xenophobia, and welfare cheats, compared to the conservative one.

Figure 4.5 finds a positive association between higher social expenditures and the total generosity of the welfare state on the one hand and the belief that immigrants are welfare cheats on the other. This may be explained by a welfare chauvinist resentment that migrants are treated too well by the welfare state – certainly also a theme the right-wing media and politicians never seem tired of invoking. Reading the results with inverse polarity, lower social expenditures, then, would mean lower welfare cheat sentiments, suggesting that natives should be pleased, and appeased, with lower social expenditures for immigrants. This certainly does not suggest that natives are willing to retreat from the welfare state *in toto* because they, correctly or not, perceive that migrants are treated too generously. Rather, it may indicate a diffuse sense among the native-born that migrants should receive less protection via social programs, which would explain this statistical result and is of course the very origin of the concept of welfare chauvinism.

The policy implications of these findings are that if nations want to reduce xenophobia, racism, and nativism among subsections of their population, making access to social programs for immigrants more equal could reduce the racist, xenophobic, and welfare chauvinist attitudes that are visible in most of the post-industrial democracies.

This chapter offers some tantalizing results; however, two significant caveats are in order. First, since this research design necessitated fitting the dependent variables with the countries and time periods of the theoretically central predictor variable, the IESPI, in not all cases were the data available for every country and time period. Sometimes this meant that these data lacunae were filled with the same questions from a different opinion survey, and when not available from other surveys, the data were extrapolated by simply calculating averages.[9] For some years and for some countries, some of the data needed to be stitched together from responses from the World Values Survey (WVS), the International Social Survey Program (ISSP), and the European Social Survey (ESS). Care was taken to ensure that the survey queries were the same across different opinion polls. In an effort to maximize observations, opinion data that were available but were one year off were still used in the analysis even when the time point of the dependent variable did not coincide with the time point of the predictor variable. This suboptimal solution was considered to still be superior to having no datapoints at all.

Second, as mentioned earlier, for the logic of the argument to have any traction it requires that the respondents know the degree to which there is differential access to social programs between the native-born and immigrants. This is of course an unreasonable assumption. Nevertheless, native-born individuals certainly do have opinions, or narrative scripts, in their mind about immigrants and their effects on the welfare state. This is why a brief section above introduced the frames and tropes used by various media outlets to shape the discourse and thus the opinions of the native-born. It is this asserted indirect link that animates the connection between the IESPI and individual opinions about immigrants and the welfare state.

The broader implications of these findings suggest that unequal treatment in terms of accessing social programs stigmatizes immigrants, highlights differences among them, generates unequal opportunities and life chances, and leads to further "othering" by driving ever deeper wedges between natives and immigrants. The putative motive for these exclusionary policies is to reclaim a more just, misty-eyed, primordial image of "Heimat" or "folkhem" for those who are considered to be "rightful" recipients of welfare support. Paradoxically, the present findings suggest the opposite, namely that the more exclusionary treatment immigrants receive compared to natives, the more racism, xenophobia, and nativism there is. The opposite would also be true: widening the orbit of community by treating immigrants more equally with natives would result in less xenophobia, racism, and sentiments that immigrants are welfare cheats and perhaps help foster an ethic of a shared fate.

NOTES

1 In Sweden there is a term called *utanförskap*, which translates as "social alienation" and denotes a belief that migrants who are not allowed to work or study, who don't know anybody, or who don't speak the local language are in a "lamentable" position (Koning 2019, 79) and need to be treated equally as much as possible compared to natives. There are other frames that can explain why native-born citizens and immigrants have more or less equal access to social benefits. For instance, societies whose master narrative is one of being a country of immigration, such as Canada, Australia, New Zealand, and the United States, may treat immigrants more equally when it comes to accessing social benefits as compared to countries that, if anything, see themselves as countries of "emigration," such as Germany and Italy, even as they are beginning to soften their stances on this issue.

2 The creation of a social safety net starting in the late nineteenth century in many European countries was purposefully designed for two reasons: to abate class struggle and to forge a sense of national identity. In the late Gabriel Almond's (1991, 220) incisive words, "Without this welfare adaptation, it is doubtful that capitalism would have survived, or rather, its survival 'unwelfarized' would have required a substantial repressive apparatus." Similarly, Keith Banting describes how the incorporation of Newfoundland into Canada in 1949 was aided by making Newfoundlanders eligible to receive family benefits and unemployment support, thereby assisting in "making" Canadians (Banting 1999).

3 Obinger, Leibfried, and Castles (2005, 314) for instance describe the German welfare state as "the great national unifying institution of the German state." In the late nineteenth century Austria was characterized by massive ethnic heterogeneity, particularly after Bosnia and Herzegovina was incorporated into the Habsburg Empire in 1878. Obinger and his colleagues (2005, 326) argue that "the early development of the Austrian welfare state must be seen as a means to counter the strong centrifugal forces of a multi-ethnic empire."

4 A case in point for the latter is the development of the British National Health Service (NHS) after the Second World War. That service was an outgrowth of the war with Germany. Its origins are poignantly expressed by Charles Webster (2002),

who claimed that "the *Luftwaffe* achieved in months what had defeated politicians and planners for at least two decades." During the 2012 London Summer Olympics Opening Ceremony, the British National Health Service was described as "the institution which more than any other unites our nation" (Adams 2012). Similarly, the Canadian experience of the Second World War triggered the development of social security programs that the Liberal government in 1945 argued had the potential to "strengthen true Canadian unity ... [and provide] ... a vital contribution to our development of the concept of Canadian citizenship and to the forging of lasting bonds of Canadian unity" (Jenson and Papillon, n.d., 38).

5 In Titmuss's words, "If men are treated as a burden to others – if this is the role expected of them – then, in time, they will behave as a burden" (1968, 26).

6 Sweden, for instance, is known to have a society that has a strong sense of "folkhemmet," that is, a "good home" characterized by mutual support and equality of opportunity. Certainly, when Per Albin Hansson developed these concepts in 1928, Sweden was a much more homogenous society than it is today. Nevertheless, would it be unreasonable to assume that some of that altruism that motivated the establishment of national welfare states during periods of high social homogeneity spills over into how outsiders are included today, now that societies have become more heterogenous?

7 The Hausman specification test revealed a chi^2 test larger than .05 (i.e., .27) which rejects the hypothesis that a fixed effects model is appropriate.

8 The first of the two items on this variable technically does not measure racist sentiment directly. However, the correlation with the second item is so striking that it seems reasonable to assume it functions as a latent variable for such sentiment. In any event, the results are not an artefact of the composite nature of the "racism" variable. The higher the value on the IESPI, the higher the value on either variable.

9 Extrapolations were calculated simply by averaging the existing observations. However, of the four time points, at least three had to be observed in order to calculate the remaining fourth one.

APPENDIX

Appendix Table 4.1. Tabular presentation of linear regression results (random effects models) as shown in Figures 4.3, 4.4, and 4.5 (robust standard errors in parentheses)

Variables	(1) racism	(2) xenophobia	(3) welfare cheats
IESPI	0.03***	0.15**	0.20**
	(0.01)	(0.06)	(0.08)
Multiculturalism	–0.00	–0.06	0.35
	(0.05	(0.50)	(0.39)
Total generosity	0.01	–0.09	0.70**
	(0.04)	(0.14)	(0.31)
Percentage foreign-born	–0.11***	–0.15	–0.32
	(0.02)	(0.16)	(0.29)
Social expenditure	0.07**	0.29	0.42**
	(0.03)	(0.18)	(0.20)
Liberal	0.78	–2.34	7.30**
	(0.50)	(2.66)	(3.71)
Social democratic	–0.68**	–4.11**	–5.89***
	(0.28)	(1.65)	(1.96)
Southern	0.46	–3.39	–1.60
	(0.40)	(3.41)	(2.01)
Observations	59	76	56
Number of countries	15	19	16
R-square:			
Within	0.12	0.02	0.13
Between	0.86	0.70	0.73
Overall	0.59	0.40	0.35

* $p < 0.1$; ** $p < 0.05$; *** $p < 0.01$

5 Closing the Gaps: The Positive Effects of Welfare Inclusion on Immigrants' Labour Market Integration

ANIL DUMAN, MARTIN KAHANEC, AND LUCIA MÝTNA KUREKOVÁ

In recent decades we have witnessed a significant rise in global migration flows accompanied by changes in national migration policies (De Haas, Natter, and Vezzoli 2015).[1] Given that projections anticipate that migration flows into developed countries will increase in the coming years (UN-DESA 2016), it is crucial for us to understand which factors contribute to successful labour market integration of immigrants in host countries. Most evidence to date reveals that immigrant labour market performance systematically falls behind that of native-born citizens (Barrett and Duffy 2008; Chiswick and Miller 2011; Kahanec and Zimmermann 2011; Zimmermann et al. 2008). This is important from the perspective of the overall contribution migration makes to well-being in home and host countries, which has been widely studied in terms of economic, social, cultural, and religious impacts (Kaczmarczyk 2013), and also given the link between exclusion of immigrants and negative public opinion (see chapter 4 in this volume). One of the most heated debates today concerns the role of the welfare state in shaping migration dynamics in terms of numbers, selection and integration of immigrants, and the resulting fiscal impacts on host countries.

So far, most research on the link between welfare states and migration has focused on two broad areas. First, welfare states have been examined from the perspective of the fiscal impact of immigration conditional on different models of welfare and levels of social spending (Kaczmarczyk 2013; Nannestad 2007; Österman, Palme, and Ruhs 2019). Some of this literature has focused on understanding how the self-selection of migrants into host countries may be impacted by welfare state generosity (Borjas 1999). Second, a growing body of research has looked at the role of welfare states, or institutions more generally, in facilitating or hindering immigrants' integration (Guzi, Kahanec, and Kureková 2014; Huber 2015; Koopmans 2010). This chapter contributes to the latter debate, addressing the sixth hypothesis presented in chapter 1 of this volume regarding the impact of exclusionary policies on immigrant integration (see Figure 1.1 in chapter 1). We ask two related questions: (1) What is the relationship between social welfare inclusiveness and labour market outcomes of immigrants in host countries? and (2) In which social policy areas does inclusion encourage the labour market integration of immigrants?

We find evidence that at the aggregate level, greater social policy inclusiveness supports the labour market integration of immigrants both in terms of accessing the labour market (labour market participation) and in terms of finding a job (unemployment rate). However, our findings also point to the need to open the "welfare state black box" and carefully consider the often conflicting effects of greater inclusiveness across social policy areas. On the one hand, we find evidence that inclusiveness plays an especially positive role in housing benefits schemes, which seem to increase immigrants' participation *and* stability in the labour market. On the other hand, greater inclusion in social assistance programs seems to lock immigrants out of the labour market, decreasing their labour market activity and increasing their unemployment rates relative to native-born citizens. The impact of these two social policy areas on immigrants' labour market integration outcomes appear to be immune to general economic conditions, skill composition of immigrants and native-born citizens, the size of the immigrant population, and changes to migration policy restrictiveness.

The contribution of our work lies in a systematic historical and comparative approach that enables us to evaluate the impact of social welfare inclusiveness on immigrants' labour market integration across different institutional contexts and over time. We analyse 19 developed economies around the world[2] for which social policy programs targeting immigrants were mapped from 1990 to 2019. We construct a panel dataset mapping almost 30 years of social policy inclusiveness documented in the IESPI dataset as well as migration dynamics to study whether higher social inclusiveness contributes to better labour market integration of immigrants relative to native-born citizens, measured as gaps in unemployment rates and labour market participation between immigrants and native-born citizens. To the best of our knowledge, the time and country coverage of our work is unique and will enrich current debates over the role of welfare state policies in immigrant labour market integration.

In the next section we review two bodies of literature relevant to our study: factors influencing labour market gaps between immigrants and native-born citizens, and the link between the welfare state and immigration. After stating our hypotheses, we present the data sources we utilized to construct our panel dataset as well as the econometric methodology. The subsequent section discusses our findings on the relationships among social policies, labour force participation gaps, and unemployment gaps. The final section offers brief concluding remarks.

Literature Review

There is abundant literature on the reasons for immigrant underperformance in the labour market. There is also a growing body of research investigating the role of welfare states, and institutions more generally, in facilitating or hindering immigrant integration in host countries. Next we review these literatures in turn.

Determinants of Immigrant Labour Market Integration

Labour market integration is a key vehicle of integration, for it enables immigrants to earn a living. Starting with seminal works by Chiswick (1978) and Borjas (1985), who examined immigrant adjustment in the US labour market, this topic has received extensive scholarly attention. These studies have concluded that labour market gaps tend to shrink over time spent in the receiving country and that they may vary in terms of outcome variables (employment, unemployment, job quality, wages), individual characteristics (e.g., gender, age, education, ethnicity), legal status, receiving countries, and the region of origin of immigrants (Adsera and Chiswick 2007; Blume and Verner 2007; Cangiano, 2014; Felbo-Kolding, Leschke, and Spreckelsen 2019; Gorinas 2014; Gorodzeisky and Semyonov 2017; Kahanec and Zaiceva 2009; Voitchovsky 2014). Several studies show that gaps seldom disappear entirely and that some of them are transferred across generations of immigrants; indeed, some of these gaps may even widen in subsequent generations (Connor and Koenig 2015; Kahanec and Zimmermann 2011).[3] Additional evidence points out that discriminatory attitudes toward immigrants may pose barriers to their labour market integration (Carlsson and Rooth 2007; Connor and Koenig 2015; Constant, Kahanec, and Zimmermann 2009; Luthra 2013).

Labour market gaps may be attributable to various other factors besides observable socio-demographic differences between immigrants and native-born citizens. Differences manifesting themselves at the micro-level include the market value of the education acquired in different sending countries (Chiswick and Miller 2003; Stangej et al. 2019); the level of (host) country-specific human capital, such as skills and language (Chiswick and Miller 2003, 2005); and social contacts and social norms (Gorinas 2014; Leschke and Weiss 2020). Spatial or occupational segregation (Andersson et al. 2018; Felbo-Kolding, Leschke, and Spreckelsen 2019; Kogan 2004) and the business cycle's differential impact on immigrants (Blume and Verner 2007) have also been identified as explanations for immigrant underperformance.

Recent scholarship has paid increasing attention to macro-level policy and institutional factors, such as receiving countries' labour market institutions (Devitt 2018) as well as other institutional factors (Huber 2015; Kahanec, Kim, and Zimmermann 2013). Of key relevance in this respect are admission policies, which regulate access to the labour market and the composition of immigrants; and integration policies, which aim to smooth the transition into the host country's labour market and society (Cangiano, 2014). Czaika and de Haas (2011) conclude that changes in admission policies have a small but significant effect on the volume of migration relative to other economic and political determinants of migration. They show that admission policies may well affect the composition of migration flows in the long term, and they call for more research to confirm this. According to Cangiano (2014), the potential impact of admission policies is twofold. First, they may influence the number and skill levels of immigrant workers (points-based systems, quotas, bilateral agreements, asylum policies, student-targeted migration, etc.). Second, they may impact labour market dynamics through labour market access restrictions and regulations, such as the requirement for various types of residence and employment permits.

Many European countries have in recent years implemented policies facilitating the entry and stay of highly skilled foreigners as well as foreigners with skills deemed scarce in the labour market (De la Rica, Glitz, and Ortega 2015), with the aim of attracting immigrants favourable to the host country's needs. Koettl, Holzmann, and Scarpetta (2006) posit that immigration policies with a strong demand-driven component seem best able to ensure the most suitable composition of immigrants for destination countries' labour markets. Yet the effect of selective admission policies on the skill composition of immigrants is not always positive. For example, Anderson and Ruhs (2008) argue that the employment restrictions in the UK (e.g., its temporary seasonal agricultural worker scheme) limit migrant mobility across occupational sectors and also keep workers in unattractive jobs with low wages, or in remote geographical regions. This may explain immigrants' poorer labour market outcomes.

Looking deeper into the role of integration policies, Ramos, Matano, and Nieto (2015) show that wage gaps between immigrants and the native-born are lower in countries with more favourable integration policies, measured by the MIPEX migration policy index. In an EU-wide analysis of immigrants' responsiveness to labour and skill shortages, Guzi, Kahanec, and Kureková (2018) find that immigrants respond more fluidly to changing skill shortages in countries with more open immigration and integration policies.

In sum, various individual-level as well as macro-institutional and structural factors come into play in explaining labour market gaps between immigrants and the native-born and in shaping the prospects of successful immigrant integration. Immigration and integration policies may affect employment type through work permits and other regulatory norms; they may also influence immigrants' labour market outcomes, including the quality of their employment. A particular interest in this chapter is the role of the welfare state and social policies in shaping immigrant integration, which we review more extensively in the next section.

Welfare State, Social Policies, and Immigration

Recent years have seen growth in the academic literature about welfare systems as a potential pull factor of immigration (Borjas, 1999; De Jong, Graefe, and Pierre 2005). Migration theories propose a diversity of factors influencing migration patterns. While welfare generosity in host countries may be a factor, immigration is driven primarily by wage and unemployment differentials between the home and host countries, geographical proximity, migration policy, and social and migrant networks (Barrett and McCarthy 2008; Brettell and Hollifield 2008; Massey et al. 1993). Sending-country factors and policies, including welfare policies, may also play a role (Koettl, Holzmann and Scarpetta 2006; Kureková 2013). Some scholars have argued that on a systemic level there are relatively strong institutional complementarities between minimalist welfare provisions, open migrant admission policies, and underdeveloped integration policies (Bommes and Geddes 2000; Menz 2003, 2009; Ruhs 2011; Sainsbury 2006).

Evidence on migrants' relative resort to welfare, and on the fiscal effects of immigration, remains inconclusive. Various review studies provide a comprehensive theoretical and empirical overview of this issue and conclude that numerous factors, including the type of migration, labour market incorporation, and the structure of the welfare state in the host country, combine to determine the fiscal impact of migration and migrants' resort to welfare (Giulietti and Wahba 2013; Kaczmarczyk 2013). Comparative large-N studies tend to show that the impact of welfare generosity on migration is negligible (Giulietti et al. 2013; Pedersen, Pytlikova, and Smith 2008). Interestingly, Kerr and Kerr (2011) find that migrants rely more on welfare benefits in Europe than in the US or Canada. Rigzin and Kaushal (chapter 6 in this volume) find no evidence that higher social welfare inclusiveness of immigrants has had a statistically robust impact on overall government expenditure over the past three decades.

There are several countries where immigrants turn to social benefits more than the native-born population, such as Denmark (Zimmermann et al. 2012), Sweden (Hansen and Lofstrom 2003), and the UK (Barrett and McCarthy 2008). On the other hand, Barrett and Maître (2013) find that immigrants in the EU are not more likely to be receiving welfare than native-born citizens. Even regarding unemployment benefits, it has been found that immigrants are *less* likely to resort to them than comparable native-born citizens when individual characteristics and unemployment propensity are controlled for. When immigrants are found to use welfare more intensively than native-born citizens, the gap is often attributable to differences in social and demographic characteristics between the two groups and possibly also to more limited access to insurance-based social policies linked to past employment, such as sickness insurance or unemployment insurance.

One possible reason why studies about the impact of the welfare state on immigrants' labour market outcomes are inconclusive and at times contradictory is that welfare systems are complex regimes with several functions and composed of various sub-policies, with possibly opposing effects on labour market outcomes of immigrants (Guzi, Kahanec, and Kureková 2022). Welfare systems are in effect sets of institutions and policies that directly or indirectly intervene in the functioning of labour markets in addressing various market failures (Devitt 2011; Eugster 2018; Kureková 2013).

Access to social programs, whether in the form of services (education, healthcare), social insurance (unemployment benefits, pensions, active labour market policies), or social assistance (minimum income schemes, family benefits), is highly regulated by various eligibility criteria. Even for the native-born, the right to draw on such programs is a function of many factors, such as previous legal employment, history of social security contributions, age, labour market status, and marital status. Advanced economies often place additional restrictions on immigrants' access to welfare based on criteria related to immigrant status, type of labour migration scheme, citizenship, and country of origin (Carrera 2005; Curtis et al. 2017; Kubal 2009; Kvist 2004). These factors result in a fluidity of inclusion and exclusion for different immigrant groups, so that immigrants and their families face different barriers across countries and over time (Hemerijck, Palm, Entenmann, and Van Hooren 2013; Sainsbury 2012).

Existing research also seems to suggest that inclusion in various welfare and social policies may have different impacts on the labour market integration of immigrants relative to the native-born. Much research so far has focused on access to social assistance, including minimum income schemes or family benefits. Some scholars argue that access to these programs may have a lock-in effect and disincentivize labour market integration, especially at the low-skilled spectrum of the labour market (Borjas and Hilton 1996; Hagelund 2005). Koopmans (2010) argues that countries that combine generous welfare policies with strong multiculturalism policies in which there are no clear incentives for interethnic interaction and language acquisition create an environment that results in negative labour market outcomes for immigrants.

Yet other scholars have pointed out that immigrants tend to assimilate out of welfare with time (Blume and Verner 2007). Various studies also reveal that immigrants have higher poverty rates than native-born citizens, which explains their higher reliance on income support (Bárcena-Martín and Pérez-Moreno 2017; Blume et al. 2007). Furthermore, both monetary and in-kind family benefits (access to child care, maternity leave, etc.) can have a strong poverty-alleviating effect and contribute to positive labour market outcomes for immigrants (Eugster 2018). In fact, active welfare policy can reduce the duration of social assistance use by immigrants (Heinesen, Husted, and Rosholm 2013), especially if it helps them gain country-specific skills.

Active labour market policies (ALMPs) are of particular interest in investigating labour market gaps between immigrants and the native-born. ALMPs generally target unemployed, inactive individuals and various disadvantaged groups of native-born individuals as well as immigrants; they include tools such as job search assistance, wage subsidies, and training. ALMPs may strengthen knowledge of the receiving country's official languages, which is key to success in the labour market as well as to meaningful participation in other types of training in host countries. The participation of immigrants in active labour market measures has been shown to have a significant positive impact on their prospects for labour market inclusion; this is much less convincingly the case for the general population (Butschek and Walter 2014; Clausen et al. 2009; Heinesen et al., 2013; Sarvimäki and Hämäläinen 2016).

To date, the impact of immigrant inclusion (or a lack thereof) in other social and welfare instruments, such as the health care system (Fortuny and Chaudry 2011), housing benefits (Magnusson Turner and Hedman 2014; Wimark, Haandrikman, and Nielsen 2019), and pensions, on labour market outcomes appears to be less researched. Indirectly, however, we can anticipate that better health and adequate housing contribute to the participation of immigrants in labour markets. Similarly, access to tax-based as well as contributory pensions is typically linked to labour market participation, and this may incentivize immigrants to engage with the labour market.

Another macro-level structural and institutional factor that has been found to shape immigrant labour market integration is labour market regulation, which includes employment protection regulations and industrial relations systems (Devitt 2018; Eugster 2018; Migali 2018; Sá 2011; Ulceluse and Kahanec 2018). While we acknowledge the possible intervening role of these other parameters, it is beyond the scope and data possibilities of this chapter to investigate them fully.

Hypotheses

The above literature leads us to propose two opposing hypotheses, which we will investigate empirically. The *welfare trap perspective* anticipates that access to benefits disincentivizes immigrants from labour market integration and contributes to higher levels of inactivity. Based on this line of reasoning, we should expect welfare exclusion to *improve* immigrants' labour market integration outcomes – that is, more exclusion is associated with less unemployment and higher labour market participation of immigrants relative to the native-born.

The *welfare access perspective* argues that access to (some) social programs helps mitigate the barriers immigrants face in labour market integration in host countries and thereby facilitates their access to the labour market and improves their labour market outcomes relative to the native-born. So we would anticipate that exclusion will *reduce* immigrants' labour market integration – that is, greater levels of welfare exclusion is associated with higher unemployment and lower labour market participation of immigrants relative to the native-born.

The IESPI dataset measures the inclusion of immigrants in various social policy areas, thus allowing us to investigate the competing hypotheses both on a general level and with respect to specific social policy areas. We test the overall score as well as all seven sub-indices to clarify whether the effect of exclusion varies by specific social policy domain.

Regarding the seven social policy areas that construct the overall IESPI index, the literature is more extensive about the effect of immigrant inclusion on labour market outcomes with respect to social assistance, contributory unemployment benefits, and active labour market policies, but much thinner about – for example – inclusion in housing benefits, or pensions. We anticipate, however, that welfare trap hypotheses will be less useful in explaining the differences between immigrant and native-born labour market participation for those policies where previous labour market activity typically conditions access (contributory pensions, contributory unemployment benefits) or which aim directly to activate those who are more distant from the labour market (active labour market policies). Access to decent housing and health care protect against social risks and are preconditions for labour market activity, so we anticipate that more inclusion in these social sub-policies will result in greater labour market participation and less unemployment. Other policies may have different effects on immigrants' relative unemployment levels. For example, we hypothesize that greater inclusion in social assistance and unemployment benefits may cement immigrants outside the labour market, given that those benefits may offer some a suitable alternative to employment.

Data and Methodology

To examine the impact of exclusion from social programs on immigrants' labour market integration, we construct a panel dataset covering 19 countries[4] for the years 1990–2019. We measure immigrant labour market integration as immigrant/native-born gaps in labour force participation and in unemployment rates; those gaps are calculated by subtracting the respective value of the indicator for the native-born from the value for the foreign-born. These two measures capture two key areas in which immigrants' labour market integration occurs (or not): whether immigrants seek employment (or have a job), and whether they, participation granted, succeed in securing a job. This study's key independent variables come from the Immigrant Exclusion from Social Programs Index (IESPI), which collects comparative data about immigrant exclusion in seven policy areas: tax-paid pensions, health care, contributory unemployment, contributory pension, housing benefits, social assistance, and active labour market policies. The IESPI measures formal rules and legislation, not the actual implementation of policies. Its value ranges from 0 to 100 where 0 is the most inclusionary approach and 100 is the most exclusionary approach to social welfare inclusion. A composite summary index is calculated from respective sub-indices (see chapter 2).

Our primary independent variable, the IESPI, has been calculated for a limited number of years: 1990, 2000, 2010, and 2015. To increase the frequency of the data, we employed the linear interpolation technique[5] to construct new data points for each year in the period 1990–2019.[6] All of the control variables have been interpolated to reach the maximum number of observations. The description, data sources, and explanations are provided in Table A5.1.

With its wide country and time coverage, the IESPI enables us to systematically compare various social policies in terms of their accessibility for immigrants across a number of countries with different welfare regimes. The wide geographical coverage and lengthy periodization make it impossible to include individual-level factors and work with micro-level data. Even so, the dataset enables us to test the merits of the welfare trap and welfare access hypotheses at the country level, accounting for the cross-country time-invariant variation in the data in fixed-effects models.

The selection of control variables is driven by the existing literature but limited by data constraints. We include GDP growth, total unemployment rate, public spending on welfare, stock of migrants, education levels for native-born and foreign-born populations, bureaucratic quality, and migration policy. It is well-established in the literature that the level of income and the performance of the labour market in the host and home countries are related to migration decisions and can also affect the labour market integration of immigrants (Borjas 1985; Morley 2006). Migrant characteristics matter as well, but due to data restrictions we can only control for education in our estimations; however, education can be taken as a proxy for skills, using the share of tertiary-educated among the native-born and the share of tertiary-educated among immigrants. Public spending on social policies can influence the integration of migrants by generating different employment opportunities and varied degrees of protection against objective and subjective risks (Brady and Finnigan 2014; Eugster 2018). We also control for bureaucratic quality, which is argued to have a positive impact on the net inflow of highly educated migrants (Ariu, Docquier, and Squicciarini 2016) and can also be considered a general proxy for policy implementation.

Lastly, we include a variable measuring change in migration policy restrictiveness over time. We include this variable because the existing literature points to its role in shaping migrant composition and selectivity, which are non-trivial for actual labour market outcomes. The variable measuring the restrictiveness of migration policy is constructed from the DEMIG migration policy database in a way that focuses on those groups of immigrants from whom labour market attachment is expected; thus it excludes measures of policy restrictiveness with respect to, for example, refugees or asylum seekers, who are often subject to specific social and labour market regimes.

Due to data limitations, we are unable to control for various individual-level characteristics such as gender, age, ethnicity, time since arrival, and the region of origin of immigrants, even though these can be highly relevant with regard to labour market gaps between immigrants and the native-born. Statistically speaking, we control for country-specific, time-invariant variation by introducing country-fixed effects in the models. We also acknowledge a possible reverse causality – that welfare and social policies are historically shaped in response to immigration (Brady and Finnigan 2014; Devitt 2010). This is also examined in chapter 3 of this volume, which looks at the possible impact of social expenditures and immigrants' welfare dependency on inclusionary policies. To alleviate this issue at least in part, in the analysis we lag the variables measuring socio-economic conditions and policies; this also reflects that these variables can be expected to influence the labour market only after a certain period. Nevertheless, the empirical strategy employed in this study does not permit a causal interpretation of the findings.

An additional limitation of our study is that we have only four data points in the IESPI dataset (1990, 2000, 2010, 2015), the rest being extrapolated. Linear interpolation is one of the most widely used techniques for predicting unobserved high-frequency values of a variable using observed frequency values and trend terms, hence allowing researchers to conduct analysis even when time series data are incomplete (Chow and Lin 1971). However, as with any forecasting technique, it makes strong assumptions, including that the rate of change between the known values is constant and there are no sudden jumps in the values we interpolate. Given the slow-changing nature of the IESPI index from year to year, it is likely that these assumptions hold. We should note here that without interpolation (and thus with far fewer data points), the coefficients estimated with the overall IESPI index become insignificant. However, we do find statistically significant results for one sub-index: exclusion from active labour market policies is positively linked to immigrants' relative labour market participation. Tables A5.2 and A5.3 present the results without interpolation.

Table 5.1. Summary statistics

	N	Mean	St.dev.	Min.	Max.
Labour force participation gap (%)	484	3.41	8.00	−11.13	20.33
Unemployment gap (%)	479	4.20	3.33	−2.60	20.00
GDP growth (%)	567	2.30	2.67	−8.27	26.28
Unemployment (%)	525	7.33	3.84	1.48	26.09
Share of tertiary educated (Native born)	401	26.82	8.54	9.62	57.59
Share of tertiary educated (Foreign born)	403	23.50	7.51	5.97	44.66
Public spending on social expenditure (%)	565	21.52	4.65	10.49	34.18
Bureaucratic quality	567	3.82	0.40	2.00	4.00
Migrant stock (% of population)	133	12.49	7.69	1.27	43.96
Migration policy restrictiveness	251	2.08	4.61	−15.00	16.00
IESPI summary score	88	42.65	12.51	17.82	73.90
Tax pensions	88	55.31	19.68	20.54	100.00
Healthcare	88	51.56	18.09	18.75	100.00
Contributory unemployment benefits	79	47.42	12.14	25.00	75.00
Contributory pensions	78	16.29	19.86	0.00	86.07
Housing benefits	88	39.70	26.16	0.00	100.00
Social assistance	88	43.36	20.81	0.00	81.25

Finally, our measures of social welfare inclusiveness toward immigrants are based on formal rules and legislation. However, the actual inclusiveness of social welfare may depend on many procedural, cultural, and other factors and deviate from the formally defined measures. With the data at hand, the analysis can only measure formal, not actual, inclusiveness of welfare.

Table 5.1 presents summary statistics for all the variables used in the regression models. As can be seen, there is significant variation across countries and over the years. This is confirmed in Figure 5.1, which shows the relationship between the IESPI index and the difference in labour force participation between immigrants and the native-born. The first observation is that in 2015, immigrants outperformed the native-born in most of the countries studied in their levels of labour force participation. Second, no clear relationship appears to exist between the degree of immigrant exclusion and labour market participation – more inclusionary and more exclusionary countries are quite comparable in terms of how migrants perform. For example, in Sweden and the Netherlands, native-born labour force participation is 1.35 and 2.28 percentage points higher than for the foreign-born respectively, even though these countries differ vastly in social policy inclusion. A similar point can be made

Figure 5.1. Relationship between exclusion from social programs and labour force participation gap, 2015.

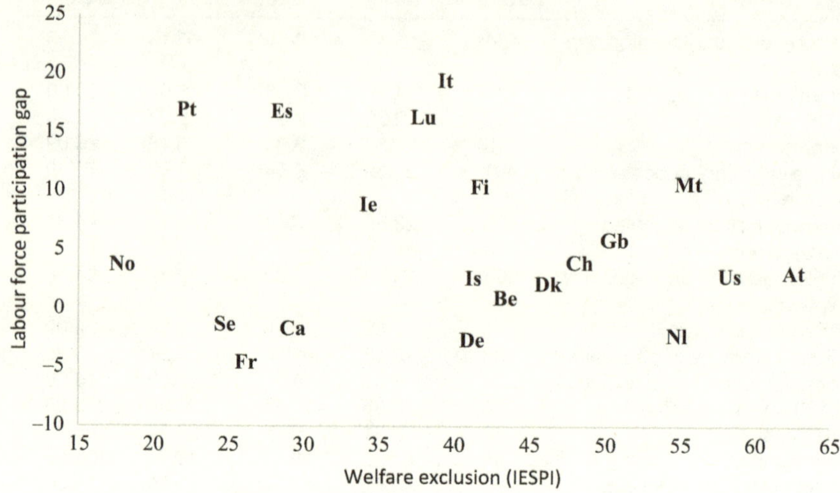

Source: Authors' estimations based on IESPI and panel data set.
Note: A positive labour force participation gap means that immigrants have higher labour force participation than native-born citizens.

about Norway and Austria, which are the most and least inclusive states in our sample. In these two countries, migrants' labour force participation is very similar (3.76 and 3.11 percentage points higher than the domestic population, respectively).

Figure 5.2 displays the gap between unemployment rates for the same year, 2015. Once again, no immediate relationship can be detected between exclusion from social programs and labour market outcomes for unemployment. Except in Malta and the US, immigrants' unemployment rate is consistently higher than the rate for the native-born. However, there is variation among the countries in terms of the magnitude of the gap. For example, in Portugal, which takes an inclusionary approach, the unemployment gap between the native-born and foreign-born populations is only 2.6 percentage points whereas that gap is more than 10 percentage points in Belgium, where social policies are more exclusionary of immigrants.

We use a standard fixed-effect panel regression technique to explore the relationship between social policy inclusiveness and labour market integration. To control for unobserved heterogeneity, we allow the intercept to vary from country to country (entity effects). The model is as follows:

$$y_{i,t} = \alpha_i + X_{i,t}\beta + \phi_i + \varepsilon_{i,t}$$

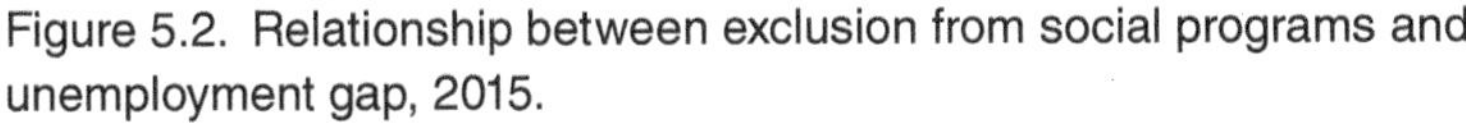
Figure 5.2. Relationship between exclusion from social programs and unemployment gap, 2015.

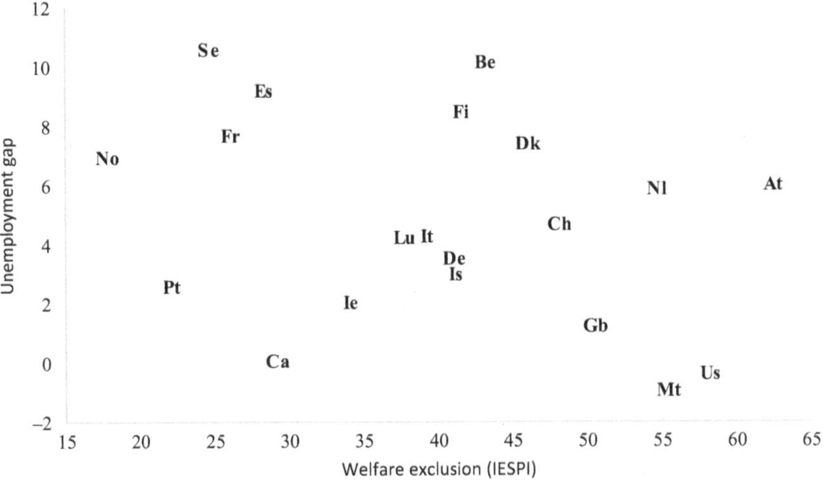

Source: Authors' estimations based on IESPI and panel data set.
Note: A positive unemployment gap means that immigrants have a higher unemployment rate than the native-born population.

where $y_{i,t}$ is the gap in labour force participation or unemployment between native-born and foreign-born in each country i and year t. The intercept α_i is the vector of individual effects c. $X_{i,t}$ is a design matrix with β being a column vector of estimated coefficients. The disturbance term is denoted with $\varepsilon_{i,t}$. To take time effects into account, 1-year lagged values of GDP growth, unemployment rate, migrant stock, and public spending are used in the regression models. The fixed-effect term ϕ_i enables us to control for the variation across countries that is time-invariant within countries. Besides the variation in economic, political, geographic, historical, policy, and other variables, this encompasses the possible effects of immigrant selection, to the extent that it is time-invariant within countries.

Results

Table 5.2 presents the estimation results of our panel data covering 19 countries and the period 1990–2019.[7] The estimated coefficients in the specification with control variables (column II) indicate that welfare exclusion reduces the immigrant–native-born gap in labour force participation, suggesting that the more inclusionary the social policies are, the easier it gets for immigrants to enter the labour market. For example, when we look at the conditional marginal effects,[8] a 1-point increase in the IESPI index brings about a 0.27-point reduction in the participation difference. In other words, moving from the most inclusionary country (Norway) to the most exclusionary one (Austria) would decrease the labour force participation gap between immigrants and native-born by 12.7 points. Our results, therefore, suggest that inclusionary social policy is positively associated with immigrants' labour force participation.

Looking at the relationship between the IESPI and the unemployment gap, more exclusionary social policy increases the gaps between the two groups, by 0.14 percentage points for every one-unit increase in the IESPI in the specification with control variables (IV). In other words, less access and narrower coverage of social programs for immigrants augments the unemployment differences between foreign- and native-born populations. If we compare the least and most inclusionary social policy environments (Austria versus Norway), these coefficients translate into a 6.5-point change in the unemployment gap in the preferred specification. Similar to our findings regarding labour force participation, we also observe that the IESPI is significantly related to the unemployment gap even in the absence of covariates. It is worth emphasizing that the findings are robust in terms of changes in the restrictiveness of migration policy. In other words, whether the countries are getting more open does not affect the impact of social policy inclusion.[9]

The coefficients of control variables are in line with our expectations. Lagged GDP growth does not appear to affect either immigrants' relative labour force participation or unemployment. Lagged unemployment is negatively associated with the labour force participation gap but has a positive association for the unemployment gap. This may suggest that higher overall unemployment in the country discourages immigrants from entering the labour market and reduces their labour market prospects once they participate.

We find that larger immigrant populations and a higher percentage of tertiary-degree holders among immigrants both reduce the labour force participation of the immigrant population in comparison to native-born citizens as well as their relative unemployment rate. Conversely, a higher share of tertiary-educated native-born citizens has an improving effect on the labour market participation of immigrants relative to native-born individuals, but no effect on immigrants in terms of unemployment rate. As expected, we find that the educational structure of the native-born population as well as of immigrants significantly shapes the relative standing of these two groups in the labour market.

Bureaucratic quality and lagged social spending both increase the labour force participation difference and reduce unemployment gaps (although the association between bureaucratic quality and the unemployment gap is not significant). This could indicate that as social spending and quality of public services go up, immigrants benefit from them through better opportunities to enter the labour market as well through lower unemployment.

Table 5.2. Effect of IESPI overall score on LFP and UR gaps

	LFP (I)	LFP (II)	UR (III)	UR (IV)
IESPI	−0.34***	−0.27***	0.07*	0.14***
	0.07	0.07	0.04	0.05
Lagged GDP growth		0.14		0.03
		0.09		0.06
Lagged unemployment rate		−0.95***		0.24**
		0.16		0.11
Lagged migrant stock		−0.07*		−0.06**
		0.04		0.03
Lagged social spending		2.10***		−0.41***
		0.25		0.16
Share of tertiary educated (FB)		−0.26***		−0.27***
		0.07		0.04
Share of tertiary educated (NB)		0.12***		0.00
		0.04		0.03
Bureaucratic quality		0.47***		−0.12
		0.21		0.14
Migration policy restrictiveness Change		−0.03		0.03
		0.04		0.03
R-squared	0.08	0.28	0.05	0.45
N	576	527	606	557

Notes: Dependent variable is the difference between immigrant and native-born LFP and UR rates. Second rows represent standard errors. ***, **, and * denote 0.01, 0.05 and 0.1 significance levels respectively. Hausman tests confirm FE model specification.

To get a more fine-tuned understanding of the effect of specific social programs, we also inspect the sub-indices of the IESPI database separately. In Table 5.3, we present how sub-indices of social policy that are used to construct the IESPI summary score shape the labour market outcomes for immigrants in relation to the native-born population.[10] A key message of the disaggregated approach is that once we consider different social policy areas, we find that the relationship between social policy inclusiveness and labour market integration outcomes of immigrants relative to the native-born population varies across policy areas. First, more exclusion from tax-paid pensions, housing benefits, and active labour market policies is associated with worse labour force participation outcomes for immigrants, providing support for the welfare access hypothesis.

Second, more exclusion from contributory unemployment benefits and social assistance increases the labour force participation gap between immigrants and the native-born, implying support for the welfare trap hypothesis. This is partly against our expectation that inclusion in policies where benefits are conditioned on previous employment (contributory unemployment benefits, contributory pensions) would enhance immigrant labour market participation.

With respect to contributory unemployment benefits, the coefficient is also relatively large. For example, a one-point increase in exclusion from contributory unemployment benefits increases the labour force participation gap by 0.62 percentage points in our model without control variables and raises the gap by 0.41 percentage points with covariates. Given that to be eligible for these kinds of benefits one already must pay into social security, it is hard to derive precise conclusions about the implications. Exclusion from contributory pensions and health care does not have a robust association with the difference in labour force participation between foreign and native-born individuals, considering we find contradicting results in the specifications with and without control variables for these programs.

Next, we explore the association between each social policy and the unemployment performance of immigrants relative to native-born groups in models III and IV in Table 5.3. We find systematic and stable results for sub-policies except for tax-paid pensions. Exclusion from health care, contributory unemployment benefits, social assistance, and active labour market policies reduces immigrants' relative unemployment rate and hence favours immigrants, implying evidence for the welfare trap hypothesis. On the other hand, exclusion from contributory pensions and housing benefits is associated with higher unemployment rates of immigrants relative to the native-born population, which could be taken as support for the welfare access hypothesis.

Conclusions

In this chapter we have studied how social welfare inclusiveness is associated with the labour market integration of immigrants in a range of developed countries. Exploiting the novel IESPI dataset and various macroeconomic datasets to construct a panel covering 19 developed countries over three decades (1990–2019), we found that more inclusive social welfare is associated with more favourable labour market integration outcomes for immigrants: in countries with more inclusive welfare regimes, immigrants have higher labour force participation rates and lower unemployment rates relative to the native-born population. This result suggests that more inclusive social welfare approaches not only foster more equality of opportunity between immigrants and the native-born but seem in fact to result in more favourable outcomes for immigrants as well.

However, we document important variations in the estimated effects across various social welfare instruments that shed more light on the above finding. Regarding labour force participation gaps between immigrants and the native-born, more inclusive contributory unemployment benefits and social assistance work against immigrants' economic integration. Conversely, more inclusive active labour market policies, housing benefits, and tax-paid pensions improve immigrants' standing. With regard to native-born–immigrant

Table 5.3. Joint effect of different social policies' exclusiveness on labour market integration

	LFP (I)	LFP (II)	UR (III)	UR (IV)
Tax-paid pensions	−0.09*	−0.11**	0.05***	0.03
	0.05	0.04	0.02	0.02
Health care	−0.01	0.24***	−0.09***	−0.13***
	0.06	0.07	0.02	0.03
Contributory unemployment benefits	0.62***	0.41***	−0.15***	−0.13***
	0.10	0.08	0.04	0.04
Contributory pensions	0.12*	−0.38***	0.24***	0.33***
	0.07	0.11	0.03	0.05
Housing benefits	−0.25***	−0.23***	0.35***	0.38***
	0.06	0.07	0.02	0.03
Social assistance	0.18***	0.24***	−0.19***	−0.26***
	0.06	0.05	0.02	0.02
Active labour market policies	−0.33***	−0.22***	−0.06***	−0.05***
	0.04	0.04	0.02	0.02
Lagged GDP growth		0.16**		0.00
		0.08		0.03
Lagged unemployment rate		−1.30***		0.21
		0.14		0.06
Lagged migrant stock		−0.10**		−0.05***
		0.04		0.02
Lagged social spending		2.62***		−0.16*
		0.21		0.09
Share of tertiary educated (FB)		0.26***		0.09***
		0.08		0.03
Share of tertiary educated (NB)		−0.01		−0.07***
		0.04		0.02
Bureaucratic quality		0.47**		−0.08
		0.22		0.10
Migration policy restrictiveness Change		0.05		0.07***
		0.03		0.01
R-squared	0.08	0.25	0.53	0.44
N	514	465	544	495

Notes: Dependent variable is the difference between immigrant and native-born LFP and UR rates. Second rows represent standard errors. ***, **, and * denote 0.01, 0.05 and 0.1 significance levels respectively. Hausman tests confirm FE model specification.

unemployment rate gaps, more exclusionary health care, contributory unemployment benefits, social assistance, and active labour market policies seem to favour immigrants, increasing (or decreasing less) the native-born unemployment rate vis-à-vis immigrants' unemployment rate. Moreover, exclusionary housing benefits and contributory pensions worsen the situation of immigrants by decreasing (or increasing less) the unemployment rate of the native-born vis-à-vis immigrants. We hence find only partial support for our initial hypotheses regarding the effects of exclusion from specific programs. While the findings that exclusion from housing benefits worsens, and exclusion from social assistance improves, immigrants' labour market integration are in line with our expectations, the findings for other programs are less expected.

This variation in the estimated effects across social welfare instruments indicates that greater inclusiveness of some instruments plays an enabling role for immigrants with regard to their labour market integration. But other instruments may be trapping them in welfare or actually enabling native-born citizens more; on average, the latter tend to command greater economic and social resources that gain them an advantage in the labour market. This seems to be the case with contributory unemployment benefits, for example, where inclusiveness seems to favour the native-born relative to immigrants in terms of both unemployment and labour force participation.

Importantly, we find some evidence to contest the suggestion that social policy inclusion hurts immigrants' economic integration. A welfare trap may manifest itself with respect to some programs, but this does not hold when the full welfare state apparatus and external conditions are taken into account. In practice, this means that governments need to carefully consider different social welfare policies, as well as their design and interactions, to fully understand how these might provide desirable incentives and conditions for positive labour market outcomes for immigrants.

We also call for further research to help us understand precisely how immigrant inclusion in different social policy areas incentivizes or disincentivizes immigrant behaviour in labour market, relative to other factors. Beyond those covered here, the role of multiculturalism policies could be considered more systematically, and micro-level analysis could shed light on a range of other issues we were unable to study in greater detail. Future research should also carefully consider the possible endogeneity in the interlinked relationship between migration and social policies in Western democracies.

NOTES

1 L.M. Kureková acknowledges the financial support of VEGA [2/0079/21] from the Scientific Grant Agency of the Ministry of Education, Science, Research and Sports of the Slovak Republic, and the Slovak Academy of Sciences. The authors also appreciate the research assistance of Hannah Taylor.

2 Austria, Belgium, Canada, Denmark, Finland, France, Germany, Iceland, Ireland, Italy, Luxembourg, Netherlands, Norway, Portugal, Spain, Sweden, Switzerland, UK, and USA.

3 In addition to the studies that take a pan-European perspective, there are numerous country studies, including Clark and Drinkwater (2008) on the UK, Amuedo-Dorantes

and De la Rica (2007) on Spain, Venturini and Villosio (2008) on Italy, Voitchovsky (2014) on Ireland, and Biavaschi and Zimmermann (2014) on Germany.

4 The original IESPI data set has values for 22 countries over all policy areas and summary scores for the years 1990, 2000, 2010, and 2015. Due to lack of data on labour market outcomes, Australia and New Zealand are excluded from fixed-effect regressions. Malta was also excluded due to the lack of data on several control variables.

5 For details, see Chow and Lin (1971).

6 We also tried to exclude the last three years (2016–19) from interpolation as a robustness check; our findings remained the same.

7 In the baseline estimations without interpolation, the IESPI score is found to have an insignificant effect on both labour market outcomes. This can be due to the low number of observations; 62 and 53 for specifications with and without covariates, respectively. See Appendix Tables 5.2 and 5.3 for detailed results.

8 Full estimation results for marginal effects are not presented in the chapter but can be requested from the authors.

9 We also performed this analysis with adding Banting and Kymlicka's (2020) Multiculturalism Policy index and its interaction with the IESPI as control variables. Our results of the IESPI overall index remain robust, whereas multiculturalism policies and their interaction with the IESPI turn out to be mostly insignificant. This analysis can be considered a robustness check, but also a test of Koopmans's (2010) argument about a negative role of multiculturalism policies on labour market outcomes of immigrants in countries with generous welfare systems. Results are available upon request.

10 We test for multicollinearity to check whether sub-indices are linearly related to one another. However, there is no problem of multicollinearity, and each sub-index has potential explanatory power on its own.

APPENDIX

Appendix Table 5.1. Data sources and definitions

Description	Source	Notes
Labour force participation rate (%)	ILO and OECD	Separate rates for native-born and foreign-born populations.
Unemployment (%)	ILO and OECD	Separate rates for native-born and foreign-born populations.
GDP growth (%)	GLOW dataset	Annual change in GDP.
Unemployment (%)	GLOW dataset	Unemployment refers to the share of the labour force that is without work but available for and seeking employment.
Share of population by education across migrants and native-born	ILO	Aggregate education levels; less than basic, basic, intermediate, and advanced.

(Continued)

Appendix Table 5.1. Data sources and definitions (*Continued*)

Description	Source	Notes
Migrant stock (% of population)	GLOW dataset	International migrant stock is the number of foreign-born individuals (including refugees).
Public spending (% of GDP)	GLOW dataset	Social expenditure comprises cash benefits, direct in-kind provision of goods and services, and tax breaks with social purposes.
Bureaucratic quality	GLOW dataset	"Bureaucratic quality" combines responses on the quality of public service provision, the quality of the bureaucracy, the competence of civil servants, the independence of the civil service from political pressures, and the credibility of the government's commitment to policies.
Migration policy	DEMIG	Weighted and grouped summary score for change in migration policy restrictiveness.
IESPI scores (sum score and program scores)	IESPI dataset	Values ranging from 0 to 100, where 0 is maximally inclusionary and 100 is maximally exclusionary.

Appendix Table 5.2. Results without interpolation (IESPI overall score)

	LFP (I)	LFP (II)	UR (III)	UR (IV)
IESPI	0.00	0.02	–0.05	–0.03
	0.08	0.08	0.08	0.08
Lagged GDP growth		0.05		0.21
		0.25		0.25
Lagged unemployment rate		–0.21		0.74***
		0.21		0.22
Lagged migrant stock		–0.08		–0.07
		0.05		0.05
Lagged social spending		0.70*		–0.63
		0.35		0.38
Share of tertiary educated (FB)		0.11		0.01
		0.10		0.12
Share of tertiary educated (NB)		–0.43		0.09
		0.26		0.28
Bureaucratic quality		0.49*		–0.37
		0.26		0.27
R-squared	0.54	0.69	0.05	0.41
N	54	52	54	52

Notes: Dependent variable is the difference between immigrant and native-born LFP and UR rates. Second rows represent standard errors. ***, **, and * denote 0.01, 0.05, and 0.1 significance levels respectively. Hausman tests confirm FE model specification.

Appendix Table 5.3. Results without interpolation (sub-indices)

	LFP (I)	LFP (II)	UR (III)	UR (IV)
Tax-paid pensions	–0.05	0.00	0.04	0.01
	0.05	0.07	0.06	0.07
Health care	–0.10	–0.03	–0.08	–0.15
	0.07	0.09	0.09	0.10
Contributory unemployment benefits	0.20	0.03	–0.17	–0.12
	0.12	0.16	0.14	0.16
Contributory pensions	–0.03	–0.12	–0.03	0.02
	0.07	0.09	0.09	0.09
Housing benefits	–0.11	–0.13	0.12	0.12
	0.13	0.15	0.15	0.16
Social assistance	0.08	–0.03	–0.04	0.14
	0.08	0.12	0.10	0.13
Active labour market policies	0.10*	0.13*	–0.04	0.01
	0.05	0.06	0.06	0.06
Lagged GDP growth		0.34		0.29
		0.29		0.30
Lagged unemployment rate		–0.23		0.84***
		0.25		0.25
Lagged migrant stock		–0.12*		–0.09
		0.06		0.07
Lagged social spending		0.57		–0.57
		0.45		0.46
Share of tertiary educated (FB)		0.13		–0.03
		0.18		0.18
Share of tertiary educated (NB)		–0.32		–0.15
		0.44		0.45
Bureaucratic quality		0.69		–0.91*
		0.45		0.46
R-squared	0.70	0.80	0.16	0.60
N	48	46	49	47

Notes: Dependent variable is the difference between immigrant and native-born LFP and UR rates. Second rows represent standard errors. ***, **, and * denote 0.01, 0.05, and 0.1 significance levels respectively. Hausman tests confirm FE model specification.

6 It Ain't about the Money: A Cross-Country Study of the Fiscal Implications of Immigrant Exclusion

TSEWANG RIGZIN AND NEERAJ KAUSHAL

In recent decades, immigration has become a major source of population growth in many wealthy countries. For example, between 1990 and 2015 the share of foreign-born increased nearly fourfold in Italy (from 2.5% to 9.7%); more than threefold in Norway (from 4.5% to 14.2%); by 80% in Germany (from 7.5% to 13.5%), and by over 70% in the US (from 7.9% to 13.5%) (OECD, 2020). Immigrants encounter diverse sets of social policies from one country to the next. Some host countries have programs that are inclusive of immigrants (e.g., Canada, Norway, Sweden), while others have policies that explicitly exclude immigrants or certain groups of immigrants from a range of social programs (e.g., the UK, the US, Switzerland).

One widely held argument in favour of less inclusive policies toward immigrants is that exclusionary policies reduce the fiscal burden of immigration. Yet little research has been done to empirically investigate this argument. Extant research has studied the impact of immigration on public expenditures in general and on social expenditures in particular (see, e.g., Huddle and Simcox 1994; Fix and Passel 1994; Borjas and Hilton 1996; Rodrik 1998; Marcelli et al. 1998; Lee and Miller 1998, 2000; Soroka et al. 2006, 2015; Meinhard and Potrafke 2012; Gaston and Rajaguru 2013; Xu 2017; Blau et. al. 2017; Fenwick 2019). Several researchers have examined the impact of inclusive policies on the integration of immigrants (see, e.g., Kahanec, Kim, and Zimmerman 2013; Zhu and Xu 2015; Condon, Filindra, and Wichowsky 2015). But there has been much less research on the fiscal effects of specific policies, and none using cross-national panel data.

This chapter aims to test the seventh hypothesis of this volume, that is, the effect of welfare exclusion on government social spending (see also Figure 1.1 in chapter 1). To do so, we examine the fiscal consequences of policies toward immigrant inclusion or exclusion from social programs using data from 21 OECD countries[1] covering 25 years, from 1990 to 2015. We take advantage of the variation by year in the degree of social policy exclusion across countries, using models with country- and year-fixed effects, to estimate its association with social expenditures. We distinguish between overall exclusion and variation across program types. This research is important because if immigrant inclusionary policies have significant (adverse) fiscal impacts, they will be unsustainable in the long run. Furthermore, if immigrant inclusionary policies encourage an influx of low-skilled immigrants, who are more likely to receive social programs, it may accentuate adverse fiscal impacts. However, if immigrant exclusion has no fiscal effects or only marginal ones, this will increase the administrative costs of implementing programs that distinguish between native-born and immigrant populations, create discriminatory policies toward immigrants, hamper immigrant integration (i.e., by treating them differently and restricting their access to social programs), and in turn lower immigrant productivity and long-term tax contributions.

Immigrant exclusion from social programs and policies affects social expenditures via a number of direct and indirect channels, with varying long- and short-term impacts. The effects also differ by program type. In general, between two countries with similar economies, similar social welfare and tax systems, and similar demographics and immigrant characteristics, the country with a more exclusive set of safety net programs – in particular, cash transfer programs – will likely spend a lower proportion of its GDP on these programs in the short run. Furthermore, if more exclusionary policies discourage the immigration of populations that are more likely to receive social benefits, their fiscal costs will be lower. In periods of high immigration, inclusionary policies may also increase the pressure on host country finances, and this may result in countries paring down their welfare systems to lower their overall costs. (Fiscal pressures would be weaker where social programs are contributory and stronger where social programs are tax-based.) In such a scenario, immigrant inclusion may lead to weaker social welfare systems, in turn lowering social expenditures.

Importantly, the fiscal impact of inclusionary policies will differ by program type. Certain means-tested programs may induce behaviours that increase long-term dependence on welfare. Access to certain other types of programs may reduce public expenditures. For instance, access to public health care and health insurance may reduce health care expenditures by ensuring timely health care and thus avoiding expensive emergency public health care of the sort that is generally available to immigrants in most OECD countries (Ku and Matani 2001; Mohanty et al. 2005; Sommers 2013). Public health insurance may also reduce participation in means-tested programs, as found in studies in the US, where Medicaid expansions under the Affordable Care Act increased immigrant access to public health insurance (Medicaid), reduced participation in Supplemental Security Income,[2] and increased labour force participation (Burns and Dague 2017; Soni et al. 2017; Muchomba and Kaushal 2021).

Furthermore, immigrant inclusion in certain types of programs will have negligible cost implications if immigrants are less likely to use them. This applies to public health care because immigrants are generally healthier and younger than the native-born and therefore have lower health care utilization (Antecol and Bedard 2006; Kennedy et al. 2015; Riosmena, Kuhn, and Jochem 2017). This also applies to public pension programs. Because immigrants, on average, are younger than the native-born, their inclusion in contributory public pension schemes may create fiscal windfalls because they will have contributed for several years before receiving any benefits. In short, the effect of immigrant inclusivity on public expenditures differs across programs. In the empirical analysis, we estimate these effects across programs and expense types.

In the long run, more inclusionary policies will likely increase immigrant integration, thus enhancing immigrant productivity and contributions to the economy and the state exchequer; they will also reduce immigrant dependence on welfare, thus lowering social expenditures. The long-term impacts of inclusionary policies are important; however, due to data limitations, we confine our study to short-term impacts. In defence, we argue that short-term impacts are important, for they impact influence policies, and that our research design increases the probability of finding cost-saving effects of exclusionary policy approaches.

The fiscal effect of immigration on countries with similar degrees of inclusivity may vary depending on the overall generosity of their social programs. In our empirical analysis, we apply country-fixed effects to control for time-invariant differences in social programs across countries. Furthermore, year-fixed effects capture the effect of factors that may be influencing social expenditures globally (e.g., the 2008 financial crisis, which increased social spending in OECD countries).

Our research is hampered by the fact that policies regarding immigrant exclusion from social benefits are likely endogenous to immigration trends as well as social expenditures. Countries experiencing large-scale immigration may adopt exclusionary policies to limit the impact of immigration on social expenditures. Furthermore, as chapter 3 investigated, levels of welfare exclusion could be impacted by the structure of the welfare regime (and thus indirectly by welfare expenditure). While we are unable to directly address the endogeneity, we estimate models using lagged policy variables and control for the foreign-born share in the population and overall government revenue, in some models, to control for the size of the welfare state. Furthermore, in supplementary analyses, we estimate models of the association between exclusionary policies and immigration. We measure exclusion using the newly constructed Immigrant Exclusion from Social Programs Index (IESPI) (see chapter 2). That index is based on policies related to seven specific programs: tax-paid pension benefits, public health care or health care subsidies, contributory unemployment benefits, contributory pension benefits, housing benefits, social assistance, and labour market policies. We first study the association between total social expenditure and the overall index and then between the index and each of the seven programs; we follow this with estimates of the association between specific programs and corresponding public expenses, which are divided into five categories: expenditure on family benefits, pension expenditure, disability benefit expenditure, public health expenditure, and unemployment expenditure.

Overall, our analysis finds little evidence that exclusionary arrangements lead to savings on social expenditures. While exclusionary approaches are associated with modest reductions in social expenditure, in most of our models these effects are statistically insignificant. We also find no evidence that inclusionary arrangements attract immigrants who are particularly likely to turn to the state for support.

Literature Review

A large body of literature has spawned around the question of the fiscal effects of immigration. Researchers have used two different approaches: a static method measuring short-term fiscal effects of immigration (see, e.g., Huddle 1993; Passel and Clark 1994; Borjas 1995; Lee and Miller 1998), and a holistic, life cycle approach (see, e.g., Fix and Passel 1994; Marcelli, Smith, and Edmonston 1998; Lee and Miller 2000; Blau and Mackie 2017). Using a static approach, Huddle (1993) estimated that in 1992 immigrants in the US added a total net cost to all levels of government of $42.5 billion (Huddle 1993). Fix and Passel (1994) questioned Huddle's assumptions[3] and re-estimated the net fiscal impact of immigration after dropping Huddle's generalizations, concluding that annual taxes paid by immigrants in the US are higher than the combined costs of services they receive, generating a net annual surplus of US$25–$30 billion. Using a similar approach, Lee and Miller 1998) estimated the net fiscal contribution of existing immigrants and their concurrent descendants in the US in 1994 to be a surplus of US$23.5 billion, or 0.35% of GDP.

Studies taking similar static approaches have been conducted in other immigrant-receiving countries as well. Weber and Straubhaar (1996) estimated that in 1990 immigrants in Switzerland made an annual fiscal contribution of US$460 million, or 0.2% of GDP. Grady and Grubel (2015) estimated the fiscal impact of immigrants arriving in Canada between 1985 and 2009 and found that on average, in the fiscal year 2005–6, immigrants received an excess of C$5,329 in benefits over taxes paid. Hansen and colleagues (2015) in their study of Denmark found that the fiscal impact of immigration varied by immigrants' country of origin. They concluded that in 2014, non-Western immigrants residing in Denmark caused a deficit of around 1% of GDP, but that immigrants from Western countries represented a net fiscal benefit.

Taking a holistic, life cycle approach, Marcelli, Smith, and Edmonston (1998) estimated the heterogenous fiscal impacts of immigration in the US as a function of the skill levels of immigrants. They found that an immigrant with less than a high school education would incur a lifetime cost of $89,000 in terms of net services received (i.e., services received minus taxes paid). In contrast, an immigrant with more than a high school education would contribute $105,000 more in taxes over what they would receive in public services (Marcelli, Smith, and Edmonston 1998). Lee and Miller (2000) estimated the fiscal effect of raising net immigration in the United States and found that 100,000 more immigrants per year would initially raise taxes for the native-born, and later reduce them, by amounts less than 1% of current tax levels (Lee and Miller 2000).

In an extensive evaluation of the economic and fiscal effects of immigration in the US, Blau and Mackie (2017) concluded that on average over 75 years, an immigrant contributed $92,000 in net fiscal revenue. But the contribution differed greatly with educational attainment: the average immigrant with a BA degree contributed just over $200,000; the average immigrant with an MA or higher contributed over $500,000. Conversely, immigrants who lacked a high school diploma were a net liability, with an average cost of $115,000 per immigrant. The report concluded that while less-educated immigrants were a fiscal drag, more educated ones were a net gain, as were young and recent immigrants because they were better educated than earlier arrivals and had a long working life ahead of them. Using a similar approach for Sweden, Storesletten (2003) estimated that the average net government gain from a new immigrant who is 20 to 30 years old at the time of immigration is about 200,000 SEK, or about US$23,500. For immigrants older than 50 or younger than 10, the net cost is more than 1.5 million SEK, or about US$169,588. The study concluded that on average, a new immigrant represented a net government loss of 175,000 SEK, or about US$20,500 (Storesletten 2003).

In the UK, Dustmann and Frattini (2014) found that between 1995 and 2011, immigrants were generally less likely than the native-born living in the same region of the country to receive state benefits or tax credits or to live in social housing. They found that immigrants from the European Economic Area (EEA) contributed 10% more than people born in the UK and that non-EEA immigrants contributed 9% less. They also found that recent immigrants made a much larger fiscal contribution than older immigrants. Immigrants who had been in the UK for fewer than 10 years contributed £20 billion to the UK exchequer: those from EEA countries contributed £5 billion and those from non-EEA countries £15 billion. Of great importance was their contribution during the financial crisis of 2007–11: in those years, recent EEA immigrants contributed £2 billion and recent non-EEA immigrants £8.6 billion.

Evidence from other OECD countries suggests that the overall fiscal effect of immigration – positive or negative – is modest. OECD (2013) found that immigration to OECD countries over the past 50 years on average has had a negligible fiscal impact, rarely rising above 0.5% of GDP.

Several cross-national studies have examined the fiscal impact of immigration on government welfare spending, with mixed findings. Soroka and colleagues (2006) studied 18 OECD countries over four decades (1960–2000) and found that increasing migration was associated with decreasing social welfare expenditure. Gaston and Rajaguru (2013), using social expenditure data for 25 OECD countries from 1980 to 2008, found no association between social expenditure and immigration. Fenwick (2019), on the other hand, studied the impact of immigration on social welfare spending in 16 European countries for the years 1990 to 2010 and found that increased immigration led to increased welfare expenditures.

The OECD's *International Migration Outlook 2013* reported that for most OECD countries, the average net direct fiscal contribution of immigrant households was positive, albeit with wide variation between countries owing to the different age profile of immigrants and differences in tax and welfare systems (OECD 2013). Soroka and colleagues (2015) built on their 2006 paper, studying the impact of immigration on nine subdomains of welfare programs, and provided further evidence of a slower increase in social welfare spending in countries with more immigration.

Several researchers have examined the impact of immigrant inclusivity in welfare programs on immigrant well-being, most notably with regard to health, education, and income. Leveraging substantial variation in welfare inclusivity across states in the US, Condon and colleagues (2015) studied the impact of immigrant inclusion on the educational attainment of youth from racial and ethnic minority groups. They found that low-income Latinos were more likely to graduate from high school in states that had more inclusive welfare policies (Condon, Filindra, and Wichowsky 2015). Kaushal and Kaestner (2005, 2007) studied the effect of immigrant exclusion from Medicaid in the 1996 welfare reform in the US and variation in immigrant inclusivity across states regarding health insurance coverage and the health of immigrants and their children. They found that while the policy change lowered the insurance coverage of immigrants and their children in states that did not allow these groups access to Medicaid, it had no effect on the self-reported health of immigrants and their children. Researchers have also examined the consequences of immigrant exclusion from accessing safety net programs in the post-PRWORA era and found that state policies excluding immigrants from Medicaid widened the Medicaid coverage gap between immigrants and the native-born (Zhu and Xu 2015; Huang, Kaushal, and Wang 2020).

Building on previous research, we specifically address this question: do immigrant inclusivity policies have fiscal consequences?

Data

The empirical analysis draws data from several sources, as described in detail below.

Dependent Variables

We study six primary outcome variables: aggregate social expenditure expressed as a proportion of GDP, as well as five subdomains of social expenditures, namely expenditures on pension, family benefit, unemployment, disability, and health care. These expenditures are from the OECD Social Expenditures Database (SOCX). The OECD defined aggregate social expenditure as cash benefits or direct in-kind provision of goods and services, as well as tax breaks with social purposes that may be targeted at low-income households, the elderly, the disabled, the sick, the unemployed, or young persons. Social benefits are classified as public when the government (central, state, or local) controls the relevant financial flows. Several previous studies of the impact of immigration on the welfare spending of host countries have used these data (see, e.g., Soroka et al. 2006; Gaston and Rajaguru 2013; Fenwick 2019).

Expenditures on pensions as a subdomain of social expenditure are defined as all cash expenditures on old-age and survivors' pensions. This category also includes early retirement pensions, supplements for dependents paid to old-age pensioners with dependents under old-age cash benefits; expenditures on elderly daycare and rehabilitation and home-help services, and provision of residential care in an institution. It excludes programs related to early retirement for labour market reasons (OECD 2020).

Family benefits expenditures refer to public spending on family benefits, including financial support that is exclusively for families and children. This comprises both cash benefits and in-kind benefits, including child allowances, supplementary income support for single parents, child tax allowances and child tax credits, public spending on assistance for young people and residential facilities, public spending on family services such as centre-based facilities and home help services for families in need, and financial support for families provided through the tax system, including tax exemptions (e.g., income from child benefits that is not included in the tax base). Spending recorded in other social policy areas, such as health and housing, also assists families, but not exclusively, so it is not included in this indicator (OECD 2020). Unemployment expenditure refers to cash benefits for individuals to compensate for unemployment. This includes redundancy payments from public funds, as well as the payment of pensions to beneficiaries before they reach the standard pensionable age if these payments are made because the beneficiaries are out of work or for other labour market policy reasons (OECD 2020).

Disability expenditures refer to cash and in-kind benefits that are provided on account of complete or partial inability to participate gainfully in the labour market due to disability. They include spending on occupational injury and disease, which records all cash payments such as paid sick leave, special allowances, and disability-related payments such as pensions, as well as expenditures on services for disabled people, which encompasses services such as daycare and rehabilitation services, home-help services, and other in-kind benefits. They exclude paid leave related to the sickness or injury of a dependent child, which is recorded under family cash benefits.

Health care expenditures measure the final consumption of health care goods and services, including personal health care (curative care, rehabilitative care, long-term care, ancillary services, and medical goods) and collective services (prevention and public health services as well as health administration), but excluding spending on investments. OECD health spending includes a mix of financing arrangements, including government spending and compulsory health insurance ("Government/compulsory"), as well as voluntary health insurance and private funds ("Voluntary"). In this analysis, we have only considered government spending and compulsory health insurance. All of the above indicators are measured as a proportion of GDP. Data on pension, unemployment, family benefit, and disability spending are missing for the year 2018; these missing values are interpolated using linear interpolation.[4]

Table A6.1 shows the average aggregate social expenditure as a proportion of GDP in the countries under study from 1990 to 2015, and Table A6.2 presents the average social expenditures (proportion of GDP) across the five subdomains. An important point to note about both tables is that there are large-scale variations in expenditures within countries and across years.

Explanatory Variable

Our measure of immigrant exclusion is based on the IESPI, described in detail in chapter 2. We merge the aggregate IESPI and sub-indices across programs with the OECD Social Expenditures Database by country and year.

Control Variables

Following previous research, in our regression analysis we run models controlling for host-country demographic, macroeconomic, and social variables. Demographic control variables include share of immigrants in the host-country population, the share of the host-country population below 18 years and above

65 years of age, and mean years of schooling (Soroka et al. 2006; Gaston and Rajaguru 2013; Soroka et al. 2015; Fenwick 2019).

Share of the immigrant population is from the OECD database (OECD 2020). Population data are also obtained from the OECD database (OECD 2020). Data on mean years of schooling are from the World Bank database (World Bank 2019).

The macroeconomic control variables are labour force participation rate (taken from the World Bank) and general government revenue (% GDP) by country and year. The government revenue data are obtained from the OECD database. Revenue data are missing for fourteen countries[5] for the year 1990; these missing values are interpolated with linear interpolation using data for later years.

We also control for globalization and development levels across countries. The UNDP's Human Development Index (HDI) is based on three variables: life expectancy at birth, expected years of schooling, and the GNI per capita. It varies from 0 (low human development) to 1 (high human development). We control for the HDI because previous research suggests that HDI is positively associated with public spending (UNDP 2014). We also control for the KOF globalization index, which measures the rate of globalization across countries. The index is based on economic, social, and political dimensions of globalization and varies between 0 and 100 (with higher scores indicating more globalization) (Gygli et al., 2019).

Descriptive Results

Figure 6.1 presents trends in social expenditures as a proportion of GDP and immigration (proportion of the foreign-born in the host-country population) in the 21 OECD countries that are the focus of our study. There are four points to note. First, in seven countries, barring short-term fluctuations, there is a general upward trend in social expenditures over the 25 years covered in this study: France, Italy, Great Britain, the US, Portugal, Denmark, and Spain. In two countries – Sweden and the Netherlands – the overall trend suggests a decline in social expenditures. In the remaining 12 countries, while there are tremendous fluctuations in expenditures, there is no discernible trend. Second, in the majority of countries, social expenditures fell in the early 1990s, capturing a wave of fiscal conservatism in the OECD countries at the end of the Cold War, and increased during 2008–10, capturing stimulus expenditures by governments in response to the global financial crisis and the Great Recession.

Third, while the proportion of foreign-born in national populations differs substantially across countries, there has been a general rising trend over the past quarter-century. In most countries, the increase in immigration has been slow but steady, with a few exceptions. For example, Spain, Ireland, and Iceland registered

Figure 6.1. Immigrant population as a percentage of the population and social expenditure as % of GDP, 1990–2015

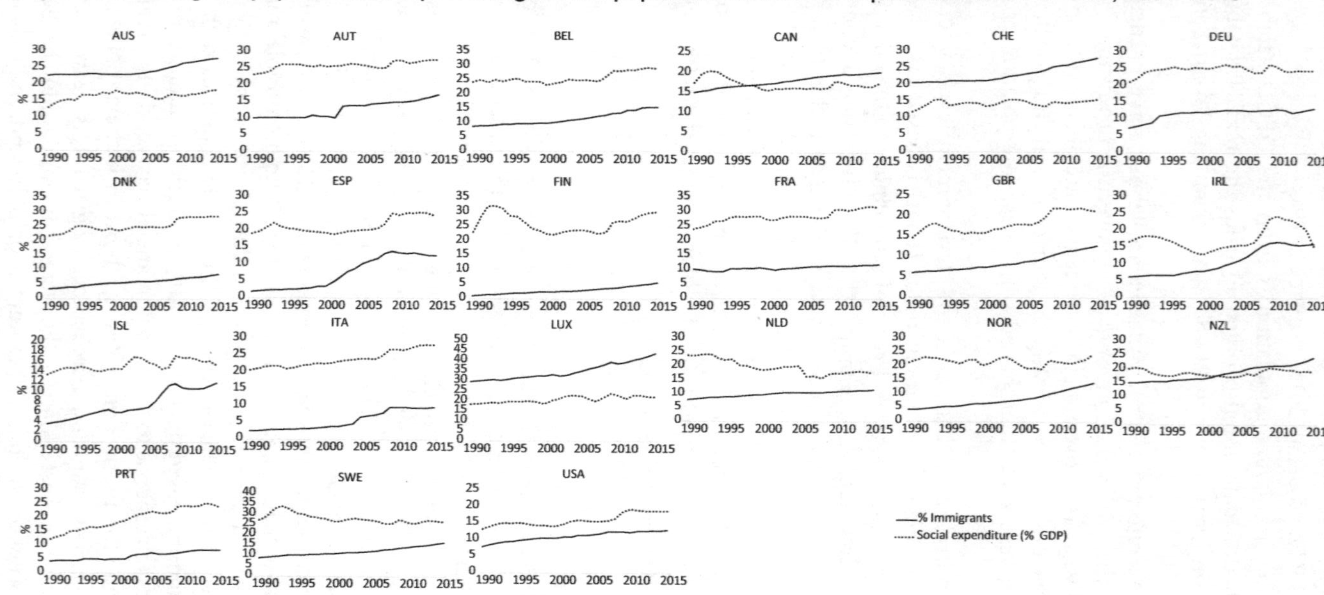

a sharp increase in immigration between 2000 and the global financial crisis and stagnation after that. Fourth, and perhaps most important for the purpose of this chapter, the levels and long-term trends in social expenditures and immigration fail to provide any clear insight into the relationship between the two.

Figure 6.2 presents the trend in social expenditures and the IESPI. Because we have the IESPI score for four years, the figure is based on four points in the data. There is little evidence of a uniform trend across countries. In six countries (Spain, Germany, France, Finland, Norway, and Portugal), the two variables trend in the opposite direction. However, in at least four countries (Australia, Belgium, the US, and the UK) the two variables trend in the same direction.

In Figure 6.3, we plot social expenditures and IESPI summary scores across countries for each year separately. Here too, there is little indication of a one-to-one relationship between the two variables in any single year.

These descriptive trends in Figures 6.1 to 6.3 are useful in that they provide a crude overview of the data, but they do not control for factors that vary across countries and years and are likely to confound the association between social expenditures and the exclusion index. In the multivariate analysis we present below, we control for these factors.

Multivariate Analysis

Table 6.1 presents the association between aggregate social expenditure (as a proportion of GDP) and the IESPI summary score. We estimate three models. Model 1 controls for year- and country-fixed effects. Country-fixed effects allow us to control for certain cultural and other time-invariant factors that cause expenditures to differ between countries; they also adjust for time-invariant differences in measurements (or errors) between countries. Year-fixed effects allow us to control for global changes in expenditures (e.g., global fiscal conservatism in the early 1990s, or global increases in stimulus during the Great Recession). Model 2 adds controls for a set of time-varying demographic and economic variables in the host country. In the final model (Model 3), we add a further control for the gross state revenue as a proportion of GDP to capture changes in revenue streams, within countries and across years, that may be correlated with the immigrant exclusion index.

We use two measures of social expenditures: current and expenditure in year t + 3. Ideally, we would like to estimate models with current and lagged policies using expenditures for the same years. Unfortunately, our IESPI data are specific to four years. However, we have expenditure data for the entire period. Therefore, in the empirical analysis, we first use expenditure data for the same year as the policy index and then use expenditure data with a three-year lead. For convenience, in the presentation here, we describe the second set of expenditure models (three-year lead) as models with lagged policy.

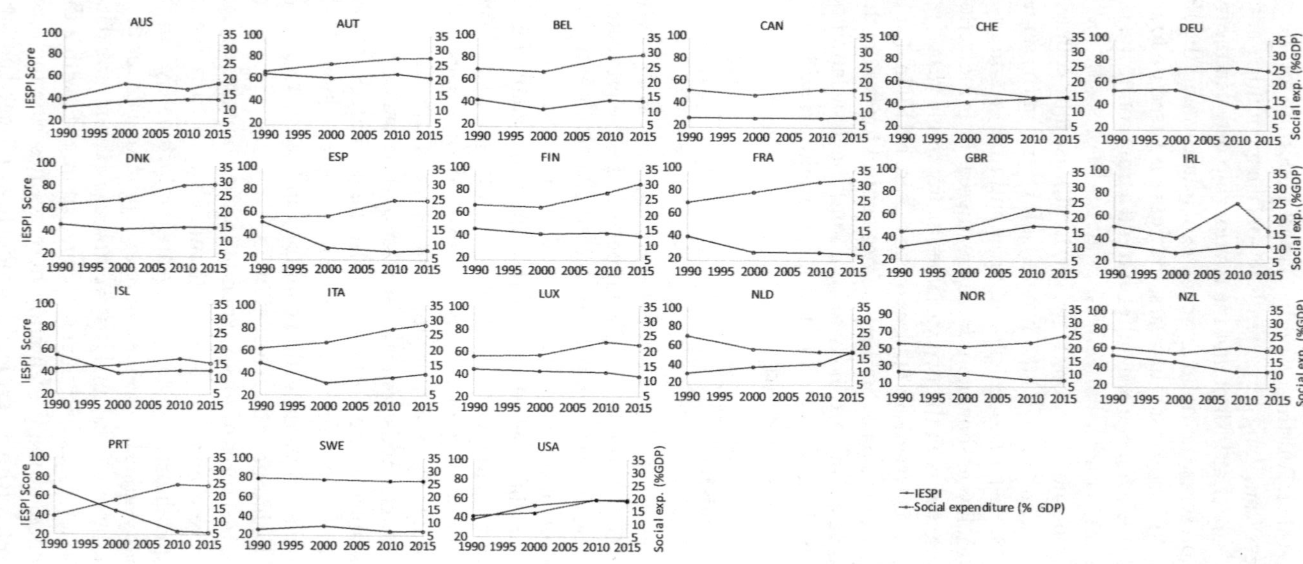

Figure 6.2. Social expenditure as a percentage of GDP and IESPI summary score, 1990–2015

Figure 6.3. Policy exclusivity index (*x*-axis) and social expenditure (*y*-axis) across countries, 1990, 2000, 2010, and 2015

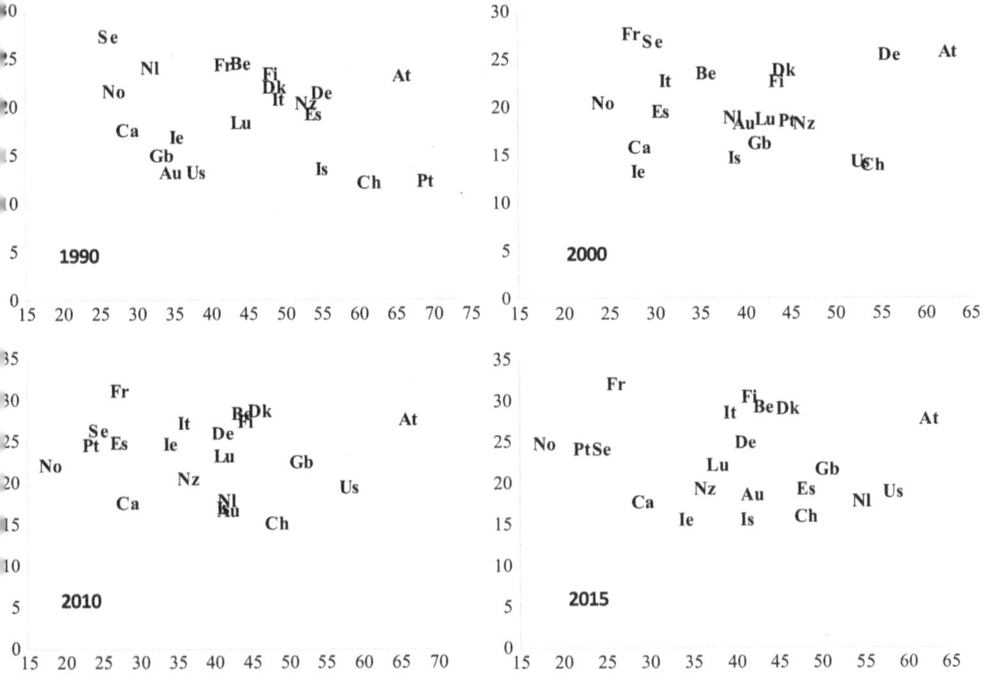

Estimates in Table 6.1 suggest a modest and statistically insignificant effect of immigrant exclusion policies on social expenditures. Estimates remain generally modest and mostly statistically insignificant across models. These estimates imply that a 10-point increase on the exclusion index lowered social expenditure as a proportion of GDP by 0.22 to 1.05 percentage points (or 1% to 4.7%). In our data, the IESPI summary score is highest (the most exclusive) for Austria (64.21) and lowest (the most inclusive) for Norway (21.73). Our analysis, therefore, suggests that increasing the IESPI score from Norway's to Austria's will lower social expenditure by 0.9 to 4.5 percentage points (or 4% to 21%).

In Table 6.2, we estimate models using the seven different IESPI sub-indices. The estimated coefficients on all sub-indices are modest and statistically insignificant, with one exception: an increase in the exclusion sub-index for contributory unemployment benefit raised overall social expenditure (in Model 3), but the effect turned insignificant with the lagged policy variable.

Next, we estimate models with expenditures on specific items as the dependent variables; the results are in Table 6.3. The only statistically significant effect

Table 6.1. Association between social expenditure and social policy exclusion index

	Social expenditure (as the proportion of GDP)					
	Current	t + 3	Current	t + 3	Current	t + 3
	Model 1		Model 2		Model 3	
Aggregate exclusion index (0–100)	−0.067 (0.054)	−0.072 (0.050)	−0.055 (0.055)	−0.105* (0.059)	−0.022 (0.051)	−0.074 (0.056)
Population (in millions)			0.091** (0.038)	0.129*** (0.040)	0.081** (0.034)	0.120*** (0.033)
Foreign-born share			0.401 (0.256)	0.281 (0.246)	0.540** (0.251)	0.414* (0.226)
Share of population below 18 years			0.451 (0.303)	0.605** (0.292)	0.312 (0.290)	0.473* (0.279)
Share of population above 65 years			0.275 (0.324)	0.370 (0.434)	0.366 (0.320)	0.457 (0.405)
Labour force participation rate			−0.334** (0.163)	0.049 (0.216)	−0.431*** (0.147)	−0.044 (0.194)
Mean years of schooling			0.232 (0.668)	0.190 (0.631)	0.012 (0.559)	−0.020 (0.555)
Human Development Index			26.672 (25.890)	12.452 (28.281)	24.366 (20.424)	10.248 (23.438)
KOF Globalization Index			0.308* (0.157)	0.076 (0.171)	0.230 (0.149)	0.001 (0.159)
General government revenue (% GDP)					0.385*** (0.119)	0.368*** (0.132)
Number of observations	84	84	84	84	84	84
Mean aggregate social exp. (% GDP)	21.338	22.256	21.338	22.256	21.338	22.256
Country and year fixed-effect	Yes	Yes	Yes	Yes	Yes	Yes

Note: The dependent variable is aggregate government social expenditure as a percentage of GDP. The general government revenue data for AT, BE, CH, DE, DK, ES, IE, IS, IT, LU, NL, NO, PT, and SE for 1990 are interpolated based on data for the years 1994 to 2000. Robust standard errors are in parentheses, *** $p < 0.01$, ** $p < 0.05$, * $p < 0.1$.

is when the dependent variable is expenditure on pension, but the effect dissipates in Models 2 and 3. Note that the estimated coefficients on the exclusion index for all other outcomes are modest, sometimes even positive (suggesting exclusion may lead to more spending), and always insignificant.

Next, we link subdomain expenditures with policies that are most likely to influence these expenditures; the results are in Table 6.4. There are five

Table 6.2. Association between social expenditure and exclusion index, by program type

	Social expenditure (as a proportion of GDP)					
	Current	t + 3	Current	t + 3	Current	t + 3
	Model 1		Model 2		Model 3	
Tax-paid pensions index	0.014	0.001	0.008	0.009	−0.012	−0.013
	(0.028)	(0.027)	(0.027)	(0.035)	(0.029)	(0.035)
Public health care index	0.019	0.062	0.024	0.035	0.056	0.071
	(0.028)	(0.037)	(0.034)	(0.045)	(0.034)	(0.044)
Contributory unemp. benefits index	0.014	0.032	0.069	0.040	0.070*	0.041
	(0.036)	(0.046)	(0.045)	(0.050)	(0.041)	(0.043)
Contributory pensions index	−0.035	−0.049	−0.010	−0.069	0.024	−0.032
	(0.041)	(0.043)	(0.059)	(0.078)	(0.053)	(0.068)
Housing benefits index	−0.051	−0.045	−0.035	−0.040	−0.044	−0.049
	(0.036)	(0.040)	(0.049)	(0.060)	(0.041)	(0.048)
Social assistance index	0.009	−0.036	0.000	−0.057	0.018	−0.036
	(0.024)	(0.033)	(0.032)	(0.037)	(0.026)	(0.031)
Lab. market policies index	−0.005	−0.004	−0.019	−0.022	0.022	0.023
	(0.031)	(0.042)	(0.045)	(0.058)	(0.036)	(0.046)
Population (in millions)			0.039	0.137**	0.002	0.096
			(0.060)	(0.067)	(0.060)	(0.064)
Foreign-born share			0.420	0.188	0.672*	0.468
			(0.358)	(0.365)	(0.345)	(0.331)
Share below 18 yrs			0.664	0.863	0.293	0.450
			(0.466)	(0.520)	(0.450)	(0.515)
Share above 65 yrs			0.502	0.628	0.625	0.765
			(0.489)	(0.649)	(0.424)	(0.553)
Labour force participation rate			−0.225	0.106	−0.394**	−0.082
			(0.206)	(0.256)	(0.186)	(0.216)
Mean years of schooling			−0.400	−0.281	−0.086	0.069
			(1.078)	(1.083)	(0.739)	(0.873)
Human development index			25.987	33.073	32.546	40.367
			(39.082)	(41.272)	(32.278)	(32.389)
KOF Globalization Index			0.440*	−0.001	0.356*	−0.094
			(0.220)	(0.287)	(0.201)	(0.247)
General govt. revenue (% GDP)					0.442**	0.492**
					(0.162)	(0.182)

(Continued)

Table 6.2. Association between social expenditure and exclusion index, by program type (*Continued*)

	Social expenditure (as a proportion of GDP)					
	Current	t + 3	Current	t + 3	Current	t + 3
	Model 1		Model 2		Model 3	
Number of observations	68	68	68	68	68	68
Mean social exp. (as % GDP)	21.34	22.26	21.34	22.26	21.34	22.26
Country and year fixed-effect	Yes	Yes	Yes	Yes	Yes	Yes

Note: The dependent variable is aggregate government social expenditure as a % of GDP. Data on contributory unemployment benefit index for Australia and New Zealand are not available and data for the contributory pension index are not available for Iceland and the Netherlands. The 1990 data for general government revenue (as % GDP) for AT, BE, CH, DE, DK, ES, IE, IS, IT, LU, NL, NO, PT, and SE are interpolated based on data for the years 1994 to 2000. Robust standard errors are in parentheses, *** $p < 0.01$, ** $p < 0.05$, * $p < 0.1$.

important findings in this analysis. First, exclusion from social assistance policies reduces expenditures on family benefits. Increasing the exclusion index in social assistance by 10 points lowers family benefit expenditure by 0.06 to 0.1 percentage points (2.6% to 4.3% of the mean family expenditure). Second, exclusion of social assistance reduces expenditures on disability benefits. A 10-point increase in the exclusion index decreases disability benefit expenditure by 0.09 (statistically insignificant) to 0.16 percentage points (3.5% to 6% of the mean). Third, exclusion from health care increased health care expenditure in Model 1, but the effect turns modest and insignificant in Models 2 and 3. Fourth, contributory unemployment benefits increase current public expenditure on unemployment benefits in Model 1, but the estimated coefficient turns modest and statistically insignificant in Models 2 and 3 and in models where the policy variable is lagged by three years. Fifth, exclusion in contributory pension lowers pension expenditures, but the coefficient is significant in only one model.

Expenditures on family benefits and disability are most directly affected by housing benefits and social assistance. Therefore, we also estimated models in which we combined the two expenditures. The results are in panel 3 of Table 6.4. Estimates suggest that while social assistance exclusion lowered the combined expenditures on the two items, exclusion from housing benefits increased these expenditures.

In additional analyses, we link subdomain expenditures with the seven subdomain policy indices. Overall, estimates from these models suggest that the

Table 6.3. Association between social expenditure and exclusion index, by program type, and exclusion index

	Current	t + 3	Current	t + 3	Current	t + 3
	Model 1		Model 2		Model 3	
Expenditure on family benefits						
Aggregate immigrant exclusion index	0.003	–0.004	0.009	–0.002	0.013	0.002
	(0.006)	(0.007)	(0.010)	(0.014)	(0.010)	(0.015)
Mean family benefit expenditure	2.273	2.367	2.273	2.367	2.273	2.367
Unemployment expenditure						
Aggregate immigrant exclusion index	–0.004	–0.004	0.003	–0.022	0.008	–0.009
	(0.008)	(0.013)	(0.009)	(0.016)	(0.009)	(0.016)
Mean unemployment expenditure	1.097	1.304	1.097	1.304	1.097	1.304
Expenditure on disability benefits						
Aggregate immigrant exclusion index	–0.002	0.000	–0.001	–0.038	0.003	0.000
	(0.010)	(0.009)	(0.011)	(0.015)	(0.012)	(0.015)
Mean disability benefit expenditure	2.562	2.656	2.562	2.656	2.562	2.656
Pension expenditure						
Aggregate immigrant exclusion index	–0.060**	–0.054*	–0.038	–0.040	–0.021	–0.026
	(0.029)	(0.036)	(0.024)	(0.036)	(0.019)	(0.031)
Mean pension expenditure	7.436	7.794	7.436	7.794	7.436	7.794
Public health expenditure						
Aggregate immigrant exclusion index	0.032	0.023	0.017	–0.012	0.015	–0.008
	(0.024)	(0.020)	(0.018)	(0.013)	(0.016)	(0.014)
Mean public health expenditure	6.642	6.870	6.642	6.870	6.642	6.870
Number of observations	84	84	84	84	84	84
Country and year fixed-effect	Yes	Yes	Yes	Yes	Yes	Yes

Note: Dependent variables in all models are subdomains of government social spending as a percentage of GDP (listed as row headings). Expenditures on pension, unemployment, family benefit, and disability spending for the year 2018 are linearly interpolated based on the trend from 2010 to 2015. Model 1 controls for year and country fixed effects. Model 2 includes additional controls for population, foreign-born share, share of population below 18 years, share of population above 65 years, labour force participation rate, mean years of schooling, HDI, and KOF globalization index. Model 3 includes general government revenue (% GDP) as an additional control. The 1990 data for general government revenue (as % GDP) for AT, BE, CH, DE, DK, ES, IE, IS, IT, LU, NL, NO, PR, and SE are interpolated based on data for the years 1994 to 2000. Robust standard errors are in parentheses, *** $p < 0.01$, ** $p < 0.05$, * $p < 0.1$.

Table 6.4. Association between social expenditure and exclusion index, by program type and social program exclusion

	Current	t+3	Current	t+3	Current	t+3
	Model 1		Model 2		Model 3	
Expenditure on family benefits						
Housing benefits index	0.005	0.004	0.007	0.008	0.008	0.005
	(0.003)	(0.004)	(0.005)	(0.006)	(0.006)	(0.006)
Social assistance index	–0.008***	–0.010**	–0.006*	–0.009**	–0.006*	–0.009**
	(0.003)	(0.004)	(0.003)	(0.004)	(0.003)	(0.004)
Mean family benefit expenditure	2.273	2.367	2.273	2.367	2.273	2.367
Number of observations	84	84	84	84	84	84
Expenditure on disability benefits						
Housing benefits index	0.000	0.005	0.004	0.008	0.005	0.010
	(0.004)	(0.004)	(0.005)	(0.006)	(0.006)	(0.006)
Social assistance index	–0.009	–0.014*	–0.010	–0.016**	–0.009	–0.016**
	(0.008)	(0.007)	(0.006)	(0.006)	(0.006)	(0.006)
Mean disability benefit expenditure	2.562	2.656	2.562	2.656	2.562	2.656
Number of observations	84	84	84	84	84	84
Family and disability expenditure						
Housing benefit index	0.005	0.010*	0.011	0.015**	0.013	0.016**
	(0.005)	(0.006)	(0.007)	(0.007)	(0.008)	(0.008)
Social assistance index	–0.017*	–0.023**	–0.016*	–0.024***	–0.015*	–0.024***
	(0.010)	(0.009)	(0.009)	(0.008)	(0.009)	(0.008)
Number of Observations	84	84	84	84	84	84
Unemployment expenditure						
Contri. Unemp. benefits index	–0.010*	–0.002	–0.000	–0.006	0.000	–0.003
	(0.005)	(0.009)	(0.006)	(0.010)	(0.006)	(0.009)
Labour Market policies index	0.001	0.007	–0.001	0.007	0.002	0.010
	(0.004)	(0.007)	(0.004)	(0.006)	(0.004)	(0.006)
Mean unemployment expenditure	1.097	1.304	–0.000	–0.006	–0.000	–0.006
Number of Observations	75	75	75	75	75	75

(*Continued*)

Table 6.4. Association between social expenditure and exclusion index, by program type and social program exclusion (*Continued*)

	Current	t+3	Current	t+3	Current	t+3
	Model 1		Model 2		Model 3	
Pension expenditure						
Tax-paid pensions index	−0.012	−0.005	0.001	0.006	0.003	0.007
	(0.015)	(0.020)	(0.011)	(0.015)	(0.009)	(0.013)
Contri. Pensions index	−0.022	−0.014	−0.031*	−0.023	−0.019	−0.017
	(0.017)	(0.020)	(0.016)	(0.025)	(0.013)	(0.021)
Mean pension expenditure	7.436	7.794	7.436	7.794	7.436	7.794
Number of Observations	74	74	74	74	74	74
Public health expenditure						
Public health care index	0.038**	0.021	0.017	−0.005	0.017	−0.004
	(0.017)	(0.014)	(0.016)	(0.012)	(0.015)	(0.012)
Mean public health expenditure	6.642	6.870	6.642	6.870	6.642	6.870
Number of Observations	84	84	84	84	84	84
Country and Year fixed-effect	Yes	Yes	Yes	Yes	Yes	Yes

Note: Dependent variables in all models are subdomains of government social expenditure as percentage of GDP (listed as row headings). Expenditures on pension, unemployment, family benefit, and disability spending for the year 2018 are linearly interpolated based on the trend from 2010 to 2015. Model 1 controls for year- and country-fixed effects. Model 2 includes additional controls for population, foreign-born share, population share below 18 years, population share above 65 years, labour force participation rate, mean years of schooling, HDI, and KOF globalization index. Model 3 includes general government revenue (% GDP) as an additional control. The 1990 data for general government revenue (% GDP) for AT, BE, CH, DE, DK, ES, IE, IS, IT, LU, NL, NO, PT, are SE are interpolated based on data for the years 1994 to 2000. Data for the contributory unemployment benefit index for Australia and New Zealand and for contributory pension index for Iceland and the Netherlands are not available. Robust standard errors in parentheses, *** $p < 0.01$, ** $p < 0.05$, * $p < 0.1$.

exclusion is correlated across programs and that effects therefore often spill over across social expenditure sub-domains. The results are presented in Table A6.3.

As mentioned earlier, social inclusion policies are not made in a vacuum. Countries experiencing large-scale immigration may decide to implement more exclusionary policies to control for future immigration flows. (This is partly why models 2 and 3 in the estimates presented in Tables 6.1 to 6.4 control for foreign-born population share.) Next, we study whether exclusionary policies affect immigrant flows. Here too, we study three models. Model 1 controls for year- and country-fixed effects; models 2 and 3 include additional control variables that are known to influence the share of immigrants in the host country. Estimates are presented in Table 6.5.

The two main findings are, first, that estimates suggest that the overall exclusion index has no effect on immigration, and second, that estimates of the association between specific measures of exclusion and immigration are mixed. For instance, while an increase in the exclusion index in tax-paid pension and housing benefit increases the share of the immigrant population (statistical significance dissipates in models 2 and 3), exclusion in social assistance, contributory pension, and health care policies decreases the immigrant population (the effect turns statistically insignificant in some models). The coefficients on other inclusivity indices are modest and statistically insignificant.

Conclusions and Discussion

This chapter examines the fiscal consequences of immigrant exclusion policies using cross-national data for 21 OECD countries covering 25 years, from 1990 to 2015. Previous chapters in this volume suggested that immigrant exclusion policies are associated with worse public opinion (see chapter 4) and by and large with worse labour market outcomes (see chapter 5). Yet one might still be motivated to pursue exclusionary policies if such policies could lead to savings.

Using the IESPI, we first studied the association between total social expenditure and the overall index and then with the index for the seven programs separately. We then estimated the association between specific programs and corresponding public expenses, which were divided into five categories: expenditures on family benefits, pension expenditure, disability benefit expenditure, public health expenditure, and unemployment expenditure.

Descriptive results indicate a general upward trend in government social expenditures (as a proportion of GDP), except in Sweden and the Netherlands, which register a decline. The countries covered in our study exhibit diverse trends in exclusiveness toward immigrants. But the descriptive data do not point to any clearly discernible association either between immigration and aggregate public social expenditure or between the exclusion index and aggregate social expenditures.

Results from our multivariate analyses suggest that immigrant exclusion from welfare programs has a modest and mostly statistically insignificant

Table 6.5. Association between immigrant share and exclusion index

	Foreign-born population (as a proportion of host country population)		
	Model 1	Model 2	Model 3
Aggregate immigrant exclusion index	−0.011 (0.029)	−0.022 (0.029)	−0.028 (0.028)
Number of observations	84	84	84
Exclusion sub-indices			
Tax-paid pensions index	0.055***	0.030	0.029
	(0.017)	(0.021)	(0.021)
Public health care index	−0.036	−0.042**	−0.041*
	(0.024)	(0.020)	(0.021)
Contributory unemployment benefits index	0.014	−0.023	−0.025
	(0.023)	(0.025)	(0.026)
Contributory pensions index	−0.028	−0.051**	−0.052**
	(0.018)	(0.024)	(0.026)
Housing benefits index	0.029*	0.028	0.025
	(0.016)	(0.025)	(0.025)
Social assistance index	−0.035*	−0.016	−0.017
	(0.018)	(0.019)	(0.020)
Lab. market policies index	−0.020	−0.005	−0.007
	(0.015)	(0.017)	(0.017)
Mean immigrant share	14.084	14.084	14.084
Number of observations	68	68	68
Country and year fixed-effect	YES	YES	YES

Note: The dependent variable is foreign-born population as a percentage of host country population. The foreign-born data for the year 1993 are linearly interpolated for Australia, Belgium, Canada, Switzerland, Germany, Spain, Finland, France, Iceland, Italy, Luxemburg, New Zealand, Portugal, and Sweden based on each country's immigrant share data for 1990 and 2000. Model 1 controls for year- and country-fixed effects; model 2 includes additional control variables, namely GDP per capita, KOF Globalization Index, Human Development Index, share of host country population less than 18 years and share more than 65 years, labour force participation rate, and mean years of schooling. Model 3 includes general government revenue (% GDP) as an additional control. Data on contributory unemployment benefit index for Australia and New Zealand and for contributory pension index for Iceland and the Netherlands are not available. Robust standard errors in parentheses: *** $p < 0.01$, ** $p < 0.05$, * $p < 0.1$

impact on aggregate government social spending. Our statistically insignificant estimates show that a 10-point increase in the exclusion index lowered social expenditure as a proportion of GDP by 0.22 to 1.05 percentage points (or 1% to 4.7%). In our data, the IESPI summary score is highest (the most exclusive) for Austria (64.21) and lowest (the most inclusive) for Norway (21.73). Our analysis, therefore, suggests that increasing the IESPI score from Norway's to Austria's will lower social expenditure by 0.9 to 4.5 percentage points (or 4% to 21%).

We also find that increasing the exclusion index in social assistance by 10 points lowers family benefit expenditure by 0.06 to 0.1 percentage points (2.6% to 4.3% of the mean family expenditure). Furthermore, we find that while social assistance exclusion lowers the combined expenditure on family benefits and disability, exclusion from housing benefits increases these expenditures. Importantly, we find that inclusion in health care lowers health care expenditure, but the effect turns modest and insignificant in models where the policy variable is lagged. These results suggest that immigrant exclusion from certain programs (such as health care) could be detrimental to the exchequer as well as to immigrant health. Our analysis suggests that the overall exclusion index has no statistically significant association with the proportion of foreign-born in the host country. The association between foreign-born share and specific policies is mixed.

A limitation of our analysis is that our primary explanatory variable – IESPI – is not exogenous to the outcomes of interest and that social expenditures may themselves impact IESPI. While we have lagged the IESPI index to avoid reverse causation and in some models control for the general social revenue, we acknowledge that more rigorous research is needed to establish causality. Nevertheless, our findings suggest that immigrant exclusion does not have a significant fiscal effect and therefore should not be defended on the grounds of its fiscal implications.

NOTES

1 These countries are Australia, Austria, Belgium, Canada, Denmark, Finland, France, Germany, Iceland, Ireland, Italy, Luxembourg, Netherlands, New Zealand, Norway, Portugal, Spain, Sweden, Switzerland, United Kingdom, and the United States.

2 In the US, participation in Supplemental Security Income involves a long and arduous process of disability establishment. But adults receiving SSI are automatically eligible for Medicaid (Burns and Dague 2017; Soni et al. 2017).

3 Huddle used income estimates for legal immigrants in Los Angeles County who entered the US during the 1980s, generalizing these to represent the earnings of all legal immigrants who entered the United States during the period 1970–1992. Fix

and Passel argued that estimating tax revenues from immigrants requires a dynamic picture that includes all immigrants, not just recent arrivals, as was done by Huddle.

4 We conducted the lagged policy analysis in two ways: using four years of data (with 2018 interpolated) and three years of data (without interpolation). Estimated results were similar. For brevity we do not present the results using three years of data. These results are available upon request.

5 Austria, Belgium, Denmark, Germany, Iceland, Ireland, Italy, Luxembourg, Netherlands, Norway, Porgual, Spain, Sweden, and Switzerland.

Appendix Table 6.1. Annual aggregate social expenditure as a percentage of GDP

	AUS	AUT	BEL	CAN	CHE	DEU	DNK	ESP	FIN	FRA	GBR	IRL	ISL	ITA	LUX	NLD	NOR	NZL	PRT	SWE	USA
1990	13.14	23.15	24.42	17.55	12.09	21.35	21.95	19.2	23.32	24.28	14.9	16.84	13.49	20.7	18.33	23.99	21.55	20.31	12.22	27.24	13.16
1991	14.31	23.47	25.18	19.78	13.06	22.39	22.4	19.93	28.23	24.91	16.39	17.74	13.95	21.08	18.63	23.94	22.46	20.73	13.1	29.07	14.13
1992	15.29	24.16	24.19	20.43	14.42	24.11	22.6	21.07	32.17	25.64	17.82	18.5	14.49	21.81	18.97	24.38	23.35	20.37	13.76	32.67	14.81
1993	15.55	25.47	25.24	20.35	15.75	24.77	23.79	22.32	32.26	27.02	18.42	18.47	14.86	22.07	19.28	24.49	23.26	18.89	15.12	34.18	15.07
1994	15.27	26.32	24.65	19.26	15.69	24.91	25.42	21.32	31.57	27.06	17.76	18.08	14.77	22.05	19.11	23.14	23.08	18.19	15.24	32.94	15.02
1995	16.92	26.28	25.17	18.35	14.03	25.21	25.51	20.69	28.9	28.33	16.72	17.54	15.05	21.12	19.88	22.45	22.47	17.69	16.02	30.56	15.06
1996	17.03	26.4	25.74	17.55	14.4	25.81	24.95	20.58	28.74	28.62	16.52	16.57	14.74	21.52	19.73	22.54	21.68	17.64	16.6	30.09	14.86
1997	16.79	25.85	24.72	16.94	14.91	25.38	24.16	20.01	26.62	28.49	15.81	15.51	14.15	22.22	19.86	20.5	21.18	18.58	16.44	28.87	14.43
1998	17.62	25.63	24.73	17.03	14.87	25.35	23.74	19.91	24.53	28.71	16.24	14.56	14.25	22.38	20.15	20.25	22.63	19.08	16.83	28.52	14.49
1999	17.25	25.95	24.54	16.05	14.65	25.61	24.55	19.75	23.84	28.68	16.06	13.71	14.53	22.81	19.5	19.45	22.55	18.49	17.24	27.98	14.23
2000	18.25	25.69	23.49	15.76	13.88	25.39	23.77	19.48	22.61	27.58	16.19	13.19	14.63	22.68	18.7	18.85	20.4	18.23	18.47	26.77	14.25
2001	17.55	25.75	23.99	16.2	14.18	25.41	24.29	19.11	22.44	27.58	17.03	14.02	14.67	22.94	20.39	18.91	21.23	17.63	18.95	26.81	14.84
2002	17.36	26.05	24.34	16.21	15.06	26.04	24.8	19.34	23.16	28.3	17.13	14.91	16.05	23.35	21.43	19.32	22.72	18.03	20.28	27.52	15.69
2003	17.56	26.59	25.49	16.29	15.95	26.53	25.33	19.93	23.89	28.67	17.88	15.41	17.13	23.68	22.81	20.09	23.66	17.51	21.32	28.2	15.95
2004	17.26	26.33	25.25	16.29	15.85	25.94	25.12	20.14	24.01	28.75	18.38	15.68	16.76	23.93	23.08	19.98	22.3	17.21	21.65	27.67	15.81
2005	16.71	25.95	25.23	16.14	15.62	26.24	25.2	20.41	23.97	28.73	18.34	15.91	15.95	24.17	22.83	20.23	20.75	17.78	22.29	27.33	15.65
2006	15.74	25.67	25.11	16.29	14.7	25.02	24.96	20.43	23.72	28.28	18.24	15.89	15.5	24.3	21.4	16.47	19.49	18.48	22.02	26.61	15.73
2007	15.9	25.09	24.89	16.2	14.09	24.07	24.98	20.8	22.82	28.07	18.81	16.76	14.62	24.14	20.21	16.58	19.6	18.25	21.73	25.48	15.86
2008	17.09	25.52	26.26	16.28	13.82	24.2	25.37	22.19	23.28	28.33	20.11	19.79	15.06	25.08	21.94	15.73	19.21	19.64	22.18	25.55	16.5
2009	16.93	27.47	28.55	18.02	15.26	26.64	28.25	25.38	26.87	31.02	22.24	23.74	17.29	27.11	24.04	17.36	22.44	20.69	24.54	27.63	18.6

2010	16.59	27.56	28.28	17.53	15.06	25.9	28.59	24.72	27.34	31.04	22.42	24.57	16.9	27.12	23.14	17.78	22.03	20.43	24.47	26.26	19.37
2011	17.05	26.74	28.73	17.03	14.93	24.66	28.63	25.4	27.09	30.82	22.16	23.67	17.03	26.8	21.19	17.75	21.5	20.04	24.39	25.59	19.08
2012	17.29	27.11	28.69	17.06	15.29	24.53	28.75	25.34	28.35	31.36	22.23	23.36	16.67	27.59	22.89	18.21	21.43	20.14	24.53	26.51	18.83
2013	17.64	27.51	29.21	16.78	15.44	24.69	28.78	25.56	29.42	31.88	22.45	22.19	16.21	28.17	23.08	18.45	21.89	19.48	25.57	27.17	18.8
2014	18.27	27.74	29.45	16.69	15.5	24.71	28.82	25.23	30.19	32.21	21.86	20.4	16.33	28.36	22.37	18.1	22.83	19.62	25.07	26.8	18.78
2015	18.54	27.7	29.19	17.63	15.89	24.86	28.99	24.66	30.39	31.98	21.61	15.51	15.48	28.48	22.1	17.73	24.7	19.21	24.04	26.34	18.85

Source: OECD Social Expenditure data

Appendix Table 6.2. Social spending as a percentage of GDP by program type

Country	Pension spending	Unemployment spending	Family benefit	Disability spending	Health care (public)
Australia	3.96	0.80	2.41	2.29	5.41
Austria	12.36	0.97	2.76	2.44	7.00
Belgium	9.56	3.00	2.57	2.50	7.27
Canada	4.35	0.98	1.07	0.93	6.75
Denmark	6.92	0.00	3.45	4.22	7.66
Finland	8.95	1.87	3.08	3.84	6.22
France	12.23	1.57	2.82	1.74	7.75
Germany	10.25	1.13	2.06	2.05	8.06
Iceland	1.99	0.62	2.89	2.18	6.76
Ireland	4.04	1.90	2.45	1.70	5.49
Italy	14.12	0.70	1.34	1.70	6.23
Luxembourg	7.82	0.83	3.04	2.73	5.04
Netherlands	5.34	1.63	1.51	4.09	6.79
New Zealand	5.39	1.01	2.79	2.60	6.62
Norway	5.49	0.61	3.02	4.42	7.08
Portugal	9.49	0.79	1.06	2.06	5.57
Spain	9.06	2.44	0.98	2.36	5.72
Sweden	7.16	0.76	3.45	4.61	7.05
Switzerland	5.93	0.59	1.41	2.13	7.03
United Kingdoms	5.45	0.37	2.91	2.02	5.93
United States	6.28	0.48	0.66	1.19	8.04

Appendix Table 6.3. Association between social expenditure and exclusion index, by program type and detailed social policy exclusion index

	Current	t + 3	Current	t + 3	Current	t + 3
	Model 1		Model 2		Model 3	
Expenditure on family benefits						
Tax-paid pensions	−0.000	0.002	−0.004	−0.003	−0.006	−0.003
index	(0.004)	(0.005)	(0.005)	(0.007)	(0.005)	(0.008)
Public health care	0.003	0.013*	0.004	0.011	0.008	0.012
index	(0.007)	(0.007)	(0.009)	(0.011)	(0.009)	(0.011)
Contri. unemp.	0.020**	0.015*	0.023**	0.012	0.023**	0.013
benefits index	(0.009)	(0.008)	(0.009)	(0.010)	(0.009)	(0.010)
Contri. Pensions index	−0.007	−0.010	0.001	0.004	0.004	0.005
	(0.007)	(0.006)	(0.012)	(0.015)	(0.013)	(0.016)
Housing benefits index	−0.004	−0.003	−0.004	−0.006	−0.005	−0.006
	(0.005)	(0.005)	(0.008)	(0.010)	(0.007)	(0.010)
Social assistance	−0.005	−0.012***	0.002	−0.009	0.004	−0.009
index	(0.004)	(0.004)	(0.005)	(0.006)	(0.005)	(0.006)
Lab. Market policies	0.000	−0.004	0.004	0.001	0.008	0.002
index	(0.006)	(0.007)	(0.008)	(0.008)	(0.007)	(0.008)
Mean Family benefit exp.	2.273	2.367	2.273	2.367	2.273	2.367
Unemployment expenditure						
Tax-paid pensions	0.008	−0.007	0.003	−0.011	−0.000	−0.015
index	(0.006)	(0.008)	(0.006)	(0.011)	(0.007)	(0.011)
Public health care	−0.015**	0.004	−0.014*	−0.007	−0.010	−0.002
index	(0.006)	(0.012)	(0.008)	(0.014)	(0.007)	(0.012)
Contri. unemp.	−0.010	−0.001	−0.003	−0.012	−0.003	−0.009
benefits index	(0.007)	(0.012)	(0.009)	(0.013)	(0.009)	(0.014)
Contri. pensions	−0.007	−0.025*	0.000	−0.035	0.005	−0.026
index	(0.010)	(0.014)	(0.015)	(0.025)	(0.015)	(0.022)
Housing benefits	−0.003	−0.016	−0.007	−0.016	−0.008	−0.017
index	(0.006)	(0.010)	(0.009)	(0.016)	(0.009)	(0.014)
Social assistance	0.012**	−0.004	0.013**	−0.005	0.016**	−0.003
index	(0.005)	(0.011)	(0.006)	(0.012)	(0.006)	(0.010)
Lab. market policies	0.001	0.023	0.002	0.023	0.007	0.030*
index	(0.007)	(0.014)	(0.009)	(0.018)	(0.008)	(0.015)
Mean unemployment exp.	1.097	1.304	1.097	1.304	1.097	1.304
Expenditure on disability benefits						
Tax-paid pensions	0.006	0.005	0.010**	0.009	0.009*	0.008
index	(0.004)	(0.007)	(0.005)	(0.009)	(0.005)	(0.009)
Public health care	0.003	0.007	0.004	0.008	0.007	0.010
index	(0.006)	(0.009)	(0.008)	(0.011)	(0.007)	(0.011)
Contri. unemp.	−0.004	−0.011	−0.001	−0.006	−0.001	−0.005
benefits index	(0.007)	(0.009)	(0.007)	(0.012)	(0.007)	(0.012)

(Continued)

Appendix Table 6.3. Association between social expenditure and exclusion index, by program type and detailed social policy exclusion index (*Continued*)

	Current	t + 3	Current	t + 3	Current	t + 3
	Model 1		Model 2		Model 3	
Contri. pensions index	0.007	0.010	0.013	0.001	0.015*	0.005
	(0.005)	(0.008)	(0.009)	(0.016)	(0.009)	(0.016)
Housing benefits index	0.006	0.011	0.008	0.007	0.007	0.006
	(0.005)	(0.006)	(0.007)	(0.011)	(0.007)	(0.010)
Social assistance	0.000	–0.010	–0.002	–0.013	–0.001	–0.012
index	(0.005)	(0.008)	(0.006)	(0.009)	(0.006)	(0.009)
Lab. market policies	–0.004	–0.001	–0.011	–0.004	–0.008	–0.001
index	(0.005)	(0.006)	(0.007)	(0.011)	(0.007)	(0.012)
Mean disability benefit exp.	2.562	2.656	2.562	2.656	2.562	2.656
Pension expenditure						
Tax-paid pensions	0.002	0.012	0.012	0.015	0.004	0.010
index	(0.014)	(0.017)	(0.012)	(0.018)	(0.011)	(0.017)
Public health care	–0.006	0.001	–0.010	–0.013	0.003	–0.007
index	(0.018)	(0.021)	(0.016)	(0.029)	(0.017)	(0.030)
Contri. unemp.	0.000	–0.015	0.020	–0.010	0.021	–0.006
benefits index	(0.019)	(0.023)	(0.021)	(0.028)	(0.019)	(0.028)
Contri. pensions	–0.044*	–0.040	–0.031	–0.054	–0.018	–0.040
index	(0.025)	(0.026)	(0.025)	(0.042)	(0.021)	(0.033)
Housing benefits index	-0.038**	–0.031	–0.014	–0.020	–0.017	–0.022
	(0.019)	(0.021)	(0.020)	(0.025)	(0.017)	(0.023)
Social assistance	–0.001	–0.016	–0.020	–0.031	–0.013	–0.028
index	(0.014)	(0.014)	(0.012)	(0.019)	(0.010)	(0.017)
Lab. market policies	–0.001	0.002	–0.017	0.001	–0.001	0.012
index	(0.015)	(0.018)	(0.018)	(0.029)	(0.015)	(0.027)
Mean Pension exp.	7.436	7.794	7.436	7.794	7.436	7.794
Public health expenditure						
Tax-paid pensions	–0.018*	–0.013	–0.032**	–0.011	–0.033***	–0.015*
index	(0.010)	(0.008)	(0.013)	(0.009)	(0.012)	(0.009)
Public health care	0.048**	0.023	0.020	–0.011	0.023	–0.005
index	(0.019)	(0.016)	(0.028)	(0.024)	(0.027)	(0.024)
Contri. unemp.	0.003	0.008	0.012	0.002	0.012	0.002
benefits index	(0.014)	(0.016)	(0.020)	(0.015)	(0.020)	(0.014)
Contri. Pensions	0.060	0.047	–0.009	–0.038	–0.006	–0.032
index	(0.044)	(0.045)	(0.033)	(0.034)	(0.033)	(0.033)
Housing benefits	–0.018	–0.009	–0.016	–0.012	–0.017	–0.014
index	(0.015)	(0.013)	(0.018)	(0.015)	(0.018)	(0.014)
Social assistance	0.008	0.005	0.008	–0.011	0.010	–0.008
index	(0.009)	(0.009)	(0.014)	(0.012)	(0.014)	(0.012)
Lab. market policies	0.009	0.008	0.032**	0.017	0.035**	0.024*
index	(0.012)	(0.011)	(0.014)	(0.013)	(0.014)	(0.014)

(*Continued*)

Appendix Table 6.3. Association between social expenditure and exclusion index, by program type and detailed social policy exclusion index (*Continued*)

	Current	t + 3	Current	t + 3	Current	t + 3
	Model 1		Model 2		Model 3	
Mean public health exp.	6.642	6.87	6.642	6.87	6.642	6.87
Number of observations	68	68	68	68	68	68
Country and year fixed-effect	YES	YES	YES	YES	YES	YES

Note: Dependent variables in all models are subdomains of government social spending as a percentage of GDP (listed as row sub-headings). Expenditures on pensions, unemployment benefits, family benefit, and disability spending for the year 2018 are linearly interpolated based on trend from 2010 to 2015. Model 1 controls for year- and country-fixed effects. Model 2 includes additional controls for population, foreign-born share, population share below 18 years, population share above 65 years, labour force participation rate, mean years of schooling, HDI, and the KOF globalization index. Model 3 includes general government revenue (% GDP) as an additional control. The 1990 data for general government revenue for AT, BE, CH, DE, DK, ES, IE, IS, IT, LU, NL, NO, PT, and SE are interpolated based on data for the years 1994 to 2000. Data on contributory unemployment benefit index for Australia and New Zealand and for contributory pension index for Iceland and the Netherlands are not available. Robust standard errors in parentheses, *** $p < 0.01$, ** $p < 0.05$, * $p < 0.1$.

SECTION THREE

Case Studies

7 Between Equality and Exclusion: Migrant Integration in Austria's Bismarckian Welfare System

OLIVER GRUBER

"Stop immigration to the welfare system" – this demand by Austria's right-wing coalition in its 2018 government program follows a long tradition. Similar claims have been popularized in particular by one of the most successful populist radical-right parties in Western Europe, the Austrian Freedom Party (FPÖ), since the late 1980s, coinciding with a period of general transformation of the Austrian welfare system. Long described as a prototypical Bismarckian model, the Austrian welfare system has seen retrenchment with disadvantageous effects for socio-economically deprived population groups, among them immigrants. Political parties have tried to keep immigrants' access limited, even while European Union regulations and court decisions have compelled more inclusion of selected groups in particular welfare segments.

For a thorough understanding of migrant integration in Austria's welfare system and, more specifically, the country's position in the IESPI comparison, this chapter describes the historic evolution of the Austrian welfare state and its connection with immigration patterns during the Cold War. It then elucidates the drivers that have led not only to a transformation of the Austrian welfare regime but also to stronger differentiation in benefit access between native-born and immigrants, as well as between different immigrant groups. It demonstrates that in an era of a steadily increasing immigrant population coupled with a hardening political climate, the welfare system had to become more inclusive for some groups (in particular, EU migrants and permanent residents); others have faced not only the indirect effects of an increasingly retrenched welfare system but also more deliberate barriers, as well as calls to further tighten access for EU citizens and third-country nationals alike.

The Evolution of the Austrian Welfare State and the Role of Immigration

Historical Roots and Characteristics of the Austrian Welfare System

In comparative welfare system research, Austria has long been viewed as one of the prototypes for the continent's Bismarckian welfare system (Esping-Andersen 1990; Castles and Mitchell 1993). It was founded in the late nineteenth century under Habsburg monarchical rule against the backdrop of a growing workers' movement, copying from the German model of social insurance under Bismarck. Hence, its original focus was on addressing the workforce's social security needs (Kapuy 2016). Core pillars of the Austrian welfare system were established at that time, in particular its system of compulsory insurance and its strong links with employment. The system was expanded during the First Austrian Republic (1919–34), which fostered the role of corporatist interest groups as brokers for welfare policies. But the growing social and political conflicts alongside the dominant labour/capital-cleavage eventually led to a civil war, the collapse of the First Republic, and the establishment of an authoritarian state in 1934, prior to the country's annexation by Nazi Germany in 1938 (Gerlich and Campbell 2000).

After the Second World War, the inclusionary design of general social insurance[1] was an expression of the dominant political forces of the time. Austria emerged as a model of consociationalist democracy, in which two major political camps – the centre-left Social Democrats (SPÖ) and the centre-right Christian-Democrats (ÖVP) – aspired to settle political conflicts by turning consensual politics into a central pillar of government – a compromise that was further entrenched through a corporatist system of social partnership. This counterbalancing of interests also shaped the composition of the Austrian welfare system during the postwar decades, fostering its classification as a consociationalist model characterized by three key features.

First was the *dominance of social insurance* as the primary welfare net. To this day, the social insurance principle dominates in the sectors of old age security, health, and unemployment, financed through income-contingent contributions by employers and employees alike. Hence, it is strongly tied to formal employment, even more so because it embraces an equivalence principle – that is, the duration of employment and the amount of income from which insurance contributions are deducted together prescribe the amount and duration of benefits, especially when it comes to pensions or unemployment benefits. Thus it is considered a status-conservative model, in the sense that the social hierarchy within the workforce is largely reproduced through social insurance; this has also earned it the characterization of being a male-breadwinner model. *Universal programs*, the second key feature of the Austrian welfare regime, have been slowly introduced in some policy areas, such as family and long-term care, though they remain curtailed by various deductibles. Third and finally, a *social assistance* benefit covers basic needs for those who cannot support themselves (solely) through the first two instruments (Heitzmann and Österle 2008, 49f.).

Until the 1980s this model experienced a period of expansion (to other sectors and target groups) (see Figure 7.1), with costs increasing in tandem (Obinger and Tálos 2010; Heitzmann and Österle 2008). By the 1980s, Austria ranked above average in terms of annual public spending on social programs, investing more than half its state budget in this policy area. The dominant sector by far was the tax-financed pension system (where Austria ranked among the most cost-intensive OECD countries); in other sectors, such as unemployment and health care, it ranked only at the median among OECD countries (Obinger 2015, 2).

Immigrants' Role within the (Expanding) Welfare System

A welfare system's inclusivity vis-à-vis immigrants depends greatly on the country's pattern of immigration and its immigration regime, hence the immigration/welfare nexus. In Habsburg Austria already, access to social services had been predicated on national origin and homeland. Despite free movement rights between the Crown lands and municipal voting rights for intra-monarchical immigrants at their main place of work and tax payments, the "principle of residence" (*Heimatprinzip*) had directed destitute subjects of the monarchy to their hometowns if they wished to make claims for social service (Bauböck 1996, 21). During the interwar years, emigration from the remaining Austrian territories exceeded the number of immigrant newcomers. It was only during the *trente glorieuses* with its expansion of the welfare state that the turn from an emigration country to an immigration country set in again (see Figure 7.1).

Due to Austria's location in the centre of Europe, in the Second Republic one early source of immigration (with recurring peaks over the following decades) was refugees from the Soviet Union. During the Cold War, three major Eastern European refugee movements shaped the Austrian population the most: refugees from the Hungarian Uprising in 1956, from the Prague Spring in 1968, and from the 1981 declaration of martial law in Poland. Though most of them used Austria only as a transit country or a temporary refuge, those who decided to stay (not more than 10%) were considered legal refugees almost automatically due to their Soviet origin (Volf 1995). The same was true for smaller contingents of refugees from Asia, Africa, and South America who arrived during the 1970s and 1980s. In accordance with the Geneva Convention on Refugees (Article 24), these recognized refugees enjoyed the same access as Austrian citizens to social insurance and welfare benefits (Pfeil 2018, 124f).[2] This immediate

Figure 7.1. Migration balance and size of foreign population, welfare system developments, and government coalitions, 1961–2019

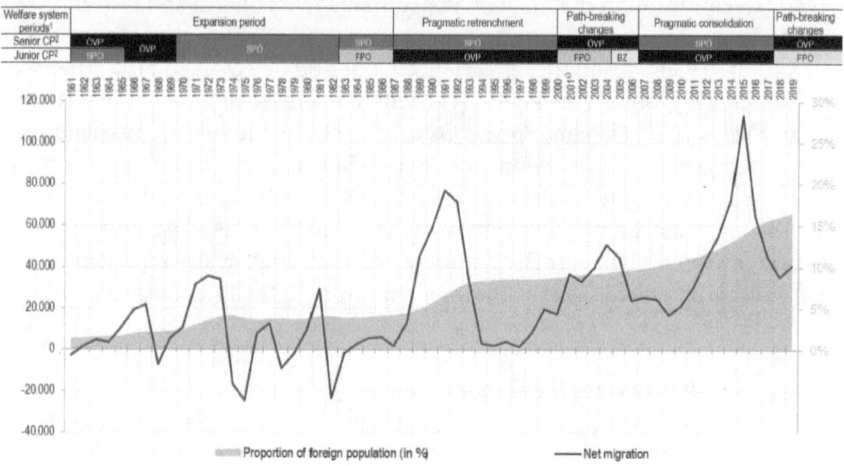

Source: Statistics Austria, Migration statistics.
Note 1: Periods of welfare system policy based on Obinger and Tálos 2010; Tálos and Obinger, 2020.
Note 2: Government coalitions (senior and junior coalition partners) based on Gruber 2014.

access was not granted to other types of immigrants, such as those entering for economic reasons.

Since the 1960s, the second important contributor to a more systematic shift in the net migration balance has been labour migration. The establishment of a temporary labour migration regime to rotate "guestworkers" in the 1960s and 1970s contributed to a growing share of foreign residents in Austria (from 1% in the early 1960s to roughly 4% by the end of the 1970s). Guestworkers from Turkey and Yugoslavia were recruited predominantly for blue-collar jobs in the industrial and construction sectors (Marik-Lebeck and Wisbauer 2017). Yet targeted welfare support for labour migrants did not materialize. For one thing, unlike in traditional countries of immigration, Austria's immigration experience has long been overshadowed by a reluctance of political elites to consider Austria a country of immigration (Fassmann and Münz 1995). Moreover, the guestworker system's rotational character meant that no need was seen for specific integration measures; it relied instead on the inclusiveness of the fine-meshed welfare system, which was based on employment, without distinction being made for nationality or ethnic background (Biffl and Faustmann 2013, 51). Unlike the more universal Scandinavian welfare systems, which are based on residence (see chapter 8 on Norway in this volume), in

Austria the early predominance of an employment-based provision of social programs kept labour migrants' participation within narrow bounds (Pfeil 2011).

Hence, early guestworker migration did not impose a burden on the Austrian welfare budget: employment among guestworkers was ensured by definition, and its temporary nature did not create long-term claims to welfare contributions anyway – on the contrary, labour immigrants were net fiscal contributors during the 1960s and 1970s, and their labour contributed greatly to the country's economic growth, the consolidation of the welfare state, and the upward mobility of native-born workers (Bauböck 1996, 24; Biffl 1997, 561). The gap between immigrants and the native-born did not widen until the Austrian government ended the rotational system in 1974, at which point temporary migration became permanent, family reunification increased the number of non-employed spouses and children, and the first immigrant generation turned from working age to pension age.

Thus, the country's economic development became intertwined with the general welfare system and the patterns of immigration: as long as immigration was adapted to the country's economic needs and the economy thrived, employment of labour immigrants was largely assured and so was the security provided by the welfare system. However, when the economic situation deteriorated (as happened during the global economic crisis of 1973–74), job security vanished and so did the security provided by the welfare system. In the case of immigrants, for some this led to expulsion, while those who remained and eventually brought their families faced much greater difficulties than nationals (Biffl and Faustmann 2013, 51): they could neither rely on the same ties and networks as most Austrians could, nor on the income and/or insurance of their relatives. With regard to insurance-based instruments, guestworkers had to pay the same contributions to unemployment insurance as Austrian employees, yet their claims to it expired more quickly than those of Austrian citizens (Gächter 1995, 435). And though formally employed labour migrants were covered by the insurance, until 1989 immigrants were explicitly excluded from access to unemployment assistance before they obtained a limited form of access (Kargl 2004, 4).

However, as the number of immigrants remained relatively small, during the 1970s the absorption capacity of both the labour market and the welfare system was not strained severely by their presence. In fact, some observers concluded that the Austrian welfare state had fostered the social integration of most immigrants even more effectively in some regards than traditional immigration countries that offered more formal equality but at the same time generally weaker systems of social security (Bauböck 1996, 24). This picture had changed by the end of the 1980s, as migrant demography underwent a transformation and the unemployment rate of foreign nationals doubled in the span of a decade. In this changing economic and political climate, immigrants' disproportionately positive economic contribution to the welfare budget diminished (Biffl 1997, 561). That was when the political debate about the relationship between immigration and the welfare state budget started to gain intensity (Biffl 1997, 561; Felderer et al. 2004). Once the fall of the Iron Curtain kicked off a new era of immigration to Austria, its role in welfare state reform became increasingly and negatively politicized.

Welfare System Reform and Migrant Integration in Austria Since the 1990s

Changing Contexts for the Immigration/Welfare Nexus

The relationship between the welfare state and immigration changed against the background of three sets of economic and political transformations. *Macroeconomic changes (globalization)* tied to economic stagnation in Austria were the first and strongest source of pressure. Although debates about the welfare system's long-term financial viability had already started during the economic recession of the 1970s, in the 1980s the combination of economic stagnation, growing unemployment, and increasing budget deficits triggered a reorientation of social policy (Heitzmann and Österle 2008, 48). That reorientation, however, was possible only because of *changes in government.* The end of the SPÖ's absolute majority brought about an SPÖ/FPÖ-coalition government, which began to halt the expansion of the welfare state in some of its facets and to even gradually retrench it in others. After the coalition's collapse, the return of six centrist grand coalition governments of SPÖ and ÖVP from 1987 to 1999 brought even stronger momentum to welfare state retrenchment, for now two political parties of equal size sought to forge a compromise on the rescaling of welfare services and the fiscal stabilization of the increasing budget deficit. These tasks became ever more pressing as a third transformation loomed over Austrian politics: *institutional changes* tied to the country's preparations for accession to the European Union. Its realization in 1995 marked a watershed with regard to Austria's institutional structure, its traditional patterns of postwar politics, and its sovereignty in key areas of domestic policy-making (Obinger and Tálos 2010, 108).

Regarding the specific role immigrants played in these transformations and in the welfare state reforms tied to them, two further transformations came to be of striking importance. First, the growing debate over the role of immigrants was accelerated by decisive *changes in immigration patterns*, again owing to Austria's location in Central Europe (and in sharp contrast to the more postcolonial patterns of immigration in peripherally located Portugal, which led to more sympathetic public opinion and political approaches there – see chapter 10). When the Iron Curtain fell, an abrupt increase in (South)Eastern European

Figure 7.2. Annual immigration to Austria by nationality since EU accession, 1996–2019.

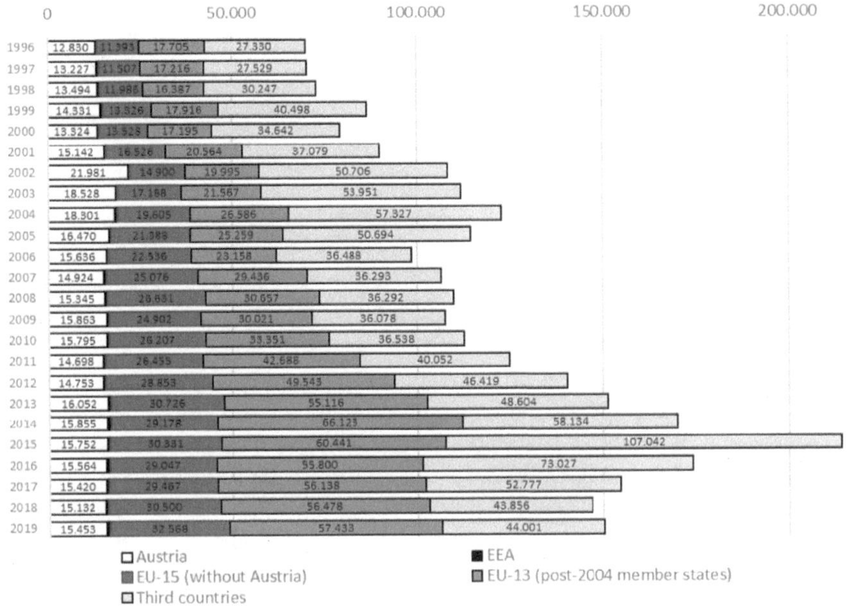

Source: Statistics Austria, migration statistics.

immigration almost doubled the share of the foreign population within a few years (from 1989 to 1993, it grew from 4% to 8%). After restrictive immigration laws were introduced in 1992–93, which established a new system of residence permits and briefly reduced immigration, the country's EU accession further accelerated the influx of EU citizens based on freedom-of-movement principles, in particular after the EU's enlargement into (South)Eastern Europe in 2004. Since then, as shown in Figure 7.2, immigration to Austria has become predominantly EU-internal migration, which makes up around two-thirds of the total annual immigration (Rosenberger and Gruber 2020, 32ff). The European influx was accompanied by two higher peaks of refugee migration (from Southeastern Europe due to the Balkan wars of the 1990s, as well as from Syria, Iraq, and Afghanistan between 2015 and 2017). Altogether, over the past two decades the percentage of foreign residents has again almost doubled (from 8.7% at the turn of the century to 16.5% in 2019) (see Figure 7.1).

Second, not only increasing immigration contributed to growing politicization of the issue. *Party system changes* in Austria now catalysed political contestation as well. With a shift from a (limping) two-party system toward moderate

Figure 7.3. Austria's place in the IESPI comparison, 1990–2015

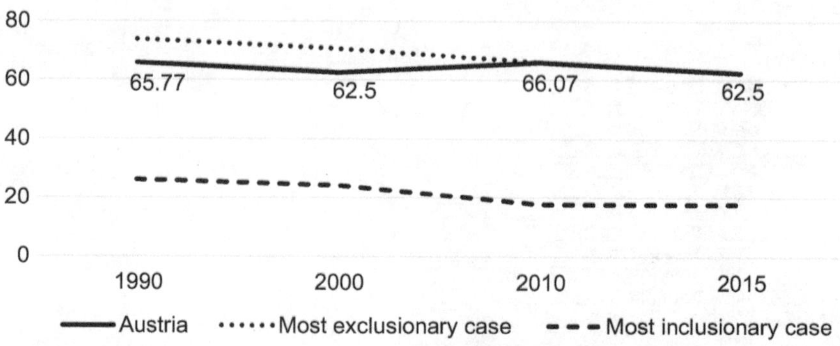

pluralism featuring a Freedom Party (FPÖ) that had been reorganized from liberal-national to populist radical right, and the entrance of left-libertarian Greens into parliament in 1986, political contestation over immigration issues grew ever more intense (Gruber 2014). The radical-right FPÖ, growing steadily at the expense of the governing mainstream parties, championed welfare chauvinist arguments, pushing hard for a halt to immigration and for the targeted exclusion of immigrants from welfare benefits (Ennser-Jedenastik 2016). Even though the governing parties initially treated the Haider-led FPÖ as a pariah, its platform influenced mainstream parties' policy positions. Eventually, the FPÖ joined two right-wing coalitions between 2000 and 2006, the Second Republic's first of their kind,[3] before centrist grand coalitions returned from 2006 to 2017, only to be toppled by yet another (short-lived) right-wing coalition from 2017 to 2019 (Gruber 2014; Rosenberger and Gruber 2020). These changes in government composition not only kicked off a period of path-changing welfare state reform but also intensified the attempts to erect targeted barriers for immigrants.

In a nutshell, since the 1990s immigration has been debated much more strongly than in previous decades, precisely at the time when the scope for national immigration control or targeted exclusion of immigrant groups from social welfare has become narrower due to supranational EU-regulations (Peyrl 2019). This tension has since become a characteristic pattern in Austrian politics, with the result that immigrants have been assigned an ambivalent position in the Austrian welfare system: some categories of migrants are now treated more or less as coequal insiders, while other categories remain disadvantaged outsiders, with varying nuances in different welfare segments identified by the IESPI. When we set all of this atop an already status-conservative and selective tradition, this helps explain Austria's position as one of the most exclusionary welfare systems among the countries selected by the IESPI.

Gradual Welfare Retrenchment to Immigrants' Disadvantage

What has been the consequence of these changing contexts for the immigration/welfare nexus? To begin with the most general impact, the retrenchment of the Austrian welfare system in the 1990s and even more so in the 2000s came at a specific disadvantage to immigrants, in particular with regard to insurance-based contributory benefits.

As Austria's public *pension system* was "one of the most expensive in the world" (Obinger and Tálos 2010, 109), it was the specific focus of initially slight but later more far-reaching reforms. Between 1987 and 1999, the centrist grand coalition engaged in pragmatic retrenchment, passing reforms on a regular basis (e.g., raising the early retirement age, raising the general assessment basis from 5 to 15 contribution years, and locking in the increment factor for all pension types). In 2000, the right-wing coalition government kicked off a period of path-breaking changes in the welfare system with pension reforms, introducing additional cuts (e.g., raising the years required for a maximum pension to 45 years, abolishing certain types of early retirement benefits, lowering the increment factor) but also systemic changes (e.g., stretching the assessment basis from 15 to 40 years, that is, the full lifetime work record, and introducing a system of "corridor pensions" between the ages of 62 and 68 or a "three-pillar system" of public, occupational, and private pensions) (Mairhuber 2009, 210; Obinger and Tálos 2010, 115). All reforms in that period strengthened the insurance-based logic of the public pension system, in that they tied pensions more strongly to employment and wage levels while also worsening the situation for non-continual and atypical forms of employment (Mairhuber 2009, 210). With the return of the grand coalition between 2007 and 2017, the general trend of cutbacks was halted in favour of pragmatic consolidation; the reforms that followed focused predominantly on specialized regulations for premature pensions (Wöss 2020, 238; Tálos and Obinger 2020, 113ff).

A second area of prominent curtailment concerned *unemployment benefits.* While Austria had prided itself on its low unemployment rates in the economic golden age, during the centrist grand coalition of the 1990s rising numbers of unemployment catalysed a trend toward activating social policy (Unger 2001). Reforms of unemployment benefits reduced benefit levels by changing the basis of assessment, restricted access through harsher criteria for entitlement, expanded the number and range of sanctions against recipients, and cut back on unemployment assistance (Obinger and Tálos 2010, 110). After the turn of the millennium, the right-wing coalition further cut unemployment benefits (e.g., by reducing family surcharges and extending the qualifying period) and tightened sanctions. Measures to "activate" the unemployed were intensified, for example, by increasing the pressure to accept a job (e.g., by expanding the parameters of reasonable commuting time or job suitability) and by introducing a "service check" designed to create (legalized) jobs in the low-wage sector (such as housekeeping or cleaning) (Atzmüller 2009, 29f; Obinger and Tálos 2010, 116f.).

These reforms have indirectly exacerbated immigrants' generally disadvantaged position: not only are resource-poor groups of immigrants (see the section on "Outcomes" below) at higher risk of discontinuous and atypical forms of employment, they also suffer disproportionally from extensions of assessment periods. Moreover, since immigrants' pension claims are suspended if they stay abroad for more than two months, there is also a limitation for them to export their pensions. Finally, as entitlements to pension benefits depend on contribution periods and contribution size, third-country nationals who move to Austria later in their careers have to expect lower pension levels and may not even attain the waiting period of 15 contribution years at all (since only insurance periods completed in Austria, EU/EEA member states, and countries with bilateral agreements can be credited) (Davy and Çinar 2001, 612ff.).

With regard to unemployment benefits, similar mechanisms disadvantaging immigrants are at work. Necessary periods of employment function as a filter, especially considering that the requirements for entering and remaining in the country (and thus for being able to take a job on a permanent basis) are continuously being raised (Peyrl and Bruckner 2017). For example, in 2003 the right-wing coalition introduced an "integration agreement" for third-country nationals that required them to demonstrate German-language competence at level A1 or to attend a language course in order to be entitled to permanent residency (Mourão Permoser 2012). These language criteria were raised to level A2 in 2005 and to B1 in 2011 and have since been bolstered by the obligation to pass "value courses" organized by the Austrian Integration Fund in 2017. Indeed, language competence has now become a criterion for entering the country at all: in 2011 the grand coalition established proof of German-language competence at level A1 as a condition for first-time applications for certain types of residence permits (mostly related to labour migration and family reunification).

Courts and EU as Drivers for Targeted Inclusion

Despite the overall restrictive political climate, since the 1990s some steps toward greater inclusion of immigrants have been initiated as well. Much in line with the book's overall theoretical framework (see chapter 1), however, their provenance were judicial actors and the EU rather than elected politicians.

One prominent example of liberalization spurred by court decisions relates to *unemployment assistance*, a last-resort mechanism for bridging periods of hardship for the long-term unemployed. Until 1989, unemployment assistance was limited to Austrian citizens, but after years of debate it was expanded to include foreigners who could demonstrate eight years of employment history in Austria or who had obtained a current work allowance (Kargl 2004, 4). In 1992, another amendment passed by the grand coalition extended entitlement to other immigrant groups (refugees and stateless persons) while lowering the required duration of employment to five years. However, the decisive steps for equal treatment were the result of a court ruling by the ECHR,[4] which compelled Austria to expand the entitlement to foreigners as long as they were EU citizens and/or permanent residents and had met the same insurance criteria as Austrian nationals (Ataç 2019). Tellingly, however, after a "citizenship-neutral" regulation was implemented by the centrist government in 1998, the Austrian Constitutional Court invalidated this regulation a year later, on the basis that the government had maintained the discriminatory character of the regulation by simply referencing the place of birth instead. This ruling forced the government to finally eliminate all references to nationality (Davy and Çinar 2001, 609). Nonetheless, the Austrian legislature has found alternative ways to limit immigrants' access, in particular by focusing on specific residence statuses, which themselves require a minimum duration of residence or employment (Brameshuber 2018, 263–4). As put by Verschueren (2016, 193): "Economic activity serves as a sort of 'master key' that unlocks redistributive arrangements in the host State for migrants, which is justified by their participation in the employment market of that State."

This also applies to EU citizens, even though they have become an increasingly heterogeneous and important group since 1995. Austria's accession to the EU turned out to be the most impactful source of pressure for inclusionary reform: it has forced the country to conform to the EU's *acquis communautaire* and to establish the since then characteristic trichotomy between Austrian citizens, EU citizens, and third-country nationals (Bauböck 1996, 19). The European Community's principles of free movement of workers (and their families)[5] and their access to social security benefits[6] has meant that, for example, Austria now grants EU citizens access to contributory unemployment benefits from day one and factors in contribution periods accrued in other member states (Peyrl and Bruckner 2017, 3). Similarly, insurance periods acquired from pension systems in other member states are recognized reciprocally when calculating eventual pension claims in Austria.[7] Yet with regard to social assistance benefits, the Maastricht Treaty's expansion of the principle of non-discrimination to non-working EU citizens and subsequent rulings of the European Court of Justice (ECJ)[8] have kicked off a protracted debate led by some member states, Austria among them, who fear "benefit tourism" (Felten 2018, 236f.).[9] With the "Citizens' Rights Directive" (2004/38), the European Commission settled on a three-stage system of equal treatment regarding social assistance benefits: equal treatment can be suspended for stays of less than three months; it has to be granted after a residence of more than five years, whereas for the period in between, access can be limited for non-employed EU citizens (Kapuy 2016, 399). Since then, Austria (like other member states) has started to grant access to social assistance only to those EU citizens who can provide the necessary economic means to receive a legal residence status (and therefore not require social assistance measures in the first place) (Felten 2018, 239). More recent rulings by the ECJ[10] have confirmed this practice and have gone even further by confirming similar restrictions regarding certain social security benefits as well.[11] This has led the European Commission to propose a respective amendment of regulation 883/2004 – a proposal that is still being crafted at the time of writing.[12]

Non-Contributory Benefits as Constant Object of Political Conflict

Non-contributory benefits are the most controversial programs at the European level – indeed, at the domestic level as well. The most fiercely debated instrument in Austria is social assistance, a protection against poverty that is taxpayer-funded rather than insurance-based (Pratscher 1992). Introduced by the Social Democratic government in the 1970s, it was placed under the administration of the nine Austrian provinces, resulting in different designs and implementations, though throughout moulded as an income-contingent and needs-based instrument (Heitzmann and Österle 2008, 60). Ongoing debate about the need for harmonization led to its replacement with "needs-based minimum benefits" in 2010, which harmonized the different provincial regulations; but in 2018, it was once again restructured under its old name (social assistance) by the right-wing coalition. In terms of immigrant access, the instrument is selective. As early as the nineteenth century, precursors of social assistance were tied to permanent residence (*Heimatrecht*), and nowadays the status and residence requirements perform a similar function (Tálos 2004, 6). EU/EEA citizens have unrestricted access only if they have been permanent residents for more than five years or are actively employed in Austria, and third-country nationals have access only after five years of rightful residence in Austria and only if they have attained permanent residence (for which German-language competence at level B1 is currently required) (Peyrl and Bruckner 2017, 6). Asylum seekers are excluded since they are covered by another, refugee-specific instrument of primary care, yet once asylum is officially granted, they lose access to primary care and instead gain equal access to social assistance.

Social assistance remains a popular target for restrictive immigration policy proposals, and since it is under the jurisdiction of the Austrian provinces, it has also become subject to interprovincial competition. Despite harmonization, right-wing parties' demands for further restrictions have not receded; for example, in 2016 the right-wing coalition in the province of Upper Austria curtailed the needs-based minimum for refugees with temporary recognition, only to be overturned shortly afterwards by the ECJ.[13] At the national level, after it gained power in 2018, a right-wing coalition followed a similar path by reducing social assistance for refugees with subsidiary protection status to the level of basic primary care payments. Moreover, "to curb incentives for an immigration into the Austrian welfare system," the government introduced a "labor market qualification bonus."[14] This amounted to a targeted cutback of social assistance for claimants who could not demonstrate language competence in either German (B1) or English (C1); the savings from the cuts were earmarked to finance language courses instead. However, this time it was the Austrian Constitutional Court that eventually overturned that regulation, stating that it violated the principle of equality. Thus, high courts had overruled political attempts at further exclusion once more (Verfassungsgerichtshof Österreich 2019).

Another area in which provincial jurisdiction has led to recurring conflict is housing. Here, the most important support instrument is the housing allowance – that is, cash benefits, which are tied to the rental agreement and the size of the household. Over the past five decades, these benefits have evolved into very different regulations across the nine provinces. With regard to immigrants, the varying regulations for access should have been brought into alignment with the minimum level of equality for EU citizens and permanent residents as established by EU directive 2003/109/EG. However, some provinces continue to maintain their own regulations, such as criteria of current employment or continuous employment in the past, which make it hard for some third-country nationals to access the housing allowance. These regulations are especially challenging for recognized refugees who no longer have access to state-funded primary care but who are unable to show previous employment after having been excluded from the labour market during the asylum-granting process. Some provinces even require as many as 25 years' local residence, which presents a challenge for most immigrants (Mundt 2015, 7). Still, housing allowance continues to be controversial in Austria. In a recent example, in 2017 the right-wing coalition in the province of Upper Austria added German language competence at level A2 or proof of course attendance as a criterion for third-country nationals and raised the required duration of previous employment to 54 months. The Austrian Ombudsman Board described the reform as discrimination incompatible with EU law and as a violation of human rights, and it urged the provincial government to revise the amendment,[15] an assessment that was supported by an expert opinion issued by the Advocate General of the ECJ.[16]

Immigrants' access to social housing is another controversial issue in the area of housing policy. It is regulated by the provinces as well, but generally there are limitations for immigrants, as social housing is available only to EU/EEA citizens and third-country nationals who have obtained permanent resident status or are recognized as refugees. These limitations are not strict enough for the radical right, as demonstrated by their frequent objections. Most recently, during the Viennese provincial elections of 2020, the FPÖ called for "delinquent foreigners" to be barred from further entitlement to social housing.[17] Related claims have also become talking points among Austria's centre-right. In the same election campaign, the ÖVP frontrunner revitalized an old FPÖ claim by demanding that German language competence be made a prerequisite for access to social housing. Little surprise, then, that during their joint coalition at the national level, the ÖVP/FPÖ government drafted a bill clarifying that social housing was "dedicated primarily to serve the housing supply of Austrian citizens and citizens with equal rights," and introducing integration certificates from the Austrian Integration Fund as a requirement to access social housing.[18] The government collapsed before the bill could be enacted; even so, this example demonstrates that similar thrusts can be ratcheted up in an endless spiral.

The conflicts just described underscore that non-contributory benefits are the most controversial welfare instruments when it comes to immigrants. They are not designed as insurance instruments to which the equivalence principle (of contribution and benefits) can be applied; rather, their availability is based on considerations of overall deservingness, so they are much more prone to controversy over which groups are "deserving" in the first place. Immigration-related factors such as duration of residence are politically popular eligibility criteria, the implication being that those immigrants who have not satisfied sufficient requirements are not immediately viewed as deserving (Fernández de la Hoz and Pflegerl 2000). On a similar note, the amount of primary care provided to immigrants during the asylum procedure is also regularly contested. For example, in response to increasing numbers of asylum applications since 2015, the right-wing coalition introduced an amendment to the asylum law in 2018 that divested asylum seekers of a significant share of their cash possessions as a form of "cost sharing" of the procedural costs. Hence, non-contributory benefits will likely remain the most controversial social programs in relation to immigrants.

Less Controversial and Growingly Inclusive Segments

In contrast to the programs reviewed above, access to basic health care is a less controversial topic despite being the second-highest line item in the Austrian social budget (Heitzmann and Österle 2008, 53). For statutory health care, employment insurance also plays an important role, though in contrast to pension insurance or unemployment benefits, the system is more strongly oriented toward universal inclusion. General access to the Austrian health care system is organized through social security as compulsory health insurance for everyone in the labour force (or for registered jobseekers) and their dependent relatives (Muckenhuber, Freidl, and Rásky 2011, 559). In addition to employees, health insurance covers specific social groups, such as students and immigrants (Heitzmann and Österle 2008, 54). Through this arrangement, the vast majority of the population is covered by basic health care: only about 2% of the population has no insurance, most of these being unemployed individuals (in particular unemployed women), asylum seekers who are ineligible for national primary care, and migrants without legal residence status. Undocumented migrants are the most vulnerable group, since even if they can afford insurance, they are not legally entitled to comprehensive insurance and are not even allowed to secure private health insurance (Anzenberger, Bodenwinkler, and Breyer 2015; Muckenhuber, Freidl, and Rásky 2011, 599; Bachner et al. 2013). Hence, undocumented migrants often avoid medical institutions out of fear of being expelled from the country. Their only access to health care is through "informal solidarity" – that is, professionals in the medical or social system treat them *pro bono*, or they turn to various charitable programs (Anzenberger, Bodenwinkler, and Breyer 2015, 56).

As numerous studies have documented, though, formal access does not ensure equal participation in the health care system (Wimmer-Puchinger, Wolf, and Engleder 2006; Mayer 2011). For a number of reasons (e.g., language barriers, information deficits, lack of intercultural competence, institutional barriers, socio-economic deficits), migrants tend to participate less actively in the Austrian health care system (Anzenberger, Bodenwinkler, and Breyer 2015; Spahl, Weiss, and Kohlenberger 2017). As a consequence, health care providers themselves have increasingly introduced measures to promote intercultural sensitivity among medical staff, besides providing multilingual services and personnel to facilitate information provision and communication with patients. At the government level, in 2012 the grand coalition presented ten framework goals designed to structure the Austrian health care strategy for the next 20 years. One of those goals was to reduce health inequity for various disadvantaged groups, among them people of different national origins (Bundesministerium für Gesundheit und Frauen 2012). In a similar vein, in 2010 the government tabled its "National Action Plan for Integration" (NAP.I), which identified health as a central field of action, and it has since promoted a variety of measures in this direction (such as increasing information for recipients, strengthening cultural sensitivity training for medical staff, and promoting more diversity among employees in health institutions).

As employment plays such a central role in the Austrian social security regime, since the 1990s the government has expanded active labour market policies to help the unemployed re-enter the labour market. This expansion is in part the result of Austria's accession to the EU and the availability of European structural funds that can be used for active labour market instruments (Heitzmann and Österle 2008, 59). The total budget for active labour market integration policies steadily increased after the 1990s, in particular for those that target vulnerable groups, including immigrants. In 2010, in the aftermath of the global financial crisis, Austrian expenditures on active labour market policy (relative to the level of unemployment) reached an all-time high, ranking in the top third among OECD countries (Grand 2009; Bösch et al. 2012). Since then, the Austrian Labor Market Service (AMS) has steadily developed a more and more fine-meshed system of measures to "activate" the unemployed (e.g., through client counselling, qualification measures, supports for job applications, or instruments to pressure clients toward job searches) as well as financial incentives for employers to hire or maintain employees supervised by the AMS (such as co-payments and reductions of non-wage labour costs) (Atzmüller 2009, 30f). Since the NAP.I was tabled in 2010, clients with a migrant background have been identified, studied, and supported as a target group more specifically.

Yet even these gradual measures for targeted labour market integration can become subject to partisan politics, as recent years have shown. In 2017, in response to the abrupt increase in refugees seeking employment, the grand coalition introduced a specific labour market integration package (the "integration year") targeting refugees (and even asylum seekers who had a high likelihood being granted asylum); however, this package was cut only one year later when the centrist grand coalition ceded power to a right-wing coalition (Rosenberger and Gruber 2020).

Public Opinion and Outcomes

With regulations upholding various ways to block certain groups of immigrants (at least for some time), the question remains: how does this relate to public opinion on immigrants' welfare integration as well as to outcomes?

Attention to immigration in Austria has long been above the EU average, and this has been even more the case in the aftermath of the 2015–16 refugee peaks. In the biannual Eurobarometer the questions about the most important challenges the country is facing show that immigration was the most salient issue in Austria from 2015 to 2018, and its score has ranked consistently above the EU average (see Figure 7.4). Regarding preferences, immigration-sceptic stances have usually outweighed pro-immigrant stances, making Austria one of the more immigration-critical countries among Western European democracies (Rosenberger and Seeber 2011). This is reflected in support for radical-right populist parties and has also influenced mainstream parties' stances on the welfare integration of immigrants. It helps explain, for example, the centre-right's clear shift toward a tougher integration stance (including more restricted welfare integration) under party leader Sebastian Kurz (Rosenberger and Gruber 2020; Heinisch, Werner, and Habersack 2020).

Figure 7.4. Public views on most important challenge the country is facing, 2003–2019.

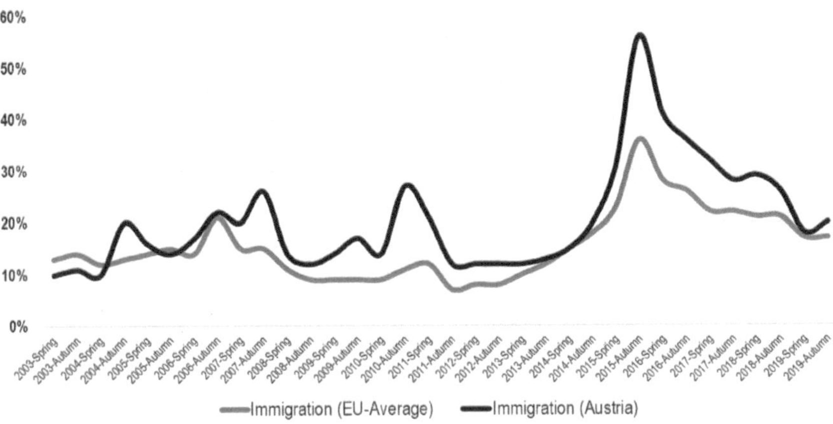

Source: Eurobarometer, 2003–2019.

Let us now turn to the outcomes of Austria's welfare system retrenchment and targeted exclusion for the economic status of immigrants in Austria. Various outcome variables indicate a rough hierarchy of socio-economic integration, with Austrian citizens and migrants from the EU's 15 member states at the top, immigrants from the post-2004 EU member states in the middle, and third-country nationals at the bottom. Obviously, this generalization obscures some variance within these three groups; nevertheless, it reveals the importance of the specific combination of resource capacities on the one hand and legal types of immigration on the other for understanding the Austrian case.

Starting with unemployment (see Figure 7.5), since 2004 there has been a remarkably consistent unemployment rate among Austrian citizens of about 5% or below. Citizens from the (old) EU-15 countries have a similar rate of around 5%, with occasional increases to 6% at most. Considerably higher unemployment rates can be observed among citizens from the (new) post-2004 accession states (EU-13), for whom the average is around 9%. The two biggest immigrant communities (Germany excluded) in Austria, citizens from Yugoslavia's successor states and Turkey, perform even worse, with rates of 11% and 17% respectively. Moreover, there are discrepancies in terms of gender (immigrant women are significantly less employed than men) and generation (second-generation immigrants exhibit higher unemployment rates than first-generation immigrants) (Huber 2010). These patterns of unemployment coincide with patterns of living space, another indicator of socio-economic integration. Austrians and residents with a migrant background in the old EU-15 member states have access to the

Figure 7.5. Unemployment rate among population 15–64 (in % of the labour reserve), by nationality, 2004–2019.

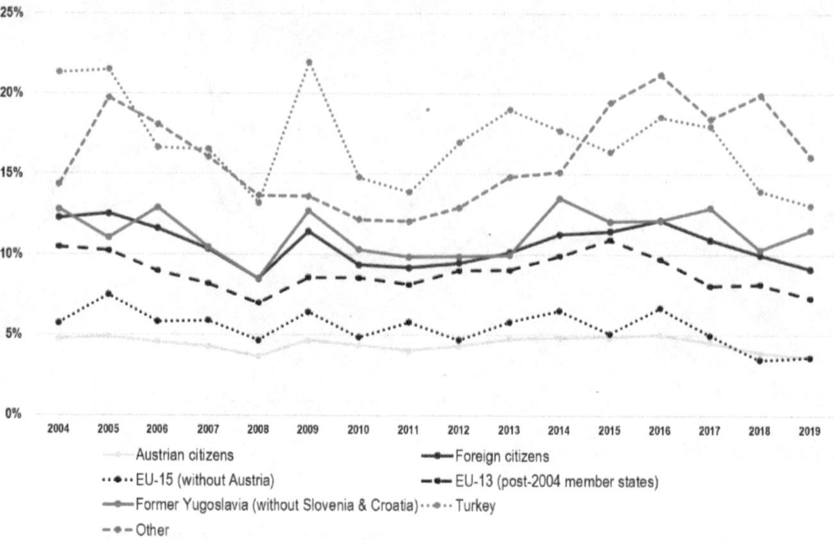

Source: Statistics Austria, Micro-census.
Note: Annual mean value over all weeks. Definition of unemployment according to the International Labor Organization.

same amount of square metres per capita in their homes (47–48 m^2), whereas residents with a migrant background in an EU-13 member state have to get by with about 10 square metres less (36 m^2). Far more cramped housing conditions can be observed among residents with a background in Yugoslavian successor states and other third-country nationals (26–27 m^2 per capita), in particular among residents with a Turkish background (who have less than half the space at their disposal than their counterparts of Austrian origin). While among all immigrant groups the second generation is better off in terms of living space than the first generation, this generational improvement is much larger for EU-13 immigrants and third-country nationals than for former Yugoslavian or Turkish immigrants.

A useful indicator of the degree of welfare integration is the risk of poverty, both before and after considering welfare support (see Figure 7.6). Austrian citizens face the lowest risk of poverty (roughly 20%); that risk is considerably higher for foreign citizens in general (on average 44%). However, again we see the characteristic pattern of EU citizens being better off (poverty risk 35%) than immigrants from former Yugoslavian countries (about 45%) and Turkey (roughly 48%), who in turn are in a better position than other third-country nationals (poverty risk as high as 60%). Given that Austria is a welfare state with segmented support mechanisms for different categories of residents, it is

Figure 7.6. Risk of poverty before and after welfare benefits, 2004–2019.

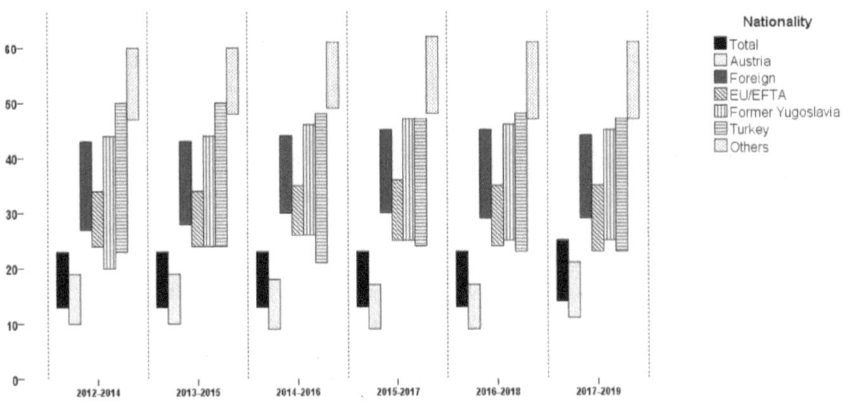

Source: Statistical Yearbooks of Migration (Statistics Austria), EU-Silc.
Note: Values based on three-year averages, expressing the percentage of people within each group of nationality at risk of poverty. Top end of bar indicates risk of poverty before; bottom end of the bar indicates risk of poverty after receiving welfare support.

important to consider the effect of those mechanisms on poverty alleviation. As shown in Figure 7.6, welfare support reduces the risk for all categories of residents, but this effect is smaller for Austrian citizens (–10%) and EU citizens (–11%) than for the long-standing migrant communities from former Yugoslavia (–21%) and Turkey (–25%). Here, the confluence of a weaker socio-economic background and a more common status of permanent residence leads to a larger effect of welfare benefits. Conversely, while the socio-economic situation for many other third-country nationals is at least as precarious as for ex-Yugoslavian or Turkish immigrants, their residence status is more often characterized by temporary permits coupled with tougher restrictions regarding their access to welfare benefits, resulting in a much lower risk-reducing effect (–13%).

Conclusion: Differential Integration and Persistent Reluctance in a Constrained Scope of Action

Austria's position at the exclusive end of the IESPI can be read as the result of an interplay between its welfare system's heritage, its modern-day retrenchment in light of substantial economic, demographic, and political transformations, and its differential treatment depending on legal residence status.

Austria has long been viewed as a model Bismarckian welfare system. Core pillars of that system, such as social insurance as the dominant mode of financing, labour market participation as the predominant path to insurance, and status preservation as the inherent effect of earnings-related transfers, remain to this day (Obinger and Tálos 2010). These characteristics traditionally implied a considerable gap between insiders and outsiders, since "in employment-based social security systems like the Austrian, exclusion is structurally inherent" (Tálos 2004). However, the implications for immigrants did not become truly apparent during the Cold War, because Austria admitted a relatively small number of immigrants and the guestworker regime by definition fostered employment-based integration into social insurance, making immigrants net contributors to the welfare budget.

Fast forward, ever since the *trente glorieuses* Austria has undergone significant demographic changes, among them increasing immigration and a growing number of foreign residents. This has fuelled political debate over their access to the welfare system (Heitzmann and Österle 2008). The general retrenchment of welfare system generosity under centrist grand coalitions, and even more so under right-wing coalitions, underscores the importance of government constellations and of right-wing party strength as explanatory factors, echoing anti-immigrant sentiments in the population that are hard to appease (as discussed in depth in chapter 4 of this volume). These general reforms have clearly hurt inherently disadvantaged groups with limited socio-structural resources and discontinuous or part-time employment records – among them in particular certain categories of immigrants (Obinger and Tálos 2010, 127).

Conversely, the country's EU accession and various high court rulings have constrained national political ambitions by promoting further inclusion, in particular for EU citizens but also for permanent residents from third countries. Other examples of more inclusive steps have been targeted support measures vis-à-vis residents with a migrant background, such as active labour market support measures for (re-)employment and culture- and language-sensitive measures in the health care sector in the past decade. These have been encouraged by an evolving national approach to systematic migrant integration, in particular since the adoption of a National Action Plan for Integration by the centrist grand coalition in 2010. This approach was encouraged by the European Union but was also a response to ongoing evidence of weaker performance by certain migrant groups with regard to the labour market, the education system, and social security – a pattern that has remained challenging to this day.

The result is a retrenched but (in contrast to other exclusionary cases in the IESPI dataset, like the US – see chapter 9) relatively still generous welfare system that has become more inclusive for some categories of immigrants yet has retained barriers vis-à-vis others and that continues to seek ways to further restrict access. All this occurs in the context of an increasingly contentious political debate over the future design of the country's immigration/welfare nexus (in contrast to the Portuguese example in chapter 10) – a debate that is not limited to the national level but in some welfare segments is pursued at the subnational level as well. Risking an outlook to the immediate future, the various recent attempts by right-wing political parties and coalition governments documented in this chapter indicate a trend toward further attempts to limit welfare access for various categories of immigrants. These attempts no longer arise solely from the radical right; they are also encountered among the centre-right. Hence, even though a right-wing coalition was replaced by an ÖVP/Green coalition in 2020, given this new coalition's balance of power – already apparent in the coalition's program[19] – a continuation of restrictive thrusts is to be expected. As the past three decades have demonstrated, the most decisive impediment to such attempts has not been the party-political system but rather the national or European courts and EU legislation.

Since immigration will continue to shape Austria's demographics, as will the necessity to integrate socio-economically disadvantaged groups of migrants, the controversy over the welfare system's role in this broader task will continue to impact Austrian political competition. As the leeway for decisions at the national level has become narrower, conflicts will increasingly go beyond the mere national arena and may even confront the foundations of the supranational European framework. The Austrian government's recent attempt to index family benefits for EU citizens working in Austria, which has led the European Commission to launch an infringement procedure, may be a foretaste of what is on the horizon in the years to come.

NOTES

1 The "General Law on Social Insurance" (Allgemeines Sozialversicherungsgesetz, ASVG) unified the hitherto fragmented regulations. Originally the ASVG considered only workers and employees; during the 1960s the social insurance law also integrated the agricultural sector and the self-employed (Heitzmann and Österle 2008, 47).

2 A commitment to equality, later also enforced by EU law (Directive 2011/95/EU).

3 In 2005 and 2006 the coalition was maintained by the FPÖ's splinter party, the Alliance for the Future of Austria (BZÖ), which took over ministerial seats from the FPÖ.

4 ECHR, 16.9.1996, 39/1995/545/631, *Gaygusuz vs Austria.*

5 Art. 48–51 EEC-Treaty.

6 Council Regulation no. 1408/71 (now no. 883/2004).

7 The Council Directive 2003/109/EC extended the principle of equal treatment even to long-term residents with legal and uninterrupted residence of at least five years without recourse to the social assistance system, but it allowed for member states to limit access that went beyond the level of core benefits.

8 ECJ 12.5.1998, C-85/96, *Martínez Sala*; ECJ 20.9.2001, C-184/99, *Grzelczyk*; ECJ 7.9. 2004, C-456/02, *Trojani*.

9 In fact, once handed the chance to co-create EU policy-making in that regard, Austria soon positioned itself among the hardliners in immigration and migrant integration policy-making. During the first right-wing coalition government, Austria blocked the commission's draft for an equalization of long-term residents, pushed for limits in family reunification, and demanded longer transition periods for new member states in Eastern Europe (Perchinig and Valchars 2019, 420). But also during the centrist grand coalition era Austria maintained a restrictive stance, for example, when in April 2013 the Interior Minister, together with German, Dutch, and British colleagues, issued a letter to the European Council insisting that abuse of free movement rights strained the welfare systems of those countries (Kapuy 2016, 401).

10 See ECJ 11.11.2014, C-333/13, *Dano*; ECJ 15.9.2015, C-67/14, *Alimanovic*; ECJ 25.2.2016, C-299/14, *García-Nieto*.

11 ECJ 14.6.2016, C-308/14, *Commission v United Kingdom*.

12 See COM(2016) 815 final.

13 See ECJ 21.11.2018, C-713/17, Ayubi.

14 Amendment to the Social Assistance Law [173/BNR (XXVI.GP)], 25.04.2019.

15 Austrian Ombudman Board (2019): "Missstandsfeststellung und Empfehlung der Volksanwaltschaft - VA-OÖ-SOZ/0134-A/1/2017 & VA-OÖ-BT/0062-B/1 /2018", 24.06.2019, https://volksanwaltschaft.gv.at/downloads/5cljn /Missstandsfeststellung_und_Empfehlung_der_Volksanwaltschaft _-_Wohnbeihilfen_OÖ_-_19.06.19.pdf.

16 N.N. "EuGH-Generalanwalt hält Deutscherfordernis für Wohnbeihilfe für rechtswidrig." In *Der Standard*, 02.03.2021, https://www.derstandard.at/story /2000124589305/europaeischer-gerichtshof-entscheidet-ueber-deutschnachweis -fuer-wohnbeihilfe.

17 Krutzler, David; Winkler-Hermaden, Rosa (2020): "ÖVP fordert Deutsch für Gemeindewohnung". In *Der Standard*, 06.09.2020, https://www.derstandard.at /story/2000119820899/oevp-fordert-deutsch-fuer-gemeindewohnung.

18 Ministerial draft bill, "Wohnungsgemeinnützigkeitsgesetz, Änderung (140/ME)," 18 April 2019, https://www.parlament.gv.at/PAKT/VHG/XXVI/ME/ME_00140 /index.shtml.

19 In fact, the government program even lays down that in the event of an immigration crisis, the parties – after repeated consultation – are allowed to seek other majorities for bills adressing this topic, without endangering the continuity of the coalition (Österreichische Bundesregierung 2020, 200). Given the majority situation in the Austrian parliament (the first chamber majority leans to the right), this option is *de facto* only available to the senior coalition partner, the ÖVP.

8 Inclusion under Pressure: The Case of Norway

GRETE BROCHMANN

The crowning of Norway as the most immigrant-inclusionary welfare state in the West (see Figure 8.1) comes as no big surprise to experienced students of comparative welfare politics. Norway and Sweden usually lead on such international indexes. Denmark used to be part of the club, but as reflected in this IESPI study, a more dualized – exclusionary – development has taken place in the Danish context, shifting the country down the scale. The contrast between Sweden and Norway on the one hand and Denmark on the other invites reflection on the challenges facing the renowned "Nordic Model" in relation to comprehensive immigration in the twenty-first century. So far Sweden and Norway have more or less sustained the original universalistic approach to welfare – including for legal newcomers – whereas Denmark has undertaken reforms in a more differentiated direction. This contrast is interesting, for the three advanced welfare states share basic features as to the dynamics of the welfare state/labour market nexus.

I will in this chapter analyse the case of Norway,[1] making sense of why the inclusionary approach has prevailed throughout the last three decades of crises and challenges. My main argument is that a combination of systemic necessities from the outset –the basic features of the immigration regulation were established in the mid-1970s – followed by pragmatic adjustments after the late 1980s explain why a rather path-dependent pattern has predominated, so that Norway (until recently) has not embarked on the Danish path. The fiscal resources generated by the comprehensive oil economy have clearly also played a part: the pressure for retrenchment has been weaker than in the neighbouring states. There are, however, indications in the political climate since the 2015 refugee crisis that Norway may introduce more differentiated mechanisms in order to make its welfare institutions more "immigration robust," as the political argument goes. Such adjustments are, however, highly controversial, and a more open and generous approach to immigration still enjoys support among parts of the population. Immigration policy has been a focal issue among

Figure 8.1. Social policy differentiation between immigrants and native-born, Norway scores compared with lowest and highest IESPI scores, 1990–2015

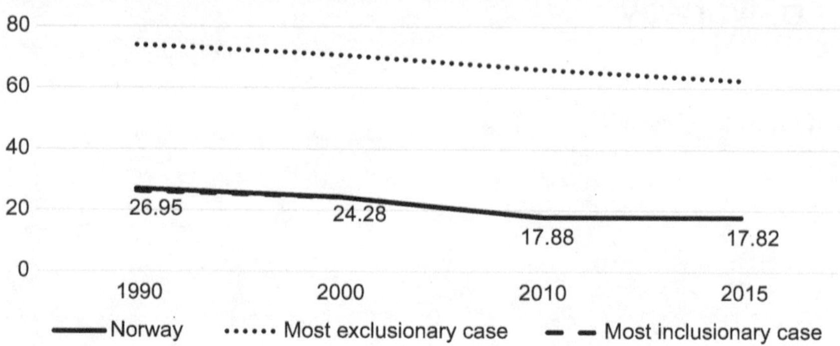

the Norwegian public over the past few decades. Governments across party cleavages nevertheless tend to end up pursuing an ostensibly balanced approach, catering to humanitarian conventions *and* labour-market/welfare-state concerns – a mixture of principles and interests.

The Historical Legacy

According to one Norwegian historian (Seip 1994), it took 100 years to build the collectivist culture that gave birth to the welfare model. That comprehensive structure, finalized in the 1960s, emerged through a long and complex process in which economic, cultural, and political elements interacted. The welfare model was inspired by the concept of "productive social policy," involving an ethos of equal opportunity; income security via economic redistribution and empowerment of the disadvantaged through public education; high-quality (and free) health care; and active labour market policies. This system – which was tax-based – was regarded as a means to invest in people and their productivity. It was believed that what created equality and social security also stimulated economic growth; good social policy was also smart economics. Basic security and equal opportunity generated individual freedom – a fact often disregarded in Anglo-Saxon contexts. The interaction of freedom and security drove collective investments in welfare provision, forming the basis for the social integration of the population across class and geography.

The small, rather homogeneous postwar country was characterized by a high level of trust. Indeed, trust in public institutions and the state has long been higher in Scandinavia generally than anywhere else in the world. Institutionally embedded equality, trust, and security – often labelled "generalized trust" or "impersonal reciprocity" (Rothstein 2017; Ferrera 2005; Brochmann and Dølvik 2018) – are essential components of the Norwegian political economy. The central institutional characteristics of the Norwegian model can be summed up as follows: it is a small, open-market economy relying on an interplay between stability-oriented macroeconomic policies, an organized working life with coordinated wage-setting, and a comprehensive public welfare structure. The system implies the pooling of risks through extensive social insurance, public services, corporatist coordination with strong social partners, and low inequality. Labour relations and the welfare system have served mutual buffer functions, with a high rate of employment as the building block; employment is essential in order both to fund welfare and to reduce public expenditures (Dølvik 2013). The model has enjoyed high legitimacy among the Norwegian people over the years, across party lines.

These basic features remain intact, yet today the Norwegian economy risks being eroded by myriad forces, many of which are related to globalization. The central challenges are fiscal and demographic: the aging population makes it difficult to keep up high-quality benefits and services without raising taxes to levels that are bound to be contested. Meanwhile, the sizable immigration of people with low qualifications has added to worries whether the Norwegian model as we know it today can be sustained,[2] and there are economic, institutional, and political reasons for those worries.

The historical chronology is important here. When the Norwegian model was completed in the mid-1960s, international migration was not yet a topic of concern. Very few people actually arrived, the issue was not politicized, and none of the politicians at the time knew the degree to which immigration would increase in the years to come. The Norwegian welfare model assumed the character of "bounded universalism" (Benhabib 2002), based on institutionalized solidarity within the nation-state. That solidarity was rooted in social norms, subtly developed, and based on peer pressure according to a do-your-duty-claim-your-right logic, anchored in the labour movement.

Why Choosing the Inclusive Avenue?

When labour immigrants from the global South started arriving in the early 1970s, the Norwegian welfare model became an important premise for generating a brand-new immigration policy. As long as the population by and large remained resident within the national borders and there were few new arrivals from outside the country, it was politically possible to go far in the direction of making social programs universal – that is, to cover the entire population – without subnational variation. It could be plausibly assumed that investments in education, health, and living conditions would benefit society as a whole in the form of later contributions through work and the payment of taxes. The basic principles of social security benefits – and of other legislation in the social field in Norway – became premised on residency, though a number of exemptions would be added to the legislation later on. The flip side of this was that the only eligibility requirement was legal residency, that is, basic income security was available from day one for newcomers. The composition of the Norwegian welfare model was thus different in important ways from that of more contribution-based models, such as the Austrian one (see chapter 7), or more market-based models like the one in the US (see chapter 9).

The Norwegian welfare state's economic transfers to weak groups and the principle of equal treatment to all had two basic implications for immigration. First, it became crucial to *regulate* immigration to Norway. The welfare model, all-embracing and generous in principle, might be undermined if too heavily exposed, so some selection and limitation of new members from outside would have to be conducted.

Second, it was essential to *integrate* newcomers, especially into working life but also into society at large. If the fundamental social structure was to be maintained, new inhabitants would have to be made part of it. Well-functioning welfare systems like Norway's are vulnerable to large arrivals of people outside the bounds of regulated work, who may drive down wages and labour standards or burden budgets and thus potentially challenge the nation's unity and consensus. A concept developed later – absorption capacity (Collier 2013; Brochmann and Grødem 2019) – was indirectly what it was about, that is, society's ability and capacity to include new members as well-functioning and equally treated citizens, particularly in productive work.

The "immigration stop" in 1975 was intended to address all of this. Most immigration at the time was low-skilled labour migration, particularly from Pakistan but also from Morocco and Turkey. The new regulation quite effectively tamped down that influx. People were no longer arriving *as* labour immigrants. A changed immigration pattern now developed that escaped the newly installed tools for governance: asylum seekers and family migrants, given access for humanitarian reasons, were now the dominant categories. Consequently, since the initial phase of the "new immigration era" (Brochmann and Kjeldstadli 2008) and the "stop-policy" of the 1970s, the preconditions for addressing the dual policy concerns of regulation and integration have changed.

The legacy of this "access control *cum* integration" policy-making has met its basic challenges in recent decades, due to developments in international human rights legislation and to later obligations attached to the EEA agreement.[3] As we saw in the case of Austria (chapter 7), policy-makers in Norway have since faced legal constraints in managing migration and its implications.

Before 2004 these challenges were associated with immigrants coming to the region from the global South, almost exclusively as refugees and family migrants. One of the greatest challenges facing these people – who were being admitted on humanitarian grounds – was labour market inclusion. Typically,

Figure 8.2. Migration to Norway, by motive for migration

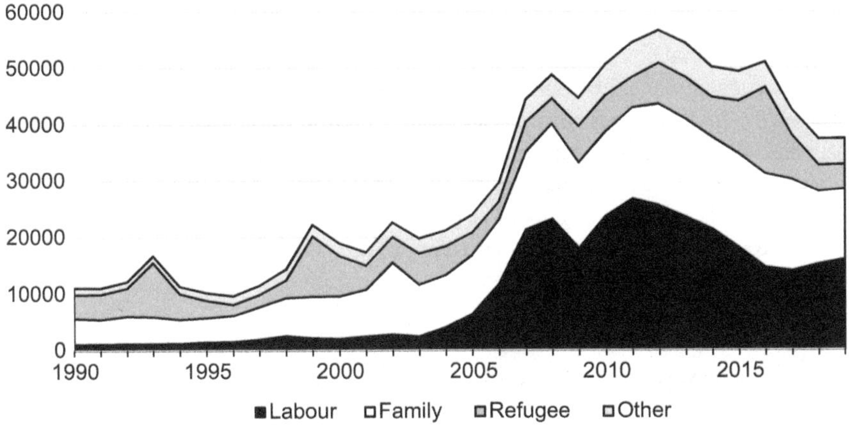

Source: Statistics Norway

they were low-skilled and had difficulties in the highly paid and skill-demanding labour market; consequently, they faced the problem of persistent welfare dependence. During the 1990s, cultural issues also arose on the political agenda. In particular, Muslim immigrants were increasingly seen by some of the native-born as a challenge to the Norwegian way of life. "Humanitarian migrants" should not be regulated with "absorption capacity" in mind; nevertheless, control and integration rhetoric found its way into public discussions in relation to these groups.

After 2004, a major change occurred. The EU extension eastward resulted in the largest influx ever of semi-skilled and low-skilled labour migrants, who took advantage of the free labour market within the European Union (see Figure 8.2).[4] This EU mobility has so far served the Norwegian economy well,[5] in that it has boosted economic growth and increased flexibility in the private sector. Yet it has also called attention to some major challenges ahead: the EU's labour mobility disturbs the basic premises of the Norwegian approach to immigration, with its relative social closure. Norway has renounced immigration control over EU migrants through the EEA agreement; a free market system is being imposed from outside, through EU legislation. This large and unfettered influx of workers has resulted in low-wage competition, which has contributed to labour market segmentation and the erosion of collective institutions in the labour market, thus disturbing central mechanisms in the labour model. There are also concerns related to increased circumvention of labour laws and regulations as well as the long-term effects on vocational training and the national pool of skilled labour (NOU 2017:2; Bratsberg and Raaum 2020).

In practice, these externalities have brought about significant liberalization of immigration to Norway. The rate of immigration has in fact been in the upper tiers internationally since the turn of the century, at times higher than that of the traditional champions – the US, Canada, and Australia.[6]

As a consequence, immigration governance has faced notable pressure since the 1970s. Inclusiveness through equal treatment and the extension of rights is still essential for the functioning of the labour market and welfare state in Norway, yet it can be argued that the country's absorption capacity has been tested over the years, and limitations have been placed on the size and composition of the influx. One outcome has been rising social inequality – significant in that equality is often viewed as key to the sustainability of the Norwegian welfare model.

This description of how the labour/welfare model operates in relation to immigration serves as a backdrop for the following analysis of the Norwegian score in the IESPI database, in particular regarding the extent to which the policy approach followed by governments since the 1990s has succeeded, and whether inclusiveness on paper has materialized in practice. But before I turn to these questions, I first briefly describe how the approach works in practice.

The Norwegian Integration Approach

As we have seen, the inclusiveness of the welfare model has been pivotal to its *modus operandi*. Broad strata of the population, including legal migrants, are covered by the same programs. But the system's basic universality is somewhat modified by the fact that some transfers are contribution-based, such as unemployment and sickness benefits. Important transfers, such as the old age and disability pensions, are also linked to income. Basic income security through social assistance is universal but also subject to need-testing. Norwegian benefits are generally high by international standards, as is the quality of public services, many of which are free of charge.

Since the initiation of integration policies in Norway, the approach taken for immigrants has mixed general measures (in line with programs for the rest of the population) with measures specifically for them. The tendency over the years has been to gradually mainstream that approach as much as possible to lower public cost and avoid stigmatization. Nevertheless, targeted schemes have endured, in the belief that they are necessary to promote integration – that is, genuine inclusion of newcomers in society beyond the general access to rights. These targeted policies cover a number of areas, such as the labour market, social benefits, housing, education, language instruction, and funds for organizational activities. In the years immediately following the 1975 regulation (the "immigration stop") integration measures were meagrely developed. In the cultural sphere, "freedom of choice" was the prevailing ideology (largely influenced by Sweden), and "integration" basically meant equal rights combined with a lax attitude as to the form of adaptation to Norwegian society.

In the 1990s, this approach began to change. The authorities became aware (through increased knowledge and experience) that the results of integration efforts were far from satisfactory. Rising concern about problems of living conditions, at least in some immigrant communities, made authorities step up the scale and quality of the targeted programs. This new line of thinking was bolstered by a changing political climate – by a growing dedication to the "duty-line" in relation to new members of society. A more demanding attitude came to be seen as more respectful than turning recipients into long-term welfare clients through unconditional social benefits. The "work-line" approach started engaging the entire spectrum of welfare measures during the 1990s. Intervention and activation became the standard approach. Thus, Norway has, like other European welfare regimes, made adjustments in order to become more "employment friendly" and "make work pay."

By the end of the 1990s an important change was in the making, inspired by policy-making in two neighbouring countries, Sweden and Denmark. The authorities in all three countries had realized that the immigrant population was highly heterogeneous in terms of basic qualifications and capacities and that a more differentiated approach to integration was necessary. A line was drawn between a specially designed program for new arrivals (refugees and their family members) and a general policy for labour immigrants, their families, and descendants of immigrants. The special program for new arrivals was in Norway named The Introductory Act, finalized in 2004. This targeted and financially demanding program was driven by the fact that a worryingly high proportion of refugees and their families had become dependent on long-term social assistance. A pattern had developed whereby the refugee population (albeit with internal variation) had significantly lower employment rates than the native-born. The term "outsidership" (*utenforskap*) was cropping up more and more in the integration debate.

The new program was aimed at preparing these newcomers for more rapid inclusion, whether this meant finding a job or pursuing an education through a comprehensive training program. This program was to include language instruction, a course in "Norwegian life and society," and, not least, preparation for employment. The program combines rights and obligations in new ways. Participation is mandatory, but newcomers are paid to attend, at rates higher than the equivalent social assistance. This "salary" is subject to cuts in cases of absence without cause. At the same time, the participants have a right to an individual plan, which is supposed to reflect an overall assessment of their educational profile, their general qualifications, and their personal aspirations in the job market.

This new invention is clearly part of the new work-oriented perspective in social policy, but it is also a socialization project and, as such, a break with the former, more liberal take on social adjustment. It is part of a steadily more demanding approach to granting permanent residency and eventually citizenship. The past decade has seen new requirements related to economic self-sufficiency, language skills, and country knowledge in order to pass through this final gate to the nation-state.

Whether this new approach to integration reflects retrenchment logic or a more advanced form of social investment and individual "empowerment" is a matter for debate. It is, however, beyond doubt that the authorities have changed policy in order to generate better-functioning citizens, who are to be integrated first and foremost through labour market participation.

Migrant workers (mostly EU workers) and refugees (including their families) now face different sets of rules regarding both immigration and integration. Immigrants from the EU, who have free access in accordance with the market-driven EEA, in principle do not qualify for special assistance or any inclusion programs. Conversely, humanitarian migrants face constrained access to the country but, once they do enter, qualify for comprehensive integration programs. This is so, even though the two groups face similar problems in Norwegian society, and even though there is systemic interaction between the groups. People with low qualifications tend to compete for the same low-paid jobs. Migrant workers who lose their jobs face much the same problems as refugees: social marginalization, the risk of permanent low income, and the need for either skills development or support for living costs. Yet while EU migrants are in many ways privileged as migrants, they are still supposed to leave if they become a welfare burden.

Regarding general welfare entitlements, Norway – with its solid oil economy – has been able to adjust and retrench more gradually than its neighbours. It ranks first in sickness compensation within the OECD, and only minor adjustments have been undertaken (caps on benefit levels as well as a requirement imposed on recipients to follow an activation program). Because Norway has one of the highest rates of sickness leave in Europe, the authorities have tried to involve its social partners through an "inclusive labour life" agreement, in which graded sick leave, and follow-up agreements in cooperation with the doctor and the employer, have been important mechanisms. The same approach has been applied to other benefits in the system. The ruling premise in the current welfare thinking is that work – however limited – is good for the individual and for the healing process. "Residual work capacity" has become a prominent line in welfare governance. Sanctions have been introduced to a larger extent, as have tighter follow-up routines and tailor-made plans for individuals. All of this is still, however, strongly influenced by social investment thinking.

These minor adjustments reflect growing worry over the long-term sustainability of the attractive and popular welfare model at a time of decreasing oil revenues, an aging society, and persistently low employment rates among segments of the population, especially immigrants.

Successful Inclusion?

Viewed from afar, there is no doubt that Norway deserves a high score on immigrant inclusion. The immigrant population has over the years benefited both economically and physically from a well-functioning liberal democratic and highly secure society. The generally high living standard and the inclusive approach to social rights have undoubtedly contributed to well-being for newcomers and have made Norway a highly attractive destination country. Notwithstanding all of this, and particularly in a national context in which equal treatment is the *sine qua non* for the functioning of the political economy, structurally driven inequality has become a major challenge. Immigrants continue to lag behind the population at large in economic terms (see Figure 8.3). As we saw in chapter 5, therefore, the Norwegian case illustrates that welfare inclusion does not automatically result in equal labour market outcomes.

Despite the strong economic growth since the turn of the century, with increasing labour demand and low unemployment rates, Norway has had the same problems as its Scandinavian neighbours when it comes to the inclusion of low-qualified immigrants in productive work. This has made relative poverty, by and large associated with immigrants, a fraught issue on the public agenda. The part of the population characterized by persistent low income[7] increased from 9.6% to 11.2% between 2011 and 2017. That same year, 10.7% of all children in Norway were living in a family marked by relative poverty, and a clear majority of them had an immigrant background. Children with immigrant parents are only 16% of all children in Norway, yet they account for 56% of children in families with persistent low income. Increases in the most recent years have also been significant.[8] There is, however, marked variation between immigrant groups. In the Indian minority there is slightly less poverty than in the majority population, whereas in the Somali, Iraqi, and Syrian populations, (relative) poverty is widespread. These three groups are large immigrant communities in Norway. Today, 79% of Somali children live in families with persistent low income, reflecting an increase in recent years. The figures for Iraqis and Syrians are 51% and 80% respectively.[9] Generally speaking, one of the main reasons for increased income inequality in Norway in recent years has been increased immigration from low-income countries.[10]

Norway today has among the highest employment rates in Europe, but also the largest employment gap between the native-born and immigrant populations. Of the immigrant population between 20 and 66 years, 67% are employed, compared to 79% for the native-born. There are, however, large differences between immigrant groups, and there is also variation in terms of gender. EU immigrants, a large group, contribute strongly to this general level of participation – 78% are employed. For refugees and family migrants, the figures are 52% and 62% respectively. On aggregate, immigrant men are 8 percentage points

Figure 8.3. Poverty, employment, and welfare receipt for immigrants and the overall population, 2010–2019

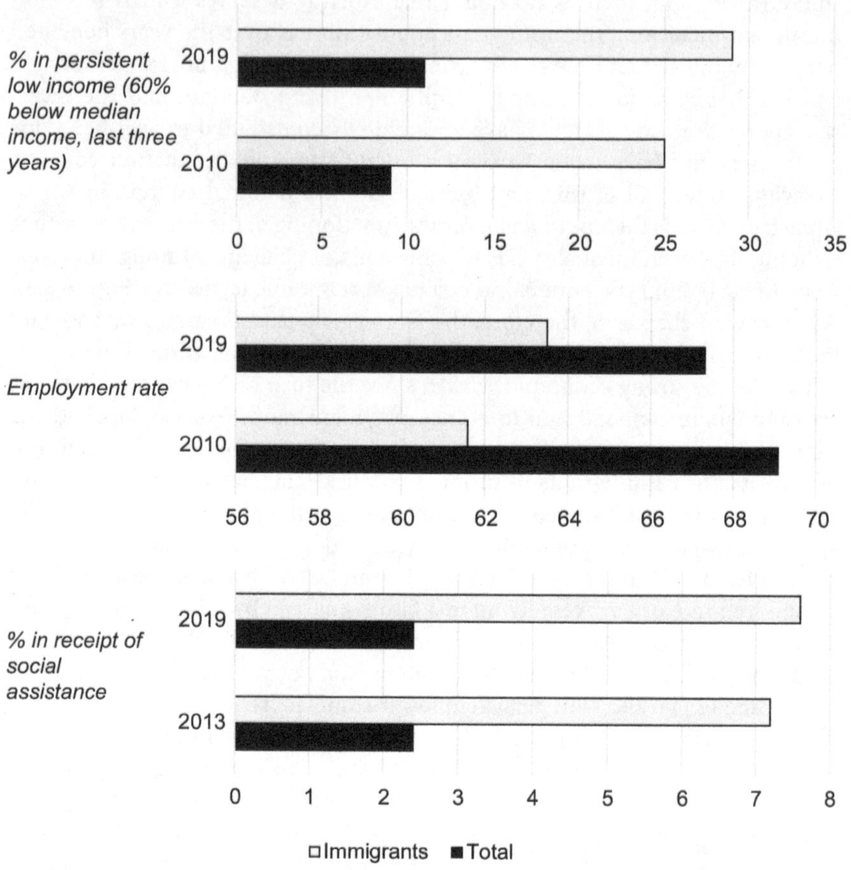

Note: Data for low income include both first- and second-generation immigrants; the other data are for first-generation immigrants only.
Source: Statistics Norway.

more likely to be employed than immigrant women. The equivalent difference among the native-born is 4 percentage points. Only 10% of Somali women and 5% of Syrian women (15 to 74 years) are working full-time. Actual unemployment is usually more than three times as high for the immigrant population than it is for the native-born (Imdi 2020).

Refugees are a particularly vulnerable group, in that they have been allowed residence despite their lack of qualifications in demand. Productive employment is nevertheless seen as essential for their inclusion in society and for their long-term standard of living. Years of residence do account for an improvement in employment rates for these groups, yet a counter-tendency has been discovered: employment increases the first years after arrival, and after five years the employment rate is at its highest: 60% to 70% for men and 40% to 50% for women. Yet after seven to ten years' residence, the rates tend to fall again, particularly among refugee men (Bratsberg, Raaum, and Røed 2011, 2017).

In the Norwegian welfare system, low employment means that a larger share of income will be welfare transfers. Since many immigrants have had no connection to the labour market, they tend to rely on social assistance – often on a long-term basis.[11] This means that immigrants account for a disproportionately large part of social assistance transfers: in 2017, 56% of all this assistance went to immigrants (71% of the total in the capital, Oslo), and of this, 86% went to persons from Africa or Asia. There has been an increase in social assistance spending of 30% since 2013, and the larger part of this is explained by immigration (Statistics Norway).[12]

A mix of factors explain this overall picture. People with low education have initial (and increasing) problems accessing the labour market.[13] The welfare model and the (interlinked) compressed wage structure are such that they pose a specific challenge in relation to immigrants who are misaligned with the demand structure.

Low-skilled immigrants thus tend to rely on public transfers, and this tends to reinforce a number of other social problems, such as poor language skills, problems of participation in civil society, poor health, and lack of capacity to assist children in schoolwork (NOU 2011: 7).

A number of public investigations (NOU 2011: 7, 2017: 2, 2019: 7) have pointed to comprehensive labour immigration from the EU as part of the explanation for the difficulties integrating marginalized newcomers from other parts of the world, despite the expanding economy and increased demand in the labour market. Norwegian employers have since 2004 had an abundant supply of workers from the new EU member states, who are relatively well-educated and willing to work long hours.

When evaluating the overall "success" of the Norwegian inclusion endeavour, a broader set of factors should be considered. Immigrants and their offspring clearly have worse living conditions than the rest of the population, yet from an international perspective they have a good material standard of living. Most immigrants have experienced a significant improvement in their lives in terms of security, health, level of consumption, education facilities, and access to various welfare services. The inclusiveness of the welfare model – that is, the equal access to the key institutions – plays an essential role in this regard.

Norwegian society has witnessed increased inequality in recent years, but the country still ranks as one of the most egalitarian in the world. That immigrants score lower on most indicators of living standards is nevertheless of increasing concern. In particular, some refugee groups face significantly poorer housing and health conditions than the average population. In 2020, one-third of the residents of Oslo had an immigrant background, and in some residential areas more than 50% of the inhabitants were immigrants and their offspring (Statistics Norway). Steps have been taken to address residential segregation which is a result of complex and cumulative forces, among which housing prices figure prominently. These segregated areas offer higher living standards than are possible in many other national contexts; even so, social research has found that these areas have brought about reduced life chances as a consequence of a "concentration of social problems" (Staver, Brekke, and Søholt 2019). There are also indications of discrimination in the housing and labour markets. Generally speaking, connections have been found between causes of immigration, settlement patterns, living conditions, and participation in civil society (NOU 2017:2). The persistent link between segregation and social problems may be especially worrisome in a country with strong egalitarian norms, in that deviation from core values may only strengthen feelings of marginalization. Moreover, lasting differences among population groups may indicate that the integration measures are not effective enough.

The Problem and the Solution

Overall, there is an intergenerational divide – what has been labelled a paradox (Hermansen 2016, 2017) – in the Norwegian integration approach. The labour market/welfare state nexus seems to be having an ambiguous effect on newcomers' performance across generations. Low-skilled immigrants in the productivity-demanding Norwegian labour market have substantial barriers to overcome. The compressed wage structure implies relatively high salaries even for the lower segments in the market, making employers cautious in hiring people whose qualifications are uncertain. As a result, immigrants face inclusion problems when it comes to regular work and end up as long-term low-income earners or benefit recipients. Yet at the same time, the social investment approach – the high quality and the accessibility of institutions, especially health and education – has made social mobility possible for the second generation. Indeed, that mobility has taken root to a remarkable degree in today's Norway. Recent research reveals (Friberg 2016; Hermansen 2016) that even though this second generation in Norway is still quite young, thus making it difficult to judge the long-term robustness of the findings, there are clear indications that children of immigrants (by and large) make a great leap upwards on the social scale. There has been a clear uptake in terms of both education[14] and labour market participation. Descendants also tend to adapt to Norwegian liberal democratic values to a large extent.[15] Not all economic differences disappear, but the social mobility of this second generation is significantly higher than it is for young people from the native-born population with a similar background. These recent reports suggest that ethnic background is gradually being eradicated as a factor in one's life opportunities.

Seen from the authorities' point of view, it is promising that the long-term prospects are good for a large proportion of immigrant children. Financially, however, this is far from satisfactory, as the sheer size of the first generation is so much larger.[16] Regarding remedies for existing integration problems, the authorities seem to be continuing the mixed approach they embarked on in the 1990s. They have gradually taken on a practice in which guaranteed basic maintenance has been replaced by increased emphasis on the work-line: more activation, more conditionality. At the same time, when it comes to the long-term inclusion of the next generation, the state is counting on slow processes of socialization through the country's basic societal institutions. It is believed that integration will work the same way for newcomers as for the population at large: economic, social, and democratic co-citizenship will develop through education, employment, social rights, and the right to vote, thus reducing cultural and value-related tensions over time.

The first part of this dual track – the work-line policy – has been summed up as only "moderately successful" both by the National Commission on Welfare and Immigration (NOU 2017: 2) and by a Nordic comparative study undertaken for the Nordic Council of Ministers (Calmfors and Gassen 2019). Even during the economic boom of the early 2000s, there was no significant change in the employment gap between immigrants and the native-born (NOU 2017: 2).

These unsatisfactory results have led the authorities to add some retrenchment mechanisms to the dominant social investment line in recent years. Various conditionalities have been introduced in order to prod benefit recipients into activity. Most benefits have been revised with this principle in mind – also involving basic social assistance. And the duration of some of the transfers has been reduced. The disability pension has been subject to a cap on total transfers, obviously with the immigrant population in mind (after all, families with many children sometimes used to receive more through transfers than their likely salary level in the labour market) (Pedersen, Grødem, and Wagner 2019). In the past few years – especially since 2015 – clearly inspired by Danish policies, the authorities have introduced waiting times (residency) for access to some social benefits. Five years' residency is now required to access the attractive (for immigrant families) family cash allowance for families who do not utilize public kindergartens. Since 2020, waiting times have been introduced for a number of other arrangements as well (elderly pensions, disability pension, child pension, benefits for single parents, and the so-called Work Assessment Allowance). Limiting access through waiting times on this greater scale clearly constitutes a new line of thinking in the welfare system, obviously targeted at the immigrant population. This breach with the earlier universalistic approach is justified by the need to sustain the welfare model and the work-line policy.

Attitudes in the Majority Population

The principles of equal treatment, equality, and conformity have fostered ambiguities in relation to multicultural immigration in Norway. Until late in the twentieth century, Norway was characterized by high levels of economic and cultural homogeneity. Equality as a value with a variety of expressions has been central for achieving support and legitimacy in Norwegian politics ever since the key welfare institutions were founded. It is still a pertinent value, yet inequality is increasing on many dimensions.

This equality/conformity package, partly as a social fact, partly as a normative ideal, can pose a challenge for people from other cultural backgrounds in which such values are less entrenched. At the same time, parts of the Norwegian majority express concerns about the erosion of economic equity and cultural "core values" as a result of increasing heterogeneity. These types of issues have sparked a great deal of engagement in Norwegian society. Public debates about multicultural Norway tend to become quite contentious.

In Norway, the Progress Party (*Fremskrittspartiet*) began to play a central role in immigration policy in the late 1980s after the issue became politicized. The party was able to find support among the segments of the population critical of immigration, and it grew considerably, especially after the turn of the century. In the years since, the Progress Party has gained "ownership" over immigration issues among the Norwegian public. Its followers had named immigration as their top issue in most elections. In 2013 the party entered government for the first time, together with the Conservative Party (Høyre).[17]

The other political parties long tried to distance themselves from the Progress Party's approach, which they viewed as indecent. Yet the traditional two main parties – the Social Democrats (Arbeiderpartiet) and the Conservatives – have gradually moved in a more restrictive direction on immigration policy. During the 2015 refugee crisis, most parliamentary parties joined a policy front in order to get control over immigrant inflows; this included steps to retrench welfare policy for newcomers. But when the inflow decreased in 2016, the Progress Party was unable to secure a parliamentary majority for a number of its proposed retrenchments.

Despite heated public discourse about immigration and integration in Norway, various coalition governments have tended to land on a version of the consensus-driven dual policy line as first developed by the Social Democrats: substantial regulation when possible, combined with equal treatment and social investment. But since the turn of the century, the different governments have gradually looked more to restrictive Denmark than to liberal Sweden for

Figure 8.4. Negative attitudes about immigration in Norway, 2002–2019 (Statistics Norway)[18]

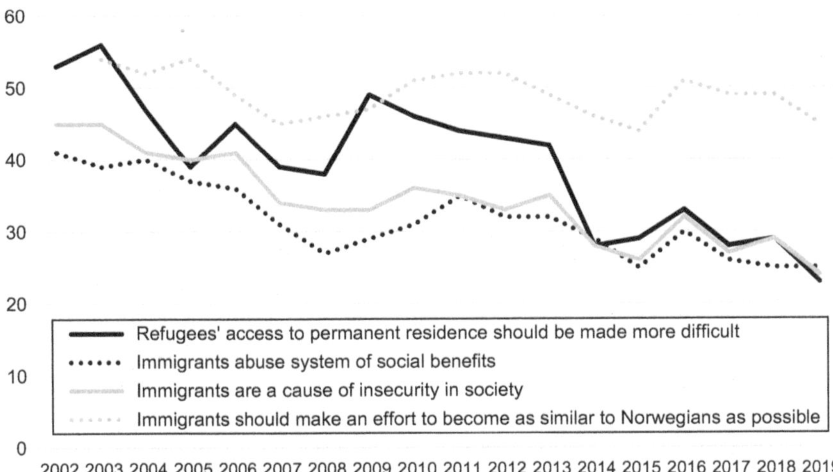

inspiration. This tendency intensified while the Progress Party was in government between 2013 and 2020. In other words, the entire political spectrum has turned more restrictive (particularly) since 2015, although still within the bounds of attempts to balance access and control issues against humanitarian ideals and commitment to the EU *acquis*. By and large, there has been continuity in Norwegian governance on this issue, yet in public discourse it seems as if polarization has been heightened regarding both immigration control (access) and welfare state generosity. The question "Is the welfare state too kind or not kind enough?" has captured much of the public debate in Norway over the past two decades. Much of this is driven by the dynamics of party politics, with the Progress Party in the lead as it tries to maintain ownership over a restrictive line, thus escalating efforts at retrenchment by the other parties.

The significant (yet fluctuating) growth of the Progress Party is an indication of a more immigration-critical constituency in Norway. Yet centrally conducted opinion polls suggest a different picture, albeit a mixed one. Statistics Norway has since 1993 undertaken an attitudinal survey of the Norwegian population, testing the same statements consistently. Figure 8.4 shows the results from four such questions that have been asked since 2002. The polls show that Norwegians have become steadily more positive toward immigration. Fewer and fewer people believe that access to permanent residence should be more difficult, that immigrants abuse the social benefits system, or that immigrants are a source of insecurity in society. Also, there is more and more social contact between immigrants and the rest of the population (Strøm 2019). On the other hand, almost half (49%) of the respondents state that immigrants should try to become as Norwegian as possible, and there is little sign of this sentiment decreasing over time. In addition, various investigations have found that immigrants experience discrimination in the labour and housing markets (NOU 2017: 2).

On the whole, opinion polls on Norwegians' attitudes toward immigration and immigrants' rights in their country's welfare system reveal a stable yet highly ambiguous picture.[19] A quite striking feature over time has been the stability in terms of support for the authorities' line of conduct when it comes to access to residency in Norway (immigration policy proper). According to a long-term opinion poll, based on the question "Should refugees' and asylum seekers' access to residency in Norway become easier, more difficult or as it is today?," a quite stable majority want things to continue as they are, regardless of variations in the strictness of these policies over time. Occasionally, though, the majority want them stricter than they are, never more liberal (indeed, the share of respondents who support easier access to residency has never surpassed 18%). Consequently, Norwegians' attitudes toward immigration and integration policies can overall be read as quite system-loyal, basically supporting the dual-policy baseline of the authorities over time: rather strict access control combined with lenient policies related to inclusion and equal rights. The latter part of the dual-policy approach has become a target for adjustments, as we have seen. Indirectly, this gradual change can be perceived as anchored in public opinion as well.

Investigations that ask more specific questions about people's attitudes toward the inclusiveness of the welfare model reveal a more mixed and less positive picture than the general surveys, which may help to explain the *de facto* political support for the retrenchments that have been undertaken over the last two decades.

Overall, there seems to be no negative correlation between immigration and popular support for the Norwegian welfare model. This is in line with findings in other national contexts (Banting and Kymlicka 2006). It seems that welfare states that were entrenched before immigration started to grow have a robustness against such negative effects; the intertwined institutional configuration seems to raise buffers against system erosion in the wake of enhanced immigration. In addition, possible distress in parts of the population related to (real or imagined) low-wage competition, as well as job insecurity stemming from more immigrants in the market, may even increase support for the welfare security system (Finseraas 2008). Since 2011, various studies in Norway and Scandinavia have revealed a discrepancy between support for the welfare system as such and the endorsement of giving newcomers direct and equal access to the very same system. An investigation after the 2013 parliamentary election asked respondents to consider the following statement: "Refugees and immigrants should have equal access to social security benefits as Norwegians, even if they are not citizens." It was found that 52% disagreed with the statement, up from 39% in 2005 – a quite clear increase in selective restrictionism (Kleven et al. 2015). A 2013 study found that 37% of the population agreed that the state should withhold social assistance from immigrants (Bay, Finseraas, and West Pedersen 2013).

A move toward welfare dualism, as we have witnessed in Denmark, is slowly gaining ground in Norway as well. This approach resembles a two-tier welfare system in which access to welfare goods and/or level of compensation is being systematically differentiated between immigrants and the population at large (Bay, Finseraas, and West Pedersen 2013). It is possible that people prefer this approach to a more general weakening of the welfare system. It is nevertheless a deviation from the universalistic, inclusive policy tradition of the Norwegian welfare model (Finseraas, West Pedersen, and Bay 2016).

Inclusiveness under Strain: Concluding Remarks

The central idea of the Scandinavian welfare model is that economic equality is a prerequisite for equal social citizenship. A high degree of social and economic equality is furthermore seen as necessary for social cohesion and stability. The centrality of the welfare model, both in terms of constituting nationhood and as a vehicle for social well-being and mobility, is beyond dispute in Scandinavia. As a consequence of this legacy, the dual-policy approach to immigration was a necessity in order to sustain the model's basic mechanisms. The pace, volume, and composition had to be manageable in order to secure the continuation of a well-regulated labour market, social integration, and political stability.

Immigrants, particularly those from the global South, have injected a new (sometimes extremely) low-skilled element into Scandinavia's "middle class societies" (Kuhnle and Alestalo 2018, 18). The reintroduction of enduring low-income groups, marginalized economically, residentially, and socially, has been a systemic challenge, and there has been public worry over the pace and direction of this social change.

Today there is growing tension between "conflicting logics of solidarity" attached to three levels of governance: global solidarity through the human rights regime; regional solidarity through the EU, and traditional solidarity through the pressed nation-states – the bounded social contract (Brochmann and Dølvik 2018, 509). For the Nordic welfare model, the systemic necessity is still there for a productive balance between an orderly labour market and a redistributive welfare state. The substantial inflow of people with a strong need for higher qualifications or basic education to match the demand side of the labour market will definitely influence future policy-making in Norway. This extraordinary situation comes on top of already existing challenges and may trigger more reforms to the basic social rights approach of the welfare systems. The endeavour of getting people productively absorbed in work as soon as possible will be *the* public task ahead.

The prospects are uncertain. The major trend is that there will be fewer jobs for people with low qualifications in the years to come. The salary level even in low-skilled jobs in Norway is so high that the push toward replacing people with machines is strong. Thus, there could be a move toward even more people on benefits.

An underlying assumption of Norwegian welfare model has been that social rights contribute to societal integration and economic growth. Hannah Arendt's much quoted "right to have rights" has been accommodated for both systemic and humanitarian reasons. Only in recent years have we seen a competing thesis, one that states that too easily accessible rights to welfare benefits can be an impediment – at least, an impediment to getting low-skilled people into productive employment. Thus, "inclusion" and "integration" are not necessarily the same. "Subsidized isolation" is increasingly viewed as an unforeseen consequence of a too lenient approach. "The right to have duties" seems to be the new *doxa,* that is, the right to enabling resources for participation through work and through civil society.

What may happen in the near future is retrenchment at the margins, possibly moving toward a more contribution-based welfare system, leading to a more multitiered social model. If that is the case, Norway's top position in the IESPI inclusion index may be in for a change. In such a scenario the core majority will basically maintain their welfare, but there will be increasing divisions between insiders and outsiders as we have seen in other places in Europe. How this may feed into the social and cultural spheres is a fraught question.

The pace and composition of new inflows in the years to come will strongly affect outcomes in this regard. The Norwegian inclusive labour and welfare model is institutionally well-equipped to fend off challenges, but it is equally vulnerable if its capacity is stretched too far.

NOTES

1 See Brochmann and Hagelund 2012 for a full comparative analysis of all three Scandinavian countries.

2 See English summary of the governmental commission report NOU 2011:7 *Velferd og migrasjon. Den norske modellens framtid*, https://www.regjeringen.no/globalassets/upload/bld/ima/nou_2011_7_perspective_andsummary.pdf.

3 EEA stands for "European Economic Agreement" – a treaty regulating Norway's relation to the EU as a non-member country.

4 The influx from the EU has first and foremost been from Poland (52%) and Lithuania (21%). Migrants from these countries have been largely employed in construction work.
5 From 2003 to 2017, employment in Norway increased by approximately 730,000 persons. Of these, 74% were immigrants. Approximately 15% of those employed in Norway today are immigrants (Bratsberg and Raaum 2020).
6 NOU 2011:7. In 2019, the immigrant share of the population in Norway was 15%, an increase from 5% in 1992.
7 This term is used to refer to income that is below 60% of the median national income, three years in a row.
8 In 2006, immigrants' share of children in families experiencing relative poverty was 38.8%.
9 The Syrian minority has lived the shortest period of all in Norway, which explains this extraordinary figure.
10 All data are taken from Statistics Norway – www.ssb.no.
11 Social assistance is the basic income security entity in Norway and is supposed to be a short-term alleviation when no other income possibility is available.
12 There was in the same period a reduction of 5% in the use of social assistance by the native-born population.
13 51.4% of refugees have only basic education. The same is true for 70% of the refugees who arrived in 2015–16 (Statistics Norway).
14 In fact, children of immigrants today participate in higher education to a higher degree than what is the case in the majority population (NOU 2017:2). Despite this fact, the transition from education to work is less smooth among second-generation immigrants as compared to peer groups in the majority. Discrimination in the employment process seems to be an important explanation for this discrepancy (Hermansen 2017).
15 The Friberg report (2016) measured important values such as acceptance of gender equality and homosexuality. The adjustment process occurred at a different pace across dimensions, and the question of "social trust" showed slower adaptation than the other dimensions.
16 In 2019, immigrants represent 14.4% of the population, descendants only 3.4%.
17 In 2018 the Liberal Party (Venstre) joined in, followed by the Christian Democrats (Kristelig Folkeparti) in 2019. Then in 2020, the Progress Party left the government again.
18 Figure 8.1 shows the percentage of respondents answering "more difficult" to the question "Compared to today, should refugees' and asylum seekers' access to residence permits be easier, more difficult or remain the same?" (solid black line); and the percentage of respondents who "agree" or "strongly agree" with the statements "Most immigrants abuse the system of social benefits" (dotted black line), "Most immigrants are a cause of insecurity in society" (solid grey line), and "Immigrants should make an effort to become as similar to Norwegians as possible" (dotted

grey line). See https://www.ssb.no/en/statbank/table/08778/ and https://www.ssb.no/en/statbank/table/08783.

19 There is also significant variation among respondents along different dimensions: women, young people, educated respondents, and people living in cities tend to have more favourable views of immigrants. People on welfare programs are more sceptical, as are people with hardly any contact with immigrants (Strøm 2019).

9 From Exclusion to More Exclusion: Immigration and Social Welfare Access in the United States

JASON E. KEHRBERG, ADAM M. BUTZ, AND MIKHALA L. WEST

The relationship in the US between immigration, citizenship, and social welfare provision is complicated and exclusionary. The US is an immigrant nation and is often referred to as a "melting pot" because of its ethnic diversity – Americans and their forebears hail from every part of the world. At the same time, many Americans would prefer that social welfare benefits be provided only to members of their perceived shared community (Theiss-Morse 2009). As a result of the "racialization" (Gilens 1999) and, more recently, "immigrationalization" (Garand, Xu, and Davis 2015) of welfare attitudes in the US, minorities and immigrants are often barred from that shared community.

Among the countries included in the Immigrant Exclusion from Social Programs Index (IESPI), the US is the second-most exclusionary today (after Austria). Also, for the period covered in the database, the US has the second-highest rate of exclusionary change (after the Netherlands). The US case study provides insight into the role of bipartisan support for the exclusionary politics and policies of the 1990s and how a growing partisan divide since 2000 has resulted in legislative gridlock that has prevented any further dramatic movement in social policy. In this chapter, we demonstrate how and why selective solidarity has functioned in the US over the past 25 years under "welfare reform" and how social welfare benefits, which remain across-the-board relatively underdeveloped compared with European countries, are often distributed on the basis of citizenship boundaries that exclude immigrants and non-citizen refugees as a consequence of immigrant-excluding welfare reforms (IEWRs). Our focus will primarily be on welfare policy reforms instituted in the 1990s and the current uncertain future of immigrants' role in the US social welfare system in the aftermath of a Donald Trump administration that exuded anti-immigrant posturing and openly advocated for IEWRs. After briefly discussing the historical development of the US social welfare system, we demonstrate that except for relatively brief periods of policy liberalization, both public opinion and policy-making elites have driven US welfare policy as it relates to immigrant access in a decidedly exclusionary direction. The discussion then shifts to more recent changes in immigration access to welfare programs at the federal level and examines state-level differences. We also explore changing American attitudes toward immigration, as well as the partisan sorting around immigration that has induced more recent congressional gridlock and presidential executive orders that have led to relatively incremental changes to immigrants' access to welfare. The US remains a deeply divided nation over issues of immigrant access to social benefits, and a relatively restrictive social welfare posture toward immigrants remains entrenched there.

The American Context

Most of the early post-indigenous settlers in what became the United States were British and European and had been driven to immigrate by principles of Protestantism and minimal government involvement in public affairs and social benefit provision. The latter was left to private charity and religious institutions (Daniels 2002; Trattner 2007). This dynamic of private, localized governance, including austere social welfare provision rooted in the British Poor Laws, would broadly hold for a century and a half (Trattner 2007). From time to time, some individual colonies or states attempted to implement public goods such as public education (in Massachusetts) or workers' compensation (in Wisconsin), but a formal welfare state of guaranteed social benefits at the national level would not develop in the US until the 1930s (Fox 2012). It is here that we start to see the formal development of the welfare state at the federal level and expanding social benefits for the citizenry; it is here too that we also observe backlash and anti-immigrant restrictions – a dynamic still visible in contemporary American social policy debates. The past half-century has seen broadly expanding social benefits, but also a series of historic and modern IEWRs in US social welfare policy.

In tandem with the rugged individualist ethos in the US there ran a system of selective solidarity in the form of white supremacy and selective citizenship benefits for white individuals and families (Feagin 2020; Kendi 2018). Citizenship and its rights and privileges in the early US were fundamentally determined by skin colour; non-Whites (and immigrants) were cast as genetically inferior, and this resulted in overtly racist policies of oppression and apartheid that lasted well into the 1960s. The idea that racial minorities, especially Indigenous and Black people, were inherently savage, criminogenic, and lacking a proper work ethic pervaded the early US and arguably remains entrenched (Peffley and Hurwitz 2010). Racial minorities were perceived as "undeserving" of citizenship and were excluded from benefits. Indeed, recent research demonstrates that US social welfare policy remains strongly racialized and rooted in negative stereotypes of Black citizens as welfare-dependent and lacking a work ethic (Gilens 1999; Soss, Fording, and Schram 2011). Negative stereotyping and perceptions of incompatible values routinely arise today with regard to immigrant populations of colour and arguably work to shape welfare access for immigrants. For instance, when he announced his bid for the presidency in 2015, Donald Trump referred to Mexican immigrants as "bringing drugs and bringing crime," accused them of being "rapists," and framed them more generally as dangerous and undeserving. So it is not surprising that the Trump administration attempted on multiple occasions to curtail welfare benefits for immigrant populations. Clearly, the social construction of race (Schneider and Ingram 1993) continues to play a potent role in welfare policy debates and development.

While chattel slavery and Jim Crow segregation against Blacks were the most obvious manifestations of white supremacy in action, immigrant populations – especially non-White immigrant populations – have faced similar unflattering stereotypes and attempts to curtail their citizenship rights and social welfare benefits (Fox 2012). With the current immigration wave being primarily from Latin America, stereotypes of criminality, welfare dependency, and undeservingness have again resurfaced in the rhetoric of US elites, shaping welfare reform debates and IEWRs in the contemporary US (Chavez 2008). The rich diversity of the country's sizable immigrant population has arguably enlivened the US and made it more innovative and dynamic both culturally and economically, but it has also stifled welfare state development and saddled newly arriving immigrants – both legal and undocumented – with unique burdens and restrictions on social benefits.

Immigration and the Development of the US Welfare State

Both social welfare provision and immigration to the US changed rapidly following the Great Depression. Perceptions that poverty had to be an individual's own fault were shifting as a result of unprecedented unemployment levels, and there were calls from the populace, often riotous, for national action on social benefit provision (Trattner 2007). In 1932, Democrat Franklin Delano Roosevelt was elected to the presidency at a time of economic ruin; in short order he ushered in a formalized federal-level welfare state, most significantly with the cornerstone Social Security Act of 1935 (Trattner 2007). That act provided social insurance in the form of cash benefits to elderly and unemployed individuals. Additionally, the first cash benefits to low-income families were instituted in the form of Aid to Dependent Children (ADC), now known as Temporary Assistance to Needy Families (TANF). This forever changed the federal government's role in providing social welfare benefits, but it did not provide universal coverage, and it included aspects of selective solidarity that favoured native-born White people. For instance, while not explicitly outlawing benefits for immigrants, the Social Security legislation exempted agriculture and domestic workers from public benefits – occupations held disproportionately by immigrants and African Americans.

Just a few decades later, in the 1960s, immigration levels in the US rose significantly with the Immigration and Nationality Act of 1965 (INA), the same year that Medicare and Medicaid programs were passed. These expanded the reach of the US social welfare system to include guaranteed health benefits for elderly and low-income families. This third era of American immigration federalism, generally defined as 1965 to the present, has been characterized by three main pillars: (1) increasing levels of immigration as the INA abolished country quotas and expanded immigration from Asian and Latin American countries; (2) increasing selective solidarity and IEWRs in social welfare programs, restricting immigrants' welfare access and social rights; and (3) the devolution of immigration policy-making to state and local governments, resulting in significant variation in immigrant social welfare access at subnational levels of government (Gulasekaram and Ramakrishnan 2015). The INA abolished strict country-based or ethnic-based quotas, which led to a significant increase in the flow of immigrants into the United States and a shift in the countries of origin from mostly European countries to primarily Asian, South American, and Central American ones. The share of immigrants in the US population rose from 4.7% to 13.7% between 1970 and 2017. Simultaneously, Europe declined as an immigration source: in 1960, over 70% of immigrants were from Europe, by 2013, less than 20%, while the share of immigrants from the Americas increased from roughly 20% to over 50% (Radford 2019).

In the 1960s, while America was diversifying and inviting increased immigration, the welfare state was expanding into areas such as health care, food assistance, and education assistance. As discussed by Koning (2019), this scenario presents the progressive's dilemma – the tensions and trade-offs, real or perceived, between immigrant accommodation and welfare state expansion. The expanding US welfare system would soon respond to real and imagined pressures from rising immigration levels. The trope of immigrant undeservingness now began to take hold among the political elites of both major parties, eventually leading to a bipartisan set of federal-level IEWRs in the 1990s.

The 1996 Personal Responsibility Work Opportunity Reconciliation Act (PRWORA) formalized a restrictive set of IEWRs and limited the ability of both legal and undocumented immigrants to access social welfare benefits. Nearly a quarter-century later, layered on top of an already restrictive and ungenerous US welfare system for immigrant populations, anti-immigrant fervour was accelerated by President Donald Trump and the Republican Party elites, who sought to further restrict social benefits for non-citizens and for immigrant populations more generally. Overall, US welfare programs became more restrictive toward immigrants in the 1990s, and that trend has largely continued to this day. Data from the IESPI in Figure 9.1 show this abrupt 1990s shift toward welfare restrictiveness, followed by a plateauing pattern from 2000 to the present.

Figure 9.1. The increase and stabilization of American IESPI

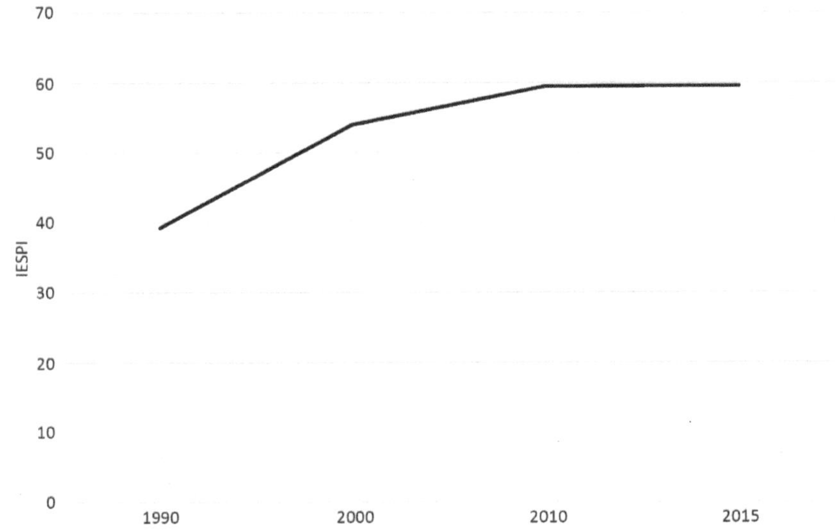

Note: Higher values indicate an overall more restrictive environment for immigrants to access welfare programs.

Increasing American Exclusion with IEWRs: The Personal Responsibility and Work Opportunity Reconciliation Act of 1996

After decades of increased immigration and welfare state expansion, in 1996 the PRWORA fundamentally changed the US welfare system. It represented a compromise between a Democratic president, Bill Clinton, and a Republican-controlled Congress. In the 1980s and 1990s, the Democrats advocated for fewer immigrants and strengthened border security to reduce the economic threat that immigrants were perceived to be posing to US labour interests. The Republican Party wanted to build on California's popular Proposition 187, a state-level ban on undocumented immigrants accessing state programs, by implementing it at the national level through a narrower policy that focused on exclusion from welfare programs. At this point in time, the two major political parties found common ground, adopting exclusionary immigrant welfare policies supported by the majority of Americans (Kehrberg 2020a).

The PRWORA ended cash welfare payments as an entitlement program by replacing Aid to Families with Dependent Children (AFDC) with Temporary Assistance for Needy Families (TANF). TANF created work requirements, imposed time limits on cash assistance, restricted eligibility requirements, and increased the role of the states in policy formation (e.g., Fellowes and Rowe 2004; Soss et al. 2001; Soss, Fording, and Schram 2011). In addition, the PRWORA instituted a series of IEWRs that restricted immigrants' access to welfare programs like TANF and Medicaid. Most significantly, the legislation barred many non-citizens from accessing federal welfare programs for five years after entering the country. The PRWORA also granted states greater power in administering new welfare programs and implementing unique requirements and restrictions to welfare benefits, which often included additional state-level measures to restrict immigrants' welfare access (Butz and Kehrberg 2015; Filindra 2012; Hero and Preuhs 2007; Kehrberg 2017). The immigration access restrictions in the PRWORA were passed primarily on the premise that immigrants were being drawn to the US by ready access to welfare benefits (Fix, Capps, and Kaushal 2010), the so-called magnet effect (Borjas and Hilton 1996). This sentiment was expressed by Dave Camp, Republican congressman from Michigan: "We don't want to be a welfare magnet for the world." The federal government thus set out to "fix" the supposed dependence of non-citizens on federal programs by barring unnaturalized foreigners almost entirely from all possible benefits. Gone were the welfare entitlements that were perceived as attracting dependent non-citizens, whom the Clinton administration and congressional Republicans believed were plaguing American society. Under the PRWORA, self-sufficient and hard-working immigrants with good standing would now be drawn to naturalize into the United States in order to gain access to federal programs – or at least that was the dominant narrative spun for the average US citizen during the 1990s policy debate (Fix, Capps, and Kaushal 2010).

Before the 1996 reforms, legal permanent non-citizen residents were generally allowed to access and utilize the same welfare benefits under the same conditions and requirements as US citizens. The PRWORA and other welfare reforms now pushed the importance of citizenship and legal status as prerequisites for welfare program access. This citizenship barrier approach was mirrored in crackdowns on immigrants' use of federal programs, with new restrictions placed on TANF, Medicaid, Supplemental Security Income, and the Food Stamp program (Butz and Kehrberg 2015; Fix, Capps, and Kaushal 2010; Hero and Preuhs 2007). Following the PRWORA, many post-enactment authorized and unauthorized immigrants in the US found themselves without the vital support they needed to alleviate material hardships. Unauthorized immigrants in particular were completely shut out, ineligible for most if not all means-tested benefit programs. In short, this period saw the passing of several IEWRs, and not only at the national level.

The PRWORA drew a clear line between desirable and undesirable immigrants. Those deemed desirable included naturalized citizens and long-term legal residents, who were allowed access to federal programs and welfare benefits. Any requirements and non-citizen restrictions created by the PRWORA, including state-level decisions to restrict non-citizens, did not apply to them. To limit welfare program access for immigrant populations constructed as undeserving, states took it upon themselves to increase requirements and conditions for access to certain welfare benefits. Mirroring federal-level approaches, states used their new powers to direct TANF monies, often with an eye toward exclusion, cracking down on immigrants' access to benefit programs by adopting work requirements, time limits on federal and state monetary assistance, and family caps (Hero and Preuhs 2007). All of this resulted in the "hardening" of immigration policy, in that it weakened the social rights of immigrants in the states (Boehme 2011; Bosniak 2006).

Instead of providing federal-level entitlement grants under the AFDC, the PRWORA divided TANF funding between the federal government and the states through fixed federal-level block grant allocations (Trattner 2007). Fiscal pressures now increased at the state level, and this incentivized the states to enact their own restrictive welfare measures, especially toward immigrant populations. The PRWORA allowed state governments to block immigrants from receiving state welfare funds. States' decisions to restrict or expand access to benefits have had racial undertones (Butz and Kehrberg 2015; Hero and Preuhs 2007), in that minorities have been disproportionately affected by changes in the welfare system. Regarding TANF, states with more authoritarian values were more likely to enact more restrictive policies to keep immigrants from using welfare benefits (Kehrberg 2017).

Impact of the PRWORA on Non-Citizen Caseloads across Four US Social Welfare Programs

The residency and citizenship barriers placed on social welfare programs have significantly increased the material hardships facing immigrant populations in the US. In 2019, immigrants had a lower unemployment rate than the native-born; even so, they were more likely to be living in poverty than native-born Americans (14.6% to 11.8%) and more likely to lack health insurance (19.6% compared to 8%) (Budiman et al. 2020). This section investigates the impact of the PRWORA on immigrants' use of the major US social welfare programs. We provide a brief overview of those programs and then examine evidence of reductions in immigrants' welfare use, which is what the PRWORA's architects hoped would happen. In particular, we examine immigrants' use of four major redistributive social welfare programs that were targeted by the PRWORA: Supplemental Security Income (SSI), the Supplemental Nutrition Assistance Program (SNAP), Temporary Assistance to Needy Families (TANF), and Medicaid benefits.

SSI

SSI is a federal program designed to help poor elderly and/or low-income disabled people by providing cash assistance. Those who fit the eligibility criteria are typically viewed as "deserving" by the general public (Schneider and Ingram

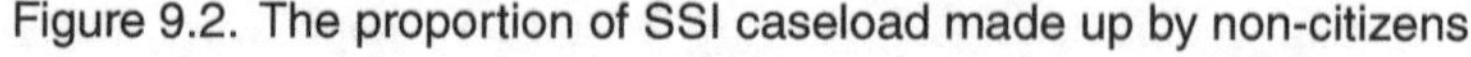

Figure 9.2. The proportion of SSI caseload made up by non-citizens

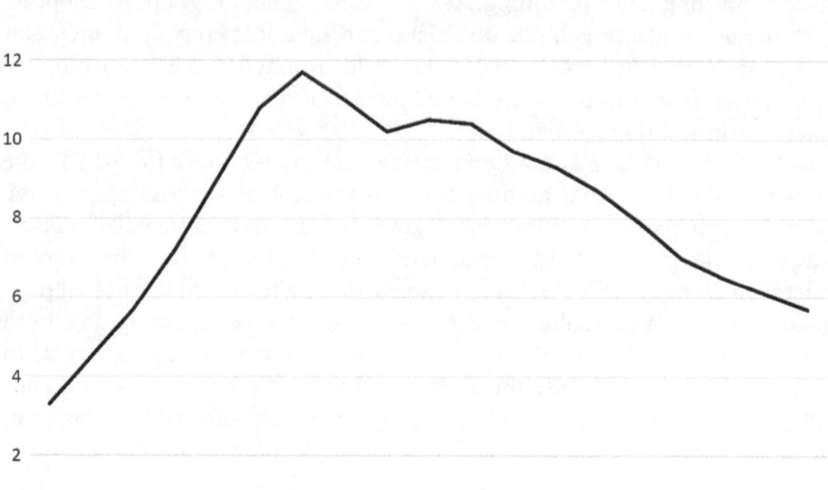

Source: SSI Annual Statistical Report, 2018. Social Security Administration.

1993). Yet eligible immigrants are viewed by some political elites as "undeserving" of SSI benefits (Yoo 2008). Reflecting the negative frame that immigrants are a drain on social resources, the PRWORA restructured immigrants' access to SSI. The consequences of these changes can be seen in Figure 9.2, on which we have graphed the proportion of SSI program participants who are non-citizens between 1982 and 2018. As the data show, this proportion more than tripled from the early 1980s to the mid-1990s. Since the passage of the PRWORA in 1996, the proportion of immigrants accessing SSI cash benefits has slowly declined.

SNAP

SNAP is the primary American food assistance program for low-income individuals, especially children. SNAP eligibility thresholds are more generous than for other benefit programs like SSI or TANF, and tens of millions of working-class American families are enrolled in the program (Ziliak 2015). Eligible families receive monthly non-cash, in-kind resources to purchase select food and grocery items. In Figure 9.3, we have graphed the proportion of eligible non-citizen immigrants who are participating in SNAP.[1]

Figure 9.3. The percentage of eligible non-citizen families receiving food stamps

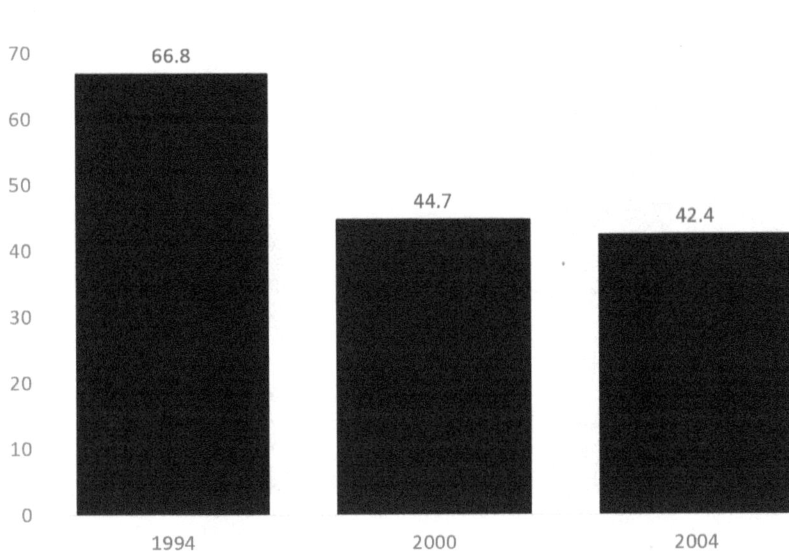

Source: Ku 2009.

As the data in Figure 9.3 show, the proportion of eligible non-citizen participants receiving SNAP benefits decreased precipitously from 66.8% in 1994 to 44.7% in 2000. After 2000, the number remained relatively stable, with a 42.4% participation rate among eligible non-citizens in 2004. With the passage of the PRWORA, the participation rate decreased to roughly two-thirds of the pre-enactment participation rate. The decline in SNAP participation rates likely has a significant impact on the material hardship of non-citizens and their children. Previous studies have found that 25.1% of children with immigrant parents who have been in the US for less than five years live with food insecurity, yet only 12.1% of the families with this immigration characteristic participate in SNAP (Kaushal, Waldfogel, and Wight 2014). In comparison, 9.7% of children with native-born parents live with food insecurity and 16.3% of children with native-born parents receive SNAP benefits. Non-citizen SNAP participation rates increase the longer parents have lived in the US, but the percentage of children living with food insecurity stays roughly the same for immigrant families regardless of their length of residence in the US (Kaushal et al. 2014). In short, the PRWORA has starkly reduced immigrants' access to SNAP benefits, with likely significant

Figure 9.4. The percentage of non-citizen families with incomes below 200% of the poverty line receiving TANF

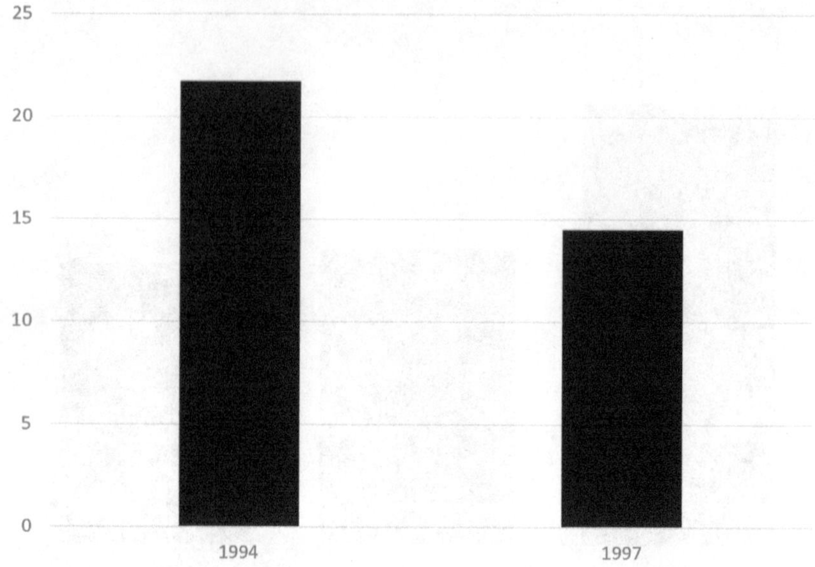

Source: Fix and Passel 1999.

consequences for the material hardships experienced by low-income immigrants (Bartfeld et al. 2015).

TANF

TANF is the primary cash assistance program for non-disabled low-income families in the United States. Replacing AFDC with the TANF program was the cornerstone of the 1996 PRWORA legislation; that change instituted time limits and strict work requirements, besides reducing access for immigrant populations. As a result, immigrants' use of TANF cash assistance has declined in recent decades. In Figure 9.4, we graph the proportion of poor non-citizens who receive TANF benefits. Non-citizen use of TANF declined from 21.7% in 1994 to 14.5% by 1997 – nearly a one-third decrease in program enrolment. The decline in TANF enrolment has been mainly among post-enactment immigrants and in states that deny state-funded TANF benefits to non-citizens. The disparate impact of the PRWORA reforms is highlighted by the fact that 18% of children in poor families with native-born parents receive TANF, compared to only 11% of children in poor families with foreign-born parents (Hanson, Koball, and Fortuny 2014).

Figure 9.5. The percentage of non-citizen families with incomes below 200% of the poverty line receiving Medicaid benefits

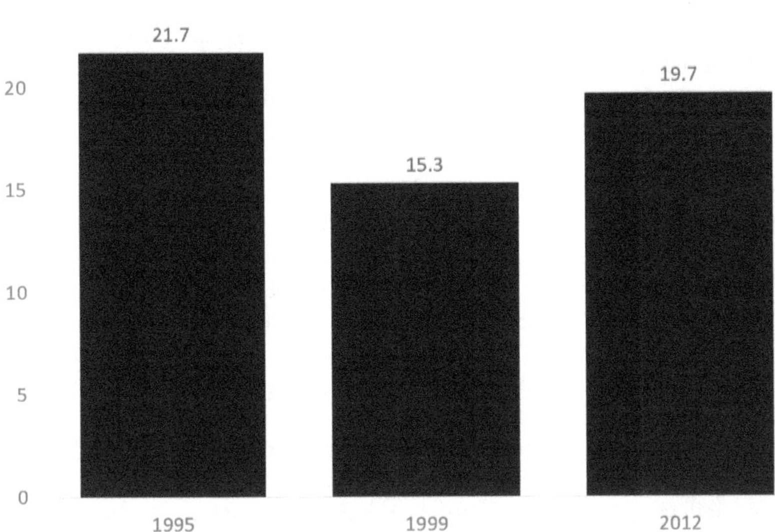

Source: data for 1995 and 1999 are drawn from Ku and Blaney 2000; 2012 data are from Ku and Bruen 2013.

Medicaid

Medicaid was established in 1965 to provide health coverage for the low-income elderly, disabled individuals, pregnant women, and needy families. The welfare reforms of 1996 changed the Medicaid eligibility requirements for non-citizens. In particular, the reforms created a waiting period for post-enactment immigrants and gave the states greater control of eligibility for state funds (Filindra 2012). Thus, Medicaid coverage is totally unavailable to unauthorized immigrants as well as to newly arrived legal immigrants who are seeking affordable medical coverage through the government. This means that immigrant populations have been less likely to access Medicaid benefits since the 1996 IEWRs. As with SNAP, this is likely increasing the hardships faced by immigrant families, for they are less likely to be able to access health care benefits and services. In Figure 9.5, we graph non-citizen use of Medicaid benefits. Before the PRWORA, 21.7% of non-citizen families with incomes under 200% of the poverty line – the income limit for the federal Basic Health Program – received Medicaid benefits. That percentage had declined to 15.3% by 1999. As the pool of post-enactment immigrants who meet that federal waiting period increased, the percentage grew to 19.7% by 2012. The pattern of non-citizen exclusion is not as dramatic for the Medicaid program, which remains available in several states, but still indicates a modest drop in immigrant usage. While non-citizens are not denied emergency medical treatment, non-citizen immigrants are more likely than citizens to lack health care insurance and as a result have a lower quality of life, because they avoid regular and preemptive medical care (Prentice, Pebley, and Sastry 2005). Clearly, the IEWRs instituted in the PRWORA have significantly reduced non-citizen use of major welfare programs in the US since 1996.

Congressional Gridlock, Rise of Sub-National Actors, and Executive Action: 2000 to 2020

In this section we discuss the emerging federal gridlock over immigration reform and the rise of sub-federal immigration policies in the US states since the passage of the PRWORA. Soon after the terrorist attacks of 11 September 2001, bipartisan support for federal immigration reform, along both restrictive and liberal policy dimensions, collapsed both at the elite level (Monogan 2007) and among the public at large (Kehrberg 2020b). With the Democrats adopting more liberal immigration policy preferences and the Republicans supporting restrictive policies, immigration legislation ground to a halt in Congress as the parties polarized on this salient political issue. As the IESPI data show, the US has roughly the same level of immigrant welfare exclusion at the federal level in 2015 as it did in 2000. Put another way, the eruption of reforms in the mid-1990s was followed by a period of policy stasis over the following two decades. During those decades, federal immigration reform has been polarized in Congress. There are some exceptions to the stalemate, such as the Patient Protection and Affordable Care Act (ACA) of 2010, which included restrictions on undocumented immigrants and some legal immigrants from receiving benefits on the Medicaid expansion and insurance exchanges (Joseph 2015, 2016, 2017). The ACA represents a bipartisan expansion of social benefits in the US that broadly excludes immigrant populations. In a rare example of immigrant inclusion, the 2002 Farm Security and Rural Investment Act (FSRIA) increased the number of immigrant children who are eligible for SNAP (Kaushal et al. 2014). Overall, the US government has failed to adopt immigration reforms; in regard to IEWRs, newer policies remain restricted to the existing PRWORA framework, with a few additional restrictions on immigrant access to social benefits.

A Patchwork of Immigration Policies: American Federalism

The 1996 immigration and welfare reforms, the PRWORA, brought about a major shift in policies regarding both immigrant rights to social welfare policies and the enforcement of immigration policies. As discussed earlier, the

PRWORA limited welfare access to federal funds for non-citizen immigrants on the national level. At the same time, it granted states the authority to include or exclude immigrants from social programs, thus inviting subnational variation in welfare approaches. Thus, 19 states granted immigrants access to TANF benefits during the five-year federal ban, and 37 allowed access after the federal ban. Of the 19 states that grant immediate access to welfare programs, only Utah and Georgia limit TANF access by immigrants to state funds after the federal five-year waiting period. Also, 17 states provided SNAP to the immigrant population during the federal five-year ban (Butz and Kehrberg 2015).

In the early 2000s, the states became very active in adopting immigration legislation. The National Conference of State Legislatures (NCSL) reports that in 2005 alone, state representatives introduced 300 bills on immigration, 45 of which passed. By 2010, state legislatures had introduced 1,400 bills, of which 208 were enacted. Examples of more inclusive policies include Colorado's HB 05-1086, which reinstated access to SSI and Medicaid for certain immigrant groups, and Vermont's HB 523, which provided funds for social welfare programs to provide benefits for immigrants who were ineligible for federal funds. Restrictive legislation at the state level can range from requiring state agencies to verify the citizenship or immigrant status of applicants (such as Pennsylvania H 960 in 2011), to limiting when immigrants can gain access to benefits (such as Kansas HB 2157 did with unemployment benefits in 2006), to restricting immigrant groups' access to benefit programs (such as Maine HB 1651, which cuts access to SNAP after immigrants are no longer eligible for federal funding). Over time, immigrants' experience with social welfare in America has become markedly varied in that access to social benefits nearly always depends on the state where an immigrant resides. While individual states have the flexibility to restrict narrow cash and food benefits under TANF and SNAP, the federal district courts in the US have shown a willingness to uphold a legal regime that protects immigrant populations under federal law. For instance, California's Proposition 187, which restricted health care, SSI, and education benefits for undocumented populations, was struck down as unconstitutional by a US district court, which reasoned that federal-level immigration rules preempted state action. This demonstrated that the legal regime allowed for state-level variation, but only under a federal-level umbrella that set baseline legal contours for social benefits. Put another way, states must stay within federal policy contours when crafting reforms and cannot further restrict immigrants' rights in other ways (e.g., by eliminating access to public education), because a legal regime of federal-level supremacy still defines legal protections and precedence in the US.

That said, the nature of the US federal system, in which 50 states hold substantive policy-making and implementation powers, has resulted in greater regional variation than in the other federal country studied in this volume,

Austria (see chapter 7). This almost unique federal system provides an opportunity for future research. The IESPI dataset was developed to compare exclusion of immigrants from welfare programs across countries based on national-level legislation. This approach may help us compare the US welfare system with welfare states elsewhere in the world quite well, but it obfuscates the considerable variation within the US. With the US federal policy framework being stagnant, the development of a state-level IESPI may provide new insights into the differences among the states and offer a more nuanced subnational view of US social welfare policy toward immigrants.

Diverging Attitudes toward Immigration

US political elites (Levendusky 2009; Monogan 2007) and the media (Haynes, Merolla, and Ramakrishnan 2016) have become more polarized on the issue of immigration over the past few decades. The public at large has responded in kind, with diverse attitudes toward the issue (Abrajano and Hajnal 2015). In this section we briefly examine that polarization, which often follows partisan lines and has contributed to today's legislative gridlock in the US Congress.

We use the American National Election Study (ANES) to graph changes in immigration preferences from 1992 to 2016. Unfortunately, the question concerning immigrants' access to welfare programs that was asked in the 1990s was dropped from the ANES after 1996 (Kehrberg 2020a). So instead, we use a question asking people whether the US should admit more immigrants, the same number, or fewer immigrants. This question is commonly used in scholarly research on attitudes toward immigration.

In Figure 9.6, we graph the percentage of respondents who want to decrease immigration by partisanship. Partisanship is an important predictor of attitudes and political behaviour; some even argue it is the most important identity marker in American politics, for it tends to be powerful and long-lasting (Bartels 2002; Green, Palmquist, and Schickler 2002). Starting in 2008, we observe a marked partisan split on immigration, with Democrats holding more positive attitudes toward immigrants and Republicans becoming increasingly more negative. These findings are important in that many public opinion studies from the 1990s and early 2000s found at best a weak relationship between partisanship and attitudes toward immigration (Citrin et al. 1997; Espenshade and Hempstead 1996; Nieman, Johnson, and Bowler 2006; Scheve and Slaughter 2001), but more recent studies have found a strong relationship (Abrajano and Hajnal 2015; Hajnal and Rivera 2014; Knoll, Redlawsk, and Sanborn 2011). As the partisan gap on immigration has increased, so has the importance of immigration as a wedge issue in politics, to the point that some research argues that immigration attitudes may be driving individuals to fully change their partisanship and/or ideology (Abrajano and Hajnal 2015; Hajnal and Rivera

Figure 9.6. Partisanship and support for decreasing immigration levels, 1992–2016

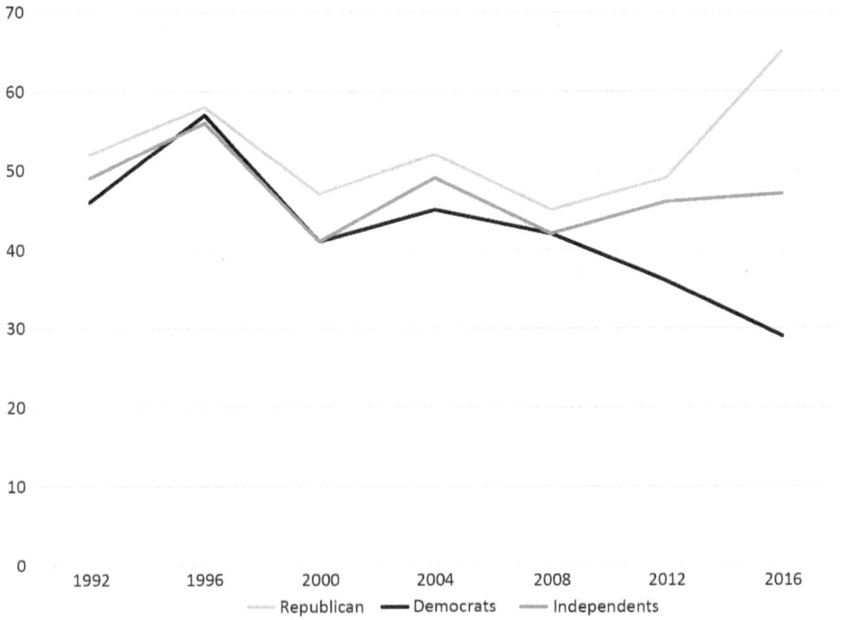

Note: The lines represent the proportion of Democrats, Republicans, and Independents respectively who want the number of immigrants to be "decreased a little" or "decreased a lot."
Source: American National Election Study, and authors' calculations.

2014). The combination of an increasing partisan divide on immigration and the heightened salience of immigration as a divisive political issue can create the necessary and sufficient conditions for gridlock in the American political system (Brooks and Manza 2008). In the end, the partisan polarization of immigration attitudes among the mass public in the US is apparent, creating an additional barrier to passing immigration reform among elites, and allowing for the status quo of restrictive social rights to be maintained.

Immigration Levels in a Period of Congressional Gridlock and Sub-Federal Activity

Over the past five decades, the US immigrant population has changed in several important respects. Overall, the foreign-born population has continued to grow since 1970, from an estimated 4.7% to 13.7% in 2017, but this measure of the proportion of foreign-born includes undocumented immigrants, along with naturalized citizens, who are treated the same as the native-born regarding access to welfare programs. As Figure 9.1 shows, the US became more restrictive on immigrant access to welfare programs in the 1990s. In 1990, 38% of immigrants were naturalized citizens. This increased to 56% by 2011 (Taylor et al. 2012) but has since declined to 45% in 2017 (Budiman 2020). During the same time frame the undocumented immigrant population increased from 5.7 million in 1995 to an estimated 12.2 million in 2006. The number of undocumented immigrants has since declined, to 10.5 million in 2017.

It is unclear how, if at all, these trends in US immigration have influenced the level of immigrant welfare exclusion. After all, while the number of undocumented immigrants decreased and the proportion of legal immigrants obtaining citizenship increased, federal legislation has remained more or less unchanged. This seems to undercut the so-called group threat hypothesis (Blalock 1960; Key 1949), which predicts that a larger or faster-growing immigrant population will result in more restrictive social programs (Filindra 2012; Hero and Preuhs 2007). For the same reason, the findings in this chapter do not support the theoretical expectation that growing populations can create inclusive policy outcomes as politicians attempt to incorporate these groups into their political coalitions (Provine and Chavez 2009). More recent studies have found that growing immigrant populations can simultaneously predict restrictive *and* inclusive state-level policies (Filindra 2019). States with growing immigrant populations are potentially more likely to adopt restrictive policies; however, states where Latinos are politically mobilized adopt fewer restrictive policies (Avery, Fine, and Márquez 2017). In the end, it is difficult to determine the influence of the Latino and immigrant population flows on US federal welfare policy due to the lack of fundamental change in those policies since 1996.

Two Sides of the Same Coin: Obama and Trump Executive Action

Frustration over congressional inaction at the federal level has motivated the US states to adopt their own immigration policies and IEWRs in recent decades. It has also motivated the US president to engage in executive actions, usually in the form of Executive Orders, to shape the flow of immigrants into and out of the US as well as immigrant access to social welfare programs. In this section, we examine a subset of presidential executive actions – those that impact immigrant access to welfare programs – by Presidents Obama and Trump. Presidents have limited power to create IEWRs, which are usually drafted by legislative bodies; however, presidents do have the power to direct the federal bureaucracy to adopt certain priorities and to shape how social benefit legislation is interpreted. The cases of Presidents Obama and Trump show a clear contrast between the former's attempt to protect "Dreamers" and undocumented immigrants whose children are US citizens on the one hand, and the latter's executive policies that sought to create new IEWRs or to punish immigrants who chose to access social welfare programs on the other.[2]

In the summer of 2013, the stage was seemingly set for comprehensive immigration reform and bipartisan federal legislative action that would increase immigration levels as well as immigrant access to US social welfare programs. President Obama came to power in the 2008 election with a somewhat mixed rhetorical and policy approach: he consistently exulted the promise and contributions of immigrants, including the undocumented; yet under his watch, immigrant deportations reached record levels. A "Gang of Eight" immigration bill known as the Border Security, Economic Opportunity, and Immigration Modernization Act of 2013 would have increased levels of border security while extending protections and welfare rights to more classes of immigrants and promising a pathway to citizenship.[3] The legislation passed the US Senate on 27 June 2013 with 68 votes – a rare supermajority in contemporary American governance. However, the legislation ultimately failed in the US House of Representatives, which was controlled by a recalcitrant Republican Party and a strict anti-immigrant gatekeeper, Republican Speaker John Boehner. Despite public opinion favouring legislative action, and seemingly widespread congressional support for immigration reform (at least in the US Senate), formal legislation would never reach President Obama's desk for final signature.

When Congress failed to pass immigration reform or create a pathway for citizenship for undocumented immigrants, President Obama used his executive power to create two programs: (1) Deferred Action for Childhood Arrivals (DACA), and (2) Deferred Action for Parents of Americans and Lawful Permanent Residents (DAPA). DACA and DAPA are most commonly known for creating a temporary registration system allowing certain unauthorized immigrants to defer deportation. These executive orders did not explicitly increase the social rights of undocumented immigrants or immigrants in general. The policies do allow for undocumented immigrants participating in DACA and DAPA to potentially receive social insurance such as Social Security and/or Medicare benefits, but these undocumented immigrants are still denied access to other redistributive social welfare programs, such as TANF and SNAP, because earlier legislative restrictions from the PRWORA remain in place. In short, President Obama's executive orders shielded certain immigrants from deportation but did very little to expand immigrant access to social welfare programs. The period of the Obama administration (2008–2016) can best be characterized as maintaining stasis, allowing certain immigrant groups shelter from deportation through executive actions but without any dramatic movement toward either immigrant welfare exclusion or expansion. This would soon change as political winds shifted sharply in 2016.

President Trump came to power following the 2016 election on an explicit platform of immigrant exclusion and welfare chauvinism. For instance, he was quick to distribute federal resources to "favoured" groups such as farmers and industry, while advocating for welfare restrictions for less favoured groups like immigrants, especially undocumented immigrants and refugees. However, bombastic rhetoric and overtly restrictionist appeals from Trump's bully pulpit did not yield significant legislative successes. His most ambitious anti-immigration plans, including the construction of a southern border wall, met with congressional resistance and minimal legislative action. In the 2018 midterm election, Democrats took majority control of the US House of Representatives, further stymying Trump's anti-immigrant agenda. Much like Obama, Trump subsequently turned to unilateral executive action. However, in contrast to Obama's, the Trump administration drafted policies and orders that more explicitly restricted some immigrant groups from access to social programs and that punished immigrants for receiving public benefits.

For instance, in August 2019, the Trump administration published a new rule through the US Department of Homeland Security that sought to curtail immigrants' use of public benefit programs. The primary policy change involved the concept of a "public charge" and eligibility for Green Card status (Evelly 2020). "Public charge" refers to an immigrant who is expected to become or becomes dependent on government welfare programs. Under this regulatory change, any immigrant who used 12 months of social welfare benefits (within a 36-month period), such as SNAP, TANF, Medicaid, or a public housing allowance could be denied permanent residency. This represented a significant new development in terms of immigrant welfare exclusion. Historically, authorized immigrants could utilize certain welfare programs such as SNAP and Medicaid, because these programs were deemed essential for health and nutrition purposes. Enrolment in these programs would not discount or hinder an immigrant's permanent citizenship case (Evelly 2020). With Trump's new rule, enrolment in food assistance, medical programs, and traditional forms of cash assistance could count against an immigrant's citizenship. When announcing the rule, Trump reiterated his disdain for immigrants who used welfare: "I am tired of seeing our taxpayer paying for people to come into the country and immediately go onto welfare and various other things. So I think we're doing it right" (White House 2019).

The Trump administration also moved to end DACA. This would have ended the already minimal access to social programs that had been granted under Obama's executive orders. Although Trump's legislative successes were scant, he succeeded in moving immigration policy and immigrant access to social welfare benefits in a restrictive and exclusionary direction. In the November

2020 presidential election, he was defeated by Democrat Joseph Biden, who had been Obama's vice-president. The future of immigration and US social welfare policy remains very much in flux under the new president.

Conclusion: The Future of Immigration and Welfare Exclusion in the US

This chapter has demonstrated that modern US immigration and social welfare politics are being shaped by a culture of individualism and self-reliance, deep partisan conflict, racial conflict, and recent policy stalemate. The country's relatively underdeveloped federal welfare state offers paltry social benefits and routinely bars immigrants from social programs. This trend continued with the election of Donald Trump, whose executive actions restricted immigrants' access to social welfare programs through "public charge" rules. This trend could well continue as a result of ongoing legislative stalemate. Anti-immigrant sentiment could also be fuelled by recent economic decline and the COVID-19 pandemic. Rivalries around economic opportunity, taxation, and redistribution could continue to define immigrant/native-born dynamics, and the US welfare state could well continue its underdeveloped and restrictive pattern toward immigrants in particular.

On the other hand, the widespread unpopularity of the recently defeated Trump presidency may signal a seismic shift in US politics – a movement toward a more genuine multiracial democracy that demonstrates greater tolerance and inclusion of non-White people, including immigrants. As persons of colour continue to expand their share of the US electorate and begin holding elected office with greater frequency, we may see broad shifts toward welfare accommodation for newcomers, especially authorized immigrants. An ascendant Democratic coalition of younger, more urban, more educated, more minority voters, including those favouring immigration expansion, could yield long-term fundamental changes in US welfare policy and how immigrants access the social safety net. In many ways, the Trump administration's slogan to "Make America Great Again" hearkens back to a likely soon to be extinct form of White identity politics. That said, the forces of restriction and exclusion remain potent. At its core, America remains "symbolically" conservative – rooted in principles of individualism and free enterprise, with minimal government involvement in public affairs. "Socialism" remains a term of invective and is unlikely to take hold in governing institutions and welfare policy outcomes. Also, while the Democratic Party diversifies and advocates for immigration expansion, the Republican Party is conversely becoming whiter (Abrajano and Hajnal 2017), more authoritarian (Hetherington and Weiler 2009), and more anti-immigrant (Kehrberg 2020b). Now that the Republicans have started embracing exclusionary social policies toward immigrants, it is coming to resemble many of Europe's populist anti-immigrant parties (such as Norway's

Progress Party; see chapter 8). For example, former President Trump modelled some of his rhetoric after these political parties, using a similar call to develop a "worker's party" rooted in opposition to immigrant labour. This may well yield continued legislative stalemate, with stasis favouring restricted social welfare provision for immigrants. There may not be new 1996-style shifts that impose additional burdens on immigrant populations or exclude them more than at present; however, there will also likely not be dramatic shifts toward immigrant inclusion in US social welfare programs. In our view, the most likely scenario is policy stalemate and continued immigrant exclusion from US social welfare programs. Occasionally, individual states like California may undertake expansive welfare reforms for non-citizens, such as extending Medicaid benefits to undocumented immigrants, but the broad national posture still tilts toward exclusion. Given the current American fault lines of demographics, culture, and institutions, it would seemingly take something much more revolutionary to produce a welfare state with greater inclusion of immigrant populations. We remain sceptical that this will happen in the short or medium term; longer-term prospects for fundamental change in the US are somewhat rosier. The centre of gravity in the US continues to pull in the direction of immigrant welfare exclusion.

NOTES

1 This measure has advantages and disadvantages. When possible, we picked non-citizens since citizenship is one of the barriers preventing many immigrants from accessing SNAP. An additional difficulty in measuring SNAP participation is that benefits can be awarded to the citizen-children of non-citizen immigrants.

2 "Dreamers" refers to unauthorized immigrants who were brought to the US as children.

3 "Gang of Eight" refers to a bipartisan group of eight U.S. senators – four Republicans and four Democrats – who drafted the Immigration Modernization Act of 2013.

10 Why Choose the Inclusionary Path? Social Policy in a Recent Welfare and Immigration Country: The Case of Portugal

CATARINA REIS OLIVEIRA AND JOÃO PEIXOTO

Academics and policy-makers have long discussed the potential tension between immigration and welfare, arguing about the consequences of social policy differentiation between immigrants and the native-born in host societies. However, welfare politics and responses to immigrants' social benefit dependence are not straightforward: whether they become less or more inclusive toward immigrants depends on the host country's welfare conditions, socio-economic and political characteristics, and experience with immigrants. As we will highlight in this chapter, and against what could be expected (and as Koning 2019 also concluded), the politics of immigrant welfare exclusion or inclusion are not straightforward and have to do with other factors besides economic ones.

While its experience with immigration has been only recent (positive net migration dates back only to 1993), and while its immigrant population today is relatively small (in 2020, only 6.4% of residents), several international comparative reports and studies over the past decade have named Portugal as having one of the best integration policies in the world and as one of the most inclusionary countries for immigrants (see, e.g., MIPEX scores for 2007, 2010, and 2015; IOM 2010; UNDP 2009). So it is no surprise that Portugal is the second most inclusive country in the Immigrant Exclusion from Social Programs Index (IESPI).

The IESPI dataset indicates that Portugal is the country that has undergone the most spectacular transformation. After ranking as the second-most exclusionary country in 1990 (after Malta), it became the second most inclusionary in 2010 and 2015 (after Norway; see Figure 10.1). The general evolution of the Portuguese welfare system and various contextual factors help explain not only why Portugal is presently inclusionary but also why it has become so much more inclusionary over the past three decades. Those factors include the end of the dictatorial regime in 1974; the end of colonialism in the 1970s and increased inflows from former colonies; the country's entry into the EU in 1986; positive net migration after 1993; a negative natural balance since 2007;

Figure 10.1. Social policy differentiation between immigrants and native-born, Portugal scores compared with lowest and highest IESPI scores, 1990–2015

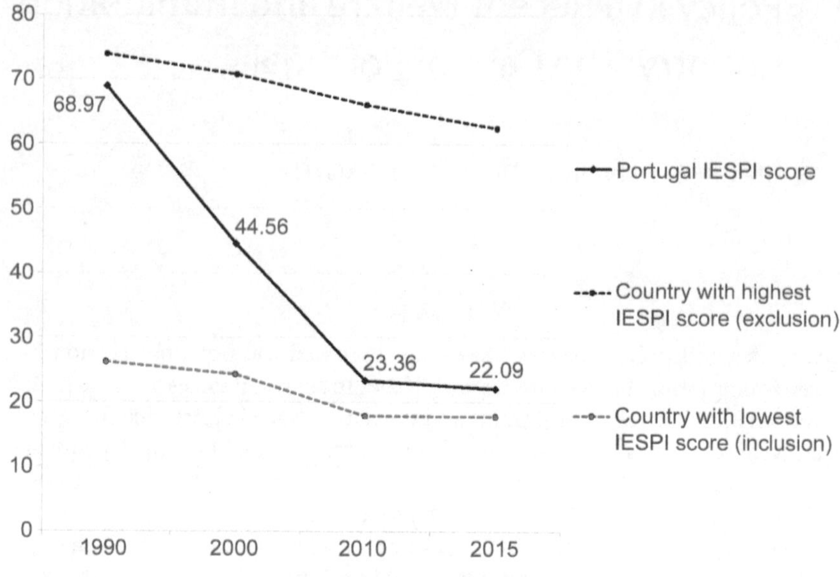

economic and financial crises; relatively favourable public opinion about immigration; and a lack of divisive political actors.

This change did not happen without difficulties. For one thing, the welfare regime is very recent. Portugal was part of the third wave of democratization worldwide (after the military coup on 25 April 1974 and a long history of colonization). Both the national health system (created only in 1979) and the welfare system (the first basic law dates back to 1984) were direct consequences of an aspiring democratic country that wished for more economic and social equality after a long authoritarian regime.

At the same time, though, the country has endured successive and prolonged economic crises, such as the one that started after the world economic crisis in 2008, which led to a financial bailout and an outside intervention that directly affected the welfare system's ability to take care of all residents (both native-born and foreigners). Moreover, Portugal faces an aging population that will make its welfare system harder to sustain. Despite this, Portugal has embraced humanitarian social policies and has avoided differentiating between immigrants and the native-born, as defined in the 1976 Constitution, which marked the advent of democracy in the country.

Portugal's migratory experience has its own particularities that explain its inclusionary welfare path. Most of the inflows have a postcolonial character, with the result that the cultural, linguistic, and religious diversity that immigration has brought about is limited. Immigration to the country has been driven mainly by economics, with immigrants showing high labour participation rates and lower social benefit dependency.

Nonetheless, equality and inclusion are not synonymous with welfare state generosity and high social expenditure. This chapter analyses the determinants for the increased social policy homogenization between immigrants and native-born in Portugal in recent decades. In documenting that the Portuguese welfare system has become inclusionary toward immigrants, we are not suggesting there has been an increase in welfare state spending, as clearly Portugal is not among the most generous welfare states in Europe.[1]

Taken together, these contextual factors and legacies explain the politics of welfare for immigrants. The chapter begins by characterizing the Portuguese welfare regime, taking into account the chronology of social policies since the end of the 1970s and underscoring the factors that led to the present inclusionary setting. After that, we revisit Portugal's immigration history; then we briefly describe the immigrant population and the evolution of integration policies targeting them. We then identify the main immigrant social inclusion outcomes, considering achievements and challenges. To explain the factors that led to Portugal's integration policies and the extension of social rights to foreign residents, a further section highlights the favourable political climate, which is characterized by relatively pro-immigration attitudes among both politicians and the Portuguese public. Finally, some concluding remarks will be made.

Creating the Inclusionary Portuguese Welfare State

In *The Three Worlds of Welfare Capitalism*, Esping-Andersen (1990) placed Portugal among the generally "conservative" group of Continental European countries, which emphasize family as a means of social support, but also classified it as a Southern European type of welfare regime, acknowledging the impact of a relatively late democracy and the role of the informal economy. Although countries have deviated from Esping-Andersen's original classification over the past thirty years, especially since the policy changes of the last decade arising from the 2008 economic crisis (Eurofound 2015, 8), several regime characteristics are still apparent.

Portugal's colonial and authoritarian legacies played a role in the country designing an inclusionary welfare state, especially after 1974, when the country joined the "third wave of democratization" and developed several social policies (Esping-Andersen 1993). Portugal's accession to the EU in 1986 also encouraged the quick build-up and consolidation of a modern welfare regime.

In relation to social policy differentiation toward immigrants, Portugal has undergone much change (Figure 10.1). First, it is important to understand that because Portugal is a relatively recent country of immigration, most social policy differentiation between native-born and immigrants until the 1990s was not necessarily evidence of an exclusionary policy orientation; mainly, it was a consequence of immigration being absent from policy-makers' attention (e.g., the first Immigration Act dates back only to 1981 and was tabled in the context of the country's entry into the EU, and the first steps in developing immigrant integration policies were taken only in 1996). Indeed, at no point has Portugal introduced exclusionary frameworks deliberately aimed at differentiating between immigrants and native-born.

A description of the main elements in the making of the Portuguese welfare system, along with changes in several contextual factors, explain not only why Portugal is inclusionary now but also why it has become so much more inclusionary over the past three decades.[2]

The existence of the national health system, public education system, and social protection in Portugal is a direct consequence of the revolution of 25 April 1974 that ended the authoritarian regime and induced several revolutionary social dynamics, the end goal being more economic, political, and social equality. All of this led to the 1976 Constitution, which underscored the general principle of equality and ample social rights as part and parcel of the advent of democracy in the country (González and Figueiredo 2014, 291).

Over the past four decades, the country has launched successive basic laws in social security, health, and education. Those legal frameworks, while reflecting different governments' interpretations of the country's constitutional ambitions, its socio-economic situation, and its capacity to finance public expenditure, have together strengthened the principle of universality of social rights enshrined in the Constitution. Since then, national citizenship has not been a precondition for accessing fundamental rights in Portugal. Foreigners and stateless persons residing in the country enjoy the same rights[3] as the native-born and are subject to the same duties (Oliveira and Carvalhais 2017, 793). Moreover, the conditions that immigrants encounter in Portugal are uniform across the country (much like what we saw in Norway in chapter 8, and in contrast to what we saw in Austria and the United States in chapters 7 and 9 of this volume).

Under the new democratic government established in 1974, Portugal began transitioning to a unified model of social security that expanded social protection. It did so through a series of concrete measures related to social pensions, unemployment protection, family subsidies, and social protection for self-employed and domestic workers. In 1977, the country enacted the first legal framework for social security, based on three fundamental principles – integration, decentralization, and participation. Seven years later, in 1984, followed the first Social Security Act.

It was also under constitutional principles that in 1979 Portugal created the National Health System, which made explicit that access should be guaranteed "to all citizens, no matter their economic and social conditions," and that "the access is guaranteed to foreigners in reciprocity, to stateless and to refugees residing in the country" (Oliveira and Gomes 2018, 107–8).

The 1976 Constitution identified housing as a fundamental social right. However, housing has always had a peripheral place in Portuguese public policy, receiving far fewer public resources than education, health, and social security. Portugal has reduced its public intervention in housing, as have other Southern European countries. Hence, housing has been dominated by the private sector, and there are very few available public housing units. In 1993, Portugal launched a special program of social housing in several municipalities. Since then, many social housing programs and rent assistance policies have been promoted throughout the country, for which foreign residents have been eligible on the same terms as Portuguese nationals. Over the past two decades, specific measures aimed at more vulnerable groups, such as the homeless, the elderly, and immigrants, have been defined in Housing Action Plans (Malheiros and Fonseca 2011, 81–3), and action plans for immigrants' integration today are part of several measures on housing tailored to immigrants. Nonetheless, given that immigrants find it harder to access credit for private housing, the available social supports and housing programs are often seen as not enough for their needs.

The 1990s were characterized by increased financial strains and numerous initiatives to reform social protection. These led to the introduction of contributory fees and penalties for infractions against the national social security system. Since 1995, general social assistance benefits have been available to foreigners residing legally in Portugal. Foreign residents' access to social welfare entitlements was reinforced in the 1990s to encourage formal labour market integration and to discourage work in the informal economy as well as irregular stay in the country. In 1996, on the recommendation of the European Commission, the Portuguese government launched the "minimum income subsistence."[4] This benefit was made accessible for foreign residents after one year of residence. After 1998, access to unemployment insurance and to labour market programs was extended to foreigners who had worked and paid social security for a minimum period of time in the country (presently a minimum of six months is required).

The new century saw a rapid transformation of the immigrant population in Portugal: between 1999 and 2002, the foreign population residing in the country more than doubled, from 190,000 to 413,000. Moreover, that population became much more diverse, in particular because more immigrants arrived from non-Portuguese-speaking countries and from countries with which Portugal had no historical links. All of this pressured the country to invest in integration policies and to pay closer heed to immigrants' social protection. Hence most inclusionary welfare policies date back to the beginning of this century.

Until 2001, health services were available solely to nationals and foreigners from countries with which Portugal had reciprocal health agreements. That year, the national health system was opened to all foreign residents, including undocumented immigrants residing in the country for more than 90 days. Nonetheless, depending on migrants' legal status, the treatments have to be paid entirely or partly with established fees, with exemptions for minors under 12, pregnant women, and those for whom the denial of treatment would risk public health (for an overview see Oliveira and Gomes 2018, 95–117).

A legislative reform in 2003 disentitled a large number of immigrants residing in Portugal from minimum income subsistence.[5] These changes were not entirely implemented, however, in part because they were rejected by the Constitutional Court and in part because the left-wing government that took office in 2005 revoked those changes, including the restrictions to immigrants' access.

In 2007, under the same centre-left government, a new Social Security Act adjusted the system to align it with the country's aging population;[6] this meant that the old-age pension system now reflected the life expectancy of the population. Also in 2007, the new Immigration Act (still in force) underscored that foreigners with legal residence in Portugal have social rights; it also made enrolment in the social security system a precondition for obtaining or renewing residence in the country.

The 2007 Social Security Act was revised again in 2013 in the context of a financial and economic crisis and a population decrease. In addition to demographic pressures, the Portuguese welfare system has been especially impacted over the past decade by economic and financial crises, mainly between 2011 and 2014, when the Troika[7] intervened in the country. This period was marked by fewer contributors and growing numbers of beneficiaries of social protection. In 2012, several changes were introduced in the social protection regime, with the main argument that the most vulnerable could not be allowed to undermine the financial sustainability of the social security system (stated in the decree law; see Oliveira and Gomes 2019, 212). As a consequence, economic support for very low income families decreased, which increased the number of families at risk of poverty and material deprivation, including immigrant families (Eurofound 2015, 60; Oliveira and Gomes 2019, 203, 212)

Also as a result of the 2011–14 crisis, Portugal made several reactive political decisions regarding the management of its national health system. These have focused on reducing costs, limiting access to services, and increasing user fees for public health services. These measures were especially problematic in a context in which the population at risk of poverty had grown, and they led to an increase in health inequality (Sakellarides et al. 2014, 31; Padilla et al. 2018, 319; Oliveira and Gomes 2018, 113–17). These changes triggered many complaints to the National Ombudsman, and in 2014 they were partly reversed though an expansion of exceptions to users' charges for health services (Oliveira and Gomes 2018, 128–36).

Between 2012 and 2015, a centre-right government implemented explicit social policy differentiation according to the nationality of residents: nationals and EU citizens residing in Portugal could benefit from minimum income subsistence after one year of residence, but non-EU citizens would have to wait three years. These differentiations were overturned by the Constitutional Court in 2015 (judgment 296/2015) based on the argument that social rights are universally protected in Portugal and that all foreign residents have the same rights and duties as nationals. Hence, at the end of 2015, under a centre-left government, the welfare system returned to its previous framework and social security allowances were revised and increased.

During the 2011–14 crisis the sustainability of the welfare and health systems was debated, both in relative economic terms (costs as a percentage of GDP) and in absolute financial terms (public expenses). So far, however, the constitutional principles of equality and universality have prevailed against attempts to differentiate between immigrants and the native-born.

Foreign residents in Portugal, once legalized, have the same rights and duties as national citizens when it comes to social security. However, they still need to satisfy certain eligibility requirements, such as minimum residence and contributions. They also need to be registered in the national social security system in order to obtain or renew their residence permits. In 2019 the Portuguese parliament approved a law that mandated that one year of payments to the welfare system gave a foreigner the right to obtain a residence permit, even if he/she had not entered the country legally. Centre-right parties voted against this law, arguing that it would open the door to all sorts of immigrants. However, the centre-left majority in parliament insisted that this new law would "dignify" labour immigrants, who at the time were paying for national welfare without being able to legalize their residence in the country or gain social protection as residents.

In short, the Portuguese welfare system is a new and at times troubled one. It has set out to grant public support to all citizens and residents in an era marked by global and national economic challenges. The national public debt and financial tensions, in particular those arising from the global economic crisis and the subsequent intervention by the Troika, have together limited Portugal's ability to guarantee welfare for all residents and resulted in a revision of certain welfare characteristics. The Portuguese welfare system is relatively inclusionary (as the IESPI demonstrates), and by constitutional principle it is universal to all residents (including foreign residents), but these characteristics do not mean it is able to address all needs effectively and consistently.

Explicit restrictions on immigrants' access to social programs and benefits have been consistently condemned in Portugal. Instead, constraints have been imposed on the overall population in times of crisis. As such, although the social policy differentiation between immigrants and the native-born has not increased, the overall population at risk of poverty and welfare dependence has grown larger. Thus, during the crisis, welfare state protections in Portugal decreased generally in scope and efficacy, meaning that the inclusionary outcomes in the IESPI dataset in the crisis years of 2010 and 2015 may not necessarily reflect that the welfare state gave immigrants more (in terms of an increase of generosity), but instead that it gave the native-born less.

Portugal's Migratory Experience and Immigrants' Characteristics

Researchers today are trying harder to determine how welfare state politics and policies of social redistribution are influenced by the levels and patterns of immigration flows and stocks (for a synthesis, see Burgoon and Rooduijn 2020). Many have debated whether welfare states can cope with increasing numbers of immigrants (including refugees), expressing concerns that they may weaken support for welfare redistribution and increase exclusion and social policy differentiation between immigrants and the native-born.

Here, as a contribution to this debate, we consider Portugal's experience with migration as a determinant of the politics of welfare. An immediate apparent contradiction arises from this analysis: according to the IESPI dataset, Portugal moved from one of the most exclusionary countries (in 1990) to one of the most inclusionary (in 2010 and 2015), precisely at a time when it was increasing its immigration flows and stock. That is, Portugal moved in an inclusionary direction even while increasing immigration.

The increase in the foreign population has been very sharp since the 1980s (see Figure 10.2) – from around 100,000 individuals in the early 1990s, representing around 1% of the population, to 589,000 in 2019, representing 5.7% of the population.[8] Although to a lesser degree than other European host countries,[9] Portugal has become an immigration country.

However, the effects of the migratory experience on social policy differentiation may not be fully captured by aggregate data on stocks and flows. Portugal is an experienced emigration country and has only recently attracted large-scale immigration – for every non-citizen resident in Portugal, there are 5 non-resident Portuguese citizens abroad (Pires 2010). Emigration and immigration have coexisted in recent decades. Like other Southern European countries, Portugal underwent a migration turn in the 1990s during which immigration increased and became structural. Even so, emigration never ceased: after the massive flows of the 1960s and early 1970s, it resumed in the mid-1980s – mainly, after 2011, during the economic and financial crisis (Peixoto et al. 2016). Emigration and immigration have also been intertwined, in that many flows occur along the same geographical corridor – for example, uniting Portugal and Brazil in opposite directions.

Figure 10.2. Number of foreign residents in Portugal, including foreign residents from Portuguese-speaking countries, and net migration and natural balance, 1980 to 2019 (thousands)

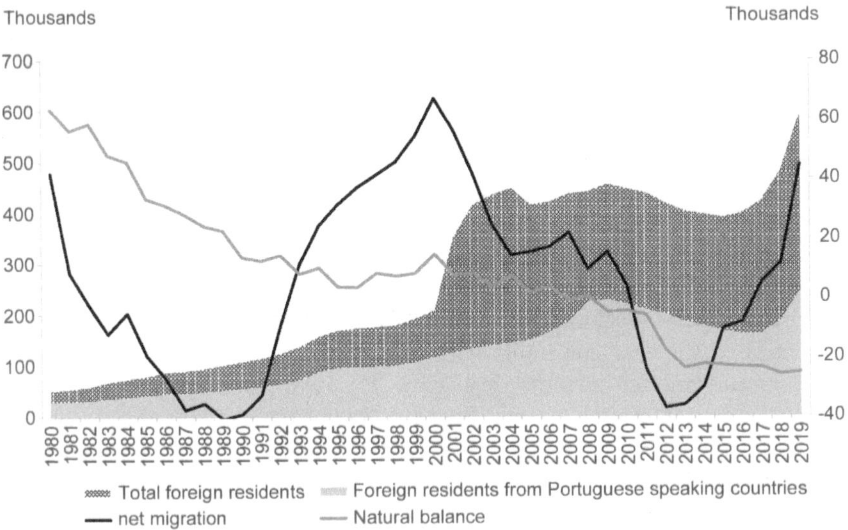

Source: INE and Aliens and Border Service.

This migratory experience has left its mark on the country's attitudes and policies regarding immigration. Policy-makers on issues of immigrant integration often turn to the argument that the rights claimed for Portuguese emigrants living abroad are the same as those advocated for immigrants residing in Portugal (Oliveira 2012, 294). In this way, the emigration experience has fostered a pro-migrant narrative, including in the provision of social rights.

From the mid-1970s to the early 1980s, inflows spiked because of the abrupt return from the ex-colonies after the democratization and decolonization in 1974, as well as the return of emigrants from Europe. Except for this, however, positive net migration only became a reality in 1993. After a new period of net emigration between 2011 and 2016 as a consequence of the economic crisis, net immigration increased again, before coming to an abrupt halt in 2020 as a result of the COVID-19 pandemic.

Foreign inflows to Portugal date back to the 1960s, when immigrants from Cape Verde, then a Portuguese colony, started arriving in sizable numbers. They came to fill the needs of the labour market, which had been partly depleted by emigration. After decolonization in 1974, inflows of Africans from the former colonies continued. Cape Verde was always predominant, followed by Angola and Guinea-Bissau. In the early 1990s, immigration from Brazil started to increase, so that today, after successive waves, Brazilians are the main foreign nationality in Portugal. Data on the foreign population illustrate these trends. As Figure 10.2 shows, foreigners from Portuguese-speaking countries have consistently accounted for the bulk of all foreign residents in Portugal.

In the late 1990s, Eastern European immigration began as well, bringing in Ukrainians, Romanians, Moldavians, and others. Asian immigration, from China, Pakistan, Nepal, Bangladesh, and other countries, was steady but grew more significantly in the new century. The same period saw a steady inflow from Western Europe, mainly the United Kingdom (for a synthesis, see Pires 2010).

Three characteristics of immigration to Portugal are worth emphasizing, given their importance for the country's inclusionary approach. First, most of the flows have a postcolonial character. Among the main foreign nationalities, the proportion of former colonies is impressive: Brazil, Cape Verde, and other Portuguese-speaking countries were always a large majority. Foreign immigration has a clear continuity with the country's past, and in many cases, currents and counter-currents are evident. The Portuguese-speaking countries are united by a migration system (Baganha 2009; Góis and Marques 2009) and share a history, culture, and language. Despite the many hurdles to successful integration that still exist, this is crucial for explaining the development of Portuguese immigration policy.

Second, economic drivers predominate. Except for the large migration stream from Africa in the mid-1970s, which gathered more ethnic Europeans than ethnic Africans and had an obvious political drive, most newcomers to Portugal migrated for economic reasons. The evolution over the years reveals a close relationship between immigration and economic cycles: it increases in times of prosperity and decreases in times of hardship (Peixoto 2002). Immigrants' labour participation rates have always been high (OECD 2008; Oliveira and Gomes 2019): men and women are both strongly engaged in the market and are viewed by the population as hard workers and not welfare leeches.

Third, the cultural and religious diversity among newcomers to Portugal is low. Immediately after Brazil and the African Portuguese–speaking countries, the largest group of immigrants comes from Eastern Europe. This inflow has no previous links to Portugal, but its integration has proved not to be hard. Besides being European, most of them have quickly learned the language and entered the labour market as wage earners, further enhancing their living conditions. Asian immigrants have increased in number and live in relatively closed communities, but rank as the minority with the highest entrepreneurial rates, operating businesses used by the entire population (Oliveira 2010). Regarding religion, the number of Muslims is rather limited, and most have a Portuguese background or come from former colonies, particularly Guinea-Bissau. The relationship between the Muslim community and mainstream religious groups has been quite smooth.

In brief, the long coexistence of emigration and immigration and the characteristics of immigration help explain the evolution of inclusionary policies in Portugal. In contrast to other immigrant-receiving countries (see, for example, the previous three chapters of this volume), some particularities emerge: most immigrants share a language and history with the host society; economically motivated flows largely exceed refugee flows; and cultural and religious backlashes are rare. Unlike other Southern European host countries, Portugal is not a popular destination for land or maritime irregular flows. Given the economic hardships of the country and the recurrent emigration waves, it is not hard for native-born citizens to understand immigrants.

The Development and Achievements of Immigrant Integration Policies over Time

Portugal's experience with migration has framed the policy options toward immigrants' integration. However, it would be incomplete to end our explanation there. As a wide literature has demonstrated (e.g., Zincone 2006), the making of immigration policies is complex, with dynamic strategies developed by several stakeholders leading to unique and often unexpected results. Similar contexts can lead to contrasting policies, as demonstrated by a comparison with other Southern European countries.

Regarding the general legal framework, the first immigration law in Portugal was tabled in 1981, aimed at tackling the first foreign inflows and anticipating the accession to the EU (which happened in 1986). The endemic difficulty of controlling inflows was already evident with this law and continued afterwards, since irregular migration never ceased. The second law dates from 1993, this time anticipating membership in the Schengen Agreement (implemented in 1995). This law was more restrictive; even so, the high number of irregular immigrants at the time led to the country's first extraordinary regularization, in 1992–93.

The 1990s witnessed an increasingly progressive approach toward immigration. In 1996, a second regularization process was launched. As with the former, most applicants came from Portuguese-speaking countries. A less restrictive approach was evident in a new law, introduced in 1998, and was reinforced with a subsequent law in 2001. The latter accepted the principle of granting temporary residence rights (*autorizações de permanência*) to irregular immigrants who had overstayed but had a labour contract and were paying social security.[10] Family reunion was treated as a right in both laws. The granting of temporary rights corresponded, in practice, to regularization – the most sweeping the country has known to this day (184,000 immigrants). This time, Eastern Europeans joined Portuguese-speaking immigrants in acquiring legal status.

A less progressive law was adopted in 2003, but it did not block two additional regularization processes, in 2003 and 2004. In 2007, a more progressive immigration law was approved that is still in effect today (although there have been some revisions and updates over the years). This law simplified procedures and bureaucracy in order to stimulate legal migration; embraced a principle of relative openness, given economic or human rights considerations; and reaffirmed the fight against illegal migration. A notable point was the introduction of a mechanism of "ordinary" regularization, based on the principle of *de facto* integration, such as labour insertion and having children at local schools (Peixoto and Sabino 2009).

In terms of the IESPI framework, the most important changes occurred in the realm of integration policy. During the 1980s, policies targeting immigrants centred mainly on the regulation of flows; since the earlier 1990s, policies have also started to cover mechanisms of integration. The first measure that can be named as such was launched by the Ministry of Education in 1991: the creation of an agency devoted to developing multicultural education programs.

After the mid-1990s, a series of ambitious and coherent policies were launched, and they have remained in place to this day. In 1996, the government created the position of High Commissioner for Immigration and Ethnic Minorities (ACIME) with the objective of promoting immigrants' integration. This was based on five principles:

> first, the positive impact of immigrants on Portuguese society was acknowledged; second, integration was underlined as an inter-ministerial intervention, in other words as a holistic action; third, the promotion of immigrants' integration underlined the consultation and dialogue with entities that represent immigrant communities; fourth, integration meant achieving better life conditions in Portugal with respect to immigrants' identity and culture of origin; and, finally, integration of immigrants also implied equal opportunities and combating racial discrimination. (Oliveira 2012, 295)

In 2002, with the upsurge of immigration to the country (particularly of non-Portuguese speakers), this policy gathered strength when the High Commissioner's cabinet was converted into a High Commission. In 2007 the agency's resources were further reinforced and the designation changed: it was renamed the High Commission for Immigration and Intercultural Dialogue (ACIDI). The intent here was to reinforce cultural dialogue and the involvement of all stakeholders. Finally, in 2014, the name was again changed, this time to High Commission for Migration (ACM). The objective was to combine integration, immigration, asylum, and emigration policies under the same administrative umbrella.

Throughout its existence under left- and right-wing governments, the High Commission has taken a sound approach to immigration issues. To start, it adopted a comprehensive approach. Instead of observing the implications of immigration for home affairs, social security, and labour separately, the agency involved all governmental sectors simultaneously. The principle was that immigration was a complex and multidimensional reality that could only be addressed by a holistic approach (i.e., by "joined-up government") (Oliveira 2012). The High Commission has always reported directly to the Minister of the Presidency and involved representatives from many ministries.

The agency has enacted several policy measures. Since 2004, there has been direct provision of services to immigrants through specialized support centres – the "one-stop-shop approach" (Oliveira, Abranches, and Healy 2009). National and Local Immigrant Support Centres exist in the main cities and municipalities, joining various public services in the same location. The establishment of protocols with civil society organizations (e.g., immigrant associations) has guaranteed the presence of intercultural mediators (many of them immigrants themselves). Notably, these centres provide services to all immigrants, regardless of their legal status. Despite the presence of the Aliens and Borders Service (SEF) – the police for foreigners – on the premises, it is not uncommon for irregular immigrants to visit. This approach to irregular immigration has a longer history. For example, since 2001 access to health care has been granted to both legal and illegal immigrants, and since 2004 all children, regardless of the legal situation of their parents, have the same access to schools. The overarching goal has been to improve immigrants' living conditions, regardless of their legal status.

Some instruments add further coherence to Portugal's integration policies. Since 1998, a Consultative Council for Immigration Affairs (later called Council for Migration) has been in place, joining representatives from different ministries, immigrant associations, other civil society organizations, employers, and trade unions. Also since 2002, an Observatory for Migration has monitored the immigration situation, recruiting academics and researchers to evaluate policy impacts and thus encouraging the development of informed policy. Since 2014 this Observatory has been responsible for publishing annual statistical reports with indicators of immigrant integration (Oliveira and Gomes 2019), in partnership with the National Statistical Institute (INE).

To encourage further coherence, in 2007 and 2010 two Action Plans for Immigrant Integration were launched. They contained a series of specific integration measures (including for welfare), involving several ministries, with the aim of achieving consistency among different areas of intervention (Oliveira 2012). The design of both plans counted on the support of other stakeholders, particularly immigrant associations. In 2015, Portugal launched the Strategic Plan for Migrations 2015–2020, aiming to coordinate both emigration and immigration political guidelines and interventions within the same action plan. In 2019, Portugal launched a National Plan to implement the Global Pact on

Migration, becoming the first country in the world to convert the pact into a national action plan, with political commitments on migration to be implemented by different public institutions.

Over the years, Portugal has approached immigrant integration in very broad terms. The intervention areas have included education, labour, health, housing, welfare, immigrants' participation, religion, anti-discrimination measures, awareness-raising in relation to immigration and cultural diversity, and holistic integration services and measures (for a detailed description, see Oliveira 2012). Most of these measures have directly targeted immigrants and their descendants; others had addressed the mass media and the entire population with a view to framing attitudes toward immigration.

Other areas have been crucial to developing the Portuguese inclusive model. Some pertain to the general legal framework described earlier. Despite the endemic difficulty of controlling migration, opening the possibility that legal status will be granted on certain grounds has been a way of integrating foreigners. Others involve the nationality law: a series of changes, which culminated in the 2006 law, have given way to a relatively liberal stance toward the acquisition of nationality. This liberal approach has been observed ever since (Oliveira, Gomes, and Santos 2017). For example, in 2020, in the midst of the COVID-19 pandemic, a change in the law implied that children born in Portugal of foreign parents would be able to acquire Portuguese citizenship provided that they resided legally in the country for more than one year.

The High Commission has been in place for many years, working with governments of different political orientations, which have accepted the same broad integration principles. Moreover, the immigration and nationality laws have often been approved with a broad political consensus. This has not been achieved without negotiations, compromises, and individual leadership.

Immigrants' Inclusion Outcomes: Achievements and Challenges

In most European countries, some of the most persistent critiques of immigration relate to levels of immigrant welfare dependence and fears of "welfare migration" (Koning 2017). There is evidence that the combination of generous welfare-state protections and widespread perceptions that immigrants rely more than the native-born on welfare can harden anti-immigration attitudes and thereby increase social policy differentiation between immigrants and the native-born (Burgoon and Rooduijn 2020).

In Portugal, as in many other immigration countries, the risk of poverty or social exclusion is higher among foreigners than among nationals (see Figure 10.3). That risk is much greater for non–EU nationals than for EU nationals (for whom the risk is even lower in some years than for Portuguese citizens). The risk of poverty or social exclusion increased during the years

Figure 10.3. People at risk of poverty or social exclusion by broad category of citizenship (population aged 18 and over), 2010 to 2019

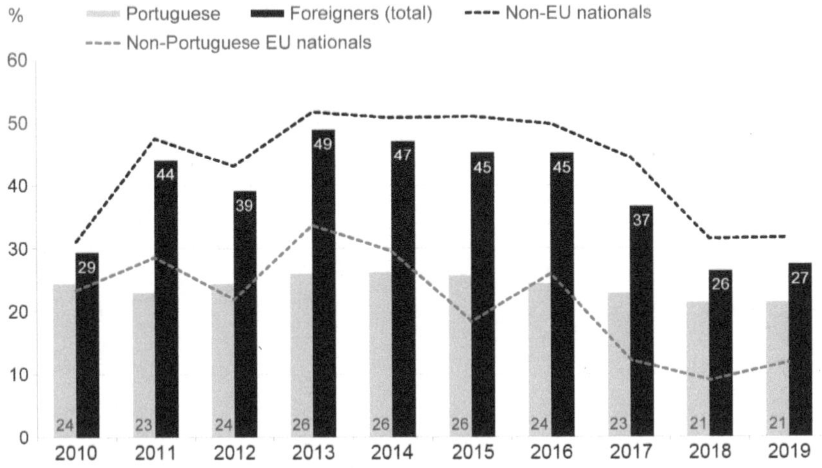

Source: Oliveira and Gomes 2019: 195; using EUROSTAT data.

of the recent financial crisis in Portugal, reaching a peak in 2013 with 52% of non–EU national residents at risk, 34% of EU nationals, and 26% of Portuguese citizens.

Foreign residents' place in the labour market partly explains their higher risk of poverty or social exclusion. Portugal has a segmented labour market (Peixoto 2002). Compared to Portuguese nationals, foreigners (mainly non–EU nationals) are overrepresented in low and unskilled activities (in 2017, 50% of foreign workers versus 39% of national workers), earn lower salaries (foreigners received on average 3% less than nationals in 2017, and 9% less in 2011), and show higher unemployment rates (in 2018 these rates were 12% for foreigners but only 7% for nationals, and in 2013 the gap was as great as 30% versus 16%; see Figure 10.4). Moreover, as analysed in detail by Oliveira and Gomes (2019, 189–90), because immigrants traditionally have lower-income jobs, they tend to receive lower unemployment benefits than the native-born, and for shorter periods of time.

The recent crisis especially affected the economic sectors in which immigrants traditionally are employed (e.g., construction, accommodation, and food service activities), resulting in both a greater increase in unemployment rates among foreign workers and a widening of the gap between foreigners (especially non-EU foreigners) and the country's overall population. This unemployment growth had direct consequences for the welfare system, because it

Figure 10.4. Unemployment rates in Portugal, total population and non-EU foreign residents, 2001 to 2019

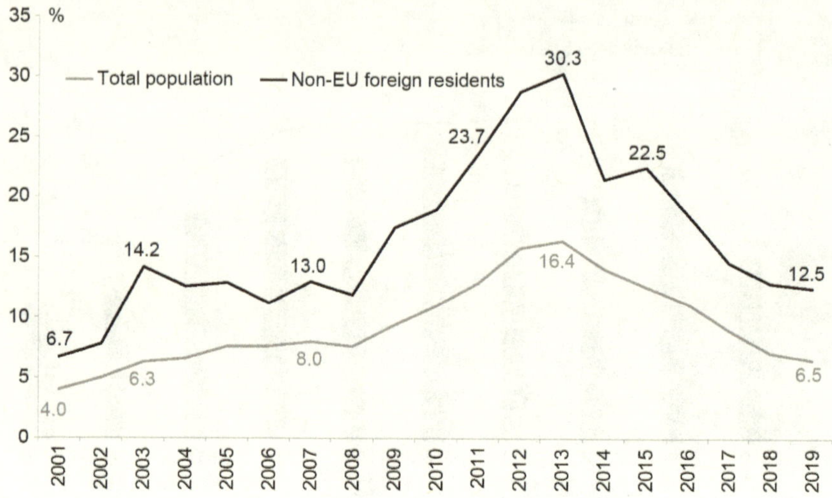

Source: Oliveira and Gomes 2019: 195; using Labour Force Survey – INE.

both reduced foreigners' payments to social security and increased social benefit expenditures.

Regarding other indicators, immigrants also show higher social vulnerability than the native-born. Foreigners describe their own health in more favourable terms than native Portuguese (61% versus 49% in 2019), have fewer work absences due to health problems (20% for foreigners but 26% for native-born Portuguese, in 2019), use fewer social protection subsidies in the event of illness, and face more health risks. Yet they also self-report more unmet needs for medical examination and less use of health services (Oliveira and Gomes 2019, 234–76). Foreign residents are also more likely to reside in overcrowded housing (25% in 2019) than nationals (8%) (Oliveira and Gomes 2019, 224–33).

Because immigrants to Portugal are more vulnerable to challenging economic and social conditions, one might expect them to sometimes be seen as a threat to the welfare state, because they would be expected to rely more on social benefits and to thereby increase social expenditures (Koning 2017). Yet this has never been the case; indeed, the evidence contradicts any suggestion that the overall effect of immigration on the Portuguese welfare state has been negative.

The Portuguese welfare system has always had a very positive financial balance with respect to foreign residents: their payments into social security have consistently been much higher than the social benefits they receive. The

Figure 10.5. Foreign residents' payments to social security, social benefits received, and social security balance with foreign residents in Portugal (in millions euros), 2002 to 2019

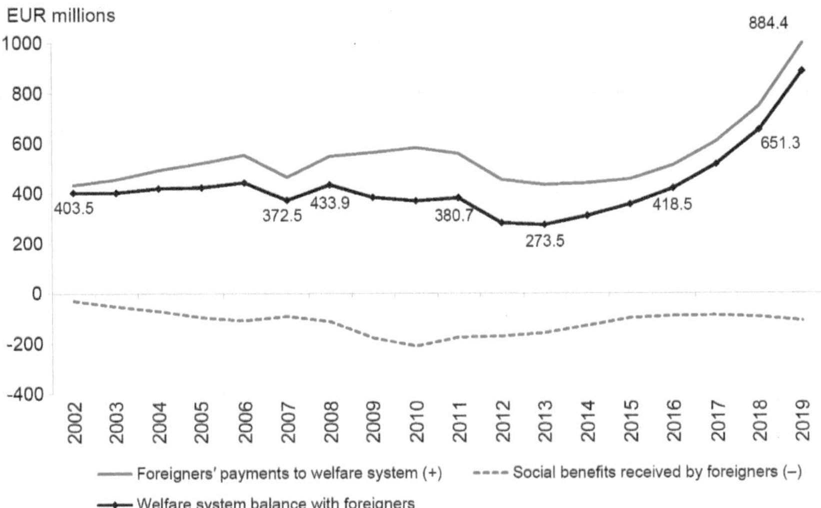

Source: Oliveira and Gomes 2019, 200, using data of the Ministry of Labour, Solidarity and Social Security of Portugal.

aforementioned crisis has somewhat reduced this surplus: foreigners' payments to the welfare state have decreased and the social benefits they receive have increased. Yet even in these years, the balance in the welfare system between expenditure and revenue was positive. In other words, foreigners have lightened the burden on the Portuguese welfare system even during the most difficult times (Figure 10.5).

In 2019, for every 100 foreign residents there were 67 contributors to the Portuguese welfare system (compared to 45 for the total population) and 19 recipients of social benefits (compared to 26 for the total population) (see also in Oliveira and Gomes 2019, 203). Foreign residents in Portugal have also received lower rates of social benefits per total payments to the welfare system than the native-born. Except between 2010 and 2014, the relative importance of social benefits received by foreigners in total payments by the welfare system has been lower than for the country's total population: in 2002, social benefits for foreigners represented only 7% of their payments into the system (9 percentage points lower than for the total population), and the gap between foreigners and Portuguese citizens in this respect was even larger in 2005 (when it was as high as 11 percentage points) (detailed in Oliveira and Gomes 2019, 201–2).

All in all, official data indicate that immigrants to Portugal rely much less than the native-born on the welfare state. The same was shown by Burgoon and Rooduijn (2020), who, using aggregated data from seven waves of the European Social Survey (ESS; between 2002 and 2014), identified Portugal as one of only three countries (along with Italy and Hungary) where migrants are less likely to depend on social benefits than the native-born.

The impacts of the financial crisis in Portugal could have led to welfare retrenchment after 2011; however, the policy responses for alleviating welfare pressure and dependence took another approach: amending some social policies (e.g., reducing assigned values of social benefits, differentiating access to social benefits according to time of payments to social security, increasing the payments to health care, and reducing exceptions); and expanding immigrant-targeted labour market policies (e.g., entrepreneurship support programs, training programs, language courses, tax incentives to foreigner investors). The reduction of social benefits per total payments to social security after 2014 alleviated the welfare pressure, and this allowed Portugal to return to some of the rules and frameworks prior to the Troika intervention, although it continued to face the most negative effects of austerity, specifically regarding access to education and health care (González and Figueiredo 2014, 333).

So if Burgoon and Rooduijn (2020) are correct that "where migrants rely disproportionately more on social benefits, anti-immigration attitudes can more readily awaken opposition to welfare redistribution," we would expect the opposite to occur in Portugal, where immigrants are not a burden on the welfare system and where crises affect all equally in terms of social protection.

Immigration Endorsement in Portugal

Immigration is becoming an increasingly politicized and divisive issue in many host societies (Koning 2019). Growing segments of the electorate and the political elite are showing hostility toward immigrants. In Portugal, although tensions between immigration and welfare sustainability are continuously being monitored (Oliveira and Gomes 2019), and immigration is an increasingly debated topic, a remarkable convergence has taken place since the 1990s among the dominant political parties (Peixoto and Sabino 2009; Oliveira and Carvalhais 2017). This is in stark contrast to the polarization on this issue in other countries (see the other chapters in this volume, in particular chapter 9 on the United States).

The most revealing examples of Portuguese convergence were the votes taken on the citizenship regime (in 2006), and the Immigration Act (since 2007), which saw broad political consensus among the right- and left-wing parties in parliament (Oliveira and Carvalhais 2017). Furthermore, extraordinary regularization programs and expanded integration policies between 1992 and 2004 were carried out under governments of both political orientations, and the current regime of ordinary regularization has been accepted by governments of all political stripes. Action plans for immigrants' integration have been developed and implemented since 2007 by both ends of the political spectrum. All politicians seem to agree on the importance of successfully integrating immigrants and their descendants, and tend to see immigration issues as non-divisive (Oliveira and Carvalhais 2017).

Policy-makers have frequently based their arguments on evidence supporting the positive impacts of inflows. Although it is clear that immigration will not on its own resolve the country's challenges of an aging population and consequent welfare sustainability (Peixoto et al. 2017, 259–60), this argument has often been used in public debate. Many policy-makers have recognized the potential contributions of immigrants to the birth rate, the labour market, and the welfare system. These ideas have been used to promote inclusive policies, including investment in integration. As could be read in the introduction to the National Action Plan for Migrations 2015–2020, written under a centre-right government that was lifting the country out of an economic crisis:

> In recent years the net migration in Portugal no longer compensates the negative birth rates. Thus, Portugal is in a situation of demographic fragility. It is in this context that the migratory phenomenon in Portugal must be analysed and a transversal policy drawn up to account for the evolution of this system. Portugal's immigration policy must reflect the changes that occurred in the migratory profiles. Studies show the positive effect of immigration on public finances and how immigrants are net contributors.[11]

The situation may have changed recently. The extreme right has begun promoting racist attitudes and xenophobia, but this did not bring them any significant electoral gains until 2019. That year, a new party entered the Portuguese parliament that injected stronger anti-immigrant rhetoric into public debate. Paradoxically, this right-wing party entered parliament at the same time that left-wing parties increased the representation of African descendants in parliament. Such results seem to reflect voters' lack of enthusiasm for xenophobic and anti-immigration agendas. Unlike in other European countries, the extreme-right and nationalistic agendas in Portugal have had no influence on policy-making, and such parties have not been part of any coalition government (Oliveira and Carvalhais 2017).

Findings from the ESS confirm this: Table 10.1 compares the attitudes of surveyed people in Portugal according to their political self-placement on a left/right scale. We focus on their attitudes toward migration from poorer countries outside Europe and their perceptions as to whether immigrants are bad or good for the country's economy. Regardless of the political self-identification of respondents in Portugal, the majority believe that the country should allow in some immigrants from poorer non-European countries and that immigration

Table 10.1. Public attitudes on immigration, according to political self-placement on left–right scale,* 2016 and 2018.

	Left	Centre-left	Centre	Centre-right	Right	Total (%) ***
Allow many/few immigrants from poorer countries outside Europe to come and live in Portugal (Round 9, 2018)						
Allow many	19.9	18.7	15.2	17.0	12.2	16.2
Allow some	64.0	63.6	66.6	57.1	53.9	62.3
Allow few	14.0	15.8	14.3	19.0	24.3	16.8
Allow none	2.2	1.9	4.0	6.8	9.6	4.7
Total (N)	136	209	329	147	115	1029
Immigrants bad or good for Portugal economy (Round 9, 2018)**						
Bad for the economy	10.9	12.3	15.0	24.0	18.1	15.3
Not bad nor good	13.0	24.5	23.0	18.7	19.8	20.8
Good for the economy	76.1	63.2	61.9	57.3	62.1	64.0
Total (N)	138	212	339	150	116	1055
When should immigrants obtain rights to social benefits/services in Portugal (Round 8, 2016)						
Immediately on arrival	19.9	19.9	20.1	14.9	17.0	18.9
After a year, whether or not have worked	9.5	7.9	5.5	5.8	5.7	6.8
After worked and paid taxes at least a year	52.7	48.5	52.4	56.5	53.2	52.3
Once they have become a citizen	15.4	19.1	18.4	20.8	19.9	18.5
They should never get the same rights	2.5	4.6	3.7	1.9	4.3	3.5
Total (N)	201	241	403	154	141	1140

Note: * Political placement is in a scale from 0 (left) to 10 (right), being the variable recoded to this analysis in the scale: left (0, 1, 2), centre-left (3, 4), centre (5), centre-right (6,7) and right (8, 9, 10). ** The variable is a scale from 0 (bad) to 10 (good), being recoded to this analysis as "bad for the economy" (0 to 4), "neither bad nor good" (5) and "good for the economy" (6 to 10). *** The total includes refusals and "no answers" to political self-placement.
Source: ESS Rounds 8 and 9.

is good for the economy. More than half the respondents, whatever their political self-identification, agree that Portugal should allow some immigration from poorer countries; however, those who identify as right-wing (53.9%) or centre-right (57.1%) are somewhat less likely to say so than self-identified left (64%) and centre-left (63.6%) respondents. Slight differences are also identified regarding the perception that immigrants are good for the Portuguese economy: such sentiment is more pervasive among left and centre-left respondents

(76.1% and 63.2%) than among those who identify as centre-right (57.3%) and right (62.1%). Similar results were identified on the question of when immigrants should obtain rights to social benefits or services. Around half the respondents of each political self-placement agree that immigrants should obtain such social rights after having worked and paid taxes for at least one year, and here, the differences in response patterns are relatively small. For example, those who self-identify as left, centre-left, and centrist are slightly more likely to say that immigrants should obtain social rights immediately after arrival than those who identify as centre-right and right.

Despite this consensus around immigration and integration policies, the differences among political parties on the granting of social rights to immigrants should not be overlooked. As highlighted earlier in this chapter, the successive changes in the structure of the welfare system have followed the governing parties' overall programs, toward slightly fewer restrictions during centre-left governments and slightly more restrictions during centre-right governments (Peixoto and Sabino 2009, 191).

Nonetheless, many restrictions that have taken place can be understood more as a consequence of the impacts of the economic and financial crisis (which increased unemployment and the number of social beneficiaries) and of demographic aging on the sustainability of the welfare system than as evidence of a tension between immigration and welfare. This is confirmed in the results of the EU's annual standard Eurobarometers: immigration has been shown repeatedly in recent years to be a minor national concern for Portuguese respondents (in the spring of 2019,[12] only 4% viewed immigration as a challenge to the country – fully 13 percentage points lower than the EU average).

In longitudinal surveys, Portuguese respondents express increasingly positive views about the impacts of immigration on Portugal, although a potential conflict arising from perceived competition in the labour market may be latent (Peixoto and Sabino 2009; Oliveira and Gomes 2019). In the ESS, Portuguese respondents have become slightly more positive about the effect of migration over the years: between 2002 and 2018 (and especially in the years of the economic and financial crisis), the percentage who considered that the country had become a better place to live since the arrival of foreigners and who perceived the economy as having improved as a result of immigration increased considerably. Among the factors identified to explain the variances in Portuguese public opinion about immigration over time are age (younger adults more favourable), intensity of contacts with residents of different backgrounds (regular contacts increase sympathy), political positioning (left or centre more favourable), education level, and socio-professional status and income (the higher the above-mentioned factors, the more favourable the attitude) (Peixoto and Sabino 2009, 194).

The ESS also examined attitudes toward redistribution and equal treatment. Data from the ESS 2018 indicate that attitudes in Portugal are highly egalitarian:

the majority of respondents agree or agree strongly that a society is fair "when it takes care of those who are poor and in need, regardless of what they give back" (62.4% and 21.4%, respectively) and "when income and wealth is equally distributed" (51.4% and 26.1%, respectively), and consider it to be "important that people are treated equally and have equal opportunities" (32.3% stated that people who have that opinion are "very much like me" and 33.8% stated they are "like me").

Small variations are observed when we cross-tabulate attitudes toward redistribution and equal treatment with attitudes toward immigration from poorer countries. Generally, respondents mainly agree or agree strongly with redistribution and equal treatment (even among the minority of respondents who believe that Portugal should allow just few or no immigrants from poorer countries outside Europe). Hence, although generally the Portuguese case confirms that individuals with pro-immigration attitudes are more likely to support redistribution and equality in society (similar to the findings of Burgoon and Rooduijn 2020), it is also relevant that even individuals with anti-immigration attitudes are largely supportive of redistribution and equality in society. In other words, in Portugal anti-immigration sentiments do not undermine support for welfare redistribution or equal treatment.[13]

To understand the support for welfare redistribution and equal treatment even among those who show anti-immigration sentiments, one should again consider the particular characteristics of Portugal's migration experience discussed earlier (a comparatively small foreign population, which largely consists of individuals who are culturally aligned and do not depend on social benefits). Moreover, Portugal's social welfare spending is limited, so welfare redistribution and equal treatment do not mean greater generosity of the national welfare system toward immigrants relative to native-born. Thus, as Burgoon and Rooduijn (2020, 22) also concluded, it may be that welfare distribution and equal treatment are undermined by anti-immigration sentiments only "when and where *ex ante* foreign-born stocks, actual social-welfare spending, and migrant dependency on social benefits (relative to native) are all high. Yet such anti-immigration sentiments can actually undergird support for redistribution (compensation effect) where foreign-born stocks, social spending and migrant welfare dependency are low."

Conclusions

The inclusionary trend in Portugal in recent decades is such that it has gone from being the second most exclusionary country in 1990 to the second most inclusionary one in 2010 and 2015 in the IESPI dataset. This is quite remarkable.

This change suggests that welfare politics and responses to immigrant welfare dependence are not straightforward; rather, they are shaped by several determinants that may vary over time and across social contexts. The Portuguese case highlights several such determinants: (1) migratory experience (including not only inflows, but also outflows and diaspora claims, which foster a pro-migrant narrative) and immigrant population characteristics (e.g., labour participation, cultural proximity to the native-born, low social benefit dependency); (2) contextual legacies (in particular the colonial past and the relatively recent democratization), which have framed the definition of the welfare system; (3) legal framework (e.g., constitutional principles, EU guidelines); (4) characteristics of the welfare system (e.g., degree of generosity of welfare state protections, welfare sustainability); (5) country characteristics that make it more or less dependent on immigrants (e.g., demographic structure, labour market, economy, and the effect of crisis); and (6) the general endorsement of immigration (lack of divisive political actors and relatively favourable public opinion).

Nonetheless, these explanatory factors arising from the Portuguese case provide no definitive conclusion on how welfare politics become more inclusionary to immigrants over time. We cannot rule out that similar legacies or migratory experiences will lead to the opposite response (i.e., exclusionary welfare) elsewhere. It would be naive to establish a causal link between context and policies, as similar contexts can lead to contrasting policies (this seems to be confirmed by the mostly inconclusive results in chapter 3, which suggest that explanations for welfare inclusion and exclusion do not apply uniformly to all countries).

The fact is that Portugal has chosen an inclusionary path, both in welfare policies and in integration policies for immigrants, especially since the beginning of this century, with immigration increasing as much as the percentage of the foreign residents in the total population. Still, we cannot rule out the possibility that even after two decades of inclusion, Portugal may one day take an exclusionary turn. The changes in the Portuguese political arena, in particular the arrival in 2019 of a right-wing party in parliament and growing racist and anti-immigration rhetoric in public debate, may create uncertainty about the inclusionary approach, threatening pro-immigration public opinion and the political consensus on immigration and integration.

Over the course of this inclusionary path of almost two decades, Portugal has maintained relatively favourable public opinion and a consensual approach to immigration issues among mainstream political parties. By and large, immigration is acknowledged as a necessity for the country's welfare, demography, and economy. Accessible social and integration policies are thus perceived as investments, and the positive outlook on immigration is maintained even in unfavourable economic and financial moments such as the one observed in Portugal more recently.

The impact of immigrants' cultural and historical affinities on the host country (a consequence of past colonial experience and return migration) should also not be overlooked. Other socio-economic characteristics of the immigrant population in Portugal, including the predominant economic motivation, higher labour market participation, and lower social benefit dependency, should also be considered to explain the Portuguese politics of welfare for immigrants.

Welfare conditions and their legacies also play a role. The Portuguese welfare state is relatively young (around 40 years), and its inclusionary approach is rooted in the 1976 Constitution. Since then, welfare redistribution and equal treatment to all residents (including non-citizens) have been advocated as a touchstone of democracy. This does not mean, however, that the original principles (e.g. equality and non-discrimination) have not been challenged over the years. Those principles have encountered contradictions and vicissitudes, in particular related to demography, public finances, and the economy as a whole.

Additionally, the Portuguese inclusionary welfare principles of equality and non-discrimination in social benefits redistribution should not be mistaken as welfare generosity and high social expenditure. Immigrants, as much as the native-born, are affected by Portugal being among the European countries with the lowest social protection expenditures as a percentage of GDP.

While Portugal stands out for its integration policies for immigrants and inclusionary welfare system, that does not mean immigrants are at lower risk of poverty or have the same social and economic conditions as the native-born. Inequalities persist (e.g., immigrants are more likely to be poor, to be unemployed, to earn low income, to work in risky and dirty jobs, to live in worse housing, and to have less accessibility to public health services than the native-born), and those inequalities have been exacerbated in years of economic crisis.

The Portuguese welfare system aimed to grant public support to all citizens in an era marked by global and national economic difficulties. The national public debt and financial tensions had direct consequences for the effectiveness of social protection for all residents. Today, Portuguese income levels and living standards are still below average for the EU, and levels of poverty and social exclusion are higher. The welfare state is incapable of closing these gaps. If this applies to the whole population, it also applies to immigrants. Although the Portuguese welfare system is fairly inclusionary (as the IESPI underscores), and by constitutional principle is universal to all residents (including foreign residents), that does not mean that in practice it can address all the needs of the native-born *and* immigrants.

NOTES

1 When compared to other member states of the European Union (EU28), Portugal tends to be below the average on social protection expenditure (in percentage of GDP): in 2018, its general government expenditure on social protection represented 17.1% of GDP, compared to an EU28 average of 18.6%.

2 See Appendix Table 10.1 for a chronology of selected social support policies since 1976, with contextual factors.
3 The only exceptions regard political rights.
4 For an overview see Mendes (2011) and Peixoto (2011).
5 This has since been renamed "social insertion income" as a consequence of successive changes starting in 2003.
6 Portugal stands out as one of the most aged countries in Europe, having a negative natural balance since 2007. A recent study by the European Commission (2018) highlighted the impacts of population aging on the evolution of the labour force, pensions, the health system, and welfare, finding that there are serious challenges to the sustainability of European social protection systems.
7 "Troika" was the decision group formed by the European Commission, the European Central Bank, and the International Monetary Fund as the consequence of Cyprus, Greece, Ireland, and Portugal entering risk of insolvency after the world financial crisis of 2008. The financial bailout and associated austerity measures were in force in Portugal between 2011 and 2014.
8 However, these figures must be read cautiously, since they do not count immigrants who have acquired Portuguese citizenship. Over the years, a large proportion of foreigners have become Portuguese (more than half a million since 2006; see Oliveira and Gomes 2019, 277–300).
9 In the 28 EU member states, Portugal is still among the countries with the lowest percentage of foreigners as residents (it is in twentieth position among the EU28). One might hypothesize, therefore, that the relatively small size of the foreign population explains the host society's attitudes toward immigration and support for an inclusionary welfare state.
10 The regularization was justified by this contradiction: immigrants in an irregular situation were residing in the country and paying social security, believing that they would have rights, but they did not due to the absence of legal status as residents; thus, the Portuguese state was earning from these contributions without providing social rights.
11 The tradition of Portugal as an emigration country has also been used in the past. In 2004, Portugal launched a campaign to raise awareness of the positive contributions made by immigrants. The campaign had the motto "We have been for many centuries a country of emigrants. Now it is our turn to welcome, as only we know how, all those immigrants who work together with us to construct a better Portugal." This was associated with images of immigrants to whom was written "Thank you."
12 Data from Standard Eurobarometer 91.
13 Burgoon and Rooduijn (2020, 15) concluded that "respondents harbouring anti-immigration sentiments tend to be less likely to support redistribution than those with more pro-immigration attitudes," though the effect they found was quite modest.

APPENDIX

Appendix Table 10.1. Chronology of selected social support policies, since 1976, with contextual factors

Year	Policy developments	Main content	Contextual factors
1976	Constitution	Equality principle: foreigners and stateless persons residing in Portugal enjoy the same rights and are subject to the same duties as Portuguese citizens	End of dictatorial regime in 1974, which induced several revolutionary social dynamics, aspiring for more economic, political, and social equality. Centre-left government from 1976 till 1978.
1977	First legal act that defined the organic structure of welfare system	Three fundamental principles: integration, decentralization, and participation. Transition to a unified model of social protection. Underscored the universality of the system: universal guarantee of access to health and social security benefits to all residents.	
1979	Ministerial order to create the national health system	Conceived as a free service, although with the possibility of introducing health fees as means of rationalizing demand. Health fees seen as an instrument to encourage users to share national health system costs and avoid unnecessary demand on services.	From 1978 to 1980 several independent governments.
1981	New Immigration Act	Focus on border control and visa issuing. No reference to social rights or duties of the resident.	Centre-right government from 1980 till 1983.
1984	First Social Security Act	Established a budget for the general social security regime funded by the contributions of both employers and employees and the state budget financing of the non-contributory system.	Socialist government (centre-left) from 1983 till 1985.
1985	Creation of the unemployment insurance system	General regime based on both duration (period worked) and amount (workers' contributions and wages).	From 1985 till 1995 centre-right government.
1986	First basic law on education	Generalized and universal access to education	Portugal entrance to EU in 1986.

(*Continued*)

Appendix Table 10.1. Chronology of selected social support policies, since 1976, with contextual factors (*Continued*)

Year	Policy developments	Main content	Contextual factors
1990	Reform of the regimes of social protection	Introduction of contributory fees and penalties for infractions and crimes against the welfare system. Foreign residents' access to social welfare entitlements was reinforced in the 1990s to encourage formal labour market integration and to discourage work in the informal economy or irregular stay in the country. Social assistance benefits are available for foreigners after three years of residence in Portugal.	
1991	Creation of EntreCulturas agency – Ministry of Education	Public agency named "Between Cultures" devoted to developing multicultural education programs.	
1993	Launch of public special programs of social housing in several municipalities	Foreign residents eligible on the same terms as Portuguese nationals.	
1993	New Immigration Act	Focus on border control and visa issuing. No reference to social rights or duties of the resident.	Transition to Schengen agreement of 1995.
1992/1993 & 1996	Immigrants' regularizations	Extraordinary regularizations of illegal immigrants in the country	Since 1993: positive net migration rate.
1995 and following years	Reforms of the social protection regime	Increase of financial strains: introduction of contributory fees and penalties for infractions. General social assistance benefits become available for foreigners after 3 years of residence in Portugal. Unemployment insurance and labour market programs extended to foreigners who paid social security	From 1995 till 2002 centre-left government.

(*Continued*)

Appendix Table 10.1. Chronology of selected social support policies, since 1976, with contextual factors (*Continued*)

Year	Policy developments	Main content	Contextual factors
1996	Creation of the minimum guaranteed income	Ambitious social measure involving both a monetary allowance and a social integration program. All residents benefit from the measure (including immigrants residing legally in the country).	
1996	Creation of the cabinet of the High Commissioner for Immigration and Ethnic Minorities	Immigrants' integration in focus as an inter-ministerial intervention.	
1998	Creation of the Consultative Council for Immigration Affairs	Council presided by the High Commissioner.	
1998	New Immigration Act	Still focused on border control.	
1998	Revisions to welfare entitlements to foreign residents to encourage their formal labour market integration	Access to unemployment insurance and to labour market program support is extended to foreigners who had worked and paid social security for a minimum period of time in the country.	
2000	Second Framework Law on Social Security (centre-left government)	Introduction of efficiency and effectiveness goals, combined with reinforcement of the system's equity (social protection citizenship, contributory social protection and complementary protection modalities). Access to unemployment insurance and to labour market program support was extended to foreigners who had worked and paid social security for a minimum period of time in the country (presently a minimum of six months is required).	

(*Continued*)

Appendix Table 10.1. Chronology of selected social support policies, since 1976, with contextual factors (*Continued*)

Year	Policy developments	Main content	Contextual factors
2001	National health system opened to all foreign residents	All foreigners with legal and illegal residence (in the country for more than 90 days) have the right to health care.	
2002	Third revision of social security law		From 2002 till 2005 centre-right government.
2002	High Commissioner's cabinet converted into High Commission	Political cabinet converted into a public institution focused on immigrants' integration: High Commission for Immigration and Ethnic Minorities. Reports directly to the Minister of the Presidency.	
2003	Minimum guaranteed income revised into "social insertion income"	Restrictions introduced to foreigners. Constitutional Court considers restrictions on immigrants' access unconstitutional (revoked in 2005).	
2003–4	Regularization processes to immigrants	Temporary residence rights to irregular immigrants that overstayed with a labour contract and were paying for the Portuguese welfare system.	
2004	Access to education to all children regardless of legal residence	All children, regardless of the legal situation of their parents, have the same access to mandatory school levels.	
2006	New Citizenship Act	Relatively liberal stance toward acquisition of Portuguese nationality.	From 2005 till 2011 centre-left government.
2007	New Social Security Act	Focus on the sustainability of the system according to the country's aging demographic, adjusting the old-age pension system to the life expectancy.	

(*Continued*)

Appendix Table 10.1. Chronology of selected social support policies, since 1976, with contextual factors (*Continued*)

Year	Policy developments	Main content	Contextual factors
2007	Renamed and reinforced: High Commission for Immigration and Intercultural Dialogue	Reinforcement of the public institution for immigrants' integration. Reinforce several services and programs for immigrants (e.g., national and local centres for immigrants integration since 2004 with a branch of Social Security in the one-stop-shops).	
2007	Portugal launches the first integration action plan for immigrants	Implemented between 2007 and 2009, involving several ministries. Specific measures of immigrants' integration (including on welfare).	Since 2007 Portugal with negative natural balance and positive net migration
2007	New Immigration Act	Progressive immigration law: simplified procedures and bureaucracy. Explicit references to the rights and duties (including social protection) of legal residents.	
2008	Creation of a public capitalization regime	Stimulate beneficiaries to invest in complementary schemes.	Economic and financial crisis starts (2008/2014).
2010		Social assistance benefits become available for foreigners after one year of residence in Portugal.	Decrease of payers to welfare and increase of beneficiaries.
2010	Second integration action plan for immigrants	Implemented between 2010 and 2013, involving several ministries. Specific measures of immigrant integration (including on welfare).	Negative natural balance not compensated by net migration from 2010 to 2018.
2012	Austerity measures: changes in the social protection regime	Reduced the number of beneficiaries of social benefits and the amounts conceded: increase of selectivity and eligibility criteria. Also defined a differentiated treatment on the extension of social benefits according to the nationality of the beneficiary.	From 2011 till 2015 centre-right government. Troika intervention between 2011 and 2014 associated with austerity measures.

(*Continued*)

Appendix Table 10.1. Chronology of selected social support policies, since 1976, with contextual factors (*Continued*)

Year	Policy developments	Main content	Contextual factors
2013	Revisions to Social Security Act	Constitutional court deliberated unconstitutional applicability to foreigners	
2014	High Commission for Migration	Public institution for migrants integration revised: join immigration, asylum and emigration policies in the same administrative body.	
2015	Strategic plan for migrations	Coordinate in the same plan measures for both immigrants, refugees and Portuguese emigrants.	
2015	Revisions to austerity measures		Since the end of 2015 centre-left government.
2018	New social protection framework	New framework to beneficiaries of social protection in case of illness, unemployment, or parenthood.	
2019	National plan to implement the Global Pact on Migration	Portugal is the first country in the world to convert the UN pact into a national action plan with political commitments.	In 2017 Portugal return to positive net migration
2019	New legal framework for foreign contributors to the welfare system	Law approved in parliament that underscores that one year of payments to the welfare system gives the right to foreigners to obtain a residence permit, even if they did not enter the country legally.	

SECTION FOUR

Concluding Reflections

11 Welfare and Immigration: Factoring In the Neoliberal Order

CHRISTIAN JOPPKE

In a classic paper, Gary Freeman (1986, 51) argued that "national welfare states" are "closed systems" that "cannot coexist" with the "free movement of labor," and he feared that too much migration would inevitably lead to the "Americanization of European welfare politics." Thirty-five years later, with global migrations vastly extended, this dark outcome has yet to materialize. Certainly, for half a century now, there has been persistent pressure to make welfare states leaner and meaner. However, migration has *not* been among its major causes. The crisis of the welfare state predates the politicization of migration. This crisis was first addressed as an endogenous problem of too much social democracy endangering the profitability of capitalism (see Crozier, Huntington, and Watanuki 1975). Two decades later, in the context of globalization, not inflation but austerity was the impetus for welfare restructuring, with capital threatening to move abroad if labour continued to be too costly and states becoming "competition states" for attracting footloose money and investment (Genschel and Seelkopf 2015). What Freeman did not anticipate is that the free movement of capital, not of labour, has made the crisis of the welfare state a recurrent topic.

However, Freeman was right to insist on the philosophical incompatibility of welfare and immigration. To try your luck elsewhere (discounting forced migration), whether pushed by misery or pulled by the hope of plenty, is ultimately an individual choice, for it implies severing your ties with the society into which you were born and socialized. Unless it is directly responsible for the misery or lack of opportunity abroad (which, of course, is the claim of critical or postcolonial migration theories), why should another society carry the cost? The developed postwar Western welfare states, in which welfare is conceived as a right, not a charity (see Wilensky 1975, 1), are the historical product of strong national solidarities, a sense of shared fate that is the fruit not just of nationhood but of having shouldered risk and suffered for it, typically in war. To die for your country, as compensation for which the mid-20th-century redistributive "society of equals" needs to be understood (Rosanvallon 2013), is the exact opposite of extracting yourself from your country in search of improvement just for yourself (and your family). Welfare and immigration are principled antagonists at the motivational level, even if institutionalized welfare schemes become decoupled from the motivations that brought them into existence. The world's proverbial immigration country, the United States, has understood this better than others. Its rediscovery of anti-welfarist "deeming" in the 1990s, which holds the migrating individual and her family, but not society and state, responsible for the risks of migration, while seemingly neoliberal, is only a return to its historical roots (see Zolberg 2006, 411).

Welfare and immigration, apparently, are not easily reconciled. Today's "welfare chauvinism" of the populist right only articulates the deep antagonism and tension between the two. Having said that, reality is more mundane. Welfare chauvinism, the impulse of which is not even national but tribal, to limit social benefits to putative co-ethnics, rests on a double error. The first error is to assume that citizenship is an ethnic construct. In reality, as long as naturalization is possible, as it always was even in the German ethnic nationalist past (which some date as recent as pre-1990), citizenship is true to its etymological roots, which is to be civic and to associate strangers. The second error is to assume that the dividing line with respect to welfare as a right could ever be between citizens and all others. In reality, the dividing line is between long-term residents and citizens, on the one hand, and all others, on the other. This results from the territoriality principle of the welfare state, for which legal residence, often in combination with work, is decisive, but not nationality. This principle has been reinforced by the postwar human rights regime, under which rights and protections, except in the political realm, are grounded in "personhood," not citizenship (Soysal 1994). Accordingly, legal residence, not citizenship, is the central hurdle and battle line, also with respect to welfare. Increasingly, access to permanent residence, even in classic immigration countries, is limited to high-skilled immigrants and/or the meeting of formal integration requirements, such as language competence and civic knowledge (both demonstrated by course- and test-taking), and ironically but perfectly logically, welfare dependence may exclude you from its ambit.

The perhaps most interesting finding in this volume is that among rich Western countries there is a high degree of variation in the inclusiveness of their welfare systems for immigrants. Among the top five inclusive countries on the IESPI are Norway, Portugal, and France, while among the top five exclusive countries are Austria, the United States, and the Netherlands (see chapter 2 in this volume). This motley distribution cuts across the known welfare-state typologies, with a certain exception for universalistic welfare state regimes, which (apart from Denmark) are on the inclusive end of the scale. It suggests that randomness and contingency – "contingent political dynamics" as Edward Koning appositely writes (chapter 1 in this volume) – are the main drivers. More importantly perhaps, to be on the inclusive or exclusive side of the IESPI tells you little to nothing about the relative attractiveness of the respective country for immigrants. While Canada ranks among the more inclusive countries on the IESPI, its frozen grounds – rightly or wrongly – are the unquestionable second choice for immigrants to North America, behind the United States, irrespective of the fact that the latter is the second most exclusive country on the index.

A further interesting finding is that "extremely exclusionary measures seem to become less common," even though there may be "new barriers" here and there, and, of course, there is "large cross-national variation" (chapter 1). This communality becomes understandable when we turn our attention to a deliberate blind spot of this volume. How generous a respective welfare system is, and under what conditions it offers or denies services, is unrelated to its relative inclusiveness for immigrants: "The indicators (of the IESPI) do not convey any information about the generosity of the programs in absolute terms" (chapter 2). Fair enough, choices must be made. However, as I would like to suggest in the remainder of my contribution, to throw light on this blind spot may help explain the stated greater inclusiveness of welfare systems over time.

In the neoliberal era, in which market principles have invaded the realm of the state with respect to its internal functioning (in terms of New Public Management, etc.) and the delivery of its services and output, Western welfare systems have changed from being solidarity-based to becoming more contract-based. This is bad for all, because it entails less generosity and more behaviour-based conditionality. However, it is good for immigrants, because nationalist hurdles for access have been lowered or even cleared – in contrast to solidarity, contract is nationality-blind. In his contribution to this volume, Will Kymlicka implicitly acknowledges this when arguing that "immigrants accept the premise that access to welfare programs must be 'earned'" (chapter 12 in this volume), thus invoking (in a surprisingly affirmative way, I think) the lodestar of neoliberal social policy (see Joppke 2021a).

What Kymlicka fails to see is that this condition is recent, and more importantly still: that citizens also are subjected to it. Access to the classic welfare state did not have to be "earned." Instead, it was based on the idea of solidarity and shared fate. Even when dependent on own contributions, as in social insurance, the principle was individual-blind "risk pooling," which required the trust and solidarity that flows from shared nationhood. There is an element of contract in social insurance, which distinguishes it from charity in the 19th-century poor law tradition. But it is subdued by the principle of risk pooling, which operates "regardless of risk profiles" (Garland 2014, 341). The classic welfare state "[made] each person a part of the whole" (Ewald 1986, 390), without attributing responsibility to the individual for a bad outcome. That is the whole point of "liberal nationalism" (though always more an academic than a political movement): to argue that the premise of risk-pooling is to be member of a "community of fate" (Tamir 1993, 19). No nationalism, no welfare state. As another liberal nationalist explicates the nexus, "social justice" requires "trust," which in turn depends on "solidarity," which only the bonds of "nationality" can provide (Miller 1995, 140).

A distinct feature of current welfare schemes, particularly the "active labor market" policies that are part of the IESPI, is the foregrounding of the contractual element. Individual "responsibilization" is the key feature of neoliberal social policy (see Mounk 2017, ch. 2). This is most visible in workfare policies, where unemployment compensation is tied to ever more exacting behavioural requirements. An extreme example is the "claimant commitment" in the UK's Universal Credit policy for the unemployed, which requires its beneficiaries to be actively looking for work, 35 hours per week, and to also accept low-paid work below one's legitimate expectations, or even to do unpaid community work, so as not to fall out of the "habit" of work. The logic of behaviour-conditioned and responsibilizing social policy is to move society, in this case the "structural causes of unemployment" (Veitch 2013: 148), out of the picture. But once society is out, everyone is in. Neoliberal social policy blurs the distinction between citizen and immigrant: both are met with suspicion. As Mark Freedland and Desmond King noted (2003, 471), "welfare contractualism" rests on a pejorative picture of welfare claimants as "shirking" and always ready for "fraud." Now through the negative, immigrants are easily brought on board. The intention is to create a "hostile environment for both migrants and welfare claimants" whereby "the 'illegal' migrant and the 'benefit scrounger' are intimately connected" (Morris 2020, 247). More than classic welfare, neoliberal workfare and kindred social policies "cut across the citizen/non-citizen divide" (Morris 2020, 252).

It is noteworthy that the element of contract is foregrounded not only in neoliberal social policy but also in similarly behaviour-tracking and conditionalizing immigrant integration policies, which are often issued in terms of an explicit "integration contract." As in welfare policy, in integration policy the notion of contract camouflages the vast power asymmetry between individual and state as the principal contract parties. Even though the difference must be acknowledged that no one is forced to immigrate (bracketing, again, the special case of forced migration), to be in need is not something the individual chooses, which makes the injection of contract elements into welfare a tad more devious. The family resemblance of neoliberal social policy and immigrant integration policy is most openly visible in Germany, where the identical slogan *Fördern und Fordern* (Supporting and Demanding) has been applied to both (see Joppke 2021b, 172–81).

In workfare and active labour market policies, the distinction between immigrant and citizen is blurred because *all* are expected to be productive "worker citizens" (Anderson 2015). Of course, this is only one of several types of welfare policy. In addition, there are pensions, health care, housing, and social assistance, to mention only some that have gone into the IESPI. However, workfare best expresses the general direction of neoliberal social policy, which is not to "decommodify" the individual, as had been the purpose of classic welfare (see Esping-Andersen 1990), but on the contrary, to recommodify her, to make her self-providing and not a burden on society, in tandem with a disciplining sense that coercion is the most effective way to get there.

Importantly, workfare, while originating in social insurance–based unemployment compensation, is often empirically fused with tax-based social assistance that seeks to guarantee a minimum level of subsistence. Tax-based and thus redistributive social assistance is a relatively late development in the fully developed welfare state, and it has been one of the few welfare schemes originally tied to nationality, as it flows directly from a sense of national solidarity. In Europe, it had to be opened up to citizens of other member states in order to be compatible with the requirement under EU law not to discriminate on the basis of nationality (see Ferrera 2005). If this was a first attack on its nationalist shell, social assistance's fusion with demoted unemployment compensation is a second. If being in work or looking for work is a condition for receiving minimum benefits, the functionality of this nexus is at odds with a nationality requirement. Germany is a special case because social assistance (*Sozialhilfe*) had never been contingent on citizenship there (though non-citizens applying for it could lose their residence status). However, the alignment between citizens and immigrants in social policy reached a new level with the introduction of workfare. Since the early-millennium Hartz IV labour market reforms, the long-term unemployed, after one year of status-preserving and insurance-based unemployment compensation, while naturally still required to look for work or to accept low-paid work, have been demoted to bare life–preserving social assistance (dubbed *Arbeitslosengeld II*), which is the same low rate for all. And since a benchmark decision by the Federal Constitutional Court in 2012, asylum seekers, even those whose claims have been rejected, are due the same level of social assistance under the Hartz IV rules, based now on the upbeat notion that "human dignity cannot be relativized for purposes of migration policy."[1] The two developments follow different paths: downbeat for the long-term unemployed and upbeat for precarious migrants. But they share a common message: citizens and migrants are to be treated alike, and that at low level.

The tendency of neoliberal social policy to blur the citizen–immigrant distinction, but in a downgrading rather than upgrading direction, takes some of the drama out of a dilemma that all rich immigrant-receiving societies now face: an open immigration policy, including one that is open to the low-skilled, is known to be the most effective means to alleviate global inequality, but may require lesser rights for (certain) migrants, including their exclusion from social benefits and the hope of citizenship. In a provocative work, Martin Ruhs has called this the "numbers v. rights" dilemma (2013). It has been resolved most blatantly in the oil-producing Gulf States, where a vast migrant worker population is categorically excluded from the possibility of permanent residence and citizenship. Branko Milanovic (2019, 147) has argued similarly that "citizenship light," which is his term for "differential rights to different categories of residents," with a "robust and possibly violent enforcement of exits when the time is up," is the only realistic possibility for rich societies to keep their doors open to large numbers of migrants, which in his view – and that of most economists – is good for global wealth production.

The problem is that to ditch the mantra of "equal participation," which is the liberal gold standard for immigrant integration, and which Ruhs, Milanovic, and other economists see as the price to pay for open immigration policies, may come easily in the Gulf States (and in South Korea, which has recently embraced the same illiberal logic); but it comes much less easily in Western states that are beholden to a universalist ethic and human rights principles, and where "equal participation" is the gold standard of immigrant integration. Note that Ruhs himself, after deftly attacking the hypocrisy of the most underratified of all UN human rights treaties, the 1990 Migrant Workers Convention, which protects the rights of "existing migrants" at the cost of "potential future migrants" (Ruhs 2013: 9), quickly loses his nerve: after only four years of temporary residence, he argues, the low-skilled also should have access to permanent residence and the social perks that go along with it; this would be an even lesser requirement than is current practice in most Western states.

Because the assumption that populist radical-right parties "will lead to more exclusion" (chapter 1) is among the lead hypotheses of this volume, it is apposite to return to the issue of welfare chauvinism. Radical-right parties have adjusted to the liberal constraint on crude welfare chauvinism in demanding, not to exclude immigrants from welfare benefits *per se*, but to greatly prolong the residence requirement before welfare can be accessed. The Dutch PVV, for instance, the party of populist maverick Geert Wilders, wants that immigrants must live and work in the Netherlands for ten years before they become eligible for social benefits, which is double the residence time required for legal permanent residence (which, as in most countries, triggers equal treatment on Dutch lands). An analysis of populist party manifestos in four European countries with a notorious radical-right presence – Sweden, the Netherlands, the UK, and Switzerland – found that their restrictive claims are mainly "directed at groups that have no contribution history" (Ennser-Jedenastik 2018, 307), most notably asylum seekers and illegal immigrants. By contrast, social policies that strictly or mainly operate on the basis of prior contributions, such as unemployment compensation or old-age pensions, have seen little or no welfare chauvinist claims. It is true that "Henk and Ingrid are paying for Ali and Fatima" was a notorious line in the 2010 PVV party program. Nevertheless, if Ennser-Jedenastik is right, actually existing welfare chauvinism, despite the posturing, operates less on an ethnic or racial agenda than on a strong sense of "equity" or "reciprocity," that is, according to the notion that not need but merit or desert triggers social rights (Ennser-Jedenastik 2018, 296). This is the principle that benefits must be "earned," which, to reiterate Kymlicka (chapter 12 in this volume), "immigrants themselves seem to accept."

But the idea that the "benefit one receives from the community should be in proportion to one's contribution" (Ennser-Jedenastik 2018, 216), the flip-side of which is self- or personal responsibility, is a neoliberal idea. It constitutes, for instance, the philosophical underpinnings of the UK's Universal Credit policy: "real fairness," said David Cameron, "is about the link between what you put in and what you get out" (in Morris 2018, 7). Fairness, above all, is fairness to the "Taxpayer" (with a capital T), who has replaced the citizenry as the collective subject to which public policy is to be held accountable. This implies a neoliberal nationalism that assembles all "hard-working people," the "aspiration nation," in Cameron's diction. Such a "nation" is indifferent to the citizen–immigrant distinction. When introducing the Universal Credit welfare reform in 2012, Cameron tellingly depicted welfare reform and immigration restriction as "two sides of the same coin," the implication being that a mutually reinforcing "'something for nothing' culture" of freeloaders had to be ended: "Migrants are filling gaps in the labour market left wide open by a welfare system that for years has paid British people not to work … [We] will never control immigration properly until we tackle welfare dependency" (Cameron, qtd. in Morris 2016, 693). Cameron in this way subtly combined anti-welfare with anti-immigrant resentment, with cleverly inverted sets of culprits that neutralize any possible charge of racism or of ethnic favouritism on his part. On the welfare front, the "go-getting migrant" is taken as model for the "lazy Brit" (Anderson 2015, 189), while on the immigration front the "genuine concerns of hard-working people" about "uncontrolled immigration" have to be heard, whereby the native-born are posited above the immigrant.[2] This deliberate confusion, one must suspect, is not without a populist motive: one must consider that Cameron's austerity-mongering welfare reform has been hugely popular in the UK (see Deeming 2015). The bottom line is still that "the experience of citizens and migrants moves closer together" (Morris 2016, 696), because the rights or prerogatives of both are subject to restriction, for the sake of "fairness to the taxpayer" (2016, 703). As Lydia Morris has demonstrated in a lucid analysis of recent British court cases, citizens' rights no longer serve as a "normative yardstick" for immigrants' rights; instead, legal contestation is increasingly in terms of "human rights … for both groups" (2016, 606).

My point is that reflection on the relative inclusiveness or exclusiveness of immigrants as it relates to welfare policies must factor in the general direction these policies are taking in neoliberal societies. Given that neoliberalism endorses a merit-based social order, in which rank and reward should be open equally to all irrespective of an individual's origins or other ascriptive features, immigrants are in principle included on grounds of a strong antidiscrimination norm. But substantive equality, the lodestar of what T.H. Marshall had called social citizenship rights, is not among its priorities, to say the least. While its causes must not be confused with its functions, meaner and leaner welfare, for which the citizen–immigrant distinction is increasingly irrelevant, may be the price to pay for the fundamental openness and the resultant "diversity" to which Western societies have enduringly committed themselves.

NOTES

1 "Menschenwürde ist migrationspolitisch nicht zu relativieren", in: *1 BvL 10/10*, German Federal Constitutional Court decision of 18 July 2012, at para. 95.

2 David Cameron, "The Age of Austerity," speech to the Conservative Party on 26 April 2009, https://conservative-speeches.sayit.mysociety.org/speech/601367.

12 Philosophies of Inclusion and Exclusion

WILL KYMLICKA

The Immigrant Exclusion from Social Programs Index (IESPI) reveals striking diversity in the ways that Western countries include or exclude newcomers from access to the welfare state. While all of these countries are constitutionally committed to upholding core liberal democratic values of freedom, equality, and democracy, they nonetheless reach very different conclusions about what these values permit or require in relation to immigrants' inclusion in the welfare state. A shared commitment to liberal democratic values seems to radically underdetermine policy choices in this area.

For political philosophers, this raises an interesting challenge. Are liberal democratic values really so indeterminate? Or can we argue that some countries are failing to live up to the values enshrined in their constitutions and that they are betraying or violating core principles of liberal democratic justice?

We can think about liberal democratic justice as creating three zones or domains of public policy: some policies are required by principles of justice, some policies are prohibited by principles of justice, and then some policies fall into an intermediate zone, neither required nor prohibited by justice, subject to legitimate democratic discretion, and hence appropriately varying from country to country. Drawing the boundaries of these three zones is contested, not least in relation to issues of immigration. Given the harsh consequences of exclusion, we may be tempted to shrink the zone of discretion, putting tight limits on how and when states can legitimately exclude immigrants from social programs. But on the other hand, we do not want principles of justice to occupy the entire policy space, leaving no room for political communities to exercise collective autonomy regarding the kind of society they want to live in. A robust democracy arguably depends on maintaining a healthy zone of discretion in which policies are responsive to the will of the people, not just mechanically implementing the conclusions of a theory of justice.

We can see this balancing act at work in the related field of access to citizenship for immigrants. In the past, many Western countries had racially discriminatory laws about who could naturalize, precluding Asians for example from becoming citizens. Many Western countries also had blood-based definitions of citizenship that precluded newcomers from ever becoming citizens, no matter how long they had lived in a country. Such policies are now seen as falling outside the bounds of legitimate discretion: justice prohibits racially discriminatory naturalization laws, and justice requires some path for permanent residents to become citizens. This is a dramatic shrinking of the zone of discretion regarding naturalization policy. But this still leaves a very healthy dose of discretion, reflected in varying policies across the Western democracies regarding the required length of residency (e.g., three years or five years or eight years), whether knowledge of the national language is required, whether citizenship tests or citizenship oaths are required, and so on. And very few political philosophers would want to shrink this space entirely. There is a range of legitimate values to consider when making these choices, and it is understandable and appropriate for different political communities to come to different decisions about how to weigh these different values. While political philosophers disagree about the upper and lower bounds of this zone of discretion, most would agree that justice does not pick out one naturalization policy as the only legitimate way for newcomers to become citizens.[1]

Similarly, when reflecting on the IESPI, we might look to political philosophy to help us determine what justice requires in terms of immigrants' access to social programs, what justice prohibits, and what falls into the zone of legitimate discretion. Unfortunately, political philosophers have had very little to say about this. The issue of what justice requires in relation to newcomers' access to welfare programs is a bit of a black hole. This is perhaps because, as Koning notes in the introduction to this volume, the politicization of this issue is relatively recent, and political philosophy has simply not yet caught up to this emerging debate.

But I would argue that this gap reflects a deeper feature of contemporary political philosophy. At its most general, contemporary political philosophy explores what we owe one another by way of justice, but in practice, political philosophers have focused primarily on two specific domains or levels of justice, two different grounds on which we can make claims on one another.

First, there are claims we can make simply on the basis of our shared humanity, often articulated in the language of universal human rights. These claims are grounded in ideas of respect for "human dignity" or respect for "human personhood." To be denied these rights is to be treated as less than fully human, to be dehumanized. These rights are universal and portable – we take them with us as we move around the face of the world – and are not owed solely to our co-citizens. Everyone – whatever their legal or political status as tourists, refugees, or native-born citizens – must be treated in ways that respect our common humanity and human dignity.

Second, there are claims we can make on the basis of our shared membership in a specific society, often articulated in the language of citizenship rights. These claims are grounded in the idea that people who have made their life in a particular society – the long-term, non-transient residents who have set down roots in a society – have a distinctive stake in that society that gives them distinctive rights to share in the fruits of society's scheme of cooperation as well as distinctive responsibilities toward the future of that society. Citizenship rights, in T.H. Marshall's famous and evocative words, rest on "a direct sense of community membership based on loyalty to a civilisation that is a common possession" (Marshall 1950: 96). This metaphor of society as a "common possession" is vague, but we can think of it in terms of bidirectional belonging. If someone is a member of society, then they belong there, but equally society belongs to them, and they become the rightful custodians or stakeholders of this common possession. Membership rights, unlike universal human rights, go through allegiance to some bounded "we." My obligations to you as a fellow member depend on the perception that we share an allegiance – or "loyalty," to use Marshall's word – to a shared society.

For Marshall, social rights – what he called "social citizenship" – is both a cause and an effect of this "direct sense of community membership." Because citizens see one another as sharing an allegiance or attachment to society as a common possession, they feel a distinctive sense of solidarity and shared fate towards one another, above and beyond what we owe to all humans. But the welfare state, once in place, also serves to cement this sense of national loyalty: it orients people toward shared institutions and a shared public life, it visibly embodies and expresses the idea that this shared society is a common possession of its members, and it gives members reasons to feel allegiance and loyalty to it. The welfare state is a tool of societal integration, or, if you prefer, nation-building, and claims to citizenship are therefore claims to equal belonging in this society.

Contemporary political philosophy has explored in depth these two domains or vocabularies of political claims-making. There are bookshelves full of learned discussions of what we humans owe one another in virtue of our shared humanity, and of what citizens owe one another in virtue of their shared membership in society as a common possession. Unfortunately, neither of these registers adequately addresses the specific issues raised by the IESPI. The issue of newcomers' access to social programs falls in between the two. When newcomers claim social benefits, they are typically asking for more than the universal human rights owed to all human beings. As I move across the face of the globe, I carry certain universal rights with me – such as the right not to be tortured or subject to degrading treatment – but these universal portable rights do not typically include access to a country's social welfare programs. And indeed, surveys show that immigrants themselves do not believe that access to welfare programs is an unconditional human right. They stake their claim to access welfare programs not just on their humanity but on some further characteristic or qualification relating to their participation or contribution to society.[2]

So immigrants' claim to access to welfare programs involves more than the register of universal human rights, but at the same time, it involves less than claims to full membership rights. Most immigrants covered by IESPI are not naturalized citizens – that is, they have not gone through the process by which society formally recognizes immigrants as part of the "we" who hold society as a common possession. They are still, formally speaking, foreigners or aliens, and while some may hope to become citizens, others have no desire or intention to naturalize, viewing their stay as temporary. They may have what Ottonelli and Torresi (2012) call "temporary migration projects," seeking only temporary stays in another country in order to advance life-projects that are tied to their country of origin. It is no part of their project to make their life in another country, or to become members or citizens of another country: they simply want to temporarily work or learn in a foreign country in order to advance their life-projects back home.[3]

So immigrants' claims to access to welfare programs rest on something more than common humanity but less than full membership. This is underexplored territory in political philosophy. In fact, we don't even have a clear term or label for this sort of claims-making. Immigrants are making claims to welfare programs not as human beings or as citizens, but as what? Workers? Taxpayers? Residents? Denizens? Guests?[4]

It is interesting to speculate about why political philosophy has been so reluctant to theorize (or even to name) this domain of claims-making. One possible answer is that political philosophers – at least in the contemporary Western world – are deeply committed to ideals of equality and so are comfortable with registers of claims-making that are fundamentally egalitarian. Both universal human rights and citizenship rights are egalitarian in this sense: human rights appeal to the idea of equal moral status of all human beings, while citizenship rights appeal to the idea of equal political status, that is, equality in our status as members of the *demos* that governs our shared society. The moral vocabulary for immigrants claiming access to the welfare state seems harder to frame in these egalitarian terms. It seems to be a kind of semi-citizenship or partial citizenship status, a kind of junior or inferior level of membership – a claim to some but not all of the rights and responsibilities that flow from participating in a shared society.[5] Contemporary political philosophers are uncomfortable with such inegalitarian second-class statuses and so tend to simply ignore them and focus instead on claims-making tied to equal humanity or to equal citizenship.[6]

Insofar as political philosophers have discussed these issues, therefore, they have tended to do so indirectly, through the filters of either human rights or citizenship rights, asking what sorts of policies are required or prohibited by our ideals of human rights and/or equal citizenship. First, then, we might ask whether any of the forms of exclusion captured by the IESPI can plausibly be categorized as violations of universal human rights. For example, it is widely accepted that children have a human right to an education, regardless of the legal status of the parents. So any welfare exclusion policy that denied access to education to the children of refugees or irregular immigrants would be a violation of human rights. Similarly, international human rights law prohibits forced labour or degrading working conditions, so any policy that rendered immigrants vulnerable to coercion or abuse would be a violation of human rights.[7] There is also a human right to emergency health care, and a human right not to have families broken up.

These are all important constraints, and Western countries need to do a better job upholding and enforcing these human rights requirements. But in principle at least, most Western countries accept these human rights norms, and it is not clear that the specific policies tracked by the IESPI violate them. Even the most exclusionary country in the IESPI – Austria – does not obviously violate these fundamental human rights. We might think it is unduly harsh of Austria to restrict access to housing benefits to those immigrants who have lived in the country for five years. But as I noted earlier, immigrants themselves seem to accept that such benefits must be "earned," and while we can debate about what are legitimate or reasonable criteria for earning housing benefits, for example, this takes us outside the domain of unconditional human rights arguments.

Second, we might ask how the forms of exclusion captured by the IESPI affect the ideal of equal citizenship. Indeed, I would argue that ideals of citizenship are always hovering in the background of these debates, but in two fundamentally different ways, depending on whether we view migrants primarily as future citizens in their new country of residence or as temporarily absent citizens of their country of origin. Citizenship matters in both cases, but in different ways.

Consider first those immigrants who are long-term residents and have made their life in a different country than where they were born. As I noted earlier, political philosophers today almost unanimously agree that such immigrants must have a path to citizenship. Citizenship cannot be restricted to those with a particular blood or ancestry and must instead be available to all who are long-term residents. If so, then a crucial question is whether immigrants have an escalator to citizenship: is there a reliable and accessible route to becoming recognized and accepted as one of the "we"?

From this perspective, a central question is not only the extent to which immigrants are excluded from social programs but also whether these exclusions operate to impede the escalator to equal citizenship. This could happen in at least two different ways. First, these exclusions could trap people in a second-class status, unable to get on the escalator to citizenship (or even worse, leaving them at risk of slipping backwards into a more precarious status).[8] Without adequate economic support, health care, and educational or economic opportunities, they may never be able to pass the thresholds needed to become citizens. Second, welfare exclusions might reflect and perpetuate the stigmatizing perception of immigrants as lazy or dishonest or incompetent or unruly, and hence undeserving of membership rights. If so, then even those immigrants who are able to naturalize may discover that they are not in fact accepted by their co-citizens as truly belonging (de Waal 2020). Where welfare exclusions have these effects, they operate to undermine the fundamental principle that long-term residents should have reliable access to equal citizenship.

Which forms of welfare exclusion might have these citizenship-corroding effects? This would require a separate investigation in its own right, but we might start by comparing IESPI rankings with some of the existing citizenship indexes – such as Sara Goodman's Civic Integration Index (CIVIX) (Goodman 2014). She measures the extent to which different countries facilitate or impede the ability of immigrants to become members of society and ranks them on a continuum from "enabling" to "prohibitive." If we compare the top and bottom of the IESPI and CIVIX rankings, unsurprisingly, we see a lot of overlap (Figure 12.1).[9] Those countries that are most inclusionary regarding access to social programs also tend to be most enabling of access to citizenship (e.g., Portugal, Sweden). Conversely, those countries that are most exclusionary regarding social rights also tend to be quite prohibitive in terms of access to citizenship (e.g, Austria and the Netherlands).

However, there is interesting variation in the middle of the IESPI. Countries with similar mid-level scores in the IESPI have wildly variable scores on the CIVIX. Consider the four countries highlighted by the shaded area in Figure 12.1, in the middle of the IESPI. Germany and Finland have a similar score on the IESPI, but on the CIVIX, Germany ranks as one of the more prohibitive states whereas Finland is one of the more enabling. Similarly, Denmark and Belgium score similarly on the IESPI, but Denmark is in fact the most prohibitive of all EU-15 countries on the CIVIX, whereas Belgium is one of the most enabling.

This suggests that similar IESPI scores can mean quite different things in different countries, at least in terms of their impact on fundamental liberal democratic principles of equal citizenship. Two countries may have similar IESPI scores in the 30s or 40s, but the exclusions may not be equally "sticky." In countries with more prohibitive CIVIX scores, not only are immigrants excluded from certain social rights, they cannot easily move out of that status into full citizenship either. In other countries, immigrants who are currently excluded from social rights are nonetheless on a secure escalator out of that status to citizenship.

The fact that immigrants in some countries can quickly move out of a particular immigration status does not mean of course that the exclusions from

Figure 12.1. Relationship between IESPI 2015 (*x*-axis) and CIVIX 2014 (*y*-axis, taken from Goodman 2014)

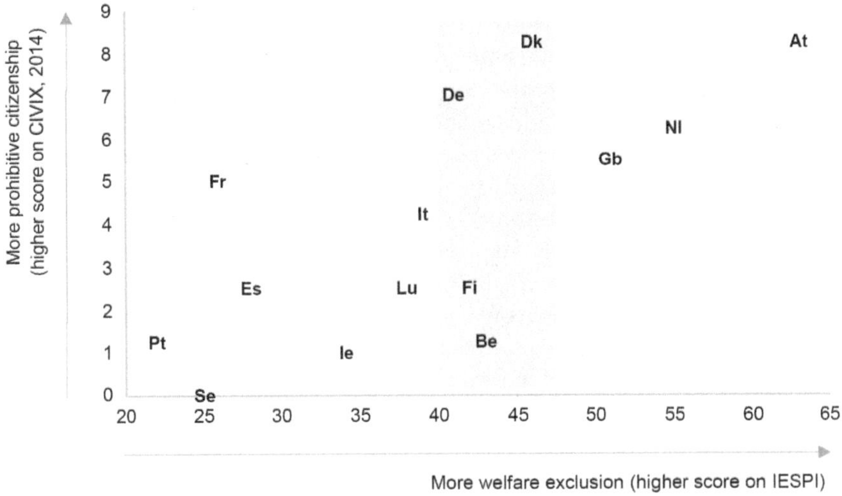

welfare benefits attached to that status are benign, or fair, or reasonable. As I said earlier, we don't in fact have well-developed theories to evaluate the justice of these exclusions tied to immigration statuses. But if immigrants have escalators out of the status that carries exclusions, then these exclusions are less likely to generate "durable inequalities" in Tilly's sense (Tilly 1998).

Moreover, this is also likely to affect how the policies are perceived, both by immigrants and the native-born. Countries that enable access to citizenship are saying to immigrants: "we view you as future citizens and look forward to you becoming one of us." In this context, immigrants are less likely to view temporary exclusions from social programs as stigmatizing or as evidence that the larger society does not care about their needs or wishes them to leave the country. Temporary exclusions from social programs may reflect some mixture of cost concerns as well as beliefs about what are appropriate incentives to encourage integration, and/or beliefs about how the costs of integration should be shared between immigrants and the larger society. But if there is an escalator to citizenship, then the trajectory is clear: immigrants are seen as future citizens, and their current status is a temporary proto-citizenship.

By contrast, in countries that have prohibitive approaches to citizenship, it is natural for immigrants to interpret exclusions from social programs as part and parcel of the same overall exclusionary philosophy. If the state is saying, "We don't see you as future citizens," then it is natural to interpret exclusions from social programs as stigmatizing, as a further way to mark their fundamental and unalterable otherness. While Denmark and Belgium have similar IESPI scores, how this exclusion is experienced is surely very different in the two countries.

Put another way, whether exclusions tied to a category are likely to be stigmatizing – whether they mark the person in enduring and damaging ways – depends on the stickiness of the category. Where people can quickly move out of a status, and are given ladders and escalators out of that status, exclusions are more likely to be experienced as temporary inconveniences or burdens, not assaults on their sense of dignity or self-respect or belonging.

We can see this dynamic at work, I think, in the related field of access to local voting rights for immigrants. Some countries provide local voting rights to immigrants, others do not. We might think that immigrants who live in countries that provide local voting rights will feel more welcome and more at home, and that immigrants living in countries that deny local voting rights will feel excluded and stigmatized. But in fact, the meaning of local voting rights depends on how those rights relate to broader philosophies of inclusion. Many of the countries that provide local voting rights – such as Denmark and Switzerland – make it virtually impossible for immigrants to become citizens. Immigrants are therefore stuck in a subordinate status, and they experience this as exclusionary. By contrast, some of those countries which do not grant local voting rights – such as Canada – encourage immigrants to naturalize quickly and thereby acquire full and equal voting rights. All of the evidence suggests that immigrants to Canada care more about the escalator to citizenship than about whether they have local voting rights at the first step of the escalator. The lack of local voting rights does not lead them to feel stigmatized or discriminated against or unwelcome; on the contrary, they feel a sense of belonging because they see themselves on a secure ladder to equal citizenship (Bloemraad 2006).

Of course we might think that social rights are of more tangible immediate benefit to immigrants than local voting rights and that hopes and beliefs about future trajectories toward citizenship cannot take the place of meeting material needs now. As I said earlier, the fact that immigrants in some countries can quickly move out of a particular immigration status does not mean that the exclusions from welfare benefits attached to that status are benign, or fair, or reasonable. But from a normative perspective, durable inequalities matter more than temporary ones, and stigmatizing inequalities matter more than non-stigmatizing ones. And these differences only become visible when we step back and situate IESPI scores in relation to broader trajectories of "citizenization" (Tully 2001), which are themselves tied to broader philosophies of inclusion.[10]

So insofar as we are focusing on the case of permanently settled long-term immigrants, political philosophers are likely to be concerned first and foremost with their path to citizenship and will evaluate IESPI exclusions at least in part on whether they interfere with that path. If long-settled immigrants are penalized by their lack of citizenship status, then political philosophers are likely to argue that the ultimate remedy is to facilitate citizenship. This should not be surprising, since contemporary political philosophy, at least its Western liberal democratic strand, is fundamentally "citizenist" (Bloom 2017). The field of political philosophy has often understood its fundamental task and historical calling as a matter of turning subjects into citizens.[11]

But of course not all immigrants want to settle permanently or make a life in their new country. As I noted earlier, many immigrants have "temporary migration projects" that are tied to their country of origin. They have made a life in their country of origin, and they seek temporary access to another country simply in order to advance life-projects that are located back in their home country. In this case, we cannot argue that temporary exclusions from social programs are somehow offset by escalators to citizenship. For temporary migrants, exclusions cannot be seen as a kind of down payment on future citizenship; they are just pure loss.

How then should we think about the justice of IESPI exclusions for those who do not want to stay and become citizens? Political philosophy has few resources for thinking about this. Obviously, as I stated earlier, there are the constraints set by universal human rights, but what more or what else is required by justice? Where the duration of stay is very brief – say, someone spends a month in the country as an intern or au pair or tourist, or on a family visit or academic sabbatical – we might think this is too temporary or transient to generate claims to social programs (beyond the requirements of universal human rights). But if someone's temporary migration projects involves, say, two years of full-time labour and paying taxes, they clearly have legitimate claims to access social programs.

But precisely because they are not future citizens, it is not clear that the most appropriate form of access is inclusion in existing general programs. As I noted earlier, social programs have always had an integrative function. They are not just about meeting the humanitarian needs of abstract or disconnected individuals; rather, they are about orienting people toward a shared society and thereby creating that "direct sense of community membership" (Marshall 1963, 96) that underpins the welfare state. This is reflected not only in rules about who qualifies for social programs but also in how programs are administered, often focusing on ideas of social inclusion, civic literacy, language skills, and participation, all defined with reference to the national society. Social policies are intended to enable people to feel at home in society and to make a home in society, to feel a sense of belonging to the society and of the society belonging to them.

Those who have temporary migration projects have little or no interest in this integrative aspect of the welfare state. They do not want to make a home here, and they often resent any implication that they should devote their time and energy to mastering the sort of civic literacy needed to do so. In Ottonelli and Toressi's words,

> temporary migrants display reduced engagement with the host society at the level of civic, political and social participation. They do not participate in the political life of the receiving country and do not entertain plans to advance their social and economic conditions in the host society. Socially, they invest little time in making themselves at home in the new country, and there is little chance or willingness on the part of these migrants to build stable relationships. This has been described as an "apnea strategy": the hard toil, little leisure, and very reduced social space of these workers is part of an investment plan that postpones the fulfilment of the most fundamental dimensions of emotional, social and civic life. These paths, not being aimed at permanent settlement, generally do not and cannot lead to happy endings as a matter of social integration … in the receiving countries. (Ottonelli and Toressi 2012, 210)

It is not obvious, therefore, that temporary migrants want or need "inclusion" in those social programs that have been designed to promote social integration. Ottonelli and Toressi suggest instead that we should think about special policies designed specifically for their status, which start from the premise that their citizenship and social integration in fact lies elsewhere:

> Various measures could be put in place in order to achieve the distinctive goals of temporary migrants and make their rights effective: being able not only to change jobs but also to return whenever they wish would provide temporary migrants guarantees that conventional social rights, aimed toward local workers, might be unable to provide; temporary immigrants could be allowed to divert part of their income taxes and social security payments to private health insurance or other forms of social guarantee to be used in their home countries; pension and social security benefit portability could be granted; programs could be developed to further the establishment of the returnees' private business in the sending countries; special funds could be created for voluntary repatriation; forms of savings and money transfers could be established that are specifically devoted to investments back in countries of origin; finally, other legal provisions could be arranged to make frequent visits to, and long-distance interactions with, home countries possible, in order to keep ties to the sending society alive. (Ottonelli and Toressi 2012, 220)

It's an interesting question how policies designed along these lines would affect IESPI scores.[12] In some respects, they can be seen as countering the exclusion of migrants from existing social programs, but in other respects these proposals arguably involve a greater degree of exclusion from, or at least an opting out of, general social programs. Perhaps, for at least some purposes, justice for the truly temporary migrants lies in disengaging from the embrace of the national welfare state, not further inclusion in it.

As Ottonelli and Toressi acknowledge, we would need to make sure that any such disengagement would not leave migrants in a vulnerable and precarious situation. But in their view, when thinking about justice for those with temporary migration projects, we need to take seriously the idea that the life they've made is back in their sending society, and not adopt a model of "inclusion" that would implicitly or explicitly try to reorient them toward our society.

Conclusion

As we've seen, contemporary political philosophy does not provide us with clear or well-developed guidelines for evaluating the sorts of policies captured in the IESPI. Political philosophers focus overwhelmingly on either the logic of universal human rights or the logic of equal citizenship, and neither provides the tools we need to evaluate IESPI exclusions. This is a significant shortcoming of the field.

However, I think these disciplinary preoccupations with universal human rights and equal citizenship can, in their own way, shed interesting light on how to think about these exclusions. There is a broad consensus that any such policies must uphold universal human rights, and this sets an important lower limit on what is permissible. Beyond that, however, how political philosophers respond to IESPI exclusions is likely to be shaped by how these exclusions relate to the broader disciplinary focus on citizen-making. Since the field defines itself, at least in part, by the imperative of turning subjects into citizens, political philosophers will want to know how IESPI exclusions either enable or erode the theory and practice of equal citizenship. And this in turn is likely to focus our attention on the difference between long-settled immigrants and those with temporary migration projects. The former should be on a secure escalator to citizenship; the latter hold their citizenship elsewhere. In both cases, some of the exclusions captured in the IESPI are likely to be unjust and corrosive. But not all. Long-settled immigrants may not object to all IESPI exclusions if they can quickly transition out of that status into citizenship. And temporary migrants may not object to all IESPI exclusions if the resulting disengagement enables them to more effectively pursue their life-projects in their country of origin. In both cases, assessing the exclusions attached to a particular status requires attending to the trajectories by which individuals enter and exit that status.

Of course, this presupposes that we have some way of distinguishing temporary from permanent immigrants, and many people have said that what distinguishes our new "era of mobility" from the older "era of migration" is precisely that this distinction is breaking down. I don't have space to address that worry here, except to simply assert that any plausible conception of democratic citizenship and of the welfare state requires distinguishing long-term members from those who are simply passing through. If that distinction is indeed no longer one we can draw, then it is not just IESPI policies that will need to be rethought, but our entire architecture of democratic politics.[13]

NOTES

1 For a good overview of these debates, see Joppke and Bauböck (2010).
2 For evidence that immigrants accept the premise that access to welfare programs must be "earned," not claimed simply as unconditional human rights, see Osipovič (2015), Reeskens and Van Oorschot (2015), and Kremer (2016). The evidence also suggests that immigrants accept the premise that access to citizenship must be earned (Midtbøen, Brochmann, and Erdal 2020).
3 Ottonelli and Torresi define temporary migration projects this way: "Temporary migration projects consist in migrating to a foreign country for a limited span of time, with the purpose of sending money home or acquiring knowledge and expertise needed to advance specific aims once back in one's country (children's education, building a house, supporting a family, starting a new business activity, etc.). The decision to migrate is usually motivated by greater economic opportunity in the host country, but it specifically aims to take advantage of this differential to achieve personal ends in the society of origin; the aim is never to create a whole new life in the host society … Temporary migration means bracketing many essential components of one's life while living and working in the host society in order to advance an overall life plan and long-term goals that will be realized at another time and in a different social space" (Ottonelli and Torresi 2012, 208-9).
4 For a brief period in the 1990s, there was speculation that the category of "citizen" might fade into insignificance, given the tendency across the West to grant an increasing number of rights – including social rights – to long-term residents. Citizenship, it was speculated, might become a purely honorific status, irrelevant to the actual dynamics of claims-making in society (see, most famously, Soysal 1994). And indeed, it remains true that residence not citizenship is the predominant criterion for access to social benefits (Koning forthcoming). Nonetheless, citizenship has not faded into political significance. On the contrary, we have seen the return of "citizenship with a vengeance" (Dauvergne 2007), tied in part to post-9/11 preoccupations with security and social cohesion. In any event, political philosophy's commitment to citizenship is very deep, for reasons I discuss below.
5 On partial citizenship, see Baubock 2011; Spinner-Halev 1999.
6 On the failure of political theorists to acknowledge and address the enduring realities of what she calls "semi-citizenship," see Cohen 2009.

7 It is a long-standing criticism of Canada's foreign temporary worker programs that they leave migrant workers vulnerable to human rights abuses from their employers (e.g., Khan 2009).

8 In some cases, this is the result of regulations that deny citizenship or revoke residence permits on the basis of welfare uptake, as measured by indicator SA3 on the IESPI. But in other cases, even where immigrants may not be formally barred from ascending the escalator to citizenship, they may not have the resources or support needed to take that step.

9 Indeed, the correlation between the two policy indexes in Figure 12.1 is as high as 0.69.

10 I've focused so far on how IESPI scores relate to access to citizenship, since citizenship is so central to contemporary political theories of justice, but we could make the same point by exploring the stickiness of other immigration statuses prior to naturalization. In many countries, a crucial step in avoiding precarity is to gain the status of "permanent residence," even if not yet a naturalized citizen. So here too we can ask not only what exclusions attach to the status of being a temporary resident, but also whether that status is sticky or whether immigrants have an escalator to a more secure permanent residence status. And this too would reveal important – and morally significant – variations between countries with similar IESPI scores. See Appendix Figure 12.1, which shows considerable variation in the mid-range of IESPI scores in terms of ease of accessing permanent residence. The ability to move out of a status can be as important, from the perspective of justice, as the particular mix of benefits/burdens tied to that status.

11 Of course, there are dissenting voices – Linda Bosniak famously proposed "giving up on citizenship as an aspirational project altogether" (1998), and Tendayi Bloom (2017) has more recently argued for at least supplementing "citizenism" with what she calls "noncitizenism." But they both note that their proposals run headlong into the deep and abiding commitment of liberal political theory to citizen-making.

12 It is worth noting that the IESPI scores policies that allow temporary migrants to opt out of insurance programs as inclusionary (see CUB3, CP1). It also defines portability of benefits as inclusionary (see TPP4, CP2). In these respects, "inclusionary" in the IESPI sense does not necessarily mean "integrative" in the Marshallian sense.

13 For further reflections on this, see Kymlicka 2015, 2017.

APPENDIX

Appendix Figure 12.1. Relationship between IESPI 2015 (*x*-axis) and access to permanent residence (*y*-axis, MIPEX 2014, inverted)

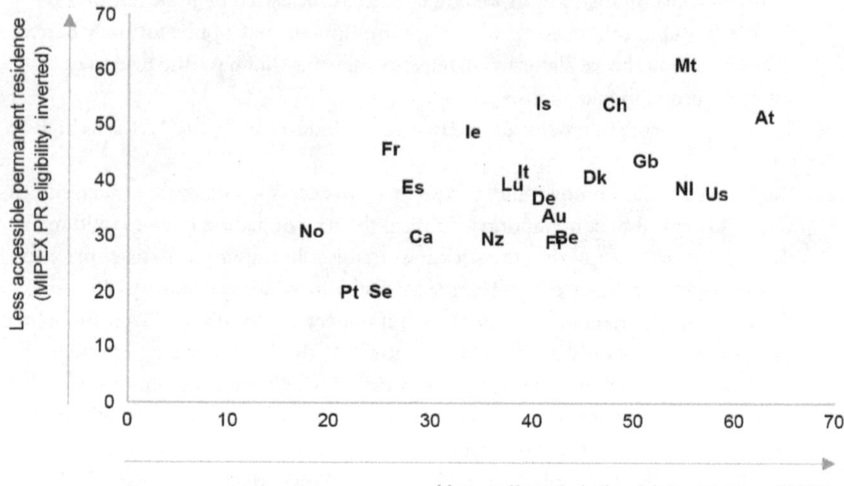

13 Conclusions: Is an Inclusive Multicultural Welfare State a Feasible Project?

KEITH G. BANTING

Is a robust welfare state still a feasible project?[1] In particular, is a robust and *inclusive* welfare state feasible given contemporary patterns of immigration and the ethnic diversity they bring in their wake? In the first decades of the twenty-first century, scholarly and public discourse has become increasingly pessimistic about the answers to these questions. This concluding chapter pulls together the evidence gathered in this volume, focusing on the seven hypotheses set out in the introduction. The main conclusion is that, in addition to providing an impressive analysis of the politics of exclusion, this volume provides the basis for greater optimism about the prospects for an inclusive welfare state in the twenty-first century.

Anxiety about the impact of immigration-induced diversity on the redistributive state first emerged in the early decades of this century. Redistribution, analysts reasoned, rests on the foundation of a shared sense of community. Growing ethnic, racial, and religious diversity, however, seemed likely to weaken the bonds that tie. A substantial literature has investigated the effects of diversity on support for the welfare state, but with mixed results. Some studies have found a negative impact, but just as many studies have found no impact or even positive effects. In addition, effects – whether positive or negative – tend to be small. In retrospect, it seems strange to assume that citizens would readily abandon major social programs they value in their daily lives. Citizens have not turned their backs on the welfare state *en masse*.

The second version of the debate, which has followed quickly on the first, holds that although citizens of contemporary democracies remain committed to major social programs, the inclusion of newcomers and minorities in the benefits of the welfare state is problematic. In this version, the underlying sense of a shared community continues to provide support for the welfare state, but it also establishes sharp boundaries that define who is included and who is excluded from social protection. The welfare state supports members of the historic community, thereby protecting "us," rather than newcomers, who are seen as "strangers" and not part of "us." In this view, a redistributive state may remain a feasible political project, but an inclusive redistributive state is not.

Is such pessimism warranted? The chapters in this volume shed new light on this central issue of our time. This chapter pulls together the evidence presented in the substantive chapters and reflects on its implications for the feasibility of an inclusive welfare state as a societal goal. As we shall see, the evidence gathered here provides the basis for greater optimism about the prospects before us.

The organization of the chapter follows the logic of the theoretical framework set out in chapter 1, and the discussion pays particular attention to the seven hypotheses set out there. The first section summarizes the pattern of exclusion revealed by the IESPI. The second section turns to the *drivers* of welfare exclusion, drawing together the themes that emerge across the substantive chapters. The third section focuses on the *consequences* of welfare exclusion, summarizing the conclusions that emerge across the chapters regarding levels of xenophobia in society, immigrant integration, and the fiscal position of the state. The final section then steps back and reflects on the implications of the evidence here for the prospects for an inclusive welfare state as a societal goal.

Inclusion and Exclusion: The Trajectory

Political discourse might leave the impression that the arc of history is moving against the inclusion of immigrants and that welfare chauvinism is increasingly pervasive throughout democratic societies. Until recently, there has been no instrument with which to test such assumptions by providing a comprehensive view of the extent of exclusion over time. Hence the importance of the IESPI, which provides consistent evidence on the extent to which 22 democratic countries differentiate between immigrants and native-born citizens in granting access to social programs. The result is a much more nuanced description of the pattern and trajectory.

Chapter 2 sets out three major patterns (see Figures 2.2–2.4). First, welfare chauvinism is not a new phenomenon. In most countries covered by the index, the level of immigrant welfare exclusion was greater in 1990 than in 2015. Some countries introduced both inclusionary and exclusionary measures over that period, but only four countries – Australia, the Netherlands, the UK, and the US – have become significantly more exclusionary overall during the last 25 years. Second, there is dramatic and persistent variation in the levels of welfare exclusion across countries. Third, the level of exclusion varies significantly across types of programs. Most countries have gradually extended access to health care and active labour market programs to immigrants, but access to social assistance is clearly controversial, with most countries restricting access over time, dramatically in some cases.

The Drivers of Inclusion/Exclusion

Understanding the factors that drive the inclusion and exclusion of immigrants in the welfare state is an urgent task. The introduction to this volume sets out four hypotheses about the drivers, which we consider here.

The characteristics of the welfare state regime. Following the insights of institutionalist theory, the first hypothesis posits that the structure of a welfare regime shapes the entitlements of immigrants. The expectation is that universal welfare systems will be more inclusionary because they encourage solidarity between taxpayers and those who receive benefits. In contrast, immigrants are likely to fare less well in conservative welfare states that rely heavily on contributory insurance programs, as these create informal barriers for immigrants who have limited work experience in the country. Finally, liberal welfare states rely more heavily on selective programs, which can underscore immigrants' reliance on support, provoking stronger political backlash.

What does the evidence presented in this volume say? In chapter 3, Friederike Römer and Liv Bjerre provide a quantitative analysis of this debate. They start from the intuition that "it seems obvious that immigrants' welfare access will be affected by the institutional and normative frame" provided by the overall generosity of the welfare state. To test the idea, they analyse the relationship between the generosity of the welfare state and the level of immigrant exclusion, and their results come down firmly on the importance of the welfare state regime. The size of the welfare state, as measured by spending on welfare as a proportion of GDP, has a robust, sizable, and significant positive effect on immigrants' access to social benefits.

Beyond spending levels, does the design of the welfare state matter?[2] The country case studies in this volume make clear that it does. The cases include classic examples of each of Esping-Andersen's regime types: social democratic, conservative, and liberal. Norway built a social democratic welfare state, and Grete Brochmann argues in chapter 8 that its egalitarian and universal nature resulted "almost naturally in an inclusionary approach to immigrant entitlements." Her emphasis on path dependency goes even deeper: she holds that "systematic necessities" of the Norwegian model shaped the adaptations that have occurred. The universal welfare state was built on the foundation of a high rate of employment, and growing numbers of low-skilled, unemployed refugees place a strain on the logic of the system. Over time, governments have adopted a serious of pragmatic adjustments designed to enhance immigrants' labour market participation. In recent years, growing political contestation has intensified debates. Nonetheless, for Brochmann, the underling logic of the welfare state helps explain why "a rather path-dependent pattern has predominated" so that Norway remains our most inclusionary country.

In contrast, Austria is a classic example of a conservative or Bismarckian welfare state, with its heavy reliance on contributory programs. In chapter 7, Oliver Gruber argues that the gulf between contributory and non-contributory programs continues to shape immigrants' ability to access social benefits. Contributory programs have been relatively accessible to EU migrants and permanent residents, but third-country immigrants with weaker employment records have much more difficulty accessing support. They have benefited from growing inclusion in health care (unless they are undocumented migrants) and new active labour market programs. However, their access to non-contributory programs such as social housing and social assistance generates constant political conflict. As a result, Austria remains our most exclusionary country.

Finally, the United States is a classic liberal welfare state. In contrast to European welfare states, which were founded by relatively homogenous societies, the US welfare state was plagued from the outset by the politics of race. The regime that emerged in the middle of the 20th century was comparatively modest and relied more heavily on means-tested programs. The primary social assistance program, Aid to Families with Dependent Children, highlighted the greater dependence of Black and Hispanic Americans on benefits, which fueled a toxic politics of welfare. In 1996, political backlash over Black dependence on welfare culminated in legislation to "end welfare as we know it," which ultimately was signed by Bill Clinton, a Democratic president. Although the politics of immigration did not generate the political anger that drove the legislation, immigrants were the major victims, for their access to a range of benefits was now restricted, especially for the elderly.[3]

In sum, quantitative analysis and qualitative country cases point in the same direction, confirming our first hypothesis. The structure of the welfare state built during the 20th century has structured the context in which contemporary political contests over the inclusion/exclusion of immigrants are now playing out. This is not to minimize the role of other factors, especially political dynamics. A glance at the full range of countries covered by the IESPI suggests that when it comes to immigrant exclusion, there is considerable variation within Esping-Andersen's regime categories: social democratic regimes in Norway and Denmark differ; conservative regimes in France and Austria differ; liberal regimes in the United States and Canada differ. Clearly, other things matter as well.

Characteristics of immigration and immigrants. The second hypothesis holds that migration patterns and the characteristics of immigrants themselves can trigger exclusion from social programs. Two related propositions are worth separating here. The first holds that a large surge in immigration triggers political backlash and exclusion. The issue is not so much the *level* of immigration as the speed of *change* in the level. The second holds that the characteristics of the immigrants themselves matter: a substantial flow of immigrants who are likely to struggle economically and/or to be perceived as culturally different by the majority population is likely to result in exclusionary responses.

What does our evidence say about these propositions? Chapter 3 provides a quantitative analysis of the second proposition, focusing on the economic success of immigrants. Many countries fear that low-skilled immigrants will experience high levels of unemployment and rely heavily on social assistance, and this triggers exclusionary responses. Römer and Bjerre test whether higher relative immigrant unemployment is associated with more immigrant welfare exclusion. The results suggest it is not. None of their measures of immigrant unemployment are significantly associated with immigrant exclusion, as measured by the summary IESPI scores. Nor do they find a significant association for six of the seven program sub-indicators. Overall, therefore, they conclude that immigrant unemployment is not a powerful driver of welfare exclusion.

The country case studies provide a more complex view. In the chapters on Norway, Austria, and the US, the size of immigration flows and the skill levels of immigrants pervade the analysis, although the particular friction points vary. Regarding Norway and Austria, the proportion of their populations born outside the country has risen significantly in recent decades, and the 2015 surge of refugees sparked political conflict. Beyond that particular shock, these countries have struggled over the economic integration of low-skilled immigrants. As we have seen, the policy response has included active labour market programs as well as restrictions on access to social assistance and related benefits. The details differ in the US, where the toxic politics have been driven more by the legal status of immigrants – legal/illegal/undocumented – than by their employment levels.

In the reverse way, Portugal offers fascinating confirmation of the importance of the cultural *and* economic dimensions of immigration. The country has successfully transformed itself from one of the most exclusionary countries on the IESPI to one of the most inclusionary. Since 1995, for example, general social assistance benefits have been available for all foreigners with legal residence in Portugal. This transition has been eased by the cultural proximity of immigrants to Portuguese society. Most immigrants have come from former Portuguese colonies, and the cultural, linguistic, and religious diversity that immigration has brought about is limited. The number of Muslims is also small, and most have a Portuguese background. As a result, cultural and religious backlash is rare. In addition, there are vastly more economic immigrants than refugees, and immigrants overall have high labour market participation, ensuring that benefit dependency is limited.

In short, our second hypothesis about the size of the immigration flow and the characteristics of the immigrants themselves finds mixed support. Cross-national analysis stands as a caution against simple arguments, finding no evidence that immigrants' unemployment drives their exclusion from social benefits. However, these factors pervade the country studies in complex and various ways. Below, we will further discuss the differing results from the quantitative and qualitative chapters.

Political parties. Our third hypothesis holds that political hostility to immigration and immigrants ultimately drives the exclusion of immigrants from social benefits. Public hostility must be mobilized, and anti-immigrant parties are often seen as the critical force bearing down on immigration issues. Their influence does not depend solely on participation in governing coalitions; more often, they generate pressure on mainstream governments on both the right and the left to introduce restrictions.

What does the evidence here suggest? The cross-national analysis of Römer and Bjerre finds mixed evidence regarding the role of political parties generally. They analyse the impact of anti-immigrant parties' share of the vote, as well as the dominance of left parties and right parties in the cabinet. Overall, they find little support for the influence of both mainstream and anti-immigrant parties. They do qualify this conclusion by noting some evidence that political parties influence different social benefits differently. Overall, however, their results caution against assuming that anti-immigrant parties are the main drivers of exclusion everywhere.

Our country studies provide more nuanced analyses of political parties, but once again, simple conclusions are elusive. Party conflict has generated controversy over immigration and welfare access in many countries, but the actual impact on exclusion varies considerably. Austria is a country in which political parties have had a major impact on the exclusion of immigrants from welfare benefits. During the 1990s, the populist radical-right FPÖ grew steadily at the expense of the governing mainstream parties, and pushed fiercely for both an immigration halt and targeted exclusion of immigrants from welfare benefits. In chapter 7, Oliver Gruber concludes that this pressure shaped the policies of mainstream governments and grew stronger when the FPÖ joined two right-wing coalitions between 2000 and 2006. The IESPI rankings seem consistent with his analysis. Austria became more exclusionary between 2000 and 2010 and then moved back again over the following decade.

Elsewhere, partisan effects are more difficult to detect. For example, the experience in Norway seems consistent with Römer and Bjerre's ambiguous conclusions. The Progress Party has long opposed immigration and emphasized the "burden" on the welfare state. Initially, the mainstream Social Democrats and Conservatives sought to distance themselves from their populist rival, but between 2013 and 2020 the Progress party joined a Conservative coalition. During the 2015 refugee crisis, parliamentary parties coalesced around efforts to control the inflow of newcomers and reduce the welfare benefits they received. However, Brochmann points out that when the inflow weakened in 2016, the Progress Party could not secure a parliamentary majority for a number of its proposed retrenchments, and the party resigned from the government in 2020 over an immigration-related question. Despite the heightened partisan conflict generated by the Progress Party, the Norwegian welfare state remains highly inclusionary, and its summary ranking on the IESPI does not change between 2000 and 2015.

The US presents another ambiguous pattern. As we saw earlier, the big exclusionary moment came with the 1996 legislation, in a shift driven overwhelmingly by the historic politics of race. More recently, a renewed anti-immigrant campaign driven by President Donald Trump and the Republican Party has continually sought to restrict eligibility for benefits, targeting non-citizens and immigrant populations more generally. The Trump administration had a major impact on the lives of people attempting to cross the Mexican border. Nonetheless, when we focus on immigrants' access to welfare benefits, the authors of chapter 9 conclude that the policy framework established in 1996 has held during the subsequent 20 years without pronounced change. Once again, this conclusion is supported by the IESPI, which captures the abrupt 1990s shift toward welfare restrictiveness, followed by a plateauing pattern from 2000 to the present.

Finally, in a different way, Portugal offers evidence of the importance of political parties. Under the new democratic regime, established in 1974, Portugal began transitioning to a unified model of social security through a series of concrete measures related to social pensions, unemployment protection, family subsidies, and social protections for self-employed and domestic workers. As noted earlier, these Portuguese programs are highly inclusive of immigrants. All of the major parties support this inclusionary approach, and the anti-immigrant party has never had a significant presence (although it did win its first seat in the legislative elections of 2019 and significantly increased its parliamentary presence in 2022).

In short, our third hypothesis finds mixed support. In many countries, political parties have certainly generated conflict over immigrants' access to social benefits. However, the impact on actual exclusion levels has varied enormously from one country to another, consistent with the more ambiguous findings in the cross-national quantitative analysis.

Public opinion. The discussion of political parties leads naturally to the fourth hypothesis, which posits that inclusion and exclusion are reflections of prevailing public attitudes. Studies have measured public conceptions of the deservingness of different groups for social benefits and have found that immigrants rank at the bottom of the deservingness hierarchy everywhere in Europe and beyond (Van Oorschot 2006; Jaeger 2007; Buss 2019). The wider literature offers different explanations for this. Some analysts see anti-immigrant attitudes as a direct reflection of xenophobia, racism, and/or Islamophobia. Others point to the role of nationalism and national identity in shaping the response to outsiders. Appealing to a sense of shared nationhood might be effective in promoting redistributive solidarity for the native-born, but it can also exclude minorities and immigrants.

What do the chapters here say about the role of public attitudes? The quantitative chapters do not address the relationship in this form. In chapter 5, Markus Crepaz examines the relationship between prejudice and exclusion from the other direction, asking whether including immigrants in the social benefit structure can reduce levels of racism and xenophobia as well as perceptions that immigrants abuse welfare. We return to his contribution below. The country cases do not address the implications of political culture and national identity but do address public attitudes about immigration and immigrant access to benefits.

Comparative opinion polls such as the Eurobarometer reveal that Austria is one of the countries most concerned about immigration. Gruber contends that this climate has fuelled support for radical-right populist parties and influenced mainstream party positions regarding social welfare benefits for immigrants. In contrast, Brochmann sees Norwegians' attitudes toward immigration and integration policies as consistent with the logic of the welfare regime, which combines support for a rather strict approach to admission to the country with lenient policies related to inclusion and equal rights. The views in Portugal are even more supportive. In longitudinal surveys, Portuguese respondents have expressed increasingly positive views about the impacts of immigration. Beyond the average level of support for immigration in a country, the degree of consensus or polarization within the population matters. In the US, voters are increasingly at odds, which helps explain the difficulty in reversing the exclusionary moment of 1996.

In summary, the patterns here seem similar to those related to the role of political parties discussed earlier, suggesting it is difficult to disentangle the separate effects of party mobilization and public attitudes in shaping the exclusion of immigrants from the benefits of the welfare state. We return to the implications of the differences below.

Legal structures. The final hypothesis about the drivers of exclusion focuses on the scope and robustness of legal protections. To what extent do legal structures insulate immigrants' access from shifts in the political winds? Many scholars have noted that immigrant inclusion is less likely to emerge from politicians and legislatures and more likely to flow from judicial interpretations of human rights legislation as well as international and supranational rights protections.

Only one the quantitative studies in this volume includes an analysis of legal regimes. In chapter 3, Friederike Römer and Liv Bjerre control for the number of veto points inherent in the legal structure, which they operationalize as the sum of measures for federalism, a presidential system, single-member district plurality electoral systems, the strength of bicameralism, the frequency of referendums, the strength of judicial review, and EU integration. In their results, this aggregate measure of veto points does not show consistently significant effects. However, the influence of the legal regime pervades the country chapters. For countries such as Austria and Norway, the EU and EEA framework is critical. The primary beneficiaries have been immigrants from EU countries, but also permanent residents from third countries in some segments of the welfare system. In Austria, for example, Gruber argues that the most decisive barrier to excluding immigrants from benefits "has not come from within the party-political system but rather from national or European courts and from EU legislation in general." As a result, immigrants live in various ambivalent positions: some categories of migrants are treated more or less as coequal insiders, while other categories remain disadvantaged outsiders. In Portugal, the role of the EU regime is less determinative, for access to social benefits is embedded in the country's constitution, and national courts have struck down several efforts by conservative governments to constrain immigrant access. The legal regime figures less prominently in the chapter on the US, but the authors emphasize the extent to which other political structures, such as congressional veto points and federalism, are impediments to inclusionary change. Overall, the evidence in this volume supports the fourth hypothesis.

Consequences of Inclusion/Exclusion

The impact of including immigrants in the welfare state regime has been a subject of immense political controversy. Does immigrants' access to benefits weaken their incentive to work? Does the "burden" of immigrants place unbearable stress on the finances of the country and the sustainability of a generous welfare state? Does immigrants' dependence on welfare excite xenophobic backlash? These are standard tropes in the discourse of anti-immigrant politicians and common justifications for excluding immigrants from welfare benefits. Are those justifications valid? Our final three hypotheses probe these issues.

Public opinion. The fifth hypothesis addresses whether existing arrangements on immigrants' welfare access shape public opinion. Institutionalists argue that political institutions and policy regimes influence how people think about the world around them. From this perspective, the inclusion of immigrants in benefit regimes implicitly defines them as legitimate members of the community and facilitates more positive attitudes toward them. The alternative view is that immigrant access to benefits is likely to exacerbate xenophobic sentiment and backlash against immigration. Many politicians seem to operate on the premise that exclusion is a price to be paid for public support of a robust immigration program.

Markus Crepaz tackles this issue in chapter 5. He concludes that exclusionary policies stigmatize immigrants, highlight differences among them, generate unequal opportunities and life chances, and lead to further "othering" by driving ever deeper wedges between immigrants and the native-born. In contrast, making access to social programs for immigrants more equal reduces racist, xenophobic, and welfare chauvinist attitudes. Clearly, untangling cause and effect between racism and exclusion is difficult, but the findings cast doubt on the idea that exclusion can appease a public that otherwise might object that support for immigrants is unduly generous. This conclusion is echoed in the country chapters. For example, there is no evidence that the 1996 exclusionary changes in the US reduced public concerns about the "welfare burden" of immigration; instead, the issue seems to have become *more* salient and polarizing. Nor have the inclusionary changes in Portugal led to a nativist backlash, at least so far. The evidence in this volume consistently points to the importance of the legitimating effects of inclusion.

Economic integration. Our next hypothesis dives into the intense debates over how to build economic self-reliance among newcomers. One proposition is that exclusion hinders immigrants' chances for economic integration by leaving them on the margins of the labour market with little opportunity to pursue upward social mobility. A counterview is that inclusion discourages economic activity, based either on the general view that transfer benefits reduce employment or the more specific argument that immigrants are especially likely to linger on benefits, which may to them seem plentiful compared to the standard of living they could expect in their country of origin.

Chapter 5 finds that at the aggregate level, greater social policy inclusiveness *supports* the labour market integration of immigrants. However, Kananec, Kureková, and Duman find that the effects differ from one policy to another. For example, inclusiveness in housing benefits plays an especially positive role, enhancing immigrants' participation and stability in the labour market. However, greater inclusion in social assistance programs seems to decrease immigrants' labour market activity and increase their unemployment rates relative to the native-born. Overall, their chapter concludes that fears that social policy inclusion hurts immigrants' economic integration are greatly exaggerated.

This evidence is significant because the country studies report many politicians and political parties expressing the alternative view that immigrants' dependence on social benefits weakens their labour market integration. This has often generated a two-part strategy: active labour market programs (ALMPs) designed to stimulate immigrant employment; and barriers to immigrants' use of social assistance. Indeed, ALMPs have become dramatically more inclusive over the period tracked by the IESPI, whereas social assistance reveals an overall trend in an exclusionary direction. The country studies add detail here. It seems clear that the 1995 exclusionary legislation in the US hurt the integration of American immigrants and that immigrants in Norway have benefited from its inclusionary welfare regime (although they still struggle in its rather protective labour market). The Austrian chapter shows that the most welfare-excluded categories of immigrants have the highest unemployment rates and are at the highest risk of living in poverty. Moreover, it seems that the gaps in Austria between EU migrants and third-country nationals are larger in that respect than in Portugal, although admittedly the data in chapters 7 and 10 are not strictly comparable.

The evidence on this hypothesis from the quantitative and qualitative studies suggests that, whatever many politicians believe, benefit inclusion is not a major barrier to immigrants' economic integration.

Social spending. Our final hypothesis tackles a related issue: the relationship between welfare exclusion and social spending. Does immigrant inclusion raise social spending and represent a burden on the wider society? Or does immigrant inclusion produce positive economic effects, especially in the long run? Populist anti-immigrant rhetoric in many countries, including several discussed in our country chapters, aggressively asserts that immigrants represent a burden on the welfare state.

Chapter 6 provides systematic cross-national evidence here. Rigzin and Kaushal find little support for the proposition that excluding immigrants reduces social expenditures. The aggregate savings their models predict are very small and statistically insignificant. As in chapter 5, the conclusions vary across program types. Exclusion from housing and health care may actually be detrimental to the exchequer. In contrast, exclusion from social assistance does lower combined expenditures on family benefits and disability benefits. Overall, they conclude that "immigrant exclusion does not have a significant fiscal effect and therefore it should not be defended on grounds of its fiscal implications." Given the populist rhetoric on these issues, this is a useful finding. In large part, the country studies do not address the impact of immigrant integration on the finances of the state, except for its influence on political rhetoric. The only dissent from the conclusions of Rigzin and Kaushal comes in the chapter on Norway, which is titled "Inclusion under Pressure." In Brochmann's view, costs feature prominently as a source of pressure in our most inclusive welfare state.

The Overall Patterns

All of our hypotheses find some support in the chapters in this volume. In some cases, the evidence from quantitative analysis and country studies points in the same direction, as in the discussion of the first hypothesis on the impact of welfare state regimes. In other cases, such as the second hypothesis on the characteristics of immigrants and the third hypothesis on political parties, the quantitative and qualitative chapters point in different directions. Nevertheless, such results are useful, highlighting the complexity of the issues and the advantages of a multimethod approach to big questions. The different conclusions also likely reflect the choice of case studies, since the countries analysed in depth here represent extremes of inclusion or exclusion among democratic states. The quantitative results are also influenced by the many countries in the middle.

Our evidence also highlights the difficulties inherent in trying to tease out the different impacts of closely related factors. For example, the pattern in the impact of political parties overlaps significantly with the pattern in public attitudes, confirming that parties and public attitudes are highly interactive in practice. A fine-grained longitudinal analysis would be required to try to determine whether political parties simply mobilize pre-existing attitudes or whether party contestation shapes the attitudes of the electorate. Both are likely at work. Similarly, the analysis of the relationship between inclusionary policies and racist attitudes is complicated by their endogenous nature and by the probability that causality runs in both directions.

In contrast to the complex interweaving of the drivers of inclusion/exclusion, the results of the analyses of the consequences of inclusion all point in the same reassuring direction. Inclusion reduces xenophobia, supports labour market integration, and does not impose a major financial burden on the state. Given the political mythology surrounding each of these issues, these are reassuring findings. There is no reason to fear inclusion.

Finally, the evidence is clear that drivers and consequences vary in complex ways across different social programs. Exclusion has not happened across the board, but has fallen disproportionately on some programs, especially social assistance. It is worth noting that chapters 5 and 6 find that exclusion from social assistance is associated with better labour market outcomes and (modest) reductions in spending. This could be taken as indicating that we need not worry about patterns of immigrant welfare exclusion. We return to the normative question below.

The richness and intricacies in the findings point to the need for continued research. Moreover, the evidence gathered here makes a strong case for continuing to rely on the model that structures this volume. All of the hypotheses set out in Figure 1.1 resonate in our chapters. In addition, despite the contextual complexity of specific countries, none of our authors pointed to major explanatory factors completely outside that model. In combination with the IESPI, this model provides a solid foundation for further work.

Concluding Reflections: The Feasibility of an Inclusive Multicultural Welfare State

Finally, what do our findings imply for the larger question, which is whether an inclusive welfare state represents a realistic project in a multicultural democracy? As noted at the outset, considerable pessimism swirls around the prospects for the redistributive state in ethnically diverse societies. The original argument that diversity erodes the welfare state has faded, and current debate focuses on the pervasiveness of welfare chauvinism. The exclusion of immigrants from social benefits seems to represent a significant departure from the original ideals underpinning a welfare state. The implication would seem to be that the redistributive welfare state may be durable, but only for the historic community of native-born citizens. Given that immigrants represent a rising proportion of the population in contemporary democracies, exclusion creates new status hierarchies of membership and deservingness inconsistent with egalitarian aspirations. The worry is that a redistributive state may remain possible, but an *inclusive* redistributive state may not.

Is exclusion from the welfare state normatively important? In chapter 12, Will Kymlicka addresses this issue from the perspective of liberal democratic thought. He argues that immigrant welfare inclusion/exclusion falls in between the logic of universal human rights on the one hand and the logic of equal citizenship on the other. As a result, political philosophers have had little to say about the issues. As an initial proposition, Kymlicka argues that in the case of settled immigrants who are making their lives in their new country, exclusion from full social benefits may be less objectionable *if* they have a secure, rapid escalator to citizenship. In such circumstances, exclusions are less likely to generate durable inequalities. As he demonstrates, some countries do provide such a rapid escalator. Many, however, do not. Moreover, Kymlicka acknowledges that "the fact that immigrants in some countries can quickly move out of a particular immigration status does not mean that the exclusions from welfare benefits attached to that status are benign, or fair, or reasonable … We don't in fact have well-developed theories to evaluate the justice of these exclusions tied to immigration status."[4] The issue of whether exclusions rest uneasily with egalitarian aspirations remains.

On the question of whether an inclusive welfare state is a feasible social project, this volume provides grounds for optimism. First, the IESPI puts the reality of welfare chauvinism in greater context. First, as we have seen, the most extreme forms of welfare exclusion have declined since the late 20th century. Second, not all policy adaptations to the presence of immigrants have been punitive. Many countries have expanded active labour market programs for newcomers. To be sure, some of these programs are mandatory and enforced through punitive measures. But not all. Third, and most importantly, there is dramatic variation in the levels of welfare exclusion. Exclusion is not an inevitable price to pay for a robust welfare state. The variation across countries confirms the importance of different choices.

On its own, the IESPI cannot provide a full answer to our question, for it does not measure the generosity or redistributive ambition of the welfare state. Full inclusion in a neoliberal regime of paltry social benefits would not represent a reassuring response to the pessimism about the prospects for the redistributive state. Indeed, in chapter 11, Christian Joppke argues that the distinction between citizens and immigrants is fading precisely because of a neoliberal reordering of the welfare state. In his view, the neoliberal order treats "citizens and migrants alike – and that at a low level." In this neoliberal order, welfare programs are based not on the logic of solidarity but on the logic of a contract, with access depending on prior contributions through employment. In his view, the idea of workfare best expresses the general direction of neoliberal social policy, with retrenchment directed particularly at groups with no contribution history. Presumably, the inclusion of immigrants in ALMPs and the greater barriers to their accessing social assistance are consistent with this interpretation. In the long term, Joppke expects this trend to drain the heat from the distinction between citizens and immigrants: the welfare state will treat both with equal suspicion.

In this context, however, it is important to remember that although neoliberalism has been a force in welfare politics for several decades, the IESPI demonstrates that the distinction between citizens and immigrants is alive and well. In some countries, the distinction is growing, not shrinking, including in the US, where the spirit of neoliberalism seems particularly advanced. Whatever the long-term prospects, neoliberalism has yet to fulfil Joppke's expectations of the future.

Indeed, on balance, this volume serves as a source of optimism about the prospects for an inclusive welfare state with redistributive ambitions. Several indicators point in this direction. Recall that in chapter 3, Römer and Bjerre found compelling evidence that the generosity of welfare benefits and the inclusion of immigrants are positively related. If it were impossible to combine welfare inclusion and welfare generosity, they would not have found that welfare generosity predicts more inclusionary approaches to immigrant welfare access.

Additional support comes from analysis of the relationship between inclusion and redistribution, as well as the relationship between inclusion and overall inequality. Consider Figure 13.1, which includes IESPI scores and a measure of the redistributive impact of taxes and transfers. Clearly, some countries do manage to combine above-average inclusion with above-average redistribution, most obviously Sweden, Portugal, and France. There are also countries that combine exclusion and limited redistribution, most clearly Switzerland, the UK, and the US. More generally, the graph does not suggest that inclusion and redistribution are necessarily at odds. If that were the case, we should see evidence of a positive relationship between exclusion and redistribution in the graph. Instead, there is little of a relationship at all. If anything, there is a slightly negative pattern between exclusion and redistribution (the correlation coefficient for this plot is –0.102).

Measuring the impact of redistribution through taxes and transfers does not fully capture the social role of the state, for it misses the ways in which social and labour policies influence the original wage distribution, often referred to as predistribution. Figure 13.2 therefore provides a complementary analysis,

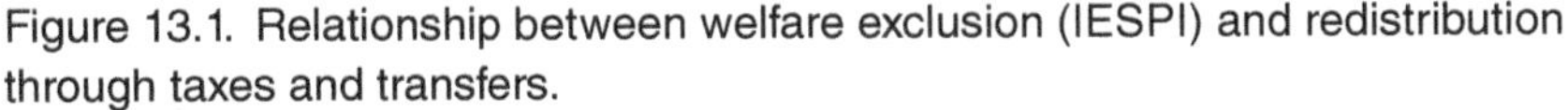

Figure 13.1. Relationship between welfare exclusion (IESPI) and redistribution through taxes and transfers.

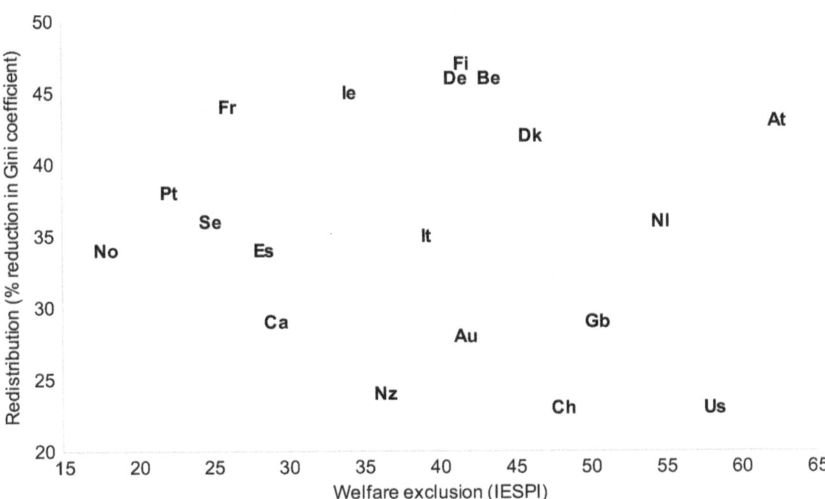

Notes and sources: IESPI data are for 2015. Redistributive impact is calculated from data on inequality pre-tax/transfer and inequality post-tax/transfers drawn from OECD Income Distribution Database. Redistribution data are for 2018 or near year.

Figure 13.2. Relationship between welfare exclusion (IESPI) and inequality in disposable income.

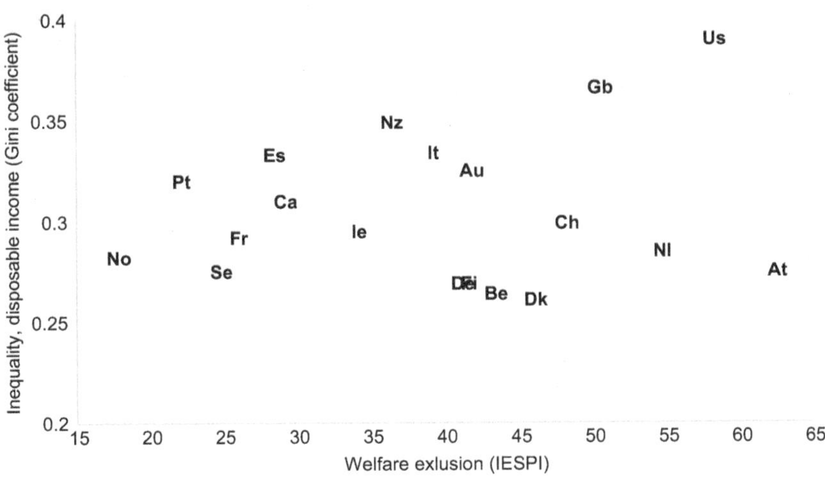

Notes and sources: Disposable income includes the effects of taxes and transfers. IESPI data are for 2015. Inequality data are drawn from OECD Income Distribution Database and are for 2018 or near year.

examining the relationship between IESPI scores and the level of inequality in disposable incomes, a measure that incorporates the effects of both predistribution and redistribution. Once again, the overall patterns are similar. Here, there is no systematic relationship suggesting that welfare exclusion improves a state's ability to foster equality. If anything, there is more inequality in countries that practise more welfare exclusion (the correlation coefficient for this plot is 0.131). The same set of countries as in the first figure manage to combine inclusion and above-average levels of economic equality.

The answer is clear. Welfare chauvinism is not the inevitable price to pay to protect the welfare state. There is no inherent tension between inclusion of immigrants in social programs and the robustness of the welfare state, whether we conceive of that robustness in terms of benefit generosity, redistribution, or inequality. The future is never driven exclusively by impersonal, structural forces. Political choices matter. Thus, the future is shaped by perceptions of what is possible and what is impossible. This volume stands as evidence that the ideal of an inclusive redistributive state remains a feasible project in a multicultural world.

NOTES

1 I would like to thank Edward Koning for his incredibly helpful comments on an early draft of this chapter.

2 Elsewhere, Edward Koning (2020) has added a time dimension to this issue. He presents preliminary evidence that in the late twentieth century, differences between welfare state regimes explained much of the variation in the inclusion or exclusion of immigrants in social benefits. However, as the twenty-first century has unfolded, he contends, institutional determinants have faded, with political factors, especially anti-immigrant parties and anti-immigrant public attitudes, increasingly explaining punitive forms of immigrant exclusion.

3 Portugal, a Mediterranean welfare state, is building its welfare state and defining immigrant access simultaneously, making it more difficult to tease out the relationship between the two.

4 Kymlicka also addresses the status of temporary immigrants who have no interest in making their lives in the country. This case is less central to the above discussion.

Appendix: Detailed Country Descriptions

Australia

(data collection by Besarta Kajmolli and Edward Koning)

	Tax-paid pensions	Health care	Contr. unempl.	Contr. pension	Housing	Social assist.	Active labour market	Average
1990	51	44	n/a	13	44	19	38	35
2000	51	38	n/a	13	50	31	56	40
2010	57	38	n/a	13	56	31	56	42
2015	57	38	n/a	13	56	31	56	42

Tax-paid pensions

TPP1: *Residence requirements for universal tax-paid pension*
1990–2015: ***–8*** *(no universal public pension)*

The only tax-paid pension in Australia is the Age Pension, which is means-tested (Social Security Act, 1991).

TPP2: *Availability of means-tested program for those with incomplete benefit*
1990–2015: ***3*** *(yes, with residence requirement of ten or more years)*

The means-tested Age Pension is available to anyone who has been an Australian resident for at least ten years. Individuals who have been an Australian resident for more than one period must have at least been a resident for five continuous years, and the aggregate of the periods must at least equal ten years. Exemptions from this residence requirement exist for refugees, former refugees, recipients of widow or partner allowances, and widows born before July 1955. (Social Security Act, 1991, ss. 23 and 243.)

TPP3: *Status requirement for access to (means-tested or universal) tax-paid pension*
1990–2015: ***1*** *(citizens and all permanent residents)*

The only claimants who are eligible for the Age Pension are Australian residents. According to 1947 law, this includes citizens and all legal residents except undocumented migrants and temporary permit holders (Social Security Act, 1947, section 3). The Social Security Act of 1991 defines Australian residents as citizens, permanent visa holders, and holders of a protected Special Category Visa (Social Security Act, 1991, s. 7). Between 1994 and 2001, migrants from New Zealand were issued a protected Special Category Visa, which gives privileged access to the Age Pension (Spinks & Klapdor, 2016).

TPP4: *Export possibilities of (means-tested or universal) tax-paid pension*
1990: ***2.1*** *(without restrictions, to designated countries only)*
2000: ***2.1*** *(without restrictions, to designated countries only)*
2010: ***2.9*** *(without restrictions, to designated countries only)*
2015: ***2.8*** *(without restrictions, to designated countries only)*

Emigrants can receive the Age Pension in any country with which Australia has bilateral social security agreements, without deductions or additional requirements. It is not possible to export the Age Pension to other countries. Australia had bilateral social security agreements with four countries in 1990 (Canada, Italy, New Zealand, United Kingdom), ten countries in 2000 (Cyprus, Ireland, Malta, Netherlands, Portugal, Spain added), 23 countries in 2010 (agreement with United Kingdom terminated; Belgium, Chile, Croatia, Czech Republic, Denmark, Finland, Germany, Greece, Japan, Korea, Norway, Slovenia, Switzerland, United States added), and 28 countries in 2015 (Latvia, North Macedonia, Poland, Slovak Republic added) (Department of Human Services, n.d.-a). The proportion of the foreign-born population from these countries was 0.47 in 1990 (1,822,400/3,885,600), 0.46 in 2000 (2,021,740/4,369,450), 0.29 in 2010 (1,635,730/5,729,880), and 0.29 in 2015 (1,912,770/6,557,650) (OECD, 2017).

Health care

HC1: *Residence requirements for public health care (subsidies)*
1990–2015: ***0*** *(no waiting period)*

All eligible migrants (see HC2) have immediate access to Medicare upon arrival (Young, 1994). The only exception is that since 1994, there is a two-year waiting period before newcomers can access the means-tested Low Income Health Care Card (Department of Human Services, n.d.-b).

HC2: *Status requirements for public health care (subsidies)*
1990–2015: ***4** (undocumented and some categories of legal migrants excluded entirely)*

For the entire duration under study, Medicare has been available only to Australian citizens, permanent residents, and temporary residents who are in the process of applying for permanent residence and have either the right to work or a partner, parent, or child who is an Australian citizen. Other temporary migrants can only access Medicare if they are from a country with which Australia has a Reciprocal Health Care Agreement. All others are expected to secure private health care (interview AUS-01; Department of Immigration and Border Protection, n.d.-a). Ineligible migrants might access health care services under the Status Resolution Support Services Programme, but accessing this program requires applicants to cooperate with the Department of Immigration to resolve their immigration status (Department of Immigration and Border Protection, n.d.-b).

HC3: *Health care accessibility services*
1990: ***1** (state-funded translation services)*
2000–2015: ***0** (state-funded translation services and health services with cultural sensitivity)*

Since 1973, migrants in Australia have been able to access free translation services in the health care sector (Kelaher & Manderson, 2000; Department of Immigration and Border Protection, n.d.-c). Since the early 1990s, Australian states have developed state-specific health care accessibility services. New South Wales established a Multicultural Health Communication Service in 1997, which provides multilingual health resources, translation services, and cultural sensitivity programs (NSW Ministry of Health, n.d.).

HC4: *Additional health care benefits*
1990–2015: ***2** (specialized services for refugees, in particular in the area of mental health)*

The Program of Assistance for Survivors of Torture and Trauma (PASTT), funded by the federal Department of Health, funds several mental health services targeted specifically at refugees and humanitarian migrants. These services started in New South Wales in 1988 with the founding of the Service for the Treatment and Rehabilitation of Torture and Trauma Survivors (STARTTS, n.d.), and since the mid-1990s have been offered in all other provinces as well. Beyond these services, there are no health care benefits that are exclusively available to refugees or other migrants (Buckmaster, 2012).

Contributory unemployment

There are no contributory unemployment programs in Australia. Instead, all programs for the unemployed, such as the Unemployment Benefit, the Job Search Allowance, and the New Start Allowance, are means-tested (Ey, 2012; Young, 1994). All values for this social program in Australia are, therefore, **–8** (no contributory unemployment benefit).

Contributory pension

CP1: *Status requirement*
1990–2015: ***0** (all legal residents included)*

Since 1983, the mandatory contributory pension Superannuation requires employers to make payments to a superfund for all their employees who earn more than a very low threshold (about 5 hours of minimum wage per week). This means that everyone who is legally working in the country is entitled to this program (OECD, 2009; Australian Taxation Office, n.d.-a).

CP2: *Export possibilities*
1990–2015: ***1** (some can export without restrictions, others subjected to additional taxation)*

Permanent residents and Australian citizens can claim their Superannuation upon retirement from abroad without any restrictions. Temporary residents can apply for the Departing Australia Superannuation Payment, which allows them to claim their Superannuation when they leave the country. However, in that case the funds are subject to significant taxation (up to 47%) (Australian Taxation Office, n.d-b).

Housing

HB1: *Residence requirements for housing benefits*
1990: ***0** (no residence requirement)*
2000–2015: ***2** (residence requirement of two years)*

There was no residence requirement on access-to-rent assistance until 1993. Since 1996, the requirement has been two years, as per the so-called Newly

Arrived Residents Waiting Period (Department of Social Services, n.d.-a). Social housing is administered at the state level, but no state imposes additional requirements apart from the normal wait times to which all applicants are subjected.

HB2: *Status requirements for housing benefits*
1990: ***3*** *(citizens and permanent residents)*
2000: ***2*** *(some but not all temporary migrants)*
2010–2015: ***3*** *(citizens and permanent residents)*

Only citizens and permanent residents are eligible for rent assistance. In New South Wales, social housing was available to temporary migrants from New Zealand between 1994 and 2001, but has otherwise been exclusively available to citizens and permanent residents. In exceptional cases, the state temporarily accommodates temporary migrants escaping violent situations (NSW Family and Community Services, n.d.).

HB3: *Integration requirements for housing benefits*
1990–2015: ***0*** *(no integration requirements)*

Australia has never placed any integration requirements on accessing housing benefits.

HB4: *Preferential treatment in housing*
1990–2015: ***4*** *(no privileged access for migrants)*

Humanitarian entrants (let alone other groups of migrants) do not receive preferential treatment in the system of social housing. They have to stay on the same wait lists as native-born Australians, and as a result, most find accommodation in the private market (Department of Social Services, n.d.-b).

Social assistance

SA1: *Residence requirements*
1990: ***0*** *(no residence requirement)*
2000–2015: ***3*** *(between 1 and 5 years)*

There was no residence requirement on access to social assistance until 1993. Since 1996, the requirement has been two years, as per the so-called Newly Arrived Residents Waiting Period. Refugees and holders of certain humanitarian visas are exempted from this requirement, as well as migrants who experience severe hardship for reasons beyond their control (Department of Social Services, n.d.-c). Since the proportion of new arrivals under these conditions is very small (about 2% in the period under study, Australian Bureau of Statistics, 2019), these scores do not incorporate the exemptions.

SA2: *Status requirements*
1990: ***3** (all permanent residents)*
2000–2015: ***2** (all permanent residents and some temporary residents)*

All permanent residents and citizens have access to social assistance. Only some categories of temporary visa holders have been eligible since the 1990s. Migrants from New Zealand were between 1994 and 2001, and since 1992 there are special social assistance benefits for asylum seekers (Department of Social Services, n.d.-c; Department of Human Services, n.d.-c; Department of Immigration and Border Protection, n.d.-b; Millbank, 2007; Refugee Council of Australia, n.d.).

SA3: *Consequences of uptake for status*
1990–2015: ***0** (no consequences)*

Drawing on social assistance benefits cannot affect a migrant's legal status in Australia. Migrants with precarious status who seek social assistance through the Status Resolution Support Services Programme are required to cooperate with the Department of Immigration to resolve their immigration status, but this cannot result in the loss of an already acquired status. (Department of Immigration and Border Protection, n.d.-b).

SA4: *Integration requirements for social assistance*
1990–2015: ***0** (no integration requirements)*

Australia has never placed any integration requirements on accessing social assistance benefits.

Active labour market policies

1990: ***1** (funded language programs, but not freely available to all categories of migrants)*
2000–2015: ***2** (visa fee levied for access to language programs)*

Australia has offered funded English-language training to immigrants since the 1940s (Pietsch, 2013). Since 1971, this has consisted of 510 hours of tuition, available to all permanent visa holders and some classes of temporary migrants (Immigration Education Act, 1971). Since 1993, however, the government charges a higher upfront visa fee for migrants who lack basic proficiency in English to offset the costs of the "free" language training (Pietsch, 2013).

ALM4: *Other immigrant-targeted employment assistance*
1990: ***3** (some programs offered, but offered ad hoc or inconsistently across the country)*
2000: ***2** (programs available, but only for refugees and/or asylum seekers)*
2010–2015: ***1** (programs available for some but not all categories of migrants)*

Until the 1990s, most of the efforts to help immigrants on the labour market were uncoordinated and small in scope (Spinks, 2009). In 2000, the Department of Immigration and Multicultural and Indigenous Affairs launched the Integrated Humanitarian Settlement Strategy (since renamed Humanitarian Settlement Program), an extensive range of settlement services for new arrivals targeted specifically at refugees and other entrants through the humanitarian streams of Australia's admission system (Leibig, 2007). Later programs, such as the Settlement Grants Program launched in 2004, also provide employment assistance to family migrants (Spinks, 2009). There is no targeted employment assistance, however, for temporary migrants and skilled labour market migrants.

Austria

(data collection by Edward Koning)

	Tax-paid pensions	Health care	Contr. unempl.	Contr. pension	Housing	Social assist.	Active labour market	Average
1990	58	75	58	50	75	69	75	66
2000	58	75	42	50	75	63	75	63
2010	58	69	42	50	94	81	69	66
2015	58	69	42	50	94	81	44	63

Tax-paid pensions

TPP1: *Residence requirements for universal tax-paid pension*
1990–2015: ***–8** (no universal public pension)*

There is no universal public pension in Austria. The most important public pension is contributory, and the only tax-paid pension benefits are small in scope and means-tested in benefit structure (Obinger & Tálos, 2010).

TPP2: *Availability of means-tested program for those with incomplete benefit*
1990–2015: ***3** (yes, with residence requirement 10+ years)*

In 1965, the government introduced the so-called "Ausgleichszulage," a means-tested top-up benefit for low-income pensioners (Obinger et al., 2010). Eligibility depends on at least 180 months (15 years) of contributions (General Social Security Act, 236.1). Low-income pensioners with at least 360 months of contributions are eligible for an "Ausgleichszulage" at a higher level (General Social Security Act, 293.1). The only benefit that is available for low-income elderly without such contribution history (or without a spouse with such a history) is the residual social assistance benefit, "Sozialhilfe."

TTP3: *Status requirement for access to means-tested or universal tax-paid pension*
1990–2015: ***1** (citizens and all permanent residents)*

There are no specific status requirements for access to the "Ausgleichszulage." Since it requires a work history of at least fifteen years, however, it is only accessible to citizens and permanent residents (General Social Security Act, 236.1).

TTP4: *Export possibilities of (means-tested or universal) tax-paid pension*
1990–2015: ***3** (during very short stay abroad only)*

The Ausgleichszulage cannot be exported abroad (General Social Security Act, ss. 292.1 and 292.14). Nevertheless, recipients can retain their benefit during temporary stays abroad of up to two months per year (Chamber of Labor, n.d.).

Health care

HC1: *Residence requirement for public health care*
1990–2015: *0 (no waiting period)*

There is no waiting period before newcomers can access public health insurance (General Social Security Act, ss. 10 and 117; Government of Austria, n.d.-a).

HC2: *Status requirements for public health care*
1990–2000: ***4** (undocumented and some categories of legal migrants excluded entirely)*
2010–2015: ***3** (undocumented migrants excluded entirely)*

Most residents in Austria are mandatorily insured, and everyone else is eligible for voluntary insurance. Until a 2004 health care agreement between the federal government and the *Länder*, however, asylum seekers only had access to private insurance. Since then, the federal government has funded health care services for asylum seekers during the time that their claim is being processed (Marth, 2005). Undocumented migrants do not have access to any public health care. They might not be reported to immigration when they use medical services, but they will be charged for the costs (Hofbauer, Mayr, & Laubacher-Kubat, 2005: 93–96). Apart from that, they have to rely on charity services, such as the Marienambulanz-funded by NGO Caritas, which provides medical services to uninsured individuals (Muckenhuber, Freidl, & Rásky, 2011).

HC3: *Health care accessibility services*
1990–2015: ***4** (nothing available)*

There are no publicly funded translation or cultural sensitivity services in Austria. Indeed, several studies criticize the absence of such services (Dressler & Pils, 2009; Pöchhacker, 2000).

HC4: *Additional health care benefits*
1990–2015: ***4** (no additional health care benefits)*

Austria does not offer any special health care services or benefits exclusively for immigrants. Asylum seekers have access to a tax-paid health care package before they are included in the mandatory insurance system, but this package is decidedly less generous than what the general system offers (Department of Internal Affairs, n.d.).

Contributory unemployment

CUB1: *Status requirements for access to contributory unemployment benefits*
1990–2015: ***3** (permanent residents, citizens, and very few temporary migrants)*

During the period under study, there have not been explicit status requirements for accessing "Arbeitslosengeld," the contributory unemployment benefit. (The situation is different for the means-tested unemployment program "Notstandshilfe"; see discussion under "Social assistance" below.) However, because access requires a contribution history ranging between one and two years during the period under study as well as availability for work, certain groups of migrants are *de facto* ineligible. Asylum seekers are only allowed to work in seasonal labour or community service jobs, neither of which generates access to unemployment benefits (Asylkoordination Österreich, n.d.). International students, seasonal migrants, and holders of temporary permits that are tied to a specific employer are in a similar situation: they either are not allowed to build up entitlement or are forced to leave the country when they become unemployed (Afonso, 2013, Gächter, 1995, Perchinig, 2009).

CUB2: *Integration requirements for access to contributory unemployment benefits*
1990–2015: ***0** (no integration requirements)*

Eligibility for unemployment benefits does not depend on satisfying integration requirements (Arbeitsmarktservice, n.d.-a).

CUB3: *Export possibilities*
1990: ***4** (no export possible)*
2000–2015: ***2** (export possible to limited number of states for short period of time)*

Unemployment benefits are generally only available to residents of Austria. However, since Austria joined the European Union in 1995 job seekers have been able to bring the benefit to any state in the European Economic Area or Switzerland for up to three months, albeit under additional conditions (Arbeitsmarktservice, n.d.-b).

Contributory pension

CP1: *Status requirement*
1990–2015: ***4** (all temporary migrants excluded)*

The public pension has undergone significant reform over the last two decades, but eligibility has always depended on 15 years of contributions (Obinger & Tálos, 2010). While there are no specific status requirements, this effectively means that the pension is inaccessible to temporary migrants (General Social Security Act, 236.1).

CP2: *Export possibilities*
1990–2015: ***0** (export possible without restrictions)*

There are no restrictions on exporting Austrian pension benefits. They can be exported to any country in the world (Government of Austria, n.d.-b).

Housing benefits

HB1: *Residence requirements for housing benefits*
1990–2015: ***4** (residence requirement of more than 4 years)*

All minimum-income benefits, including housing allowances and rent benefits, have a residence requirement of five years (Social Affairs Ministry, 2016). The eligibility requirements for social housing differ across Austrian provinces, but since permanent residency is required everywhere and there is a five-year residence requirement for accessing permanent residency, there is effectively a five-year residence requirement on access to social housing as well (Immobilienscout, n.d.). Recognized refugees, on the other hand, are eligible for social housing and housing benefits as soon as their asylum claim has been accepted. Since this group makes up only a small proportion of the migrant population (between 2% and 7% in the period under study, Statistics Austria, n.d.), the scores reported here do not reflect these exemptions.

HB2: *Status requirements for housing benefits*
1990–2000: ***4** (only some permanent residents and privileged nationals)*
2010–2015: ***3** (citizens and permanent residents)*

For a long time, only citizens and (since 1995) EU nationals were eligible for social housing in Austria (Reinprecht, 2007, Richter & Pflegerl, 2001). In 2006, however, the European Union forced Austria to grant access to third-country nationals with a permanent residence permit as well. Since then, all citizens and permanent residents have been eligible (Immobilienscout, n.d.).

HB3: *Integration requirements for housing benefits*
1990–2000: ***0** (no integration requirements)*
2010–2015: ***4** (integration and/or language requirements)*

There are no direct integration requirements for access to social housing or housing benefits. However, since 2003 there have been both integration and language requirements for accessing a permanent residence permit (Pöschl, 2006), and therefore access to housing benefits also depends on meeting those requirements.

HB4: *Preferential treatment in housing*
1990–2015: ***4** (no privileged access for housing)*
There is no immigrant-targeted housing assistance in Austria.

Social assistance

SA1: *Residence requirements for social assistance benefits*
1990–2015: ***3*** *(residence requirement between one and five years)*

All minimum-income benefits have a residence requirement of five years (Social Affairs Ministry, 2016). Recognized refugees are eligible for social assistance as soon as their asylum claim has been accepted. Since this group makes up only a small proportion of the migrant population (between 2% and 7% in the period under study, Statistics Austria, n.d.), the scores reported here do not reflect these exemptions.

SA2: *Status requirements for social assistance benefits*
1990: ***4*** *(only citizens and some permanent residents)*
2000–2015: ***3*** *(all permanent residents and EU citizens)*

Until the mid-1990s, most means-tested benefits were exclusively available to Austrian citizens (Gächter, 1995; Sensenig-Dabbous, 1999). In 1995, the European Court of Human Rights forced Austria to make the emergency benefit "Notstandshilfe" accessible to non-citizens as well (Gortázar Rotaeche, 1998). Since then, all means-tested cash benefits in Austria have been available to both citizens and permanent residents (Social Affairs Ministry, 2016).

SA3: *Consequences of uptake for status*
1990–2015: ***4*** *(revocation of residence permit)*

A central element of Austria's immigration regime is that non-citizens can lose their right of residence when they become unable to support themselves. Drawing on social assistance is usually considered evidence of this (Gächter, 1995).

SA4: *Integration requirements for social assistance*
1990–2000: ***0*** *(no integration requirements)*
2010–2015: ***3*** *(access tied to permits with integration requirements)*

There are no direct integration requirements for access to social assistance benefits. However, access is tied to at least a permanent residence permit, which since 2003 has come with both integration and language requirements (Pöschl, 2006).

Active labour market

ALM1: *Residence requirements*
1990–2015: ***2*** *(access tied to unemployment benefits requiring a work history)*

Most unemployment benefits are available only to recipients of unemployment benefits, which are available only to residents with a work history ranging between one and two years during the period under study (Ludwig-Mayerhofer & Wroblewski, p. 487).

ALM2: *Status requirements*
1990: ***4*** *(citizens and privileged non-nationals only)*
2000–2015: ***2*** *(all citizens and permanent residents)*

Since access to active labour market programs is tied to unemployment benefits, the same status requirements apply as for unemployment benefits: contributory unemployment benefits are *de facto* unavailable to most temporary migrants (see CUB1), and until 1995 the means-tested unemployment benefit "Notstandshilfe" was exclusively available to Austrian citizens (see SA2).

ALM3: *Immigrant-targeted language programs*
1990–2000: ***4*** *(no funded language programs)*
2010–2015: ***3*** *(only some discount and only if completed successfully)*

Before the integration reform in 2003, language training for migrants received little attention in Austria, mostly because proficiency in German was a precondition for admission in the first place. Since then, however, there have been mandatory language classes for migrants, which since 2005 have had to be funded almost entirely by migrants themselves (Duncan, 2010; Perchinig, 2009). In some cases, immigrants can receive a rebate if they complete the course successfully (City of Vienna, n.d.).

ALM4: *Other immigrant-targeted employment assistance*
1990–2010: ***4*** *(no immigrant-targeted active labour market policies available)*
2015: ***0*** *(programs available to any migrant)*

Austria has long had no immigrant-targeted employment assistance programs; this has occasionally been criticized by academics (Kaloianov, 2012; Perchinig, 2009). This changed in 2011, however, when the government established the State Secretariat for Integration, which among other activities rolled out a number of employment services, including welcome desks aiming to help immigrants on the labour market and job support programs for migrants in certain professions (Gruber, Mattes, & Stadlmair, 2016; Speer, 2018). By now, there are several employment services available to newly arrived migrants who are not yet eligible for the more general active labour market policies (Arbeitsmarktservice, 2018: 18–25).

Belgium

(data collection by Zina Bibanovic, Liam Thompson, and Edward Koning)

	Tax-paid pensions	Health care	Contr. unempl.	Contr. pension	Housing	Social assist.	Active labour market	Average
1990	58	56	25	38	25	50/25	56/81	44
2000	50	44	42	18	13	50/31	44	36
2010	67	44	58/42	18	44/19	69/44	38/44	44
2015	67	44	58/42	14	44/19	69/44	38/44	43

Tax-paid pensions

TPP1: Residence requirements for universal tax-paid pension
*1990–2015: **–8** (no universal public pension)*

There is no universal public pension program in Belgium. The only tax-paid pension is means-tested (see below).

TPP2: Availability of means-tested program for those with incomplete benefit
*1990–2000: **0** (yes, with no or very short residence requirement)*
*2010–2015: **2** (yes, with residence requirement of 3–10 years)*

Pensioners with incomplete pension income have been able to avail themselves of a means-tested benefit. Before 2001, this benefit was called the "Gewaarborgd Inkomen voor Bejaarden" (GBI). It had a one-month residence requirement, which was abolished in 1999 (Lewis, 1969; Seniorennet, n.d.). A 2001 reform replaced this benefit with the "Inkomensgarantie voor ouderen / Garantie de revenus aux personnes âgées" (IGO). This is only accessible to pensioners who receive some form of pension income, which requires at least 312 days of work history in Belgium or five years of residence (Mussche, Corluy, & Marx, 2014; Loi instituant la garantie de revenus aux personnes âgées, 2001).

TTP3: Status requirement for access to means-tested or universal tax-paid pension
*1990–2015: **3** (citizens and specially designated groups only)*

Access to both the GBI and IGO is restricted to Belgian citizens, EU citizens, and refugees (Lewis, 1969; Loi instituant la garantie de revenus aux personnes âgées, 2001, Seniorennet, n.d.).

TTP4: *Export possibilities of (means-tested or universal) tax-paid pension*
1990: ***4** (no export possibility at all)*
2000–2015: ***3** (during very short stay abroad only)*

The means-tested pension benefit could not be exported at all until 1992, when receipt abroad was made possible for stays of less than 90 days per calendar year (Seniorennet, n.d.). The introduction of the IGO changed this to a maximum stay abroad of 30 days, and a 2014 provision added that any uninterrupted stay abroad of more than six months would make claimants lose their eligibility altogether (Federale Pensionsdienst, n.d.)

Health care

HC1: *Residence requirement for public health care*
1990–2015: ***3** (1 year of contributions)*

Health care benefits only become available after patients have made compulsory health care insurance contributions for at least one year (Gerkens & Merkur, 2010; Mussche, Corluy, & Marx, 2014; Loi relative à l'assurance obligatoire soins de santé et indemnités, 1994).

HC2: *Status requirements for public health care*
1990–2015: ***1** (restrictions for undocumented migrants, but no barriers to urgent care)*

All legal residents are eligible for public health care (Gerkens & Merkur, 2010; Mussche, Corluy, & Marx 2014; Loi relative à l'assurance obligatoire soins de santé et indemnités, 1994). Undocumented migrants have had access to urgent medical care at least since 1976, when a law explicitly granted access to this category of residents, and indirectly since 1964, when a law ensured that insurance coverage would not be checked until after health care had been administered (Loi organique des centres publics d'action sociale, 1976; Romero-Ortuno, 2004: 255).

HC3: *Health care accessibility services*
1990: ***4** (nothing available)*
2000–2015: ***2** (services exist, but not are not fully funded and/or not run directly by government)*

Public funding for translation services in the Belgian sector was first introduced in 1991. But since hospitals have to apply for federal funding and arrange the translation services themselves, these services are far from universally available (Lorant & Bhopal, 2010: 237; Verrept, 2008). Indeed, it is far more common that patients with low language proficiency rely on family members than on professional translators (Van Eechoud et al., 2017). Moreover, several observers have criticized a lack of cultural sensitivity in the extension of health care services in Belgium (Ahaddour, Van den Branden, & Broeckaert, 2016).

HC4: *Additional health care benefits*
1990–2015: ***1*** *(extra coverage only for some refugees or refugee claimants)*

Asylum seekers and refugees receive coverage for some medical expenses that are not normally covered under Belgian insurance schemes, such as glasses for children and specific prescription drugs (Druyts et al., 2013; Frydryszak & Macherey, 2016).

Contributory unemployment

CUB1: *Status requirements for access to contributory unemployment benefits*
1990: ***1*** *(all legal residents except international students and/or seasonal workers)*
2000–2015: ***3*** *(Permanent residents, citizens, and very few temporary migrants)*

In 1990, access to unemployment benefits were accessible to all legal residents except international students (interview BEL-01; Agentschap Integratie en Inburgering, n.d.). Since then, however, the requirements have been tightened: many temporary migrants have been granted either a closed permit (which means that when they lose their job they will not be eligible for unemployment benefits, but instead lose their right of residence), or a permit with a very short duration (which means that they are unable to build up entitlement to unemployment benefits) (Forem, n.d.; Mussche, Corluy, & Marx, 2014).

CUB2: *Integration requirements for access to contributory unemployment benefits*
1990–2000: ***0*** *(no integration requirements)*
2010–2015: ***Flanders: 2*** *(access tied to permits with integration requirements)*
Wallonia: 0 *(no integration requirements)*

Before 2003, there were no integration requirements for accessing unemployment benefits. In 2003, however, Flanders introduced integration requirements for obtaining long-term residency in Flanders, which is necessary in order to access unemployment benefits (Dierkx & Van Dam, 2014; Adam & Jacobs, 2014). Such requirements have never been introduced in Wallonia (Mandin, 2014).

CUB3: *Export possibilities*
1990–2015: ***2*** *(export possible to limited number of states for short period of time)*

Unemployment benefits can be exported to countries of the EU, the European Economic Area, and Switzerland, for a maximum period of 3 months (interview BEL-01).

Contributory pension

CP1: *Status requirement*
1990–2015: ***0*** *(all legal residents included)*

There are no status requirements for accessing contributory pension benefits: everyone who is eligible to work is eligible to participate in the contributory pension scheme (Mussche, Corluy, & Marx, 2014, MISSOC 2004–2018).

CP2: *Export possibilities*
1990: ***3*** *(citizens only)*
2000: ***1.4*** *(no restrictions for citizens of designated countries only)*
2010: ***1.4*** *(no restrictions for citizens of designated countries only)*
2015: ***1.2*** *(no restrictions for citizens of designated countries only)*

Before 1993, only Belgian citizens were able to export their pension abroad. Since then, however, pension export has become possible for an increasing share of the migrant population. Since 1993, this has become a possibility for all citizens of EU member states, and since 1996 of all member states of the European Economic Area and any country with which Belgium had signed a bilateral social security agreement as well (Mussche, Corluy, & Marx, 2014; Corluy & Verbist, 2010). By 2000, this included a total of 23 covered countries, and these numbers have gone up to 47 by 2010, and 53 by 2015 (Socialsecurity.be, n.d.).

Housing benefits

HB1: *Residence requirements for housing benefits*
1990–2015: ***0*** *(no residence requirement)*

There has never been a waiting period before one can register for social housing anywhere in Belgium (interview, BEL-02; Notre Maison, n.d.; Societé Wallonne du Logement, n.d.).

HB2: *Status requirements for housing benefits*
1990–2000: ***0*** *(any resident)*
2010–2015: ***1*** *(all legal residents)*

For a long time, there was no test of legal residency to access social housing. Since the 2000s, however, applicants need to be registered in the national population register or the aliens register, which effectively bars undocumented migrants (Decreet behoudende de Vlaamse Wooncode, Art. 93; interview, BEL-02; Notre Maison, n.d.; Societé Wallonne du Logement, n.d.).

HB3: *Integration requirements for housing benefits*
1990–2000: ***0*** *(no integration requirements)*
2010–2015: ***Flanders: 4*** *(integration and/or language requirements)*
Wallonia: 0 *(no integration requirements)*

There have never been integration requirements for accessing social housing in Wallonia. In Flanders, however, since 2008 immigrants for whom integration courses are compulsory (i.e., recent third-country nationals, asylum seekers, and non-citizens who are dependent on social assistance) must at least be in the process of taking integration classes before they can access social housing (Decreet behoudende de Vlaamse Wooncode, Art. 95; interview, BEL-02; Vlaamse Maatschappij voor Sociaal Wonen, n.d.-a)

HB4: *Preferential treatment in housing*
1990: ***4*** *(no privileged access for migrants)*
2000–2015: ***2*** *(housing assistance for recognized refugees)*

No group of migrants receives privileged access to social housing – social housing companies work through waiting lists in order of application, regardless of the status of the applicant (Vlaamse Maatschappij voor Sociaal Wonen, n.d.-b). Since 1999, however, asylum seekers whose claim is accepted have received some assistance to finance the costs of settling into independent housing (interview, BEL-02; Openbaar Centrum voor Maatschappelijk Welzijn, 2008-a).

Social assistance

SA1: *Residence requirements for social assistance benefits*
1990–2000: ***0*** *(no residence requirement for anyone)*
2010–2015: ***2*** *(residence requirement of 1 year or less)*

Between 1976 and 2002, the social assistance benefit in Belgium did not stipulate any minimum length of residence. Since a comprehensive reform in 2002, migrants need to have resided in the country for at least 3 months before they can access the program, with the exception of refugees and stateless persons (Mussche, Corluy, & Marx, 2014, pp. 33–34, 43–44).

SA2: *Status requirements for social assistance benefits*
1990: ***Flanders: 4*** *(only citizens and some permanent residents)*
Wallonia: 0 *(all residents)*
2000: ***Flanders: 4*** *(only citizens and some permanent residents)*
Wallonia: 1 *(all legal residents)*
2010–2015: ***1*** *(all legal residents)*

In Flanders, until 2002 the social assistance benefit was available to citizens, EU nationals, and refugees and stateless persons (MISSOC, 2009). Since the 2002 welfare reform, social assistance has been available to all immigrants who are registered in the population register, i.e., all documented residents (Openbaar Centrum voor Maatschappelijk Welzijn, 2008-b). In Wallonia, until the 1990s social assistance was available even to undocumented migrants. Since then, only legal residents have been able to apply for the benefit, although exceptions are made for undocumented migrants who are in financial hardship and are unable to leave the country for reasons beyond their control (FRA, 2011; Mussche, Corluy & Marx, 2014, p. 43).

SA3: *Consequences of uptake for status*
1990–2015: ***4*** *(revocation of residence permit)*

Immigrants on temporary permits can lose their status or not see their permit renewed if they apply for social assistance. Similarly, migrants who rely on welfare are unlikely to meet the requirements related to economic activity for naturalization (Loi sur l'accès au territoire, le séjour, l'établissement et l'éloignement des étrangers, 1980; Mussche, Corluy, & Marx, 2014; Stadlmaier, 2018).

SA4: *Integration requirements for social assistance*
1990–2000: ***0*** *(no integration requirements)*
2010–2015: ***Flanders: 4*** *(compulsory integration for benefit recipients)*
Wallonia: 0 *(no integration requirements)*

There have never been any integration requirements associated with benefit access in Wallonia (Adam & Jacobs, 2014; Martiniello, 2012). In 2006, however, Flanders made the completion of an integration course, consisting of language training, cultural orientation, and career advice, mandatory for benefit recipients (Gysen, Kuijper, & Van Avermaet, 2009; Mussche, Corluy, & Marx, 2014).

Active labour market

ALM1: *Residence requirements*
1990–2015: **4** *(more than 1 year)*

Most active labour market programs in Belgium are available only to permanent residents, which in practice means that for most migrants (except refugees), these programs are unavailable in the first five years they reside in the country (Mussche, Corluy, & Marx, 2014). Since 2013, EU citizens have been able to access active labour market programs after 3 months (Loi concernant le droit à l'integration sociale, 2002).

ALM2: *Status requirements*
1990: **4** *(citizens and privileged non-nationals only)*
2000–2015: **2** *(all citizens and permanent residents)*

Most active labour market programs in Belgium were inaccessible to third-country nationals until the 1990s, even those with permanent residence. Since then, all citizens and permanent residents have had access to active labour market programs (Mussche, Corluy, & Marx, 2014).

ALM3: *Immigrant-targeted language programs*
1990–2000: **1** *(funded programs, but not freely available to all categories of migrants)*
2010–2015: ***Flanders: 0*** *(funded programs available to all migrants)*
Wallonia: 1 *(funded programs, but not freely available to all migrants)*

Language programs in Belgium have long been run by local centres, which need to apply for federal funding. This has resulted in uneven availability across the country. Since 2003, however, Flanders has offered fully funded integration courses, which are compulsory for certain categories of immigrants (recent third-country nationals, asylum seekers, and non-citizens who are dependent on social assistance) (Mandin, 2014; Yanasmayan & Foblets, 2010).

ALM4: *Other immigrant-targeted employment assistance*
1990: ***Flanders: 0*** *(programs available to any migrant)*
Wallonia: 4 *(no public integration programs available)*
2000–2015: **0** *(programs available to any migrant)*

Flanders has offered immigrant-targeted employment assistance since at least 1984, when it initiated services to facilitate the recognition of foreign credentials. Since then, it has expanded the range of available programs, most dramatically since the launch of mandatory integration programs in 2003 (Naric, n.d.; Van de Voorde & De Bruijn, 2010). Wallonia, by contrast, has never run immigrant-targeted active labour market policies (interview, BEL-03), even though since 1996 it has offered immigrant-targeted employment services out of welcome centres (Mandin, 2014; Décret relatif à l'intégration des personnes étrangères ou d'origine étrangère, 1996).

Canada

(data collection by Camila Rivas-Garrido and Edward Koning)

	Tax-paid pensions	Health care	Contr. unempl.	Contr. pension	Housing	Social assist.	Active labour market	Average
1990	47	38	42	0	31	19	25	29
2000	50	38	42	0	31	19	19	28
2010	50	38	42	0	31	19	19	28
2015	50	44	42	0	31	19	19	29

Tax-paid pensions

TPP1: *Residence requirements for universal tax-paid pension*
1990–2015: ***3** (40 years for complete benefit, with prorated benefits for shorter residency)*

The federal universal tax-paid pension in Canada, Old Age Security, is available to anyone aged 65 who has resided legally in Canada for 40 years after the age of 18. Seniors with residency of at least 10 years are eligible for a prorated benefit (Koning & Banting, 2013).

TPP2: *Availability of means-tested program for those with incomplete benefit*
1990: ***2.6** (yes, with residence requirement 10+ for most but not all)*
2010–2015: ***3** (yes, with residence requirement 10+ years)*

There is a means-tested pension benefit for low-income elderly with incomplete pension income, called the Guaranteed Income Supplement. The benefit is only available for recipients of some level of Old Age Security, which means that the GIS is not accessible until migrants have resided in the country for at least 10 years. Since 1984, the benefit has been available earlier in cases where the applicant had resided for 10 years in Canada and one of the countries with which Canada has a bilateral security agreement; since then, however, a 1996 reform has denied this early access to the largest group of recently arrived elderly migrants, i.e., those under a sponsorship agreement (Koning & Banting, 2013). The score for 1990 is weighted to reflect the relative number of migrants who arrived in Canada in the 1980s who were from one of the 19 countries with which Canada had a bilateral agreement at the time (and who therefore could access the GIS upon arrival in cases where they were at least 65) (Statistics Canada, 1996).

TTP3: *Status requirement for access to means-tested or universal tax-paid pension*
1990–2015: ***1*** *(citizens and all permanent residents)*

While immigrants can use the years they spent in Canada on a temporary permit in determining their eligibility for tax-paid pension benefits, these programs are only accessible by those who are permanent residents or citizens at the time of retirement (George & George, 2013; Koning, 2019).

TTP4: *Export possibilities of (means-tested or universal) tax-paid pension*
1990–2015: ***1*** *(with additional residence requirements)*

Old Age Security is payable anywhere abroad, but only for beneficiaries who have resided in Canada for at least 20 years after the age of 18. The Guaranteed Income Supplement can only be received abroad for a short period (up to 6 months), and only in countries with which Canada has a bilateral social security agreement (Social Security Administration 2003, 2015).

Health care

HC1: *Residence requirement for public health care*
1990–2015: ***2*** *(6 weeks-3 months)*

The provinces that receive the largest numbers of immigrants (Ontario, Quebec, and British Columbia) have a 3-month waiting period before new arrivals can access their health care systems. Certain groups of migrants (such as protected persons) are exempted from this requirement (Caulford & Vali, 2006; Koning & Banting, 2013; Ontario Health Insurance Act, 2017).

HC2: *Status requirements for public health care*
1990–2015: ***2*** *(restrictions for undocumented and some categories of legal migrants, but no barriers to urgent care)*

Most legal residents, except international students and holders of a temporary work permit of a very short duration, are eligible for provincial health care (Koning & Banting, 2013; Ontario Health Insurance Act, 2017), or in the case of refugee claimants, for a federal health care program (see HC4). Individuals who are ineligible for provincial health care coverage (including undocumented migrants) can, however, access subsidized emergency health care services (Koning, 2019).

HC3:	*Health care accessibility services*
1990–2015:	***2** (services exist, but not are not fully funded and/or not run directly by government)*

Since the 1970s, community health centres have been set up across the country that provide accessibility services for immigrants in health care, including culturally sensitive care, and translation services. These centres are government-funded but autonomous non-profit organizations, and therefore the range and availability of services differ dramatically across the country (Alliance for Healthier Communities, n.d.; BCACHC, n.d.).

HC4:	*Additional health care benefits*
1990–2010:	***0** (expanded coverage available for refugees or refugee claimants)*
2015:	***1** (extra coverage only for some refugees or refugee claimants)*

Since 1957, Canada has run a federal health care program specifically designed for refugees and refugee claimants, the Interim Federal Health Program. This program can grant access to services that are usually not covered under provincial health care packages, such as dental and ophthalmological care (Koning, 2019; Merry et al., 2011). A 2012 reform, however, cut access to this program for some categories of active asylum seekers and all rejected refugee claimants (including those awaiting appeal decisions). And while many of the 2012 changes were reversed in 2015, the program is still decidedly less accessible now than it was before 2012 (Machery, Simonnot, & Vanbiervliet, 2015).

Contributory unemployment

CUB1:	*Status requirements for access to contributory unemployment benefits*
1990–2015	***3** (Permanent residents, citizens, and very few temporary migrants)*

Everyone who is employed in Canada pays contributions to an unemployment insurance benefit. However, most temporary residents have a permit that is tied to a specific employer, which means that when they lose their job they lose their right of residence and cannot draw from unemployment benefits (Banting & Koning, 2017; Nakache & Kinoshita, 2010; Rodriguez-Garcia, 2012).

CUB2: *Integration requirements for access to contributory unemployment benefits*
1990–2015: ***0*** *(no integration requirements)*

There have never been any integration requirements to accessing unemployment benefits.

CUB3: *Export possibilities*
1990–2015: ***2*** *(export possible for short period of time)*

In principle, the export of unemployment benefits is not possible. However, recipients can continue to receive their benefits if they are abroad for up to seven days in case of personal emergencies, or up to fourteen days in order to pursue an international job opportunity (Government of Canada, n.d.-a).

Contributory pension

CP1: *Status requirement*
1990–2015: ***0*** *(all legal residents included)*

The contributory Canada Pension Plan (CPP) is accessible to anyone 65 or older with at least one valid annual contribution. There are no other requirements, and therefore all legal residents are in principle eligible for the program (Koning, 2019; Social Security Administration, 2015).

CP2: *Export possibilities*
1990–2015: ***0*** *(export possible without restrictions)*

There are no residence requirements for the Canada Pension Plan: eligible retirees can claim this benefit from anywhere in the world, without additional restrictions (Canada Pension Plan Act, 1985; Social Security Administration, 2015).

Housing benefits

HB1: *Residence requirements for housing benefits*
All years: ***0*** *(no residence requirement)*

In the province of Ontario, there is no length-of-residence requirement before someone becomes eligible for subsidized housing or rent assistance (City of Toronto, n.d.; interview, CAN-01; OCASI, n.d.-a).

HB2: *Status requirements for housing benefits*
1990–2000: ***2*** *(some but not all temporary migrants)*

In the province of Ontario, all permanent residents and refugee claimants are eligible for subsidized housing and rent assistance. Other temporary migrants (temporary workers and international students who are not in the process of applying for permanent residence) are ineligible (City of Toronto, n.d.; OCASI, n.d.-a).

HB3: *Integration requirements for housing benefits*
1990–2015 ***0*** *(no integration requirements)*

There have never been any integration requirements to accessing housing benefits.

HB4: *Preferential treatment in housing*
1990–2015: ***3*** *(some services available but are not fully funded and/or not run by government)*

The federal Resettlement Assistance Program helps refugees find a place to live when they first get to Canada. The services and programs offered under this program, however, are highly decentralized and are managed by local service provider organizations. As a result, the range and availability of services differ dramatically across the country (Government of Canada, n.d.-b).

Social assistance

SA1: *Residence requirements for social assistance benefits*
1990–2015: ***1*** *(residence requirement only for specific categories, such as family migrants)*

Federal funding for provincial assistance programs prohibit any residence requirement to accessing social assistance. Sponsored family migrants are the only category of immigrants who face some form of residence requirement. In the first years in the country (3–10 years, depending on their relationship to the sponsor), they are technically eligible for social assistance, but any benefits they take up during that period will have to be paid back by their sponsor, except in exceptional circumstances (Department of Finance, n.d.; Koning & Banting, 2013).

SA2: *Status requirements for social assistance benefits*
1990–2015: ***2*** *(all permanent residents and some temporary residents)*

All citizens and permanent residents (with the exception of family migrants during their first years in the country, see SA1) are eligible for social assistance. The eligibility of temporary migrants differs between provinces. In some, international students and temporary workers can access welfare, whereas in others access is more restricted. Refugee claimants can access some form of cash benefit in every province (Koning & Banting, 2013).

SA3: *Consequences of uptake for status*
1990–2015: ***0*** *(no consequences)*

Taking up social assistance does not have consequences for residency in Canada.

SA4: *Integration requirements for social assistance*
1990–2015: ***0*** *(no integration requirements)*

There are no integration or language requirements associated with accessing social assistance.

Active labour market

ALM1: *Residence requirements*
1990–2015: ***2*** *(access tied to unemployment benefits requiring a work history)*

Canadian provinces offer a wide variety of active labour market programs, such as job counselling, training programs, and internships. In most cases, access to these programs is reserved for recipients of unemployment benefits, and by extension for those with a work history in Canada (Morden, 2016).

ALM2: *Status requirements*
1990–2015: ***1*** *(all permanent residents and some temporary residents)*

Since access to most active labour market policies is tied to unemployment benefits, only those migrants who are eligible for those benefits can access active labour market programs: permanent residents and temporary migrants with an "open" permit whose residence is not tied to a specific employer (see CUB1).

ALM3: *Immigrant-targeted language programs*
1990: ***1** (funded programs, but not freely available to all categories of immigrants)*
2000–2015: ***0** (fully funded language programs, available to any immigrant)*

In 1985, the federal government launched the Canadian Jobs Strategy, a program designed to help economic migrants succeed on the labour market, including by offering them language training (Ricento et al., 2008). In 1992, Language Instruction for Newcomers, which made language training available to all permanent residents, replaced this program (OCASI, n.d.-b; Rodriguez-Garcia, 2012).

ALM4: *Other immigrant-targeted employment assistance*
1990–2015 ***0** (programs available to any migrant)*

In 1974, the federal government launched the Immigrant Settlement and Adaptation Program to fund services aimed at assisting the integration of immigrants. The services are delivered primarily by not-for-profit organizations and local partners and include employment assistance, referrals, counselling, and orientation services (Biles, 2008; Government of Canada, 2011, n.d.-c). Since the early 2000s the federal government has also expanded its services aimed at facilitating the recognition of foreign credentials (Koning, 2019).

Denmark

(data collection by Camila Rivas-Garrido and Edward Koning)

	Tax-paid pensions	Health care	Contr. unempl.	Contr. pension	Housing	Social assist.	Active labour market	Average
1990	63	56	58	38	19	50	56	49
2000	63	56	42	38	19	50	44	44
2010	56	50	42	38	31	81	25	46
2015	56	50	42	38	31	81	25	46

Tax-paid pensions

TPP1: *Residence requirements for universal tax-paid pension*
1990–2015: ***3** (40 for complete, with pro-rated benefits for shorter residency)*

The universal tax-paid pension in Denmark, the Folkepension, is available to anyone aged 65 who has resided at least 40 years in the country. People with a shorter residency can receive a prorated benefit if they have spent at least

3 years (in case they are citizens) or 10 years (in case they are not) in the country (Andersen, 2007; Social Security Administration 2002, 2016).

TPP2: *Availability of means-tested program for those with incomplete benefit*
1990–2000: ***4** (no program)*
2010–2015: ***3** (yes, with residence requirement 10+ years)*

Since 2004, low-income recipients of the Folkepension can receive a pension supplement. Since non-citizens need at least 10 years of residence before they are eligible for any level of Folkepension (and the residence requirement for accessing citizenship and therefore a reduced waiting period is about equally long), in practice there is a residence requirement of 10 years to accessing the pension supplement (Blume and Verner 2007; Koning, 2011; MISSOC, 2014–2018; Sørensen, Olesen, & Olesen, 2018).

TTP3: *Status requirement for access to means-tested or universal tax-paid pension*
1990–2015: ***1** (citizens and all permanent residents)*

The Folkepension can only be accessed by citizens and long-term residents (of more than 10 years) (Andersen, 2007; European Commission, 2013; Social Security Administration 2002, 2016).

TTP4: *Export possibilities of (means-tested or universal) tax-paid pension*
1990–2015: ***2** (with cuts in benefits)*

The Danish Folkepension can be exported anywhere in the world. However, for Danish citizens this is only possible after 10 years of permanent residence in the country after the age of 15. Moreover, none of the tax-paid pension supplements (including the means-tested supplement, see TTP2) can be exported (Consolidated Act on Social Pensions, 2010; Government of Denmark, n.d.-a).

Health care

HC1: *Residence requirement for public health care*
1990–2015: ***2** (6 weeks to 3 months)*
2010–2015: ***0** (no waiting period)*

There used to be a 6-week waiting period for new residents after registering in the national register (Cuadra, 2010; Social Security Administration, 2002).

A 2007 reform, however, abolished this requirement, and new residents now have immediate access as soon as they register (MISSOC, 2004–2018).

HC2: *Status requirements for public health care*
1990–2015: ***2** (restrictions for undocumented migrants and some categories of legal migrants, but no barriers to urgent care)*

All those who are registered in the national register are eligible for public health care. Those who stay in Denmark temporarily must pay for the services they receive. Undocumented migrants are entitled to state-funded acute care but not to any other health care services (Cuadra, 2010; Ministry of Health, 2017).

HC3: *Health care accessibility services*
1990–2000: ***1** (state-funded translation services only)*
2010–2015: ***2** (services exist, but are not fully funded)*

State-funded translation services are available when a doctor determines a patient needs an interpreter. A 2004 policy change, however, introduced fees on such services for residents who have resided in the country for 7 years or more, and a subsequent reform expanded this to anyone who has resided in Denmark for more than 3 years (Act to Amend the Hospital Organisation Act and the Public Health Insurance Act, 2004; Ministry of Health, n.d.).

HC4: *Additional health care benefits*
1990–2015: ***4** (no additional health care benefits)*

No categories of immigrants have access to health care benefits that are unavailable to native-born citizens. Some health care providers have recently started pilot projects in providing refugee-targeted care, but those did not start until after the period under investigation.

Contributory unemployment

CUB1: *Status requirements for access to contributory unemployment benefits*
1990–2015 ***3** (permanent residents, citizens, and very few temporary migrants)*

The Danish unemployment insurance scheme is voluntary and therefore can only be accessed by those who have voluntarily paid into it. It becomes available after one year of contributions, as long as the recipient is available to take up work (Blume & Verner, 2007; Nannestad, 2004; Pedersen, 2013; Social Security Administration, 2002, 2016). As a result, the scheme is not accessible to holders of a permit that is tied to a specific employer or that is too short in duration to make it possible to build up entitlement (A-kasser, n.d.-a, n.d-b).

CUB2: *Integration requirements for access to contributory unemployment benefits*
1990–2015: ***0*** *(no integration requirements)*

There are no integration requirements to join the unemployment insurance scheme (A-Kasser, n.d.-b).

CUB3: *Export possibilities*
1990: ***4*** *(no export possible)*
2000–2015: ***2*** *(export possible for short period of time)*

Unemployment benefits are generally only available to residents of Denmark. However, since the mid-1990s job seekers have been able to bring the benefit to any state in the European Economic Area for up to 3 months, albeit under additional conditions (A-Kasser, n.d.-c).

Contributory pension

CP1: *Status requirement*
1990–2015: ***3*** *(some temporary migrants excluded)*

The contributory pension, the ATP Livslang Pension, is available to retirees with a long work history in Denmark. Those who have worked on a short-term permit are usually not eligible, unless the Minister of Employment decides otherwise (Supplementary Labour Market Pension Act, 2014: s. 3).

CP2: *Export possibilities*
1990–2015: ***0*** *(export or cash-out possible without restrictions)*

Residence in Denmark is not a requirement to receive the ATP Livslang Pension. It can be exported anywhere in the world (Government of Denmark, n.d.-b; Supplementary Labour Market Pension Act, 2014).

Housing benefits

HB1: *Residence requirements for housing benefits*
All years: ***0*** *(no residence requirement)*

There is no waiting period before one becomes eligible for housing benefits. Apart from the regular waiting lists, there is no additional wait period before newcomers can access social housing either (Act on Individual Housing Support, 2019; Ministry of Housing, 2000).

HB2: *Status requirements for housing benefits*
1990–2000: ***2** (some but not all temporary residents)*

Permanent residents, EU nationals, and some categories of temporary permit holders are eligible for housing support (Aarhus University, n.d.; Act on Individual Housing Support, 2019; Ministry of Housing, 2000).

HB3: *Integration requirements for housing benefits*
1990–2015 ***0** (no integration requirements)*

There are no integration requirements associated with accessing either social housing or housing assistance (Act on Individual Housing Support, 2019; Ministry of Housing, 2000).

HB4: *Preferential treatment in housing*
1990–2000: ***1** (earmarked housing for refugees)*
2010–2015: ***3** (some services available but are not fully funded)*

Municipalities used to have a duty to provide refugees with housing within three months. The government abolished this requirement in 2002, however, encouraging municipalities to prioritize Danish citizens (Borevi & Bengtsson, 2015). During their first three years in the country, refugees can receive a loan, however, to help finance the costs of settling in (such as paying for a deposit) (Act on Individual Housing Support, 2019).

Social assistance

SA1: *Residence requirements for social assistance benefits*
1990–2000: ***3** (residence requirement between 1 and 5 years)*
2010–2015: ***4** (residence requirement of more than 5 years)*

Before 2002, there was no formal residence requirement for accessing social assistance, but because the benefit was reserved for permanent residents and there was a 3-year waiting period before one could access permanent residency, the residence requirement for accessing social assistance was effectively 3 years. A 2002 reform both increased the residence requirement for accessing permanent residence to 7 years and placed a formal 7-year residence requirement on social assistance (Borevi & Bengtsson, 2015; Pedersen, 2013; Andersen, Larsen, & Møller, 2009).

SA2: *Status requirements for social assistance benefits*
1990–2015: ***3** (all permanent residents and EU citizens)*

Only permanent residents and EU citizens are able to access social assistance. Other categories in need can only access a much less generous cash benefit (Andersen, Larsen, & Møller, 2009; Groenendijk, Guild, & Barzilay 2000).

SA3: *Consequences of uptake for status*
1990–2015: ***2** (inaccessible permanent residence or citizenship)*

Taking up social assistance in Denmark means that immigrants are ineligible for permanent residence permits for at least four years, and ineligible for citizenship, although exceptions are made for some categories of immigrants (Government of Denmark, n.d.-c; Neerup, 2012; Stadlmair, 2018).

SA4: *Integration requirements for social assistance*
1990–2000: ***0** (no integration requirements)*
2010–2015: ***4** (compulsory integration for recipients)*

Until the 2000s, there were no integration requirements to accessing social assistance. Since then, there have been not only stringent integration requirements for accessing permanent residency – the necessary permit to become eligible for general social assistance – but also formal integration requirements directly associated with receiving cash benefits, such as signing an integration contract that commits recipients to certain activities and taking mandatory language classes (Government of Denmark, n.d.-c; Jørgensen & Thomsen, 2016; Neerup, 2012).

Active labour market

ALM1: *Residence requirements*
1990–2015: ***2** (access tied to unemployment benefits requiring a work history)*

The Danish welfare state offers a wide range of active labour market policies. These are only accessible by those who receive either social assistance or unemployment benefits (Ahmad, Svarer, & Naveed, 2019). The residence requirement for social assistance is quite long (see SA1), but unemployment benefits can in principle be accessed after one year of contributions (see CUB1).

ALM2: *Status requirements*
1990–2015: ***1** (all permanent residents and some temporary residents)*

Since active labour market programs are available to recipients of unemployment benefits, any resident who is eligible for unemployment benefits, including some categories of temporary residents, can access these programs (see CUB1).

ALM3: *Immigrant-targeted language programs*
1990–2000: ***4** (no funded language programs)*
2010–2015: ***1** (funded programs, but not freely available to all categories)*

Since 2003, certain categories of newcomers are required to attend language programs. This can entail up to 3 years of free language training. However, the training is not accessible to newcomers who are not required to take it (Clausen et al., 2009; Neerup, 2012, OECD, 2007).

ALM4: *Other immigrant-targeted employment assistance*
1990 ***2** (programs available, but only available for refugees and/or asylum seekers)*
2000–2015 ***0** (programs available to any migrant)*

Denmark first established integration programs to assist immigrants' prospects on the labour market, but until 1999 these were available only to refugees (OECD, 2007). Since then, Denmark has run several programs to improve the employment prospects of immigrants in general, including wage subsidies for employers who hire newcomers, public-sector employment programs, training opportunities, and job counselling services (Clausen et al. 2009; Jørgensen & Thomsen, 2016).

Finland

(data collection by Edward Koning)

	Tax-paid pensions	Health care	Contr. unempl.	Contr. pension	Housing	Social assist.	Active labour market	Average
1990	35	75	58	38	38	19	75	48
2000	63	44	42	38	19	75	25	43
2010	62	44	42	38	19	81	25	44
2015	43	44	42	38	19	81	25	42

Tax-paid pensions

TPP1: *Residence requirements for universal tax-paid pension*
1990: ***1*** *(between 5 and 10 years)*
2000–2015: ***3*** *(40 for complete, with pro-rated benefits for shorter residency)*

Before 1994, the residence requirement for accessing the tax-paid national pension was 5 years for foreigners, but nothing for Finnish citizens. When Finland joined the EU, however, its pension was reorganized such that full access was available only after 40 years, and reduced prorated access became possible after 3 years for citizens and 5 years for foreigners. Since 2007, the requirement for early access has been 3 years of residence for all categories of applicants (Kela, n.d.-a; Kotkas, 2016).

TPP2: *Availability of means-tested program for those with incomplete benefit*
1990: ***–8*** *(no program)*
2000–2010: ***4*** *(no program or not accessible program)*
2015: ***1*** *(yes, with residence requirement of 1–3 years)*

Before the pension reform in 1994, the absence of any means-tested supplement was understandable considering that everyone would be able to access the full national pension benefit after 5 years' residence in the country. Since the reform, however, people with a relatively short history of residence in the country have seen their benefit level drop considerably. A 2011 reform introduced a guaranteed pension aimed at guaranteeing a minimum pension income for anyone with at least 3 years' residence in the country (Airio & Nurminen, 2016; Kela, n.d.-b; Kotkas, 2016).

TTP3: *Status requirement for access to means-tested or universal tax-paid pension*
1990–2015: ***1*** *(citizens and all permanent residents)*

Tax-paid pensions are only available to residents who have settled permanently in Finland. Other categories of migrants, such as seasonal workers, au pairs, students, asylum applicants, and undocumented migrants, are explicitly excluded (Kela, n.d.-a; Könönen 2018b).

TTP4: *Export possibilities of (means-tested or universal) tax-paid pension*
1990: ***2.2*** *(possibilities for export depend on country of residence)*
2000: ***2.0*** *(possibilities for export depend on country of residence)*

2010: **1.9** *(possibilities for export depend on country of residence)*
2015: **1.9** *(possibilities for export depend on country of residence)*

Before the 1994 pension reform, the national pension could only be exported without restrictions to the Nordic countries, as well as to Canada (albeit with additional residence requirements). Pensioners in other countries could only receive the benefit for the first year after leaving the country. Since then, the rules have differed even more. The pension is exportable without restrictions to Switzerland and all EU and EEA member states. To export the benefit to United States, Canada, Chile, and Israel, the recipient needs to satisfy additional residence requirements. Exporting the benefit to Australia usually implies a benefit cut. Exporting the national pension to any other country is only possible for a period of up to one year. The guaranteed pension (see TPP2) is not exportable (Kela, n.d.-c, n.d.-d; Koikkalainen et al., 2012; Ministry of Social Affairs and Health, 1956).

Health care

HC1: *Residence requirement for public health care*
1990–2015: **0** *(no waiting period)*

There is no residence requirement for accessing health care in Finland. Anyone with the necessary permits to be eligible is covered immediately (Helander, Holley, & Uuttana, 2016; Kela, n.d.-e; MISSOC 2004–2018).

HC2: *Status requirements for public health care*
1990–2015: **4** *(undocumented and some categories of legal migrants excluded entirely)*

The public health care system is available to all permanent residents and, since 2004, all EU citizens. Since 2011, third-country nationals with a job and work permit as well as registered job seekers with a 6-month employment history can also access the basic system. Asylum seekers are covered by a parallel system that is decidedly less generous. Third-country nationals who are seasonal workers, au pairs, students, or undocumented migrants are only eligible to receive emergency care and can be charged for the costs of such care afterwards (Kela, n.d.-e; Könönen, 2018a, 2018b; Kotkas, 2016; Martikainen, Valtonen, & Wahlbeck, 2012; Tuomisto et al., 2019).

HC3: *Health care accessibility services*
1990: **4** *(nothing available)*
2000–2015: **1** *(state-funded translation services only)*

Since 1992, patients have had the right to interpreter services, and since 1999, the costs for those services have been covered by the (national or municipal) authorities (Eklöf, Hulpi, & Leino-Kilpi, 2014; InfoFinland, n.d.-a).

HC4: *Additional health care benefits*
1990: ***4** (nothing available)*
2000–2015: ***2** (specialized services for refugees, in particular in mental health)*

Since the mid-1990s, there have been psychiatric clinics in Finland specifically aimed at helping refugee survivors of torture and their family members (Deaconess Foundation, n.d.; EU-healthcare, n.d.).

Contributory unemployment

CUB1: *Status requirements for access to contributory unemployment benefits*
1990–2015: ***3** (permanent residents, citizens, and very few temporary migrants)*

Unemployment benefits are available to all unemployed job-seeking permanent residents and citizens who are fit for work, looking for a full-time job, and meet the work requirement. Labour migrants whose permits are tied to a specific employer or sector of employment, recently arrived asylum seekers, au pairs, and international students all have restricted access to the labour market and are therefore excluded (Kela, n.d.-f; Koikkalainen *et al.*, 2012; Könönen, 2018b; Kyyrä, Pesola & Rissanen, 2017).

CUB2: *Integration requirements for access to contributory unemployment benefits*
1990–2015: ***0** (no integration requirements)*

There are no specific immigrant-targeted integration requirements associated with accessing unemployment benefits in Finland. Recipients of unemployment benefits can be asked to participate in training programs in order to improve their standing on the labour market, but this applies to native-born Fins as well (Kela, n.d.-f; Kyyrä, Pesola & Rissanen, 2017).

CUB3: *Export possibilities*
1990: ***4** (no export possible)*
2000–2015: ***2** (export possible for short period of time)*

Unemployment benefits can only be accessed by those who reside in Finland. However, since the country joined the EU in 1995, recipients can retain the benefit for a period of up to 3 months while searching for employment in a different member state (Kela, n.d.-g).

Contributory pension

CP1: *Status requirement*
1990–2015: ***3** (some temporary migrants excluded)*

Anyone who works legally in Finland builds up entitlement to the earnings-related pension, but some workers, such as seasonal workers and au pairs, will never be able to access the pension despite making contributions (Finnish Centre for Pensions, n.d.; Könönen, 2018b).

CP2: *Export possibilities*
1990–2015: ***0** (export possible without restrictions)*

The earnings-related pension is payable anywhere in the world (Finnish Centre for Pensions, n.d., Koikkalainen et al., 2012).

Housing benefits

HB1: *Residence requirements for housing benefits*
All years: ***0** (no residence requirement)*

There is no residence requirement for accessing housing benefits in Finland. However, long-term residence is a criterion in the allocation of municipal social housing (Kaupinen, 2002; Kela, n.d.-h; Koikkalainen et al., 2012).

HB2: *Status requirements for housing benefits*
1990–2015: ***2** (some but not all temporary migrants)*

Housing benefits are only available to those who are considered to be settling or have been settled permanently in Finland. Labour migrants with a permit of less than one year, au pairs, and international students are excluded. Social housing is similarly only available to those who have a permit to reside for at least one year. (InfoFinland, n.d.-b; Kela, n.d.-h; Könönen, 2018b).

HB3: *Integration requirements for housing benefits*
1990–2015 ***0** (no integration requirements)*

There are no integration requirements associated with accessing social housing or housing benefits in Finland (Kaupinen, 2002; Kela, n.d.-i).

HB4: *Preferential treatment in housing*
1990: ***4** (no privileged access for immigrants)*
2000–2015: ***1** (earmarked housing for refugees)*

Since the 1990s, quota refugees have had privileged access to social housing. (Kaupinen, 2002; InfoFinland, n.d.-c).

Social assistance

SA1: *Residence requirements for social assistance benefits*
1990: ***0** (no residence requirement for anyone)*
2000–2015: ***3** (residence requirement between 1 and 5 years)*

Initially, social assistance in Finland was available to any municipal resident, without any residence requirement. Reforms in the 1990s, however, made access more restrictive. Accessing municipal services usually requires a 2-year history of working or studying in Finland and uninterrupted residence in the municipality for at least one year, and accessing national social assistance requires permanent residence, which in most cases comes with a 4-year residence requirement (Helander, Holly, & Uuttana, 2016; Koikkalainen et al., 2012; Kotkas, 2016).

SA2: *Status requirements for social assistance benefits*
1990: ***1** (all legal residents)*
2000–2015: ***3** (all permanent residents)*

Initially, social assistance in Finland was available to any municipal resident, including those on a temporary permit. Since 1997, however, only permanent residents can access social assistance. Temporary residents can only receive emergency assistance in the form of vouchers (Dalli, 2019; Kela, n.d.-j; Kotkas, 2016).

SA3: *Consequences of uptake for status*
1990–2000: ***2** (inaccessible permanent residence or citizenship)*
2010–2015: ***3** (non-renewal of residence permit)*

Until 2003, welfare uptake has been an explicit ground to deny access to Finnish citizenship. Since 2004, repeated welfare uptake can be grounds to deny migrants the renewal of a residence permit (Kotkas, 2016; Stadlmaier, 2018).

SA4: *Integration requirements for social assistance*
1990: ***0*** *(no integration requirements)*
2000–2015: ***4*** *(compulsory integration for benefit recipients)*

Since 1999, immigrants on welfare have seen cutbacks in their benefits in cases where they refuse to participate in integration plans (Van Aerschot, 2014).

Active labour market

ALM1: *Residence requirements*
1990: ***–8*** *(no active labour market policies)*
2000–2015: ***2*** *(access tied to benefits requiring a work or residence history)*

Finland only introduced activation policies in the 1990s. Since then, access to virtually all of these policies has been tied to receipt of either unemployment benefits or social assistance, and therefore comes with an indirect residence requirement (Karjalainen and Saikku, 2011; Krivinos, 2019).

ALM2: *Status requirements*
1990: ***–8*** *(no active labour market policies)*
2000–2015: ***1*** *(all permanent residents and some temporary residents)*

Since most active labour market policies are only accessible to recipients of social assistance or unemployment benefits, they can only be accessed by residents who are able to demonstrate (the intent of) permanent residence in Finland. Short-term residents, such as seasonal workers, au pairs, international students, and asylum applicants are excluded (Karjalainen & Saikku, 2011; Könönen, 2018b; Krivinos, 2019).

ALM3: *Immigrant-targeted language programs*
1990: ***4*** *(no funded language programs)*
2000–2010: ***1*** *(funded programs, but not freely available to all migrants)*
20115: ***0*** *(fully funded, available to all migrants)*

Finland did not adopt any formal integration policy until 1999. Since then, municipalities have been required to develop individualized integration plans for all migrants who are unemployed and in receipt of income support, which include language, education, and work training. Since an integration policy reform was adopted in 2010, integration programs including language training are available to all migrants who are able to demonstrate (the intent of) permanent residence in Finland (Martikainen, Valtonen, & Wahlbeck, 2012; Masoud, Holm, & Brunila, 2021; Sagne & Saksela-Bergholm, 2014; Van Aerschot, 2014).

ALM4: *Other immigrant-targeted employment assistance*
1990: ***2** (only for refugees and/or asylum seekers)*
2000–2015: ***0** (programs available to any migrant)*

Before the first integration act of 1999, the few integration programs that were available in Finland exclusively targeted refugee migrants. Since then, municipalities have been required to develop individualized integration plans, including language, education, and work training, for all migrants who are unemployed and in receipt of income support, (Martikainen, Valtonen, & Wahlbeck, 2012; Masoud, Holm, & Brunila, 2021; Sagne & Saksela-Bergholm, 2014; Van Aerschot, 2014).

France

(data collection by Yuriko Cowper-Smith and Edward Koning)

	Tax-paid pensions	Health care	Contr. unempl.	Contr. pension	Housing	Social assist.	Active labour market	Average
1990	75	38	n/a	13	6	44	75	42
2000	59	44	17	5	13	44	13	27
2010	59	56	17	4	19	38	0	27
2015	59	56	17	2	13	38	0	26

Tax-paid pensions

TPP1: *Residence requirements for universal tax-paid pension*
1990–2015: ***–8** (no universal public pension)*

France does not have a universal public pension.

TPP2: *Availability of means-tested program for those with incomplete benefit*
1990–2015: ***3** (yes, with residence requirement 10+ years)*

Before 2006, France offered a number of different means-tested pension supplements, which all came with a residence requirement of at least 10 years (Bolderson & Gains, 1993). These benefits were replaced by a single program in 2006, the Allocation de Solidarité aux personnes agées, which also requires 10 years' residence (Walraet & Mahieu, 2007).

TTP3: *Status requirement for access to means-tested or universal tax-paid pension*
1990: ***3*** *(citizens and specially designated groups only)*
2000–2015: ***1*** *(citizens and permanent residents)*

Before 1998, only French nationals and citizens of countries that had reached an agreement with France could access the means-tested pension supplement (Conseil d'orientation des retraites, 2006). A reform in May 1998, however, made this benefit available to all permanent residents as long as they met the residence requirement (Kondo, 2001: 86).

TTP4: *Export possibilities of (means-tested or universal) tax-paid pension*
1990–2015: ***3*** *(During short stay abroad only)*

"'Stable residence" in France is a requirement for accessing the pension supplement. However, residing 181 days per year in the country is already enough to satisfy this requirement (EMN, 2012; Government of France, n.d.).

Health care

HC1: *Residence requirement for public health care*
1990–2000: ***0*** *(no waiting period)*
2010–2015: ***2*** *(6 weeks–3 months)*

A 2003 reform established a waiting period of three months of legal and uninterrupted residency before newcomers have access to regular health care benefits. Before then, no such residence requirement existed (André & Azzedine, 2016; Carde, 2009; Sargent & Kotobi, 2017).

HC2: *Status requirements for public health care*
1990: ***0*** *(full access to all residents)*
2000–2015 ***1*** *(restrictions for undocumented migrants, but no barriers to urgent care)*

Before 1993, all residents regardless of legal status were able to access health care. Since then, adult undocumented migrants have been barred from the regular health care system. Nevertheless, those who have resided for at least 3 months in the country can make use of a specific health care program for low-income undocumented migrants, the Aide Medicale Etat, which covers all basic health care services (but is not quite as comprehensive as the regular system). And even undocumented migrants who do not satisfy the requirements for the AME can access urgent care in hospitals, including perinatal care (André & Azzedine, 2016; Carde, 2009; Frydryszak & Macherey, 2016; Gray & Van Ginneken, 2015; Sargent & Kotobi, 2017).

HC3: *Health care accessibility services*
1990–2015: ***2*** *(services exist but are not fully funded and are not run directly by government)*

There is no central policy guiding how services should be made available to migrants. Accessibility services, including translation, are offered either by individual hospitals or by non-governmental organizations (André & Azzedine, 2016; Department of Health, 2018; ISM Interprétariat, n.d.).

HC4: *Additional health care benefits*
1990–2015: ***4*** *(no additional health care benefits)*

No categories of immigrants have access to health care benefits that are unavailable to native-born citizens.

Contributory unemployment

CUB1: *Status requirements for access to contributory unemployment benefits*
1990: ***–8*** *(no contributory unemployment benefit)*
2000–2015: ***0*** *(all legal residents)*

Before 1992, the only unemployment benefits in France were means-tested and not contributory (Bolderson & Gains, 1993). Since then, all residents who have access to the labour market, including seasonal workers, are eligible for contributory unemployment benefits as long as they meet the general requirements (Holzmann & Pouget, 2010; Palier, 2004).

CUB2: *Integration requirements for access to contributory unemployment benefits*
1990: ***–8*** *(no contributory unemployment benefit)*
2000–2015: ***0*** *(no integration requirements)*

Ever since the introduction of contributory unemployment benefits, there have been no integration requirements for accessing them.

CUB3: *Export possibilities*
1990: ***–8*** *(no contributory unemployment benefit)*
2000–2015: ***2*** *(export possible for short period of time)*

Residence in France (or the overseas departments, Saint Pierre and Miquelon, Saint Barthelemy, Saint Martin, and Monaco) is a requirement for receiving unemployment insurance. However, since the mid-1990s job seekers have been able to bring the benefit to any state in the European Economic Area for up to three months, albeit under additional conditions (CLEISS, n.d.-a, n.d.-b).

Contributory pension

CP1: *Status requirement*
1990–2015: ***0** (all legal residents)*

All legal residents are eligible for the contributory pay-as-you go system. While one needs to have contributed to the scheme for at least 10 years, at least theoretically even temporary workers can draw from the benefit based on multiple periods of making contributions to the benefit (Brickenstein, 2015; Holzmann, Koettl, & Chernetsky, 2005; Holzmann & Pouget, 2010; Leger, 2011).

CP2: *Export possibilities*
1990: ***1** (export possible when already in receipt, but not claimable from abroad)*
2000: ***0.4** (export claimable from some countries but not from others)*
2010: ***0.3** (export claimable from some countries but not from others)*
2015: ***0.1** (export claimable from some countries but not from others)*

The pension benefit cannot be exported in cases where the applicant emigrated before reaching retirement age. Since the mid-1990s, however, this restriction has not applied to countries with which France has social security agreements, i.e., member states of the European Union and countries with which France has bilateral agreements (23 countries in 2000, 32 in 2010, and 39 in 2015) (Bolderson & Gains, 1993; CLEISS n.d.-c; Holtzmann, Koettl & Chernetsky, 2005).

Housing benefits

HB1: *Residence requirements for housing benefits*
All years: ***0** (no residence requirement)*

As a result of the 1990 Besson Law, the national government launched the *Fonds Solidarité de Logement* to fund housing assistance services at the departmental level. This funding comes with an explicit prohibition against mandating a certain prior residence in the department (Assemblée des departements de France, 2015; Loi n° 90–449: article 6.1). Nevertheless, some departments offer additional housing assistance benefits that do come with residence requirements (City of Paris, n.d.).

HB2: *Status requirements for housing benefits*
1990–2000: ***1*** *(all legal residents)*
2010: ***2*** *(some but not all temporary migrants)*
2015: ***1*** *(all legal residents)*

Social housing and housing assistance have been intended for all legal residents of France ever since the adoption of the Besson Law in 1990 (Fougère et al. 2013; Loi n° 90–449: article 1; Wong & Goldblum, 2016). A 2007 reform excluded some categories of temporary migrants, such as international students, but this restriction was lifted again in 2013 (Huddleston et al., 2015).

HB3: *Integration requirements for housing benefits*
1990–2015 ***0*** *(no integration requirements)*

There have never been any integration requirements attached to accessing housing assistance in France.

HB4: *Preferential treatment in housing*
1990: ***0*** *(earmarked housing for various groups of immigrants)*
2000–2015: ***1*** *(earmarked housing for refugees)*

As early as the 1950s, France developed housing units specifically earmarked for temporary foreign workers, but these units have been redeveloped as social housing units since 1997 (UNAFO, 2017). Since 1991, France has also reserved specific accommodation, so-called *centres provisoires d'hébergement*, for recognized refugees during their first years in the country (Lévy-Vroelant, 2015).

Social assistance

SA1: *Residence requirements for social assistance benefits*
1990–2015: ***3*** *(residence requirement between 1 and 5 years)*

Non-citizens cannot access French social assistance benefits during their first years in the country. The residence requirement was 3 years until 2003, when it was increased to 5 years (Allwood & Wadia, 2010; Bergmann, 1996; Kondo, 2001; Paraschivescu, 2013).

SA2: *Status requirements for social assistance benefits*
1990–2000: ***1*** *(all legal residents)*
2010–2015: ***3*** *(all permanent residents)*

The social assistance benefit Revenu Minimum d'Insertion (RMI), created in 1988, was available to all legal residents of France (Kondo, 2001; Paraschivescu, 2013). A major overhaul of the social assistance system in 2009, however, created a new social assistance benefit, the Revenu de Solidarité Active (RSA), which is in practice altogether inaccessible to temporary migrants (Legros, 2015; UNAFO, 2016; Vlandas, 2012).

SA3: *Consequences of uptake for status*
1990–2000: ***3*** *(non-renewal of residence permit)*
2010–2015: ***0*** *(no consequences)*

Under the system of RMI, temporary residents could not renew their work permit in cases where they were drawing from the RMI (Bergmann, 1996; Kondo, 2001). For the RSA benefit, however, only migrants with a long-term residence permit are eligible, and welfare uptake has no consequences for their status (RSA, n.d.).

SA4: *Integration requirements for social assistance*
1990–2015: *0 (no integration requirements)*

There are no integration requirements associated with accessing social assistance in France.

Active labour market

ALM1: *Residence requirements*
1990–2000: ***–8*** *(no active labour market policies)*
2010–2015: ***0*** *(no residence requirements)*

France did not offer much in terms of specific active labour market policies until 2008, when it created the Pôle emploi, an agency aimed at facilitating the entry of the unemployed in the labour market (Schulte et al., 2018). There is no residence requirement associated with accessing the services this agency provides – indeed, new migrants are invited to contact it upon arrival for career counselling, information services, and training opportunities (Pôle emploi, n.d.).

ALM2: *Status requirements*
1990–2000: ***–8*** *(no active labour market policies)*
2010–2015: ***0*** *(all legal residents)*

All legal residents can register with Pôle emploi (Pôle emploi, n.d.).

ALM3: *Immigrant-targeted language programs*
1990: ***4*** *(no funded language programs)*
2000: ***1*** *(funded programs, but not freely available to all migrants)*
2010–2015: ***0*** *(fully funded, available to all migrants)*

Since the 1990s, some departments have offered language training to immigrants. Since the mid-2000s, integration has taken on a more centralized and mandatory character, and all newcomers from outside the European Union with low language proficiency are required to complete French language classes as part of a more general integration trajectory (Guibentif, 2004; EMN, 2012).

ALM4: *Other immigrant-targeted employment assistance*
1990: ***2*** *(programs available, but only for refugees and/or asylum seekers)*
2000–2015: ***0*** *(programs available to any migrant)*

France has offered employment assistance programs to refugees since 1990. Since the late 1990s, a more general set of integration programs has been developed. As of 1995, all departments have the legal obligation to develop and implement a local plan for the reception of newcomers, including services aimed at improving their standing in the labour market. These kinds of services have been further developed over time, but as mentioned above, have taken on a more mandatory character since the mid-2000s. (Guibentif, 2004; IOM 2013; Shields, Valenzuela and Drolet, 2016).

Germany

(data collection by Madison Milne-Ives and Edward Koning)

	Tax-paid pensions	Health care	Contr. unempl.	Contr. pension	Housing	Social assist.	Active labour market	Average
1990	100	56	67	13	25	56	69	55
2000	100	50	67	13	38	56	69	56
2010	42	50	42	11	38	81	25	41
2015	42	50	42	11	38	81	25	41

Tax-paid pensions

TPP1: *Residence requirements for universal tax-paid pension*
1990–2015: ***–8*** *(no universal public pension)*

There is no universal tax-paid pension benefit in Germany: the main pillar of its public pension system is contributory (Bridgen & Meyer, 2014).

TPP2: *Availability of means-tested program for those with incomplete benefit*
1990–2000: ***4*** *(no program)*
2010–2015: ***0*** *(yes, with residence requirement of less than 1 year)*

Before 2001, social assistance was the only benefit available to low-income pensioners. A comprehensive reform in that year, however, introduced a means-tested pension benefit, the so-called Grundsicherung im Alter. There is no waiting period before newcomers can access this benefit (Busemeyer, 2005; Conrad & Fukuwa, 2003; EMN, 2014; Holzmann, 2016).

TTP3: *Status requirement for access to means-tested or universal tax-paid pension*
1990–2000: ***–8*** *(no tax-paid programs)*
2010–2015: ***1*** *(citizens and all permanent residents)*

All residents with a long-term permit are eligible for the Grundsicherung im Alter as long as they meet the income-based eligibility requirements (Busemeyer, 2005; Conrad & Fukuwa, 2003; EMN, 2014; Holzmann, 2016).

TTP4: *Export possibilities of (means-tested or universal) tax-paid pension*
1990–2000: ***–8*** *(no tax-paid programs)*
2010–2015: ***4*** *(no export possible)*

The Grundsicherung im Alter cannot be exported. People who reside outside of Germany can only receive it in exceptional circumstances (Sozialgesetzbuch, 2019).

Health care

HC1: *Residence requirement for public health care*
1990–2015: ***0*** *(no residence requirement)*

All holders of a residence permit have immediate access to the mandatory health insurance program (Huschke, 2014; Lindert et al., 2008).

HC2: *Status requirements for public health care*
1990–2015: ***2*** *(restrictions for undocumented and some other migrants, but no barriers to urgent care)*

Both undocumented migrants and newly arrived asylum seekers are barred from the regular health care system. Asylum seekers have access to emergency medical care, treatment for acute conditions, vaccinations, and perinatal care. (They gain access to the regular health care system after a waiting period, which ranged between 12 and 48 months during the period under study.) Undocumented migrants are technically eligible for the same services but in practice can only access emergency care because all other services require providers to report migrants to the immigration authorities (Bozorgmehr & Razum, 2015; Castañeda, 2012; Frydryszak & Macherey, 2016; PICUM, 2001; Pross, 1998).

HC3: *Health care accessibility services*
1990: ***4** (nothing available)*
2000–2015: ***3** (some incidental programs or translated written documents)*

The German health care system offers little help to patients with language barriers. Some hospitals have developed their own translation services since the mid-1990s, but the responsibility for providing an interpreter remains the legal responsibility of the patient. Since the 2000s, the health care system has also started to provide more written documents in languages of large immigrant populations (Castañeda, 2012; Spallek, Zeeb, & Razum, 2010).

HC4: *Additional health care benefits*
1990–2015: ***3** (incidental services but nothing guaranteed)*

While immigrants are overrepresented among the patients in some facilities, such as centres for torture victims, there are no public health care services immigrants can use that are unavailable to native-born citizens. Nevertheless, the Federal Department for Health Education has run occasional migrant-targeted health care prevention projects throughout the period under study (AIDA, n.d.; Bauhoff & Göpffarth, 2018; Borgschulte et al., 2018; KGC, n.d.; Spallek, Zeeb, & Razum, 2010).

Contributory unemployment

CUB1: *Status requirements for access to contributory unemployment benefits*
1990–2000: ***4** (only permanent residents and citizens)*
2010–2015: ***3** (permanent residents, citizens, and very few temporary residents)*

The contributory unemployment benefit Arbeitslosengeld was exclusively available to permanent residents and citizens (Faist & Haüßermann, 1996). A major policy reform replaced this benefit with the unemployment benefit I, for which temporary residents are technically eligible but in practice is only available to few. Most temporary residents cannot access the benefit either because their residence permit expires when they fall unemployed or because their permit does not allow them to work long enough in Germany to satisfy the contributory requirements (Müller, Mayer, & Bauer, 2014).

CUB2: *Integration requirements for access to contributory unemployment benefits*
1990–2015: ***0*** *(no integration requirement)*

There are no integration requirements to accessing contributory unemployment benefits in Germany – such requirements only exist for means-tested benefits (see SA4).

CUB3: *Export possibilities*
1990–2000: ***4*** *(no export possible)*
2010–2015 ***3*** *(export possible for short period of time)*

Contributory unemployment benefits cannot usually be exported. Since June 2003, however, recipients can continue to receive benefits while searching for employment elsewhere in the European Union for a period of up to three months (EMN, 2014; Müller, Mayer, & Bauer, 2014).

Contributory pension

CP1: *Status requirement*
1990–2015: ***0*** *(all legal residents)*

There is no specific status requirement for accessing the contributory pension in Germany. Everyone who has had sufficient legal employment in the country is eligible (EMN 2014).

CP2: *Export possibilities*
1990–2000: ***1.0*** *(without restrictions to some countries, at reduced rate to others)*
2010–2015: ***0.9*** *(without restrictions to some countries, at reduced rate to others)*

Pension benefits can be exported without any restrictions to EU member states and countries with which Germany has signed a bilateral social security agreement. The benefits can be exported to other countries as well, but in cases where the applicant is not a citizen of the EU or one of the countries with which Germany has signed a bilateral social security agreement, the benefits are reduced by 30% (Holzmann, Koettl, & Chernetsky, 2005). The number of countries to which pensions could be exported without restrictions totalled 18 in 1990, 26 in 2000, 39 in 2010, and 41 in 2015 (Deutsche Rentenversicherung, n.d.). (Because of limited availability of data on the number of foreign-born by country of birth, the data for 1990 and 2000 are very rough estimates.)

Housing benefits

HB1: *Residence requirements for housing benefits*
1990–2015: ***1** (residence requirement of 1 year or less)*

There is no residence requirement for accessing housing allowance in Germany, except a 3-month waiting period for EU migrants (Bruzelius, Ehata, & Seeleib-Kaiser, 2015). Since 2006, when social housing was decentralized, the eligibility requirements have differed between the German *Länder*. North Rhine–Westphalia did not change the previous residence requirement of one year, but other *Länder* did (interview, GER-01; Ponzo, 2010).

HB2: *Status requirements for housing benefits*
1990: ***3** (citizens and permanent residents)*
2010–2015: ***1** (all legal residents)*

Until the 1990s, access to social housing and housing benefits was denied to temporary migrants. Since then, all legal residents have been eligible for housing benefits, even though since the decentralization of social housing policy in 2006 the precise eligibility requirements have differed between the *Länder* (Faist & Haüßermann, 1996; interviews, GER-01 & GER-02). Newly arrived asylum seekers do not have access to the regular system of housing benefits, but are accommodated in asylum centres during that time (Bozorgmehr & Razum, 2015; Liedtke, 2002).

HB3: *Integration requirements for housing benefits*
1990–2015: ***0** (no integration requirements)*

There are no integration requirements for accessing housing benefits or social housing in Germany (interview, GER-01).

HB4: *Preferential treatment in housing*
1990: ***0** (earmarked housing for various groups of migrants)*
2000–2015: ***4** (no privileged access for migrants)*

Until 1992, *Aussiedler* (immigrants with German ancestry) were given privileged access to housing: they received aid in finding accommodation and received the highest priority for accessing social housing, even before native-born German citizens. Since then, however, no groups of residents in Germany have had priority in accessing social housing (Faist & Haüßermann, 1996; interview, GER-01).

Social assistance

SA1: *Residence requirements for social assistance benefits*
1990–2015: ***2*** *(residence requirement of less than 1 year)*

There are no formal residence requirements for accessing social assistance in Germany. However, in the first 3 months EU migrants can be denied access and referred to their country of origin for assistance (Bruzelius, Ehata, & Seeleib-Kaiser, 2015: Müller, Mayer, & Bauer, 2014). Since 1993, asylum seekers have gained access to social assistance only after a waiting period, which ranged between 12 and 48 months during the period under study (Leidtke, 2002; Söhn, 2013).

SA2: *Status requirements for social assistance benefits*
1990: ***2*** *(all permanent residents and some temporary residents)*
2000–2015: ***3*** *(all permanent residents and EU citizens)*

All holders of a long-term residence permit are eligible for social assistance. Other groups of migrants can receive such benefits only on a discretionary basis (EMN 2014; Müller, Mayer, & Bauer, 2014). Before 1993, newly arrived asylum seekers were also eligible for social assistance benefits, but since then they only receive a minimum benefit that is about 20% lower than the level of general social assistance and is usually provided in kind or with vouchers (Bosswick, 2000; Leidtke, 2002; Söhn, 2013).

SA3: *Consequences of uptake for status*
1990–2015: ***4*** *(revocation of residence permit)*

Migrants who claim social assistance over a long period run serious risks: their permit may not be renewed, they may become ineligible for naturalization, and they may even be subject to expulsion (Faist & Haüßermann, 1996; Muller, Mayer, & Bauer, 2014; Sainsbury, 2006; Stadlmaier, 2018).

SA4: *Integration requirements for social assistance*
1990–2000: ***0*** *(no integration requirements)*
2010–2015: ***4*** *(compulsory integration for benefit recipients)*

Since 2005, participation in or completion of an integration course has been obligatory for migrants who are claiming social assistance (Doerschler & Jackson, 2010; Joppke, 2007; Rother, 2010).

Active labour market

ALM1: *Residence requirements*
1990–2015: ***2*** *(access tied to unemployment benefits requiring a work history)*

Since at least the 1980s, (West) Germany has offered a wide range of active labour market policies, including vocational training, wage subsidies, and employment subsidies. Most of these are only available to recipients of unemployment benefits and therefore indirectly require a work history (Zoellner, Fritsch, & Wyrwich, 2018).

ALM2: *Status requirements*
1990–2000: ***2*** *(all citizens and permanent residents)*
2010–2015: ***1*** *(all permanent residents and some temporary residents)*

Because access to most active labour market policies is reserved for recipients of unemployment benefits, the status requirements are the same as for unemployment benefits (see CUB1).

ALM3: *Immigrant-targeted language programs*
1990–2000: ***4*** *(no funded language programs)*
2010–2015: ***1*** *(funded programs, but nominal fees and/or not freely available to all migrants)*

Before 2005, the only funded language training was a small program exclusively available to *Aussiedler.* An elaborate integration reform in 2005, however, introduced language classes that are accessible to all newcomers unless they already have sufficient proficiency in German. While the lessons are heavily subsidized, migrants still need to pay nominal fees. These fees are waived, however, for migrants who experience financial difficulties (Doerschler & Jackson, 2010; Joppke, 2007; Rother, 2010).

ALM4: *Other immigrant-targeted employment assistance*
1990–2000 ***3*** *(some programs offered, but offered ad hoc or inconsistently across the country)*
2010–2015 ***0*** *(programs available to any migrant)*

Before the integration reform of 2005, Germany offered little publicly funded integration assistance, except for small-scale civic orientation programs for *Aussiedler* (Joppke, 2007). Since the reform, however, there have been several programs that aim to assist immigrants' prospects in the labour market, including vocational training programs, referral services, assistance with foreign credential recognition, and job application counselling (Burkert and Haas, 2014; OECD, 2017).

Iceland

(data collection by Edward Koning)

	Tax-paid pensions	Health care	Contr. unempl.	Contr. pension	Housing	Social assist.	Active labour market	Average
1990	43	69	50	n/a	38	31	100	55
2000	43	69	33	n/a	19	31	38	39
2010	39	69	58	n/a	19	38	25	41
2015	39	69	58	n/a	19	38	25	41

Tax-paid pensions

TPP1: *Residence requirement for universal tax-paid pension*
1990–2015: ***3** (40 for complete, with prorated benefits for shorter residency)*

The small tax-paid pension in Iceland is available to anyone who has resided in the country for at least 3 years between the ages of 16 and 66. The complete benefit is available after 40 years of residence (Gudmundsson, 2001; Social Security Administration, 2002, 2016; State Social Security Institute, n.d.).

TPP2: *Availability of means-tested program for those with incomplete benefit*
1990–2015: ***2** (yes, with residence requirement 3–10 years)*

A recipient of an incomplete pension (which requires at least 3 years of residence) can receive a pension supplement in case their total pension income falls below a certain minimum (Gudmundsson, 2001, Social Security Administration, 2002, 2016; State Social Security Institute, n.d.).

TPP3: *Status requirement for access to (means-tested or universal) tax-paid pension benefit*
1990–2015 ***1** (citizens and all permanent residents)*

All residents who are registered in the population registry (which is only mandatory for those who stay more than 6 months) who meet the residence requirements are covered by the public pension program (Gudmundsson, 2001, Social Security Administration, 2002, 2016; State Social Security Institute, n.d.).

TPP4: *Export possibilities of (means-tested or universal) tax-paid pension benefit*
1990: ***1.9** (exportable only to some countries)*
2000: ***1.9** (exportable only to some countries)*
2010: ***1.2** (exportable only to some countries)*
2015: ***1.2** (exportable only to some countries)*

Accrued entitlement to the tax-paid pension can only be exported to EEA/EFTA member states and Canada (with which Iceland struck a bilateral agreement in 1989).

Health care

HC1: *Residence requirement for public health care*
1990–2015: ***2** (more than 6 weeks but less than one year)*

Every legal resident is automatically insured after 6 months of residence. Migrants from EEA countries can apply for immediate coverage, and the residence requirement is waived for recognized refugees (Icelandic Health Insurance, n.d.-a; Irving, 2011; MISSOC, 2004–2018).

HC2: *Status requirements for public health care*
1990–2015: ***4** (undocumented and some categories of legal migrants excluded entirely)*

Since regular health care is only available to those who are registered in the population registry, several categories of migrants (including asylum seekers, migrants on short-term permits from outside the EEA, and undocumented migrants) are excluded. Asylum seekers receive care from the Icelandic Red Cross while their claim is being processed, but there are concerns about the quality of care they receive. Other excluded groups can access health care services but will have to foot the entire bill. However, the state will finance emergency services in cases where the patient is unable to pay for them (Fontaine, 2019; Icelandic Health Insurance, n.d.-a, n.d.-b; Shields et al., 2004).

HC3: *Health care accessibility services*
1990–2015: ***1** (state-funded translation services only)*

All insured patients have free access to interpretation services if they require them (Halldorsdottir, Jonsson, & Gudmundsson, 2016; Icelandic Health Insurance, n.d.-c; Shields et al., 2004).

HC4: *Additional health care benefits*
1990–2015: ***4*** *(no additional health care benefits)*

There are no categories of migrants who have access to more or more generous health care services than native-born Icelandic people. Recognized refugees have access to the exact same system as native-born people (Directorate of Immigration, n.d.-a; Shields et al., 2004).

Contributory unemployment

CUB1: *Status requirements*
1990–2000: ***2*** *(all legal residents except some temporary migrants)*
2010–2015: ***3*** *(permanent residents, citizens, and very few temporary migrants)*

One of the requirements to access unemployment benefits is to be available for work, which cannot be satisfied by migrants whose permits do not allow them to take up employment (such as international students and asylum seekers) or whose permit expires once employment is terminated (such as seasonal workers). Since 2002, all temporary work permits have been tied to a specific employer, which effectively means that the only migrants who do not need a permanent residence permit for accessing unemployment benefits are migrants from EEA countries (Directorate of Labor, n.d.-a, n.d.-b; Ministry of Welfare, 2002; Trygvadóttir & Skaptadóttir, 2018).

CUB2: *Integration requirements*
1990–2000: ***0*** *(no integration requirements)*
2010–2015: ***2*** *(access tied to permits with integration requirements)*

Since 2002, participation in at least 150 hours of Icelandic language training has been a requirement for obtaining a permanent residence permit, and thus an indirect requirement for accessing unemployment benefits (Directorate of Immigration, n.d.-b; Hilmarsson-Dunn & Kristinsson, 2013; Skaptadóttir & Loftsdóttir, 2009).

CUB3: *Export possibilities*
1990: ***4*** *(no export possible)*
2000–2015: ***2*** *(export possible for short period of time)*

Residence in Iceland is a requirement for receiving unemployment benefits, but since Iceland joined the EEA in 1994 recipients can retain their benefits while looking for a job in another EEA member state for a period of up to 3 months (Directorate of Labor, n.d.-c).

Contributory pension

There is no public contributory pension program in Iceland. Apart from the universal pension, most pensioners draw income from mandatory occupational pension programs that have been set up by their employers and are run by private pension funds and insurance companies (Gudmundsson, 2001). For that reason, the score for all indicators regarding contributory pension benefits is **–8** (no contributory pension benefit).

Housing benefits

HB1: *Residence requirement for housing benefits*
1990–2015: ***0** (no residence requirement)*

Means-tested rent benefits and (the relatively limited number of) social housing units are available to anyone who is registered in the population registry and meets the income tests, without any additional residence requirement (Björnsson, Kposch, & Zoega, 2018; Housing Financial Fund, n.d.; Irving, 2011; Sveinsson, 1996).

HB2: *Status requirement for housing benefits*
1990–2015: ***2** (some but not all temporary migrants)*

Since only those who are registered in the population registry are eligible for housing benefits, temporary migrants who are on a permit for less than 6 months and asylum seekers are excluded (Housing Financial Fund, n.d; Ministry of Social Affairs, 2003; Multicultural and Information Centre, n.d-a).

HB3: *Integration requirements for housing benefits*
1990–2015: ***0** (no integration requirements)*

There are no immigrant-targeted integration requirements associated with accessing housing benefits in Iceland. As long as immigrants are registered, they can access housing benefits on the same terms as native-born Icelandic people (Housing Financial Fund, n.d; Ministry of Social Affairs, 2003; Multicultural and Information Centre, n.d.-a).

HB4: *Preferential treatment in housing*
1990: ***4** (no privileged access for migrants)*
2000–2015: ***1** (earmarked housing for refugees)*

Since 1996, Iceland has offered convention refugees a furnished apartment upon arrival. Other categories of migrants do not have privileged access to housing in Iceland (Björnsson, Kposch, & Zoega, 2018; Government of Iceland, 2016; Shields et al., 2004).

Social assistance

SA1: *Residence requirements*
1990–2015: ***0*** *(no residence requirement for anyone)*

There is no formal residence requirement for accessing social assistance in Iceland. It is worth noting, however, that the necessary permit to be eligible for social assistance is only granted and retainable in cases where applicants can demonstrate financial self-sufficiency. For that reason, few migrants can in practice access social assistance before they obtain permanent residence, which in most cases comes with a residence requirement of 4 years (City of Reykjavik, n.d.; Jonsson, 2001; Multicultural and Information Centre, n.d.-b).

SA2: *Status requirements*
1990–2015: ***2*** *(all permanent residents and some temporary residents)*

Municipal authorities only extend welfare to those who are domiciled in their jurisdiction, which means that only migrants who are registered in the population registry can access social assistance (European Committee of Social Rights, 2001: 13.4; Jonsson, 2001).

SA3: *Consequences of uptake for status*
1990–2015: ***3*** *(non-renewal of residence permit)*

Uptake of social assistance in Iceland can have serious consequences for one's status: it can be grounds for not renewing existing permits and denying permanent residence or citizenship (Althingi, 2002, 2016; Directorate of Immigration, n.d.-b, n.d.-c).

SA4: *Integration requirements*
1990–2000: ***0*** *(no integration requirements)*
2010–2015: ***1*** *(integration requirements can be requested at discretion of local authorities)*

There are no formal integration requirements for accessing social assistance in Iceland. However, municipal authorities can require recipients to participate in reintegration measures, which since the introduction of Icelandic language courses for foreigners can imply language training for migrants (City of Reykjavik, n.d.; Multicultural and information Centre, n.d.-b).

Active labour market

ALM1: *Residence requirements*
1990–2000: ***–8*** *(no active labour market policies)*
2010–2015: ***0*** *(no residence requirement)*

Active labour market policies were virtually absent in Iceland until the mid-2000s. Since 2006, however, several programs (including reschooling opportunities, job introduction programs, and employment counselling) have been rolled out. These programs are in principle open to any job seeker in Iceland, without any residence requirement (Agnarsson, 2010; Althingi, 2006; Irving, 2011).

ALM2: *Status requirements*
1990–2000: ***–8*** *(no active labour market policies)*
2010–2015: ***1*** *(all permanent residents and some temporary residents)*

Active labour market policies (in existence only since the mid-2000s) are accessible for any job seeker in Iceland. That means that the only category of migrants who are excluded from them are those whose permits do not allow them to change or find employment (Agnarsson, 2010; Althingi, 2006).

ALM3: *Immigrant-targeted language programs*
1990: ***4*** *(no funded language programs)*
2000–2015: ***1*** *(funded programs, but not freely available to all categories of migrants)*

Iceland has only started offering Icelandic courses specifically for immigrants since the 1990s. These courses are not run by the state directly, but organizers can apply for state funding. Unemployed individuals and recently arrived refugees can access these courses free of charge, but others will have to pay nominal fees (Government of Iceland, 2016; Shields et al., 2004; Skaptadóttir & Innes, 2017).

ALM4: *Other immigrant-targeted employment assistance*
1990: ***4*** *(no integration programs or immigrant-targeted active labour market policies)*
2000–2015: ***2*** *(programs available, but only for refugees)*

Since 1999, there have been several programs aimed at improving refugees' chances in the labour market, such as preparation courses and the provision of "guides" who help them find their way in Iceland. Beyond this, Iceland only adopted an integration policy aimed at all immigrants in 2007, and this has mostly taken the form of anti-discrimination and diversity awareness initiatives (Irving, 2011; Shields et al., 2004; Skaptadóttir & Innes, 2017).

Ireland

(data collection by David Markle and Edward Koning)

	Tax-paid pensions	Health care	Contr. unempl.	Contr. pension	Housing	Social assist.	Active labour market	Average
1990	33	38	33	0	31	13	100	35
2000	33	31	33	0	38	13	50	28
2010	50	31	33	0	38	38	50	34
2015	50	31	33	0	38	38	50	34

Tax-paid pensions

TPP1: *Residence requirements for universal tax-paid pension*
1990–2015: ***-8** (no universal public pension)*

Ireland does not offer a universal pension. The only tax-paid pension is a means-tested benefit (see below).

TPP2: *Availability of means-tested program for those with incomplete benefit*
1990–2000: ***0** (yes, with no residence requirement)*
2010–2015: ***1** (yes, with residence requirement 1–3 years)*

Low-income pensioners can receive a means-tested state pension. Initially, there was no residence requirement associated with this benefit, but since the introduction of the Habitual Residence Condition in the mid-2000s EU citizens can only access the benefit after 3 years' residence in the country (Citizens Information, n.d.-a; Department of Employment Affairs and Social Protection, n.d.-a; MRCI, 2005; Quinn et al., 2014).

TTP3: *Status requirement for access to means-tested or universal tax-paid pension*
1990–2000: ***0** (all legal residents)*
2010–2015: ***1** (all citizens and permanent residents)*

The means-tested pension was available to any legal resident until the introduction of the Habitual Residence Condition in 2004, which effectively restricted access to long-term residents (Citizens Information, n.d.-a; Department of Employment Affairs and Social Protection, n.d.-a; MRCI, 2005).

TTP4: *Export possibilities of (means-tested or universal) tax-paid pension*
1990–2015: ***4*** *(no export possibility)*

The non-contributory state pension is only accessible to those who reside in Ireland. It cannot be exported (Department of Employment Affairs and Social Protection, n.d.-a; Social Security Administration, 2002).

Health care

HC1: *Residence requirement for public health care*
1990–2015: ***0*** *(no waiting period)*

There is no formal waiting period before residents can access public health care benefits. Anyone who can demonstrate the intention to live in Ireland for at least a year is eligible (Citizens Information, n.d.-b; MISSOC 2004–2018; Quinn et al., 2014).

HC2: *Status requirements for public health care*
1990–2000: ***0*** *(full access for all residents)*
2010–2015: ***2*** *(restrictions for undocumented and some other migrants, but no barriers to urgent care)*

Public health care was available to all residents regardless of status until the mid-2000s. Since then, undocumented migrants and short-term visitors are ineligible for any health services except emergency care (Citizens Information, n.d.-b; MISSOC 2004–2018; MRCI, 2005).

HC3: *Health care accessibility services*
1990–2000: ***2*** *(services exist, but are not fully funded and/or not run directly by government)*
2010–2015: ***0*** *(translation services and health services with specific cultural sensitivity)*

Before the 2000s, there were few interpretation or cultural sensitivity services in the Irish health care system. While some medical practitioners hired professional interpreters and were able to claim the costs from regional health authorities, this practice was rare and there were frequent concerns about the quality of available interpreters. In 2007, however, the national health authority launched a National Intercultural Health Strategy, which involved the promotion of more culturally sensitive health services and the expansion of translation services. And while concerns remain about the reach and quality of available services, the changes since 2007 signal a clear commitment to expand health care accessibility services for immigrants in Ireland (MacFarlane 2018; MacFarlane et al., 2008, 2009).

HC4: *Additional health care benefits*
1990: ***4*** *(no additional health care benefits)*
2000–2015: ***3*** *(incidental services but nothing guaranteed)*

There are no public health care services or programs that are exclusively available to immigrants. Refugees and asylum seekers are covered by the same system that native-born Irish make use of. Since 1999, an NGO called Spiritas has provided specialized treatment for refugees and asylum seekers who are trauma and torture victims (Irish Refugee Council, n.d.).

Contributory unemployment

CUB1: *Status requirements for access to contributory unemployment benefits*
1990–2015 ***2*** *(all legal residents except some temporary migrants)*

There are no formal status requirements to access the contributory unemployment benefit in Ireland, the Jobseeker's Benefit. However, several categories of newcomers, including asylum seekers, will in practice never be able to access the benefit, because their residence permit would not enable them to satisfy the contributory requirements (Citizens Information, n.d.-c; Quinn et al., 2014).

CUB2: *Integration requirements for access to contributory unemployment benefits*
1990–2015: ***0*** *(no integration requirements)*

There are no integration requirements for accessing the Jobseeker's Benefit (Citizens Information, n.d.-c).

CUB3: *Export possibilities*
1990–2015: ***2*** *(export possible for short period of time)*

The benefit is only available to residents of Ireland, but recipients can stay abroad for up to 4 weeks and receive the payment for those weeks upon their return. Moreover, since 2003, recipients can continue to receive benefits while searching for employment elsewhere in the European Union for a period of up to 13 weeks (Citizens Information, n.d.-d; EMN, 2014).

Contributory pension

CP1: *Status requirement*
1990–2015: ***0*** *(all legal residents included)*

There are no status requirements for accessing the contributory pension benefit in Ireland. The only eligibility requirements relate to the applicant's age and record of social insurance contributions (Department of Employment Affairs and Social Protection, 2017, n.d.-b).

CP2: *Export possibilities*
1990–2015: ***0*** *(export possible without restrictions)*

The contributory pension can be exported to any country in the world, without additional restrictions (Citizens Information, n.d.-d; Department of Employment Affairs and Social Protection, 2017, n.d.-b).

Housing benefits

HB1: *Residence requirements for housing benefits*
All years: ***0*** *(no residence requirement)*

There is no specific residence requirement before newcomers can apply for social housing or housing assistance benefits. Social housing is largely operated by local authorities, and applicants can only apply to an authority with which they have a "local connection." This connection might be proven by length of residence in the area, but also by other means such as local employment or family ties to long-term residents. Refugees are eligible for housing support as soon as their claim has been accepted. (Citizens Information, n.d.-e; Department of Environment, Community, and Local Government, 2012; Norris, Healy, & Coates, 2008; Watson & Corrigan, 2019).

HB2: *Status requirements for housing benefits*
1990–2015: ***2*** *(permanent residents and some but not all temporary migrants)*

For the full duration of the period under study, local authorities determined eligibility for social housing. While there were no specific status requirements before the introduction of the Habitual Residence Condition, applicants would only be deemed eligible if they were seen to have a "local connection" (Citizens

Information, n.d.-e; Department of Environment, Community, and Local Government, 2012).

HB3: *Integration requirements for housing benefits*
1990–2015 ***0** (no integration requirements)*

There are no integration requirements associated with access to social housing.

HB4: *Preferential treatment in housing*
1990: ***3** (some services available but are not fully funded and/or are not run by government)*
2000–2015: ***4** (no privileged access for migrants)*

Before the creation of reception centres for asylum seekers in 1999, local authorities were charged with accommodating both asylum seekers and refugees, but there was no national policy on the type of assistance they should receive or the funding that would be available to the authorities in providing it. Since then, program refugees have been accommodated upon arrival in the country, but successful asylum claimants need to leave reception centres and find housing on their own, with only limited support (Citizens Information, n.d.-f; Department of Justice and Equality, 2015).

Social assistance

SA1: *Residence requirements for social assistance benefits*
1990–2000: ***1** (residence requirement only for specific categories)*
2010–2015: ***3** (residence requirement between 1 and 5 years)*

Before the introduction of the Habitual Residence Condition, there was no waiting period before newcomers could access social assistance. The only exception applied to migrants from within the European Community/European Union, who can be deemed an unreasonable burden if they claim welfare during their first 3 months in the country. Since the mid-2000s, however, applicants have needed to demonstrate "habitual residence." And while there is no explicit length of residence associated with this term, anyone who has resided in the country for less than 2 years is considered not habitually resident unless they can prove otherwise. Moreover, EU citizens lose their right to reside in cases where they claim social assistance during their first 5 years in the country, and would therefore not satisfy the Habitual Residence Condition (Department of Employment Affairs and Social Protection, n.d.-a; Irish Congress of Trade Unions, n.d.; MRCI, 2005; Quinn et al., 2014).

SA2: *Status requirements for social assistance benefits*
1990–2000: ***1** (all legal residents)*
2010–2015: ***2** (all permanent residents and some temporary residents)*

Before the introduction of the Habitual Residence Condition, the only status requirement for accessing social assistance benefits was legal residence. Now that applicants need to demonstrate being a "habitual resident," most migrants on a temporary permit will have difficulty accessing the benefit (Department of Employment Affairs and Social Protection, n.d.-a; MRCI, 2005).

SA3: *Consequences of uptake for status*
1990–2015: ***0** (no consequences)*

Claiming social assistance in Ireland does not jeopardize someone's residence status or access to citizenship (Quinn et al., 2014; Stadlmaier, 2018).

SA4: *Integration requirements for social assistance*
1990–2015: ***0** (no integration requirements)*

There are no integration requirements to access social assistance in Ireland.

Active labour market

ALM1: *Residence requirements*
1990: ***–8** (no active labour market policies)*
2000–2015: ***2** (access tied to unemployment benefits requiring a work history)*

Ireland introduced its first active labour market policies in the mid-1990s and since then has developed a wide range of programs, including job assistance, wage subsidies, and training programs. Access to almost all of these programs is tied to the receipt of unemployment benefits and therefore indirectly requires a work history (Citizens Information, n.d.-g; McGuinness, O'Connell & Kelly, 2019)

ALM2: *Status requirements*
1990: ***–8** (no active labour market policies)*
2000–2015: ***1** (all permanent residents and some temporary residents)*

Since access to active labour market policies is tied to the receipt of unemployment benefits, the same status requirements apply.

ALM3: *Immigrant-targeted language programs*
1990: ***4** (nothing available)*
2000–2015: ***1** (funded programs, but nominal fees and/or not freely available to all categories of migrants)*

Ireland first started offering language training to migrants with a pilot project in 1998 offering language programs to refugees. The successor to this program, however, was discontinued in 2008. Meanwhile, local education and training boards offer subsidized classes for speakers of other languages. These classes are not entirely free, however, and availability ranges across the country (MacCormaic, 2008; Office for the Promotion of Migrant Integration, 2017, n.d.; WRC Social and Economic Consultants, 2006).

ALM4: *Other immigrant-targeted employment assistance*
1990–2015 ***4*** *(no integration programs or immigrant-targeted active labour market policies)*

The Irish approach to integration is based on granting migrants access to the exact same services as native-born Irish. There are therefore no immigrant-targeted labour market programs, except for some small programs funded by the EU (Office for the Promotion of Migrant Integration, 2017).

Italy

(data collection by Camila Rivas-Garrido, Gloria Novovic, and Edward Koning)

	Tax-paid pensions	Health care	Contr. unempl.	Contr. pension	Housing	Social assist.	Active labour market	Average
1990	83	69	42	38	31	25	56	49
2000	33	63	42	0	56	19	6	31
2010	58	63	25	0	63	38	6	36
2015	58	63	42	0	63	38	13	39

Tax-paid pensions

TPP1: *Residence requirements for universal tax-paid pension*
1990–2015: ***–8*** *(no universal public pension)*

There is no universal public pension program in Italy. The only tax-paid pension benefit, the *pensione sociale* before 1996 and the *assegno sociale* since then, is means-tested (INPS, n.d.).

TPP2: *Availability of means-tested program for those with incomplete benefit*
1990: ***3*** *(yes, with residence requirement of 10+ years)*
2000: ***0*** *(yes, with no residence requirement)*
2010–2015: ***3*** *(yes, with residence requirement of 10+ years)*

Before 2009, there was no residence requirement associated with accessing the means-tested public pension. However, the *pensione sociale* was only available to Italian citizens and therefore was effectively inaccessible to newcomers in their first 10 years, after which they would be eligible for naturalization. Since 2009, the benefit has been available only to those with at least 10 years of residence in Italy (INPS, 2016; Parlamento Italiano, 1969, 1998, 2008).

TTP3: *Status requirement for access to means-tested or universal tax-paid pension*
1990: ***4*** *(citizens only)*
2000–2015: ***1*** *(citizens and all permanent residents)*

Only Italian citizens were eligible for the *pensione sociale*. The *assegno sociale*, on the other hand, is available to all citizens, EU citizens, and permanent residents, as long as they meet the age, income, and, since 2009, residence requirements (INPS, 2016; Parlamento Italiano, 1969).

TTP4: *Export possibilities of (means-tested or universal) tax-paid pension*
1990: ***4*** *(no export possible)*
2000–2015: ***3*** *(during very short stay abroad only)*

The *pensione sociale* could not be exported. Recipients of the *assegno sociale* can reside abroad for up to 30 days without losing the benefit (Galli, Pittau, & Ricci, 2014; INPS, n.d.; Parlamento Italiano, 1969).

Health care

HC1: *Residence requirement for public health care*
1990–2015: ***0*** *(no waiting period)*

There is no waiting period before new arrivals can access the health care system: access begins as soon as one is registered with the National Health Service (MISSOC 2004–2018; Parlamento Italiano, 1989, 1998).

HC2: *Status requirements for public health care*
1990: ***3*** *(undocumented migrants excluded entirely)*
2000–2015: ***2*** *(restrictions for undocumented and some legal migrants, but no barriers to urgent care)*

All legal residents, except for international students and some other categories of temporary permit holders, are eligible to access public health care.

Undocumented migrants used to be excluded altogether, but as a result of a 1998 reform gained access to emergency services and urgent care (Cuadra, 2010; Devillanova, 2008; Galli, Pittau, & Ricci, 2014; Parlamento Italiano, 1998).

HC3: *Health care accessibility services*
1990–2015: ***4*** *(nothing available)*

There are no public translation services or attempts to introduce cultural sensitivity in the provision of medical services in Italy. Even translated documents are very rare. Immigrants with low proficiency will have to rely on professional interpreters or, more commonly, family and friends (Falla et al., 2017).

HC4: *Additional health care benefits*
1990–2015: ***4*** *(no additional health care benefits)*

There are no health care services in Italy that are exclusively available to immigrants (Busetta, Ceterolli, & Wilson, 2018; De Luca, Ponzo, & Andrés, 2013; Devillanova, 2016; Falla et al., 2017).

Contributory unemployment

CUB1: *Status requirements for access to contributory unemployment benefits*
1990–2010: ***1*** *(all legal residents except international students and seasonal workers)*
2010–2015: ***3*** *(permanent residents, citizens, and very few temporary migrants)*

Before 2015, all legal residents were eligible to participate in the contributory unemployment benefit scheme, except for seasonal workers (and international students, who are barred from the labour market altogether). In that year, however, a large-scale reform restricted access to permanent residents and holders of long-term work permits (Galli, Pittau, & Ricci, 2014; Parlamento Italiano, 2015).

CUB2: *Integration requirements for access to contributory unemployment benefits*
1990–2015: ***0*** *(no integration requirements)*

There are no integration requirements for accessing unemployment insurance benefits in Italy.

CUB3: *Export possibilities*
1990–2000: ***4** (no export possible)*
2010–2015: ***2** (export possible for short period of time)*

Unemployment benefits are generally not exportable. Since 2004, however, recipients can retain their benefit when searching for a job in a different member state of the European Union for a period of up to 3 months (Galli, Pittau, & Ricci, 2014; INPS, 2017).

Contributory pension

CP1: *Status requirement*
1990: ***3** (some temporary migrants excluded)*
2000–2015: ***0** (all legal residents included)*

All residents who have worked in Italy will have built up entitlement to a contributory pension. Seasonal workers used to be unable to claim pension benefits after multiple spells of employment in Italy, but the immigration reform of 1998 (Turco-Napolitano) explicitly specified their eligibility (Galli, Pittau, & Ricci, 2014; Parlamento Italiano, 1998).

CP2: *Export possibilities*
1990–2015: ***0** (export possible without restrictions)*

The contributory pension can be claimed from any country in the world. The 2002 Bossi-Fini law made it impossible for emigrants to countries with which Italy has no social security agreements to receive a refund of the contributions they paid upon leaving the country, but they are still eligible for the pension benefit when they reach retirement age (Galli, Pittau, & Ricci, 2014; Ministero del lavoro e delle politiche sociale, n.d.; Parlamento Italiano, 2002).

Housing benefits

HB1: *Residence requirements for housing benefits*
1990: ***0** (no residence requirement)*
2000–2015: ***4** (residence requirement of more than 4 years)*

The 1990 Martelli law established the right to housing for foreigners in Italy, although it mostly focused on temporary solutions for a large inflow of newcomers. The 1998 Turco-Napolitano law formally integrated immigrants into Italian housing programs. And while the law did not specify any residence requirements, local authorities did – the province of Lombardy established a requirement of at least 5 years of residence or work history in the province. A 2008 law established that immigrants would only be eligible for the full slate of housing support after having spent at least 10 years in the country or 5 years in the same province (Parlamento Italiano, 1990, 1998, 2008; Pompei & Cutini, 2009; Regione Lombardia, 2013).

HB2: *Status requirements for housing benefits*
1990–2000: ***1*** *(all legal residents)*
2010–2015: ***2*** *(some but not all temporary migrants)*

Housing assistance was available to all legal migrants until the passing of the 2002 Bossi-Fini Law, which required at least a residency permit of 2 years (Parlamento Italiano, 2002; Pompei & Cutini, 2009).

HB3: *Integration requirements for housing benefits*
1990–2015 ***0*** *(no integration requirements)*

There are no integration requirements associated with accessing housing benefits in Italy.

HB4: *Preferential treatment in housing*
1990–2015: ***4*** *(no privileged access for migrants)*

There is no immigrant-targeted housing assistance or other form of privileged access to housing and housing benefits for immigrants.

Social assistance

SA1: *Residence requirements for social assistance benefits*
1990–2015: ***1*** *(residence requirement only for specific categories)*

There are no residence requirements for accessing social assistance. All foreigners with a residence permit of at least one year are eligible for social assistance if they meet the other eligibility criteria. Some municipalities have tried to implement residence requirements, but they have been overturned by the judiciary. The only exception applies to migrants from other EU states. They can be refused social assistance during their first 3 months in the country on the basis that they would constitute an unreasonable burden on the system (Galli, Pittau, & Ricci, 2014; Saraceno, 2006).

SA2: *Status requirements for social assistance benefits*
1990: ***3*** *(all permanent residents)*
2000–2015: ***2*** *(all permanent residents and some temporary residents)*

Since 1990, social assistance has been reserved for citizens and those who have registered as permanent residents. The 1998 Turco-Napolitano Law established that social assistance is available to anyone with a residence permit of at least one year. A subsequent law in 2000 aimed to once again disentitle temporary permit holders, but this restriction was deemed unconstitutional by the Constitutional Court and overturned shortly afterwards (Galli, Pittau, & Ricci, 2014; Parlamento Italiano 1990, 1998).

SA3: *Consequences of uptake for status*
1990–2015: ***0** (no consequences)*

Uptake of social assistance does not have consequences for migrants' residence status or access to citizenship.

SA4: *Integration requirements for social assistance*
1990–2000: ***0** (no integration requirements)*
2010–2015: ***3** (access tied to permits with integration requirements)*

There are no formal integration requirements for accessing social assistance in Italy. However, since 2007, there have been language requirements, and since 2012, there have been integration requirements for accessing long-term residence permits in Italy. Immigrants who fail to live up to these requirements will not see their residence permit renewed and will thus become ineligible for social assistance (Campomori & Caponio, 2016; Cuttita, 2016; OECD, 2014).

Active labour market

ALM1: *Residence requirements*
1990–2015: ***0** (no residence requirements)*

There are several active labour market policies in Italy, including training programs and job orientation. They are usually available to recipients of unemployment benefits, but the 1990 Martelli law and the 1998 Turco-Napolitano law specified that foreigners with legal work permits have the right to register as job seekers and as such participate in employment programs (OECD, 2014; Parlamento Italiano, 1990, 1998).

ALM2: *Status requirements*
1990–2015: ***1** (all permanent residents and some temporary residents)*

All foreigners who are legally entitled to work in Italy are eligible to participate in employment programs. The only categories that are ineligible are migrants on short-term permits that do not grant access to the Italian labour market, such as international students (OECD, 2014; Parlamento Italiano, 1990, 1998).

ALM3: *Immigrant-targeted language programs*
1990: ***4** (no funded language programs)*
2000–2010: ***0** (fully funded programs, available to any immigrant)*
2015: ***1** (funded programs, but nominal fees and/or not freely available to all immigrants)*

Free language instruction was introduced in 1997. Since a reform in 2011, only immigrants who are required to integrate (new arrivals from outside the European Union) can access these classes for free or at nominal fees (Caponio, Baucells and Cuell, 2015; OECD, 2014).

ALM4: *Other immigrant-targeted employment assistance*
1990: ***4** (no public integration programs)*
2000–2015 ***0** (programs available to any migrant)*

The first public integration programs were rolled out as a result of the 1998 Turco-Napolitano Law, which created a fund for financing integration programs. Since 2011, Italy has also offered a range of immigrant-targeted active labour market programs, such as vocational training for humanitarian migrants. And since 2012, all third-country nationals who intend to reside for the long term are required to follow public integration courses (Cuttita, 2016; OECD, 2014; Parliamento Italiano, 1998).

Luxembourg

(data collection by Liam Thompson and Edward Koning)

	Tax-paid pensions	Health care	Contr. unempl.	Contr. pension	Housing	Social assist.	Active labour market	Average
1990	100	81	33	0	6	38	50	44
2000	100	81	33	0	6	25	50	42
2010	100	56	33	0	6	44	50	41
2015	100	69	33	0	6	44	13	38

Tax-paid pensions

TPP1: *Residence requirements for universal tax-paid pension*
1990–2015: ***–8** (no universal public pension)*

The public pension system in Luxembourg is contributory. There is no tax-paid pension program (Chaput, Julienne, & Lelièvre, 2007; Social Security Administration, 2016).

TPP2: *Availability of means-tested program for those with incomplete benefit*
1990–2015: ***4*** *(no program)*

There is no tax-paid pension program in Luxembourg. The only benefit that elderly with low pension income can access is social assistance (Chaput, Julienne, & Lelièvre, 2007; EMN, 2013).

TTP3: *Status requirement for access to means-tested or universal tax-paid pension*
1990–2015: ***–8*** *(no tax-paid programs)*

See above.

TTP4: *Export possibilities of (means-tested or universal) tax-paid pension*
1990–2015: ***–8*** *(no tax-paid programs)*

See above.

Health care

HC1: *Residence requirement for public health care*
1990–2015: ***2*** *(between 6 weeks and 3 months)*

Employed residents are covered by mandatory insurance from the moment they start working. Newcomers who do not have employment can apply for voluntary insurance, which has a 3-month waiting period (Inspection Générale de la sécurité sociale, 2017).

HC2: *Status requirements for public health care*
1990–2015: ***3*** *(undocumented migrants excluded entirely)*

All legal residents are able to access health care, via either mandatory or voluntary insurance. Undocumented migrants can access emergency care but will be asked to pay for it. There is, however, the opportunity to be reimbursed by a fund specifically set up for uninsured patients, including undocumented migrants (Commission Nationale d'Éthique, 2007; EMN, 2013; FRA, 2011, Inspection générale de la sécurité sociale, 2017).

HC3: *Health care accessibility services*
1990–2000: ***3** (some incidental services and/or translated documents)*
2010: ***0** (state-funded translation and health care services with cultural sensitivity)*
2015: ***2** (services exist, but not fully funded and/or not run directly by government)*

Intercultural interpretation services in the health care sector were established in 2008. Before then, all that was available was a telephone translation service in a limited number of languages. In 2011, however, the demands on the intercultural interpretation services increased while the government did not increase their funding. As a result, the service was transferred to the Luxembourgish Red Cross and was no longer available free of charge (interview. LUX-01).

HC4: *Additional health care benefits*
1990–2015: ***4** (no additional health care benefits)*

There are no health care benefits or services in Luxembourg that are exclusively available to (certain categories of) immigrants.

Contributory unemployment

CUB1: *Status requirements for access to contributory unemployment benefits*
1990–2015: ***2** (all legal residents except asylum seekers, international students, and/or seasonal workers)*

In order to be eligible for unemployment benefits, one must be allowed to work legally in Luxembourg, be registered as a job seeker, and have worked continuously in the country for at least 26 weeks out of the past 12 months. This effectively disentitles international students, whose permits do not allow access to the labour market. Asylum seekers can take up employment under very strict conditions, but they are nevertheless ineligible for unemployment benefits (EMN 2013; Government of Luxembourg, 1976, 2016, n.d.-a; MISSOC 2004–2018).

CUB2: *Integration requirements for access to contributory unemployment benefits*
1990–2015: ***0** (no integration requirements)*

There have never been integration requirements associated with accessing unemployment benefits in Luxembourg (interview, LUX-02).

CUB3: *Export possibilities*
1990–2015: ***2*** *(export possible for short period of time)*

Unemployment benefits are generally not exportable. However, recipients can retain their benefit when searching for a job in a different member state of the European Economic Area for a period of up to 3 months (EMN 2013; Government of Luxembourg, 1976, 2016, n.d.-b).

Contributory pension

CP1: *Status requirement*
1990–2015: ***0*** *(all legal residents)*

The only requirement for accessing the contributory pension in Luxembourg is a legal work history. There are no other status requirements (CNAP, 2019; Government of Luxembourg, 1987, 2016).

CP2: *Export possibilities*
1990–2015: ***0*** *(export possible without restrictions)*

The pension can be exported anywhere in the world without restrictions (EMN, 2013; Government of Luxembourg, 1987; interview, LUX-03).

Housing benefits

HB1: *Residence requirements for housing benefits*
1990–2015: ***0*** *(no residence requirement)*

There is no waiting period for immigrants other than the normal waiting period all applicants face when being placed on a waiting list (Government of Luxembourg, 1983, n.d.-c).

HB2: *Status requirements for housing benefits*
1990–2000: ***1*** *(all legal residents)*

Everyone who is registered in the population register can apply for social housing as long as they meet the income requirements. Since everyone who spends more than 3 months in the country is obliged to register, the only status requirement is legal residence (EMN, 2013; Government of Luxembourg, 1983, n.d.-c).

HB3: *Integration requirements for housing benefits*
1990–2015 ***0** (no integration requirements)*

There are no integration requirements associated with accessing social housing (Government of Luxembourg, n.d.-c).

HB4: *Preferential treatment in housing*
1990–2015: ***0** (earmarked housing for various groups of immigrants)*

Since 1972, the government of Luxembourg has committed itself to assisting immigrants in their housing needs, both by assistance in finding suitable housing and in the development and management of temporary accommodation for foreign workers and asylum seekers (Government of Luxembourg, 1972, 1993, 2008b).

Social assistance

SA1: *Residence requirements for social assistance benefits*
1990: ***4** (residence requirement of more than 5 years)*
2000–2015: ***3** (residence requirement between 1 and 5 years)*

Until 1999, there was a 10-year residence requirement for accessing social assistance in Luxembourg. Since then, the requirement has been 5 years' residence out of the past 20. This requirement is waived for refugees and stateless persons (Ametepe & Hartmann-Hirsch, 2010; EMN, 2013; Government of Luxembourg, 1986, 1999. 2009).

SA2: *Status requirements for social assistance benefits*
1990: ***2** (all permanent and some temporary residents)*
2000: ***1** (all legal residents)*
2010–2015: ***2** (all permanent and some temporary residents)*

Before a 1999 social assistance reform, all residents who were legally allowed to work in Luxembourg were eligible, which made the benefit inaccessible to some categories of temporary migrants. The 1999 law only required legal residence. A 2009 reform, however, again, specifically disentitled certain categories of migrants on a temporary permit, such as newly arrived family migrants and international students (Ametepe and Hartmann-Hirsch, 2010; EMN, 2013; Government of Luxembourg, 1986, 1999, 2009).

SA3: *Consequences of uptake for status*
1990–2000: ***0** (no consequence)*
2010–2015: ***2** (inaccessible permanent residence or citizenship)*

Before 2008, accessing social assistance did not have consequences for the recipient's residence status. Since 2008, however, people who have taken up social assistance will not be granted a long-term residence permit if they are otherwise eligible (Government of Luxembourg, 2008a; interview, LUX-04).

SA4: *Integration requirements for social assistance*
1990–2015: ***0*** *(no integration requirements)*

There are no integration requirements for accessing social assistance benefits in Luxembourg.

Active labour market

ALM1: *Residence requirements*
1990–2015: ***0*** *(no residence requirement)*

There has never been a waiting period before job seekers can access active-labour market policies. Anyone who is legally entitled to work in Luxembourg can immediately register as a job seeker and as such become eligible for job assistance programs (interview, LUX-02; Government of Luxembourg, n.d.-d).

ALM2: *Status requirements*
1990–2015: ***1*** *(all permanent residents and some temporary residents)*

Anyone who is legally entitled to work in Luxembourg can immediately register as a job seeker and as such become eligible for job assistance programs. As a result, only some categories of temporary residents, such as international students, are ineligible (interview, LUX-02; Government of Luxembourg, n.d.-d).

ALM3: *Immigrant-targeted language programs*
1990–2010: ***4*** *(no funded language programs)*
2015: ***1*** *(funded programs, but nominal fees)*

Luxembourg did not offer discounted language instruction until a law of 2008 specifying a "welcome and integration contract" came into force in 2011. Since then, immigrants have had access to subsidized language classes in one of the three official languages of Luxembourg (Government of Luxembourg, 2008b; OLAI, n.d.).

ALM4: *Other immigrant-targeted employment assistance*
1990–2010: ***3*** *(some programs offered, but offered ad hoc or inconsistently across the country)*
2015: ***0*** *(programs available to any migrant)*

While the Luxembourgish immigration service has been tasked with encouraging the integration of immigrants since 1972, this did not result in any consistent employment assistance until 2011, when the "welcome and integration contract" come into force. Since then, immigrants can take a free citizenship course and attend information sessions. Since 2015, Luxembourg has also run a specific employment assistance program for third-country nationals and refugees, which includes assistance with foreign credential recognition, assistance with job applications, job mediation, and professionalization workshops (Government of Luxembourg, 1972, 2008b ; OLAI, n.d.; Swinnen, 2016).

Malta

(data collection by Matt McBurney, Gloria Novovic, and Edward Koning)

	Tax-paid pensions	Health care	Contr. unempl.	Contr. pension	Housing	Social assist.	Active labour market	Average
1990	100	100	50	86	88	38	56	74
2000	100	100	50	64	88	38	56	71
2010	92	63	33	38	75	38	50	55
2015	92	63	33	38	75	38	50	55

Tax-paid pensions

TPP1: *Residence requirements for universal tax-paid pension*
1990–2015: ***–8** (no universal public pension)*

There is no universal public pension in Malta. The only tax-paid pension is means-tested (Government of Malta, 1987, n.d.-a).

TPP2: *Availability of means-tested program for those with incomplete benefit*
1990–2015: ***4** (yes, but in practice not accessible)*

While there is no formal residence requirement for accessing the means-tested benefit, it is exclusively available to (EU) citizens, and since citizenship can only be acquired by family members of Maltese citizens and humanitarian migrants, and only at the discretion of Minister of Foreign Affairs, the benefit is in practice inaccessible to migrants from outside the EU (Government of Malta, 1964, 1987: 66.1bi; Identity Malta Agency, n.d.).

TTP3: *Status requirement for access to means-tested or universal tax-paid pension*
1990–2000: ***4** (citizens only)*
2010–2015: ***3** (citizens and specially designated groups only)*

Only citizens are eligible for the means-tested age pension. Since Malta joined the EU in 2004, citizens of other member states who are resident in Malta have been entitled to the same rights (Government of Malta, 1987: 66.1bi).

TTP4: *Export possibilities of (means-tested or universal) tax-paid pension*
1990–2015: ***4** (no export possibility at all)*

Access to the means-tested benefit is tied to residence in Malta. It cannot be exported (Government of Malta, 1987; Social Security Administration, 2010).

Health care

HC1: *Residence requirement for public health care*
1990–2015: ***4** (five years or more)*

There is no formal waiting period before newcomers can access public health care. However, since the regular system is only available to permanent residents and there is a 5-year residence requirement before someone becomes eligible for permanent residence, there is effectively a 5-year residence requirement on public health care as well, except for refugees (Cuadra, 2010; EMN, 2014; Gauci, 2010; Government of Malta, 1987; MISSOC 2004–2018).

HC2: *Status requirements for public health care*
1990–2000: ***4** (undocumented and some categories of legal migrants excluded entirely)*
2010–2015: ***2** (restrictions for undocumented and some categories of legal migrants, but no barriers to urgent care)*

Until 2001, access to public health care was technically reserved for Maltese citizens, but in practice available to permanent residents as well. Since then, health care has been available to recognized refugees, permanent residents, and EU citizens. Irregular entrants, including asylum seekers, are detained for the first 18 months in Malta and have access to basic health care services while in detention, even though the quality and availability of these services have been frequently criticized (Cuadra, 2010; DeBono, 2013; Government of Malta, n.d.-b; Luhmann, Bouhénia, & Giraux, 2007; MISSOC, 2004–2018).

HC3: *Health care accessibility services*
1990–2000: ***4** (nothing available)*
2010–2015: ***0** (state-funded translation and services with cultural sensitivity)*

Malta did not offer any health care accessibility services until 2008, when the Department of Health established a Migrant Health Liaison Office. This office helps immigrants navigate the health care system, runs training programs for cultural mediators, and provides translated materials. Its services are unavailable, however, to asylum seekers and undocumented migrants in detention (Government of Malta, n.d.-c; UNHCR, 2013).

HC4: *Additional health care benefits*
1990–2015: ***4** (no additional health care benefits)*

There are no health care programs exclusively available to immigrants in Malta. The lack of mental health services specifically targeted to refugees has attracted criticism (Aditus and JRS Malta, n.d.; UNHCR, 2013).

Contributory unemployment

CUB1: *Status requirements for access to contributory unemployment benefits*
1990–2015 ***2** (all legal residents except asylum seekers, international students, and seasonal workers)*

Residence in Malta and a history of at least 50 weeks of contributions are required to access the contributory unemployment benefit in Malta. International students cannot access the benefit even if they meet these requirements. Denied asylum claimants who cannot legally be deported are similarly barred, even if they meet the contribution requirements (Cuadra, 2010; Government of Malta, 1987; MISSOC 2004–2018; Nimführ, 2016).

CUB2: *Integration requirements for access to contributory unemployment benefits*
1990–2015: ***0** (no integration requirements)*

There are no integration requirements associated with accessing contributory unemployment benefits.

CUB3: *Export possibilities*
1990–2000: ***4** (no export possible)*
2010–2015: ***2** (export possible for short period of time)*

Unemployment benefits are generally not exportable. However, since Malta joined the EU recipients have been able to retain their benefit when searching for a job in a different member state for a period of up to 3 months, which under certain circumstances can be extended by another 3 months (EMN 2014; MISSOC 2004–2018).

Contributory pension

CP1: *Status requirement*
1990–2015: ***3** (some temporary migrants excluded)*

The only requirement for accessing the contributory pension benefit is a work history of at least 10 years' worth of paid contributions. However, non-deportable asylum seekers are eligible to take up employment, though they cannot access pension benefits even if they meet the contribution requirements (EMN, 2014; Government of Malta, 1987; Nimführ, 2016).

CP2: *Export possibilities*
1990: ***3.9** (no export possible, except to specific countries)*
2000: ***2.1** (no export possible, except to specific countries)*
2010–2015: ***0** (export possible without restrictions)*

Before Malta joined the EU, the contributory pension was exportable only to countries with which Malta had signed a bilateral social security agreement (Libya in 1988, Canada in 1991, and the United Kingdom in 1995). Since then, the benefit has been payable anywhere in the world (Government of Malta, 1987, n.d.-d; Spiteri Gingell, 2015).

Housing benefits

HB1: *Residence requirements for housing benefits*
1990–2000: ***4** (residence requirement of more than 4 years)*
2010–2015: ***2** (residence requirement of 2 years)*

In 1976, Parliament established a Housing Authority in charge of providing housing benefits and assistance. One of the eligibility requirements for accessing rent assistance is 18 months of uninterrupted residence. Before the 2000s, however, these benefits were only available to Maltese citizens, and access to citizenship comes with a residence requirement of 10 years (Government of Malta, 1976; Housing Authority, 2017; OECD, 2009).

HB2: Status requirements for housing benefits
1990–2015: ***4*** *(only some permanent residents and privileged nationals)*

All housing benefits were originally reserved for Maltese citizens. Since the 2000s, however, EU citizens and recognized refugees have been entitled to these benefits as well (Fsadni & Pisani, 2012; Government of Malta, 1976; OECD, 2009).

HB3: Integration requirements for housing benefits
1990–2015 ***2*** *(access tied to permits with integration requirements)*

There are no integration requirements associated with access to housing benefits in Malta. However, the benefits are only available to citizens (and since the 2000s, some other categories of migrants), and citizenship comes with integration requirements (Government of Malta, 1964; Identity Malta Agency, n.d.).

HB4: Preferential treatment in housing
1990–2015: ***4*** *(no privileged housing assistance)*

Immigrants do not have privileged access to housing in Malta. Recognized refugees are able to access the same housing benefits as Maltese citizens, but there are no programs that specifically target them (Aditus, n.d.).

Social assistance

SA1: Residence requirements for social assistance benefits
1990–2015: ***3*** *(residence requirement between 1 and 5 years)*

The Social Security Act does not state any residence requirements for accessing social assistance. However, since social assistance is only available to permanent residents and there is a 5-year residence requirement for accessing permanent residency, there effectively is a 5-year residence requirement on accessing social assistance as well (Gauci, 2010; Government of Malta, 1987).

SA2: Status requirements for social assistance benefits
1990–2015: ***3*** *(permanent residents and citizens)*

Only permanent residents and (EU) citizens are eligible for social assistance in Malta (Government of Malta, 1987; McKay, 2014).

SA3: Consequences of uptake for status
1990–2015: ***0*** *(no consequences)*

Taking up social assistance does not have consequences for migrants' residence status in Malta.

SA4: Integration requirements for social assistance
1990–2015: ***0*** *(no integration requirements)*

There are no integration requirements associated with accessing social assistance.

Active labour market

ALM1: Residence requirements
1990–2015: ***0*** *(no residence requirement)*

Malta has offered a range of active labour market policies since the establishment of the Employment and Training Corporation in 1990 (since then renamed JobsPlus), including training services, individualized employment advice, internship programs, and wage subsidies, although many of these programs have been temporary in nature. Anyone can register with the ETC/JobsPlus as soon as they obtain the licence to work in Malta (Caruana and Theuma, 2012; JobsPlus, n.d.).

ALM2: Status requirements
1990–2015: ***1*** *(all permanent residents and some temporary residents)*

Anyone with a licence to work in Malta can access active labour market policies. This means that some categories of temporary residents, such as international students and temporary workers whose permit is tied to a specific employer, are ineligible (Gauci, 2010; JobsPlus, n.d.).

ALM3: Immigrant-targeted language programs
1990–2015: ***4*** *(no funded language programs)*

During the period under study, there have been no government-funded language programs specifically targeted for immigrants. The Employment and Training Corporation offers some language training, but it is not specifically targeted at immigrants. Only in 2018 did the government start to offer language training to immigrants (Dimech, 2017; Gauci, 2010).

ALM4: *Other immigrant-targeted employment assistance*
1990–2000 ***4*** *(no integration programs or immigrant-targeted active labour market policies)*
2010–2015: ***3*** *(some programs offered, but offered ad hoc or inconsistently)*

Malta did not launch a formal integration policy until 2017. However, since the 2000s it has experimented with a number of programs aimed at increasing the employability of immigrants (Dimech, 2017; Gauci, 2010).

Netherlands

(data collection by Zina Bibanovic and Edward Koning)

	Tax-paid pensions	Health care	Contr. unempl.	Contr. pension	Housing	Social assist.	Active labour market	Average
1990	56	19	17	n/a	0	0	100	32
2000	63	19	25	n/a	31	75	19	39
2010	36	19	58	n/a	31	81	25	42
2015	43	38	67	n/a	31	81	69	55

Tax-paid pensions

TPP1: *Residence requirements for universal tax-paid pension*
1990–2015: ***4*** *(more than 40 for complete, with prorated benefits for shorter residency)*

To be eligible for the universal pension AOW, one needs to have 50 years of residence in the Netherlands between 15 and 65 years of age. Applicants with a shorter history of residency receive a prorated benefit (Department of Social Affairs, 2008; MISSOC 2004–2018).

TPP2: *Availability of means-tested program for those with incomplete benefit*
1990–2000: ***4*** *(no program)*
2010–2015: ***0*** *(yes, with no residence requirement)*

A legislative reform in 2003 introduced the Supplementary Income Provision for the Elderly (AIO), a means-tested benefit for elderly with low pension income. Before that, low-income elderly were forced to rely on social assistance (interview, NET-01; SVB, n.d.-a).

TTP3:	*Status requirement for access to means-tested or universal tax-paid pension*
1990–2015:	***1*** *(citizens and all permanent residents)*

The AOW is available to all long-term residents of the Netherlands. Temporary migrants are technically able to claim benefits if they have worked in the Netherlands for long enough to build up entitlement, but such cases are rare and uptake is low (Koning, 2019; MISSOC 2004–2018).

TTP4:	*Export possibilities of (means-tested or universal) tax-paid pension*
1990:	***0*** *(without restrictions)*
2000:	***1.0*** *(without restrictions to some countries, with cuts in benefits to others)*
2010:	***0.7*** *(without restrictions to some countries, with cuts in benefits to others)*
2015:	***1.8*** *(without restrictions to some countries, with cuts in benefits to others)*

Before 2000, the AOW could be exported without restrictions anywhere. Since then, however, recipients in countries with which the Netherlands has no social security agreement have received a cut in their benefit of 50%. (In 2000, a total of 25 countries were covered by social security arrangements; this number had gone up to 61 by 2010.) Since 2014, the Netherlands has applied "the country of residence principle," which adjusts the level of the pension benefit to the standard of living in the country in which the recipient resides. Since the benefit level is never adjusted upward, and the standard of living is higher in only a small number of relevant countries (Switzerland, United States, Luxembourg, Germany, Sweden, Canada, Australia, and Finland), this effectively means that most recipients abroad see a cut in their benefit (EMN 2014; interview, NET-01; Koning, 2019; SVB, n.d.-b).

Health care

HC1:	*Residence requirement for public health care*
1990–2015:	***0*** *(no residence requirement)*

There is no residence requirement for accessing health care: insurance is mandatory for all residents, and access to health care is immediately available upon insurance (EMN 2014; MISSOC 2004–2018).

HC2: *Status requirements for public health care*
1990–2015: ***1** (restrictions for undocumented migrants, but no barriers to urgent care)*

All legal residents have access to health care. Undocumented migrants do not have access to the regular health care system but are offered medically necessary care as defined by a general practitioner (interview, NET-02; Frydryszak & Macherey, 2016; Van der Bijl *et al.*, 2013).

HC3: *Health care accessibility services*
1990–2010: ***1** (state-funded translation services)*
2015: ***4** (nothing available)*

The Netherlands used to subsidize interpretation services in hospitals. However, this subsidy was discontinued in 2012 (Devillé et al., 2011; interview, NET-02).

HC4: *Additional health care benefits*
1990–2015: ***1** (extra coverage only for some refugees or refugee claimants)*

Refugee claimants in asylum centres have access to the same services as are covered by the basic health care system, but also to additional services, such as dental care, eye care, and physiotherapy. Since 2009, these services have been managed by a private health care insurance provider, but this reorganization has not affected the range of services asylum seekers can access (Minderhoud, 1999; Van der Bijl *et al.*, 2013).

Contributory unemployment

CUB1: *Status requirements for access to contributory unemployment benefits*
1990: ***0** (all legal residents)*
2000–2010: ***1** (all legal residents except international students and/or seasonal workers)*
2015: ***2** (all legal residents except asylum seekers and international students)*

The only formal status requirement for accessing contributory unemployment benefits is legal residence. However, the 2000 Alien Act stipulated that benefit access would only be granted to immigrants in cases where the benefits "harmonize with the nature of their residence," thereby effectively disentitling international students. Moreover, a 2011 reform limited the number of weeks asylum seekers were allowed to work to 24 to ensure they would not build up entitlement to unemployment benefits (EMN 2014; Koning, 2019).

CUB2: *Integration requirements for access to contributory unemployment benefits*
1990–2000: ***0** (no integration requirements)*
2010–2015: ***4** (civic integration and language requirements)*

The Netherlands introduced integration requirements for accessing unemployment benefits in 2006. In particular, it forced all migrants on unemployment benefits to either acquire language skills and knowledge of Dutch society or lose their benefits (Koning, 2019).

CUB3: *Export possibilities*
1990–2015: ***3** (export possible for short period of time)*

Contributory unemployment benefits are generally not exportable. However, recipients can retain their benefit while looking for employment in other member states of the EU or EEA for up to 3 months (EMN, 2014; UWV, n.d.).

Contributory pension

There is no centralized contributory pension program in the Netherlands. Apart from the universal pension, most pensioners draw income from supplementary pension programs that are set up by their employers and are run by private pension funds and insurance companies (Government of the Netherlands, n.d.-a). For that reason, the score for all indicators regarding contributory pension benefits is **–8** (no contributory pension benefit).

Housing benefits

HB1: *Residence requirements for housing benefits*
1990–2015: ***0** (no residence requirement)*

During the period under study, there have not been any residence requirements related to access to either rent subsidies or social housing (Belastingdienst, n.d.; Government of the Netherlands, n.d.-b; Parliament of the Netherlands, 1984; Ponzo, 2010).

HB2: *Status requirements for housing benefits*
1990: ***0** (any resident)*
2000–2015: ***1** (all legal residents)*

The 1984 law on rent subsidy did not specify any status requirements – anyone renting a property could be eligible for rent subsidy. The introduction of the 1998 Linking Act, however, made legal residence a requirement. The Linking Act had the same implication for access to social housing (Koning, 2019; Parliament of the Netherlands, 1984; Ponzo, 2010; Van Parys & Verbruggen, 2004).

HB3: *Integration requirements for housing benefits*
1990–2015 ***0*** *(no integration requirements)*

There are no integration requirements associated with accessing rent subsidy or social housing in the Netherlands.

HB4: *Preferential treatment in housing*
1990: ***0*** *(earmarked housing for various groups of migrants)*
2000–2015: ***4*** *(no privileged access for migrants)*

Between 1975 and 1995, the Netherlands ran a preferential housing scheme for migrants from former colonies. Since then, however, no groups of immigrants have had privileged access to housing (Ponzo, 2010).

Social assistance

SA1: *Residence requirements for social assistance benefits*
1990: ***0*** *(no residence requirement)*
2000–2015: ***3*** *(residence requirement between 1 and 5 years)*

There was no formal residence requirement for accessing social assistance in the Netherlands until the 1999 Decision Expansion and Reduction Insurance Sphere Public Insurance Programs and the 2000 Aliens Act, which established, respectively, that social assistance is only available to permanent residents and that permanent residence can only be granted after 5 years of residence. Since then, there has effectively been a 5-year residence requirement for access to social assistance, although that residence requirement was only 3 years for family migrants until 2012, and exceptions are regularly made in individual cases where the applicant has a demonstrable "durable connection" to the Netherlands (Koning, 2019, Parliament of the Netherlands, 2000).

SA2: *Status requirements for social assistance benefits*
1990: ***0*** *(all residents)*
2000–2015: ***2*** *(all permanent residents and some temporary residents)*

Before the introduction of the 1998 Linking Act, all residents were able to apply for social assistance. Subsequent reforms in 1999 and 2000 (see SA1) limited access to permanent residents. The only categories of migrants on a temporary permit who are able to access social assistance are recognized refugees and, in individual cases, migrants with a "durable connection" to the Netherlands (Koning, 2019).

SA3: *Consequences of uptake for status*
1990: ***0** (no consequences)*
2000–2015: ***4** (revocation of residence permits)*

Since the passing of the 2000 Aliens Act, temporary permit holders are at risk of losing their right of residence if they take up social assistance. And as a result of a 2003 welfare reform, the same applies to EU citizens who have resided in the country for more than 3 months but less than 5 years (Parliament of the Netherlands, 2000, 2003).

SA4: *Integration requirements for social assistance*
1990: ***0** (no integration requirements)*
2000: ***3** (access tied to permits with integration requirements)*
2010–2015: ***4** (compulsory integration for benefit recipients)*

A 1998 reform made 600 hours of language and social orientation classes mandatory for all permanent residents, and as such an indirect requirement for access to social assistance. A subsequent reform in 2006 explicitly tied access to social assistance to successful participation in language and integration classes (Ersanilli, 2007; Koning 2019).

Active labour market

ALM1: *Residence requirements*
1990: ***–8** (no active labour market policies)*
2000–2015: ***2** (access tied to benefits requiring a work history or residence history)*

Active labour market policies were first introduced in the 1990s. In 2002, all reintegration programs were transferred to private providers, which receive additional government funding if they are able to place participants in a contract of at least 6 months. Most programs are available only to recipients of either social assistance or unemployment benefits and therefore are not immediately available to newcomers (Bruttel and Sol, 2006; Lindsay and McQuaid, 2009).

ALM2: *Status requirements*
1990: ***-8** (no active labour market policies)*
2000–2015: ***1** (all permanent residents and some temporary residents)*

Active labour market policies were first introduced in the 1990s. Most programs are available only to recipients of either social assistance or unemployment benefits, and therefore residents who are ineligible for those benefits (such as asylum seekers, international students, or newly arrived family migrants), cannot avail themselves of active labour market policies either (Bruttel & Sol, 2006; Lindsay & McQuaid, 2009).

ALM3: *Immigrant-targeted language programs*
1990: ***4** (no funded language programs)*
2000: ***0** (fully funded language programs, available to any immigrant)*
2010: ***1** (funded programs, but nominal fees)*
2015: ***4** (no funded language programs)*

The Netherlands first started offering funded language programs in 1998. In 2007, these services were privatized and immigrants were required to pay part of the expenses. A reform in 2012 abolished all government funding for language programs (Ersanilli, 2007; Koning, 2019).

ALM4: *Other immigrant-targeted employment assistance*
1990: ***4** (no integration programs or immigrant-targeted active labour market policies)*
2000–2010: ***0** (programs available to any migrant)*
2015 ***4** (no integration programs or immigrant-targeted active labour market policies)*

The Netherlands started to develop specific tools to assist immigrants' employment opportunities in 1998, when it began offering publicly funded integration courses and introduced a law specifically designed to trace and increase the employment of ethnic minorities (the Samen Law). These programs disappeared quickly, however: the Samen Law was abolished in 2004, and in 2012 the government stopped all funding for integration courses. By that time all other immigrant-targeted employment assistance programs had been cancelled as well (Ersanilli, 2007; Koning, 2019; Shaw, 2002).

New Zealand

(data collection by Josh Pedersen and Edward Koning)

	Tax-paid pensions	Health care	Contr. unempl.	Contr. pension	Housing	Social assist.	Active labour market	Average
1990	33	63	n/a	n/a	44	38	88	53
2000	33	31	n/a	n/a	44	38	88	47
2010	31	25	n/a	38	44	38	44	36
2015	31	25	n/a	38	44	38	44	36

Tax-paid pensions

TPP1: *Residence requirements for universal tax-paid pension*
1990–2015: ***1** (5–10 years)*

Throughout the period under study, the residence requirement for accessing the universal pension program has been 10 years since the age of 20 (and at least 5 years since the age of 50) (Ministry of Social Development, 2003, n.d.-a; Sinclair, 1990).

TPP2: *Availability of means-tested program for those with incomplete benefit*
1990: ***-8** (no program)*

There is no specific program for elderly who are ineligible for the universal public pension. They will have to rely on social assistance programs in cases where they have low income. Since the residence requirement for the universal pension is relatively short, however, this indicator will be scored as inapplicable (-8) rather than as maximally exclusionary (4) (interview, NZE-1; Ministry of Social Development, n.d.-b).

TTP3: *Status requirement for access to means-tested or universal tax-paid pension*
1990–2015: ***1** (citizens and all permanent residents)*

All citizens and permanent residents are eligible for the pension program as long as they meet the age and residence requirements (Ministry of Social Development, 2003, n.d.-a; Sinclair, 1990).

TTP4: *Export possibilities of (means-tested or universal) tax-paid pension*

1990: **2** *(with cuts in benefit)*
2000: **1.9** *(exportable to some countries, extra requirements to others, not possible to UK)*
2010: **1.7** *(exportable to some countries, extra requirements to others, not possible to UK)*
2015: **1.7** *(exportable to some countries, extra requirements to others, not possible to UK)*

Until 1990, the universal pension could be exported anywhere in the world, but recipients would receive a hefty 50% cut in their benefit. Since then, New Zealand has reformed its portability regime. The pension can be exported to some agreement countries without any restrictions (Canada, Denmark, Greece, Ireland, Jersey, and Guernsey since the mid-1990s; Australia since 2002, and Malta since 2013) and can be exported to other countries after additional residence requirements are satisfied. As specified in a bilateral agreement, however, the universal pension cannot be exported at all to the United Kingdom (Ministry of Social Development, 2003, n.d.-c; Sinclair, 1990).

Health care

HC1: *Residence requirement for public health care*
1990–2015: **0** *(no waiting period)*

Eligible residents can access public health care services in New Zealand immediately, without any waiting period (Ashton, 1996; Ministry of Health, 1994; 2011).

HC2: Status requirements for public health care
1990–2015: **2** *(restrictions for undocumented and some legal migrants, but no barriers to urgent care)*

All residents who have resided in New Zealand for more than 2 years or possess a permit allowing a residence of at least 2 years are eligible for public health care. Most other residents are ineligible for the public health care system but can receive emergency care free of charge (Ashton, 1996; Ministry of Health, 1994, 2011).

HC3: *Health care accessibility services*
1990: **4** *(nothing available)*
2000: **1** *(state-funded translation services only)*
2010–2015: **0** *(state-funded translation services and services with specific cultural sensitivity)*

Health care accessibility services have received much attention in New Zealand over the past two decades. The 1996 Code of Health and Disability Services Consumers' Rights established the right to "effective communication in a form, language, and manner that enables the consumer to understand the information provided," and since then, the scope of available state-funded translation services has greatly expanded. In 2006 the Medical Council of New Zealand issued a statement on cultural competence outlining the expectations of medical professionals regarding the delivery of culturally sensitive services. The availability and scope of these services have expanded further since (Gray, Hilder, & Stubbe, 2002; Health and Disability Commissioner, 1996; HealthNavigator, n.d.-a., n.d-b; Medical Council of New Zealand, 2006).

HC4: *Additional health care benefits*
1990: ***4** (no additional health care benefits)*
2000–2015: ***2** (specialized services for refugees, in particular regarding mental health)*

Since 1995, a not-for-profit called Refugees as Survivors New Zealand has provided targeted mental health and well-being services to people of refugee background. It relies both on public funding and on private donations. Besides this, in all regions there are public health care facilities that offer specialized care for patients with a refugee background (Auckland Regional Public Health Service, n.d.; RASNZ, n.d.).

Contributory unemployment

There are no contributory unemployment programs in New Zealand. Instead, all programs for the unemployed, such as the Unemployment Benefit and the Job Seeker Support, are means-tested (Ministry of Social Development, n.d.-d). All values for this social program in New Zealand are, therefore, **–8** (no contributory unemployment benefit).

Contributory pension

CP1: *Status requirement*
1990–2000: ***–8** (no contributory pension program)*
2010–2015: ***1** (temporary excluded, but can opt out of premium payments)*

New Zealand did not run any type of contributory pension program until 2007, when it introduced the KiwiSaver pension plan. It is only available to citizens and permanent residents. Ineligible workers are able to opt out of premium payments because the scheme is voluntary (KiwiSaver, n.d.-a; Kritzer, 2007; Trampusch, 2018).

CP2: *Export possibilities*
1990–2000: ***-8** (no contributory pension program)*
2010–2015: ***2** (accrued benefits available at reduced rate)*

The KiwiSaver can be exported anywhere in the world. However, the contributions the government makes to the KiwiSaver (the member tax credits) cannot be exported, and therefore in this scenario recipients will receive a lower benefit than if they were to retire in New Zealand (KiwiSaver, n.d.-b).

Housing benefits

HB1: *Residence requirements for housing benefits*
1990–2010: ***2** (residence requirement of 2 years)*
2015: ***3** (residence requirement of 3 or 4 years)*

There was no formal residence requirement on accessing social housing and housing benefits until 2014, when a Ministerial Direction explicitly required 2 years' residence as a permanent resident. Since permanent residency is only obtainable after 2 years of residence in New Zealand, this requirement means that in most cases at least 4 years of residence are required. For the same reason, before 2014 the *de facto* residence requirement was 2 years, considering housing benefits were only available to citizens and permanent residents (Ministry of Social Development, 2014, n.d.-e; Morrison, 1995; Murphy, 1997; Parliament of New Zealand, 1992).

HB2: *Status requirements for housing benefits*
1990–2015: ***3** (citizens and permanent residents)*

During the period under study, financial assistance to cover housing costs (the housing benefit until 1992, and the accommodation supplement since then) have been available only to citizens and permanent residents. Social housing has formally become reserved for citizens and permanent residents only since 2014, but the 1992 Housing Restructuring and Tenancy Matters Act already specified that in the allocation of social housing, applicants "are treated differently on the basis of … whether or not they are … permanently resident … in New Zealand" (Ministry of Social Development, 2014, n.d.-e; Morrison, 1995; Murphy, 1997; Parliament of New Zealand, 1992).

HB3: *Integration requirements for housing benefits*
1990–2015 ***0** (no integration requirements)*

There are no integration requirements associated with accessing housing assistance in New Zealand.

HB4: *Preferential treatment in housing*
1990–2015: ***1** (earmarked housing for refugees)*

Since 1987, New Zealand has guaranteed social housing to quota refugees. Successful asylum applicants, however, need to find housing on their own terms (Human Rights Commission, 2010; New Zealand Immigration Service, 2004).

Social assistance

SA1: *Residence requirements for social assistance benefits*
1990–2015: ***3** (residence requirement between 1 and 5 years)*

The main social assistance benefits (the Special Benefit before 2006, replaced by the Temporary Additional Support since then) are only available to applicants who have been in the country as a permanent resident or a citizen for at least 2 years. Ineligible migrants with a shorter residence history might qualify for the so-called Emergency Benefit but would still need to have a permanent residence permit, which is normally not available until after 2 years in the country (interview, NZE-01; Ministry of Social Development, n.d.-f; Parliament of New Zealand, 1964).

SA2: *Status requirements for social assistance benefits*
1990–2015: ***3** (all permanent residents)*

For the full period under study, social assistance benefits have only been available to permanent residents and citizens (interview, NZE-01; Ministry of Social Development, n.d.-f; Parliament of New Zealand, 1964).

SA3: *Consequences of uptake for status*
1990–2015: ***0** (no consequences)*

Only permanent residents and citizens are able to access social assistance, and they will not face consequences for their residence status as a result of taking up such benefits.

SA4: *Integration requirements for social assistance*
1990–2015: ***0** (no integration requirements)*

There are no integration requirements associated with accessing social assistance in New Zealand.

Active labour market

ALM1: *Residence requirements*
1990–2015: ***4** (more than 1 year)*

New Zealand offers a wide range of active labour market policies. While the eligibility criteria differ between programs, they are only available to permanent residents and citizens. Since at least 2 years of residence are required to acquire permanent residency, there is a *de facto* residence requirement of two years in most active labour market programs (Johri et al., 2004; Ministry of Social Development, n.d.-g).

ALM2: *Status requirements*
1990–2015: ***2** (all citizens and permanent residents)*

New Zealand offers a wide range of active labour market policies. While the eligibility criteria differ between programs, they are only available to permanent residents and citizens (Johri et al., 2004; Ministry of Social Development, n.d.-g).

ALM3: *Immigrant-targeted language programs*
1990–2000: ***4** (no funded language programs)*
2010–2015: ***1** (funded programs, but not freely available to all categories of migrants)*

New Zealand did not start offering language training to migrants until 2008, when it started funding tertiary education organizations and private training establishments to improve the language skills of newcomers. This was formalized with the establishment of the ILN-ESOL Fund in 2012. That fund ensures that refugees and permanent residents with low language proficiency can take free language classes. Many categories of migrants, however, are required to pay for language classes as part of their visa fee, in cases where they have low levels of proficiency in English (interview, NZE-02; Tertiary Education Commission, n.d.-a, n.d.-b).

ALM4: *Other immigrant-targeted employment assistance*
1990–2000 ***4** (no public integration programs)*
2010–2015 ***0** (programs available to any migrant)*

New Zealand has never offered integration courses and only started to offer migrant-targeted employment assistance in the early 2000s. Since then, national and regional authorities, as well as funded third parties, have offered employment assistance programs, skills training, and orientation programs (Controller and Auditor-General, 2013; Shields, Drolet, & Valenzuela, 2016).

Norway

(data collection by Matt McBurney and Edward Koning)

	Tax-paid pensions	Health care	Contr. unempl.	Contr. pension	Housing	Social assist.	Active labour market	Average
1990	47	31	42	0	6	19	44	27
2000	47	19	42	0	13	19	31	24
2010	21	19	42	0	13	25	6	18
2015	21	19	42	0	13	25	6	18

Tax-paid pensions

TPP1: *Residence requirements for universal tax-paid pension*
1990–2015: ***3*** *(40 years for complete benefit, with prorated benefits for shorter residency)*

Forty years of residence are required to access the universal pension plan in Norway (called the old-age pension until 2011, when it was replaced by the guarantee pension). People with less residency can receive a prorated benefit if they have lived in Norway for at least one year (when they are citizens of an EEA country) or 3 years (when they are not) (Labour and Welfare Administration, n.d.-a; Social Security Administration, 2010).

TPP2: *Availability of means-tested program for those with incomplete benefit*
1990–2000: ***4*** *(no program or not accessible program)*
2010–2015: ***0*** *(yes, with no residence requirement)*

In 2005, Norway introduced a special pension supplement for people with low pension income because of limited residence in the country. Initially, the only requirement was being registered in the population registry, which is possible for anyone who has a permit allowing them to stay in the country for at least one year. Legislative changes in 2016 restricted the benefit to permanent residents, which in effect introduced a residence requirement, but these changes postdate the period under investigation (Labour and Welfare Administration, n.d.-b, n.d.-c; Parliament of Norway, 2005).

TTP3: *Status requirement for access to means-tested or universal tax-paid pension*
1990–2015: ***0*** *(all legal residents)*

All residents of Norway, i.e., all individuals with permission to stay in the country for at least one year, are eligible for the universal pension program (Labour and Welfare Administration, n.d.-c; Social Security Administration, 2010).

TTP4: *Export possibilities of (means-tested or universal) tax-paid pension*
1990: ***0.5*** *(without restrictions to some countries, with additional residence requirements to others)*
2000: ***0.5*** *(without restrictions to some countries, with additional residence requirements to others)*
2010: ***0.4*** *(without restrictions to some countries, with additional residence requirements to others)*
2015: ***0.3*** *(without restrictions to some countries, with additional residence requirements to others)*

The universal pension can be exported without restrictions to any EEA country or country with which Norway has a bilateral social security agreement. It can be exported to other countries as well, but only if the recipient has resided in Norway for at least 20 years. In 1990, there were 17 countries to which the pension could be exported without restrictions; this number was 18 in 2000, 30 in 2010, and 32 in 2015 (Labour and Welfare Administration, n.d.-c, n.d.-d).

Health care

HC1: *Residence requirement for public health care*
1990–2015: ***0*** *(no waiting period)*

All residents are immediately eligible for public health care as soon as they are registered in the population registry (Abebe, 2010; eHealth Directorate, n.d.; MISSOC 2004–2008).

HC2: *Status requirements for public health care*
1990–2015: ***2*** *(restrictions for undocumented and some legal migrants, but no barriers to urgent care)*

Only those who are registered in the population registry are eligible for public health care; this excludes undocumented migrants and migrants who are in Norway for a short time. Everyone in the country, however, has access to free emergency care, including perinatal care and treatment of infectious diseases (Aschehoug, 2010; eHealth Directorate, n.d.; Kvamme and Ytrehus, 2015; MISSOC 2004–2008).

HC3: *Health care accessibility services*
1990: **3** *(some incidental outreach programs or translated written documents*
2000–2015: **1** *(state-funded translation services only)*

While translation services have long been available in the Norwegian health sector, they were not formalized as a patient's right until 1999. Norway does not offer health care services with cultural sensitivity; this has been criticized in some literature (Hjörleifsson, Hammer, & Díaz, 2018; Kale, 2006; Parliament of Norway, 1999).

HC4: *Additional health care benefits*
1990–2015: **0** *(expanded coverage available for refugees and refugee claimants)*

Since 1983, refugees and asylum seekers have had access to free dental care, which native-born adult citizens have to pay for themselves (Health Directorate, 2015; Ministry of Social Affairs and Health, 1999; Parliament of Norway, 1983).

Contributory unemployment

CUB1: *Status requirements for access to contributory unemployment benefits*
1990–2015 **1** *(all legal residents except international students and/or seasonal workers)*

Ever since the 1966 Social Security Act, everyone who is registered in the population registry and meets the requirements regarding contributions and availability of work is eligible for unemployment benefits. This means that the only migrants who are ineligible are those who are residing for a short time or who are not allowed to work in Norway (Labour and Welfare Administration, n.d.-e; Parliament of Norway, 1966, 1997; Ruud, 2015).

CUB2: *Integration requirements for access to contributory unemployment benefits*
1990–2015: **0** *(no integration requirements)*

There are no integration requirements associated with accessing unemployment benefits.

CUB3: *Export possibilities*
1990–2015: **4** *(no export possible)*

Unemployment benefits are only available to recipients who reside in Norway. The exceptions to this rule are minimal (e.g., a holiday abroad is allowed for those who have been on unemployment benefits for more than 52 weeks, and job seekers are allowed to travel to another EEA country for the purpose of attending a job interview for a period of up to 3 days) (Parliament of Norway, 1997, 1998).

Contributory pension

CP1: *Status requirement*
1990–2015: ***0** (all legal residents included)*

Ever since the 1966 Social Security Act, everyone who is registered in the population registry and who meets the requirements regarding contributions is eligible for the contributory pension (called the earnings-related pension until 2011, when it was replaced by the income pension). Since anyone who would have made enough contributions to qualify for the contributory pension would necessarily be registered in the population registry, there are no *de facto* status requirements (Labour and Welfare Administration, n.d.-f, n.d.-g; Parliament of Norway, 1966, 1997).

CP2: *Export possibilities*
1990–2015: ***0** (export possible without restrictions)*

Under both the old and new system, the contributory pension has been exportable to any country in the world without additional restrictions (Labour and Welfare Administration, n.d.-d).

Housing benefits

HB1: *Residence requirements for housing benefits*
1990–2015: ***0** (no residence requirement)*

While there is municipal social housing in Norway, the sector is very small and the housing system overall is geared toward encouraging homeownership as much as possible. Housing benefits are available to all resident homeowners who meet the income requirements, and there is no waiting period for newcomers (Parliament of Norway, 2012; Sørvoll, 2011; State Housing Bank, n.d.).

HB2: *Status requirements for housing benefits*
1990–2015: ***1** (some but not all temporary migrants)*

The only status requirement for accessing housing benefits is being registered as a resident. As such, only undocumented and some categories of temporary migrants are ineligible (Parliament of Norway, 2012; Sørvoll, 2011; State Housing Bank, n.d.).

HB3: *Integration requirements for housing benefits*
1990–2015: ***0*** *(no integration requirements)*

There are no integration requirements associated with accessing housing benefits.

HB4: *Preferential treatment in housing*
1990: ***0*** *(earmarked housing for various groups of migrants)*
2000–2015: ***1*** *(earmarked housing for refugees)*

At least since 1979, Norway has reserved social housing for recognized refugees. There used to be elaborate housing assistance for other categories of migrants as well, but these services were cancelled in 1992 (Søholt, 2010; Søholt & Wessel, 2010; Sørvoll, 2011).

Social assistance

SA1: *Residence requirements for social assistance benefits*
1990–2015: ***0*** *(no residence requirement for anyone)*

There is no residence requirement for accessing social assistance. All legal residents are eligible for the benefit upon arrival, although since 2004 newly arrived refugees and their family members have been channelled into a separate program (Brochmann and Grødem, 2013; Labour and Welfare Administration, n.d.-h).

SA2: *Status requirements for social assistance benefits*
1990–2015: ***2*** *(all permanent residents and some temporary residents)*

The only requirement for accessing social assistance is habitual residence as demonstrated by inclusion in the population registry. This includes everyone on Norwegian territory except undocumented migrants, tourists, and people who are in the country for less than a year (Brochmann and Grødem, 2013; Labour and Welfare Administration, n.d.-h).

SA3: *Consequences of uptake for status*
1990–2015: ***0*** *(no consequences)*

Accessing social assistance has no consequences for residence status in Norway (Brochmann & Hagelund, 2012).

SA4: *Integration requirements for social assistance*
1990–2000: ***1*** *(integration requirements can be requested at the discretion of local authorities)*
2010–2015: ***2*** *(loss of funds for asylum seekers and/or refugees not-participating in programs)*

Since the 1980s, municipal welfare offices have been technically allowed to require recipients to participate in language and/or vocational training, but few do so in practice. Since the 2004 launch of the introductory program, newly arrived refugees receive an introduction benefit, at a higher level than social assistance, but see cuts in those benefits for every hour of language and integration training they miss (Brochmann & Hagelund, 2012).

Active labour market

ALM1: *Residence requirements*
1990–2015: ***0*** *(no residence requirement)*

There are no residence requirements for accessing active labour market policies in Norway. They are immediately available for newcomers, unless they are already covered by targeted programs (see ALM3, ALM4) (Dahl & Lorentzen, 2005; Duell, Singh, & Tergeist, 2009, Labour and Welfare Administration, n.d.-i).

ALM2: *Status requirements*
1990–2015: ***1*** *(all permanent and some temporary residents)*

The only requirement for accessing most active labour market policies is being registered in the national population registry, which includes everyone on Norwegian territory except undocumented migrants, tourists, and people who are in the country for less than a year (Dahl & Lorentzen, 2005; Duell, Singh, & Tergeist, 2009, Labour and Welfare Administration, n.d.-i).

ALM3: *Immigrant-targeted language programs*
1990: ***1*** *(funded programs, but only available for refugees and asylum seekers)*
2000–2015: ***0*** *(fully funded language programs, available to any migrant)*

Norway has offered free language classes to refugee migrants since the 1970s, and to other categories of migrants since 1994 (Brochmann & Hagelund, 2012).

ALM4: *Other immigrant-targeted employment assistance*
1990–2000: ***4** (no integration programs or immigrant-targeted active labour market policies)*
2010–2015: ***0** (programs available to any migrant)*

Initially, the Norwegian approach to encouraging labour market participation of immigrants was to include them in general services. The introductory program, launched in 2003, however, offers extensive employment assistance, including individualized employment services. This program was initially only available to refugees and asylum seekers and their family members but since 2005 has been opened up to labour migrants and family migrants (Brochmann & Hagelund, 2012; Lodovici, 2010; Søholt, 2010).

Portugal

(data collection by Silvina Antunes and Edward Koning)

	Tax-paid pensions	Health care	Contr. unempl.	Contr. pension	Housing	Social assist.	Active labour market	Average
1990	72	75	67	0	100	69	100	69
2000	72	69	33	0	31	50	56	45
2010	45	31	25	0	6	50	6	23
2015	42	31	25	0	6	44	6	22

Tax-paid pensions

TPP1: *Residence requirements for universal tax-paid pension*
1990–2015: ***-8** (no universal public pension)*

There is no universal public pension benefit in Portugal. The main public pensions are contributory (the old-age pension) and means-tested (the social old-age pension) (European Commission, n.d.; Social Security Administration, 2002, 2016).

TPP2: *Availability of means-tested program for those with incomplete benefit*
1990–2000: ***3** (yes, with residence requirement of 10+ years)*
2010–2015: ***2** (yes, with residence requirement of 3–10 years)*

The means-tested pension benefit does not come with a formal residence requirement, but because it is only available to citizens and there is a 10-year residence requirement on access to citizenship, in practice the residence requirement for the social pension is 10 years. In 2006, Portugal introduced an additional benefit, the solidarity supplement for the elderly, which is available to all low-income elderly who have resided in Portugal for at least 6 years (OECD, 2019; Segurança Social, n.d.-a, n.d.-b).

TTP3: *Status requirement for access to (means-tested or universal) tax-paid pension*
1990–2000: ***3*** *(citizens and specially designated groups only)*
2010–2015: ***1*** *(citizens and all permanent residents)*

The means-tested pension benefit is only available to citizens of Portugal, EEA member states, and 4 countries with which Portugal has bilateral social security agreements (Australia, Brazil, Cape Verde, and Canada). The solidarity supplement for the elderly, introduced in 2006, is available to all (permanent) residents who have resided in the country uninterruptedly for the past 6 years (OECD, 2019; Segurança Social, n.d.-a; n.d.-b).

TTP4: *Export possibilities of (means-tested or universal) tax-paid pension*
1990: ***2.7*** *(not possible, except to some countries)*
2000: ***2.7*** *(not possible, except to some countries)*
2010: ***2.4*** *(not possible, except to some countries)*
2015: ***2.1*** *(not possible, except to some countries)*

Residence in Portugal is normally required for accessing the social old-age pension, but it can be exported to EEA member states and 4 countries with which Portugal has bilateral social security agreements (Australia since 2002, Brazil for the full duration under study, Cape Verde since 2011, and Canada since 2011) (OECD, 2019; Social Security Administration, 2002, 2016).

Health care

HC1: *Residence requirement for public health care*
1990–2015: ***0*** *(no waiting period)*

Since the establishment of the national health service in 1979, access to health care has been immediately available to all eligible residents (MISSOC, 2004–2018; Serviço Nacional de Saúde, n.d).

HC2: *Status requirements for public health care*
1990–2000: ***4*** *(undocumented and some categories of legal migrants excluded entirely)*
2010–2015: ***0*** *(full access for all residents)*

Before 2001, health care services were exclusively available to citizens and to citizens of countries with which Portugal had reciprocal health care arrangements. A sweeping reform in that year, however, opened the system to all residents, including undocumented migrants provided they are able to demonstrate they had resided in the country for 90 days (Backstrom, 2014; Ingleby et al., 2005; Topa, Neves, & Nogueira, 2013).

HC3: *Health care accessibility services*
1990: ***4*** *(nothing available)*
2000–2010: ***3*** *(some incidental outreach programs or translated written documents)*
2015: ***1*** *(state-funded translation services only)*

There were no health care accessibility services for migrants in Portugal before the early 2000s, when the health care system started providing some translated documents and NGOs began offering incidental outreach programs. In 2015, a government agency servicing migrants launched a telephone translation service that is freely available to all migrants (ACM, n.d.-a; Ingleby et al. 2005).

HC4: *Additional health care benefits*
1990–2000: ***4*** *(no additional health care benefits)*

There are no health care services exclusively available to groups of migrants that native-born Portuguese cannot access (Ingleby et al., 2005; Portuguese Refugee Council, n.d.-a).

Contributory unemployment

CUB1: *Status requirements for access to contributory unemployment benefits*
1990: ***4*** *(only permanent residents and citizens)*
2000: ***2*** *(all legal residents except asylum seekers, international students, and seasonal workers)*
2010–2015: ***1*** *(all legal residents except international students and/or seasonal workers)*

Access to unemployment insurance was originally reserved for citizens, but a 1998 reform opened the scheme to everyone legally employed in Portugal. This means that only foreigners who do not possess a permit entitling them to work (long enough) are excluded from the benefit, such as international students and, before 2008, asylum seekers (Bover, García-Perea, & Portugal, 2000; Oliveira, 2008; Parliament of Portugal, 2008; Portuguese Refugee Council, n.d.-b; Segurança Social, n.d.-c).

CUB2: *Integration requirements for access to contributory unemployment benefits*
1990: ***2** (access tied to permits with integration requirements*
2000–2015: ***0** (no integration requirements)*

There have never been direct integration requirements for accessing unemployment insurance in Portugal. However, until 1998, unemployment insurance was available only to citizens, and thus an indirect integration requirement was in place considering there have been language requirements for accessing Portuguese citizenship since 1981 (Oliveira, 2008; Parliament of Portugal, 1981; Segurança Social, n.d.-c).

CUB3: *Export possibilities*
1990–2015: ***2** (export possible for short period of time)*

Residence in Portugal is a requirement for accessing unemployment insurance. However, recipients can reside in another EU or EEA member state for up to 3 months for the purpose of finding employment without losing their benefits, albeit under additional conditions (Segurança Social, n.d.-d).

Contributory pension

CP1: *Status requirement*
1990–2015: ***0** (all legal residents)*

At least since the establishment of the 1984 Social Security Act, all individuals with a legal work history in Portugal are eligible for the contributory pension, as long as they meet the contributory requirements (Centro Nacional de Pensões, 2019; Garcia, 2017; Parliament of Portugal, 1984).

CP2: *Export possibilities*
1990–2015: ***0** (export possible without restrictions)*

Residence in Portugal is not a requirement for receiving the contributory pension benefit. It can be exported anywhere in the world (Centro Nacional de Pensões, 2019; Peixoto, Marçalo, & Tolentino, 2011).

Housing benefits

HB1: *Residence requirements for housing benefits*
1990: ***–8*** *(no public housing benefits)*
2000–2015: ***0*** *(no residence requirement)*

While housing policy has existed for over a century, the availability of social housing and housing support was marginal until a major revitalization in the mid-1990s. Since then, several social housing programs and rent assistance policies have become available. All of these are available to legal immigrants, regardless of their residence or status, on the same terms as for native-born Portuguese (Agarez, 2018; Malheiros & Fonseca, 2011; Pato and Pereira, 2016).

HB2: *Status requirements for housing benefits*
1990: ***–8*** *(no public housing benefits)*
2000–2015: ***1*** *(all legal residents)*

While housing policy has existed for over a century, the availability of social housing and housing support has been marginal until a major revitalization in the mid-1990s. Since then, several social housing programs and rent assistance policies have become available. All of these are available to legal immigrants, regardless of their residence or status, on the same terms as for native-born Portuguese (Agarez, 2018; Malheiros & Fonseca, 2011; Pato & Pereira, 2016).

HB3: *Integration requirements for housing benefits*
1990: ***–8*** *(no public housing benefits)*
2000–2015: ***0*** *(no integration requirements)*

There have never been integration requirements associated with accessing housing support in Portugal.

HB4: *Preferential treatment in housing*
1990–2000: ***4*** *(no privileged access for migrants)*
2010–2015: ***0*** *(earmarked housing for various groups of migrants)*

The first housing programs that were rolled out in the 1990s were not targeted specifically at immigrant groups, although they relied on these benefits disproportionately. Since the early 2000s, however, Portugal has explicitly reserved social housing units for migrant groups, developed targeted assistance programs for refugees, and made efforts to increase the uptake of housing support by migrant populations (Horta & De Oliveira, 2014; Malheiros & Fonseca, 2011).

Social assistance

SA1: *Residence requirements for social assistance benefits*
1990: ***4*** *(residence requirement of more than 5 years)*
2000–2010: ***3*** *(residence requirement between 1 and 5 years)*
2015: ***2*** *(residence requirement of one year or less)*

Before 1995, social assistance benefits were available only to citizens, and thus there was a *de facto* 10-year residence requirement considering that that many years were required before one could become a citizen. Since then, the program has been opened to foreigners as well after 3 years of residence – and, since 2011, one year of residence – in the country. (Collett, 2011; EMN, 2014; Peixoto & Sabino, 2009; Segurança Social, n.d.-e).

SA2: *Status requirements for social assistance benefits*
1990: ***4*** *(only citizens and some permanent residents)*
2000–2015: ***2*** *(some but not all temporary migrants)*

Before 1995, only citizens and some privileged nationals were eligible for social assistance. Since then, the benefit has been technically available to all legal residents, but because availability for work is one of the requirements, some categories of temporary migrants (such as short-term visa holders) are not eligible (Collett, 2011; EMN, 2014; Peixoto & Sabino, 2009; Segurança Social, n.d.-e).

SA3: *Consequences of uptake for status*
1990 ***0*** *(no consequences)*
2000–2015: ***3*** *(non-renewal of residence permit)*

Ever since the benefit became available to non-citizens, migrants on temporary permits risk a refusal to renew their permits in cases where they claim social assistance (EMN, 2014; Peixoto, Marçalo, & Tolentino, 2011).

SA4: *Integration requirements for social assistance*
1990: ***3*** *(access tied to permits with integration requirements)*
2000–2015: ***0*** *(no integration requirements)*

There are no direct integration requirements associated with accessing social assistance. However, language proficiency has been a requirement for Portuguese citizenship since 1981, and therefore served as an indirect requirement for accessing social assistance when the benefit was exclusively available to citizens (Parliament of Portugal, 1981; Segurança Social, n.d.-e.).

Active labour market

ALM1: *Residence requirements*
1990: ***4*** *(more than 1 year)*
2000–2015: ***0*** *(no residence requirement)*

Before 1998, Portugal actively limited the participation of foreigners in the labour market, and only citizens were eligible for active labour market programs. Considering the lengthy residence requirement for acquiring citizenship, this meant there was a long residence requirement on accessing such programs as well. Since then, these programs have been immediately available to all legal residents whose permits allow them to take up employment in Portugal (OECD, 1998, 2013; Oliveira, 2008; Peixoto & Sabino, 2009).

ALM2: *Status requirements*
1990: ***4*** *(citizens and privileged non-nationals only)*
2000–2015: ***1*** *(all permanent residents and some temporary residents)*

Before 1998, Portugal actively limited the participation of foreigners in the labour market, and only citizens were eligible for active labour market programs. Since then, these programs have been available to all legal residents whose permits allow them to take up employment in Portugal (OECD, 1998, 2013; Oliveira, 2008; Peixoto & Sabino, 2009).

ALM3: *Immigrant-targeted language programs*
1990–2000: ***4*** *(no funded language programs)*
2010–2015: ***0*** *(fully funded language programs, available to any immigrant)*

Portugal did not develop any integration policy until the early 1990s, and the first initiatives were primarily targeted at removing exclusionary practices and policies. Language programs were first introduced in 2008 and have since been freely available to all categories of migrants (ACM, n.d.-b; Horta and De Oliveira, 2014; Matias, Oliveira, & Ortiz, 2016).

ALM4: *Other immigrant-targeted employment assistance*
1990–2000: ***4*** *(no public integration programs or immigrant-targeted active labour market policies)*
2010–2015: ***0*** *(programs available to any migrant)*

Portugal did not develop any integration policy until the early 1990s, and the first initiatives were primarily targeted at removing exclusionary practices and policies. Since the early 2000s, Portugal has introduced a large number of programs aimed at improving immigrants' standing in the labour market, including vocational training programs, information services, and a project specifically aimed to help newcomers set up their own business (Horta and De Oliveira, 2014; Oliveira, 2008; Peixoto & Sabino, 2009).

Spain

(data collection by Daniel Waring and Edward Koning)

	Tax-paid pensions	Health care	Contr. unempl.	Contr. pension	Housing	Social assist.	Active labour market	Average
1990	50	63	25	14	75	50	100	54
2000	50	50	25	15	31	25	19	31
2010	50	44	8	14	31	25	19	27
2015	50	56	8	9	31	25	19	28

Tax-paid pensions

TPP1: *Residence requirements for universal tax-paid pension*
1990–2015: ***-8** (no universal public pension)*

There is no universal public pension in Spain. The only tax-paid pension benefit is means-tested (OECD, 2015; Social Security Administration, 2002, 2016).

TPP2: *Availability of means-tested program for those with incomplete benefit*
1990: ***2** (yes, with residence requirement 3–10 years)*

There is a means-tested program for low-income pensioners. Applicants need to have resided at least 10 years in Spain since the age of 16, including at least 2 years uninterruptedly before the date of application (Institute for the Elderly and Social Services, n.d.; Parliament of Spain, 1990).

TTP3: *Status requirement for access to means-tested or universal tax-paid pension*
1990–2015: ***0** (all legal residents)*

There are no formal status requirements for the means-tested benefit apart from legal residence, although in practice the only non-citizen recipients are permanent residents because of the lengthy residence requirement (Institute for the Elderly and Social Services, n.d.; Parliament of Spain, 1990).

TTP4: *Export possibilities of (means-tested or universal) tax-paid pension*
1990–2015: ***4*** *(no export possibility)*

Legal residence in Spain is a requirement for receiving the means-tested pension. It is discontinued as soon as recipients change their country of residence (Institute for the Elderly and Social Services, n.d.; Parliament of Spain, 1990; Social Security Administration, 2016).

Health care

HC1: *Residence requirement for public health care*
1990–2015: ***0*** *(no waiting period)*

There is no waiting period to access health care in Spain. Eligible residents are covered immediately (Dalli, 2018; MISSOC, 2004–2018; Parliament of Spain, 1986).

HC2: *Status requirements for public health care*
1990: ***2*** *(restrictions for undocumented and some other migrants, but no barriers to urgent care)*
2000–2010: ***0*** *(full access to all residents)*
2015: ***2*** *(restrictions for undocumented and some other migrants, but no barriers to urgent care)*

Before 2000, undocumented migrants and some categories of temporary migrants could only access emergency care in Spain. A reform in that year included everyone with proof of an address in Spain, including undocumented migrants, in the national health care system. A 2012 reform, however, again introduced new restrictions, disentitling any resident who did not either pay social security contributions or receive social transfers (Dalli, 2018; FRA, 2011; Frydryszak & Macherey, 2016; Peralta-Gallego, Gené-Badia, & Gallo, 2018).

HC3: *Health care accessibility services*
1990–2000: ***4*** *(nothing available)*
2010–2015: ***3*** *(some incidental outreach programs and translated written documents)*

There has been little effort to make health care services more accessible to immigrants in Spain. Since the 2000s, some hospitals have offered translation and culturally sensitive services, and some information is available in other languages. For the moment, however, there are no national and publicly funded accessibility services (Quevedo & Rubio, 2010; Sandín-Vázquez, Larraz-Antón, & Río-Sánchez, 2014).

HC4: *Additional health care benefits*
1990–2015: ***4*** *(no additional health care benefits)*

There are no public health care benefits in Spain exclusively available to migrant groups. There are a few refugee-targeted mental health care centres, but they only opened their doors in 2018 (Accem, n.d.-a; Quevedo & Rubio, 2010).

Contributory unemployment

CUB1: *Status requirements for access to contributory unemployment benefits*
1990–2015 ***1*** *(all legal residents except international students and/or seasonal workers)*

The only requirements for accessing the contributory unemployment scheme are a work history with sufficient social security contributions, and an availability for work. As a result, the only residents who are ineligible are those who do not possess a permit allowing them to work (long enough), such as undocumented migrants and most international students (Accem, n.d.-b; Department of Labour, Migration, and Social Security, n.d.-a; Fuentes & Callejo, 2011).

CUB2: *Integration requirements for access to contributory unemployment benefits*
1990–2015: ***0*** *(no integration requirements)*

There have never been integration requirements associated with accessing unemployment benefits or work permits (Department of Labour, Migration, and Social Security, n.d.-a; Fuentes & Callejo, 2011).

CUB3: *Export possibilities*
1990–2000: ***2*** *(export possible for short period of time)*
2010–2015: *0 (accrued benefits available at reduced rate upon leaving)*

Residence in Spain is normally required to access contributory unemployment benefits. There are, however, two significant exceptions. Recipients can retain their benefit during short stays abroad (up to 15 days outside of the EEA, and up to 3 months within the EEA), and since 2008 migrants can receive 60% of their benefits up front when they leave the country in case they fall unemployed (Department of Labour, Migration, and Social Security, n.d.-b; Parliament of Spain, 2008).

Contributory pension

CP1: *Status requirement*
1990–2015: ***0*** *(all legal residents included)*

There are no status requirements associated with accessing the contributory pension benefit; the only requirements are related to the age and contribution history of the applicant. That said, because of the relatively lengthy contribution requirement (15 years), in practice only permanent residents and citizens end up drawing from the pension benefit (Boldrin, Jiminez-Martin, & Peracchi, 1997; Department of Labour, Migration, and Social Security, n.d.-c).

CP2: *Export possibilities*
1990: ***1.1*** *(pension exportable to many, but not all countries)*
2000: ***1.2*** *(pension exportable to many, but not all countries)*
2010: ***1.1*** *(pension exportable to many, but not all countries)*
2015: ***0.7*** *(pension exportable to many, but not all countries)*

The contributory pension can only be exported to countries with which Spain has bilateral or multilateral social security agreements. The number of such countries, however, is very high: 28 in 1990, 31 in 2000, 48 in 2010, and 54 in 2015 (Department of Labour, Migration, and Social Security, n.d.-d.).

Housing benefits

HB1: *Residence requirements for housing benefits*
1990: ***4*** *(residence requirement of more than 4 years)*
2000–2015: ***0*** *(no residence requirement)*

Since 2000, all legal residents who are registered in their municipality have had access to social housing and housing assistance on the same terms, without any waiting period for newcomers. Before then, some local authorities did offer housing assistance to non-citizens, but the formal right of foreigners to be treated like Spanish citizens in the housing system only came about as a result of a 2000 reform. Because access to Spanish citizenship comes with a residence requirement of 10 years, therefore, before the reform there was a *de facto* residence requirement for accessing housing benefits of (more than) 10 years (City of Barcelona, n.d.; Pareja-Eastway, 2009; UNHCR, 2000).

HB2: *Status requirements for housing benefits*
1990: ***4*** *(only some permanent residents and privileged nationals)*
2000–2015: ***1*** *(all legal residents)*

Since 2000, all legal residents who are registered in their municipality have had access to social housing and housing assistance on the same terms, without any waiting period for newcomers. Before then, some local authorities did offer housing assistance to non-citizens, but the formal right of foreigners to be treated like Spanish citizens in the housing system only came about as a result of a 2000 reform (City of Barcelona, n.d.; Fuentes and Callejo, 2011; Pareja-Eastway, 2009; UNHCR, 2000).

HB3: *Integration requirements for housing benefits*
1990–2015 ***0*** *(no integration requirements)*

There have never been integration requirements associated with accessing housing benefits in Spain.

HB4: *Preferential treatment in housing*
1990–2015: ***4*** *(no privileged access for migrants)*

Immigrants have never enjoyed privileged access to social housing or housing assistance in Spain (interview, SPA-01; Pareja-Eastway, 2009).

Social assistance

SA1: *Residence requirements for social assistance benefits*
1990: ***4*** *(residence requirement of more than 5 years)*
2000–2015: ***3*** *(residence requirement between 1 and 5 years)*

The Autonomous Communities of Spain have offered social assistance benefits since the late 1980s. Non-citizens were granted equal access to these benefits only in 2000, even though some Autonomous Communities granted benefits to foreigners before then. Here, we will consider the residence requirement for accessing these benefits before 2000 to be 10 years, considering the residence requirement for access to citizenship. Since 2000, the residence requirements have differed between Autonomous Communities; for example, the requirement is 2 years in Catalonia, but only 1 in Andalusia and Madrid (Andalusia Board, 2019.; Arriba & Pérez Eransus, 2007; Community of Madrid, n.d.;

Fuentes & Callejo, 2011; Government of Catalonia, 2019; Rodríguez-Planas, N., 2013).

SA2: *Status requirements for social assistance benefits*
1990: ***4** (citizens and some permanent residents only)*
2000–2015: ***1** (all legal residents)*

Non-citizens were granted equal access to social assistance benefits only in 2000, even though some Autonomous Communities granted benefits to foreigners before then. Since 2000, all legal migrants are eligible for these benefits as long as they meet the other requirements (Arriba & Pérez Eransus, 2007; Rodríguez-Planas, 2013).

SA3: *Consequences of uptake for status*
1990–2015: ***0** (no consequences)*

Uptake of social assistance does not have consequences for someone's residence permit in Spain, nor does it jeopardize access to permanent residence or citizenship at a later point (Department of Foreign Affairs, European Union, and Cooperation, n.d.; Department of Home Affairs, n.d.; Fuentes & Callejo, 2011).

SA4: *Integration requirements for social assistance*
1990–2015: ***0** (no integration requirements)*

There are no integration requirements associated with accessing social assistance benefits in Spain (Andalusia Board, 2019; Community of Madrid, n.d.; Fuentes & Callejo, 2011; Government of Catalonia, 2019).

Active labour market

ALM1: *Residence requirements*
1990: ***–8** (no active labour market policies)*
2000–2015: ***1** (access tied to benefits requiring a work or residence history)*

Spain did not offer active labour market policies until the early 1990s. These programs are available to those receiving unemployment benefits, and can alternatively be accessed by newcomers after 6 months in the country (Durán & Gutiérrez, 2008; Gago, 2016).

ALM2: *Status requirements*
1990: ***–8** (no active labour market policies)*
2000–2015: ***1** (all permanent residents and some temporary residents)*

Everyone who is legally eligible to work in Spain can access active labour market policies. This only excludes undocumented migrants and some categories of temporary migrants (such as most international students) (Durán & Gutiérrez, 2008; Gago, 2016).

ALM3: *Immigrant-targeted language programs*
1990: ***4** (no funded language programs)*
2000–2015: ***0** (fully funded language programs, available to any immigrant)*

Free language training for immigrants first became available in Spain in 1994 and has remained available since then (Department of Labour and Social Affairs, 2007; Department of Labour, Migration, and Social Security, n.d.-e).

ALM4: *Other immigrant-targeted employment assistance*
1990: ***4** (no public integration programs available)*
2000–2015 ***0** (programs available to any migrant)*

Spain first developed integration policy, including labour market support, in 1994. It has since then expanded its range of services, including a large number of tailored services for refugees and asylum seekers (Department of Labour and Social Affairs, 2007; Department of Labour, Migration, and Social Security, n.d.-e; Gago, 2016).

Sweden

(data collection by Matt McBurney and Edward Koning)

	Tax-paid pensions	Health care	Contr. unempl.	Contr. pension	Housing	Social assist.	Active labour market	Average
1990	29	56	42	0	38	13	6	26
2000	59	56	25	0	38	25	6	30
2010	34	44	25	0	38	25	6	25
2015	35	44	25	0	38	25	6	25

Tax-paid pensions

TPP1: *Residence requirements for universal tax-paid pension*
1990: ***1** (between 5 and 10 years)*
2000–2015: ***3** (40 for complete, with prorated benefits for shorter residency)*

After 1978, the universal public pension in Sweden was available to anyone who had resided in the country for at least 10 years. In order to join the EU, however, the country reformed its pension system, so that it became a prorated benefit that required 40 years' residence for complete access and deducted 2.5% for every year short of that number (Department of Health and Social Affairs, 2003; Koning, 2019; Social Insurance Agency, 2010).

TPP2: *Availability of means-tested program for those with incomplete benefit*
1990: **–8** *(no program, in presence of accessible pension system)*
2000: **4** *(no program)*
2010–2015: **0** *(yes, with no residence requirement)*

Before the overhaul of the pension system, there was no real need for a benefit to compensate those with an incomplete pension considering the system already was very accessible. Even before the pension reform was introduced, some politicians were advocating the introduction of a special benefit to mitigate its consequences for immigrant elderly, but such a benefit did not come into existence until 2003. Since then, all retirees with low pension income because of their short history of residence in the country can avail themselves of the Income Support for Elderly (*äldreförsörjningsstöd*) (Gustafsson, 2011; Koning, 2019).

TTP3: *Status requirement for access to means-tested or universal tax-paid pension*
1990–2015: **0** *(all legal residents)*

Since 1978, the tax-paid pension has been available to all legal residents as long as they meet the age and residence requirements (Department of Health and Social Affairs, 2003; Johansson, 2010; Koning, 2019).

TTP4: *Export possibilities of (means-tested or universal) tax-paid pension*
1990–2010: **2.5** *(exportable to some countries but not others)*
2015: **2.6** *(exportable to some countries but not others)*

Residence in Sweden is normally required to access the universal pension benefit, but it can be exported to any EEA country. It can also be exported to Canada, even though additional residence requirements apply (minimum of 20 years' residence in Sweden) (Banting & Koning, 2017; Social Insurance Agency, 2010; Pension Agency, n.d.).

Health care

HC1: *Residence requirement for public health care*
1990–2015: ***0*** *(no waiting period)*

There is no waiting period to access health care. Everyone who is legally entitled to stay in Sweden for more than a year is immediately covered (Koning, 2019; MISSOC, 2004–2018; Parliament of Sweden, 1982).

HC2: *Status requirements for public health care*
1990–2000: ***4*** *(undocumented and some categories of legal migrants excluded entirely)*
2010–2015: ***2*** *(restrictions for undocumented and some categories of legal migrants, but no barriers to urgent care)*

The health care system is only available to residents whose permits allow them to stay for at least a year, which means undocumented migrants and those with more temporary permits are excluded. Initially, individuals who were not covered could access emergency care but would have to pay for those services themselves. A series of reforms in the late 2000s and early 2010s, however, expanded the range of free health care services for those who are not covered by the general system, in particular undocumented migrants (Glenngård, n.d.; Koning, 2019; Van Aerschot, 2014).

HC3: *Health care accessibility services*
1990–2015: ***1*** *(state-funded translation services)*

Since at least the 1980s, patients with low proficiency in Swedish have been able to make use of state-funded interpreters. There have not been any health care services with specific cultural sensitivity during the period under study, which has occasionally been criticized by left-wing MPs in the Swedish Parliament (Koning, 2019; National Board of Health and Welfare, 2016; Parliament of Sweden, 1986; Swedish Association of Local Authorities and Regions, n.d.).

HC4: *Additional health care benefits*
1990–2015: ***4*** *(no additional health care benefits)*

There are no health care services specifically reserved for (some) migrant groups (Migrationsinfo, n.d.).

Contributory unemployment

CUB1: *Status requirements for access to contributory unemployment benefits*
1990–2015 ***1*** *(all legal residents except international students and seasonal workers)*

There are no explicit status requirements for accessing contributory unemployment benefits, but access is conditional on a work history of at least one year, which means that residents whose permit does not allow them to work (long enough) are *de facto* ineligible (Bergmark & Palme, 2003; Bergnehr, 2016; Hammarstadt, 2008).

CUB2: *Integration requirements for access to contributory unemployment benefits*
1990–2015: ***0*** *(no integration requirements)*

There are no integration requirements associated with accessing contributory unemployment benefits in Sweden – all recipients, regardless of their background, are required to undertake efforts to find employment (Bergnehr, 2016; Koning, 2019).

CUB3: *Export possibilities*
1990: ***4*** *(no export possibilities*
2000–2015: ***2*** *(export possible for short period of time)*

Residence in Sweden is normally required to access contributory unemployment benefits. However, ever since Sweden joined the EU recipients have been able to retain their benefits while looking for employment in other member states for a period of up to 3 months, which can be extended by an additional 3 months (Banting & Koning, 2019).

Contributory pension

CP1: *Status requirement*
1990–2015: ***0*** *(all legal residents)*

There is no status requirement to access the contributory pension benefit. Anyone can access the benefit as long as they meet the age and contribution requirements (Klevmarken, 2002; Koning, 2019).

CP2: *Export possibilities*
1990–2015: ***0*** *(export possible without restrictions)*

The contributory pension can be exported anywhere in the world, without additional restrictions (Palmer, 2000; Pension Agency, n.d.).

Housing benefits

HB1: *Residence requirements for housing benefits*
All years: ***0*** *(no waiting period)*

Swedish housing benefits are available to anyone from the moment they are registered in the population registry (Hanenal, Krefetz, & Vatury, 2013; Koning, 2019; Social Insurance Agency, n.d.).

HB2: *Status requirements for housing benefits*
1990–2000: ***2*** *(some but not all temporary migrants)*

The only status requirement to accessing housing benefits is to be registered in the population registry. Even though exceptions are made under special conditions, this means that in most cases temporary migrants whose permits do not allow them to stay in Sweden for at least a year are ineligible (Social Insurance Agency, n.d.; Van Aerschot, 2014).

HB3: *Integration requirements for housing benefits*
1990–2015 ***0*** *(no integration requirements)*

There are no integration requirements associated with accessing housing benefits in Sweden (Borevi, 2012; Social Insurance Agency, n.d.).

HB4: *Preferential treatment in housing*
1990–2015: ***4*** *(no privileged access)*

Immigrants in Sweden have never enjoyed privileged access to housing or housing assistance (Borevi, 2013; Sondell, 2018; Van Aerschot, 2014).

Social assistance

SA1: *Residence requirements for social assistance benefits*
1990–2015: ***0*** *(no residence requirement for anyone)*

There is no residence requirement for accessing social assistance. Everyone is immediately eligible once they are registered in the population registry, as long as they meet the other requirements (Banting & Koning, 2017; Gustafsson, 2011).

SA2: *Status requirements for social assistance benefits*
1990–2015: ***2*** *(all permanent residents and some temporary residents)*

Only residents who are registered in the population registry are eligible for social assistance. This means that temporary migrants who are in the country for less than a year are ineligible (Gustafsson, 2011; Koning, 2019).

SA3: *Consequences of uptake for status*
1990–2015: ***0*** *(no consequences)*

Uptake of welfare does not have consequences for one's residence status or access to citizenship in Sweden (Borevi, 2012; Stadlmaier, 2018).

SA4: *Integration requirements for social assistance*
1990: ***0*** *(no integration requirements)*
2000–2015: ***2*** *(loss of funds for asylum seekers and/or refugees not-participating in programs)*

Since the 1990s, there have been strict requirements for all social assistance recipients to improve their standing in the labour market, but none of those are specifically targeted at immigrants. The only exception is that since the introduction of special social assistance benefits for newly arrived refugees and asylum seekers in 1992, recipients can lose those benefits if they do not participate in integration programs (Gustafsson, 2011; Koning, 2019; Weisbrock, 2011).

Active labour market

ALM1: *Residence requirements*
1990–2015: ***0*** *(no residence requirement)*

There are no residence requirements associated with accessing active labour market policies in Sweden. Everyone who is registered in the population registry and does not have employment is immediately eligible (Bengtsson, 2014; Mathias, 2017; Public Employment Service, n.d.).

ALM2: *Status requirements*
1990–2015: ***1*** *(all permanent residents and some temporary residents)*

Everyone who is registered in the population registry and is eligible to work in Sweden is eligible to participate in active labour market programs. This means that some temporary migrants, such as those who are in Sweden for a short period of time and/or are not permitted to work, are ineligible (Bengtsson, 2014; Mathias, 2017; Public Employment Service, n.d.).

ALM3: *Immigrant-targeted language programs*
1990–2015: ***0*** *(fully funded language programs, available to any immigrant)*

Sweden has offered free language training to immigrants since 1969 (OECD, 2016; Van Aerschot, 2014).

ALM4: *Other immigrant-targeted employment assistance*
1990–2015 ***0*** *(programs available to any migrant)*

Since at least 1985, Sweden has offered a variety of integration programs targeted at improving immigrants' standing in the labour market, including orientation courses, employment assistance, and, more recently, wage subsidies (Åslund and Johannson, 2011; Gebhardt, 2016; Koning, 2019; Konle-Seidl & Bolits, 2016; Weisbrock, 2011).

Switzerland

(data collection by Daniel Waring and Edward Koning)

	Tax-paid pensions	Health care	Contr. unempl.	Contr. pension	Housing	Social assist.	Active labour market	Average
1990	50	75	58	15	100	50	81	61
2000	50	44	58	14	100	50	63	54
2010	50	44	33	11	100	63	38	48
2015	50	44	33	11	100	63	38	48

Tax-paid pensions

TPP1: *Residence requirements for universal tax-paid pension*
1990–2015: ***–8*** *(no universal public pension)*

There is no universal pension in Switzerland. The only purely public pension is contributory (Social Security Administration, 2002, 2016).

TPP2: *Availability of means-tested program for those with incomplete benefit*
1990: **2** *(yes, with residence requirement 3–10 years)*

Since 1965, low-income elderly can receive a tax-paid supplementary benefit in case their pension income does not cover the cost of living. Non-citizens can only receive this benefit after 10 years of residence; however, this residence requirement is reduced to 5 years for refugees (AHV/IV, 2018, 2019; BSV, 2013; Parliament of Switzerland, 1965, 2006).

TTP3: *Status requirement for access to means-tested or universal tax-paid pension*
1990–2015: **0** *(all legal residents)*

The supplement is available to all legal residents of Switzerland as long as they meet the residence and income requirements (AHV/IV, 2018, 2019; BSV, 2015-a; Parliament of Switzerland, 1965, 2006).

TTP4: *Export possibilities of (means-tested or universal) tax-paid pension*
1990–2015: **4** *(no export possibility at all)*

The supplement is only available to residents of Switzerland. It cannot be exported (AHV/IV, 2018, 2019; BSV, 2015-a; Parliament of Switzerland, 1965, 2006).

Health care

HC1: *Residence requirement for public health care*
1990: **–8** *(no public health care or health care subsidies)*
2000–2015: **0** *(no waiting period)*

Switzerland has had a federal mandatory health care insurance program only since 1996. Before then, health care insurance was voluntary and health services were regulated at the subnational level. Since then, everyone who resides in the country is obliged to obtain health care insurance within 3 months of their arrival, and there is no waiting period between registration and coverage (BSV, 2015-b; Navarra, 2011).

HC2: *Status requirements for public health care*
1990: **–8** *(no public health care or health care subsidies)*
2000–2015: **1** *(restrictions for undocumented migrants, but no barriers to urgent care)*

Ever since the introduction of federal health care insurance, undocumented migrants have faced some barriers to accessing health care. They are required to obtain insurance like everyone else who resides in the country for at least 3 months, but the high costs for insurance contributions and the requirement to demonstrate the payment of income tax in order to receive premium contributions makes it practically very difficult for undocumented migrants to receive health care services on the same terms as other residents. That said, all residents are eligible for emergency care and urgent care (Bilger & Hollomey, 2011; Frydryszak & Macherey, 2016).

HC3: *Health care accessibility services*
1990–2015: ***2*** *(services exist but are not fully funded and/or not run directly by government)*

Since at least the 1980s, free interpreter services have been available at some hospitals in Switzerland. However, patients in Switzerland do not have the unqualified right to an interpreter, and health care insurance does not cover the costs of making use of the several private services that are available (Hudelson et al., 2014; Jaeger et al., 2019; Navarra, 2011).

HC4: *Additional health care benefits*
1990–2015: ***4*** *(no additional health care benefits)*

There are no additional health care benefits available to migrants of which native-born Swiss cannot take advantage (Bilger & Hollomey, 2011; Frydryszak & Macherey, 2016, Swiss Refugee Council, n.d.-a).

Contributory unemployment

CUB1: *Status requirements for access to contributory unemployment benefits*
1990–2000: ***3*** *(permanent residents, citizens, and very few temporary migrants)*
2010–2015: ***2*** *(all legal residents except international students and asylum seekers)*

Since the 1982 introduction of unemployment insurance, all unemployed residents who are eligible for a job and with a work history in Switzerland are eligible for unemployment benefits. However, before 2008 very few non-citizens were eligible to change employers, which effectively made them ineligible for unemployment benefits. Since a reform in 2008, which enhanced immigrants' possibilities for within-Switzerland mobility, the most obviously excluded categories have been international students, who are not eligible to work in Switzerland, and asylum seekers, for whom access to the labour market is heavily restricted (Liebig, Kohls, & Krause, 2012; Parliament of Switzerland, 1982; State Secretariat for Economic Affairs, n.d.; Swiss Refugee Council, n.d.-b).

CUB2: *Integration requirements for access to contributory unemployment benefits*
1990–2015: ***0*** *(no integration requirements)*

All recipients may be asked to participate in active labour market policies, but there are no integration requirements immigrants have to satisfy to which native-born Swiss are not subjected (State Secretariat for Economic Affairs, 2018-a, n.d.).

CUB3: *Export possibilities*
1990–2000: ***4*** *(no export possible)*
2010–2015: ***3*** *(export possible for short period of time)*

Residence in Switzerland is a requirement for accessing unemployment benefits. However, since 2004, the benefit can be exported to EU and EEA member states for a period of up to 3 months (Parliament of Switzerland, 1982; State Secretariat for Economic Affairs, 2018-b).

Contributory pension

CP1: *Status requirement*
1990–2015: ***0*** *(all legal residents)*

All residents of Switzerland are included in the contributory pension scheme (AHV/IV, n.d.-a; BSV, 2015-c).

CP2: *Export possibilities*
1990: ***1.2*** *(without restrictions to some countries, at reduced rate to others)*
2000: ***1.1*** *(without restrictions to some countries, at reduced rate to others)*
2010: ***0.9*** *(without restrictions to some countries, at reduced rate to others)*
2015: ***0.8*** *(without restrictions to some countries, at reduced rate to others)*

The contributory pension can be exported without restrictions to EU states, EFTA states, and countries with which Switzerland has signed bilateral social security agreements (Australia since 2008, Canada since 1995, Chile since 1998, India since 2011, Israel since 1984, Japan since 2012, North Macedonia since 2002, Philippines since 2004, San Marino since 1983, South Korea since 2015, Turkey since 1972, Uruguay since 2015, and USA since 1979). Those who immigrate to other countries can receive a reimbursement of their contributions, which in effect amounts to receiving a lower pension because any public contributions will not be reimbursed (AHV/IV, n.d.-b; State Secretariat for Migration, 2018).

Housing benefits

There are no public housing programs in Switzerland that are comparable to those in the other countries under investigation. There are no tax-paid transfer benefits such as rent subsidy (low-income households have to rely on social assistance), and there is no public social housing. Instead, a network of not-for-profit but non-governmental building cooperatives manage community housing units. For that reason, all scores on the indicators for housing benefits in Switzerland are **–8** (no public housing benefits), except HB4 (preferential treatment in housing), where the absence of policy results in a score of **4** (Althaus, Schmidt, & Glaser, 2016; Bochsler et al., 2015; Housing Cooperatives Switzerland, n.d.; State Secretariat for Housing, n.d.).

Social assistance

SA1: *Residence requirements for social assistance benefits*
1990–2015: ***3** (residence requirement between 1 and 5 years)*

The operation of social assistance benefits is heavily decentralized in Switzerland, and as a result residence requirements can vary from one canton to another. Nevertheless, there are federal requirements that apply to non-citizens. As far as residence requirements are concerned, in all cantons EU citizens are barred from using social assistance until they have worked in the country for at least one year (BSV, 2016; Swiss Conference for Social Assistance, n.d.; Zürich Canton, 1981).

SA2: *Status requirements for social assistance benefits*
1990–2000: ***1** (all legal residents)*
2010–2015: ***2** (all permanent residents and some temporary residents)*

A 2004 reform reduced the welfare rights of asylum seekers and temporarily admitted individuals from outside the EU. Since then, these individuals can no longer receive *Sozialhilfe* (which guarantees a minimum standard of living), and can at most apply for *Nothilfe* (which is limited to providing clothing, shelter, food and medication in emergency situations) (Liebig, Kohls & Krause, 2012; Sanchez-Mazas, 2015; Swiss Conference for Social Assistance, n.d.).

SA3: *Consequences of uptake for status*
1990–2015: ***4** (revocation of residence permit)*

Uptake of social assistance can have serious consequences for one's status in Switzerland. Even permanent residence permits can be revoked in cases of welfare dependence (Liebig, Kohls, & Krause, 2012; MIPEX, 2014).

SA4: *Integration requirements for social assistance*
1990–2000: ***0** (no integration requirements)*
2010–2015: ***1** (integration requirements can be requested at the discretion of local authorities)*

All social assistance recipients are expected to participate in reintegration measures, and there are no specifically immigrant-targeted integration requirements. Nevertheless, since 2008 cantons can place heavier requirements on immigrants than on native-born Swiss applicants (Swiss Conference for Social Assistance, n.d.; Zürich Canton, 1981).

Active labour market

ALM1: *Residence requirements*
1990–2000: ***4** (more than 1 year)*
2010–2015: ***2** (access tied to benefits requiring a work or residence history)*

Before 2008, only those who had been in the country long enough to have secured permanent residence were able to switch jobs and as such be eligible for the benefits that come with access to ALMPs. Since then, all recipients of unemployment insurance and some social assistance recipients have been required to participate in ALMP schemes (Duell et al., 2010; Liebig, Kohls, & Krause, 2012).

ALM2: *Status requirements*
1990–2000: ***2** (all citizens and permanent residents)*
2010–2015: ***1** (all permanent residents and some temporary residents)*

Before 2008 it was difficult for any temporary migrant to take advantage of ALMPs, because of their limited eligibility to look for another job in Switzerland in case of unemployment (Duell et al., 2010; Liebig, Kohls, & Krause, 2012).

ALM3: *Immigrant-targeted language programs*
1990: ***4** (no funded language programs)*
2000–2015: ***1** (funded programs, but not freely available)*

Language training is operated by cantonal authorities, and the overall system is rather opaque. Before 2000 cantons did not receive any federal funding for language training, and as a result very little was offered. Since then, all cantons have offered some language training, but they are not fully funded and there are concerns about their availability and quality. Only in 2015 did one canton (Basel) experiment with free language classes for the first time (Liebig, Kohls, & Krause, 2012; Leybold-Johnson & Hunt, 2016; Mexi, Russi, & Fischbach, 2019).

ALM4: *Other immigrant-targeted employment assistance*
1990–2000: ***3** (some programs offered, but offered ad hoc or inconsistently across the country)*
2010–2015: ***2** (programs available, but only available for refugees and asylum seekers)*

As with language training, other integration policies are the purview of cantonal authorities, and as a result there are large differences across the country in the amount of employment support immigrants can enjoy. Since 2008, however, there have been some federal active labour market policies that specifically target refugees and asylum seekers (Liebig, Kohls, & Krause, 2012; Mexi, Russi, & Fischbach, 2019).

United Kingdom

(data collection by Matt McBurney and Edward Koning)

	Tax-paid pensions	Health care	Contr. unempl.	Contr. pension	Housing	Social assist.	Active labour market	Average
1990	25	50	33	18	25	31	50	33
2000	50	50	42	17	50	38	44	41
2010	50	69	58	15	69	56	44	52
2015	50	63	58	14	69	56	44	51

Tax-paid pensions

TPP1: *Residence requirements for universal tax-paid pension*
1990–2015: ***–8** (no universal public pension)*

The UK has not had a universal tax-paid pension benefit since the passing of the National Insurance Act in 1946. The main public pension is contributory, and there have been means-tested supplements as well (Hunter, 2015; Social Security Administration, 2002, 2016).

TPP2: *Availability of means-tested program for those with incomplete benefit*
1990: ***0** (yes, with no residence requirement)*
2010–2015: ***2** (yes, with residence requirement 3–10 years)*

Throughout the period under study, low-income elderly have been able to make use of means-tested benefits: the Income Support for Elderly since 1988, which was replaced by the Minimum Income Guarantee in 1999, which was in turn replaced in 2003 by the Pension Credit. Since 1994, means-tested benefits in the UK have only been available to those with "settled" status (indefinite leave to remain), which was usually accessible after 4 years of residence before 2006 and after 5 years since then (Bradshaw & Bennett, 2009; Citizens Advice, n.d.-a); Government of the United Kingdom, n.d.-a; Harris, 2016; Knight, 2013; Parliament of the United Kingdom, 2006).

TTP3: *Status requirement for access to means-tested or universal tax-paid pension*
1990: ***0** (all legal residents)*
2000–2015: ***1** (all citizens and permanent residents)*

Since 1994, means-tested benefits are only available to permanent residents in the United Kingdom (Bradshaw & Bennett, 2009; Citizens Advice, n.d.-a; Harris, 2016; Knight, 2013).

TTP4: *Export possibilities of (means-tested or universal) tax-paid pension*
1990–2015: ***3** (during very short stay abroad)*

While residence in the United Kingdom is a requirement for receiving means-tested income support, recipients can retain their benefit during short stays abroad (Citizens Advice, n.d.-a); Government of the United Kingdom, n.d.-b).

Health care

HC1: *Residence requirement for public health care*
1990–2000: ***3** (1 year of residence)*
2010–2015: ***4** (more than 1 year)*

While being an ordinary resident has been a formal requirement for access to health care since the creation of the NHS in 1949, before 2004 everyone who had resided in the country for at least 12 months was eligible regardless of legal status. Since a reform in 2004, however, migrants from outside the European Union can only access health care if they have "settled" status, which is usually not accessible until 5 years of residence (Banting & Koning, 2017; Bragg & Feldman, 2011; McColl, Pickworth, & Raymond, 2006).

HC2: *Status requirements for public health care*
1990–2000: ***0*** *(full access for all residents)*
2010–2015: ***2*** *(restrictions for undocumented and some legal migrants, but no barriers to urgent care)*

While being an ordinary resident has been a formal requirement of access to health care since the creation of the NHS in 1949, before 2004 everyone who had resided in the country for at least 12 months was eligible regardless of legal status. Since a reform in 2004, however, non-refugee migrants from outside the European Union can only access health care if they have "settled" status, which is usually not accessible until 5 years of residence. Nevertheless, emergency care is still freely available to anyone on UK territory (Bragg & Feldman, 2011; Jones & Gill, 1998; McColl, Pickworth and Raymond, 2006).

HC3: *Health care accessibility services*
1990–2010: ***1*** *(state-funded translation services only)*
2015: ***0*** *(state-funded translation and health services with specific cultural sensitivity)*

Even though the right to state-funded translation services has not been explicitly legislated, most medical professionals understand the requirement to provide equal services to all members of the public in the 1968 Race Relations Act as implying the right to translation services. As a result, most patients have access to state-funded translation when they request it. Also, since the 2010s, medical professionals have increasingly been exposed to cultural competence training (Adams, 2007; George, Thornicroft, & and Dogra, 2015; Parliament of the United Kingdom, 1968).

HC4: *Additional health care benefits*
1990–2015: ***4*** *(no additional health care benefits)*

There are no health care benefits that are exclusively available to some categories of migrants. Some asylum seekers and refugees have access to free dental care and eye care, but such services are freely available to several categories of non-migrant patients as well (Government of the United Kingdom, n.d.-c; NHS, n.d.; Refugee Council, n.d.).

Contributory unemployment

CUB1: *Status requirements for access to contributory unemployment benefits*
1990: ***2*** *(all legal residents except asylum seekers, international students, and seasonal workers)*
2000–2015 ***3*** *(permanent residents, citizens, and very few temporary migrants)*

Contributory unemployment benefits in the United Kingdom used to be available to anyone who had paid contributions and was available to work. Since the introduction of the habitual residence requirement in 1994, however, these benefits are only available to EU migrants and those with "settled" status. Even migrants with temporary status who are eligible to remain in the UK when they fall unemployed for the purpose of finding other employment are now ineligible for unemployment benefits (North Lanarkshire Council, 2017; Parliament of the United Kingdom, 1975, 1995; Wu, 2000).

CUB2: *Integration requirements for access to contributory unemployment benefits*
1990–2000: ***0*** *(no integration requirements)*
2010–2015: ***2*** *(access tied to permits with integration requirements)*

There are no formal integration requirements for accessing unemployment benefits. Since 2007, however, there have been integration requirements for accessing permanent residence status (or "indefinite leave to remain"), which therefore serve as indirect integration requirements for accessing unemployment benefits (Government of the United Kingdom, n.d.-a; Home Office, 2019).

CUB3: *Export possibilities*
1990–2015: ***2*** *(export possible for short period of time)*

Residence in the United Kingdom is normally required to access contributory unemployment benefits. However, recipients can retain their benefit while looking for employment in other member states of the EU for a period of up to 3 months (Government of the United Kingdom, n.d.-d).

Contributory pension

CP1: *Status requirement*
1990–2015: ***0** (all legal residents)*

There are no residence requirements associated with accessing the state pension in the United Kingdom. Everyone with a legal working history in the United Kingdom is eligible (Government of the United Kingdom, n.d.-e; Harris 2016; Vlachantoni et al., 2017).

CP2: *Export possibilities*
1990: ***1.5** (without restrictions to some countries, at reduced rate to others)*
2000: ***1.4** (without restrictions to some countries, at reduced rate to others)*
2010: ***1.2** (without restrictions to some countries, at reduced rate to others)*
2015: ***1.1** (without restrictions to some countries, at reduced rate to others)*

The contributory pension can be exported anywhere in the world. The accumulated contributions do not receive any uprating after the time of migration, however, unless the claimant has migrated to a member state of the EEA or any of the countries with which the United Kingdom has signed a bilateral agreement (Barbados since 1981, Bermuda since 1969, Canada since 1995, Chile since 2015, Israel since 1957, Jamaica since 1997, Jersey and Guernsey since 1994, Mauritius since 1981, Philippines since 1989, Turkey since 1961, United States since 1988, and Yugoslavia and the seven countries of ex-Yugoslavia since 1958 (Government of the United Kingdom, n.d.-d; Harris, 2016).

Housing benefits

HB1: *Residence requirements for housing benefits*
1990: ***0** (no residence requirement)*
2000: ***3** (residence requirement of 3 or 4 years)*
2010–2015: ***4** (residence requirement of more than 4 years)*

Since the introduction of the habitual residence test in 1994, housing benefits are available only to those with settled status, which was usually accessible after 4 years until 2006 and after 5 years since then (Dell'Olio, 2007; Harris, 2016).

HB2: *Status requirements for housing benefits*
1990: ***2** (some but not all temporary migrants)*
2000–2015: ***3** (citizens and permanent residents)*

Since the introduction of the habitual residence test in 1994, housing benefits are only available to those with settled status. Before then, housing benefits were available to most migrants on temporary permits, excluding those with very temporary purpose in the United Kingdom (Dell'Olio, 2007; Harris, 2016).

HB3: *Integration requirements for housing benefits*
1990–2000: ***0** (no integration requirements)*
2010–2015: ***2** (access tied to permits with integration requirements)*

There are no formal integration requirements for accessing housing benefits. Since 2007, however, there have been integration requirements for accessing permanent residence status (or "indefinite leave to remain"), which serve as indirect integration requirements for accessing housing benefits (Government of the United Kingdom, n.d.-a; Home Office, 2019).

HB4: *Preferential treatment in housing*
1990–2015: ***2** (housing assistance for recognized refugees)*

Since the 1980s, public and private organizations have provided targeted housing support for recognized refugees. Nevertheless, the nature of this support has been variable, and by no means guarantees social housing to every refugee in need (ACH, n.d.; Citizen's Advice, n.d.-b; Dell'Olio, 2007; Griffiths, 2019).

Social assistance

SA1: *Residence requirements for social assistance benefits*
1990: ***0** (no residence requirement)*
2000–2015: ***3** (residence requirement between 1 and 5 years)*

Since the introduction of the habitual residence test in 1994, only EU citizens and permanent residents have had access to social assistance benefits. Since the residence requirement for accessing permanent residence has ranged between 4 and 5 years during the period under study, there has been a similar residence requirement for accessing social assistance during that time (Banting & Koning, 2017; Harris, 2016).

SA2: *Status requirements for social assistance benefits*
1990: ***2** (all permanent residents and some temporary residents)*
2000–2015: ***3** (all permanent residents and EU citizens)*

Since the introduction of the habitual residence test in 1994, social assistance benefits have been available only to EU citizens and those with settled status. Before then, income assistance was available to some migrants on temporary permits, except those with closed permits or those with a very temporary purpose in the United Kingdom (Banting & Koning, 2017; Drinkwater & Robinson, 2013; Harris, 2016).

SA3: *Consequences of uptake for status*
1990: ***3** (non-renewal of residence permit)*
2000–2015: ***0** (no consequences)*

Before the introduction of the habitual residence test, some migrants could see a refusal to renew their residence permit in cases where they were deemed an unreasonable burden on the welfare system. Since the benefit is available only to permanent residents, taking up social assistance cannot have consequences for one's status in the country or for accessing citizenship in the future (Stadlmaier, 2018).

SA4: *Integration requirements for social assistance*
1990–2000: ***0** (no integration requirements)*
2010–2015: ***3** (access tied to permits with integration requirements)*

There are no formal integration requirements for accessing social assistance benefits. Since 2007, however, there have been integration requirements for accessing permanent residence status (or "indefinite leave to remain"), which therefore serve as indirect integration requirements for accessing social assistance benefits (Government of the United Kingdom, n.d.-a; Home Office, 2019).

Active labour market

ALM1: *Residence requirements*
1990: *–**8** (no active labour market policies)*
2000–2015: ***2** (access tied to benefits requiring a work or residence history)*

The UK did not develop modern active labour market policies until the mid-1990s. Since then, these policies have been available primarily to those who are receiving unemployment benefits, and therefore come with indirect residence requirements (Finn, 2000; Sage, 2015).

ALM2: *Status requirements*
1990: ***–8*** *(no active labour market policies)*
2000–2015: ***2*** *(all citizens and permanent residents)*

The UK did not develop modern active labour market policies until the mid-1990s. Since then, these policies have been available primarily to those who are receiving unemployment benefits, and therefore can only be accessed by permanent residents (Finn, 2000; Sage, 2015).

ALM3: *Immigrant-targeted language programs*
1990–2015: ***1*** *(funded programs, but nominal fees and/or not freely available to all migrants)*

The United Kingdom has long run English language classes for migrants. However, these classes were initially freely available only to Commonwealth immigrants, and in more recent years they have been offered only to refugees. Moreover, recent cuts in funding have increased wait times before immigrants can access the classes (Glover et al. 2001; McIntyre, 2017; Rutter, 2013).

ALM4: *Other immigrant-targeted employment assistance*
1990: ***3*** *(some programs offered, but offered ad hoc or inconsistently across the country)*
2000–2015 ***2*** *(programs available, but only available for refugees and/or asylum seekers)*

The United Kingdom's history of integration policy is a rather patchy one, and for a long time immigrant-targeted employment assistance only existed as ad hoc programs in response to specific groups of refugees or local initiatives. Since 2000, however, there has been national integration policy targeting asylum seekers and refugees, which includes assistance to enter the job market and the extension of loans for the purpose of re-schooling or business purchases (Gidley, 2012; Glover et al., 2001; Herrick, 2005; Rutter, 2013).

United States

(data collection by Camila Rivas-Garrido and Edward Koning)

	Tax-paid pensions	Health care	Contr. unempl.	Contr. pension	Housing	Social assist.	Active labour market	Average
1990	33	50	57	13	44	19	50	38
2000	67	75	57	14	38	69	50	53
2010	67	75	58	51	38	69	50	58
2015	67	75	58	51	38	69	50	58

Tax-paid pensions

TPP1: Residence requirements for universal tax-paid pension
*1990–2015: **–8** (no universal public pension)*

There is no universal pension in the United States. The only tax-paid benefit for low-income elderly is a means-tested benefit called Supplemental Security Income (also available for needy individuals who are blind or have other accessibility issues) (Borjas & Hilton, 1996).

TPP2: Availability of means-tested program for those with incomplete benefit
*1990: **0** (yes, with no residence requirement)*
*2000–2015: **2** (yes, with residence requirement 3–10 years)*

Before a large-scale welfare reform in 1996, SSI was available to all legal resident immigrants on the same terms as citizens, without any residence requirement. Since then, however, the benefit is exclusively available to citizens, and therefore newcomers face at least a 5-year residence requirement to access it, considering the 5-year residence requirement for naturalization (Fix & Passel, 2002; Zimmerman & Tumlin, 1999).

TTP3: Status requirement for access to means-tested or universal tax-paid pension
*1990: **1** (citizens and all permanent residents)*
*2000–2015: **3** (citizens and specially designated groups only)*

Before 1996, all permanent residents were eligible for SSI. The welfare reform restricted the benefit to citizens, and only a few groups are exempted from this restriction (military personnel, refugees, very elderly recipients, and some categories of long-term residents who were in the country before the reform took place). Some states, including California, offer a state-level benefit for needy elderly who are ineligible for SSI, but other states, including Texas, do not (Borjas, 2002; Ross, 2002; Sainsbury, 2006; Zimmerman & Tumlin, 1999).

TTP4: *Export possibilities of (means-tested or universal) tax-paid pension*
1990–2015: ***3** (during very short stay abroad only)*

SSI is only available to residents of the United States and is lost whenever a recipient is abroad for more than a month (SSA, 2015, 2019).

Health care

HC1: *Residence requirement for public health care*
1990: ***0** (no waiting period)*
2000–2015: ***4** (more than 1 year)*

Before the 1996 welfare reform, all legal permanent residents had the same access to federal and state medical benefits as native-born citizens, without any residence requirements. Since then, however, all newcomers have been barred from the federal means-tested health insurance program (Medicaid) during their first 5 years in the country. And while some states have since developed state-level benefits for newcomers, many others have not (Bronchetti, 2014; Ku & Matani, 2001; Nam, 2012; Potochnick, 2016; Zimmerman & Tumlin, 1999).

HC2: *Status requirements for public health care*
1990–2015: ***2** (restrictions for undocumented and some categories of legal migrants, but no barriers to urgent care)*

Medical benefits are unavailable to undocumented migrants, temporary migrants, and, since 1996, non-citizens. Nevertheless, all states have emergency Medicaid programs, which pay the costs of emergency procedures for patients who are ineligible because of their immigration status (Ku & Matani, 2001; Nam & Kim, 2012; Olsen, 2002).

HC3: *Health care accessibility services*
1990–2015: ***3** (some incidental outreach programs or translated written documents)*

There are very few federal programs to ensure the accessibility of health care services for people with low proficiency in English. Even though all health care providers who receive federal funding are legally obliged to provide meaningful access to non-English-speaking individuals, there is much flexibility in the state-level interpretation of this requirement, and in many states it amounts to little more than the availability of translated documents (Grubbs et al., 2006; Ku & Matani, 2001; Teitelbaum, Cartwright-Smith, & Rosenbaum, 2012).

HC4: *Additional health care benefits*
1990–2015: ***3*** *(incidental services, but nothing guaranteed)*

There are no federal public health care services that are exclusively available to immigrants. While there are special programs that provide federal funding to cover the health care costs of refugees during the first eight months in the country, the applicable services are the same as are covered by health care benefits for native-born citizens. However, some states have offered refugee-targeted health care programs on top of any federally funded services (Department of Health and Human Services, 2012; Negash, 2015).

Contributory unemployment

CUB1: *Status requirements for access to contributory unemployment benefits*
1990–2015 ***3*** *(permanent residents, citizens, and very few temporary migrants)*

Everyone with a legal work history and availability to work is eligible for unemployment benefits. This excludes migrants who are ineligible to work (such as asylum seekers or international students), as well as temporary migrants, who lose their right to residence when they fall unemployed and are therefore not available for work (Department of Labor, n.d.; SSA, 2003, 2015).

CUB2: *Integration requirements for access to contributory unemployment benefits*
1990–2015: ***0*** *(no integration requirements)*

There are no integration requirements associated with accessing unemployment benefits in the United States (Department of Labor, n.d.; State of California Employment Development Department, n.d.; Texas Workforce Commission, n.d.).

CUB3: *Export possibilities*
1990: ***3.8*** *(not possible, except to Canada)*
2000: ***3.9*** *(not possible, except to Canada)*
2010: ***3.9*** *(not possible, except to Canada)*
2015: ***3.9*** *(not possible, except to Canada)*

Residence in the United States is a requirement for accessing unemployment benefits. The only exception is that the benefits can be claimed from Canada (Department of Labor, 1974).

Contributory pension

CP1: *Status requirement*
1990–2000: ***0** (all legal residents)*
2010–2015: ***3** (some temporary migrants excluded)*

Before 2004, all legal residents with a work history were eligible for old age assistance. Since then, however, there have been stricter requirements for migrants to demonstrate work authorization throughout the work history for which they are claiming, as a result of which many temporary migrants have lost eligibility (Borjas, 2011; SSA, 2004, n.d.).

CP2: *Export possibilities*
1990: ***1.1** (much variation depending on pensioner's citizenship and country of migration)*
2000: ***1.1** (much variation depending on pensioner's citizenship and country of migration)*
2010: ***1.1** (much variation depending on pensioner's citizenship and country of migration)*
2015: ***1.1** (much variation depending on pensioner's citizenship and country of migration)*

The rules regarding the export of the contributory pension benefit are very different depending on the pensioner's citizenship and country of migration. To a small number of countries (including Kazakhstan and Ukraine), export is impossible. To others (including France and the United Kingdom), export is unrestricted. For the largest number of countries, export is possible but only if the applicant satisfies additional requirements, such as a minimum period of residence in the United States. And for yet another sizable group of countries (including Russia and Vietnam), export is only possible if the applicant is a citizen of the United States (SSA, 2018).

Housing benefits

HB1: *Residence requirements for housing benefits*
1990–2015: ***0** (no residence requirement)*

None of the housing benefits that are offered through the federal department of Housing and Urban Development come with any residence requirements.

Newcomers are eligible as soon as they obtain the necessary status (see HB2) (Department of Housing and Urban Development, n.d.; Government Printing Office, 1934; Office of the Federal Register, 2000).

HB2: *Status requirements for housing benefits*
1990–2000: ***3** (citizens and permanent residents)*

Housing benefits are only available to citizens and permanent residents. The sole exception is that refugees, who usually only become eligible for permanent residency a year after they settle in the United States, can access housing benefits as soon as they are recognized as refugees (Department of Housing and Urban Development, n.d.; Government Printing Office, 1934; Office of the Federal Register, 2000).

HB3: *Integration requirements for housing benefits*
1990–2015 ***0** (no integration requirements)*

There are no integration requirements associated with accessing housing benefits in the United States (Department of Housing and Urban Development, n.d.; Government Printing Office, 1934; Office of the Federal Register, 2000).

HB4: *Preferential treatment in housing*
1990: ***4** (no privileged access for migrants)*
2000–2015: ***3** (services exist, but are not fully funded and are not run by government)*

There are no public housing benefits that specifically target (some categories of) migrants. However, since 2000 not-for-profit organization Mercy Housing Inc. has assisted resettlement agencies, refugees, and immigrant organizations in trying to improve the housing conditions of refugees (Mercy Housing, n.d.; Olson, 2006).

Social assistance

SA1: *Residence requirements for social assistance benefits*
1990: ***1** (residence requirement only for specific categories, such as family migrants)*
2000–2015: ***3** (residence requirement between 1 and 5 years)*

Before the welfare reform of the mid-1990s, only some categories of migrants, in particular sponsored family migrants, faced a residence requirement before being able to access social assistance (called Aid to Families with Dependent Children at the time). The welfare reform, however, imposed a 5-year residence requirement on social assistance (since then called Temporary Assistance for Needy Families) for all newcomers (Butz & Kehrberg, 2015; Fix & Zimmerman, 1994; Olsen, 2002).

SA2: *Status requirements for social assistance benefits*
1990: ***2*** *(all permanent residents and some temporary residents)*
2000–2015: ***4*** *(only citizens and some permanent residents)*

Before the welfare reform of the mid-1990s, all permanent residents and some categories of temporary migrants (e.g., conditional entrants, aliens granted suspension of deportation, and asylees) were eligible for social assistance. Since the reform, however, the benefit has been restricted to citizens and long-term permanent residents (Borjas, 2003; Fix & Zimmerman, 1994; Nam & Kim, 2012; Zimmerman & Tumlin, 1999).

SA3: *Consequences of uptake for status*
1990: ***0*** *(no consequences)*
2000–2015: ***4*** *(revocation of residence permit)*

Since the introduction of the "public charge" clause in the Immigration and Nationality Act, welfare receipt can be invoked as grounds for deportation, denied re-entry in the country, or refusal of permanent residence status (Department of Justice, 1999; National Immigration Law Center, 2014).

SA4: *Integration requirements for social assistance*
1990–2015: ***0*** *(no integration requirements)*

There are no integration requirements associated with accessing social assistance in the United States. Most states require recipients to undertake efforts to improve their standing in the labour market, but immigrants do not face more of such requirements than native-born Americans.

Active labour market

ALM1: *Residence requirements*
1990–2015: ***–8*** *(no active labour market policies)*

While a flurry of active employment programs have been attempted, by and large the United States have never developed a regime of active labour market policy comparable to those of the other countries under investigation. Indeed, in cross-national comparisons of active-labour market policies, the country consistently appears at the very bottom (Bown & Freund, 2019; Bradley & Stephens, 2007; Crépon & Van den Berg, 2016).

ALM2: *Status requirements*
1990–2015: ***–8** (no active labour market policies)*

See *ALM1.*

ALM3: *Immigrant-targeted language programs*
1990–2015: ***1** (funded programs, but not available to all categories of migrants)*

While the United States have long offered English language courses, some of which are free of charge for refugee migrants, there are widespread concerns about their quality and availability (Adess et al., 2009; Bloemraad & De Graauw, 2012; Fix & Zimmerman, 1994).

ALM4: *Other immigrant-targeted employment assistance*
1990–2015 ***3** (some programs offered, but offered ad hoc and inconsistently across the country)*

Since the 1980s, there have been federal programs aimed at improving the employment prospects of refugee migrants. Most of these programs, however, are offered inconsistently across the country, leading some observers to speak of a "lottery effect," by which some refugees enjoy considerable assistance and others nothing at all (Adess et al., 2009; Bruno, 2011; Leimsidor, 1982; Mathema, 2018).

APPENDIX BIBLIOGRAPHY

Australia

Australian Bureau of Statistics (2019). *Net overseas migration, arrivals and departures, state/territory, major groupings and visa – calendar years, 2004 to 2017.* www.abs.gov.au/AUSSTATS/abs@.nsf/DetailsPage/3412.02017-18?OpenDocument.

Australian Taxation Office (n.d.-a). Working out if you have to pay super. www.ato.gov.au/business/super-for-employers/working-out-if-you-have-to-pay-super.

Australian Taxation Office (n.d.-b). Eligibility for DASP. www.ato.gov.au/ individuals/super/in-detail/temporary-residents-and-super/super-information-for-temporary-residents-departing-australia/?page = 2#Eligibility_for_DASP.

Buckmaster, L. (2012). Australian government assistance to refugees: fact versus fiction. Parliamentary Library, background note.

Department of Human Services (n.d.-a). International social security agreements. www.humanservices.gov.au/individuals/services/centrelink/international-social-security-agreements, June 2019.

Department of Human Services. (n.d.-b). Low income health care card. www.humanservices.gov.au/individuals/services/centrelink/low-income-health-care-card, June 2019.

Department of Human Services. (n.d.-c). Residence descriptions. ww.humanservices.gov.au/individuals/services/centrelink/special-benefit/eligibility-payment-rates/residence-rules/residence-descriptions.

Department of Immigration and Border Protection (n.d.-a). Medicare. www.border.gov.au/Trav/Visa/Visa/Medicare.

Department of Immigration and Border Protection (n.d.-b). SRSS Programme. www.border.gov.au/Trav/Refu/Illegal-maritime-arrivals/status-resolution-support-services-programme-srss.

Department of Immigration and Border Protection (n.d.-c). History of TIS National. www.tisnational.gov.au/en/About-TIS-National/History-of-TIS-National.

Department of Social Services (n.d.-a). Commonwealth rent assistance. www.dss.gov.au/housing-support/programmes-services/commonwealth-rent-assistance#2.

Department of Social Services (n.d-b). Settlement services for humanitarian entrants." www.dss.gov.au/settlement-and-multicultural-affairs/publications/settlement-services-for-humanitarian-entrants#are_entrants.

Department of Social Services (n.d.-c). Social security payments – residence criteria. www.dss.gov.au/about-the-department/international/policy/social-security-payments-residence-criteria#7a.

Ey, C. (2012). Social security payments for the unemployed, the sick, and those in special circumstances, 1942–2012: a chronology. Parliamentary Library, background note.

Immigration Education Act 1971. www.legislation.gov.au/Details/C2011C00051.

Interview AUS-01. Email correspondence with civil servant in Department of Health.

Kelaher, M., & Manderson, L. (2000). Migration and mainstreaming: matching health services to immigrants' needs in Australia. *Health Policy*, *54*(1), 1–11.

Leibig, T. (2007). The labour market integration of immigrants in Australia. *OECD social, employment, and migration working Ppapers*, *49*, 4–61.

Millbank, A. (2007). Asylum seekers on bridging visa E.' Parliamentary Library, Research brief no. 13, 2006–7.

NSW Family and Community Services. (n.d.). Eligibility for social housing policy. www.facs.nsw.gov.au/housing/policies/eligibility-social-housing-policy.

NSW Ministry of Health. (n.d.). Multicultural health communication. www.mhcs.health.nsw.gov.au/services.

OECD. (2009). Pension country profile: Australia. In *OECD private pensions outlook 2008*, pp. 156–162.

OECD. (2017). *International migration database.* stats.oecd.org.

Pietsch, J. (2013). Immigration and refugees: punctuations in the Commonwealth policy agenda. *Australian Journal of Public Administration*, *72*(2), 143–155.

Refugee Council of Australia (n.d.). Status resolution support services. www.refugeecouncil.org.au/srss.
Spinks, H. (2009). Australia's settlement services for migrants and refugees. Parliamentary Library, Research paper no. 29, 2008–9.
Spinks, H., & Klapdor, M. (2016). New Zealanders in Australia: a quick guide." Parliamentary Library, Research paper series 2016–2017.
Social Security Act 1947. www.legislation.gov.au/Details/C2004C06861.
Social Security Act 1991. www.legislation.gov.au/Details/C2017C00234.
STARTTS. (n.d.). About STARTTS." www.startts.org.au/about-us.
Young, C. (1994). Health and welfare of immigrants and access to services in Australia." *Scandinavian Journal of Social Welfare, 3*(3), 121–132.

Austria

Afonso, A. (2010). *Social concertation in times of austerity: European integration and the politics of labour market reforms in Austria and Switzerland.* Amsterdam University Press.
Arbeitsmarktservice. (n.d.-a). Arbeitslosengeld. www.ams.at/arbeitsuchende/ arbeitslos-was-tun/geld-vom-ams/arbeitslosengeld.
Arbeitsmarktservice. (n.d.-b). Arbeitslosengeld under Arbeitslosenversicherung in einem EWR-Land oder in der Schweiz. https://www.ams.at/arbeitsuchende/arbeitslos-was-tun/geld-vom-ams/arbeitslosengeld-und-arbeitslosenversicherung-in-einem-ewr-land.
Arbeitsmarktservice. (2018). *Living and working in Austria.* Vienna.
Asylkoordination Österreich. (n.d.). Arbeitsmarktzugang. www.asyl.at/ de/themen/arbeitsmarkt.
Chamber of Labor. (n.d.). Mindestpension (= Ausgleichszulage). www.arbeiterkammer.at/beratung/arbeitundrecht/pension/pensionshoehe/Mindestpension.html.
City of Vienna. (n.d.). Vienna language vouchers. www.wien.gv.at/english/social/integration/arriving/start-wien-migrants/language-vouchers.html.
Department of Internal Affairs. (n.d.). Grundversorgung. www.bmi.gv.at/303/start.aspx.
Dressler, D. & Pils, P. (2019). A qualitative study on cross-cultural communication in post-accident in-patient rehabilitation of migrant and ethnic minority patients in Austria. *Disability and Rehabilitation, 31*(14), 1181–1190.
Duncan, F. (2010). Immigration and integration policy and the Austrian radical right in office: the FPÖ/BZÖ, 2002-2006. *Contemporary Politics, 16*(4), 337–354.
Gächter, A. (1995). Forced complementarity: the attempt to protect native Austrian workers from immigrants. *Journal of Ethnic and Migration Studies, 21*(3), 379–398.
General Social Security Act. www.ris.bka.gv.at/GeltendeFassung.wxe?Abfrage=Bundesnormen&Gesetzesnummer = 10008147.
Gortázar Rotaeche, C. J. (1998). Racial discrimination and the European Convention on Human Rights. *Journal of Ethnic and Migration Studies, 24*(1), 177–188.

Government of Austria. (n.d.-a). Krankenversicherung. www.migration.gv.at/ de /leben-und-arbeiten-in-oesterreich/gesundheit/krankenversicherung.

Government of Austria. (n.d.-b). Pensionsansprüche in mehreren Staaten. www .oesterreich.gv.at/themen/arbeit_und_pension/pension/Seite.270218.html.

Gruber, O., Mattes, A., & Stadlmair, J. (2016). Die meritokratische Neugestaltung der österreichischen Integrationspolitik zwischen Rhetorik und Policy. *Austrian Journal of Political Science, 45*(1), 65–79.

Hofbauer, S, Gächter, A., Mayr, K., & Laubacher-Kubat, E. (2005). *Illegale Eindwanderung in Österreich – Österreichischer Beitrag zum Europäischen Forschungsprojekt II: "Illegally resident third country nationals in the EU member states,"* International Organization for Migration.

Immobilienscout. (n.d.). Sozialwohnungen in Österreich – Günstiges Wohnen für Bedürftige. www.immobilienscout24.at/wohnen/sozialwohnungen.html.

Kaloianov, R. (2012). Affirmative action und integration von MigrantInnen,' *Austrian Journal of Political Science, 41*(2): 177–194.

Ludwig-Mayerhofer, W., & Wroblewski, A. (2004). Eppur si muove? Activation policies in Austria and Germany. *European Societies, 6*(4), 485–509.

Marth, T. (2005). Grundversorgungsvereinbarung und Betreuung von Asylwerbern. Bundesbetreuungsgesetz "neu." *SIAK-Journal – Zeitschrift für Polizeiwissenschaft und polizeiliche Praxis, 1*, 12–18.

Muckenhuber, J., Freidl, W., & Rásky, E. (2011). Healthcare for migrants and for marginalized individuals: the Marienambulanz in Graz, Austria. *Wiener klinische Wochenschrift, 123*(17–18): 559–561.

Obinger, H., Starke, P., Moser, J., Bogedan, C., Gindulis, E., & Liebfried, S. (2010). *Transformations of the welfare state: small states, big lessons.* Oxford University Press.

Obinger, H., & Tálos, E. (2010). Janus-faced developments in a prototypical Bismarckian welfare state: welfare reforms in Austria since the 1970s. In B. Palier (ed.)., *A long goodbye to Bismarck?* (pp. 101–128). Amsterdam University Press.

Perchinig, B. (2009). Migration, Integration und Staatsbürgerschaft in Österreich seit 1918. *Mitteilungen der Österreichischen Geographischen Gesellschaft, 151*, 88–118.

Pöchhacker, F. (2000). Language barriers in Vienna hospitals. *Ethnicity & Health, 5*(2), 113–119.

Pöschl, M. (2006). Integrationsverienbarung alt un neu. *Migralex, 4*(1), 42–54.

Reinprecht, C. (2007). Social housing in Austria. In K. Scanlon & C. Whitehead (eds.), *Social housing in Europe* (pp. 35–44). London School of Economics.

Richter, R., & Pflegerl, J. (2001). Living in migration in Austria. *Journal of Comparative Family Studies, 32*(4): 517–531.

Sensenig-Dabbous, E. (1999). Social democracy in one country: immigration and minority policy in Austria. In G. Dale & M. Cole (eds.), *The European Union and migrant labour* (pp. 203–230). Berg.

Social Affairs Ministry (2016). *The Austrian welfare state: benefits, expenditure and financing 2016.* Vienna.
Speer, B. External and internal effects of how Austria has handled the refugee crisis. *Croatian and Comparative Public Administration, 18*(2), 247–268.
Statistics Austria. (n.d.). *Migration.* www.statistik.at/web_en/statistics/ PeopleSociety /population/migration/index.html.

Belgium

Adam, I., & Jacobs, D. (2014). Divided on immigration, two models for integration. The multilevel governance of immigration and integration in Belgium. In E. Hepburn & R. Zapata-Barrero (eds.), *The politics of immigration in multilevel states: governance and political parties* (pp. 65–85), Houndmills: Palgrave.
Agentschap Integratie & Inburgering. (n.d.). Werkloosheid. www.agii.be/thema /vreemdelingenrecht-internationaal-privaatrecht/sociaal-medisch/ ziekteverzekering -werkloosheid-gezinsbijslag/werkloosheid.
Ahaddour, C., Van den Branden, S., & Broeckaert, B. (2016). Institutional elderly care services and Moroccan and Turkish migrants in Belgium: a literature review. *Journal of Immigrant Minority Health, 18*(5): 1216–1227.
Decreet behoudende de Vlaamse Wooncode (1997). codex.vlaanderen.be/Portals /Codex/documenten/1005498.html.
Décret relatif à l'intégration des personnes étrangères ou d'origine étrangère (1996). wallex.wallonie.be/PdfLoader.php?type = doc&linkpdf = 489-476-358.
Dierkx, D., V& an Dam, S. (2014). Redefining empowerment interventions of migrants experiencing poverty: the case of Antwerp, Belgium. *British Journal of Social Work, 44*(1), 105–122.
Druyts, E., Evenepoel, V., Jassogne, S., Van der Borght, A., & Verschueren, K. (2013). *Medische kosten van vreemdelingen. Wie betaalt?* Kruispunt Migratie-Integratie.
Federale Pensionsdienst (n.d.). De Inkomensgarantie voor ouderen (IGO). www.sfpd .fgov.be/nl/recht-op-pensioen/igo#hoofdverblijfplaats.
Forem. (n.d.). Aides à l'emploi ou créer mon activité. https://www.leforem.be /particuliers/aides-financieres-emploi.html.
FRA [European Union Agency for Fundamental Rights] (2011). *Fundamental rights of migrants in an irregular situation in the European Union.* Publications Office of the European Union.
Frydryszak, D. & Macherey, A.-L. (2016). *Legal report on access to healthcare in 17 countries.* Médecins du monde.
Gerkens, S., & Merkur, S. (2010). Belgium: health systems review. *Health Systems in Transition, 12*(5), 1–266.
Gysen, S., Kuijper, H., & Van Avermaet, P. (2009). Language testing in the context of immigration and citizenship: the case of the Netherlands and Flanders (Belgium). *Language Assessment Quarterly, 6*, 98–105.

Interview BEL-01. Email correspondence with civil servant in National Employment Office.

Interview BEL-02. Email correspondence with civil servant in Flemish Social Housing Agency.

Interview BEL-03. Email correspondence with civil servant in Walloon Employment Office "Forem."

Lewis, D. K. (1969). Social security abroad: guaranteed income for the aged in Belgium. *Social Security Bulletin*, *32*(9), 30–32.

Loi concernant le droit à l'integration sociale (2002). www.ejustice.just.fgov.be/ cgi_loi /change_lg.pl?language = fr&la = F&cn = 2002052647&table_name = loi.

Loi instituant la garantie de revenus aux personnes âgées (2001). www.etaamb.be/fr /loi-du-22-mars-2001_n2001022201.html.

Loi organique des centres publics d'action sociale (1976). www.ejustice.just.fgov.be /cgi_loi/change_lg.pl?language = fr&la = F&cn = 1976070837&table_name = loi.

Loi relative à l'assurance obligatoire soins de santé et indemnités (1994). www.ejustice .just.fgov.be/cgi_loi/change_lg.pl?language = fr&la = F&cn = 1994071438&table _name = loi.

Loi sur l'accès au territoire, le séjour, l'établissement et l'éloignement des étrangers (1980). www.ejustice.just.fgov.be/cgi_loi/change_lg.pl?language = fr&la = F&cn = 1980121530&table_name = loi.

Lorant, V., & Bhopal, R. (2010). Comparing policies to tackle ethnic inequalities in health: Belgium 1 Scotland 4. *European Journal of Public Health*, *21*(2): 235–240.

Mandin, J. (2014). *An overview of integration policies in Belgium.* Interact research report, 2014/20: 1–18.

Martiniello, M. (2012). Belgium. In C. Joppke & F. L. Seidle (Eds.), *Immigrant integration in federal countries* (pp. 58–78). Montreal & Kingston: McGill-Queen's University Press.

MISSOC [Mutual Information System on Social Protection] (2009). *Guaranteeing sufficient resources.* ec.europa.eu/employment_social/soc-prot/missoc99/english/11 /index.htm.

– (2004–18). *Comparative Tables on Social Protection.* www.missoc.org/missoc -database/comparative-tables.

Mussche, N., Corluy, V., & Marx, I. (2014). Migrant access to social security and healthcare: policy and practice in Belgium. European Migration Network Belgium.

Naric. (n.d.). Erkenning buitenlands diploma. www.naricvlaanderen.be/nl /erkenningen/erkenning-buitenlands-diploma.

Notre Maison. (n.d.). Conditions d'accessibilité. www.notremaison.be/ index.php/ menu-je-suis-candidat.

Openbaar Centrum voor Maatschappelijk Welzijn. (2008a). Tegemoetkoming in de huisvestingskosten voor asielzoekers. Information brochure, 4 July, pp. 1–13.

Openbaar Centrum voor Maatschappelijk Welzijn. (2008b). Het recht op maatschappelijke integratie. Information brochure, 22 September, pp. 1–31.

Romero-Ortuno, R. (2004). Access to health care for illegal immigrants in the EU: should we be concerned? *European Journal of Health Law*, pp. 245–272.

Seniorennet. (n.d.). Gewaarborgd inkomen voor bejaarden. www.seniorennet.be/Pages/Geld_werk/gewaarborgd_inkomen.php#ho5a1b.

Socialsecurity.be. (n.d.). Internationale socialezekerheidsakkoorden. www.socialsecurity.be/citizen/nl/over-de-sociale-zekerheid/sociale-zekerheid-internationaal/internationale-socialezekerheidsakkoorden.

Societé Wallonne du Logement. (n.d.). La location d'un logement public en Wallonie. www.swl.be/index.php/accueil-particulier/louer.

Stadlmaier, J. (2018). Earning citizenship: economic criteria for naturalisation in nine EU countries. *Journal of Contemporary European Studies*, *26*(1), 42–63.

Van de Voorde, M., & De Bruijn, H. (2010). *Equal opportunities? The labour market integration of the children of immigrants.* OECD.

Van Eechoud, I., Grypdonck, M., Leman, J., Van den Noortgate, N., Deveugele, M., & Verhaeghe, S. (2017). Balanced truth-telling: relatives acting as translators for older adult cancer patients of Turkish or northwest African origin in Belgium. *European Journal of Cancer Care*, *26*(5), 1–12.

Verrept, H. (2008). Intercultural mediation: an answer to health care disparities? In C. Valero-Garcés and A. Martin (Eds.), *Crossing borders in community interpreting: definitions and Ddilemmas* (pp. 187–202). Philadelphia: John Benjamins.

Vlaamse Maatschappij voor Sociaal Wonen. (n.d.-a). Mag u een sociale woning huren? www.vmsw.be/Home/Ik-ben-particulier/Huren-van-een-sociale-woning/Mag-u-een-sociale-woning-huren/Moet-u-verplicht-inburgeren.

Vlaamse Maatschappij voor Sociaal Wonen (n.d.-b). Wachtlijsten. www.vmsw.be/Home/Ik-ben-particulier/Huren-van-een-sociale-woning/Hoe-huurt-u-een-sociale-woning/Wachtlijsten.

Yanasmayan, Z., & Foblets, M. (2010). *Country report Belgium.* INTEC report, Radboud University Nijmegen.

Canada

Alliance for Healthier Communities. (n.d.). CHC History. www.allianceon.org/CHC-History?lang=en.

Banting, K. G., & Koning, E. A. (2017). Just visiting: The weakening of social protection in a mobile world. In A. Triandafyllidou (Ed.), *Multicultural governance in a mobile world* (pp. 108–138). Edinburgh University Press.

BCACHC [British Columbia Alliance for Community Health Care Centres]. (n.d.). What are community health centres?' www.bcachc.org/what-is-a-chc.

Biles, J. (2008). Integration policies in English-speaking Canada. In J. Biles, M. Burstein, & J. Frideres (Eds.), *Immigration and integration in Canada in the twenty-first century.* McGill-Queen's University Press.

Calfourd, P., & Vali, Y. (2006). Providing health care to medically insured immigrants and refugees. *Canadian Medical Association Journal, 174*(9): 1253–1254.

Canada Pension Plan Act. (1985). laws-lois.justice.gc.ca/eng/acts/C-8/20030101 / P1TT3xt3.html.

City of Toronto. (n.d.). Subsidized housing and housing benefits. www.toronto.ca /community-people/employment-social-support/housing-support/ subsidized -housing-housing-benefits.

Department of Finance. (n.d.). History of health and social transfers. www.fin.gc.ca /fedprov/his-eng.asp.

George, P., & George, J. (2013). Interrogating the neoliberal governmentality of the Old Age Security Act: the case of sponsored immigrant seniors. *Canadian Social Work Review, 30*(1), 65–81.

Government of Canada. (2011). *Evaluation of the immigrant settlement and adaptation program.* Evaluation Division, Research and Evaluation.

Government of Canada. (n.d.-a). EI regular benefits – while on EI. www.canada.ca/en /services/benefits/ei/ei-regular-benefit/while-receiving.html, July 2019.

Government of Canada. (n.d.-b). Find help to adjust – refugees. www.canada.ca/en /immigration-refugees-citizenship/services/refugees/help-within-canada /government-assisted-refugee-program/providers.html.

Government of Canada. (n.d.-c). Funding. www.canada.ca/en/immigration-refugees -citizenship/ corporate/partners-service-providers/funding.html.

Interview CAN-01. Email correspondence with civil servant at the Housing Administration of the City of Toronto.

Koning, E. A. (2019). *Immigration and the politics of welfare exclusion: Selective solidarity in Western democracies.* University of Toronto Press.

Koning, E. A., & Banting, K. G. (2013). Inequality below the surface: reviewing immigrants' access to and utilization of five Canadian welfare programs. *Canadian Public Policy, 39*(4), 581–601.

Machery, A., Simonnot, N., & Vanbiervliet, F. (2015). *Legal report on access to health care in 12 countries.* Médecins du Monde.

Merry, L. A., Gagnon, A. J., Kalim, N., & Bouris S. S. (2011). Refugee claimant women and barriers to health and social services post-birth. *Canadian Journal of Public Health, 102*(4), 286–290.

Morden, M. (2016). *Back to work: Modernizing Canada's labour market partnership.* Mowat Centre, University of Toronto.

Nakache, D., & Kinoshita, P. J. (2010). The Canadian Temporary Foreign Worker Program. IRPP Study, 5, 1–47.

OCASI [Ontario Council of Agencies Serving Immigrants]. (n.d.-a). Am I eligible for subsidized housing? settlement.org/ontario/housing/subsidized-housing/subsidized -housing/am-i-eligible-for-subsidized-housing.

OCASI. (n.d.-b). What is the language instruction for newcomers to Canada (LINC) program? settlement.org/ontario/education/english-as-a-second-language-esl/linc -program/what-is-the-language-instruction-for-newcomers-to-canada-linc-program.

Ontario Health Insurance Act. (2017). www.ontario.ca/laws/regulation/ 900552#BK4.

Ricento, T., Cervatiuc, A., MacMillan, F., & Masoodi, S. (2008). *Insights into funded ESL programs: report on the LINC program.* University of Calgary, Faculty of Education.

Rodriguez-Garcia, D. (2012). *Managing immigration and diversity in Canada: a transatlantic dialogue in the new age of migration.* McGill-Queen's University Press.

Social Security Administration. (2003). Canada. In *Social security programs throughout the world: the Americas, 2003* (pp. 56–60). Social Security Administration, Office of Policy, Office of Research, Evaluation, and Statistics.

Social Security Administration. (2015). Canada. In *Social security programs throughout the world: the Americas, 2015* (pp. 83–89). Social Security Administration, Office of Policy, Office of Research, Evaluation, and Statistics.

Statistics Canada (1996). *Census Canada data table 93F0023XSB96003 (immigrant population by place of birth and period of immigration).*

Denmark

Aarhus University. (n.d.). Housing benefits. international.au.dk/life/locations/ housing /auhousing/housing-through-au/practical/housingbenefit.

Act on Individual Housing Support. (2019). www.retsinformation.dk/ Forms/R0710 .aspx?id = 204977#id721f26a4-dd54-443a-be79-b797a1baa03e.

Act to Amend the Hospital Organisation Act and the Public Health Insurance Act. (2004). www.retsinformation.dk/Forms/R0710.aspx?id = 9910.

Ahmad, N., Svarer, M., & Naveed, A. (2019). The effect of active labour market policies and benefit sanctions on reducing unemployment duration. *Journal of Labor Research*, *40*(2), 202–229.

A-kasser. (n.d.-a). Unemployment benefit in Denmark. www.a-kasser.dk/unemployment -insurance-in-europe/denmark.

A-kasser. (n.d.-b). Member of an unemployment insurance fund. www.a-kasser.dk /member.html.

A-kasser. (n.d.-c). Unemployment benefits. https://www.a-kasser.dk/benefits.html.

Andersen, J.G. (2007). Restricting access to social protection for immigrants in the Danish welfare state. *Benefits*, *15*(3), 257–269.

Andersen, J., Larsen, J. E., and Møller, I. H. (2009). The exclusion and marginalisation of immigrants in the Danish welfare society: dilemmas and challenges. *International Journal of Sociology and Social Policy*, *29*(5–6), 274–286.

Blume, K., & Verner, M. (2007). Welfare dependency among Danish immigrants. *European Journal of Political Economy*, *23*, 435–471.

Borevi, K., & Bengtsson, B. (2015). The tension between choice and need in the housing of newcomers: a theoretical framework and an application on Scandinavian settlement policies. *Urban Studies*, *52*(14), 2599–2615.

Clausen, J., Heinesen, E., Hummelgaard, H., Husted, L., & Rosholm, M. (2009). The effect of integration policies on the time until regular employment of newly arrived immigrants: evidence from Denmark. *Labour Economics*, *16*, 409–417.

Consolidated Act on Social Pensions. (2010). www.retsinformation.dk/ Forms/R0710 .aspx?id = 132869.

Cuadra, C. B. (2010). *Policies on health care for undocumented Migrants in EU27. Country report: Denmark.* Malmö University.

European Commission. (2013). *Your social security rights in Denmark.* European Union.

Government of Denmark. (n.d.-a). Vil du have din folke- eller førtidspension med til udlandet? www.borger.dk/pension-og-efterloen/International-pension/Dansk -pension-i-udlandet/International-pension-flytte.

Government of Denmark. (n.d.-b). ATP livslang pension i udlandet. www.borger.dk /pension-og-efterloen/International-pension/Dansk-pension-i-udlandet/ ATP-udlandet.

Government of Denmark. (n.d.-c). Apply for a permanent residence permit. www .nyidanmark.dk/en-GB/You-want-to-apply/Permanent-residence-permit /Permanent-residence.

Groenendijk, K., Guild, E., & Barzilay, R. (2000). *The legal status of third-country nationals who are long-term residents in a member state of the European Union.* University of Nijmegen.

Jørgensen, M. B., & Thomsen, T. L. (2016). Deservingness in the Danish context: welfare chauvinism in times of crisis. *Critical Social Policy*, *36*(3), 330–351.

Koning, E. A. (2011). Ethnic and civic dealings with newcomers: naturalization policies and practices in 26 immigration countries. *Ethnic and Racial Studies*, *43*(11), 1974–1992.

Ministry of Health. (n.d.). Tolkebistand. www.sum.dk/Sundhed/Patientrettigheder /Tilskud/ Tolkebistand.aspx.

Ministry of Health. (2017). *Healthcare in Denmark: an overview.* Ministry of Health.

Ministry of Housing (2000). Vejledning om individuel boligstøtte. www .retsinformation.dk/Forms/R0710.aspx?id = 19703#K1.

MISSOC [Mutual Information System on Social Protection]. (2004–2018). *Comparative tables on social protection.* www.missoc.org/missoc-database /comparative-tables.

Nannestad, P. (2004). Immigration as a challenge to the Danish welfare state? *European Journal of Political Economy*, *20*, 755–767.

Neerup, S. (2012). Denmark. In J. Nieuwenhuysen, Duncan, H., & Neerup S. (Eds.), *International migration in uncertain times* (pp. 91–108). McGill-Queen's University Press.

OECD [Organisation for Economic Co-operation and Development]. (2007). *Jobs for immigrants,* Vol. 1: *Labour market integration in Australia, Denmark, Germany, and Sweden.* OECD.

Pedersen, P. J. (2013). Immigration and welfare state cash benefits: the Danish case. *International Journal of Manpower*, *43*(2), 113–125.

Social Security Administration. (2002). Denmark. In *Social security programs throughout the world: Europe, 2002* (pp. 64–68). Social Security Administration, Office of Policy, Office of Research, Evaluation, and Statistics.

Social Security Administration. (2016). Denmark. In *Social security programs throughout the world: the Americas, 2016* (pp. 86–91). Social Security Administration, Office of Policy, Office of Research, Evaluation, and Statistics.

Sørensen, A. E., Olesen, T. B., & Olesen, N. W. (2008). Folkepension, 1956–. *Danmarkshistorien.dk*, danmarkshistorien.dk/leksikon-og-kilder/vis/materiale/folkepension-1956.

Stadlmaier, J. (2018). Earning citizenship: economic criteria for naturalisation in nine EU countries. *Journal of Contemporary European Studies, 26*(1), 42–63.

Supplementary Labour Market Pension Act. (2014). www.retsinformation.dk/Forms/R0710.aspx?id=164210&exp=1.

Finland

Airio, I., & Nurminen, M. (2016). The case of the guarantee pension reform: change of perceived income adequacy among low-income pensioners in Finland. *European Journal of Social Security, 18*(3), 248–267.

Dalli, M. (2019). Comparing the access conditions for minimum income support in four EU member states for national, EU, and non-EU citizens.' *Journal of Social Welfare and Family Law, 41*(2), 233–251.

Deaconess Foundation. (n.d.). Centre for torture survivors in Finland. www.hdl.fi/en/support-and-action/immigrants/rehabilitation-for-torture-victims/centre-for-torture-survivors-in-finland.

Eklöf, N., Hupli, M., & Leino-Kilpi, H. (2014). Nurses' perceptions of working with immigrant patients and interpreters in Finland. *Public Health Nursing, 32*(2), 143–150.

EU-healthcare. (n.d.). Medical care of refugees and asylum-seekers in Finland. www.eu-healthcare.fi/healthcare-in-finland/moving-to-finland/medical-care-of-refugees-and-asylum-seekers-in-finland.

Finnish Centre for Pensions (n.d.). New in Finland. www.tyoelake.fi/en/new-in-finland.

Helander, M., Holley, P., & Uuttana, H. (2016). Trying to secure a future in uncertain circumstances: the social security of temporary migrant workers in Finland. *Arbor,* 192(777): 1–17.

InfoFinland. (n.d.-a). Do you need an interpreter? www.infofinland.fi/en/living-in-finland/settling-in-finland/do-you-need-an-interpreter.

InfoFinland. (n.d.-b). Housing in Helsinki. www.infofinland.fi/en/helsinki/life-in-helsinki/housing-in-helsinki.

InfoFinland. (n.d.-c). Moving to Finland as a quota refugee. www.infofinland.fi/ en/moving-to-finland/non-eu-citizens/coming-to-finland-as-a-refugee.

Karjalainen, V., & Saikku, P. (2011). Governance of integrated activation policy in Finland. In R. van Berkel, W. de Graaf, & T. Sirovátka (Eds.), *The governance of active welfare states in Europe* (pp. 216–236). Palgrave.

Kaupinen, T. (2002). The beginning of immigrant settlement in the Helsinki metropolitan area and the role of social housing. *Journal of Housing and the Built Environment, 17*, 173–197.

Kela [*Kansaneläkaitos*, Finnish Social Insurance Institution]. (n.d.-a). Old-age pension from Kela. www.kela.fi/web/en/old-age-pension.

Kela. (n.d.-b). Eligibility. www.kela.fi/web/en/guarantee-pension-eligibility.

Kela. (n.d.-c). Permanent move abroad. www.kela.fi/web/en/permanent-move-abroad.

Kela. (n.d.-d). Social security agreements. www.kela.fi/web/en/from-finland-to-another-country-social-security-agreements.

Kela. (n.d.-e). Medical care in Finland. www.kela.fi/web/en/from-other-countries-to-finland-medical-care.

Kela. (n.d.-f). Right to unemployment benefits. www.kela.fi/web/en/right-to-unemployment-benefits.

Kela. (n.d.-g). Unemployment benefits in international situations. www.kela.fi/web/en/unenmployment-benefits-in-international-situations.

Kela. (n.d.-h). Social security coverage for employees and self-employed persons. www.kela.fi/web/en/from-other-countries-to-finland-employees-and-self-employed-persons.

Kela. (n.d.-i). Who can get general housing allowance? www.kela.fi/web/en/who-can-get-general-housing-allowance.

Kela. (n.d.-j). Basic social assistance in international situations. www.kela.fi/web/en/social-assistance-foreign-residents.

Koikkalainen, S., Tammilehto, T., Kangas, O., Katisko, M., Koskinen, S., & Suikkanen, A. (2012). Welfare or work: migrants' selective integration in Finland. In E. Carmel, A. Cerami, & T. Papadopoulos (Eds.), *Migration and welfare in the New Europe: social protection and the challenges of integration* (pp. 143–158). Policy Press.

Könönen, J. (2018a). Border struggles within the state: administrative bordering of non-citizens in Finland. *Nordic Journal of Migration Research*, *8*(3), 143–150.

Könönen, J. (2018b). Differential inclusion of non-citizens in a universalistic welfare state. *Citizenship Studies*, *22*(1), 53–69.

Kotkas, T. (2016). Independent choices and extrinsic pressure: EU membership and the development of residence-based social security schemes in Finland. *European Journal of Social Security*, *18*(2), 164–182.

Krivonos, D. (2019). The making of gendered "migrant workers" in youth activation: the case of young Russian-speakers in Finland. *Current Sociology*, *67*(3), 401–418.

Kyyrä, T., Pesola, H., & Rissanen, A. (2017). *Unemployment insurance in Finland: a review of recent changes and empirical evidence on behavioral responses.* VATT Institute for Economic Research.

Martikainen, T., Valtonen, K., & Wahlbeck, Ö. (2012). The social integration of immigrants in Finland.' In J. Frideres & J. Biles (Eds.), *International perspectives: integration and inclusion* (pp. 127–146). McGill–Queen's University Press.

Masoud, A., Holm, G., & Brunila, K. (2021). Becoming integrateable: hidden realities of integration policies and training in Finland. *International Journal of Inclusive Education*, 25(1): 52–65.

Ministry of Social Affairs and Health. (1956). *National Pensions Act (347/1956).* Unofficial translation. www.finlex.fi/fi/laki/kaannokset/1956/en19560347_20041023.pdf.

MISSOC [Mutual Information System on Social Protection] (2004–2018). *Comparative tables on social protection.* www.missoc.org/missoc-database/comparative-tables.

Sagne, S., & Saksela-Bergholm, S. (2014). Finland. In A. Triandafyllidou & R. Gropas (Eds.), *European immigration: a sourcebook* (2nd Ed., pp. 122–134). Ashgate.

Stadlmaier, J. (2018). Earning citizenship: economic criteria for naturalisation in nine EU countries. *Journal of Contemporary European Studies, 26*(1), 42–63.

Tuomisto, K., Tiittala, P., Keskimäki, I., & Helve, O. (2019). Refugee crisis in Finland: challenges to safeguarding the right to health for asylum seekers. *Health Policy*, 123, 825–832.

Van Aerschot, P. (2014). Shifting policy aims in the reformed Finnish and Swedish integration legislation. In P. van Aerschot & P. Daenzer (Eds.), *The integration and protection of immigrants: Canadian and Scandinavian critiques* (pp. 51–70). Ashgate.

France

Allwood, G., & Wadia, K. (2010). *Refugee women in Britain and France.* Manchester University Press.

André, J.-M., & Azzedine, F. (2016). Access to healthcare for undocumented migrants in France: a critical examination of state medical assistance.' *Public Health Review, 37*(1), 5.

Assemblée des departements de France. (2015). *Place et role des Fonds de Solidarité pour le Logement (FSL) dans la politique sociale du logement: état des lieux et perspectives.* Paris.

Bergmann, B. (1996). *Saving our children from poverty: what the United States can learn from France.* Sage.

Bolderson, H., & Gains, F. (1993). *Crossing national frontiers: an examination of the arrangements for exporting social security benefits in twelve OECD countries.* HMSO.

Brickenstein, C. (2015). Social protection of foreign seasonal workers: from state to best practice. *Comparative Migration Studies, 3*(1), 1–18.

Carde, E. (2009). Quinze ans de réforme de l'accès à une couverture maladie des sans-papiers: de l'aide sociale aux politiques d'immigration. *Mouvements la découverte,* pp. 143–156.

City of Paris. (n.d.). Pouvez-vous bénéficier d'une aide au logement de la Mairie de Paris? www.paris.fr/aidesaulogement#pouvez-vous-beneficier-d-une-aide-au-logement-de-la-mairie-de-paris_17.

CLEISS. [Centre des Liaisons Européennes et Internationales de Sécurité Sociale]. (n.d.-a.). The French social security system: unemployment insurance.' www.cleiss.fr/ docs/regimes/regime_france/an_5.html.

CLEISS. (n.d.-b). Vous partez à l'étranger pour chercher un employ. www.cleiss.fr/particuliers/je_pars_chercher_un_emploi_a_l_etranger.html.

CLEISS. (n.d.-c). Les conventions bilatérales de sécurité sociale. www.cleiss.fr/ docs/textes/index.html.

Conseil d'orientation des retraites. (2006). Minimum vieillesse. www.cor-retraites.fr/IMG/pdf/doc-680.pdf.

Department of Health. (2018). *Healthcare handbook French/English.* Department of Health.

EMN. (2012). *Annual policy report 2011.* French National Contact Point, European Migration Network.

Fougère, D., Kramarz, F., Rathelot, R., & Safi, M. (2013). Social housing and location choices of immigrants in France. *International Journal of Manpower, 34*(1), 56–69.

Frydryszak, D., & Macherey, A.-L. (2016). *Legal report on access to healthcare in 17 countries.* Médecins du monde.

Government of France. (n.d.). Allocation de solidarité aux personnes agées (Aspa). www.service-public.fr/particuliers/vosdroits/F16871.

Gray, B., & Van Ginneken, E. (2012). Healthcare for undocumented migrants: European approaches. *Issues in International Health Policy, 33*, 1–12.

Guibentif, P. (2004). Reception and integration of newly arrived immigrants: synthesis report, France. European Commission.

Holzmann, R., Koettl, J., & Chernetsky, T. (2005). *Portability regimes of pension and health benefits for international migrants: an analysis of issues and good protection.* World Bank.

Holzmann, R., & Pouget, Y. (2010). *Toward an objective-driven system of smart labor migration management.* World Bank.

Huddleston, T., Bigili, O., Joki, A., & Vankova, Z. (2015). *Migrant integration policy index: France.* www.mipex.eu/sites/default/files/downloads/pdf/files/france.pdf.

IOM [International Organization of Migration]. (2011). *Migration, employment, and labour market policies in the European Union.* IMO.

ISM Interprétariat. (n.d.). Qui sommes-nous?' www.ism-interpretariat.fr/qui-sommes-nous.

Kondo, A. (2001). *Citizenship in a global world: comparing citizenship rights for aliens.* Palgrave.

Leger, F. (2011). Some thoughts on the French pension reform in the public interest.' *In the Public Interest*, 3, 7–9.

Legros, M. (2015). *Thematic report on minimum income schemes – France.* European Social Policy Network.

Lévy-Vroelant, C. (2015). The right to housing in France: still a long way to go from intention to implementation. *Journal of Law and Social Policy*, 24, 88–108.

Loi no. 90-449 du 31 mai 1990 visant à la mise en oeuvre du droit au logement (1990). www.legifrance.gouv.fr/affichTexte.do?cidTexte = JORFTEXT000000159413.

Palier, B. (2004). French welfare reform in comparative perspective.' *Revue Française de Sociologie*, 45, 97–124.

Paraschivescu, C. (2013). Social protection and economic security of North African migrant workers in France. *Revista Romana de Sociologie, 24*(1–2), 91–99.

Pole Emploi (n.d.). Quel justificatif fournir pour s'inscrire à Pôle emploi? www.service-public.fr/particuliers/vosdroits/F24465.

RSA [Revenu de Solidarité Active], (n.d.). Quelles sont les conditions pour toucher le RSA si vous êtes étranger? rsa-revenu-de-solidarite-active.fr/conditions-rsa/72-condition-rsa-etranger.html.

Sargent, C., & Kotobi, L. (2017). Austerity and its implications for immigrant health in France. *Social Science and Medicine*, 187, 259–267.

Schulte, L., Greer, I., Umney, C., Symon, G., & Iankova, K. (2018). Insertion as an alternative to workfare: active labour-market schemes in the Parisian suburbs. *Journal of European Social Policy, 28*(4), 326–341.

Shields, J., Valenzuela, K. & Drolet, J. (2016). Immigrant settlement and integration services and the role of nonprofit service providers: a cross-national perspective on trends, issues, and evidence. RCIS working paper 2016(1).

UNAFO [Union Professionelle du Logement Accompagné]. (2016). *La protection sociale des étrangers en France.* UNAFO.

Vlandas, T. (2013). The politics of in-work benefits: the case of the "active income of solidarity" in France. *French Politics, 11*(2), 117–142.

Walraet, E., & Mahieu, R. (2007). Simulating retirement behavior: the case of France. In J. Gruber & D. Wise (Eds)., *Social security programs and retirement around the world: fiscal implications of reform* (pp. 155–200). University of Chicago Press.

Wong, T. C., & Goldblum, C. (2016). Social housing in France: a permanent and multifaceted challenge for public policies. *Land Use Policy, 54*, 95–102.

Germany

AIDA [Asylum Information Database]. (n.d.). Health care: Germany. www.asylumineurope.org/reports/country/germany/reception-conditions/health-care.

Bauhoff, S., & Göpffarth, D. (2018). Asylum-seekers in Germany differ from regularly insured in their morbidity, utilizations and costs of care. *PLoS ONE, 13*(5), 1–11.

Borgschulte, H. S., Wiesmüller, G. A., Bunte, A., & Neuhann, F. (2018). Health care provision for refugees in Germany: one-year evaluation of an outpatient clinic in an urban emergency accommodation. *BMC Health Services Research, 18*(488), 1–10.

Bosswick, W. (2000). Development of asylum policy in Germany. *Journal of Refugee Studies, 13*(1), 43–60.

Bozorgmehr, K., & Razum, O. (2015). Effect of restricting access to health care on health expenditures among asylum-seekers and refugees: a quasi-experimental study in Germany, 1994–2013. *PLoS ONE, 10*(7), 1–22.

Bridgen, P., & Meyer, T. (2014). The liberalisation of the German social model: public–private pension reform in Germany since 2001. *Journal of Social Policy, 43*(1), 37–68.

Bruzelius, C., Ehata, R., & Seeleib-Kaiser, M. (2015). EU migrant citizens' social rights in comparative perspective. *Oxford Institute of Social Policy*, 1–3.

Burkert, C., & Haas, A. (2014). *Investing in the future: labor market integration policies for new immigrants in Germany.* Migration Policy Institute and International Labour Organization.

Busemeyer, M. R. (2005). Pension reform in Germany and Austria: system change vs quantitative retrenchment. *West European Politics*, *28*(3), 569–591.

Castañeda, H. (2012). "Over-foreignization" or "unused potential"? A critical review of migrant health in Germany and responses toward unauthorized migration. *Social Science and Medicine*, 74, 830–838.

Conrad, H., & Fukuwa, T. (2003). The 2000/2001 pension reform in Germany – implications and possible lessons for Japan. *Japanese Journal of Social Security Policy*, *2*(2), 71–82.

Deutsche Rentenversicherung, (n.d.). Deutschlands Sozialsversicherungsabkommen. www.deutsche-rentenversicherung.de/DRV/DE/Rente/Ausland/Sozialversicherungsabkommen/ sozialversicherungsabkommen_detailseite.html.

Doerschler, P., & Jackson, P. I. (2010). Host nation language ability and immigrant integration in Germany: use of GSOEP to examine language as an integration criterion. *Democracy and Security*, *6*(2), 147–182.

EMN (2014). *Migrant sccess to social security and healthcare: policies and practice.* European Migration Network.

Faist, T., & Haüßermann, H. (1996). *Immigration, social citizenship and housing in Germany.* Blackwell.

Frydryszak, D. M & Macherey, A.-L. (2016). *Legal report on access to healthcare in 17 countries.* Médecins du monde.

Holzmann, R. (2016). Bilateral social security agreements and pensions portability: study of four migrant corridors between EU and non-EU countries. *International Social Security Review*, *69*(3–4), 109–130.

Holzmann, R., Koettl, J., & Chernetsky, T. (2005). *Portability regimes of pension and health benefits for international migrants: an Aanalysis of issues and good protection.* World Bank.

Huschke, S. (2014). Performing deservingness: humanitarian health care provision for migrants in Germany. *Social Science and Medicine*, *120*, 352–359.

Interview GER-01. Email correspondence with civil servant in City of Düsseldorf.

Interview GER-02. Email correspondence with civil servant in Department of the Environment.

Joppke, C. (2007). Beyond national models: civic integration policies for immigrants in Western Europe. *West European Politics*, *30*(1), 1–22.

KGC [Kooperationsverbund Gesundheitliche Chancengleichheit]. Praxisdatenbank Gesundheitliche Chancengleichheit. www.gesundheitliche-chancengleichheit.de/praxisdatenbank/?uid = 8d2fcb066de11bdea1405a71a287c2cb.

Liedtke, M. (2002). National elfare and asylum in Germany. *Critical Social Policy, 22*(3), 479–497.
Lindert, J., Schouler-Ocak, M., Heinz, A., & Priebe, S. (2008). Mental health, health care utilization of migrants in Europe. *European Psychiatry, 23*, 14–20.
Müller, A., Mayer, M. M., & Bauer, N. (2014). Social security for third-country nationals in Germany. BAMF working paper no. 57, 1–51.
OECD. (2017). *Finding their way: labour market integration of refugees in Germany.*
PICUM [Platform for International Cooperation on Undocumented Migrants]. (2001). *Health care for undocumented migrants: Germany, Belgium, the Netherlands, United Kingdom.* De Wrikker.
Ponzo, I. (2010). Immigrant integration policies and housing policies: the hidden links. *Fieri Research Reports*, 1–123.
Pross, C. (1998). Third class medicine: health care for refugees in Germany. *Health and Human Rights, 3*(2), 40–53.
Rother, N. (2010). The German integration panel – how to measure the influence of integration courses on migrants' integration? *Migration Letters, 7*(1), 43–55.
Sainsbury, D. (2006). Immigrants' social rights in comparative perspective: welfare regimes, forms in immigration and immigration policy regimes. *Journal of European Social Policy, 16*(3), 229–244.
Söhn, J. (2013). Unequal welcome and unequal life chances: how the state shapes integration opportunities of immigrants. *Archives Européennes de Sociologie, 54*(2), 295–326.
Sozialgesetzbuch XII. (2019). Sozialhilfe für Deutsche im Ausland. www.sozialgesetzbuch-sgb.de/sgbxii/24.html.
Spallek, J., Zeeb, H., & Razum, O. (2010). Prevention among immigrants: the example of Germany. *BMC Public Health, 10*(92), 1–6.
Stadlmaier, J. (2018). Earning citizenship: economic criteria for naturalisation in nine EU countries. *Journal of Contemporary European Studies, 26*(1), 42–63.
Zoellner, M., Fritsch, M., & Wyrwich, M. (2018). An evaluation of German active labour market policies: a review of the empirical evidence. *Journal of Entrepreneurship and Public Policy, 7*(4), 377–410.

Iceland

Agnarsson, S. (2010). Labour market development and policy in Iceland. EEO ad hoc request, June 2010.
Althingi. (2002). *Act on Foreigners.* 2002 no. 96.
Althingi. (2006). *Labour Market Measures Act.* 2006 no. 55.
Althingi. (2016). *Foreign Nationals Act.* 2016 no. 80.
Björnsson, D. F., Kopsch, F., & Zoega, G. (2018). Discrimination in the housing market as an impediment to European labour force integration: the case of Iceland. *Journal of International Migration and Integration, 19*, 829–847.

City of Reykjavik. (n.d.). Financial assistance. reykjavik.is/en/financial-assistance.

Directorate of Immigration. (n.d.-a). Rights and services for applicants for international protection. utl.is/index.php/en/rights-and-services-for-asylum-seekers.

Directorate of Immigration. (n.d.-b). Permanent residence permit. utl.is/index.php/en/permanent-residence-permit-xyz.

Directorate of Immigration. (n.d.-c). Basic requirements for a residence permit. utl.is/index.php/en/basic-requirements1#who-does-not-need-to-prove-support.

Directorate of Labor. (n.d.-a). Unemployment benefits. vinnumalastofnun.is/en/ unemployment-benefits.

Directorate of Labor. (n.d.-b). Work permits for third country nationals. vinnumalastofnun.is/ en/foreign-workers/work-permits-for-third-country-nationals.

Directorate of Labor. (n.d.-c). Unemployment benefits when abroad. vinnumalastofnun.is/en/ unemployment-benefits/unemployment-benefits-when-abroad.

European Committee of Social Rights. (2001). *European social charter – conclusions.* Council of Europe.

Fontaine, A. (2019). Refugees in Iceland will march from Keflavík to Reykjavík. *Reykjavik Grapevine*, 3 May.

Government of Iceland. (2016). Iceland. In *UNHRC resettlement Hhandbook.* www.refworld.org/pdfid/577a55014.pdf.

Gudmundsson, M. (2001). The Icelandic pension system. *Monetary Bulletin*, 2001/1, 42–59.

Halldorsdottir, T., Jonsson, H., & Gudmundsson, K. G. (2016). A few observations on health service for immigrants at a primary health care centre. *International Journal of Family Medicine*, 6963835.

Hilmarsson-Dunn, A., & Kristinsson, A.P. (2013). The language situation in Iceland.' In R.B. Kaplan, R. B. Baldauf Jr., & N. M. Kamwangamalu (Eds.), *Language planning in Europe: Cyprus, Iceland, and Luxembourg* (pp. 100–169). Routledge.

Housing Financial Fund. (n.d.). Housing benefits. husbot.is/are-you-entitled-to-housing-benefits.

Icelandic Health Insurance. (n.d.-a). Health insurance in Iceland. www.sjukra.is/english/social-insurance-in-iceland.

Icelandic Health Insurance. (n.d.-b). Students. www.sjukra.is/english/students.

Icelandic Health Insurance. (n.d.-c). Interpreter service. www.sjukra.is/english/social-insurance-in-iceland/interpreter-service.

Irving, Z. (2011). Waving not drowning: Iceland, kreppan, and alternative social policy futures. In K. Farnsworth & Z. Irving (Eds)., *Social policy in challenging times: economic crisis and welfare systems* (pp. 199–217). Policy Press.

Jonsson, G. (2001). The Icelandic welfare state in the twentieth century. *Scandinavian Journal of History*, *26*(3), 249–267.

Ministry of Social Affairs. (2003). Rent benefit. www.stjornarradid.is/media /velferdarraduneyti-media/media/acrobat-skjol/rent.pdf.

Ministry of Welfare. (2002). *Foreign Nationals' Right to Work Act*, no. 97/2002.

MISSOC [Mutual Information System on Social Protection]. (2004–18). *Comparative tables on social protection*. www.missoc.org/missoc-database/comparative-tables.

Multicultural and Information Centre. (n.d.-a). Housing benefits. old.mcc.is/english /housing/rent-subsidies.

Multicultural and Information Centre. (n.d.-b). Support from municipal authorities. www.mcc.is/enska-fjarhagsadstod.

Shields, L., Stathis, S., Mohay, H., Van Haeringen, A., Williams, H., Wood, D. & Bennett, E. (2004). The health of children in immigration detention: how does Australia compare? *Australian and New Zealand Journal of Public Health*, *28*(6), 513–519.

Skaptadóttir, U. D., & Innes, P. (2017). Immigrant experiences of learning Icelandic and connecting with the speaking community. *Nordic Journal of Migration Research*, *7*(1), 20–27.

Skaptadóttir, U. D., & Loftsdóttir, K. (2009). Cultivating culture? Images of Iceland, globalization, and multicultural society. In S. Jakobsson (Ed.), *Images of the North: histories – identities – ideas* (pp. 205–216). Rodopi.

Social Security Administration. (2002). Iceland. In *Social security programs throughout the world: Europe, 2002* (pp. 101–105). Social Security Administration, Office of Policy, Office of Research, Evaluation, and Statistics.

Social Security Administration. (2016). Iceland. In *Social security programs throughout the world: Europe, 2016* (pp. 147–152). Social Security Administration, Office of Policy, Office of Research, Evaluation, and Statistics.

State Social Security Institute. (n.d.). 65 years+. www.tr.is/en/65-years.

Sveinsson, J. R. (1996). Main trends of Icelandic housing in the 1980s and 1990s. *Scandinavian Housing and Planning Research*, *13*, 215–220.

Tryggvadóttir, H., & Skaptadóttir, U. D. (2018). Borders, boundaries, and xclusion in the Icelandic Aasylum system.' *Refuge*, *34*(2), 16–27.

Ireland

Citizens Information. (n.d.-a). State pension (non-contributory). www .citizensinformation.ie/en/social_welfare/social_welfare_payments/older_and _retired_people/state_pension_non_contributory.html.

Citizens Information. (n.d.-b). Entitlement to health services. www. citizensinformation.ie/en/health/health_system/entitlement_to_public_health _services.html.

Citizens Information. (n.d.-c). Jobseeker's benefit. www.citizensinformation.ie/en /social_ welfare/social_welfare_payments/unemployed_people/jobseekers_benefit .html.

Citizens Information. (n.d.-d). Going abroad or on holidays and social welfare payments . www.citizensinformation.ie/en/social_welfare/irish_social_welfare_system /claiming_a_social_welfare_payment/going_abroad_and_social_welfare_payments .html.

Citizens Information. (n.d.-e). Applying for local authority/social housing. www .citizensinformation.ie/en/housing/local_authority_and_social_housing/applying _for_local_authority_housing.html.

Citizens Information. (n.d.-f). Accommodation for people granted refugee status or subsidiary protection or given permission to remain. www.citizensinformation.ie /en/moving_country/ asylum_seekers_and_refugees/refugee_status_and_leave_to _remain/accommodation_for_refugees.html.

Citizens Information. (n.d.-g). Schemes to support employment. www .citizensinformation.ie/en/employment/unemployment_and_redundancy /employment_support_schemes/schemes_to_support_employment.html.

Department of Employment Affairs and Social Protection. (2017). *Qualifying for state pension (contributory). Frequently asked questions.* Dublin.

Department of Employment Affairs and Social Protection. (n.d.-a). HRC – guidelines for deciding officers on the determination of habitual residence. www.welfare.ie/en /Pages/Habitual-Residence-Condition--Guidelines-for-Deciding-Offic.aspx#sect6.

Department of Employment Affairs and Social Protection. (n.d.-b). State pension (contributory). www.welfare.ie/en/Pages/State-Pension-Contributory.aspx.

Department of Environment, Community, and Local Government. (2012). Housing circular 41/2012 – access to social housing supports for non-Irish nationals. www .housing.gov.ie/sites/default/files/migrated-files/en/Publications/Development andHousing/Housing/FileDownLoad%2C29412%2Cen.pdf.

Department of Justice and Equality. (2015). *Reception and integration agency: annual report 2015.* Reception and Integration Agency.

EMN. (2014). *Migrant access to social security and healthcare: policies and practice.* European Migration Network.

Irish Congress of Trade Unions. (n.d.). *A short guide to the Irish social welfare system.* www.ictu.ie/download/pdf/swenglish.pdf.

Irish Refugee Council. (n.d.). Health care: Republic of Ireland. Country report in Asylum Information Database, www.asylumineurope.org/reports/country/republic -ireland/reception-conditions/health-care.

MacCormaic, R. (2008). Language training centre for migrants to close. *Irish Times*, 13 June.

MacFarlane, A. (2018). *To develop a model for the implementation of trained interpreters in the Irish healthcare system.* Health Service Executive.

MacFarlane, A., Dzebisova, Z., Karapish, D., Kovacevic, Ogbebor, F. & Okonkwo, E. (2009). Arranging and negotiating the use of informal interpreters in general practice consultations: experiences of refugees and asylum seekers in the west of Ireland. *Social Science and Medicine*, 69, 210–214.

MacFarlane, A., Glynn, L. G., Mosinkie, P. I. & Murphy, A. W. (2008). Responses to language barriers in consultations with refugees and asylum seekers: a telephone survey of Irish general practitioners. *BMC Family Practice*, *9*(68), 1–6.

McGuinness, S., O'Connell, P. J., & Kelly, E. (2019). Carrots, no stick, no driver: the employment impact of job search assistance in a regime with minimal monitoring and sanctions. *Journal of Labor Research*, *40*, 151–180.

MISSOC [Mutual Information System on Social Protection]. (2004–18). *Comparative tables on social protection.* www.missoc.org/missoc-database/comparative-tables.

MRCI [Migrant Rights Centre Ireland]. (2005). *Social protection denied: the impact of the habitual residency condition on migrant workers.*

Norris, M., Healy, J., & Coates, D. (2008). Drivers of rising housing allowance claimant numbers: evidence from the Irish private rented sector. *Housing Studies*, *23*(1), 89–109.

Office for the Promotion of Migrant Integration. (n.d.). Learning English. www.integration.ie/en/ISEC/Pages/Mig_Info_Learning_English.

Office for the Promotion of Migrant Integration. (2017). *The migrant integration strategy: a blueprint for the future.* Department of Justice and Equality.

Quinn, E., Gusciute, E., Barrett, A., & Joyce, C. (2014). *Migrant access to social security and healthcare: policies and practice in Ireland.* European Migration Network.

Social Security Administration. (2002). Ireland. In *Social security programs throughout the world: Europe, 2002* (pp. 106–111). Social Security Administration, Office of Policy, Office of Research, Evaluation, and Statistics.

Stadlmaier, J. (2018). Earning citizenship: economic criteria for naturalisation in nine EU countries. *Journal of Contemporary European Studies*, *26*(1), 42–63.

Watson, D., & Corrigan, E. (2019). Social housing in the Irish housing market. *Economic and Social Review*, *50*(1), 213–248.

WRC Social and Economic Consultants. (2006). *Integrate Ireland language and training.* www.ihrec.ie/download/pdf/measure_17_integrate_ireland_language _and_ training_wider_equality_study_pdf.pdf.

Italy

Busetta, A., Ceterolli, V., & Wilson, B. (2018). A universal health care system? Unmet need for medical care among regular and irregular immigrants in Italy. *Journal of Immigrant Minority Health*, *20*, 416–421.

Campomori, F., & Caponio, T. (2016). Immigrant integration policymaking in Italy: Regional policies in a multi-level governance perspective. *International Review of Administrative Sciences*, *83*(2): 303–321.

Caponio, T., Baucells, O. J., & Cuell, B. (2015). Civic integration policies from below: accounting for processes of convergence and divergence in four European cities. *Ethnic and Racial Studies*, *39*(5), 878–895.

Cuadra, C. B. (2010). *Policies on health care for undocumented migrants in EU27: country report: Italy.* Malmö University.

Cuttita, P. (2016). Mandatory integration measures and differential inclusion: the Italian case. *International Migration and Integration, 17,* 289–302.

De Luca, G., Ponzo, M., & Andrés, A. R. (2013). Health care utilization by immigrants in Italy. *International Journal of Health Care Finance and Economics, 13*(1), 1–31.

Devillanova, C. (2008). Social networks, information and health care utilization: evidence from undocumented immigrants in Milan. *Journal of Health Economics, 27,* 265–286.

Devillanova, C. (2016). Inequities in immigrants' access to health care services: disentangling potential barriers.' *International Journal of Manpower, 37*(7), 1191–1208.

Falla, A. M., Veldhuijzen, I. K., Ahmad, A. A., Levi, M., & Richardus, J. H. (2017). Language support for linguistic minority chronic hepatitis B/C patients: an exploratory study of availability and clinicians' perceptions. *BMC Health Services Research, 17*(150), 1–8.

Galli, C., Pittau, F., & Ricci, A. (2014). *Migrant access to social security and healthcare in Italy: policies and practices.* European Migration Network Italy.

INPS [Istituto Nazionale Previdenza Sociale]. (n.d.). Assegno sociale. www.inps.it/nuovoportaleinps/default.aspx? itemdir = 50184.

INPS. (2016). Assegno sociale. www.inps.it/nuovoportaleinps/default.aspx?itemDir=46047.

INPS. (2017). Chiaramenti in materia di indennità di disoccupazione NASpI: beneficiari che espatriano o soggiornano all'estero per la ricercar di un lavoro o per motivi diversi dalla ricerca di un lavoro. Circolare no. 177, 28 novembre.

Ministero del lavoro e delle politiche sociale. (n.d.). Social security. www.integrazionemigranti.gov.it/en/legal-framework/domestic-law/Pages/Social-security.aspx.

MISSOC [Mutual Information System on Social Protection]. (2004–2018). *Comparative tables on social protection.* www.missoc.org/missoc-database/comparative-tables.

OECD. (2014). *Jobs for immigrants,* Vol. 4, *Labour market integration in Italy.*

Parlamento Italiano. (1969). Legge 30 aprile 1969, n. 153: Revisione degli ordinamenti pensionistici e norme in materia di sicurezza sociale. *Gazzetta Ufficiale* 1969, 111.

Parlamento Italiano. (1989). Decreto legge 30 dicembre 1989, n. 146: Norme urgenti in materia di asilo politico, di ingresso e soggiorno dei cittadini extracomunitari e di regolarizzazione dei cittadini extracomunitari ed apolidi già presenti nel territorio dello State. *Gazzetta Ufficiale* 1990, 67.

Parlamento Italiano. (1990). Legge 28 febbraio 1990, n. 39: Norme urgenti in materia di asilo politico, di ingresso e soggiorno dei cittadini extracomunitari e di regolarizzazione dei cittadini extracomunitaqri ed apolidi già presenti nel territorio dello Stato. *Gazzetta Ufficiale* 1990, n. 49.

Parlamento Italiano. (1998). Legge 6 marzo 1998, n. 40: Disciplina dell'immigrazione e norme sulla condizione dello straniero. *Gazzetta Ufficiale* 1998, 59 – supplement ordinario n. 40.

Parlamento Italiano. (2002). Legge 30 luglio 2002, n. 189: Modifica alla normative in materia di immigrazione e di asilo. *Gazzetta Ufficiale* 2002, 199.

Parlamento Italiano. (2008). Decreto-legge 25 giugno 2008, n. 112: Disposizioni urgenti per lo sviluppo economico, la semplificazione, la competitività, la stabilizzazione della finanza pubblica e la perequazione Tributaria. *Gazzetta Ufficiale* 2008, 147.

Parlamento Italiano. (2015). Decreto legislativo 4 marzo 2015, n. 23: Disposizioni sul contratto di lavoro a tutele crescenti. *Gazetta Ufficiale* 2015, 54.

Pompei, D., & Cutini, R. Immigrazione: l'accesso ai servizi sociali. In E. Codini, R. Cutini, M. Ferrero, P. Olivani, D. Panizzut, & D. Pompei (Eds.), *I diritti sociali degli stranieri: principi e disciplina in Italia e in Europa* (pp. 27–37). Utet Giuridica.

Regione Lombardia. (2013). *Living in Lombardy. Multilingual guide to renting and buying a home.* www.integrazionemigranti.gov.it/guidemultilingua/Documents/Casa/ eng.pdf.

Saraceno, C. (2006). Social assistance policies and decentralization in the countries of southern Europe. *Revue Française des Affaires Sociales, 5*, 97–117.

Luxembourg

Ametepe, S. F., & Hartmann-Hirsch, C. (2010). Eligibility and take up of social assistance for immigrants and nationals: the case of Luxembourg. *CEPS/Instead*, Working paper 2010-05.

Chaput, H., Julienne, K., & Lelievre, M. (2007). L'aide à la veillesse pauvre: la construction du minimum vieillesse. *Revue Française des Affaires Sociales, 1*, 57–83.

CNAP [Caisse Nationale d'Assurance Pension]. (2019). *Pension de vieillesse au Luxembourg.* CNAP.

Commission Nationale d'Éthique. (2007). *Les limites de l'accès aux soins au Grand-Duché de Luxembourg.* Avis 20. cne.public.lu/dam-assets/fr/publications/avis /Avis_20.pdf.

EMN [European Migration Network]. (2013). *Migrant access to social security and healthcare: policies and practice.* EMN National Contact Point.

FRA [European Union Agency for Fundamental Rights]. (2011). *Fundamental rights of migrants in an irregular situation in the European Union.* Publications Office of the European Union.

Inspection générale de la sécurité sociale. (2017). *Droit de la sécurité sociale.* Ministère de la Securité sociale.

Government of Luxembourg. (1972). Loi du 24 juillet 1972 concernant l'action sociale en faveur des immigrants. *Journal Officiel du Grand-Duché de Luxembourg*, 28 July.

Government of Luxembourg. (1976). Loi du 21 février 1976 concernant l'organisation et le fonctionnement de l'Administration de l'Emploi et portant création d'une

Commission nationale de l'Emploi. *Journal officiel du Grand-Duché de Luxembourg*, 26 February.

Government of Luxembourg. (1983). Règlement grand-ducal du 23 juillet 1983 fixant les mesures d' exécution relatives aux primes et subventions d' intérêt en faveur du logement prévues par la loi modifiée du 25 février 1979 concernant l' aide au logement. *Journal official du Grand-Duché de Luxembourg*, 28 July.

Government of Luxembourg. (1986). Loi du 26 juillet 1986 portant a) création du droit à un revenu minimum garanti; b) création d'un service national d'action sociale; c) modification de la loi du 30 juillet 1960 concernant la création d'un fonds national de solidarité. *Journal official du Grand-Duché de Luxembourg*, 25 August.

Government of Luxembourg. (1987). Loi du 27 juillet 1987 concernant l' assurance pension en cas de vieillesse, d' invalidité et de survie. *Journal official du Grand-Duché de Luxembourg*, 28 July.

Government of Luxembourg. (1993). Loi du 27 juillet 1993 concernant l'intégration des étrangers au Grand-Duché de Luxembourg ainsi que l'action sociale en faveur des étrangers. *Journal official du Grand-Duché de Luxembourg*, 28 July.

Government of Luxembourg. (1999). Loi du 29 avril 1999 portant création d'un droit à un revenu minimum garanti. *Journal official du Grand-Duché de Luxembourg*, 1 July.

Government of Luxembourg. (2008a). Loi du 29 août portant sur la libre circulation des personnes et l'immigration. *Journal official du Grand-Duché de Luxembourg*, 10 September.

Government of Luxembourg. (2008b). Loi du 16 décembre 2008 concernant l'accueil et l'intégration des étrangers au Grand-Duché de Luxembourg. *Journal official du Grand-Duché de Luxembourg*, 24 December.

Government of Luxembourg. (2009). Loi du 18 décembre 2009 organisant l'aide sociale. *Journal official du Grand-Duché de Luxembourg*, 29 December.

Government of Luxembourg. (2016). *Code du travail*. Service central de legislation Luxembourg.

Government of Luxembourg. (n.d.-a). Work for applicants for international protection. guichet.public.lu/en/citoyens/immigration/cas-specifiques/protection-internationale/ autorisation-occupation-temporaire.html.

Government of Luxembourg. (n.d.-b). Exporter les indemnités de chômage en tant que citoyen de l'UE. adem.public.lu/fr/demandeurs-demploi/demander-indemnites-chomage/ressortissants-ue.html.

Government of Luxembourg. (n.d.-c). Louer un logement subventionné. guichet.public.lu/fr/citoyens/sante-social/action-sociale/aides-logement/location-logement-subventionne.html.

Government of Luxembourg. (n.d.-d). Mesures en faveur de l'emploi. adem.public.lu/fr/demandeurs-demploi/aides-financieres-mesures/mesures-emploi.html.

Interview LUX-01. Email correspondence with the Luxembourgish Red Cross.

Interview LUX-02. Email correspondence with civil servant at the Ministry of Work, Employment and the Economy.

Interview LUX-03. Email correspondence with civil servant at the Caisse Nationale d'Assurance Pension.
Interview LUX-04. Email correspondence with civil servant at the Directorate of Immigration.
MISSOC [Mutual Information System on Social Protection]. (2004–18). *Comparative tables on social protection.* www.missoc.org/missoc-database/comparative-tables.
OLAI [Office Luxembourgeois de l'Accueil et de l'Intégration]. (n.d.). Welcome and integration contract. www.olai.public.lu/en/accueil-integration/mesures/contrat-accueil.
Social Security Administration (2016). Luxembourg. In *Social security programs throughout the world: Europe, 2016* (pp. 204–209). Social Security Administration, Office of Policy, Office of Research, Evaluation, and Statistics.
Swinnen, H. (2016). Job Integration of Refugees and Third Country Nationals in Luxembourg: The "InSitu Jobs" Project. *ESPN Flash Report,* 2016/35.

Malta

Aditus. (n.d.). Rights attached to the beneficiaries of international protection. Factsheet no. 14. aditus.org.mt/Publications/factsheet14_rightsinternationprotection.pdf.
Aditus & JRS Malta. (n.d.). Health care: Malta. Report on Asylum Information Database, www.asylumineurope.org/reports/country/malta/content-international-protection/health-care.
Caruana, C., & Theuma, M. (2012). *The next leap: from labour market programmes to active labour market policy.* UHM Voice of the Workers.
Cuadra, C. B. (2010). *Policies on health care for undocumented migrants in EU27: country report: Denmark.* Malmö University.
DeBono, D. (2013). "Less than human": the detention of irregular immigrants in Malta. *Race and Class, 55*(2), 60–81.
Dimech, T. (2017). Immigration integration strategy has been launched. *TVM News,* www.tvm.com.mt/en/news/immigration-integration-strategy-has-been-launched.
EMN. (2014). *Migrant access to social security and healthcare: policies and practice.* European Migration Network.
Fsadni, M., & Pisani, M. (2012). *"I'm not racist, but ...": Immigrant and ethnic minority groups and housing in Malta – a research study.* National Commission for the Promotion of Equality.
Gauci, J.-P. (2010). Malta. In A. Platonova & G. Urso (Eds.), *Migration, employment, and labour market integration policies in the European Union (2000–2009)* (pp. 163–172). International Organization for Migration.
Government of Malta. (n.d.-a). Non Contributory Age Pension. socialsecurity.gov.mt/en/Pensions/ Pages/Non-Contributory-Age-Pension-.aspx.
Government of Malta. (n.d.-b). Free Medical Aid (Pink Form/Karta Roza). socialsecurity.gov.mt/ en/latest_featured/Pages/Free%20Medical%20Aid%20Pink%20FormKarta%20Roża.aspx.

Government of Malta. (n.d.-c). Migrant Health Liaison Office. deputyprimeminister .gov.mt/en/ phc/mhlo/Pages/mhlo.aspx.

Government of Malta. (n.d.-d). Social Security Reciprocal Agreements. socialsecurity .gov.mt/en/about-us/Pages/Social-Security-Reciprocal-Agreements-.aspx.

Government of Malta. (1964). *Maltese Citizenship Act.* Chapter 188, pp. 1–18.

Government of Malta. (1976). *Housing Authority Act.* Chapter 261, pp. 1–17.

Government of Malta. (1987). *Social Security Act.* Chapter 318, pp. 1–171.

Housing Authority. (2017). Rent subsidization on privately owned dwellings. housingauthority.gov.mt/en/Documents/Schemes/Sussidju%20fuq%20il-Kera %20-%20English%202016.pdf.

Identity Malta Agency. (n.d.). Acquisition of Maltese citizenship by naturalization. identitymalta.com/acquisition-of-maltese-citizenship-by-naturalisation.

JobsPlus (n.d.). Third country nationals (non-EU) seeking employment in Malta . jobsplus.gov.mt/job-seekers-mt-MT-en-GB/guidance-services/tcns-seeking -employment.

Luhmann, N., Bouhénia, M., & Giraux, F. (2007). *Access to health care and human rights of asylum seekers in Malta: experiences, results, and recommendations.* Médecins du Monde.

McKay, L. (2014). *European minimum income network country report: Malta.* European Minimum Income Network.

MISSOC [Mutual Information System on Social Protection]. (2004–18). *Comparative tables on social protection.* www.missoc.org/missoc-database/comparative-tables/, July 2019.

Nimführ, S. (2016). Living Liminality. Ethnological Insights into the Life Situation of Non-Deportable Refugees in Malta. *Österreichische Zeitschrift für Volkskunde, 119*(3–4), 245–271.

OECD. (2009). *Country chapter – Malta.* OECD Social Policy Division. www.oecd.org /els/soc/47346537.pdf.

Social Security Administration. (2010). Malta. In *Social security programs throughout the world: Europe, 2010* (pp. 205–210). Social Security Administration, Office of Policy, Office of Research, Evaluation, and Statistics.

Spiteri Gingell, D. (2015). Stronger pension system. *Times of Malta,* 20 July 20.

UNHCR [United Nations High Commissioner for Refugees]. (2013). Universal periodic review: Malta. www.humanrightsmalta.org/uploads/1/2/3/3/12339284 /unhcr_ submission_by_the_unhcr_for_the_office_of_the_high_commissioner _for_human_rights_compilation_report_universal_periodic_review_malta_2013 _refugees.pdf.

Netherlands

Belastingdienst. (n.d.). Huurtoeslag. www.belastingdienst.nl/wps/wcm/ connect /bldcontentnl/belastingdienst/prive/toeslagen/huurtoeslag.

Bruttel, O., & Sol, E. (2006). Work first as a European model? Evidence from Germany and the Netherlands. *Policy and Politics, 34*(1), 69–89.

Department of Social Affairs (2008). *The old age pension system in the Netherlands.* Publication no. SZW-74R610. Rijksoverheid.

Devillé, W., Graecen, T., Bogic, M., Dauvrin, M. Dias, S., Gaddini, A., Koitzsch Jensen, N., Karamanidou, C., Kluge, U., Mertaniemi, R., Puigpinós i Riera, R., Sárváry, A., Soares, J.J.F., Stankunas, M., Strassmayr, C., Welbel, M., & Priebe, S. (2011). Health care for immigrants in Europe: is there still consensus among country experts about principles of good practice? A Delphi study. *BMC Public Health, 11*(699), 1–10.

EMN. (2014). *Migrant access to social security and healthcare: policies and practice in the Netherlands.* European Migration Network and Immigratie- en Naturalisatiedienst.

Ersanilli, E. (2007). Netherlands. *Focus Migration,* country profile no. 11.

Frydryszak, D., & Macherey, A.-L. (2016). *Legal report on access to healthcare in 17 countries.* Médecins du monde.

Government of the Netherlands. (n.d.-a). Opbouw pensioenstelsel. www.rijksoverheid .nl/onderwerpen/pensioen/opbouw-pensioenstelsel.

Government of the Netherlands. (n.d.-b). Hoe kom ik in aanmerking voor een sociale - huurwoning? www.rijksoverheid.nl/onderwerpen/huurwoning/vraag-en -antwoord/sociale-huurwoning-voorwaarden.

Interview NET-01. Email correspondence with civil servant at SVB.

Interview NET-02. Email correspondence with civil servant at Department of Health.

Koning, E. A. (2019). *Immigration and the politics of welfare exclusion: selective solidarity in Western democracies.* University of Toronto Press.

Lindsay, C., & McQuaid, R. W. (2009). New governance and the case of activation policies: comparing experiences in Denmark and the Netherlands.' *Social Policy and Administration, 43*(5), 445–463.

Minderhoud, P. E. (1999). Asylum seekers and access to social security: recent developments in the Netherlands, United Kingdom, Germany, and Belgium. In A. Bloch & C. Levy (Eds.), *Refugees, Citizenship, and Social Policy in Europe.* Houndmills: Macmillan.

MISSOC [Mutual Information System on Social Protection], (2004–18). *Comparative tables on social protection.* www.missoc.org/missoc-database/comparative-tables.

Parliament of the Netherlands. (1984). Wet individuele huursubsidie. Document 18539-2, parliamentary year 1983–84.

Parliament of the Netherlands. (2000). Vreemdelingenwet 2000. wetten.overheid.nl/ BWBR0011823/2019-02-27.

Parliament of the Netherlands. (2003). Invoeringswet Wet werk en bijstand. wetten. overheid.nl/BWBR0015704/2006-01-01/#Hoofdstuk2.

Ponzo, I. (2010). Immigrant integration policies and housing policies: the hidden links. *Fieri Research Reports,* 1–123.

Shaw, G. (2002). *Ethnic minority employment through partnership.* Copenhagen Centre.

SVB [Sociale Verzekeringsbank]. (n.d.-a). Compleet overzicht AIO. www.svb.nl/int/nl/aio/sitemap.jsp.

SVB. (n.d.-b). Verdragslanden. www.svb.nl/int/nl/algemeen/verdragslanden.jsp.

UWV [Uitvoeringsinstituut Werknemersverzekeringen]. (n.d.). Met een uitkering naar het buitenland. www.uwv.nl/particulieren/internationaal/met-uitkering-naar-buitenland/detail/met-een-ww-uitkering-naar-het-buitenland/ik-zoek-werk-in-de-eu-eer-of-zwitserland-met-een-volledige-ww-uitkering.

Van der Bijl, N., Van der Kleij, M. B., Tuzgöl-Broekhoven, A. J. H., Van Dorst, P. C., Saeijs, J. J., De La Rambeije, I., & De Beer, S. (2013). *Medische zorg vreemdelingen: Over toegang en continuïteit van medische zorg voor asielzoekers en uitgeprocedeerde asielzoekers.* Report no. 2013/125. De Nationale Ombudsman.

Van Parys, R., & Verbruggen, N. (2004). *Report on the housing situation of undocumented migrants in six European countries: Austria, Belgium, Germany, Italy, the Netherlands, and Spain.* PICUM.

New Zealand

Ashton, T. (1996). Health care systems in transition: New Zealand. Part I: an overview of New Zealand's health care system. *Journal of Public Health Medicine, 18*(3), 269–273.

Auckland Regional Public Health Service. (n.d.). Services for refugees and asylum seekers. www.arphs.health.nz/health-professionals/refugee-health/services-for-refugees-and-asylum-seekers.

Controller and Auditor-General. (2013). *Immigration New Zealand: supporting new migrants to settle and work.* Office of the Auditor-General.

Gray, B., Hilder, J., & Stubbe, M. (2002). How to use interpreters in general practice: the development of a New Zealand toolkit. *Journal of Primary Health Care, 4*(1), 52–61.

Health and Disability Commissioner. (1996). *Code of health and disability services consumers' rights, regulations 1996.* www.hdc.org.nz/your-rights/about-the-code/code-of-health-and-disability-services-consumers-rights.

HealthNavigator. (n.d.-a). Interpreter services. www.healthnavigator.org.nz/languages/i/interpreter-services.

HealthNavigator. (n.d.-b). What is cultural competence? www.healthnavigator.org.nz/clinicians/c/cultural-competence/#Overview.

Human Rights Commission. (2010). *Human rights in New Zealand.* Human Rights Commission.

Interview NZE-01. Email correspondence with civil servant in Ministry of Social Development.

Interview NZE-02. Email correspondence with civil servant in Tertiary Education Commission.

Johri, R., De Boer, M., Pusch, H. Ramasamy, S., & Wong, K. (2004). *Evidence to date on the working and effectiveness of ALMPs in New Zealand.* Department of Labour and Ministry of Social Development.

KiwiSaver. (n.d.-a). KiwiSaver in a nutshell. www.kiwisaver.govt.nz/new/about/summary.

KiwiSaver. (n.d-b). Moving overseas permanently. www.kiwisaver.govt.nz/already/get-money/early/moving.

Kritzer, B. E. (2007). KiwiSaver: New Zealand's new subsidized retirement savings plan. *Social Security Bulletin*, *67*(4), 113–119.

Medical Council of New Zealand. (2006). Statement on cultural competence. www.mcnz.org.nz/assets/standards/c64c8a6ae1/Statement-on-cultural-competence.pdf.

Ministry of Health. (1994). *Health and disability services eligibility direction 1994*, 30 June.

Ministry of Health. (2011). *Health and disability services eligibility direction 2011*, 16 April.

Ministry of Social Development. (n.d.-a). New Zealand superannuation (NZ Super) overview. www.workandincome.govt.nz/eligibility/seniors/superannuation/superannuation-overview.html#null.

Ministry of Social Development. (n.d.-b). Emergency benefit. www.workandincome.govt.nz/products/a-z-benefits/emergency-benefit.html.

Ministry of Social Development. (n.d.-c). Living overseas. www.workandincome.govt.nz/pensions/travelling-or-moving/going-overseas-super/residing-overseas.html#null.

Ministry of Social Development. (n.d.-d). Qualifications. www.workandincome.govt.nz/map/income-support/main-benefits/jobseeker-support/qualifications.html.

Ministry of Social Development. (n.d.-e). Accommodation supplement. www.workandincome.govt.nz/ products/a-z-benefits/accommodation-supplement.html#null.

Ministry of Social Development. (n.d.-f). Temporary additional support. www.workandincome.govt.nz/ products/a-z-benefits/temporary-additional-support.html#null.

Ministry of Social Development. (n.d.-g). A-Z benefits and payments. www.workandincome.govt.nz/products/a-z-benefits/index.html.

Ministry of Social Development. (2003). A description of New Zealand's current retirement income framework. Background paper, Periodic Report Group 2003, pp. 1–15.

Ministry of Social Development. (2014). *Ministerial Direction on Eligibility for Social Housing*. Wellington, April 14.

Morrison, P. S. (1995). The geography of rental housing and the restructuring of housing assistance in New Zealand. *Housing Studies*, 10(1), 39–56.

Murphy, L. (1997). New Zealand's housing reforms and accommodation supplement experience. *Urban Policy and Research*, *15*(4), 269–278.

New Zealand Immigration Service. (2004). *Refugee voices: a journey towards resettlement.* Department of Labour.

Parliament of New Zealand. (1964). Social Security Act. Public Act 1964 no. 136, 4 December.

Parliament of New Zealand. (1992). Housing Restructuring and Tenancy Matters Act. Public Act 1992 no. 76, 18 August.

RASNZ [Refugee as Survivors New Zealand]. (n.d.). About us. rasnz.co.nz/about-us.

Shields, J., Drolet, J., & Valenzuela, K. (2016). Immigrant settlement and integration services and the role of nonprofit service providers: a cross-national perspective on trends, issues, and evidence. RCIS working paper no. 216/1.

Sinclair, J. (1990). New Zealand. *International Social Security Review, 43*(3), 345–346.

Tertiary Education Commission. (n.d.-a). Improving adult literacy and numeracy. www.tec.govt.nz/focus/our-focus/adult-literacy-numeracy.

Tertiary Education Commission. (n.d.-b). Pre-purchased English language tuition (PELT). www.tec.govt.nz/funding/funding-and-performance/funding/fund-finder/pelt.

Trampusch, C. (2018). A state-centred explanation of the finance–pension nexus: New Zealand's pension reforms as a typical case. *Social Policy and Administration, 52*(1), 343–364.

Norway

Abebe, D. S. (2010). Public health challenges of immigrants in Norway: research review. *NAKMI Report* 2/2010, 1–79.

Aschehoug, S. (2010). Rett til helsehjelp for papirløse migranter. *Tidsskriftet for den Norske Legeforening, 130*(7), 765–766.

Brochmann, G., & Grødem, A. S. (2013). Migration and welfare state sustainability: the case of Norway. In E. Jurado & G. Brochmann (Eds.), *Europe's immigration challenge* (pp. 59–76). I.B. Tauris.

Brochmann, G., & Hagelund, A. (2012). Norway: the land of the golden mean. In G. Brochmann & A. Hagelund (Eds.)., *Immigration policy and the Scandinavian welfare state* (pp. 149–224). Palgrave Macmillan.

Dahl, E., & Lorentzen, T. (2005). What works for whom? An analysis of active labour market programmes in Norway. *International Journal of Social Welfare, 14*, 86–96.

Duell, N., Singh, S., & Tergeist, P. (2010). Activation policies in Norway. OECD Social, Employment, and Migration working papers no. 78.

eHealth Directorate. (n.d.). The right to a doctor. helsenorge.no/foreigners-in-norway /the-right-to-a-doctor.

Health Directorate. (2015). *Helsetjenester til asylsøkere, flyktninger og familiegjenforente. Nasjonal veileder.* Helsedirektoratet.

Hjörleifsson, S., Hammer, E., & Díaz, E. (2018). General practitioners' strategies in consultations with immigrants in Norway – practice-based shared reflections among participants in focus groups. *Family Practice, 35*(2), 216–221.

Kale, E. (2006). *"Vi tar det vi har": om bruk av tolk i helsevesenet i Oslo en spørreskjemaundersøkelse.* Nasjonal kompetanseenhet for minoritetshelse.

Kvamme, E., & Ytrehus, S. (2015). Barriers to health care access among undocumented migrant women in Norway. *Society, Health, and Vulnerability, 6*(1), 1–17.

Labour and Welfare Administration. (n.d.-a). Garantipensjon. www.nav.no/no/Person /Pensjon/Alderspensjon/Relatert+informasjon/garantipensjon--428407.

Labour and Welfare Administration. (n.d.-b). Supplerende stønad for personer med kort botid i Norge. www.nav.no/no/Person/Pensjon/Andre+pensjonsordninger /supplerende-stønad-for-personer-med-kort-botid-i-norge.

Labour and Welfare Administration. (n.d.-c). Medlemskap i folketrygden. www.nav .no/no/Person/Flere+tema/Arbeid+og+opphold+i+Norge/Relatert+informasjon /medlemskap-i-folketrygden# chapter-1.

Labour and Welfare Administration. (n.d.-d). Alderspensjon og utland. www.nav.no/no/Person/Pensjon/Alderspensjon/Relatert+informasjon/ Alderspensjon+og+utland.

Labour and Welfare Administration. (n.d.-e). Dagpenger når du er arbeidsledig. www .nav.no/no/Person/Arbeid/Dagpenger+ved+arbeidsloshet+og+permittering /dagpenger-når-du-er-arbeidsledig--893.

Labour and Welfare Administration. (n.d.-f). Alderspension for deg født før 1954. www .nav.no/no/Person/Pensjon/Alderspensjon/alderspensjon-for-deg-født-før-1954.

Labour and Welfare Administration. (n.d.-g). Alderspension for deg født i 1963 eller senere. www.nav.no/no/Person/Pensjon/Alderspensjon/alderspensjon-for-deg-født -i-1963-eller-senere.

Labour and Welfare Administration. (n.d.-h). Økonomisk sosialhjelp. www.nav.no /sosialhjelp/slik-soker-du.

Labour and Welfare Administration. (n.d.-i). Oppfølging og tiltak for å komme i jobb . www.nav.no/no/Person/Arbeid/Oppfolging+og+tiltak+for+a+komme+i+jobb.

Lodovici, M. S. (2010). Making a success of integrating immigrants in the labour market. Discussion paper, peer review in social protection and social inclusions. European Commission.

Ministry of Social Affairs and Health. (1999). Retningslinjer for tannhelsetjenester til flyktninger og asylsøkere i statlig mottak ansvar, tjenestens faglige innhold og betalingsordninger. Circular I-23/99, 25 August.

MISSOC [Mutual Information System on Social Protection]. (2004–18). *Comparative tables on social protection.* www.missoc.org/missoc-database/comparative-tables.

Parliament of Norway. (1966). Lov om folketrygd. LOV-1966-06-17-12.

Parliament of Norway. (1983). Lov om tannhelsetjenesten. LOV-1983-06-03-54.

Parliament of Norway. (1997). Lov om folketrygd. LOV-1997-02-28-19.

Parliament of Norway. (1998). Forskrift om dagpenger under arbeidsløshet. FOR-1998-09-16-890.

Parliament of Norway. (1999). Lov om pasient-og brukerrettigheter. LOV-1999-07-02-63.

Parliament of Norway. (2005). Lov om supplerande stønad til personar med kort butid i Noreg. LOV-2005-04-29-21.

Parliament of Norway. (2012). Lov om bustøtte. LOV-2012-08-24-64.

Ruud, S. (2015). Får flyktninger mer i uføretrygd enn nordmenn? *Aftenposten*, 1 December 2015.

Social Security Administration. (2010). Norway. In *Social security programs throughout the world: Europe, 2010* (pp. 228–235). Social Security Administration, Office of Policy, Office of Research, Evaluation, and Statistics.

Søholt, S. (2010). Policy analysis related to immigrant settlement and integration. In R. Anderson et al. (Eds.), *Immigration, housing, and segregation in the Nordic welfare states* (pp. 163–175).: Helsinki University Print.

Søholt, S., & Wessel, T. (2010). Housing policy and housing market in Norway. In R. Anderson et al. (Eds.), *Immigration, housing, and segregation in the Nordic welfare states* (pp. 135-149). Helsinki University Print.

Sørvoll, J. (2011). *Norsk boligpolitikk i forandring 1970–2010. Dokumentasjon og debatt.* Norsk institutt for forskning om oppvekst, velferd og aldring.

State Housing Bank. (n.d.). Kan jeg få bostøtte? www.husbanken.no/bostotte/kan-jeg-faa-bostotte.

Portugal

ACM [Alto Comissariado para as Migrações]. (n.d.-a). Serviço de tradução telefónica . www.acm.gov.pt/-/servico-de-traducao-telefonica.

ACM. (n.d.-b). PPT program – Portuguese for all.' www.acm.gov.pt/-/programa-ppt-portugues-para-todos.

Agarez, R. C. (Ed.). (2018). *Habitação. Ce manos de políticas públicas em Portugal, 1918–2018.* Instituto da Habitação e da Reabilitação Urbana.

Backstrom, B. (2014). Migrants and health in Portugal. *Health, Culture, and Society, 7*(1), 80–93.

Bover, O., García-Perea, P., & Portugal, P. (2000). Labour market outliers: lessons from Portugal and Spain. *Economic Policy, 15*(31), 380–428.

Centro Nacional de Pensões. (2019). *Guia prático – pensão de velhicle.* Instituto da Segurança Social.

Collett, E. (2011). *Immigrant integration in Europe in a time of austerity.* Migration Policy Institute.

EMN. (2014). *Migrant access to social security and healthcare: policies and practice.* European Migration Network.

European Commission. (n.d.). Portugal – old-age pension. ec.europa.eu/social/main.jsp?catId = 1125&langId=en&intPageId=4740.

Garcia, M. T. M. (2017). Overview of the Portuguese three pillar pension system. *International Advances in Economic Research, 23*(2), 175–189.

Horta, A. P. C. B. O., & De Oliveira, M. P.G. (2014). Integration policies: Portugal country report. *Interact Research Report*, 2014/18.

Ingleby, D., Chimienti, M., Hatziprokopiou, P., Ormond, M., & De Freitas, C. (2005). The role of health in integration. In M. L. Fonseca & J. Malheiros (Eds.), *Social integration and mobility: education, housing, and health* (pp. 101–37). University of Lisbon.

Malheiros, J., & Fonseca, L. (Eds.). (2011). *Acesso à habitação e problemas residenciais dos imigrantes em Portugal.* Alto-Comissariado para a imigração e diálogo intercultural.

Matias, A. R., Oliveira, N., & Ortiz, A. (2016). Implementing training in Portuguese for speakers of other languages in Portugal: the case of adult immigrants with little or no schooling. *Language and Intercultural Communication, 16*(1), 99–116.

MISSOC [Mutual Information System on Social Protection]. (2004–18). *Comparative tables on social protection.* www.missoc.org/missoc-database/comparative-tables.

OECD. (1998). *Trends in international migration: annual report, 1998 edition.*

OECD. (2013). *Portugal: reforming the state to promote growth.*

OECD. (2019). *OECD reviews of pension systems: Portugal.*

Oliveira, C. R. (2008). The integration of immigrants in the Portuguese labour market.' *Peer Review*, June 2008, 1–8.

Parliament of Portugal. (1981). Lei n. 37/1981, de 3 de Outubro: Lei da nacionalidade.

Parliament of Portugal. (1984). Lei n. 28/1984 de 14 de Agosto da Segurança Social.

Parliament of Portugal. (2008). Lei n. 27/2008, de 30 de Junho: Concessão de asilo ou protecção subsidiária.

Pato, I., & Pereira, M. (2016). Austerity and (new) limits of segregation in housing policies: the Portuguese case. *International Journal of Housing Policy, 16*(4), 524–542.

Peixoto, J., Marçalo, C., & Tolentino, N. C. (2011). *Imigrantes e segurança social em Portugal.* Alto-Comissariado para a imigração e diálogo intercultural.

Peixoto, J., & Sabino, C. (2009). Immigration, the labour market and policy in Portugal: trends and prospects. *IDEA* working papers, no. 6, April 2009.

Portuguese Refugee Council. (n.d.-a). Health care: Portugal. Country report on Asylum Information Database, www.asylumineurope.org/reports/country/portugal /health-care-0, September 2019.

Portuguese Refugee Council. (n.d.-b). Access to the labour market: Portugal. Country report on Asylum Information Database, www.asylumineurope.org/reports /country/portugal/access-labour-market.

Segurança Social. (n.d.-a). Pensão social de velhice. www.seg-social.pt/pensao-social -de-velhice1.

Segurança Social. (n.d.-b). Complemento solidário para idosos. www.seg-social.pt /complemento-solidario-para-idosos.

Segurança Social. (n.d.-c). Subsídio de desemprego. www.seg-social.pt/subsidio-de -desemprego.

Segurança Social. (n.d.-d). Prestações de desemprego – trabalhar e residir na Europa ou noutro país. www.seg-social.pt/perguntas-frequentes?

Segurança Social. (n.d.-e.). Rendimento social de inserçao. www.seg-social.pt/rendimento-social-de-insercao.

Serviço Nacional de Saúde. (n.d.). História do SNS. www.sns.gov.pt/sns/servico-nacional-de-saude.

Social Security Administration. (2002). Portugal. In *Social security programs throughout the world: Europe, 2002* (pp. 163–167). Social Security Administration, Office of Policy, Office of Research, Evaluation, and Statistics.

Social Security Administration. (2016). Portugal. In *Social security programs throughout the world: Europe, 2002* (pp. 251–261). Social Security Administration, Office of Policy, Office of Research, Evaluation, and Statistics.

Topa, J., Neves, S., & Nogueira, C. (2013). Imigração e saúde: a (in)acessibilidade das mulheres imigrantes aos cuidados de saúde.' *Saúde e Sociedade*, *22*, 328–341.

Spain

Accem. (n.d.-a). Health care: Spain. Country report on Asylum Information Database, https://www.asylumineurope.org/reports/country/spain/health-care.

Accem. (n.d.-b). Access to the labour market: Spain. Country report on Asylum Information Database, www.asylumineurope.org/reports/country/spain/access-labour-market.

Andalusia Board. (2019). Personas titulares y beneficiarias y requisitos para acceder la renta minima de inserción social en Andalucia. www.juntadeandalucia.es/export/drupaljda/Requisitos_personas_titulares_beneficiarias_2019.pdf.

Arriba, A., & Pérez Eransus, B. (2007). La última red de protección social en España: prestaciones asistenciales y su activación. *Política y Sociedad*, *44*(2), 115–133.

Boldrin, M., Jiminez-Martin, S., & Peracchi, F. (1997). Social ecurity and retirement in Spain. NBER working paper, no. 6136.

City of Barcelona. (n.d.). El registro de solicitantes. habitatge.barcelona/es/acceso-a-vivienda/el-registro-de-solicitantes.

Community of Madrid. (n.d.). Requisitos para ser beneficiario de la prestación de renta minima de inserción. www.comunidad.madrid/sites/default/files/requisitos_rmi.pdf.

Dalli, M. (2018). Universal health coverage for undocumented migrants: the Spanish case. *International Journal on Minority and Group Rights*, *25*, 283–299.

Department of Foreign Affairs, European Union, and Cooperation. (n.d.). Nacionalidad española. www.exteriores.gob.es/Portal/es/ServiciosAlCiudadano/InformacionParaExtranjeros/Paginas/Nacionalidad.aspx.

Department of Home Affairs. (n.d.). Residencia de carácter permanente. www.interior.gob.es/web/servicios-al-ciudadano/extranjeria/ciudadanos-de-la-union-europea/residencia-de-caracter-permanente.

Department of Labour and Social Affairs. (2007). *Plan estratégico ciudadanía e integració*. Department of Labour and Social Affairs.

Department of Labour, Migration, and Social Security. (n.d.-a). He trabajado más de un año. www.sepe.es/HomeSepe/Personas/distributiva-prestaciones/quiero-cobrar-el-paro/he-trabajado-mas-de-un-ano.html.

Department of Labour, Migration, and Social Security. (n.d.-b). Me traslado al extranjero. www.sepe.es/HomeSepe/Personas/distributiva-prestaciones/estoy-cobrando-el-paro-y/me-traslado-al-extranjero.html.

Department of Labour, Migration, and Social Security. (n.d.-c). Jubilación ordinaria – requisitos. www.seg-social.es/wps/portal/wss/internet/Trabajadores/PrestacionesPensionesTrabajadores/10963/28393/28396/28472.

Department of Labour, Migration, and Social Security. (n.d.-d). Internacional. www.seg-social.es/wps/portal/wss/internet/InformacionUtil/32078.

Department of Labour, Migration, and Social Security. (n.d.-e). Programas de Integración. extranjeros.mitramiss.gob.es/es/Programas_Integracion/index.html.

Durán, C., & Gutiérrez, J. H. (2008). An evaluation of training programmes for the unemployed in Spain using causal inference. dialnet.unirioja.es/descarga/articulo.

FRA [European Union Agency for Fundamental Rights]. (2011). *Fundamental rights of migrants in an irregular situation in the European Union.* Publications Office of the European Union.

Frydryszak, D., & Macherey, A.-L. (2016). *Legal report on access to healthcare in 17 countries.* Médecins du monde.

Fuentes, F. J. M., & Callejo, M. B. (2011). *Immigration and the welfare state in Spain.* "La Caixa" Welfare Projects.

Gago, E. G. (2016). *Labour market integration of asylum seekers and refugees.* European Commission, Directorate-General for Employment, Social Affairs and Inclusion.

Government of Catalonia (2019). Renta garantizada de ciudadanía – requisitos y documentación para la cita previa. treballiaferssocials.gencat.cat/web/.content/03ambits_tematics/06pobresa_i_inclusio_social.

Institute for the Elderly and Social Services. (n.d.). PNC de jubilación: normativa y requisitos. www.imserso.es/imserso_01/prestaciones_y_subvenciones/pnc_jubilacion/normativa_requisitos/index.htm.

Interview SPA-01. Email correspondence with civil servant at Housing Secretariat of Andalucia.

MISSOC [Mutual Information System on Social Protection]. (2004–18). *Comparative tables on social protection.* www.missoc.org/missoc-database/comparative-tables.

OECD. (2015). *Pensions at a glance 2015: OECD and G20 indicators.*

Pareja-Eastway, M. (2009). The effects of the Spanish housing system on the settlement patterns of immigrants. *Tijdschrift voor Economische en Sociale Geografie, 100*(4), 519–534.

Parliament of Spain (1986). Ley 14/1986, de 25 de abril, General de Sanidad. BOE-A-1986-10499.

Parliament of Spain. (1990). Ley 26/1990, de 20 de diciembre, por la que se establecen en la Seguridad Social prestaciones no contributivas. BOE-A-1990-30939.

Parliament of Spain. (2008). Real Decreto-ley 4/2008, de 19 de septiembre, sobre abono acumulado y de forma anticipada de la prestación contributive por desempleo a trabajadores extranjeros no comunitarios que retornen voluntariamente a sus países de origen. BOE-A-2008-15278.

Peralta-Gallego, L., Gené-Badia, J., & Gallo, P. (2018). Effects of undocumented immigrants exclusion from health care coverage in Spain. *Health Policy, 122*, 1155–1160.

Quevedo, C. H., & Rubio, D. J. (2010). New citizens, new challenges for the Spanish National Health System. *Eurohealth, 16*(1), 24–26.

Rodríguez-Planas, N. (2013). Determinants of immigrants' cash-welfare intake in Spain. *International Journal of Manpower, 34*(2), 167–180.

Sandín-Vázquez, M., Larraz-Antón, R., & Río-Sánchez, I. (2014). Immigrant patient care inequalities: the importance of the intercultural approach. *Procedia – Social and Behavioral Sciences, 132*, 277–284.

Social Security Administration. (2002). Spain. In *Social security programs throughout the world: Europe, 2002* (pp. 190–194). Social Security Administration, Office of Policy, Office of Research, Evaluation, and Statistics.

Social Security Administration. (2016). Spain. In *Social security programs throughout the world: Europe, 2002* (pp. 297–305). Social Security Administration, Office of Policy, Office of Research, Evaluation, and Statistics.

UNHCR. (2000). Organic law on rights and freedoms of aliens in Spain and their social integration: summary and comments by UNHCR. www.refworld.org /pdfid/3b20e810e.pdf.

Sweden

Åslund, O., & Johansson, P. (2011). Virtues of SIN: can intensified public efforts help disadvantaged immigrants? *Evaluation Review, 35*(4), 399–427.

Banting, K., & Koning, E. A. (2017). Just visiting? The weakening of social protection in a mobile world. In A. Triandafyllidou (Ed.), *Multicultural governance in a mobile world* (pp. 108–138). Edinburgh University Press.

Bengtsson, M. (2014). Towards standby-ability: Swedish and Danish activation policies in flux. *International Journal of Social Welfare, 23*, S54–S70.

Bergmark, A., & Palme, J. (2003). Welfare and the unemployment crisis: Sweden in the 1990s. *International Journal of Social Welfare, 12*, 108–122.

Bergnehr, D. (2016). Unemployment and conditional welfare: exclusion and belonging in immigrant women's discourse on being long-term dependent on social assistance. *International Journal of Social Welfare, 25*, 18–26.

Borevi, K. (2012). Sweden: The flagship of multiculturalism. In G. Brochmann & A. Hagelund (Eds.), *Immigration policy and the Scandinavian welfare state 1945–2010* (pp. 25–96). Houndmills: Palgrave Macmillan.

Department of Health and Social Affairs (2003). *The Swedish national pension system.*

Gebhardt, D. (2016). When the state takes over: civic integration programmes and the role of cities in immigrant integration. *Journal of Ethnic and Migration Studies, 42*(5), 742–758.

Glenngård, A. (n.d.). The Swedish healthcare system. international.commonwealthfund.org/countries/sweden.

Gustafsson, B. (2011). Disparities in social assistance receipt between immigrants and natives in Sweden. IZA discussion paper, no. 6129, pp. 1–37.

Hammarstadt, M. (2008). Assimilation and participation in social assistance among immigrants. *International Journal of Social Welfare, 18*(1), 85–94.

Hanenal, R., Krefetz, S. P. M., & Vatury, A. (2013). Housing matters: public housing policy in Israel, the United States, and Sweden. Gazit-Globe Real Estate Institute, working paper GG5/2013.

Johansson, P. (2010). *Sociala rättigheter och migration. Det svenska pensionssystemet i internationella situationer 1946–1993.* Institutet för Framtidsstudier.

Klevmarken, A. (2002). Swedish pension reforms in the 1990s. Conference paper, prepared for Fundacion Ramon Areces conference on Pensions in Europe. core.ac.uk/download/pdf/7089045.pdf.

Koning, E. A. (2019). *Immigration and the politics of welfare exclusion: selective solidarity in Western democracies.* University of Toronto Press.

Konle-Seidl, R., & Bolits, G. (2016). *Labour market integration of refugees: strategies and good practices.* European Parliament (Policy Department A: Economic and Scientific Policy).

Mathias, J. (2017). Reforming the Swedish employment-related social security system: activation, administrative modernization, and strengthening local autonomy. *Regional and Federal Studies, 27*(1), 23–39.

Migrationsinfo. (n.d.). Tillgång till vård. www.migrationsinfo.se/valfard/halsa/tillgang-till-vard.

MISSOC [Mutual Information System on Social Protection], (2004–18). *Comparative tables on social protection.* www.missoc.org/missoc-database/comparative-tables.

National Board of Health and Welfare. (2016). Tolkar för hälso- och sjukvården och tandvården.

OECD. (2016). *Working together: skills and labour market integration of immigrants and their children in Sweden.*

Palmer, E. (2000). *The Swedish pension reform model: framework and issues.* OECD.

Parliament of Sweden. (1982). Hälso- och sjukvårdslag. 1982: 763.

Parliament of Sweden. (1986). Förvaltningslag. 1986: 223.

Pension Agency. (n.d.). Du som är bosatt utanför Sverige. www.pensionsmyndigheten.se/for-pensionarer/pensionar-utanfor-sverige/du-som-ar-bosatt-utanfor-sverige.

Public Employment Agency. (n.d.). När du blir arbetslös. arbetsformedlingen.se/for-arbetssokande/stod-och-ersattning/nar-du-blir-arbetslos.

Social Insurance Agency. (n.d.). Bostadsförmåner. www.forsakringskassan.se/myndigheter/ kommuner/bostadsformaner.

Social Insurance Agency. (2010). Förändringar inom socialförsäkrings- och bidragsområderna 1968-01-01-2010-07-01. Stockholm.

Sondell, M. (2018). *Social housing i Sverige: En paradoxal bostadspolitik?* MA thesis, Uppsala University.

Stadlmaier, J. (2018). Earning citizenship: economic criteria for naturalisation in nine EU countries. *Journal of Contemporary European Studies, 26*(1), 42–63.

Swedish Association of Local Authorities and Regions. (n.d.). Rätten till tolk . skl.se/integrationsocialomsorg/asylochflyktingmottagandeintegration/ansvarsfordelningregelverk/rattentilltolk.25879.html.

Van Aerschot, P. (2014). Shifting policy aims in the reformed Finnish and Swedish integration legislation. In P. Van Aerschot & P. Daenzer (Eds.), *The integration and protection of immigrants: Canadian and Scandinavian critiques* (pp. 51–70). Ashgate.

Weisbrock, A. (2011). The integration of immigrants in Sweden: a model for the European Union? *International Migration, 49*(4), 48–66.

Switzerland

AHV/IV [Alters- und Hinterlassenenversicherung/Invalidenversicherung]. (n.d.-a). Beiträge. www.ahv-iv.ch/de/Sozialversicherungen/Alters-und-Hinterlassenenversicherung-AHV/Beiträge#qa-738.

AHV/IV. (n.d.-b). Internationales. www.ahv-iv.ch/de/Sozialversicherungen/Internationales.

AHV/IV. (2018). *Altersrenten un Hilflosenentschädigungen der AHV.* Brochure 3.01.

AHV/IV. (2019). *Ergänzungsleistungen zur AHV und IV.* Brochure 5.01.

Althaus, E., Schmidt, M., & Glaser, M. (2016). *Nicht-monetäre Dienstleistungen im Bereich Wohnen für armutsbetroffene und -gefährdete Menschen.* Forschungsbericht nr. 2, 2016, Bundesamt für Sozialversicherungen.

Bilger, V., & Hollomey, C. (2011). *Policies on health care for undocumented migrants in Switzerland.* Federal Department of Home Affairs, Federal Office of Public Health, and International Centre for Migration Policy Development.

Bochsler, Y., Ehrler, F., Fritschi, T., Gasser, N., Kehrli, C., Knöpfel, C., & Salzgeber, R. (2015). *Wohnversorgung in der Schweiz: Bestandsaufnahme über Haushalte von Menschen in Armut und in prekären Lebenslagen.* Forschungsbericht nr. 15, 2015, Bundesamt für Sozialversicherungen.

BSV [Bundesamt für Sozialversicherungen]. (2015-a). 'Ergänzungsleistungen [EL].' Retrieved from www.geschichtedersozialensicherheit.ch/institutionen/verwaltung-der-sozialen-sicherheit/ergaenzungsleistungen-el/, September 2019.

BSV. (2015-b). Krankenkassen. www.geschichtedersozialensicherheit.ch/institutionen/kassenwesen/krankenkassen.

BSV. (2015-c). Die Verwaltung der Alters- und Hinterlassenenversicherung. www.geschichtedersozialensicherheit.ch/institutionen/verwaltung-der-sozialen-sicherheit/die-verwaltung-der-alters-und-hinterlassenenversicherung-ahv.

BSV. (2016). Organisation der Sozialhilfe. www.geschichtedersozialensicherheit.ch/institutionen/kantonale-lokale-und-private-institutionen/organisation-der-sozialhilfe.

Duell, N., Tergeist, P., Bazant, U., & Cimper, S. (2010). Activation policies in Switzerland. *OECD social employment and migration working papers.*

Frydryszak, D., & Macherey, A.-L. (2016). *Legal report on access to healthcare in 17 countries.* Médecins du monde.

Housing Cooperatives Switzerland. (n.d.). Wohnungspolitik. www.wbg-schweiz.ch/information/politik/wohnungspolitik.

Hudelson, P., Dao, M. D., Pereneger, T., & Durieux-Paillard, S. (2014). A "migrant friendly hospital" initiative in Geneva, Switzerland: evaluation of the effects on staff knowledge and practices. *PLoS ONE, 9*(9).

Jaeger, F. N., Pellaud, N., Laville, B., & Klauser, P. (2019). The migration-related language barrier and professional interpreter use in primary health care in Switzerland. *BMC Health Services Research, 19*, 1–10.

Leybold-Johnson, I., & Hunt, J. (2016). The place where migrants get free language lessons. www.swissinfo.ch/eng/voucher-scheme_the-place-where-migrants-get-free-language-lessons/42718866.

Liebig, T., Kohls, S., & Krause, K. (2012). *The labour market integration of immigrants and their children in Switzerland.* OECD.

Mexi, M., Russi, P. M., & Fischbasch, A. (2019). Switzerland. In N. Lillie (Ed.), *Policy barriers and enablers* (pp. 463–563). SIRIUS [Skills and Integration of Migrants, Refugees, and Asylum Applicants in European Labour Markets].

MIPEX. (2014). Switzerland. mipex.eu/switzerland.

Navarra, K. (2011). *Health guide to Switzerland: the Swiss healthcare system in brief – a guide for immigrants to Switzerland.* Swiss Red Cross.

Parliament of Switzerland. (1965). Bundesgesetz über Ergänzungsleistungen zur Alters-, Hinterlassenen- und Invalidenversicherung. 19 March.

Parliament of Switzerland. (1982). Bundesgesetz über die obligatorische Arbeitslosenversicherung und die Insolvenzentschädigung. 25 June.

Parliament of Switzerland. (2006). Bundesgesetz über Ergänzungsleistungen zur Alters-, Hinterlassenen- und Invalidenversicherung. 6 October.

Sanchez-Mazas, M. (2015). The construction of "official outlaws": social-psychological and educational implications of a deterrent asylum policy. *Frontiers in Psychology*, 8.

Social Security Administration. (2002). Switzerland. In *Social security programs throughout the world: Europe, 2002* (pp. 200–203). Social Security Administration, Office of Policy, Office of Research, Evaluation, and Statistics.

Social Security Administration. (2016). 'Switzerland.' In *Social security programs throughout the world: Europe, 2002* (pp. 313–319). Social Security Administration, Office of Policy, Office of Research, Evaluation, and Statistics.

State Secretariat for Economic Affairs. (n.d.). What to do if you are unemployed – FAQ. www.arbeit.swiss/secoalv/en/home/menue/institutionen---medien/faq.html.

State Secretariat for Economic Affairs. (2018a). *Ein erster Schritt zur Wiedereingliederung: Arbeitsmarktliche Massnahmen*. Brochure 716-800-2018.

State Secretariat for Economic Affairs. (2018b). *Leistungen bei Arbeitssuche im Ausland*. Brochure 716-204-2018.

State Secretariat for Housing. (n.d.). Gemeinnütziger Wohnungsbau. www.bwo.admin.ch/bwo/de/home/wohnungspolitik/gemeinnuetziger-wohnungsbau.html.

State Secretariat for Migration. (2018). *Swiss social insurance system: period of stay in Switzerland and departure*. State Secretariat for Migration.

Swiss Conference for Social Assistance. (n.d.). Sozialhilfe. skos.ch/themen/sozialhilfe.

Swiss Refugee Council. (n.d.-a). Health care: Switzerland. Country report on Asylum Information Database. www.asylumineurope.org/reports/country/switzerland/reception-conditions/health-care.

Swiss Refugee Council. (n.d.-b). Access to the labour market: Switzerland. Country report on Asylum Information Database. www.asylumineurope.org/reports/country/switzerland/ reception-conditions/employment-and-education/access-labour-market.

Zürich Canton. (1981). Sozialhilfegesetz. 14 June.

United Kingdom

ACH [Ashley Community Housing]. (n.d.). "Refugee accommodation and housing." www.ach.org.uk/refugee-accommodation-housing-uk.

Adams, K. (2007). Should the NHS curb spending on translation services? *BMJ*, *24*(334), 398.

Banting, K., & Koning, E. A. (2017). Just visiting? The weakening of social protection in a mobile world. In A. Triandafyllidou (Ed.), *Multicultural governance in a mobile world* (pp. 108–138). Edinburgh University Press.

Bradshaw, J., & Bennett, F. (2009). *Minimum income schemes in the United Kingdom*. Peer Review in Social Protection and Social Inclusion and Assessment in Social Inclusion.

Bragg, R., & Feldman, R. (2011). "An increasingly uncomfortable environment": access to health care for documented and undocumented migrants in the UK. In R. Sabates-Wheeler & R. Feldman (Eds.), *Migration and social protection: claiming social rights beyond borders* (pp. 91–116). London: Palgrave Macmillan.

Citizens Advice. (n.d.-a). Check if you can get Pension Credit. www.citizensadvice.org.uk/benefits/help-if-on-a-low-income/pension-credit/before-you-claim-pension-credit/check-if-you-can-get-pension-credit.

Citizens Advice. (n.d.-b). After you get refugee status. www.citizensadvice.org.uk/immigration/asylum-and-refugees/after-you-get-refugee-status.

Dell'Olio, F. (2007). Immigration and immigrant policy in Italy and the UK: is housing policy a barrier to a common approach towards immigration in the EU? *Journal of Ethnic and Migration Studies*, *30*(1), 107–128.

Drinkwater, S., & Robinson, C. (2013). Welfare participation by immigrants in the UK. *International Journal of Manpower, 34*(2), 100–112.

Finn, D. (2000). From full employment to employability: a new deal for Britain's unemployed? *International Journal of Manpower, 21*(5), 384–399.

George, R. E., Thornicroft, G., & Dogra, N. (2015). Exploration of cultural competency training in UK healthcare settings: a critical interpretive review of the literature. *Diversity and Equality in Health and Care, 12*(3), 104–115.

Gidley, B. (2012). Monitoring integration in the UK. In R. Bijl & A. Verweij (Eds.), *Measuring and monitoring immigrant integration in Europe* (pp. 344–360). The Netherlands Institute for Social Research.

Glover, S., Gott, C., Loizillon, A., Portes, J., Price, R., Spencer, S., Srinivasan, V., & Willis, C. (2001). *Migration: an economic and social analysis.* London: Home Office.

Government of the United Kingdom. (n.d.-a). Live permanently in the UK. www.gov.uk/browse/visas-immigration/settle-in-the-uk.

Government of the United Kingdom. (n.d.-b). Pension credit. www.gov.uk/pension-credit/eligibility.

Government of the United Kingdom. (n.d.-c). Asylum support. www.gov.uk/asylum-support/what-youll-get.

Government of the United Kingdom. (n.d.-d). Claiming benefits if you live, move, or travel abroad. www.gov.uk/claim-benefits-abroad/jobseekers-allowance.

Government of the United Kingdom. (n.d.-e). The basic state pension: eligibility. www.gov.uk/state-pension/ eligibility.

Griffiths, E. (2019). The housing crisis: UK refugees and asylum seekers. *Open Access Government,* 21 June.

Harris, N. (2016). Demagnetisation of social security and health care for migrants to the UK. *European Journal of Social Security, 18*(2), 130–163.

Herrick, C. (2004). *Integration matters: a national strategy for refugee integration.* Home Office.

Home Office. (2019). *Knowledge of language and life in the UK (version 22.0).* Home Office.

Hunter, T. (2015). A turbulent history of British pensions, since 1874. *The Telegraph,* 9 April.

Jones, D., & Gill, P. (1998). Refugees and primary care: tackling the inequalities. *BMJ, 317,* 1444–1446.

Knight, D. (2013). *State pensions, 2013 edition.* Office for National Statistics. www.ons.gov.uk/economy/investmentspensionsandtrusts/compendium/pensiontrends/2014-11-28/chapter5statepensions2013edition#non-contributory-state-pensions-and-benefits.

McColl, K., Pickworth, S., & Raymond, I. (2006). Project: London – supporting vulnerable populations. *BMJ, 332,* 115–117.

McIntyre, N. (2017). Migrants told to learn English upon entering UK face three-year wait for lessons. *The Independent,* 9 January.

NHS [National Health Service]. (n.d.). Get help with dental costs. www.nhs.uk/using-the-nhs/help-with-health-costs/get-help-with-dental-costs.

North Lanarkshire Council. (2017). *A guide to rights and entitlements to services and benefits for refugees, asylum seekers, and migrant workers.* www.northlanarkshire.gov.uk/CHttpHandler.ashx?id=4227&p=0.

Parliament of the United Kingdom. (1968). Race Relations Act 1968. UK Public General Acts, 1968 c. 71.

Parliament of the United Kingdom. (1975). Social Security Act 1975. UK Public General Acts, 1975, c. 14.

Parliament of the United Kingdom. (1995). Jobseekers Act 1995. UK Public General Acts, 1995 c. 18.

Parliament of the United Kingdom. (2006). Statement of Changes in Immigration Rules. Standing Committee on Delegated Legislation, 20 June. publications.parliament.uk/pa/cm200506/ cmstand/deleg2/st060620/60620s01.htm.

Refugee Council. (n.d.). Health care: United Kingdom. Country report on Asylum Information Database. www.asylumineurope.org/reports/country/united-kingdom/reception-conditions/health-care.

Rutter, J. (2013). *Back to basics: towards a successful and cost-effective integration policy.* Institute for Public Policy Research.

Sage, D. (2015). Do active labour market policies promote the well-being, health, and social capital of the unemployed? Evidence from the UK. *Social Indicators Research, 124*, 319–337.

Social Security Administration. (2002). United Kingdom. In *Social security programs throughout the world: Europe, 2002* (pp. 208–213). Social Security Administration, Office of Policy, Office of Research, Evaluation, and Statistics.

Social Security Administration. (2016). 'United Kingdom.' In *security programs throughout the world: Europe, 2002* (pp. 332–340). Social Security Administration, Office of Policy, Office of Research, Evaluation, and Statistics.

Stadlmaier, J. (2018). Earning citizenship: economic criteria for naturalisation in nine EU countries. *Journal of Contemporary European Studies, 26*(1), 42–63.

Vlachantoni, A., Feng, Z., Evandrou, M., & Falkingham, J. (2017). Ethnic elders and pension protection in the United Kingdom. *Ageing and Society, 37*, 1025–1049.

Wu, J. (2000). Unemployment-related benefits system in the United Kingdom. Hong Kong Legislative Council Secretariat, Research and Library Services Division.

United States

Adess, S., Goodman, J., Kysel, I., Pacyniak, G., Polcyn, L., Schau, J., Shum, K., Wala, R., & Waddell, A. (Eds.). (2009). *Refugee crisis in America: Iraqis and heir resettlement experience.* Georgetown University Law Center, Human Rights Institute.

Bloemraad, I., & De Graauw, E. (2012). Immigrant integration and policy in the United States: a loosely stitched patchwork. In J. Frideres & J. Biles (Eds.), *International perspectives: integration and inclusion* (pp. 205–234). McGill–Queen's University Press.

Borjas, G. (2002). Welfare reform and immigrant participation in welfare programs. *International Migration Review, 36*(4), 1093–1123.

Borjas, G. (2003). Welfare reform, labour supply, and health insurance in the immigrant population. *Journal of Health Economics, 22*, 933–958.

Borjas, G. (2011). Social security eligibility and the labor supply of older immigrants. *Industrial and Labour Relations Review, 64*(3), 485–501.

Borjas, G., & Hilton, L. (1996). Immigration and the welfare state: immigrant participation in means-tested entitlement programs. *Quarterly Journal of Economics, 111*(2), 575–604.

Bown, C. P., & Freund, C. (2019). Active labor market policies: lessons from other countries for the United States. Working paper, Peterson Institute for International Economics.

Bradley, D. H., & Stephens, J. D. (2007). Employment performance in OECD countries. *Comparative Political Studies, 40*(12), 1486–1510.

Bronchetti, E. T. (2014). Public insurance expansions and the health of immigrants and Native children. *Journal of Public Economics, 120*, 205–219.

Bruno, A. (2011). U.S. refugee resettlement assistance. *Congressional Research Service*, 7-5700.

Butz, A. M., & Kehrberg, J. E. (2015). Social distrust and immigrant access to welfare programs in the American states. *Politics and Policy, 43*(2), 256–286.

Crépon, B., & Van den Berg, G. J. (2016). Active labor market policies. IZA discussion paper series, no. 10321.

Department of Health and Human Services. (2012). 400-refugee resettlement program. www.acf.hhs.gov/orr/resource/400-refugee-resettlement-program.

Department of Housing and Urban Development. (n.d.). Rental assistance. www.hud.gov/topics/rental_assistance.

Department of Justice. (1999). Field guidance on deportability and inadmissibility on public charge grounds. *Federal Register, 64*(101), 28689–28693.

Department of Labor. (n.d.). State unemployment insurance benefits. oui.doleta.gov/unemploy/uifactsheet.asp.

Department of Labor. (1974). Unemployment insurance program letter no. 1276. 22 July. Retrieved from oui.doleta.gov/dmstree/uipl/uipl_pre75/uipl_1276.htm.

Fix, M., & Passel, J. (2002). *The scope and impact of welfare reform's immigrant provisions.* Urban Institute.

Fix, M., & Zimmerman, W. (1994). After arrival: an overview of federal immigrant policy in the United States. In B. Edmonston & J. S. Passel (Eds.), *Immigration and ethnicity: the integration of America's newest arrivals.* Urban Institute Press.

Government Printing Office. (1934). *42 US Code chapter 8 – low-income housing.*

Grubbs, V., Chen, A. H., Bindman, A. B., Vittinghoff, E., & Fernandez, A. (2006). Effect of awareness of language law on language access in the health care setting. *Journal of General Internal Medicine, 21*(7), 683–688.

Ku, L., & Matani, S. (2001). Left out: immigrants' access to health care and insurance. *Health Affairs, 20*(1), 247–256.

Leimsidor, B. (1982). The matching grant program. *In Defense of the Alien*, *5*, 108–111.

Mathema, S. (2018). What works: innovative approaches to improving refugee integration. www.americanprogress.org/issues/immigration/reports/2018/02/28/447283/what-works.

Mercy Housing. (n.d.). *Refugee housing technical assistance program.* Mercy Housing.

Nam, Y. (2012). Welfare reform and older immigrant adults' Medicaid and health insurance coverage: Cchanges caused by chilling effects of welfare reform, protective citizenship, or distinct effects of labour market condition by citizenship? *Journal of Aging and Health*, *24*(4), 616–640.

Nam, Y., & Kim, W. (2012). Welfare reform and elderly immigrants' naturalization: access to public benefits as an incentive for naturalization in the United States. *International Migration Review*, *46*(3), 656–679.

National Immigration Law Center (2014). Federal guidance on public charge: when is it safe to use public benefits? National Immigration Law Center.

Negash, E. (2015). Expansion of Medicaid eligibility under the Affordable Care Act and compliance with ORR regulations at 45 CFR 400.101. www.acf.hhs.gov/orr/resource/state-letter-13-10.

Office of the Federal Register. (2000). *Code of federal regulations 24: Housing and urban development.*

Olsen, G. M. (2002). *The politics of the welfare state: Canada, Sweden, and the United States.* Oxford University Press.

Olson, L. (2006). *At home with refugee housing: Resettlement to integration.* Mercy Housing.

Potochnick, S. (2016). Reversing welfare reform? Immigrant restoration efforts and food stamp receipt among Mexican immigrant families. *Social Science Research*, 60: 88–99.

Ross, C. (2002). *Immigrants and health care.* Washington and Lee University Library Special Collections and Archives.

Sainsbury, D. (2006). Immigrants' social rights in comparative perspective: welfare regimes, forms of immigration and immigration policy regimes. *Journal of European Social Policy*, *16*(3), 229–244.

Teitelbaum, J., Cartwright-Smith, L., & Rosenbaum, S. (2012). Translating rights into access: language access and the Affordable Care Act. *American Journal of Law and Medicine*, *38*, 348–373.

SSA [Social Security Administration]. (2003). United States. In *Social security programs throughout the World: the Americas* (pp. 135–140).

SSA. (2004). Additional requirements for alien workers – Social Security Protection Act of 2004. secure.ssa.gov/poms.nsf/lnx/0300301102.

SSA. (2015). United States. In *Social security programs throughout the World: the Americas* (pp. 211–218).

SSA. (2018). Your payments while you are outside the United States. Publication no. 05-10137.

SSA. (2019). What you need to know when you get supplemental security income (SSI). Publication no. 05-11011.

SSA. (n.d.). Determining insured status. www.ssa.gov/OP_Home/handbook /handbook.02/handbook-0201.html.

State of California Employment Development Department. (n.d.). Eligibility requirements. www.edd.ca.gov/unemployment/Eligibility.htm.

Texas Workforce Commission. (n.d.). Ongoing eligibility requirements for receiving unemployment benefits.' twc.texas.gov/jobseekers/ongoing-eligibility-requirements -receiving-unemployment-benefits#citizenshipOrWorkAuthorization.

Zimmerman, W., & Tumlin, K. C. (1999). *Patchwork policies: state assistance for immigrants under welfare reform.* Urban Institute.

Bibliography

Abrajano, Marisa, and Zoltan L. Hajnal. 2015. *White Backlash: Immigration, Race, and American Politics*. Princeton: Princeton University Press.

Adams, Ryan. 2012. "Danny Boyle's Intro on Olympics Programme." *Awards Daily*, 27 July.

Adsera, Alicia, and Barry R. Chiswick. 2007. "Are There Gender and Country of Origin Differences in Immigrant Labor Market Outcomes across European Destinations?" *Journal of Population Economics* 20(3): 495–526. http://doi.org/10.1007/s00148-006-0082-y.

Akkerman, Tjitske. 2012. "Comparing Radical Right Parties in Government: Immigration and Integration Policies in Nine Countries (1996–2010)." *West European Politics* 35(3): 511–29. https://doi.org/10.1080/01402382.2012.665738.

Albertazzi, Daniele. 2009. "Reconciling 'Voice' and 'Exit': Swiss and Italian Populists in Power." *Politics* 29(1): 1–10. http://doi.org/10.1111/j.1467-9256.2008.01332.x.

Alesina, Alberto, and Edward Glaeser. 2004. *Fighting Poverty in the US and Europe*. Oxford: Oxford University Press.

Alexander, Shannon. 2010. "Humanitarian Bottom League? Sweden and the Right to Health for Undocumented Migrants." *European Journal of Migration and Law* 12(2): 215–40. https://doi.org/10.1163/157181610X496885.

Allan, James P., and Lyle Scruggs. 2004. "Political Partisanship and Welfare State Reform in Advanced Industrial Societies." *American Journal of Political Science* 48(3): 496–512. https://doi.org/10.1111/j.0092-5853.2004.00083.x.

Almond, Gabriel. 1991. "Capitalism and Democracy." *PS: Political Science and Politics* 24(3): 467–74. http://doi.org/10.14738/abr.54.3076.

Amuedo-Dorantes, Catalina, and Sara De la Rica. 2007. "Labour Market Assimilation of Recent Immigrants in Spain." *British Journal of Industrial Relations* 45(2): 257–84. https://doi.org/10.1111/j.1467-8543.2007.00614.x.

Andersen, John, Jørgen Elm Larsen, and Iver Hornemann Møller. 2009. "The Exclusion and Marginalisation of Immigrants in the Danish Welfare Society: Dilemmas and

Challenges." *International Journal of Sociology and Social Policy* 29(5–6): 274–86. https://doi.org/10.1108/01443330910965804.

Andersen, Jørgen Goul. 2007. "Restricting Access to Social Protection for Immigrants in the Danish Welfare State." *Benefits* 15(3): 257–69.

Andersen, Jørgen Goul, and Tor Bjorklund. 1990. "Structural Changes and New Cleavages: The Progress Parties in Denmark and Norway." *Acta Sociologica* 33(3): 195–217. https://doi.org/10.1177/000169939003300303.

Anderson, Bridget. 2015. "'Heads I Win. Tails You Lose': Migration and the Worker Citizen." *Current Legal Problems* 68(1): 179–96. https://doi.org/10.1093/clp/cuv012.

Anderson, Bridget, and Martin Ruhs. 2008. "A Need for Migrant Labour? The Micro-Level Determinants of Staff Shortages and Implications for a Skills Based Immigration Policy." Paper prepared for the Migration Advisory Committee (MAC), London.

Andersson, Eva K., Bo Malmberg, Rafael Costa, Bart Sleutjes, Martin Jan Stonawski, and H.A.G. de Valk. 2018. "A Comparative Study of Segregation Patterns in Belgium, Denmark, the Netherlands, and Sweden: Neighbourhood Concentration and Representation of Non-European Migrants." *European Journal of Population* 34(2): 251–75. https://doi.org/10.1007/s10680-018-9481-5.

Antecol, Heather, and Kelly Bedard. 2006. "Unhealthy Assimilation: Do Immigrants Converge to American Weight?" *Demography* 43(2): 337–60. http://doi.org/10.1353/dem.2006.0011.

Anzenberger, Judith, Andrea Bodenwinkler, and Elisabeth Breyer. 2015. "Migration und Gesundheit: Literaturbericht zur Situation in Österreich." Vienna: Gesundheit Österreich GmbH.

Ariu, Andrea, Frédéric Docquier, and Mara P. Squicciarini. 2016. "Governance Quality and Net Migration Flows." *Regional Science and Urban Economics* 60: 238–48. https://doi.org/10.1016/j.regsciurbeco.2016.07.006.

Ataç, Ilker. 2019. "Gaygusuz v. Austria: Advancing the Rights of Non-Citizens through Litigation." *Österreichische Zeitschrift für Politikwissenschaft* 46: 21–31. https://doi.org/10.15203/ozp.1588.vol46iss1.

Atzmüller, Roland. 2009. "Die Entwicklung der Arbeitsmarktpolitik in Österreich." *Kurswechsel: Zeitschrift für gesellschafts-, wirtschafts-und umweltpolitische Alternativen* 4: 24–34.

Avery, James M., Jefferey A. Fine, and Timothy Márquez. 2017. "Racial Threat and the Influence of Latino Turnout on State Immigration Policy." *Social Science Quarterly* 98(2): 750–65. https://doi.org/10.1111/ssqu.12326.

Bachner, Florian, Joy Ladurner, Katharina Habimana, Herwig Ostermann, Isabel Stadler, and Claudia Habl. 2013. "Das österreichische Gesundheitswesen im internationalen Vergleich." Vienna: Gesundheit Österreich GmbH.

Baganha, Maria Ioannis. 2009. "The Lusophone Migratory System: Patterns and Trends." *International Migration* 47(3): 5–20. https://doi.org/10.4000/eces.3307.

Bale, Tim. 2003. "Cinderella and Her Ugly Sisters: The Mainstream and Extreme Right in Europe's Bipolarising Party Systems." *West European Politics* 26(3): 67–90. https://doi.org/10.1080/01402380312331280598.

Banting, Keith. 1999. "Social Citizenship and the Multicultural Welfare State." In *Citizenship, Diversity, and Pluralism*, ed. A.C. Cairns, J.C. Courtney, P. MacKinnon, H.J. Michelmann, and D.E. Smith, 108–136. Montreal: McGill-Queen's University Press.

– 2000. "Looking in Three Directions: Migration and the European Welfare State in Comparative Perspective." In *Immigration and Welfare: Challenging the Borders of the Welfare State*, ed. A. Geddes and M. Bommes, 13–33. London: Routledge.

Banting, Keith G., and Edward A. Koning. 2017. "Just Visiting? The Weakening of Social Protection in a Mobile World." In *Multicultural Governance in a Mobile World*, ed. A. Triandafyllidou, 108–35. Edinburgh: Edinburgh University Press.

Banting, Keith, and Will Kymlicka. 2006. *Multiculturalism and the Welfare State: Recognition and Redistribution in Contemporary Democracies*. Oxford: Oxford University Press.

– 2017. *The Strains of Commitment: The Political Sources of Solidarity in Diverse Societies*. Oxford: Oxford University Press.

– 2020. Banting, Keith, and Will Kymlicka. Multiculturalism Policy Index. http://www.queensu.ca/mcp.

Barbalescu, Roxana, and Adriana Favell. 2019. "Commentary: A Citizenship without Social Rights? EU Freedom of Movement and Changing Access to Welfare Rights?" *International Migration* 58(1): 151–65. https://doi.org/10.1111/imig.12607.

Bárcena-Martin, Elena, and Salvador Pérez-Moreno. 2017. "Immigrant-Native Gap in Poverty: A Cross-National European Perspective." *Review of Economics of the Household* 15(4). https://link.springer.com/article/10.1007/s11150-015-9321-x.

Barrett, Alan, and David Duffy. 2008. "Are Ireland's Immigrants Integrating into Its Labor Market?" *International Migration Review* 42(3): 597–619. https://doi.org/10.1111/j.1747-7379.2008.00139.x.

Barrett, Alan, and Bertrand Maître. 2011. "Immigrant Welfare Receipt across Europe." *International Journal of Manpower* 34(1): 8–23. http://doi.org/10.1108/01437721311319629.

Barrett, Alan, and Yvonne McCarthy. 2008. "Immigrants and Welfare Programmes: Exploring the Interactions between Immigrant Characteristics, Immigrant Welfare Dependence, and Welfare Policy." *Oxford Review of Economic Policy* 24(3): 542–59. http://doi.org/10.1093/oxrep/grn026.

Barry, Brian. 2001. *Culture and Equality*. Cambridge, MA: Harvard University Press.

Bartels, Larry M. 2002. "Beyond the Running Tally: Partisan Bias in Political Perceptions." *Political Behavior* 24(2): 117–50. https://doi.org/10.1023/A:1021226224601.

Bartfeld, Judith, Craig Gundersen, Timothy M. Smeeding, and James P. Ziliak. 2015. *Snap Matters: How Food Stamps Affect Health and Well-Being*. Stanford: Stanford University Press.

Bauböck, Rainer. 1996. "»Nach Rasse und Sprache verschieden«. Migrationspolitik in Österreich von der Monarchie bis heute." [Vienna]. *Reihe Politikwissenschaft* 31. https://www.ihs.ac.at/publications/pol/pw_31.pdf.

– 2011. "Temporary Migrants, Partial Citizenship and Hypermigration." *Critical Review of International Social and Political Philosophy* 14(5): 665–93. https://doi.org/10.1080/13698230.2011.617127.

Bay, Ann-Helén, Henning Finseraas, and Axel West Pedersen. 2013. "Welfare Dualism in Two Scandinavian Welfare States: Public Opinion and Party Politics." *West European Politics* 36(1): 199–220. https://doi.org/10.1080/01402382.2013.742757.

Beine, Michel, Anna Boucher, Brian Burgoon, Mary Crock, Justin Gest, Michael Hiscox, Patrick McGovern, Hillel Rapoport, Joep Schaper, and Eiko Thilemann. 2016. "Comparing Immigration Policies: An Overview from the IMPALA Database." *International Migration Review* 50(4): 827–63. http://doi.org/10.1111/imre.12169.

Benhabib, Seyla. 2002. "Transformations of Citizenship: The Case of Contemporary Europe." *Government and Opposition* 37(4): 439–65. http://doi.org/10.1111/1477-7053.00110.

Benish, Avishai, and David Levi-Faur. 2020. "The Expansion of Regulation in Welfare Governance." *Annals of the American Academy of Political and Social Science* 691(1): 17–29. http://doi.org/10.1177/0002716220949230.

Beveridge, William. 1942. Social Insurance and Allied Services. Report by Sir William Beveridge. London: HMSO.

Biavaschi, Costanza, and Klaus F. Zimmerman. 2014. "Eastern Partnership Migrants in Germany: Outcomes, Potentials, and Challenges." *IZA Journal of European Labor Studies* 3(1): 7. http://doi.org/10.1186/2193-9012-3-7.

Biffl, Gudrun. 1997. "Die Zuwanderung von Ausländern nach Österreich: Kosten-Nutzen-Überlegungen und Fragen der Sozialtransfers." *WIFO-Monatsberichte* 70(9): 557–65.

Biffl, Gudrun, and Anna Faustmann. 2013. "Österreichische Integrationspolitik im EU-Vergleich Zur Aussagekraft von MIPEX." Krems: Edition Donau-Universitsät Krems.

Bjerre, Liv, Marc Helbling, Friederike Römer, and Maltas Zobel. 2015. "Conceptualizing and Measuring Immigration Policies: A Comparative Perspective." *International Migration Review* 49(3): 555–600. https://doi.org/10.1111/imre.12100.

– 2016. "The Immigration Policies in Comparison (IMPIC) Dataset." Wissenschaftzentrum Berlin, discussion paper 2016–2201.

Blalock, Hubert M. 1960. "A Power Analysis of Racial Discrimination." *Social Forces* 39(1): 53–9. https://doi.org/10.2307/2573575.

Blatter, Joachim, Samuel Schmid, and Andrea S. Blättler. 2015. "The Immigrant Inclusion Index (IMIX): A Tool for Assessing the Electoral Inclusiveness of Democracies with Respect to Immigrants." Paper no. 8, working paper series "Glocal Governance and Democracy," University of Lucerne.

Blau, Francine D., and Christopher Mackie, eds. 2017. *The Economic and Fiscal Consequences of Immigration*. Washington, DC: National Academies Press.

Bloemraad, Irene. 2006. *Becoming a Citizen: Incorporating Immigrants and Refugees in the United States and Canada*. Berkeley: University of California Press.

Bloom, Tendayi. 2017. *Noncitizenism: Recognising Noncitizen Capabilities in a World of Citizens*. London: Routledge.
Blume, Kræn, Björn Gustafsson, Peder J. Pedersen, and Mette Verner. 2007. "At the Lower End of the Table: Determinants of Poverty among Immigrants to Denmark and Sweden." *Journal of Ethnic and Migration Studies* 33(3): 373–96. https://doi.org/10.1080/13691830701234517.
Blume, Kræn, and Mette Verner. 2007. "Welfare Dependency among Danish Immigrants." *European Journal of Political Economy* 23(2): 453–71. https://doi.org/10.1016/j.ejpoleco.2006.08.005.
Boehme, Eric. 2011. "Recession and the Risks of Illegality: Governing the Undocumented in the United States." *New Political Science* 33(4): 541–54. https://doi.org/10.1080/07393148.2011.619824.
Bommes, Michael, and Andrew Geddes. 2000. *Immigration and Welfare: Challenging the Borders of the Welfare State*. London: Routledge.
Boräng, Frida. 2015. "Large-Scale Solidarity? Effects of Welfare State Institutions on the Admission of Forced Migrants." *European Journal of Political Research* 54(2): 216–31. https://doi.org/10.1111/1475-6765.12075.
Borjas, George J. 1985. "Assimilation, Changes in Cohort Quality, and the Earning of Immigrants." *Journal of Labor Economics* 3(4): 463–89.
– 1995. "The Economic Benefits from Immigration." *Journal of Economic Perspectives* 9(2): 3–22. https://doi.org/10.1257/jep.9.2.3.
– 1999. "Immigration and Welfare Magnets." *Journal of Labor Economics* 17(4): 607–37.
– 2005. "The Labor-Market Impact of High-Skill Immigration." *American Economic Review* 95(2): 56–60. https://doi.org/10.1257/000282805774670040.
Borjas, George J., and Lynette Hilton. 1996. "Immigration and the Welfare State: Immigrant Participation in Means-Tested Entitlement Programs." *Quarterly Journal of Economics* 111(2): 575–604. https://doi.org/10.2307/2946688.
Bösch, Valerie, Tanja Jandl-Gartner, Robert Jellasitz, Ingrid Nagl, Sigrid Röhrich, and Johannes Schweighofer. 2012. "Aktive Arbeitsmarktpolitik in Österreich: 1994–2012." Vienna: BMASK.
Bosniak, Linda. 1998. "The Citizenship of Aliens." *Social Text* 56: 29–35.
– 2006. *The Citizen and the Alien: Dilemmas of Contemporary Membership*. Princeton: Princeton University Press.
Boso, Alex, and Mihaela Vancea. 2016. "Should Irregular Migrants Have the Right to Healthcare? Lesson Learnt from the Spanish Case." *Critical Social Policy* 36(2): 225–45. https://doi.org/10.1177/0261018315624174.
Boucher, Anna. 2014. "Familialism and Migrant Welfare Policy: Restrictions on Social Security Provisions for Newly Arrived Immigrants." *Policy and Politics* 42(3): 367–84. http://doi.org/10.1332/030557312X655602.
Brady, David, and Ryan Finnigan. 2014. "Does Immigration Undermine Public Support for Social Policy?" *American Sociological Review* 79(1): 17–42. http://doi.org/10.1177/0003122413513022.

Brady, David, Evelyne Huber, and John D. Stephens. 2020. "Comparative Welfare States Data Set." University of North Carolina and WZB Berlin Social Science Center.

Brameshuber, Elisabeth. 2018. "Soziale Rechte für Drittstaatsangehörige." In *Migration, Arbeitsmarkt and Sozialpolitik*, ed. B. Schrattbauer, W.J. Pfeil, and R. Mosler, 249–76. Austria: MANZ Verlag Wien.

Bratsberg, Bernt, and Oddbjörn Raaum. 2020. "*Utenlandsk arbeidskraft i Norge 1990–2017*." Oslo: Frischsenteret.

Bratsberg, Bernt, Oddbjørn Raaum, og Knut Røed. 2011. *Yrkesdeltaking på lang sikt blant innvandrergrupper i Norge (Frisch Rapport 1/2011)*. Oslo: Frischsenteret.

– 2017. "Immigrant Labor Market Integration across Admission Classes." *Nordic Economic Policy Review* 7: 17–54.

Brettell, Caroline B., and James F. Hollifield. 2008. *Migration Theory: Talking across Disciplines*. London: Routledge.

Brochmann, Grete, and Jon Erik Dolvik. 2018. "The Welfare State and International Migration: The European Challenge." In *Routledge Handbook of the Welfare State*, ed. B. Greve. London: Routledge.

Brochmann, Grete, and Anne S. Grødem. 2019. "Absorption Capacity as Means for Assessing Sustainable Immigration." EMN Norway Occasional Papers, European Migration Network. Oslo: Norwegian Ministry of Justice and Public Security.

Brochmann, Grete, and Anniken Hagelund. 2012. *Immigration Policy and the Scandinavian Welfare State 1945–2010*. London: Palgrave Macmillan.

Brochmann, Grete, and Knut Kjeldstadli. 2008. *A History of Immigration: The Case of Norway 900–2000*. Oslo: Universitetsforlaget.

Brooks, Clem, and Jeff Manza. 2008. *Why Welfare States Persist: The Importance of Public Opinion in Democracies*. Chicago: University of Chicago Press.

Brubaker, William Rogers. 1989. "Membership without Citizenship: The Economic and Social Rights of Noncitizens." In *Immigration and the Politics of Citizenship in Europe and North America*, ed. W.R. Brubaker, 145–62. New York: German Marshall Fund of the United States and the University Press of America.

Budiman, Abby. 2020. "Key Findings about U.S. Immigrants." Pew Research Center, 20 August. https://www.pewresearch.org/fact-tank/2020/08/20/key-findings-about-u-s-immigrants.

Budiman, Abby, Christine Tamir, Lauren Mora, and Luis Noe-Bustamante. 2020. "Facts on U.S. Immigrants, 2018." Pew Research Center, 20 August. https://www.pewresearch.org/hispanic/2020/08/20/facts-on-u-s-immigrants-current-data/.

Bundesministerium für Gesundheit und Frauen. 2012. "Gesundheitsziele Österreich. Richtungsweisende Vorschläge für ein gesünderes Österreich." Accessed June 11, 2020. https://gesundheitsziele-oesterreich.at/website2017/wp-content/uploads/2018/08/gz_kurzfassung_2018.pdf.

Burgoon, Brian. 2014. "Immigration, Integration, and Support for Redistribution in Europe." *World Politics* 66(3): 365–405. https://doi.org/10.1017/S0043887114000100.

Burgoon, Brian, and Matthijs Rooduijn. 2020. "Immigrationization of Welfare Politics? Anti-Immigration and Welfare Attitudes in Context." *West European Politics* 44(2): 177–203. https://doi.org/10.1080/01402382.2019.1702297.

Burns, Marguerite, and Laura Dague. 2017. "The Effect of Expanding Medicaid Eligibility on Supplemental Security Income Program Participation." *Journal of Public Economics* 149: 20–34. http://doi.org/10.1016/j.jpubeco.2017.03.004.

Buss, Christopher. 2019. "Public Opinion Towards Targeted Labour Market Policies: A Vignette Study on the Perceived Deservingness of the Unemployed." *Journal of European Social Policy* 29(2): 228–40. https://doi.org/10.1177/0958928718757684.

Butschek, Sebastian, and Thomas Walter. 2014. "What Active Labour Market Programmes Work for Immigrants in Europe? A Meta-Analysis of the Evaluation Literature." *IZA Journal of Migration* 3(1): 1–18. http://doi.org/10.2139/ssrn.2316258.

Butz, Adam, and Jason E. Kehrberg. 2015. "Social Distrust and Immigrant Access to Welfare Programs in the American States." *Politics and Policy* 43(2): 256–86. http://doi.org/10.1111/polp.12115.

Calmfors, Lars, and Nora S. Gassen. 2019. "Integrating Immigrants into the Nordic Labour Markets." Nordic Council of Ministers (24). Copenhagen: Nordic Council of Ministers.

Caminada, Koen, Kees Goudswaard, and Olaf van Vliet 2010. "Patterns of Welfare State Indicators in the EU: Is There Convergence?" *Journal of Common Market Studies* 48(3): 529–56. https://doi.org/10.1111/j.1468-5965.2010.02063.x.

Cangiano, Alessio. 2014. "Migration Policies and Migrant Employment Outcomes." *Comparative Migration Studies* 2(4): 417–43. https://link.springer.com/article/10.5117/CMS2014.4.CANG.

Cappelen, Cornelius, and Yvette Peters. 2018. "The Impact of Intra-EU Migration on Welfare Chauvinism." *Journal of Public Policy* 38(3): 389–417. http://doi.org/10.1017/S0143814X17000150.

Capps, Randy, Jacqueline Hagan, and Nestor Rodriguez. 2004. "Border Residents Manage the U.S. Immigration and Welfare Reforms." In *Immigrants, Welfare Reform, and the Poverty of Policy*, ed. P. Kretsedemas and A. Aparicio, 229–51. Westport: Praeger.

Carlsson, Magnus, and Dan Olof Rooth. 2007. "Evidence of Ethnic Discrimination in the Swedish Labor Market Using Experimental Data." *Labour Economics* 14(4): 716–29. https://doi.org/10.1016/j.labeco.2007.05.001.

Carrera, Sergio. 2005. "What Does Free Movement Mean in Theory and Practice in an Enlarged EU?" *European Law Journal* 11(6): 699–721. https://doi.org/10.1111/j.1468-0386.2005.00283.

Castles, Francis G., and Deborah Mitchell. 1993. "Worlds of Welfare and Families of Nations." In *Families of Nations: Patterns of Public Policy in Western Democracies*, ed. F.G. Castles, 93–128. Aldershot: Dartmouth.

Castronova, Edward J., Hilke Kayser, Joachim R. Frick, and Gert G. Wagner. 2001. "Immigrants, Natives and Social Assistance: Comparable Take-Up under

Comparable Circumstances." *International Migration Review* 35(3): 726–48. https://doi.org/10.1111/j.1747-7379.2001.tb00038.x.

Chavez, Leo R. 2008. *The Latino Threat: Constructing Immigrants, Citizens, and the Nation*. Stanford: Stanford University Press.

Chiswick, Barry R. 1978. "The Effect of Americanization on the Earnings of Foreign-Born Men." *Journal of Political Economy* 86(5): 897–921. https:///doi.org/10.1086/260717.

Chiswick, Barry R., and Paul W. Miller. 2003. "The Complementarity of Language and Other Human Capital: Immigrant Earnings in Canada." *Economics of Education Review* 22(5): 469–80. https://doi.org/10.1016/S0272-7757(03)00037-2.

– 2005. "Do Enclaves Matter in Immigrant Adjustment?" *City and Community* 4(1): 5–35. https://doi.org/10.1111/j.1535-6841.2005.00101.x.

– 2011. "The 'Negative' Assimilation of Immigrants: A Special Case." *ILR Review* 64(3): 502–25. https://doi.org/10.1177/001979391106400305.

Chow, Gregory C., and An-loh Lin. 1971. "Best Linear Unbiased Interpolation, Distribution, and Extrapolation of Times Series by Related Series." *Review of Economic and Statistics* 53(4), 372–5. https://doi.org/10.2307/1928739.

Chueri, Juliana. 2020. "Social Policy Outcomes of Government Participation by Radical Right Parties." *Party Politics*: 1354068820923496: 1–13.

Citrin, Jack, Donald P. Green, Christopher Muste, and Cara Wong. 1997. "Public Opinion toward Immigration Reform: The Role of Economic Motivations." *Journal of Politics* 59(3): 858–81. http://doi.org/10.2307/2998640.

Clark, Ken, and Stephen Drinkwater. 2008. "The Labour-Market Performance of Recent Migrants." *Oxford Review of Economic Policy* 24(3): 496–517. http://doi.org/10.1093/oxrep/grn023.

Clausen, Jens, Eskil Heinesen, Hans Hummelgaard, Leif Husted, and Michael Rosholm. 2009. "The Effect of Integration Policies on the Time until Regular Employment of Newly Arrived Immigrants: Evidence from Denmark." *Labour Economics* 16(4): 409–17. http://doi.org/10.1016/j.labeco.2008.12.006.

Cohen, Elizabeth F. 2009. *Semi-Citizenship in Democratic Politics*. Cambridge: Cambridge University Press.

Collier, Paul. 2013. *Exodus: Immigration and Multiculturalism in the 21st Century*. Oxford: Oxford University Press.

Conant, Lisa. 2006. "Individuals, Courts, and the Development of European Social Rights." *Comparative Political Studies* 39(1): 76–100.

Condon, Meghan, Alexandra Filindra, and Amber Wichowsky. 2015. "Immigrant Inclusion in the Safety Net: A Framework for Analysis and Effects on Educational Attainment." *Policy Studies Journal* 44(4): 424–48. https://doi.org/10.1111/psj.12140.

Connor, Phillip, and Matthias Koenig. 2015. "Explaining the Muslim Employment Gap in Western Europe: Individual-Level Effects and Ethno-Religious Penalties." *Social Science Research* 49: 191–201. https://doi.org/10.1016/j.ssresearch.2014.08.001.

Constant, Amelie F., Martin Kahanec, and Klaus F. Zimmermann. 2009. "Attitudes towards Immigrants, Other Integration, and Their Veracity." *International Journal of Manpower* 30: 5–14. http://doi.org/10.1108/01437720910948357.

Cox, Robert Henry. 2001. "The Social Construction of an Imperative: Why Welfare Reform Happened in Denmark and the Netherlands but not in Germany." *World Politics* 53(3): 463–98. https://doi.org/10.1353/wp.2001.0008.

Crepaz, Markus M. 2008. *Trust beyond Borders: Immigration, the Welfare State, and Identity in Modern Societies.* Ann Arbor: University of Michigan Press.

Crepaz, Markus M., and Regan Damron. 2009. "Constructing Tolerance: How the Welfare State Shapes Attitudes about Immigrants." *Comparative Political Studies* 42(3): 437–63. http://doi.org/10.1177/0010414008325576.

Crozier, Michel, Samuel Huntington, and Joji Watanuki. 1975. *The Crisis of Democracy.* New York: NYU Press.

Curtis, Josh, Weizhen Dong, Naomi Lightman, and Matthew Parbst. 2017. "Race, Language, or Length of Residency? Explaining Unequal Uptake of Government Pensions in Canada." *Journal of Aging and Social Policy* 29(4): 332–51. https://doi.org/10.1080/08959420.2017.1319452.

Cuttitta, Paolo. 2014. "Mandatory Integration Measures and Differential Inclusion: The Italian Case." *Journal of International Migration and Integration* 17(1): 289–302. https://doi.org/10.1007/s12134-014-0410-0.

Czaika, Mathais, and Hein de Haas. 2011. "The Effectiveness of Immigration Policies: A Conceptual Review of Empirical Evidence." *International Migration Institute Working Paper* 33: 1–26. https://doi.org/10.1111/j.1728-4457.2013.00613.x.

Daniels, Roger. 2002. *Coming to America.* New York: HarperCollins.

Dauvergne, Catherine. 2007. "Citizenship with a Vengeance." *Theoretical Inquiries in Law*, 8: 489–508.

Davy, Ulrike, and Dilek Çinar. 2001. "Österreich." In *Die Integration von Einwanderern. Rechtliche Regelungen im europäischen Vergleich*, ed. U. Davy, 567–708. Frankfurt am Main: Campus.

Deeming, Christopher. 2015. "Foundations of the Workfare State." *Social Policy and Administration*, 49(7): 862–86. https://doi.org/10.1111/spol.12096.

De Haas, Hein, Katharina Natter, and Simona Vezzoli. 2014. "Compiling and Coding Migration Policies: Insights from the DEMIG POLICY Database." IMI working paper series 87. Oxford: International Migration Institute, University of Oxford.

– 2015. "Conceptualizing and Measuring Migration Policy Change." *Comparative Migration Studies* 3(15): 1–21. https://comparativemigrationstudies.springeropen.com/articles/10.1186/s40878-015-0016-5.

De Jong, Gordon F., Deborah Roempke Graefe, and Tanja St Pierre. 2005. "Welfare Reform and Interstate Migration of Poor Families." *Demography* 42(3): 469–96. https://doi.org/10.1007/BF03214592.

De Lange, Sarah. 2008. "From Pariah to Power: Explanations for the Government Participation of Radical Right-Wing Populist Parties in West European Parliamentary Democracies." PhD diss., University of Antwerp.

De la Rica, Sara, Albrecht Glitz, and Francesc Ortega. 2015. "Immigration in Europe: Trends, Policies, and Empirical Evidence." In *Handbook of the Economics of International Migration*, ed. B. Chiswick and P. Miller, 1303–62. Amsterdam: Elsevier.

De Waal, Tamar. 2020. "Conditional Belonging: Evaluating Integration Requirements from a Social Equality Perspective." *Journal of Intercultural Studies* 41(2): 231–47. https://doi.org/10.1080/07256868.2020.1724906.

DEMIG. (2015). DEMIG POLICY, version 1.3, Online Edition. Oxford: International Migration Institute, University of Oxford. www.migrationdeterminants.eu.

Devitt, Camilla. 2010. "The Migrant Worker Factor in Labour Market Policy Reform." *European Journal of Industrial Relations* 16(3): 259–75. https://doi.org/10.1177/0959680110375135.

– 2011. "Varieties of Capitalism, Variation in Labour Immigration." *Journal of Ethnic and Migration Studies* 37(4): 579–96. https://doi.org/10.1080/1369183X.2011.545273.

– 2018. "Shaping Labour Migration to Italy: The Role of Labour Market Institutions." *Journal of Modern Italian Studies* 23(3): 274–92. https://doi.org/10.1080/1354571X.2018.1459408.

De Zwart, Frank. 2005. "The Dilemma of Recognition: Administrative Categories and Cultural Diversity." *Theory and Society* 34(2): 137–69. https://doi.org/10.1007/s11186-005-6234-3.

Doctors Without Borders. 2005. "Gömda i Sverige. Utestängda från Hälso-och Sjukvård [Forgotten in Sweden. Excluded from Health and Sick Care]." Stockholm: Doctors Without Borders.

Dølvik, Jon Erik. 2013. "Grunnpilarene i de nordiske modellene: Tilbakeblikk på arbeidslivs-og velferdsregimenes utvikling." Fafo-rapport no. 13 (Oslo).

Dustmann, Christian, and Tommaso Frattini. 2014. "The fiscal effects of immigration to the UK." *The Economic Journal*, 124(580), F593–F643. https://doi.org/10.1111/ecoj.12181

Edelmann, Peter. 1997. "The Worst Thing Bill Clinton has Done." *The Atlantic*, March 1997 issue.

Eger, Maureen E. 2010. "Even in Sweden: The Effect of Immigration on Support for Welfare State Spending." *European Sociological Review* 26 (2): 203–17. https://doi.org/10.1093/esr/jcp017.

EMN. 2014. "Migrant Access to Social Security and Healthcare: Policies and Practice." Brussels: European Migration Network.

Engelen, Ewald. 2003. "How to Combine Openness and Protection? Citizenship, Migration, and Welfare Regimes." *Politics and Society* 31(4): 503–36. http://doi.org/10.1177/0032329203256951.

Ennser-Jedenastik, Laurenz. 2016. "A Welfare State for Whom? A Group-Based Account of the Austrian Freedom Party's Social Policy Profile." *Swiss Political Science Review* 22(3): 409–27. https://doi.org/10.1111/spsr.12218.

– 2018. "Welfare Chauvinism in Populist Radical Right Platforms: The Role of Redistributive Justice Principles." *Social Policy and Administration* 52(1): 293–314. https://doi.org/10.1111/spol.12325.

Espenshade, Thomas J., and Katherine Hempstead. 1996. "Contemporary American Attitudes toward U.S. Immigration." *International Migration Review* 30(2): 535–70.

Esping-Andersen, Gøsta. 1990. *The Three Worlds of Welfare Capitalism*. Princeton: Princeton University Press.

– 1993. "Orçamentos e democracia: o Estado-Providência em Espanha e Portugal, 1960–1986." *Análise Social* 28(122): 589–606.

Eugster, Beatrice. 2018. *Immigrants and Poverty: The Role of Labour Market and Welfare State Access*. London: Rowman and Littlefield.

EU-Infothek (16 January 2020). "Wenn die Mindestsicherung as Sozial Hängematte missbraucht wird." http://www.eu-infothek.com/wenn-die-mindestsicherung-als-soziale-haengematte-missbraucht-wird.

Eurofound. 2015. Families in the Economic Crisis: Changes in Policy Measures in the European Union. Luxemburg: European Foundation for the Improvement of Living and Working Conditions, Publications Office of the EU.

European Commission. 2018. *The 2018 Ageing Report: Underlying Assumptions and Projection Methodologies and Economic and Budgetary Projections for EU Member States (2016–2070)*. Brussels.

Evelly, Jeanmarie. 2020. "Trump Administration's 'Public Charge' Rule, Explained. City Limits." https://citylimits.org/2020/02/27/trump-administrations-public-charge-rule-explained.

Ewald, François. 1986. "A Concept of Social Law." In *Dilemmas of Law in the Welfare State*, ed. G. Teubner, 111–73. New York: De Gruyter.

Fallend, Franz. 2004. "Are Right-Wing Populism and Government Participation Incompatible? The Case of the Freedom Party of Austria." *Representation* 40(2): 115–30. https://doi.org/10.1080/00344890408523254.

Fassmann, Heinz, and Rainer Münz. 1995. *Einwanderungsland Österreich [Vienna]*. Vienna: Jugend & Volk.

Feagin, Joe R. 2020. *The White Racial Frame: Centuries of Racial Framing and Counter-Framing*. 3rd Ed. New York: Routledge.

Felbo-Kolding, Jonas, Janine Leschke, and Thees F. Spreckelsen. 2019. "A Division of Labour? Labour Market Segmentation by Region of Origin: The Case of Intra-EU Migrants in the UK, Germany, and Denmark." *Journal of Ethnic and Migration Studies* 45(15): 2820–43. http://doi.org/10.1080/1369183X.2018.1518709.

Felderer, Bernhard, Helmut Hofer, Ulrich Schuh, and Ludwig Strohner. 2004. "Befunde zur Integration von AusländerInnen in Österreich." https://core.ac.uk/download/pdf/212120508.pdf.

Fellowes, Matthew C., and Gretchen Rowe. 2004. "Politics and the New American Welfare States." *American Journal of Political Science* 48(2): 362–7. https://doi.org/10.1111/j.0092-5853.2004.00075.x.

Felten, Elias. 2018. "Soziale Rechte für UnionsbürgerInnen." In *Migration, Arbeitsmarkt und Sozialpolitik, Soziale Rechte für UnionsbürgerInnen*, ed. B. Schrattbauer, W. Pfeil, and R. Mosler, 233–48. Vienna: Manz.

Fenwick, Clare. 2019. "The Political Economy of Immigration and Welfare State Effort: Evidence from Europe." *European Political Science Review* 11(3): 357–75. https://doi.org/10.1017/S175577391900016X.

Fernández de la Hoz, Paloma, and Johannes Pflegerl. 2000. "Ältere MigrantInnen in Österreich." In *Ältere Menschen. Neue Perspektiven. Seniorenbericht. Lebensituation älterer Menschen in Österreich*, ed. Bundesministerium für Soziale Sicherheit und Generationen. Vienna.

Ferrera, Maurizio. 1996. "The 'Southern Model' of Welfare in Social Europe." *Journal of European Social Policy* 6(1):17–37. https://doi.org/10.1080/13608749608539480.

– 2005. *The Boundaries of Welfare. European Integration and the New Spatial Politics of Protection*. Oxford: Oxford University Press.

Filindra, Alexandra. 2012. "Immigrant Social Policy in the American States." *State Politics and Policy Quarterly* 13(1): 26–48. https://doi.org/10.1177/1532440012454664.

– 2019. "Is Threat in the Eye of the Researcher? Theory, Definition, and Measurement in the Study of State-Level Immigration Policymaking." *Policy Studies Journal*, 47 (3): 517–543. https://doi.org/10.1111/psj.12264.

Finseraas, Henning. 2008. "Immigration and Preferences for Redistribution: An Empirical Analysis of European Social Survey Data." *Comparative European Politics* 6: 407–31. https://doi.org/10.1057/cep.2008.3.

– 2012. "Anti-Immigration Attitudes, Support for Redistribution, and Party Choice in Europe." In *Changing Social Equality. The Nordic Welfare Model in the 21st Century*, ed. J. Kvist, J. Fritzell, B. Hvinden, and O. Kangas, 23–44. Bristol: Policy Press.

Finseraas, Henning, Axel W. Pedersen, and Anne-Helen Bay. 2016. "When the Going Gets Tough: The Differential Impact of National Unemployment on the Perceived Threats of Immigration." *Political Studies* 64(1): 60–7. https://doi.org/10.1111/1467-9248.12162.

Fix, Michael. 2009. *Immigrants and Welfare: The Impact of Welfare Reform on America's Newcomers*. New York: Russel Sage Foundation.

Fix, Michael E., Randy Capps, and Neeraj Kaushal. 2010. "Immigrants and Welfare: Overview." In *Immigrants and Welfare: The Impact of Welfare Reform on America's Newcomers*, ed. M. Fix, 1–36. New York: Russell Sage Foundation.

Fix, Michael, and Jeffrey S. Passel. 1994. *Immigration and Immigrants: Setting the Record Straight*. Washington, DC: Urban Institute.

– 1999. *Trends in Noncitizens' and Citizens' Use of Public Benefits Following Welfare Reform: 1997–97*. Washington, DC: Urban Institute.

Flora, Peter, and Arnold J. Heidenheimer. 1981. "The Historical Core and the Changing Boundaries of the Welfare State." In *The Development of the Welfare*

State in Europe and America, ed. P. Flora and A. Heidenheimer, 17–36. Piscataway: Transaction Books.

Fortuny, Karina, and Ajay Chaudry. 2011. *A Comprehensive Review of Immigrant Access to Health and Human Services*. Washington, DC: Urban Institute.

Fox, Cybelle. 2012. *Three Worlds of Relief: Race, Immigration, and the American Welfare State from the Progressive Era to the New Deal*. Princeton: Princeton University Press.

Franchino, Fabio. 2009. "Perspectives on European Immigration Policies." *European Union Politics*, 10(3): 403–20. http://doi.org/10.1177/1465116509337835.

Freedland, Mark, and Desmond King. 2003. "Contractual Governance and Illiberal Contracts." *Cambridge Journal of Economics* 27(3): 465–77. http://doi.org/10.1093/cje/27.3.465.

Freeman, Gary P. 1986. "Migration and the Political Economy of the Welfare State." *Annals of the American Academy of Political and Social Science* 485: 51–63.

Freeman, Gary P. 2009. "Immigration, Diversity, and Welfare Chauvinism." *The Forum* 7(3): 1–16. https://doi.org/10.2202/1540-8884.1317.

Friberg, Jon Horgen. 2016. "Assimilering på norsk." Fafo-rapport no. 43.

Gächter, August. 1995. "Integration und Migration." *SWS-Rundschau* 35(4): 435–8.

Gal, John. 2008. "Immigration and the Categorical Welfare State in Israel." *Social Service Review* 82(4): 639–61. http://doi.org/10.1086/595715.

Garand, James C., Ping Xu, and Belinda C. Davis. 2017. "Immigration Attitudes and Support for the Welfare State in the American Mass Public." *American Journal of Political Science* 61(1): 146–62. https://doi.org/10.1111/ajps.12233.

Garland, David. 2014. "The Welfare State: A Fundamental Dimension of Modern Government." *European Journal of Sociology* 55(3): 327–64. http://doi.org/10.1017/S0003975614000162.

Gaston, Noel, and Gulasekaran Rajaguru. 2013. "International Migration and the Welfare State Revisited." *European Journal of Political Economy* 29(C): 90–101. https://doi.org/10.1016/j.ejpoleco.2012.08.004.

Gebhardt, Dirk. 2016. "When the State Takes Over: Civic Integration Programmes and the Role of Cities in Immigrant Integration." *Journal of Ethnic and Migration Studies* 42(5): 742–58. https://doi.org/10.1080/1369183X.2015.1111132.

Genschel, Philipp, and Laura Seelkopf. 2015. "The Competition State: The Modern State in a Global Economy." In *The Oxford Handbook of Transformations of the State*, ed. S. Leibfried et al. Oxford: Oxford University Press.

Gerdes, Christer. 2011. "The Impact of Immigration on the Size of Government: Empirical Evidence from Danish Municipalities." *Scandinavian Journal of Economics* 113(1): 74–92. http://doi.org/10.1111/j.1467-9442.2010.01629.x.

Gerken, Christina. 1990. *Immigrant Anxieties: 1990s Immigration Reform and the Neoliberal Consensus*. PhD diss., Bowling Green State University.

Gerlich, Peter, and David Campbell. 2000. "Austria: From Compromise to Authoritarianism." In *Conditions of Democracy in Europe, 1919–39: Systematic Case Studies*, ed. D. Berg-Schlosser and J. Mitchell, 1–19..Basingstoke: Macmillan.

Gilens, Martin 1999. *Why Americans Hate Welfare. Race, Media, and the Politics of Antipoverty Policy*. Chicago: University of Chicago Press.

Gilliam, Franklin D. 1999. The "Welfare Queen Experiment": How Viewers React to Images of African-American Mothers on Welfare. Niemann Foundation. https://nieman.harvard.edu/articles/the-welfare-queen-experiment.

Ginn, Jay, and Sara Arber. 1999. "Changing Patterns of Pension Inequality: The Shift from State to Private Sources." *Ageing and Society* 19(3): 319–42. https://doi.org/10.1017/S0144686X99007333.

Gingrich, Jane, and Silja Häusermann. 2015. "The Decline of the Working Class Vote, the Reconfiguration of the Welfare Support Coalition, and Consequences for the Welfare State." *Journal of European Social Policy* 25(1): 50–75. http://doi.org/10.1177/0958928714556970.

Giulietti, Corrado, Martin Guzi, Martin Kahanec, and Klaus F. Zimmermann. 2013. "Unemployment Benefits and Immigration: Evidence from the EU." *International Journal of Manpower* 34(1): 24–38. http://nbn-resolving.de/urn:nbn:de:101:1-201111212890.

Giulietti, Corrado, and Jackline Wahba. 2013. "Welfare Migration." In *International Handbook on the Economics of Migration*, ed. A.F. Constant and K.F. Zimmermann, 489–504. Cheltenham: Edward Elgar.

Góis, Pedro, and José Carlos Marques. 2009. "Portugal as a Semiperipheral Country in the Global Migration System." *International Migration* 47(3): 19–50. http://doi.org/10.1111/j.1468-2435.2009.00523.x.

González, Pilar, and António Figueiredo. 2014. "The European Social Model in a Context of Crisis and Austerity in Portugal." In *The European Social Model in Times of Economic Crisis and Austerity Policies*, ed. D. Vaughan-Whitehead, 291–340. Cheltenham: Edward Elgar.

Goodhart, David. 2004. "Too Diverse?" *Prospect* (February): 30–7.

Goodman, Sara Wallace. 2014. *Immigration and Membership Politics in Western Europe*. Cambridge: Cambridge University Press.

Gorinas, Cédric. 2014. "Ethnic Identity, Majority Norms, and the Native–Immigrant Employment Gap." *Journal of Population Economics* 27(1): 225–50. http://doi.org/10.1007/s00148-012-0463-3.

Gorodzeisky, Anastasia. 2013. "Mechanisms of Exclusion: Attitudes toward Allocation of Social Rights to Out-Group Population." *Ethnic and Racial Studies* 36(5): 795–817. https://doi.org/10.1080/01419870.2011.631740.

Gorodzeisky, Anastasia, and Moshe Semyonov. 2017. "Labor Force Participation, Unemployment and Occupational Attainment among Immigrants in West European Countries." *PLoS One* 12(5): e0176856. https://doi.org/10.1371/journal.pone.0176856.

Grady, Patrick, and Herbert Grubel. 2015. "Immigration and the Welfare State Revisited: Fiscal Transfers to Immigrants in Canada." *SSRN Electronic Journal*. https://doi.org/10.2139/ssrn.2612456.

Grand, Peter. 2009. "Wann sind "umfassende" Reformen auch ausreichend? Die janusköpfige Entwicklung der österreichischen aktiven Arbeitsmarktpolitik 1998–2007." *Österreichische Zeitschrift für Politikwissenschaft* 38(2): 213–30. https://doi.org/10.15203/ozp.672.vol38iss2.

Green, Donald P., Bradley Palmquist, and Eric Schickler. 2002. *Partisan Hearts and Minds: Political Parties and the Social Identities of Voters*. New Haven: Yale University Press.

Greenfeld, Liah. 1992. *Nationalism: Five Roads to Modernity*. Cambridge, MA: Harvard University Press.

Grubel, Herbert, and Patrick Grady. 2011. *Immigration and the Canadian Welfare State 2011*. Vancouver: Fraser Institute.

Gruber, Oliver. 2014. *Campaigning in Radical Right Heartland: The Electoral Politicization of Immigration and Ethnic Relations in Austrian General Elections, 1971–2013*. Münster: LIT Verlag.

Gruber, Oliver, and Sieglinde Rosenberger. 2021. "Between Opportunities and Constraints: Right-Wing Populists as Designers of Migrant Integration Policy." *Policy Studies*, online first, 1–19.

Guiraudon, Virginie. 1999. "The Marshallian Triptych Re-Ordered: The Role of Courts and Bureaucracies in Furthering Migrant Social Rights." Papers 99/1, European Institute - European Forum.

– 2000. "The Marshallian Triptych Reordered: The Role of Courts and Bureaucracies in Furthering Migrants' Social Rights." In *Immigration and Welfare: Challenging the Borders of the Welfare State*, ed. M. Bommes and A. Geddes, 72–89. London: Routledge.

Gulasekaram, Pratheepan, and S. Karthick Ramakrishnan. 2015. *The New Immigration Federalism*. Cambridge: Cambridge University Press.

Guzi, Martin, Martin Kahanec, and Lucia M. Kureková. 2014. "The Impact of Demand and Supply Structural Factors on Native-Migrant Labour Market Gaps." *KING Desk Research and In-depth Study* (17).

– 2018. "How Immigration Grease Is Affected by Economic, Institutional, and Policy Contexts: Evidence from EU Labor Markets." *Kyklos* 71(2): 213–43. http://doi.org/10.1111/kykl.12168.

– 2022. "What Explains Immigrant-Native Gaps in European Labor Markets: The Role of Institutions." *Migration Studies*, forthcoming.

Gygli, Savina, Florian Haelg, Niklas Potrafke, and Jan-Egbert Sturm. 2019. "The KOF Globalisation Index – Revisited." *Review of International Organizations* 14(3): 543–74. https://doi.org/10.1007/s11558-019-09344-2.

Hagelund, Anniken. 2005. "Why It Is Bad to Be Kind: Educating Refugees to Life in the Welfare State: A Case Study from Norway." *Social Policy and Administration* 39(6): 669–83. http://doi.org/10.1111/j.1467-9515.2005.00463.x.

Haidt, Jonathan. 2016. "When and Why Nationalism Beats Globalism." *Policy: A Journal of Public Policy and Ideas* 32(3): 46. https://search.informit.org/doi/10.3316/informit.405917723085484.

Hajnal, Zoltan, and Michael U. Rivera. 2014. "Immigration, Latinos, and White Partisan Politics: The New Democratic Defection." *American Journal of Political Science* 58(4): 773–89. https://doi.org/10.1111/ajps.12101.

Hammar, Tomas. 1994. *Democracy and the Nation State: Aliens, Denizens, and Citizens in a World of International Migration*. Avebury: Ashgate.

Hansen, Marianne, Frank Schultz-Nielsen, Schultz-Nielsen, Marie Louise, and Torben Tranæs. 2015. "The Impact of Immigrants on Public Finances: A Forecast Analysis for Denmark." IZA discussion papers 8844, Institute of Labor Economics (IZA). Bonn.

Hansen, Jorgen, and Magnus Lofstrom. 2003. "Immigrant Assimilation and Welfare Participation: Do Immigrants Assimilate Into or Out of Welfare? *Journal of Human Resources* 38(1): 74–98. https://doi.org/10.3368/jhr.XXXVIII.1.74.

Hanson, Devlin, Heather Koball, and Karina Fortuny. 2014. "Low-Income Immigrant Families' Access to SNAP and TANF." Washington, DC: Urban Institute.

Harris, Neville. 2016. "Demagnetisation of Social Security and Health Care for Migrants to the UK." *European Journal of Social Security* 18(2): 130–63. https://doi.org/10.1177/138826271601800204.

Haynes, Chris, Jennifer Merolla, and S. Karthick Ramakrishnan. 2016. *Framing Immigrants: News Coverage, Public Opinion, and Policy*. New York: Russell Sage Foundation.

Heinesen, Eskil, Leif Husted, and Michael Rosholm. 2013. "The Effects of Active Labour Market Policies for Immigrants Receiving Social Assistance in Denmark." *IZA Journal of Migration* 2(1): 1–22. https://doi.org/10.1186/2193-9039-2-15.

Heinisch, Reinhard. 2003. "Success in Opposition – Failure in Government: Explaining the Performance of Right-Wing Populist Parties in Public Office." *West European Politics* 26(3): 91–130. https://doi.org/10.1080/01402380312331280608.

Heinisch, Reinhard, Annika Werner, and Fabian Habersack. 2020. "Reclaiming National Sovereignty: The Case of the Conservatives and the Far Right in Austria." *European Politics and Society* 21(2): 163–81. https://doi.org/10.1080/23745118.2019.1632577.

Heitmeyer, Wilhelm. 2018. Autoritäre Versuchungen: Signaturen der Bedrohung. Berlin: Suhrkamp Verlag.

Heitzmann, Karin, and August Österle. 2008. "Lange Traditionen und neue Herausforderungen: Das österreichische Wohlfahrtssystem." In *Europäische Wohlfahrtssysteme: Ein Handbuch*, ed. K. Schubert, S. Hegelich, and U. Bazant, 47–69. Wiesbaden: VS Verlag für Sozialwissenschaften.

Hemerijck, Anton, T. Palm, E. Entenmann, and F. Van Hooren. 2013. *Changing European Welfare States and the Evolution of Migrant Incorporation Regimes*. Background paper. Amsterdam: Policy and Society (COMPAS).

Herda, Daniel. 2010. "How Many Immigrants? Foreign Born Population Innumeracy in Europe." *Public Opinion Quarterly* 74: 674–95. https://doi.org/10.1093/poq/nfq013.

– 2018. "Comparing Ignorance: Imagined Immigration and the Exclusion of Migrants in the US and Western Europe." *Societies Without Borders* 12: 3–25.

Hermansen, Are Skeie. 2016. "Moving Up or Falling Behind? Intergenerational Socioeconomic Transmission among Children of Immigrants in Norway." *European Sociological Review*, 32(5): 675–89. https://doi.org/10.1093/esr/jcw024.

– 2017. "Et egalitært og velferdsstatlig integreringsparadoks? Om sosioøkonomisk integrering blant innvandrere og deres etterkommere i Norge." *Norsk sosiologisk tidsskrift* (1): 15–34. https://doi.org/10.18261/issn.2535-2512-2017-01-02.

Hero, Rodney E., and Robert R. Preuhs. 2007. "Immigration and the Evolving American Welfare State: Examining Policies in the U.S. States." *American Journal of Political Science* 51(3): 498–517. https://doi.org/10.1111/j.1540-5907.2007.00264.x.

Hetherington, Marc J., and Jonathan D. Weiler. 2009. *Authoritarianism and Polarization in American Politics*. Cambridge: Cambridge University Press.

House of Lords. 2008. *The Economic Impact of Immigration*. London: HMSO.

Howard, Marc M. 2010. "The Impact of the Far Right on Citizenship Policy in Europe: Explaining Continuity and Change." *Journal of Ethnic and Migration Studies* 36(5): 735–51. https://doi.org/10.1080/13691831003763922.

Huang, Xiaoning, Neeraj Kaushal, and Julia Shu-Huah Wang. 2020. "What Explains the Gap in Welfare Use among Immigrants and Natives?" National Bureau of Economic Research, working papers, September (27811): 1–53.

Huber, Evelyne, and John D. Stephens. 2001. *Development and Crisis of the Welfare State: Parties and Policies in Global Markets*. Chicago: University of Chicago Press.

Huber, Peter. 2010. "Die Arbeitsmarktintegration von Migrantinnen und Migranten in Österreich." WIFO working papers no. 365.

– 2015. "What Institutions Help Immigrants Integrate?" WWWforEurope Working Paper (77).

Huddle, Donald L. 1993. *The Costs of Immigration*. Washington, DC: Carrying Capacity Network.

Huddle, Donald L., and David Simcox. 1994. "The Impact of Immigration on the Social Security System." *Population and Environment* 16: 91–7.

Huddleston, Thomas, Ozge Bilgili, Anne-Linde Joki, and Zvezda Vankova. 2015. *Migrant Integration Policy Index*. Barcelona and Brussels: CIDOB and MPG.

Imdi. 2020. "Innvandrere i arbeidslivet." https://www.imdi.no/om-integrering-i-norge/kunnskapsoversikt/innvandrere-i-arbeidslivet.

Jaeger, Mads Meier. 2007. "Are the 'Deserving Needy' Really Deserving Everywhere? Cross-Cultural Heterogeneity and Popular Support for the Old and the Sick in Eight Western Countries." In *Social Justice, Legitimacy, and the Welfare State*, ed. S. Mau and B. Veghte, 73–94. Aldershot: Ashgate.

Jenson, Jane, and Martin Papillon (n.d.). "The Changing Boundaries of Citizenship: A Review and a Research Agenda." http://www.cccg.umontreal.ca/pdf/CPRN/CPRN_Chnaging%20Boundaries.pdf.

Jepperson, Ronald L. 1991. "Institutions, Institutional Effects, and Institutionalism." In *The New Institutionalism in Organizational Analysis*, ed. P. DiMaggio and W. Powell, 143–63. Chicago: University of Chicago Press.

Joppke, Christian. 2001. "The Legal-Domestic Sources of Immigrant Rights: The United States, Germany, and the European Union." *Comparative Political Studies* 34(4): 339–66. https://doi.org/10.1177/0010414001034004001.

– 2021a. "Nationalism in the Neoliberal Order: Old Wine in New Bottles?" *Nations and Nationalism*, advance electronic publication.

– 2021b. *Neoliberal Nationalism: Immigration and the Rise of the Populist Right*. Cambridge: Cambridge University Press.

Joppke, Christian, and Rainer Bauböck, eds. "How Liberal Are Citizenship Tests?" Robert Schuman Centre for Advanced Studies (RSCAS) working paper 2010/41. Fiesole: European University Institute.

Joseph, Tiffany D. 2015. "Excluded and Frozen Out: Unauthorised Immigrants' (Non) Access to Care after US Health Care Reform." *Journal of Ethnic and Migration Studies* 41(15): 2253–73. https://doi.org/10.1080/1369183X.2015.1051465.

– 2016. "What Health Care Reform Means for Immigrants: Comparing the Affordable Care Act and Massachusetts Health Reforms." *Journal of Health Politics, Policy, and Law* 41(1): 101–16. https://doi.org/10.1215/03616878-3445632.

– 2017. "Falling through the Coverage Cracks: How Documentation Status Minimizes Immigrants' Access to Health Care." *Journal of Health Politics, Policy, and Law* 42(5): 961–84. https://doi.org/10.1215/03616878-3940495.

Kaczmarczyk, Pawel. 2013. "Are Immigrants a Burden for the State Budget? Review Paper." (November). Robert Schuman Centre for Advanced Studies Research Paper (2013/79).

Kahanec, Martin, Anna Myung-Hee Kim, and Klaus F. Zimmerman. 2013. "Pitfalls of Immigrant Inclusion into the European Welfare State." *International Journal of Manpower* 34(1): 39–55. http://doi.org/10.1108/01437721311319647.

Kahanec, Martin, and Anzelika Zaiceva. 2009. "Labor Market Outcomes of Immigrants and Non-Citizens in the EU: An East-West Comparison." *International Journal of Manpower* 30(1–2): 97–115. http://doi.org/10.1108/01437720910948429.

Kahanec, Martin, and Klaus F. Zimmermann. 2011. *Ethnic Diversity in European Labor Markets: Challenges and Solutions*. Cheltenham: Edward Elgar.

Kapsalis, Constantine. 2020. "The Fiscal Burden of Recent Immigrants to Canada." Research at a Glance, MDRA paper no. 102505.

Kapuy, Klaus. 2016. "Zugehörigkeit in der sozialen Sicherheit: Ändern sich die Zugehörigkeitskonzepte in Europa?" *Das Recht der Arbeit* 6: 396–403.

Kargl, Martina. 2004. "Gerechtigkeit im österreichischen Sozialstaat." http://www.armutskonferenz.at/files/kargl_gerechtigkeit_im_oe_sozialstaat-2004.pdf.

Kaushal, Neeraj. 2005. "New Immigrants' Location Choices: Magnets without Welfare." *Journal of Labor Economics* 23(1): 59–80. http://doi.org/10.1086/425433.

Kaushal, Neeraj, and Robert Kaestner. 2005. "Welfare Reform and Health Insurance of Immigrants." *Health Services Research* 40(3): 697–722. https://doi.org/10.1111/j.1475-6773.2005.00381.x.

– 2007. "Welfare Reform and the Health of Immigrant Women and Their Children." *Journal of Immigrant and Minority Health* 9(2): 61–74. https://doi.org/10.1007/s10903-006-9021-y

Kaushal, Neeraj, Jane Waldfogel, and Vanessa Wight. 2014. "Food Insecurity and SNAP Participation in Mexican Immigrant Families: The Impact of the Outreach Initiative." *B.E. Journal of Economic Analysis and Policy* 14(1): 203–40. https://doi.org/10.1515/bejeap-2013-0083.

Kehrberg, Jason E. 2017. "The Mediating Effect of Authoritarianism on Immigrant Access to TANF: A State-Level Analysis." *Political Science Quarterly* 132(2): 291–311. https://doi.org/10.1002/polq.12614.

– 2020a. "Authoritarianism, Prejudice, and Support for Welfare Chauvinism in the United States." *Statistics, Politics, and Policy*. https://doi.org/10.1515/spp-2019-0008.

– 2020b. "Setting the Stage for Trump: Authoritarianism and the Partisan Polarization of Undocumented Immigration Attitudes." Unpublished manuscript.

Kendi, Ibram. 2018. *Stamped from the Beginning: The Definitive History of Racist Ideas in America*. New York: Bold Type Books.

Kennedy, Steven, Micheal Kidd, James McDonald, and Nicholas Biddle. 2015. "The Healthy Immigrant Effect: Patterns and Evidence from Four Countries." *Journal of International Migration and Integration* 16(2): 317–32. https://doi.org/10.1007/s12134-014-0340-x.

Kerr, Sari P., and William Kerr. 2011. "Economic Impacts of Immigration: A Survey. National Bureau of Economic Research, working paper 16736. DOI 10.3386/w16736.

Kevins, Anthony, and Kees van Kersbergen. 2019. "The Effects of Welfare State Universalism on Migrant Integration." *Policy and Politics*, 47: 115–31. https://doi.org/10.1332/030557318x15407315707251.

Key, V.O. 1949. *Southern Politics in State and Nation*. New York: A.A. Knopf.

Khan, Sabaa. 2009. "From Labour of Love to Decent Work: Protecting the Human Rights of Migrant Caregivers in Canada." *Canadian Journal of Law and Society* 24: 23. https://doi.org/10.1017/S0829320100009753.

Kingdon, John W., and James A. Thurber. 1984. *Agendas, Alternatives, and Public Policies*. Boston: Little, Brown.

Kitschelt, H. and A.J. McGann. 1997. *The Radical Right in Western Europe: A Comparative Analysis*. Ann Arbor: The University of Michigan Press.

Kleven, Øyvin, Bernt Aardal, Johannes Bergh, Stine Hesstvedt, and Ådne Hindenes. 2015. Valgundersøkelsen 2013. Dokumentasjons-og tabellrapport. Notater 2015/29, Statistisk sentralbyrå.

Knoll, Benjamin R., David P. Redlawsk, and Howard Sanborn. 2011. "Framing Labels and Immigration Policy Attitudes in the Iowa Caucuses: 'Trying to Out-Tancredo Tancredo.'" *Political Behavior* 33(3): 433–54. http://doi.org/10.1007/s11109-010-9141-x.

Koettl, Johannes, Holzmann, Robert, and Stefano Scarpetta. 2006. *The relative merits of skilled and unskilled migration, temporary and permanent labor migration, and portability of social security benefits*. SP discussion paper no. 01614. World Bank. https://documents1.worldbank.org/curated/en/710661468135302581/pdf/380070SP061401PUBLIC1.pdf.

Kogan, Irena. 2004. "Last Hired, First Fired? The Unemployment Dynamics of Male Immigrants in Germany." *European Sociological Review* 20(5): 445–61. http://doi.org/10.1093/esr/jch037.

Koning, Edward Anthony. 2017. "Selecting, Excluding, or Investing? Exploring Party and Voter Responses to Immigrant Welfare Dependence in 15 West European Welfare States." *Comparative European Politics* 15(4): 628–60.

– 2018. "Three Hypotheses on the Relevance of Federalism for the Politics of Immigration and Welfare." In *Federalism and the Welfare State in a Multicultural World*, ed. E. Goodyear-Grant, R. Johnston, W. Kymlicka, and J. Myles, 201–22. Montreal and Kingston: McGill-Queen's University Press.

– 2019. *Immigration and the Politics of Welfare Exclusion: Selective Solidarity in Western Democracies*. Toronto: University of Toronto Press.

– 2020. "Accommodation and New Hurdles: The Increasing Importance of Politics for Immigrants' Access to Social Programmes in Western Democracies." *Social Policy and Administration*, online first. https://doi.org/10.1111/spol.12661.

– 2021. "Social Protection of Migrants and Citizenship Rights." In *Handbook on Citizenship and Migration*, ed. M. Grasso and Marco Guigni. Cheltenham: Edward Elgar.

Koning, Edward Anthony, and Keith G. Banting. 2013. "Inequality below the Surface: Reviewing Immigrants' Access to and Utilization of Five Canadian Welfare Programs." *Canadian Public Policy* 39(4): 581–601. http://doi.org/10.3138/CPP.39.4.581.

König, Jörg, and Renate Ohr. 2013. "Different Efforts in European Economic Integration." *Journal of Common Mark Studies* 51: 1074–90.

Koopmans, Ruud. 2010. "Trade-Offs between Equality and Difference: Immigrant Integration, Multiculturalism, and the Welfare State in Cross-National Perspective." *Journal of Ethnic and Migration Studies* 36(1): 1–26. https://doi.org/10.1080/13691830903250881.

Koopmans, Ruud, Ines Michalowski, and Stine Waibel. 2012. "Citizenship Rights for Immigrants: National Political Processes and Cross-National Convergence in Western Europe, 1980–2008." *American Journal of Sociology* 117(4): 1202–45. https://doi.org/10.1086/662707.

Koopmans, Ruud, and Paul Statham. 2000. *Challenging Immigration and Ethnic Relations Politics: Comparative European Perspectives*. Oxford: Oxford University Press.

Korpi, Walter. 1980. "Social Policy and Distributional Conflict in the Capitalist Democracies: A Preliminary Comparative Framework." *West European Politics* 3(3): 296–316. https://doi.org/10.1080/01402388008424288.

Korpi, Walter, and Joakim Palme. 2003. "New Politics and Class Politics in the Context of Austerity and Globalization: Welfare State Regress in 18 Countries, 1975–95." *American Political Science Review* 97(3): 425–46.

Kremer, Monique. 2013. *Vreemden in de Verzorgingsstaat [Aliens in the Welfare State]*. Den Haag: Boom Lemma.

– 2016. "Earned Citizenship: Labour Migrants' Views on the Welfare State." *Journal of Social Policy* 45(3): 395. https://doi.org/10.1017/S0047279416000088.

Kriesi, Hanspeter, Edgar Grande, Martin Dolezal, Marc Helbling, Dominic Höglinger, Swen Hutter, and Bruno Wüest. 2012. *Political Conflict in Western Europe*. Cambridge: Cambridge University Press.

Kriesi, Hanspeter, Edgar Grande, Romain Lachat, Martin Dolezal, Simon Bornschier, and Timotheos Frey. 2008. *West European Politics in the Age of Globalization*. Cambridge: Cambridge University Press.

Kros, Mathijs, and Marcel Coenders. 2019. "Explaining Differences in Welfare Chauvinism between and within Individuals over Time: The Role of Subjective and Objective Economic Risk, Economic Egalitarianism, and Ethnic Threat." *European Sociological Review* 35(6): 860–73. https://doi.org/10.1093/esr/jcz034.

Ku, Leighton. 2009. "Changes in Immigrants' Use of Medicaid and Food Stamps: The Role of Eligibility and Other Factors." In *Immigrants and Welfare: The Impact of Welfare Reform on America's Newcomers*, ed. Michael E. Fix. New York: Russell Sage Foundation.

Ku, Leighton, and Shannon Blaney. 2000. "Health Coverage for Legal Immigrant Children: New Census Data Highlight Importance of Restoring Medicaid and SCHIP Coverage." https://www.cbpp.org/archives/10-4-00health.htm.

Ku, Leighton, and Brian Bruen. 2013. "The Use of Public Assistance Benefits by Citizens and Non-Citizen Immigrants in the United States." Washington, DC: Cato Institute. https://www.cato.org/sites/cato.org/files/pubs/pdf/workingpaper-13_1.pdf.

Ku, Leighton, and Sheetal Matani. 2001. "Left out: immigrants' access to health care and insurance." *Health Affairs*, 20 (1): 247–256. https://doi.org/10.1377/hlthaff.20.1.247.

Kubal, Agnieszka. 2009. "Why Semi-Legal? Polish Post-2004 EU Enlargement Migrants in the United Kingdom." *Journal of Immigration, Asylum and Nationality Law* 23(2): 148–64.

Kuhnle, Stein, and Matti Alestalo. 2018. "The Modern Scandinavian Welfare State." In *The Routledge Handbook of Scandinavian Politics*, ed. P. Wivel Nedergaard and A. Wivel Nedergaard, 13–25. London and New York: Routledge.

Kuipers, Sanneke. 2006. *The Crisis Imperative. Crisis Rhetoric and Welfare State Reform in Belgium and the Netherlands in the Early 1990s*. Amsterdam: Amsterdam University Press.

Kumlin, Staffan, and Bo Rothstein. 2005. "Making and Breaking Social Capital: The Impact of Welfare-State Institutions." *Comparative Political Studies* 38: 339–65. http://doi.org/10.1177/0010414004273203.

Kunovich, Robert M. 2017. "Perception of Racial Group Size in a Minority-Majority Area." *Sociological Perspectives* 60: 479–96. https://doi.org/10.1177/0731121416675869.

Kureková, Lucia M. 2013. "Welfare Systems as Emigration Factor: Evidence from the New Accession States." *JCMS: Journal of Common Market Studies* 55(4): 721–39. https://doi.org/10.1111/jcms.12020.

Kvist, John. 2004. "Does EU Enlargement Start a Race to the Bottom? Strategic Interaction among EU Member States in Social Policy." *Journal of European Social Policy* 14(3): 301–18. http://doi.org/10.1177/0958928704044625.

Kvist, Jon, Johan Fritzell, Bjørn Hvinden, and Olli Kangas. 2012. *Changing Social Equality: The Nordic Welfare Model in the 21st Century*. Bristol: Policy Press.

Kymlicka, Will. 2015. "Solidarity in Diverse Societies: Beyond Neoliberal Multiculturalism and Welfare Chauvinism." *Comparative Migration Studies* 3(1): 1–19. https://doi.org/10.1186/s40878-015-0017-4.

– 2017. "Multiculturalism without Citizenship?" In *Multicultural Governance in a Mobile World*, ed. A. Triandafyllidou, 139–61. Edinburgh: Edinburgh University Press.

Lahav, Gallya. 1997. "Ideological and Party Constraints on Immigration Attitudes in Europe." *Journal of Common Market Studies* 35(3): 377–406. https://doi.org/10.1111/1468-5965.00067.

Larsen, Christian Albrekt. 2008. "The Institutional Logic of Welfare Attitudes: How Welfare Regimes Influence Public Support." *Comparative Political Studies* 41(2): 145–68. https://doi.org/10.1177/0010414006295234.

– 2020. "The Institutional Logic of Giving Migrants Access to Social Benefits and Services." *Journal of European Social Policy* 30: 48–62. https://doi.org/10.1177/0958928719868443.

Lee, Ronald, and Timothy Miller. 1998. "The Current Fiscal Impact of Immigrants and Their Descendants: Beyond the Immigrant Household." In *The Immigration Debate*, ed. J. P. Smith and B. Edmonston, 183–205. Washington, DC: National Academy Press.

– 2000. "New Issues in Immigration: Immigration, Social Security, and Broader Fiscal Impacts." *American Economic Review* 90(2): 350–4. http://doi.org/10.1257/aer.90.2.350.

Leibfried, Stephan, and Paul Pierson. 2000. "Social Policy: Left to Courts or Markets." In *Policy-Making in the European Union*, ed. H. Wallace and W. Wallace, 267–89. Oxford: Oxford University Press.

Lepianka, Dorota. 2017. "The Varying Faces of Poverty and Deservingness in Dutch Print Media." In *The Social Legitimacy of Targeted Welfare*, ed. W. van Oorschot, R. Roosma, B. Meuleman, and R. Reeskens, 127–48. Cheltenham: Edward Elgar.

Leschke, Janine, and Silvana Weiss. 2020. "With a Little Help from My Friends: Social-Network Job Search and Overqualification among Recent Intra-EU Migrants Moving from East to West." *Work, Employment, and Society*, online first, 34(1): 095001702092643. http://doi.org/10.1177/0950017020926433.

Leszczensky, Lars, and Tobias Wolbring. 2019. "How to Deal with Reverse Causality Using Panel Data? Recommendations for Researchers Based on a Simulation Study." *Sociological Methods and Research*, 1–29, online first: https://doi.org/10.1177/0049124119882473.

Levendusky, Matthew S. 2009. *The Partisan Sort: How Liberals Become Democrats and Conservatives Become Republicans*. Chicago: University of Chicago Press.

Levin, Shana, Miriam Matthews, Serge Guimond, Jim Sidanius, Felicia Pratto, Nour Kteily, Eileen V. Pitpitan, and Tessa Dover. 2012. "Assimilation, Multiculturalism, and Colorblindness: Mediated and Moderated Relationships between Social Dominance Orientation and Prejudice." *Journal of Experimental Social Psychology* 48(1): 207–12. http://doi.org/10.1016/j.jesp.2011.06.019.

Lippman, Walter. 1997. *Public Opinion* [1922]. New York: Free Press.

Luthra, Renee R. 2013. "Explaining Ethnic Inequality in the German Labor Market: Labor Market Institutions, Context of Reception, and Boundaries. *European Sociological Review* 29(5): 1095–107. http://doi.org/10.1093/esr/jcs081.

Ma, Ambrose, and Iris Chi. 2005. "Utilization and Accessibility of Social Services for Chinese Canadians." *International Social Work* 48(2): 148–60. https://doi.org/10.1177/0020872805050207.

Magnusson Turner, Lena, and Lina Hedman. 2014. "Linking Integration and Housing Career: A Longitudinal Analysis of Immigrant Groups in Sweden." *Housing Studies* 29(2): 270–90. https://doi.org/10.1080/02673037.2014.851177.

Mairhuber, Ingrid. 2009. "Entwicklung der österreichischen Alterssicherung seit den 1980er Jahren." In *Die Dynamik des "österreichischen Modells": Brüche und Kontinuitäten im Beschäftigungs-und Sozialsystems*, ed. C. Herman and R. Atzmüller, 187–212. Berlin: edition sigma.

Malheiros, Jorge, and Lucinda Fonseca (coord.) 2011. *Acesso à habitação e problemas residenciais dos imigrantes em Portugal, Observatório da Imigração*, vol. 48, Lisbon: ACIDI.

Marcelli, Enrico A., James P. Smith, and Barry Edmonston. 1998. "The New Americans: Economic, Demographic, and Fiscal Effects of Immigration." *Population and Development Review* 24(1): 166–9. https://doi.org/10.17226/5779.

March, James G., and Johan P. Olsen. 1984. "The New Institutionalism: Organizational Factors in Political Life." *American Political Science Review* 78(3): 734–49. https://doi.org/10.2307/1961840.

Marik-Lebeck, Stephan, and Alexander Wisbauer. 2017. "Flüchtlingsmigration im Spiegel der Bevölkerungsstatistik." *Statistische Nachrichten* 4: 268–75.

Markaki, Yvonni, and Simonetta Longhi. 2013. "What Determines Attitudes to Immigration in European Countries? An Analysis at the Regional Level." *Migration Studies* 1(3): 311–37. https://doi.org/10.1093/migration/mnt015.

Marshall, T.H. 1963. *Sociology at the Crossroads* [1950]. London: Heinemann.
Massey, Douglas S., Joaquin Arango, Graeme Hugo, Ali Kouaouci, Adela Pellegrino, and J. Edward Taylor. 1993. "Theories of International Migration: A Review and Appraisal." *Population and Development Review* 19(3): 431–66. http://doi.org/10.2307/2938462.
Mayer, Julia. 2011. "Migration und Gesundheit: Mögliche Wege aus dem Präventionsdilemma." ÖIF-Dossier no. 17.
Meinhard, Stephanie, and Niklas Potrafke. 2012. "The Globalization-Welfare State Nexus Reconsidered." *Review of International Economics* 20(2): 271–87. https://doi.org/10.1111/j.1467-9396.2012.01021.x.
Mendes, Fernando Ribeiro. 2011. *Segurança Social: o futuro hipotecado*. Lisboa: FFMS.
Menz, Georg. 2003. "Re-regulating the Single Market: National Varieties of Capitalism and Their Responses to Europeanization." *Journal of European Public Policy* 10(4): 532–55. https://doi.org/10.1080/1350176032000101226.
– 2009. *The Political Economy of Managed Migration: Nonstate Actors, Europeanization, and the politics of designing migration policies*. Oxford: Oxford University Press.
Messina, Anthony M. 2007. *The Logics and Politics of Post-WWII Migration to Western Europe*. Cambridge: Cambridge University Press.
Mewes, Jan, and Steffen Mau. 2013. "Globalization, Socio-Economic Status and Welfare Chauvinism: European Perspectives on Attitudes toward the Exclusion of Immigrants." *International Journal of Comparative Sociology* 54(3): 228–45. http://doi.org/10.1177/0020715213494395.
Midtbøen, Arnfinn H., Grete Brochmann, and Marta B. Erdal. 2020. "Assessments of Citizenship Criteria: Are Immigrants More Liberal?" *Journal of Ethnic and Migration Studies* 46(1): 1–22. https://doi.org/10.1080/1369183X.2020.1756762.
Migali, Silvia. 2018. "Migration and Institutions: Evidence from Internal EU Mobility." *The World Economy* 41(1): 29–58. https://doi.org/10.1111/twec.12525.
Migrant Integration Policy Index (MIPEX). http://www.mipex.eu.
Milanovic, Branko. 2019. *Capitalism, Alone*. Cambridge, MA: Harvard University Press.
Miller, David. 1995. *On Nationality*. Oxford: Oxford University Press.
Mohanty, Sarita A., Steffie Woolhandler, David U. Himmelstein, Susmita Pati, Olveen Carrasquillo, and David H. Bor. 2005. "Health Care Expenditures of Immigrants in the United States: A Nationally Representative Analysis." *American Journal of Public Health* 95(8): 1431–38. https://doi.org/10.2105/AJPH.2004.044602.
Mollenkopf, John. 2000. "Assimilating Immigrants in Amsterdam: A Perspective from New York." *Netherlands Journal of Social Sciences* 36: 126–45.
Monogan, James. 2007. "Issue Evolution and Public Opinion on Immigration." Paper presented at the Annual Meeting of the Midwest Political Science Association, Chicago.
Moon, Ailee, James E. Lubben, and Valentine Villa. 1998. "Awareness and Utilization of Community Long-Term Care Services by Elderly Korean and Non-Hispanic White

Americans." *The Gerontologist* 38(3): 309–16. https://doi.org/10.1093/geront/38.3.309.

Morley, Bruce. 2006. "Causality between Economic Growth and Immigration: An ARDL Bounds Testing Approach." *Economics Letters* 90(1): 72–6. https://doi.org/10.1016/j.econlet.2005.07.008.

Morris, Lydia. 2002. "Britain's Asylum and Immigration Regime: The Shifting Contours of Rights." *Journal of Ethnic and Migration Studies* 28(3): 409–25. https://doi.org/10.1080/13691830220146527.

– 2016. "Squaring the Circle: Domestic Welfare, Migrants Rights, and Human Rights." *Citizenship Studies* 20(6–7): 693–709. http://doi.org/10.1080/13621025.2015.1122741.

– 2018. "'Moralising Welfare' and Migration in Austerity Britain: A Backdrop to Brexit." European Societies 21(1): 76–100. https://doi.org/10.1080/14616696.2018.1448107.

– 2020. "The Topology of Welfare-Migration-Asylum: Britain`s Outsiders Inside." *Journal of Poverty and Social Justice*, 28(2): 245–64. https://doi.org/10.1332/175982720X15845259771861.

Moscarola, Flavia C. 2003. "Immigration Flows and the Sustainability of the Italian Welfare State." *Politica Economica* 19(1): 63–90. https://doi.org/10.1429/8527.

Mounk, Yascha. 2017. *The Age of Responsibility*. Cambridge, MA: Harvard University Press.

Mourão Permoser, Julia. 2012. "Civic Integration as Symbolic Politics: Insights from Austria." *European Journal of Migration and Law* 14(2): 173–98. https://doi.org/10.1186/s40878-017-0052-4.

Muchomba, Felix, and Neeraj Kaushal. 2021. "Medicaid Expansions and Participation in Supplemental Security Income by Noncitizens." *American Journal of Public Health* 111: 1106–12. https://doi.org/10.2105/AJPH.2021.306235

Muckenhuber, Johanna, Wolfgang Freidl, and Éva Rásky. 2011. "Healthcare for Migrants and for Marginalized Individuals: The Marienambulanz in Graz, Austria." *Wiener klinische Wochenschrift* 123: 559–61. https://doi.org/10.1007/s00508-011-0014-z.

Mundt, Alexis. 2015. "Mit Wohnbeihilfen und BMS zu leistbarem Wohnen?" In *Wohnopoly – Wohnen von Oben bis Unten*, ed. Otmar Amon, 65–80. Vienna: Bundesarbeitsgemeinschaft Wohnungslosenhilfe (BAWO).

Münz, Rainer, Thomas Straubhaar, Florin Vadean, and Nadia Vadean. 2007. "What Are the Migrants' Contributions to Employment and Growth? A European Approach." IAW-Report. 35.

Nannestad, Peter. 2004. "Immigration as a Challenge to the Danish Welfare State?" *European Journal of Political Economy* 20(3): 755–67. http://doi.org/10.1016/j.ejpoleco.2004.03.003.

– 2007. "Immigration and Welfare States: A Survey of 15 Years of Research." *European Journal of Political Economy* 23(2): 512–32. http://doi.org/10.1016/j.ejpoleco.2006.08.007.

Nasralla, Shadia. 2017. "Front runner in Austrian election proposes cuts to migrant benefits." *Reuters*, 4 September.

NBC News. 2019. "Ken Cucinelli Revises Statue of Liberty Poem to Defend New Immigration Rule." 13 August. https://www.youtube.com/watch?v = RMQBxBInImo.

Neiman, Max, Martin Johnson, and Shaun Bowler. 2006. "Partisanship and Views about Immigration in Southern California: Just How Partisan Is the Issue of Immigration?" *International Migration* 44(2): 35–56. http://doi.org/10.1111/j.1468-2435.2006.00363.x.

North, Douglass C. 1990. *Institutions, Institutional Change, and Economic Performance*. New York: Cambridge University Press.

NOU. 2011:7 Velferd og migrasjon. Den norske modellens framtid. Regjeringen.no.

NOU. 2017:2 Integrasjon og tillit. Langsiktige konsekvenser av høy innvandring. Regjeringen.no.

NOU. 2019:7 Arbeid og inntektssikring. Regjeringen.no.

Obinger, Herbert. 2015. "Österreichs Sozialstaat im Vergleich internationaler Makrodaten." *Österreichische Zeitschrift für Politikwissenschaft* 44(1). https://doi.org/10.15203/ozp.197.vol44iss1.

Obinger, Hans, Stefan Leibried, and Frank G. Castles. 2005. "Old and New Politics in Federal Welfare States." In *Federalism and the Welfare State. New World and European Experiences*, ed. S. Leibfried, H. Obinger, and F.G. Castles, 307–53. Cambridge: Cambridge University Press.

Obinger, Herbert, and Emmerich Tálos. 2010. "Janus-Faced Developments in a Prototypical Bismarckian Welfare State: Welfare Reforms in Austria since the 1970s." In *A Long Goodbye to Bismarck? The Politics of Welfare Reform in Continental Europe*, ed. B. Palier, 101–28. Amsterdam: Amsterdam University Press.

O'Connell, Michael. 2005. "Economic Forces and Anti-Immigrant Attitudes in Western Europe: A Paradox in Search of an Explanation." *Patterns of Prejudice* 39(1): 60–74. https://doi.org/10.1080/00313220500045287.

OECD. 2008. *Jobs for Immigrants*, vol. 2: *Labour Market Integration in Belgium, France, the Netherlands, and Portugal*. Paris.

– 2013. "International Migration Outlook 2013." http://doi.org/10.1787/migr_outlook-2013-en.

– 2020. International Migration Database. https://stats.oecd.org.

Oesch, Daniel. 2008. "Explaining Workers' Support for Right-Wing Populist Parties in Western Europe: Evidence from Austria, Belgium, France, Norway, and Switzerland." *International Political Science Review* 29(3): 349–73. http://doi.org/10.1177/0192512107088390.

Oliveira, Catarina Reis. 2010. "The Determinants of Immigrant Entrepreneurship and Employment Creation in Portugal." In *OECD, Open for Business: Migrant Entrepreneurship in OECD Countries*, 125–48. Paris: OECD.

– 2012. "Monitoring Immigrant Integration in Portugal: Managing the Gap between Available Data and Implemented Policy." In *Measuring and Monitoring Immigrant*

Integration in Europe, ed. R. Bijl and A. Verweij, 291–312. The Hague: The Netherlands Institute for Social Research (SCP).

Oliveira, Catarina Reis, Maria Abranches, and Claire Healy. 2009. *Handbook on How to Implement a One-Stop-Shop for Immigrant Integration*. Lisbon: ACIDI.

Oliveira, Catarina Reis, and Isabel Estrada Carvalhais. 2017. "Immigrants' Political Claims in Portugal: Confronting the Political Opportunity Structure with Perceptions and Discourses." *Ethnic and Racial Studies* 40(5): 787–808. https://doi.org/10.1080/01419870.2016.1259487.

Oliveira, Catarina Reis and Natália Gomes. 2018. *Migrações e saúde em números: o caso português, Observatório das Migrações*. Lisboa: ACM.

– 2019. *Indicadores de Integração de Imigrantes. Relatório Estatístico Anual 2019, Observatório das Migrações*. Lisboa: ACM.

Oliveira, Catarina Reis, Natália Gomes, and Tiago Santos. 2017. *Acesso à nacionalidade portuguesa: 10 anos da lei em números, Observatório das Migrações*. Lisboa: ACM.

Osipovič, Dorota. 2015. "Conceptualisations of Welfare Deservingness by Polish Migrants in the UK." *Journal of Social Policy* 44(4): 729–46. 10.1017/S0047279415000215.

Österman, Marcus, Joakim Palme, and Martin Ruhs. 2019. "National Institutions and the Fiscal Effects of EU Migrants." REMINDER working paper D4.3.

Österreichische Bundesregierung. 2020. Aus Verantwortung für Österreich:Regierungsprogramm 2020–2024. Vienna.

Ottonelli, Valeria, and Tiziana Torresi. 2012. "Inclusivist Egalitarian Liberalism and Temporary Migration: A Dilemma." *Journal of Political Philosophy* 20(2): 202–24. http://doi.org/10.1111/j.1467-9760.2010.00380.x.

Padilla, Beatriz, Vera Rodrigues, Jessica Lopes, and Alejandra Ortiz. 2018. "Saúde dos imigrantes. Desigualdades e crise no SNS." In *Desigualdades sociais. Portugal e a Europa*, ed. R. M. Carmo, J. Sebastiáo, J. Azevedo, and S. Martins, 315–34. Lisbon: Editora Mundos Sociais.

Passel, Jeffrey S., and Rebecca L. Clark. 1994. "How Much Do Immigrants Really Cost? A Reappraisal of Huddle's 'The Cost of Immigrants.'" Manuscript. Washington, DC: Urban Institute.

Pedersen, Axel W., Anne S. Grødem, and Ines Wagner. 2019. *Trygdepolitikk og trygdemottak I åtte europeiske land*. Oslo: Institutt for samfunnsforskning.

Pedersen, Peder, Mariola Pytlikova, and Nina Smith. 2008. "Selection and Network Effects—Migration Flows into OECD Countries 1990–2000." *European Economic Review* 52(7): 1160–86. https://doi.org/10.1016/j.euroecorev.2007.12.002.

Peffley, Mark, and Jon Hurwitz. 2010. *Justice in America: The Separate Realities of Blacks and Whites*. Cambridge: Cambridge University Press.

Peixoto, João. 2002. "Strong Market and Weak State: The Case of Foreign Immigration in Portugal." *Journal of Ethnic and Migration Studies* 28(3): 483–97. https://doi.org/10.1080/13691830220146563.

– 2011. *Imigrantes e Segurança Social, Observatório da Imigração*. Lisbon: ACIDI.

Peixoto, João, Daniela Craveiro, Jorge Malheiros, and Isabel Tiago de Olivera. 2017. *Migrações e sustentabilidade demográfica. Perspetivas de evolução da sociedade e economia portuguesas*. Lisbon: Fundação Francisco Manuel dos Santos.

Peixoto, João, and Catarina Sabino. 2009. "Immigration Policies in Portugal: Limits and Compromise in the Quest for Regulation." *European Journal of Migration and Law* 11: 179–97. http://doi.org/10.1163/157181609X440022.

Peixoto, João, Isabel Tiago de Olivera, Joana Azevedo, Pedro Candeias, and Georges Lemaître. 2016. *Regresso ao futuro. A nova emigração e a sociedade portuguesa*. Lisboa: Gradiva.

Perchinig, Bernhard, and Gerd Valchars. 2019. "Einwanderungs-und Integrationspolitik." In *Die Schwarz-Blaue Wende in Österreich: Eine Bilanz*, ed. E. Tálos, 413–42. Vienna: LIT-Verlag.

Peyrl, Johannes. 2019. "Österreich kann Zuwanderung steuern und soll sie auf das wirtschaftlich sinnvolle und gesellschaftlich akzeptable Maß begrenzen." In *Migration und Integration. Fakten oder Mythen?*, ed. M. Haller, 85–98. Wien: Verlag der Österreichischen Akademie der Wissenschaften.

Peyrl, Johannes, and Sarah Bruckner. 2017. "Die soziale Gleichbehandlung von EU-BürgerInnen – ein Eckpfeiler eines gemeinsamen Europas: ÖGfE Policy Brief 22'2017." https://oegfe.at/wordpress/wp-content/uploads/2017/10/OEGfE_Policy_Brief-2017.22.pdf.

Pfeil, Walter J. 2011. *Österreichisches Sozialrecht*. 11th ed. Vienna: Verlag Österreich.

– 2018. "Sozialleistungen (auch) für geflüchtete Personen." In *Migration, Arbeitsmarkt und Sozialpolitik*, ed. Birgit Schrattbauer, Walter Pfeil, and Rudolf Mosler, 121–40. Vienna: Manz Verlag.

Pires, Rui Pena. 2010. Portugal: An Atlas of International Migration. Lisbon: Tinta da China and Fundação Calouste Gulbenkian.

Ponce, Aaron. 2019. "Is Welfare a Magnet for Migration? Examining Universal Welfare Institutions and Migration Flows." *Social Forces* 98(1): 245–78. https://doi.org/10.1093/sf/soy111.

Pratscher, Kurt. 1992. "Sozialhilfe: Staat–Markt–Familie." In *Der geforderte Wohlfahrtsstaat: Traditionen–Herausforderungen–Perspektiven*, ed. E. Tálos, 61–95. Vienna: Löcker.

Prentice, Julia C., Anne R. Pebley, and Narayan Sastry. 2005. "Immigration Status and Health Insurance Coverage: Who Gains? Who Loses?" *American Journal of Public Health* 95(1): 109–16. https://doi.org/10.2105/AJPH.2003.028514.

Provine, Marie D., and Jorge M. Chavez. 2009. "Race and the Response of State Legislatures to Unauthorized Immigrants." *Annals of the American Academy of Political and Social Science* 623: 78–92. https://doi.org/10.1177/0002716208331014.

Putnam, Robert O. 2007. "E Pluribus Unum: Diversity and Community in the 21st Century: The 2006 Johan Skytte Prize Lecture." *Scandinavian Political Studies* 30(2): 137–74. https://doi.org/10.1111/j.1467-9477.2007.00176.x.

Radford, Jynnah. 2019. "Key Findings about U.S. Immigrants." Pew Research Center. https://www.pewresearch.org/fact-tank/2019/06/17/key-findings-about-u-s-immigrants.

Ramos, Raul, Alessia Matano, and Sandra Nieto. 2015. "EU Immigrant Integration Policies and Returns on Human Capital." *International Spectator* 50(3): 78–87. http://doi.org/10.1080/03932729.2015.1051905.

Razin, Assaf, and Efraim Sadka. 2000. "Unskilled Migration: A Burden or a Boon for the Welfare State?" *Scandinavian Journal of Economics* 102(3): 463–79. https://doi.org/10.1111/1467-9442.00210.

Razin, Assaf, Efraim Sadka, and Benjarong Suwankiri. 2011. *Migration and the Welfare State: Political-Economy Policy Formation*. Cambridge, MA: MIT Press.

Rector, Robert, and Jason Richwine. 2013. "The Fiscal Cost of Unlawful Immigrants and Amnesty to the U.S. Taxpayer." Heritage Foundation.

Reeskens, Tim, and Wim Van Oorschot. 2015. "Immigrants' Attitudes towards Welfare Redistribution: An Exploration of Role of Government Preferences among Immigrants and Natives across 18 European Welfare States." *European Sociological Review* 31(4): 433–45. https://doi.org/10.1093/esr/jcv003.

Riosmena, Fernando, Randall Kuhn, and Warren C. Jochem. 2017. "Explaining the Immigrant Health Advantage: Self-Selection and Protection in Health-Related Factors among Five Major National-Origin Immigrant Groups in the United States." *Demography* 54(1): 175–200. https://doi.org/10.1007/s13524-016-0542-2.

Rodrik, Dani. 1998. "Globalisation, Social Conflict, and Economic Growth." *World Economy* 21(2): 143–58. https://doi.org/10.1111/1467-9701.00124.

Rogers, William H. 1993. "Sg17: Regression Standard Errors in Clustered Samples." *STATA Technical Bulletin* 13: 19–23.

Römer, Friederike. 2017. "Generous to All or 'Insiders Only'? The Relationship between Welfare State Generosity and Immigrant Welfare Rights." *Journal of European Social Policy* 27(2): 173–96. https://doi.org/10.1177/0958928717696441.

Römer, Friederike, Eloisa Harris, Jakob Henninger, and Franziska Missler [in collaboration with Marcus Böhme and Erinn Crider]. 2021. "The Migrant Social Protection Data Set (MigSP)." SFB 1342 Technical Paper Series, 10. Bremen: SFB 1342.

Room, Graham J. 1981. "The End of the Welfare State?" In *The Emergence of the Welfare State in Britain and Germany*, ed. W.J. Mommsen, 408–23. London: Croom Helm.

Rosanvallon, Pierre. 2013. *The Society of Equals*. Cambridge, MA: Harvard University Press.

Rosenberger, Sieglinde, and Gilg Seeber. 2011. "Kritische Einstellungen: BürgerInnen zu Demokratie, Politik, Migration." In *Zukunft. Werte. Europa. Die Europäische Wertestudie 1990–2010: Österreich im Vergleich*, ed. R. Polak, 165–90. Vienna, Cologne, & Weimar: Böhlau.

Rothstein, Bo. 1998. *Just Institutions Matter: The Moral and Political Logic of the Universal Welfare State*. Cambridge: Cambridge University Press.

– 2017. "Solidarity, Diversity, and the Quality of Government." In *The Strains of Commitment: The Political Sources of Solidarity in Diverse Societies*, ed. K. Banting and W. Kymlicka, Oxford: Oxford University Press.

Rothstein, Bo, and Dietlind Stolle. 2003. "Social Capital, Impartiality, and the Welfare State: An Institutional Approach." In *Generating Social Capital*, ed. M. Hooghe and D. Stolle, 191–210. New York: Palgrave Macmillan.

Ruhs, Martin. 2011. "Openness, Skills, and Rights: An Empirical Analysis of Labour Immigration Programmes in 46 High- and Middle-Income Countries." COMPAS working paper no. 88.

– 2013. *The Price of Rights: Regulating International Labor Migration*. Princeton: Princeton University Press.

Sá, Filipa. 2011. "Does Employment Protection Help Immigrants? Evidence from European Labor Markets." *Labour Economics* 18(5): 624–42. http://hdl.handle.net /10419/34804.

Sainsbury, Diane. 2006. "Immigrants' Social Rights in Comparative Perspective: Welfare Regimes, Forms of Immigration Policy, and Immigration Policy Regimes." *Journal of European Social Policy* 16(3): 229–44. http://doi. org/10.1177/0958928706065594.

– 2012. *Welfare States and Immigrant Rights: The Politics of Inclusion and Exclusion*. Oxford: Oxford University Press.

Sakellarides, Constantino, Luis Castelo-Branco, Patrícia Barbosa, and Helda Azvedo. 2014. *The Impact of the Financial Crisis on the Health System and Health in Portugal: Case Study*. Copenhagen: World Health Organization.

Sanderson, Stephen K. 2004. "Ethnic Heterogeneity and Public Spending: Testing the Evolutionary Theory of Ethnicity with Cross-National Data." In *Welfare, Ethnicity, and Altruism*, ed. F. K. Salter, 25–86. London: Frank Cass.

Sarvimäki, Matti, and Kari Hämäläinen. 2016. "Integrating Immigrants: The Impact of Restructuring Active Labor Market Programs." *Journal of Labor Economics* 34(2): 479–508.

Sassen, Saskia. 1996. *Losing Control? Sovereignty in an Age of Globalization*. New York: Columbia University Press.

Scheve, Kenneth F., and Matthew J. Slaughter. 2001. "Labor Market Competition and Individual Preferences over Immigration Policy." *Review of Economics and Statistics* 83(1): 133–54. https://doi.org/10.3386/w6946.

Schierup, Carl-Ulrik, and Aleksandra Ålund. 2011. "The End of Swedish Exceptionalism? Citizenship, Neoliberalism, and the Politics of Exclusion." *Race and Class* 53(1): 45–64. http://doi.org/10.1177/0306396811406780.

Schmitt, Carina, and Céline Teney. 2018. "Access to General social protection for immigrants in advanced democracies." *Journal of European Social Policy*, 29 (1): 1–12. http://doi.org/10.1177/0958928718768365.

Schneider, Anne, and Helen Ingram. 1993. "Social Construction of Target Populations: Implications for Politics and Policy." *American Political Science Review* 87(2): 334–47. https://doi.org/10.2307/2939044.

Sciortino, Giuseppe. 2013. "Immigration in Italy: Subverting the Logic of Welfare Reform?" In *Europe's Immigration Challenge: Reconciling Work, Welfare, and Mobility*, ed. E. Jurado and G. Brochmann. London: L.B. Tauris.

Scruggs, Lyle, Detlef Jahn, and Kati Kuitto. 2017. *Comparative Welfare Entitlements Data Set 2, Version 2014-03: Codebook*. Storrs and Greifswald: University of Connecticut and University of Greifswald.

Seip, Anne-Lise. 1994. *Veiene til velferdsstaten. Norsk sosialpolitikk 1920–75*. Oslo: Gyldendal norsk forlag.

Singer, Audrey. 2004. "Welfare Reform and Immigrants: A Policy Review." In *Immigrants, Welfare Reform, and the Poverty of Policy*, edited by Philip Kretsedemas and Ana Aparicio, 21–34. Westport and London: Praeger.

Sommers, Benjamin D. 2013. "Stuck between Health and Immigration Reform – Care for Undocumented Immigrants." *New England Journal of Medicine* 369(7): 593–5. https://doi.org/10.1056/nejmp1306636.

Soni Aparna, Marguerite E. Burns, Laura Dague, and Kosali I. Simon. 2017. "Medicaid Expansion and State Trends In Supplemental Security Income Program Participation." *Health Aff (Millwood)* 36(8): 1485–88. https://doi.org/10.1377/hlthaff.2016.1632.

Soroka, Stuart N., Richard Johnston, and Keith Banting. 2006. "Immigration and Redistribution in a Global Era." In *Globalization and Egalitarian Redistribution*, ed. S. Bowles, P. Bardhan, and M. Wallerstein, 261–88. Princeton: Princeton University Press.

Soroka, Stuart N., Richard Johnston, Anthony Kevins, Keith Banting, and Will Kymlicka. 2015. "Migration and Welfare State Spending." *European Political Science Review* 8(2): 173–94. http://doi.org/10.1017/S1755773915000041.

Soss, Joe, Richard C. Fording, and Sanford F. Schram. 2011. *Disciplining the Poor: Neoliberal Paternalism and the Persistent Power of Race*. Chicago: University of Chicago Press.

Soss, Joe, Sanford F. Schram, Thomas P. Vartanian, and Erin O'Brien. 2001 . "Setting the Terms of Relief: Explaining State Policy Choices in the Devolution Revolution." *American Journal of Political Science* 45(2): 378–9. https://doi .org/10.2307/2669347.

Sowell, Thomas. 2004. *Affirmative Action around the World*. New Haven: Yale University Press.

Soysal, Yasemin N. 1994. *Limits of Citizenship: Migrants and Postnational Membership in Europe*. Chicago: University of Chicago Press.

Spahl, Wanda, Sabine Weiss, and Judith Kohlenberger. 2017. "Immigration and the Social Welfare State in Austria, Germany, and Switzerland: A Comparative Meta-Study." Vienna Institute of Demography working papers no. 18/2017.

Spencer, Sarah. 2003. *The Politics of Migration: Managing Opportunity, Conflict, and Change*. Malden: Blackwell.

Spinner-Halev, Jeff. "Cultural Pluralism and Partial Citizenship." In *Multicultural questions*, ed. C. Joppke and S. Lukes, 65–86. Oxford: Oxford University Press.

Stangej, Olga, Inga Minelgaite, Kari Kristinsson, and Margaret S. Sigrun. 2019. "Post-Migration Labor Market: Prejudice and the Role of Host Country Education." *Evidence-Based HRM: A Global Forum for Empirical Scholarship* 7(1): 42–55. http://doi.org/10.1108/EBHRM-03-2018-0019.

Staver, Anne, Jan Paul Brekke and Susanne Søholt. 2019. "Scandinavia's Segregated Cities – Policies, Strategies, and Ideals." NIBR Report.

Stenner, Karen, and Jonathan Haidt. 2018. "Authoritarianism Is Not a Momentary Madness, but an Eternal Dynamic within Liberal Democracies." In *Can It Happen Here*, ed. C.R. Sunstein, 175–219. New York: Dey Street.

Stokke, Øyvind. 2007. "Membership and Migration: Market Citizenship or European Citizenship." In *Citizenship in Nordic Welfare States*, ed. B. Hvinden and H. Johansson, 155–69. Abingdon: Routledge.

Storesletten, Kjetil. 2003. "Fiscal Implications of Immigration – a Net Present Value Calculation." *Scandinavian Journal of Economics* 105(3): 487–506. https://doi.org/10.1111/1467-9442.t01-2-00009.

Strøm, Frøydis. 2019. *Holdninger til innvandrere og innvandring 2019*. Oslo: Statistics Norway.

Tálos, Emmerich. 2004. "'Insider' und 'Outsider' – 'Inklusion' und 'Exklusion' im Sozialstaat." In *Insider und Outsider: Eine Dokumentation der internationalen Konferenz 2003 in Graz "Insider und Outsider" der Denkwerkstätte Graz*, ed. H. G. Zilian, 105–19. Graz: Hampp.

Tálos, Emmerich, and Herbert Obinger. 2020. *Sozialstaat Österreich (1945–2020): Entwicklung – Maßnahmen – internationale Verortung*. Wien: Studienverlag.

Tamir, Yael. 1993. *Liberal Nationalism*. Princeton: Princeton University Press.

Taylor, Paul, Ana Gonzalez-Barrera, Jeffrey S. Passel, and Mark Hugo Lopez. 2012. "Recent Trends in Naturalization, 2000–2011." Pew Research Center.

Theiss-Morse, Elizabeth. 2009. *Who Counts as an American? The Boundaries of National Identity*. Cambridge: Cambridge University Press.

Tienda, Marta, and Leif Jensen. 1986. "Immigration and Public Assistance Participation: Dispelling the Myth of Dependency." *Social Science Research* 15(4): 372–400. https://doi.org/10.1016/0049-089X(86)90019-0.

Tilly, Charles. 1998. *Durable Inequality*. Berkeley: University of California Press.

Timonen, Virpi, and Martha Doyle. 2008. "In Search of Security: Migrant Workers' Understandings, Experiences, and Expectations regarding 'Social Protection' in Ireland." *Journal of Social Policy* 38(1): 157–75. http://doi.org/10.1017/S0047279408002602.

Titmuss, Richard. 1968. *Commitment to Welfare*. London: Allen and Unwin.

Trattner, Walter I. 2007. *From Poor Law to Welfare State: A History of Social Welfare in America*. New York: Simon and Schuster.

Tully, James. 2001. "Introduction." In *Multinational Democracies*, ed. A. Gagnon and J. Tully, 1–34. Cambridge: Cambridge University Press.

Ulceluse, Magdalena, and Martin Kahanec. 2018. "Self-Employment as a Vehicle for Labour Market Integration of Immigrants and Natives." *International Journal of Manpower* 39(8): 1064–79. http://doi.org/10.1108/IJM-10-2018-0332.

UN-DESA. 2016. "International Migration Report 2015 Highlights." New York: UN Department of Economic and Social Affairs.

UNDP. 2014. "Human development report 2013: The rise of the South: Human progress in a diverse World." United Nations Development Programme, Neww York. http://hdr.undp.org/sites/default/files/reports/14/hdr2013_en_complete.pdf.

Unger, Brigitte. 2001. "Österreichs Beschäftigungs-und Sozialpolitik von 1970–2000." In *Arbeitsmarkt und Sozialstaat: Sozialpolitik in Europa*, ed. J. Alber and J. Kohl, 340–61. Wiesbaden: Chmieiorz.

United Nations. Department of Economics and Social Affairs, Population Division. 2017. "Trends in International Migrant Stock: The 2017 Revision" (UN database, POP/DB/MIG/Stock/Rev.2017).

Valenta, Marko, and Nihad Bundar. 2010. "State Assisted Integration: Refugee Integration Policies in Scandinavian Welfare States: The Swedish and Norwegian Experience." *Journal of Refugee Studies* 23(4): 463–83. https://doi.org/10.1093/jrs/feq028.

Van der Geest, L., and A.J.F. Dietvorst. 2010. "Budgettaire Effecten van Immigratie van Niet-Westerse Allochtonen" (Budgetary Effects of Immigration of Non-Western Migrants). Utrecht: Nyfer).

Van der Waal, Jeroen, Willem De Koster, and Wim Van Oorschot. 2013. "Three Worlds of Welfare Chauvinism? How Welfare Regimes Affect Support for Distributing Welfare to Immigrants in Europe." *Journal of Comparative Policy Analysis: Research and Practice* 15(2): 164–81. https://doi.org/10.1080/13876988.2013.785147.

Van Oorschot, Wim. 2006. "Making the Difference in Social Europe: Deservingness Perceptions among Citizens of European Welfare States." *Journal of European Social Policy* 16(1): 23–42. http://doi.org/10.1177/0958928706059829.

Van Oorschot, Wim, Femke Roosma, Bart Meuleman, and Tim Reeskens. 2017. *The Social Legitimacy of Targeted Welfare: Attitudes to Welfare Deservingness*. Cheltenham: Edward Elgar.

Van Oorschot, Wim, and Wilfred Uunk. 2007. "Multi-Level Determinants of the Public's Informal Solidarity towards Immigrants in European Welfare States." In *Social Justice, Legitimacy, and the Welfare State*, ed. S. Mau and B. Veghte, 217–38. Aldershot: Ashgate.

Van Slyke, David M. 2003. "The Mythology of Privatization in Contracting for Social Services." *Public Administration Review* 63(3): 296–315. https://doi.org/10.1111/1540-6210.00291.

Veitch, Kenneth. 2013. "Law, Social Policy, and the Constitution of Markets and Profit Making." *Journal of Law and Society* 40(1): 137–54. http://doi.org/10.1111/j.1467-6478.2013.00616.x.

Venturini, Alessandra. 2004. *Postwar Migration in Southern Europe, 1950–2000*. Cambridge: Cambridge University Press.

Venturini, Alessandra, and Claudia Villosio. 2008. "Labour-Market Assimilation of Foreign Workers in Italy." *Oxford Review of Economic Policy* 24(3): 517–41. https://doi.org/10.1093/oxrep/grn030.

Verfassungsgerichtshof Österreich. 2019. "VfGH zu Sozialhilfe-Grundsatzgesetz: Höchstsatzsystem für Kinder sowie Arbeitsqualifizierungsbonus verfassungswidrig." News release, 17 December. https://www.vfgh.gv.at/downloads/VfGH-Presseinformation_vom_17._Dezember_2019.pdf.

Verkuyten, Maykel. 2005. "Ethnic Group Identification and Group Evaluation among Minority and Majority Groups: Testing the Multiculturalism Hypothesis." *Journal of Personality and Social Psychology* 88(1): 121–38. https://doi.org/10.1037/0022-3514.88.1.121.

Verschueren, Herwig. 2016. "Being Economically Active: How It Still Matters." In *Residence, Employment, and Social Rights of Mobile Persons: On How EU Law Defines Where They Belong*, ed. H. Verschueren, 187–214. Cambridge: Cambridge University Press.

Vliegenthart, Rens, and Hajo G. Boomgaarden. 2007. "Real World Indicators and the Coverage of Immigration and the Integration of Minorities in Dutch Newspapers." *European Journal of Communication* 22(3): 293–314. http://doi.org/10.1177/0267323107079676.

Voitchovsky, Sarah. 2014. "Occupational Downgrading and Wages of New Member States Immigrants to Ireland." *International Migration Review* 48(2): 500–37. https://doi.org/10.1111/imre.12089.

Volf, Patrick-Paul. 1995. "Der politische Flüchtling als Symbol der Zweiten Republik. Zur Asyl-und Flüchtlingspolitik seit 1945." *Zeitgeschichte* 11–12: 415–35.

Vorauer, Jacquie D., and Stacey J. Sasaki. 2011. "In the Worst Rather Than the Best of Times: Effects of Salient Intergroup Ideology in Threatening Intergroup Interactions." *Journal of Personality and Social Psychology* 101(2): 307–20. https://doi.org/10.1037/a0023152.

Weber, Eugene. 1976. *Peasants into Frenchmen: The Modernization of Rural France, 1870–1914*. Stanford: Stanford University Press.

Weber, René, and Thomas Straubhaar. 1996. "Immigration and the Public Transfer System: Some Empirical Evidence for Switzerland." *Weltwirtschaftliches Archiv* 132(2): 330–55. https://doi.org/10.1007/bf02707810.

Webster, Charles. 2002. *The National Health Service: A Political History*. Oxford: Oxford University Press.

White House. 2019. "Remarks by President Trump before Air Force One Departure." 13 August 13. https://www.whitehouse.gov/briefings-statements/remarks-president-trump-air-force-one-departure-11/.

Wilensky, Harold. 1975. *The Welfare State and Equality*. Berkeley: University of California Press.

Wilkinson, Mick, and Gary Craig. 2012. "Wilful Negligence: Migration Policy, Migrants' Work, and the Absence of Social Protection in the UK." In *Migration and Welfare in the New Europe: Social Protection and the Challenges of Integration*, ed. E. Carmel, A. Cerami, and T. Papadopoulos, 177–98. Bristol: Policy Press.

Wimark, Thomas, Karen Haandrikman, and Micheal Meinild Nielsen. 2019. "Migrant Labour Market Integration: The Association between Initial Settlement and Subsequent Employment and Income among Migrants." *Geografiska Annaler: Series B, Human Geography* 101(2): 118–37. https://doi.org/10.1080/04353684.2019.1581987.

Wimmer-Puchinger, Beate, Hilde Wolf, and Andrea Engleder. 2006. "Migrantinnen im Gesundheitssystem. Inanspruchnahme, Zugangsbarrieren und Strategien zur Gesundheitsförderung." *Bundesgesundheitsblatt Gesundheitsforschung Gesundheitsschutz* 49(9): 884–92. https://doi.org/10.1007/s00103-006-0022-8.

World Bank. 2019. "Education statistics: Education attainment." https://databank.worldbank.org/reports.aspx?Id=fdfe8ea8&Report_Name=Average-years-of-schooling-age-15plus#.

– 2020. World Development Indicators (WDI). Washington, DC. wdi.worldbank.org.

Wöss, Josef. 2020. "Das östereichische Pensionssystem." In *Neustart in der Rentenpolitik: Analysen und Perspektiven*, ed. F. Blank, M. Hofmann, and A. Buntenbach, 235–57. Baden-Baden: Nomos.

Wright, Matthew, and Reeskens, Tim. 2013. "Of What Cloth Are the Ties That Bind? National Identity and Support for the Welfare State across 29 European Countries." *Journal of European Public Policy* 20(10): 1443–63. https://doi.org/10.1080/13501763.2013.800796.

Xu, Ping. 2017. "Compensation or Retrenchment? The Paradox of Immigration and Public Welfare Spending in the American States." *State Politics and Policy Quarterly* 17(1): 76–104. https://doi.org/10.1177/1532440016660536.

Yang, Joshua S., and Steven P. Wallace. 2007. "Expansion of Health Insurance in California Unlikely to Act as Magnet for Undocumented Migration." UCLA Center for Health Policy Research, Los Angeles.

Yeates, Nicola. 2009. *Globalizing Care Economies and Migrant Workers: Explorations in Global Care Chains*. Basingstoke: Palgrave Macmillan.

Yoo, Grace J. 2008. "Immigrants and Welfare: Policy Constructions of Deservingness." *Journal of Immigrant and Refugee Studies* 6(4): 490–507. https://doi.org/10.1080/15362940802479920.

Zaslove, Andrej. 2004. "Closing the Door? The Ideology and Impact of Radical Right Populism on Immigration Policy in Austria and Italy." *Journal of Political Ideologies* 9(1): 99–118. https://doi.org/10.1080/1356931032000167490.

Zhu, Ling, and Ping Xu. 2015. "The Politics of Welfare Exclusion: Immigration and Disparity in Medicaid Coverage." *Policy Studies Journal* 43(4): 456–83. https://doi.org/10.1111/psj.12106.

Ziliak, James P. 2013. "Why Are So Many Americans on Food Stamps? The Role of the Economy, Policy, and Demographics." *University of Kentucky Center for Poverty Research Discussion Paper Series, 12.*

Zimmerman, Klaus F. 2005. *European Migration: What Do We Know*? Oxford: Oxford University Press.

Zimmermann, Klaus F., Martin Kahanec, Amelie F. Constant, Don J. DeVoretz, Liliya Gataullina, and Anzelika Zaiceva. 2008. "Study on the Social and Labour Market Integration of Ethnic Minorities." IZA Research Report no. 16.

Zimmermann, Klaus F., Martin Kahanec, Corrado Giulietti, Martin Guzi, Alan Barrett, and Bertrand Maître. 2012. "Study on Active Inclusion of Migrants." IZA Research Report no. 43.

Zincone, Giovanna. 2006. "The Making of Policies: Immigration and Immigrants in Italy." *Journal of Ethnic and Migration Studies* 32(3): 347–75. https://doi.org/10.1080/13691830600554775.

Zolberg, Aristide. 2006. *A Nation by Design: Immigration Policy in the Fashioning of America*. London and Cambridge, MA: Russell Sage Foundation and Harvard University Press.

Contributors

Keith Banting is Stauffer Dunning Fellow in the School of Policy Studies and Professor Emeritus in the Department of Political Studies at Queen's University. He has a long-standing interest in the politics of social policy, and has extended this research to include multiculturalism and social solidarity. His recent contributions include *The Strains of Commitment: The Political Sources of Solidarity in Diverse Societies* (Oxford University Press), co-edited with Will Kymlicka.

Liv Bjerre is assistant professor at the Department of Political Science, Aarhus University, Denmark. Her research focuses on the effects of immigration and integration policy, and she is one of the authors behind the Immigration Policy in Comparison (IMPIC) Database, which provides a set of sophisticated quantitative indices to measure immigration policies in a comprehensive way across time, countries and policy fields.

Grete Brochmann is professor in the Department of Sociology and Human Geography at the University of Oslo. She has published several books and articles on international migration, sending and receiving country perspectives, EU policies, and welfare state dilemmas. She has served as a visiting scholar in Brussels, Berkeley, Malmö, and Boston. She has chaired two governmental commissions in Norway on the long-term consequences of immigration for the welfare model.

Adam M. Butz, is associate professor in the Graduate Center for Public Policy and Administration at California State University, Long Beach. He studies U.S. social welfare and immigration policy, cross-sectoral governance, race and social equity, and urban affairs. His research has appeared in scholarly outlets such as *Social Policy & Administration*, *Poverty & Public Policy*, *Evaluation Review*, *Policy Studies Journal*, and *Cities: The International Journal of Urban Policy & Planning*.

Markus M.L. Crepaz is the Josiah Meigs Distinguished Teaching Professor of Political Science in the Department of International Affairs at the University of Georgia. His research interests include comparative political economy, migration and the welfare state, connections between trust, multiculturalism and authoritarianism, as well as the impact of political institutions on a variety of social outcomes.

Anil Duman is an associate professor at Central European University, Vienna. She has received her M.A. and Ph.D. in Economics from University of Massachusetts, Amherst. Her broad research interests include political economy, industrial relations, welfare state policies, and redistribution. In her recent research, she has been specializing in the relation between labor market status and socio-economic inequalities.

Oliver Gruber is a post-doctoral lecturer at the Department of Political Science at the University of Vienna. His research and teaching focuses on migration and integration policy, party politics and public policy as well as political communication and language policy.

Christian Joppke holds a chair in sociology at the University of Bern. Previously he taught at the University of Southern California, European University Institute, University of British Columbia, International University Bremen, and the American University of Paris. He wrote extensively on social movements, immigration, citizenship, multiculturalism, nationalism, and populism. His most recent book is *Neoliberal Nationalism* (Cambridge University Press 2021). He is currently writing a book on the "political forms of neoliberalism."

Martin Kahanec is professor and head of the Department of Public Policy at the Central European University (CEU) in Vienna, where he acted as the Dean of its School of Public Policy in 2017–19 and 2020–21. He is a founder and Scientific Director of the Central European Labour Studies Institute, member of the Advisory Board at the Global Labor Organization, and affiliated researcher at the University of Economics in Bratislava. Kahanec has published extensively in the areas of labor and population economics, migration, EU mobility, ethnicity, and policy reforms in European labor markets.

Neeraj Kaushal is Professor of Social Policy at Columbia University and Research Associate at the National Bureau of Economic Research. Kaushal is a labor and health economist and conducts research on immigration. In her acclaimed book, *Blaming Immigrants: Nationalism and the Economics of Global*

Movement, she investigates the core causes of rising disaffection towards immigrants globally and tests common objections against immigration.

Jason E. Kehrberg, is an assistant professor in the Department of Political Science and Criminal Justice at Muskingum University. His primary research and teaching interests include political behavior, public policy, state politics, immigration, and social welfare policies. He is the author or coauthor of articles published in *Policy Studies Journal*, *Research & Politics*, *Political Science Quarterly*, *Politics & Policy*, and *Comparative European Politics.*

Edward A. Koning is an associate professor in the Department of Political Science at the University of Guelph. His main research interests are the politics of immigration and populism, in particular in Western Europe and North America. He is the author of *Immigration and the Politics of Welfare Exclusion* (University of Toronto Press) and has recent publications in the *Journal of Elections, Public Opinion, and Parties,* the *Journal of Public Policy,* and *Social Policy & Administration.*

Lucia Mýtna Kureková (PhD) works as a senior researcher at the Centre for Social and Psychological Sciences of the Slovak Academy of Sciences. Her research focuses on labor migration and labor mobility; skill formation and education systems; and innovative data sources. She has widely published in these fields, regularly participates in international collaborative research projects, and provides expertise to international organizations, including ILO, OECD, and World Bank.

Will Kymlicka is the Canada Research Chair in Political Philosophy at Queen's University. He is the author of several books on democracy and diversity, including *Multicultural Citizenship* (OUP, 1995), and co-editor with Keith Banting of *The Strains of Commitment: The Political Sources of Solidarity in Diverse Societies* (OUP, 2017).

Catarina Reis Oliveira is the Director of the Observatory for Migration of Portugal (OM/ACM) and Invited Assistant Professor at the Institute of Social and Political Sciences (ISCSP), Lisbon University (ULisboa). Her main areas of research are the sociology of migration, immigrants' integration, immigrant entrepreneurial strategies, and access to citizenship. She has coordinated and participated in several research projects and published extensively on migration issues in books as well as national and international journals. As advisor of three High Commissioners for Migration in Portugal (between 2005 and 2015), she was involved in the discussion and evaluation of several policies and services targeting immigrants.

João Peixoto is professor in the School of Economics and Management (ISEG), Universidade de Lisboa (ULisboa), Portugal, and researcher at SOCIUS/CSG – Research Centre on Economic and Organizational Sociology, ISEG/ULisboa. His main areas of interest are international migration, demography and economic sociology. He is the author or co-author of several books and articles published in national and international journals.

Tsewang Rigzin is a doctoral candidate at the Columbia University School of Social Work and Research Fellow at the Columbia Population Research Center. His research interest includes immigration, refugees, and social welfare policies.

Friederike Römer is the principal investigator of the project "Causes of Inclusion and Exclusion: Immigrant Welfare Rights in Global Comparison" at the Collaborative Research Center "Global Dynamics of Social Policy" at the University of Bremen. She is also one of the authors of the IMPIC database. In her current project, she investigates how political parties and actors from civil society shape immigrant rights.

Mikhala L. West is a recent graduate of Muskingum University with a Bachelor of Arts in International Affairs and Political Science. Her main areas of research included immigration, foreign affairs, and political biases. She now works for a small non-profit in Columbus (OH) that provides education for urban low-income and high-need students.

www.ingramcontent.com/pod-product-compliance
Lightning Source LLC
LaVergne TN
LVHW040154080826
844660LV00014B/956/J

* 9 7 8 1 4 8 7 5 4 6 3 4 2 *